MARCION AND THE MAKING OF A HERETIC

A comprehensive and authoritative account of the 'heretic' Marcion, this volume traces the development of the concept and language of heresy in the setting of an exploration of second-century Christian intellectual debate. Judith M. Lieu analyses accounts of Marcion by the major early Christian polemicists who shaped the idea of heresy, including Justin Martyr, Irenaeus, Tertullian, Epiphanius of Salamis, Clement of Alexandria, Origen, and Ephraem Syrus. She examines Marcion's 'Gospel', 'Apostolikon', and 'Antitheses' in detail and compares his principles with those of contemporary Christian and non-Christian thinkers, covering a wide range of controversial issues: the nature of God, the relation of the divine to creation, the person of Jesus, the interpretation of Scripture, the nature of salvation, and the appropriate lifestyle of adherents. In this innovative study, Marcion emerges as a distinctive, creative figure who addressed widespread concerns within second-century Christian diversity.

JUDITH M. LIEU is Lady Margaret's Professor of Divinity at the University of Cambridge. She has written numerous books, including *I, II, & III John: A Commentary* (2008); *Christian Identity in the Jewish and Graeco-Roman World* (2004); and *Neither Jew Nor Greek?: Constructing Early Christianity* (2002).

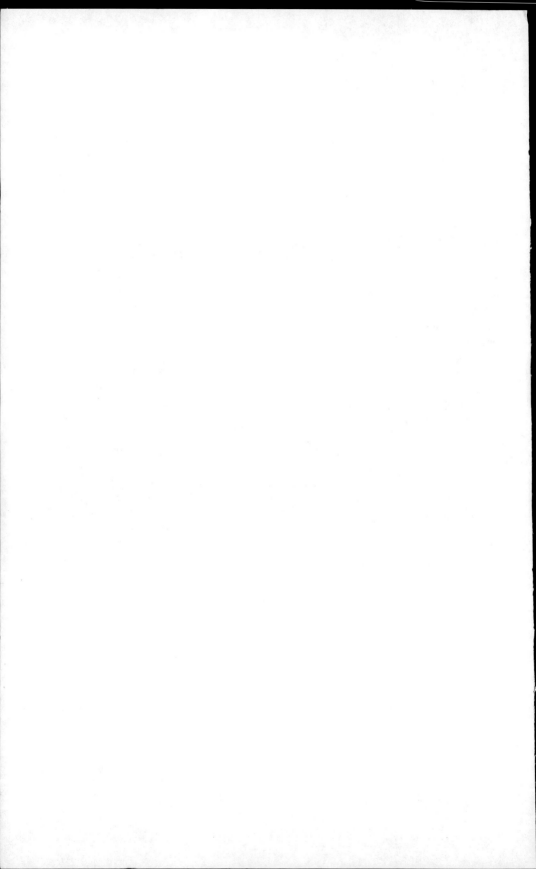

Marcion and the Making of a Heretic

God and Scripture in the Second Century

JUDITH M. LIEU
University of Cambridge

CAMBRIDGE
UNIVERSITY PRESS

University Printing House, Cambridge CB2 8BS, United Kingdom

One Liberty Plaza, 20th Floor, New York, NY 10006, USA

477 Williamstown Road, Port Melbourne, VIC 3207, Australia

4843/24, 2nd Floor, Ansari Road, Daryaganj, Delhi - 110002, India

79 Anson Road, #06-04/06, Singapore 079906

Cambridge University Press is part of the University of Cambridge.

It furthers the University's mission by disseminating knowledge in the pursuit of education, learning and research at the highest international levels of excellence.

www.cambridge.org
Information on this title: www.cambridge.org/9781108434041

First published 2015
First paperback edition 2017

A catalogue record for this publication is available from the British Library

Library of Congress Cataloging in Publication data
Lieu, Judith.
Marcion and the making of a heretic : God and scripture in the second century /
Judith M. Lieu, University of Cambridge.
pages cm
Includes bibliographical references and index.
ISBN 978-1-107-02904-0 (Hardback)
1. Marcion, of Sinope, active 2nd century. 2. Church history–Primitive and early church, ca. 30–600. 3. Theology, Doctrinal–History–Early church, ca. 30–600.
4. Theology, Doctrinal. I. Title.
BT1415.L54 2014
273′.1–dc23 2014028074

ISBN 978-1-107-02904-0 Hardback
ISBN 978-1-108-43404-1 Paperback

Contents

PART III: THE SECOND-CENTURY SHAPING OF MARCION

Preface

My fascination with Marcion dates back over more than two decades to my previous work on the emergence of Christianity out of its Jewish heritage and on the development of a distinctive 'Christian' self-definition. However, it was the award of a Leverhulme Major Research Fellowship for 2007–9 that enabled me to undertake sustained research; I am deeply grateful to the Leverhulme Trust for its generous support and for its continued recognition of the needs of those scholars whose primary requirement is uninterrupted time and access to the best research resources available. The award of the Fellowship coincided with my appointment to the Lady Margaret Professorship in Divinity at the University of Cambridge, and I am grateful to the university and to colleagues in the Faculty of Divinity for permitting me to take up the Fellowship. The unrivalled library resources at Cambridge have enriched my work on Marcion immeasurably.

Completing the research and manuscript has taken longer than I may have wished, in part owing to subsequent administrative duties as Chair of the Faculty Board. Yet this has also provided opportunity for me to read papers related to Marcion in a variety of contexts – academic and more popular – and to publish some initial articles. I am grateful to audiences for their interest and questions, to colleagues for invitations and encouragement, and particularly to colleagues at Cambridge and members of the New Testament Senior Seminar, who have had (quite properly) to include the second century in their remit. Professor C. Kingsley Barrett was a mentor ever since I undertook an MA under his supervision, and it was a particular joy on my occasional visits to Durham before his death in 2011, when he was working on the Pauline heritage, to spend time with him, discussing Marcion and his Paulinism; I join with the many students of the New Testament who acknowledge the debt they owe him.

Abbreviations

Abbreviations of ancient sources can be traced in the index of ancient authors and sources.

AARAS	American Academy of Religion Academy Series
ABRL	Anchor Bible Reference Library
AGLB	Aus der Geschichte der lateinischen Bibel (cf. VL)
AJBI	*Annual of the Japanese Biblical Institute*
ANRW	*Aufstieg und Niedergang der römischen Welt*
ANTF	Arbeiten zur neutestamentlichen Textforschung
AThR	*Anglican Theological Review*
BETL	Bibliotheca ephemeridum theologicarum lovaniensium
BFChTh	Beiträge zur Förderung christlicher Theologie
BHT	Beiträge zur historischen Theologie
BJRL	*Bulletin of the John Rylands University Library of Manchester*
BJS	Brown Judaic Studies
BSS	Black Sea Studies
BZAW	Beiheft zur Zeitschrift für die alttestamentliche Wissenschaft
BZNW	Beiheft zur Zeitschrift für die neutestamentliche Wissenschaft
CBET	Contributions to Biblical Exegesis and Theology
CB.OT	Coniectanea biblica: Old Testament Series
CBQ	*Catholic Biblical Quarterly*
CC.SA	Corpus Christianorum Series Apocrypha
CC.SL	Corpus Christianorum Series Latina
ChHist	*Church History*
Class.Phil.	*Classical Philology*
CQ	*The Classical Quarterly*
CSCO	Corpus scriptorum christianorum orientalium
CSCO Script.Arm.	CSCO Scriptores Armeniaci
CSCO Script.Syr.	CSCO Scriptores Syriaci
EAA	Collection des Études augustiniennes. Série Antiquité
EC	*Early Christianity*

EPHE	*École pratique des hautes études*
EPROER	Études préliminaires aux religions orientales dans l'empire romain
Ét.Bib.	Études Bibliques
ETL	*Ephemerides theologicae lovanienses*
ETSE	Estonian Theological Society in Exile
FC	Fontes Christiani
FKD	Forschungen zur Kirchen- und Dogmengeschichte
FoC	Fathers of the Church
GO	Göttinger Orientforschungen
HTR	*Harvard Theological Review*
JbAC	Jahrbuch für Antike und Christentum
JBL	*Journal of Biblical Literature*
JECS	*Journal of Early Christian Studies*
JMEMS	*Journal of Medieval and Early Modern Studies*
JQR	*Jewish Quarterly Review*
JSJ	*Journal for the Study of Judaism*
JSNTSup.	Journal for the Study of the New Testament Supplement Series
JSQ	*Jewish Studies Quarterly*
JTS	*Journal of Theological Studies*
LHB	Library of the Hebrew Bible
LS	Lewis, Charlton T. and Charles Short, *A Latin Dictionary* (Oxford: Clarendon Press, 1966)
LSJ	Liddell, H. G. R., R. Scott, and H. S. Jones, *A Greek-English Lexicon* (9th ed. Oxford: Clarendon Press, 1940)
Mnem.Sup.	Mnemosyne, Bibliotheca Classica Batava, Supplementum
NA27	Novum Testamentum Graece, post Eberhard and Edwin Nestle, 27th revised edition, ed. Barbara and Kurt Aland, Johannes Karavidopoulos, Carlo M. Martini, and Bruce M. Metzger (Stuttgart: Deutsche Bibelgesellschaft, 1898/ 1993)
NAPSPMS	North American Patristics Society Patristic Monograph Series
NGWGPh	Nachrichten von der Gesellschaft der Wissenschaft zu Göttingen. Philologisch-historische Klasse
NHMS	Nag Hammadi and Manichaean Studies
NHS	Nag Hammadi Studies
NovT	*Novum Testamentum*
NovTSup.	Novum Testamentum Supplements
NTOA	Novum Testamentum et Orbis Antiquus
NTS	*New Testament Studies*
NTT	*Nederlands Theologisch Tijdschrift*
NTTS	New Testament Tools and Studies
OCA	Orientalia Christiana Analecta
OCP	*Orientalia Christiana Periodica*
OECS	Oxford Early Christian Studies
OECT	Oxford Early Christian Texts
OGIS	*Orientis graeci inscriptions selectae*, ed. W. Dittenberger

OLA	Orientalia Lovaniensia Analecta
OrChr	*Oriens christianus*
OTS	Old Testament Studies
PG	Patrologia Graeca, ed. J.-P. Migne
PGL	Lampe, G. W. H., ed., *A Patristic Greek Lexicon* (Oxford: Clarendon Press, 1961)
Ph.Ant.	Philosophia Antiqua
PIRSB	Publications de l'Institut romand des sciences bibliques
PMS	Patristic Monograph Studies
PO	Patrologia Orientalis
PTS	Patristische Texte und Studien
PW	Pauly, A. F., *Paulys Realencyclopädie der classischen Altertumswissenschaft*, new edn; G. Wissowa (Stuttgart: Metzler, 1890–)
RAC	*Reallexikon für Antike und Christentum*, ed. T. Klauser et. al. (Stuttgart: Hiersemann, 1950–)
REAug	*Revue des études augustiniennes*
Rech.Aug.	*Recherches augistiniennes*
Rev.Bib.	*Revue Biblique*
RHPhR	*Revue d'Histoire et de Philosophie Religeuse*
RS	Religion and Society
RSR	*Recherches de science religieuse*
RThPh	*Revue de Théologie et Philosophie*
SAIS	Studies in the Aramaic Interpretation of Scripture
SBL	Society of Biblical Literature
SC	Sources Chrétiennes
SHCT	Studies in the History of Christian Traditions
SJLA	Studies in Judaism in Late Antiquity
SJSHR	Studien zu den Jüdischen Schriften aus Hellenistisch-Römischer Zeit
SNTSMS	Society for New Testament Studies Monograph Series
STAC	Studien und Texte zu Antike Christentum
Stud.Phil.Ann.	*Studia Philonica Annual*
SVTP	Studia in Veteris Testamenti Pseudepigrapha
TBN	Themes in Biblical Narratives
TENTS	Texts and Editions for New Testament Study
ThR	*Theologische Rundschau*
TRE	*Theologische Realenzyklopädie*
TSAJ	Textes and Studies in Ancient Judaism
TU	Texte und Untersuchungen zur Geschichte der altchristlichen Literatur
VC	*Vigiliae Christianae*
VCSup.	Supplements to Vigiliae Christianae
VL	Vetus Latina: Die Reste der altlateinischen Bibel
VTSup.	Supplements to Vetus Testamentum
WF	Wege der Forschung

WUNT	Wissenschaftliche Untersuchungen zum Neuen Testament
ZAC	*Zeitschrift für Antikes Christentum*
ZKG	*Zeitschrift für Kirchengeschichte*
ZKT	*Zeitschrift für katholische Theologie*
ZNW	*Zeitschrift für die neutestamentliche Wissenschaft und die Kunde der älteren Kirche*
ZThK	*Zeitschrift für Theologie und Kirche*

1

Introduction

It is the retrospective view that identifies the most formative moments of the past, the individuals, ideas, movements and events. Different moments, therefore, will attract attention as the point from which the viewer looks back itself moves. In recent years, the second century has emerged as decisive for the shaping of what would become the Christian Church. It is no longer seen as the period of the incubation of later institutions or when the fronts against threatening opposition from the familiar triumvirate of Judaism, paganism, and heresy were secured. Instead, it appears as a time rich in discontinuities, when straightforward development is difficult to trace or to predict, and as a time of experimentation, when ideas, structures, and patterns of behaviour are being explored. As yet, there are few securely established boundaries, even though, in one of the many contradictions characteristic of the period, a sense of sharp differentiation is being widely evoked in the literature. Among the key figures who people this landscape of opportunity or, perhaps, who are prominent in this journey of exploration stands Marcion.

MARCION IN RECENT IMAGINATION

It is not only within this new appreciation of the second century that Marcion has found a place. His significance has long been recognised; the person who did most to promote him in the modern period – and in whose shadow almost all subsequent accounts lie – was Adolf von Harnack. Harnack's earliest prize-winning publication, written before he was twenty, hailed Marcion as 'the modern believer, the first reformer'.[1] Nearly sixty

1 Adolf von Harnack, *Marcion. Der Moderne Glaübige des 2. Jahrhunderts, der erste Reformator, Die Dorpater Preisschrift* (1870) (ed. Friedemann Steck; TU 149; Berlin: de Gruyter,

years later, in a posthumously published article, he claimed that whereas on the whole a modern psychology cannot hope to truly understand the religious phenomena of the distant past, 'with Marcion that is not the case'; defending his patronage of Marcion to the last, he challenged contemporary systematic theologians: 'The most minor servant of Jesus Christ, who preaches exclusively the fatherhood of God and the forgiveness of sins, proclaims with this preaching the message of the Gospel, while the theologian with his weighty, complex and sophisticated language about God, even if he appeals to Paul, Luther and Calvin, stands in serious danger of obscuring and limiting the Gospel.'[2]

However, for Harnack, Marcion had a more immediate historical impact: He was to be credited as the first to conceive 'the idea of placing Christendom on the firm foundation of a definite theory of what is Christian', and of 'establishing this theory by a fixed collection of Christian writings with canonical authority'.[3] Marcion was the first to adopt a serious historical-critical analysis of earlier Christian tradition and thus to make possible any subsequent historical understanding of the period as well as of his own undertaking. Moreover, 'he was a man with an organising talent, such as has no peer in the early Church', and he established churches of his own, marked by their canon, by their 'fixed but free organisation', and by their strict discipline, long before the Catholic Church achieved any such solidity. Forced to defend itself against Marcion, the Catholic Church had to develop measures which in fact it had learned from Marcion himself, thus inspiring the subtitle of Harnack's most fundamental work, 'a Monograph on the History of the Foundation of the Catholic Church': These were a 'New Testament' made up of Gospel and Apostle, a formulation of teaching which could be protected from external influences or subjective interpretation, a way of understanding the place of the Old Testament and of reading it, as well as structures, discipline, and authority.[4]

2003). On the importance of Marcion for Harnack, see Wolfram Kinzig, *Harnack, Marcion und das Judentum. Nebst einer Kommentierten Edition des Briefwechsels Adolf von Harnacks mit Houston Stewart Chamberlain* (Arbeiten zu Kirchen- und Theologiegeschichte 13; Leipzig; Evangelische Verlagsanstelt, 2004).

2 Adolf von Harnack, 'Die Neuheit des Evangeliums nach Marcion [1929]', ed. Axel von Harnack, *Aus der Werkstatt des Vollendeten* (Giessen: Topelmann, 1930), 128–43, 143. The irony of the final words is that Harnack repeatedly compared Marcion to Luther.

3 On this and what follows, see Adolf von Harnack, *History of Dogma* 1 (trsl. from the 3rd German edn; Neil Buchanon; London: Williams and Norgate, 1894), 277–84.

4 Adolf von Harnack, *Marcion: das Evangelium vom Fremden Gott; eine Monographie zur Geschichte der Gundlegung der katholischen Kirche* (2nd corrected edn printed with *Neue Studien zu Marcion*; TU 45; Leipzig: Hinrichs, 1924), 209–15.

Certainly, elements and emphases in Harnack's account of Marcion changed in emphasis or nuance during his long engagement with him, and this was equally true of his core perception that Marcion's single starting point was Paul and Paul's proclamation of what is new in Christ (cf. 2 Cor. 5.17).[5] One dictum, however, is often (mis-)quoted as belonging to the essence of Harnack's portrayal: 'Marcion was the only Gentile Christian who understood Paul, and even he misunderstood him.'[6] The context of this statement, routinely ignored, is that Paul's theology was specific to Paul's own context and that it depended on the Old Testament or Judaism in a way that subsequent interpreters, especially Gentile Christians (such as Marcion was), could not hope to understand. Thus, for Harnack, Marcion was proof of the repeated need to 'reconstruct' Paulinism if it was still to inspire the Church.[7] Yet it is his account of Marcion's religious experience of the goodness and mercy of God, and of his 'opposition of faith and works, Gospel and Law', as the driving forces of his 'reforming', most fully set out in the significantly entitled *Marcion: The Gospel of the Stranger God*, that has done most to fix the reputation of the Marcion recovered by Harnack as a radical disciple of Paul.[8]

Although Harnack was reacting to earlier accounts of Marcion, as his prize-winning essay demonstrated, it is his work and, in particular, this last-named detailed comprehensive account that has shaped all subsequent studies. The continuing fascination with Marcion, 'without a doubt one of the most interesting and important figures of church history of the second century', is a fascination with the Marcion whose portrait Harnack drew and redrew across his career.[9] Even overt attempts to offer a new approach almost inevitably find themselves formulating the key questions in terms defined by his judgements.[10] These include, firstly, whether Marcion indeed can be

5 This is much more muted in *Der Moderne Glaübige*, 17, 128–30, than in 'Die Neuheit'.

6 *History of Dogma* 1, 89; quotations frequently omit or fail to realise the importance of the epithet 'Gentile Christian'.

7 *History of Dogma* 1, 282–4.

8 See Harnack, *Marcion*, 198–209, where he argues that Paul would in part have recognised Marcion as a genuine disciple but would have repulsed him in horror. For the translation 'Stranger', see below, pp. 328–30; this is preferred to 'alien' as translated by John E. Steeley and Lyle Bierma, *Marcion. The Gospel of the Alien God* (Durham, NC: Labyrinth Press, 1990) (which does not include the vital appendices of the original).

9 The quotation is from Wilhelm Schneemelcher, 'Paulus in der griechischen Kirche des zweiten Jahrhunderts', *ZKG* 75 (1964), 1–20, 10.

10 Gerhard May, 'Marcion ohne Marcion', ed. Gerhard May and Katharina Greschat, with Martin Meiser, *Marcion und seine kirchengeschichtliche Wirkung/[Marcion and His Impact on Church History]*: Vorträge der Internationalen Fachkonferenz zu Marcion gehalten vom 15.-18. August 2001 in Mainz (TU 150; Berlin: de Gruyter, 2002), 1–7; David L. Balás,

understood independently of his historical context and can be celebrated for his grasp of an essential religious idea or insight, namely as 'one of the world's great religious geniuses', as some interpreters, then and since, have done.[11]

Similar, although set within a very different confessional framework, is the debate whether Marcion can be described as a genuine disciple of Paul and as truly grasping the heart of Pauline theology, understood as 'Gospel versus Law' or as the Gospel of God's free grace – whether or not Harnack's cautions about Paul's untranslate-ability are heeded.[12] An affirmative assessment may take the form of a historical judgement about Marcion's primary inspiration, locating him within a 'radical anti-Jewish Paulinism' of the educated circles, opposing the 'catholic law-Christianity of naïve conservative communities' of the second century.[13] It may also be more consciously value-driven, implying a negative judgement on the theological trends of the post-apostolic period or on their echoes in subsequent Church history;[14] to this end, Marcion has been described as belonging to the '"logical and consistent" Paulinists who cannot call on a native Jewishness to save them from the quicksand of one-sided romanticism' or even as having instigated the 'first "protestant" schism'.[15]

Harnack was adamant that Marcion's message was fundamentally a 'biblical theology' and that he had no truck with 'the wisdom of the mysteries or with any philosophy';[16] but on this point no consensus has

'Marcion Revisited: A "Post-Harnack" Perspective', ed. W. Eugene March, *Texts and Testaments. Critical Essays on the Bible and Early Church Fathers. A Volume in Honour of Stuart Dickson Currie* (San Antonio, TX: Trinity University Press, 1980), 96–108.

11 Pierre Louis Couchoud, *The Creation of Christ: An Outline of the Beginning of Christianity* (2 vols.; ET. C. Bradlaugh Bonner; London: Watts, 1939), I, 124, who goes on to draw a contrast between Marcion's exalted if almost unachievable understanding and 'average Christianity'.

12 John W. Marshall, 'Misunderstanding the New Paul: Marcion's Transformation of the *Sonderzeit* Paul', *JECS* 20 (2012), 1–29, attempts to set the 'new perspective' on Paul and Marcion's account (largely dependent on Tertullian) in dialogue with each other as an exercise in exploring the nature of reception.

13 Hermann Langerbeck, 'Zur Auseinandersetzung von Theologie und Gemeindeglauben in der römischen Gemeinde in den Jahren 135–65', *Aufsätze zur Gnosis. Aus dem Nachlaß herausgegeben von Hermann Dörries* (AAWG Phil-hist. 3.69; Göttingen: Vandenhoeck & Ruprecht, 1967), 167–79, 173–5.

14 P. G. Verweijs, *Evangelium und neues Gesetz in der ältesten Christenheit bis auf Marcion* (Studia Theologica Rheno-Traiectina 5; Utrecht: Kemink, 1960), 349, argues that the importance of the Gospel and apostolic authority was recognised by the earliest Church but indeed lost in the post-apostolic period.

15 J. Louis Martyn, *Theological Issues in the Letters of Paul* (Edinburgh: T&T Clark, 1997), 58; Edwin C. Blackman, *Marcion and His Influence* (London: SPCK, 1948), 3.

16 Harnack, *Marcion*, 93; cf. idem, *History of Dogma*, 285, 'One thing they [the Church Fathers] could not learn from him … was how to make Christianity into a philosophical system'.

been reached, and others have located Marcion firmly 'under the spell of the God of philosophy' or at least as driven first and foremost by the challenges of a philosophical understanding of God and the world.[17] More complex has been whether to describe Marcion as a gnostic or to trace a historical relationship between his ideas and those of 'gnosticism', a debate which has been refigured as definitions of gnosticism itself have been reconceived, particularly in the wake of the discovery of the Nag Hammadi texts more than two decades after Harnack's death.[18]

A further arena of controversy has been over Marcion's historical significance. Did he indeed have a major, if not unparalleled, influence on subsequent Church doctrine, on the canon, and on ecclesial structures? Few would go so far as an unqualified affirmation; more common has been a carefully balanced attempt to question whether he had any 'direct influence on the development of the doctrine of the Great Church' while still acknowledging his considerable significance for the second century.[19] Here, still, however, it remains contested whether Marcion merely crystallised what was perhaps already inevitable, either forcing into the open the 'latent crisis of the Church' or prompting the consolidation of structures that were then in their infancy or still unstable.[20] Perhaps most important here has been whether Marcion instigated the idea of a 'canon' through his selection of a Gospel and apostolic corpus and whether he provoked the Church into its own, somewhat expanded, alternative.[21]

17 E. P. Meijering, *Tertullian contra Marcion: Gotteslehre in der Polemik Adversus Marcionem I–II* (Philosophia Patrum 3. Leiden: Brill, 1977), 160–8; Jörg Woltmann, 'Der Geschichtliche Hintergrund der Lehre Markions vom "Fremden Gott"', ed. Ernst C. Suttner and Coelestin Patock, *Wegzeichen: Festgabe zum 60. Geburtstag von Prof. Dr. Hermengild M. Biedermann, O.S.A.* (Das Östliche Christentum NF 25; Würzburg: Augustinus-Verlag, 1971), 15–42.

18 Ugo Bianchi, 'Marcion: Theologien biblique ou docteur gnostique', *VC* 21 (1967), 141–9; see also Barbara Aland, 'Marcion: Versuch einer Neuen Interpretation', *Was ist Gnosis? Studien zum frühen Christentum, zu Marcion, und zur kaiserzeitlichen Philosophie* (WUNT 239; Tübingen: Mohr Siebeck, 2009), 291–317 (= *ZThK* 70 [1973], 420–47), 300–16.

19 Aland, 'Marcion', 307.

20 The first quotation is from Gerhard May, 'Markion in seiner Zeit', ed. Katharina Greschat and Martin Meiser, *Gerhard May: Markion. Gesammelte Aufsätze* (Veröffentlichungen des Instituts für Europäische Geschichte Mainz 68; Mainz: Philipp von Zabern, 2005), 1–12, 11, referring to tension between the scriptural view of God and that of Greek contemporaries, and the variety of norms. For the second, see, for example, Alain Le Boulluec, 'Le Problème de l'extension du canon des Écritures aux premiers siècles', *RSR* 92 (2004), 45–87, 58–71, on Marcion's impact on the language and idea of an authoritative Gospel.

21 This is argued in John Knox, *Marcion and the New Testament: An Essay in the Early History of the Canon* (Chicago: University of Chicago Press, 1942), and has been taken up by many since.

These last debates have enjoyed renewed energy in recent decades. Through them, the classic model of heresy as a deviation from and a distortion of the original truth of the Gospel and of the unity of its articulation becomes open to scrutiny, to demonstration, or to fatal challenge, if not inversion. Indeed, Marcion and the history of his movement might seem to be a model of the debate over 'orthodoxy and heresy' sparked off by Walter Bauer and of its heirs in contemporary celebrations of the diversity of early Christianity.[22] Over against Harnack's 'first reformer' – on the assumption that such a role is to be positively understood – stands the 'arch-heretic'.[23]

Inevitably, such debates again bring Marcion out of his second-century context and invite assessment of his continuing significance. This indeed was why Harnack's work prompted such heated responses – one such protesting 'His strength did not lie in his character as a metaphysician or a prophet ... he was a man of action and a leader.... His Bible was a mutilated one; his theology was weak and inconsistent, and nevertheless this new sect started with tremendous energy, set out to conquer the world, and engaged in a fierce war against the Church.'[24] Most importantly, Marcion has come to be associated in particular with giving voice to the enduring and deep-seated 'question of the Old Testament' for Christian thought. Some have attributed the anti-Jewishness of much Christian theology to the convoluted efforts of the Church to retain some role for the Old Testament and a way of reading it in conscious response to Marcion's supposed rejection of it; others have recalled Harnack's own conclusion that while the preservation of the Old Testament may have been right in the second century and inevitable in the sixteenth, in the nineteenth it was 'the consequence of a religious and ecclesiastical paralysis'.[25] Since then, Marcion has retained his role as a vehicle through which the issue can be repeated, and the older solutions can even be declared no longer viable.[26]

22 Walter Bauer, *Orthodoxy and Heresy in Earliest Christianity* (ET ed. from the 2nd German edn by Robert Kraft and Gerhard Krodel; Philadelphia: Fortress Press, 1971).

23 Sebastian Moll, *The Arch-Heretic Marcion* (WUNT 250; Tübingen: Mohr Siebeck, 2010), describes Marcion as 'the first actual outcast from the Church' and the '*first actual heretic*' (p. 44; original italics).

24 J. Lebreton, *Gnosticism, Marcionism, and Manichaeism* (London: CTS, 1934), 18. That Marcion had skills as a church organiser is denied by Verweijs, *Evangelium und neues Gesetz*, 349.

25 Harnack, *Marcion*, 217.

26 Blackman, *Marcion and His Influence*, 123; Raymond Schwager, 'Der Gott des Alten Testaments und der Gott des Grekreuzigten: Eine Untersuchung zur Erlösungslehre bei Markion und Irenäus', *ZKTh* 102 (1980), 289–313, who argues that Irenaeus did not fully understand or satisfactorily address the insights of the shortcomings of the 'God of the Old Testament' and who takes recourse in the work of René Girard.

This exploration of Marcion's importance has been undertaken by means of a journey through the scholarship of the last century or more because the evidences of the impact that he made – in his immediate context and subsequently – are the only means of measuring that importance. We do not have available, either by direct transmission or by fortuitous discovery, any writings direct from Marcion's hand; he is glimpsed only through the lens of the words of others, who are for the most part engaged in an ever more heated and vigorous polemic against him. It is his shadow as much as his presence that determines the future. That this should be so is not surprising, for in one sense, any current investigation has to be content with a shadow: The Marcion who is encountered is the Marcion transmitted by those who wrote against him; possible echoes of an 'authentic' voice are always subject to testing by those cadences transmitted and probably distorted by his opponents. That the indicted Marcion is to be discovered far and wide is, as shall be seen, of little help, for the multiple voices of his opponents do not form a harmonious choir and their accounts do not always paint the same picture.

WHOSE MARCION?

As has already been indicated, the sources for Marcion and for his teaching come almost exclusively from those who opposed them. In what follows, the most significant of these shall be explored: the initial notices by Justin Martyr, the only near-contemporary of Marcion whose comments survive; Irenaeus, writing perhaps within twenty or thirty years of his death; and Tertullian, who represents the most extensive and systematic engagement with what he understood Marcion to teach, albeit now in Latin dress. With these figures, a tradition is established, but this does not prevent other writers from shaping new pictures of Marcion – whether or not these are founded on independent sources. Moving from the second to the third century, Clement of Alexandria, Origen, Hippolytus, and the author of the *Refutation of All Heresies* are the most important and witness to an expanding geographical spread. In the fourth century, Epiphanius included a long chapter on Marcion in his compendious 'medicine chest' (*Panarion*) against heresies, which was to have a decisive influence on the continuing heresiological tradition of the Church. Perhaps earlier than him but difficult to place is the anonymous *Dialogue of Adamantius* which includes among its protagonists two Marcionites as well as two followers of Valentinus and a follower of Bardaisan of Edessa. The last-named points to an eastern setting; Marcion undoubtedly did have a lasting and extensive influence in

Syriac-speaking areas. Ephraem combines Marcion with Bardaisan and with Mani in his polemics, reflecting a period when the character of the dominant form of Christianity in the region was still hotly contested; his rich poetry, together with his prose writings, paints a distinctive picture of that influence as well as of Marcion's system. Soon after him, Eznik of Kolb is forced to differentiate between their and 'our' 'covenanters', while even in the fifth century, Theodoret of Cyr still speaks of whole villages that he identifies as 'Marcionite'. Indeed, the influence of Marcion's thought can be traced further into Armenian and Arabic sources, as well as, perhaps, nourishing a new and successful religious movement: Manichaeism.

For the most part, however, this survey will finish in the fourth century. In part, this time limit can be justified by the assumption that new memories of the 'historical Marcion' are unlikely to appear thereafter; in part, it reflects the evident fact that while authentic references to Marcionite communities continue, independent accounts of their beliefs dwindle. However, the former reason is misleading if it suggests that those earlier writers are a transparent source of trustworthy memories. Study of the antiheretical literature of the early Church reveals the deceptiveness of its apparently straightforward accounts of individuals and their systems; merely to paraphrase their reports, often after collecting and harmonising them – as sometimes still happens – is wildly misleading. It was not the task of polemicists to give an unbiased account of the ideas and practices of those against whom they wished to warn their audience – at least not in this period. As shall be seen, the distinctive tradition of the description of groups deemed heretical has long roots before Epiphanius – perhaps originating with Justin Martyr himself. Within that tradition, an armoury of weapons and strategies quickly evolves; the purpose of these is to create and to present as self-evident and as incontrovertible the boundaries between 'right belief' and that being opposed, to confirm and strengthen the former far more than to refute the latter by any exercise of logic, to identify as 'outside' and as genetically illegitimate all opposing ideas, to give some explanation of their existence and origin, and to reinforce the picture of an unbroken tradition of 'right belief' and of the people and institutions which uphold it. These strategies are consistently adopted but are also adapted, as those who deploy them seek to meet their own needs and often to address issues within their own context. Meanwhile, outside this heresiological tradition, polemic against alternative views may be used to buttress the development of an exegetical argument or to help address a theological or philosophical problem, although these goals do not necessarily foster a more accurate presentation. The Marcion of Irenaeus and of Tertullian, as of Clement of

Alexandria or of Origen, has to be located within the framework of the different overarching theological templates with which each of them works.

Any picture of Marcion relies, inevitably, on those works against him that did survive. Yet in addition to these were numerous others who, at least as reported chiefly by Eusebius, did write against him but whose efforts are lost and, in many cases, were already lost in Eusebius' own time.[27] Justin Martyr himself is credited with such a compilation either against Marcion or against a wider group of 'heresies'; this and others, such as that attributed to Theophilus of Antioch, may have exercised considerable influence on their successors, although tracing such influence is a matter of guesswork. Their mere enumeration does, however, testify to the extent of influence exercised by Marcion's ideas and the concern these provoked – at least initially. In due course, however, citing Marcion as an arch-heretic may have become a standard topos, independent of any contemporary pressure; this situation is similar to the polemics 'against the Jews', which do not always prove the existence of any engagement with 'real Jews'.

What is evident in all this is that the Marcion who is met on the pages of his various opponents is a Marcion constructed by the rhetoric of each author. At the same time, through them, a tradition – or perhaps more than one – about Marcion becomes established and provides what subsequent writers 'know' about him, regardless of whether they also have access to any writings by him or by his followers, and even if they do have such, it cannot be assumed they will give them priority. Sensitivity to the strategies in use may encourage appropriate caution – a hermeneutic of suspicion – but it will not thereby ensure that the 'real Marcion' can be recovered. The Marcion who can be uncovered and described will necessarily be Irenaeus' Marcion, Tertullian's Marcion, Ephraem's Marcion....

MARCION IN HISTORY

It might be thought that to recover 'Irenaeus' Marcion' (and so on) is enough; after all, it was their perception of the implications of his teaching that inspired the responses that may (or may not) have led to the formation of a canon of Gospel and letters, to the idea of a New Testament alongside a preserved but interpreted Old Testament (and so on). Yet, if the effect of this is merely to reinscribe the developments that did ensue, little has been gained. The second century is fascinating because it was a period of

27 See Meike Willing, *Eusebius von Cäsarea als Häreseograph* (PTS 63; Berlin: de Gruyter, 2008), 188–203.

experimentation; as already noted, even if the terminology of 'heresy', if not yet 'orthodoxy', is beginning to be used in polemic and defence, it is inappropriate simply to reproduce it in any historical account and evaluation of the period. This is not only because there were no means of identifying and enforcing any such separation but also because the effort to view the period through a template of self-conscious and identifiable bounded groups distorts the actual fluidity that can be repeatedly encountered. Moreover, if some ideas, some patterns of life, and some structures did become marginalised, this may not have been because they were intrinsically flawed; neither, however, need it have been because it was only political power struggles that forced them out. Both such explanations can be and have been forwarded, but they suffer from the tendency to constrain the real complexities within rigid templates of preunderstanding. The recovery of those alternative patterns of belief and practice does not only enrich any understanding of the past, but it may also serve a fresh understanding of the present – as has been the case in studies of the representations of women and their roles. Sometimes, a clearer perception of the consequences of an excluded alternative may guide later decisions about whether to reinforce or to reconsider that alternative. It is the perceived pivotal role that Marcion has been accorded in the second century – whether as threat or as catalyst – that invites the attempt to recover his actual place therein, what he stood for, and whence he drew his inspiration. Thus, if Marcion is to make sense anywhere, it must be on the map of the second century; equally, without him, that map is incomplete.

MARCION AT THE CROSSROADS OF THE SECOND CENTURY

There are, therefore, two Marcions to recover or, rather, two stages in his recovery. First will be the Marcion who is offered by those who wrote against him. Each writer presents a different Marcion, although there are obvious continuities between them and, sometimes, literary dependence. It would be a mistake to conflate them into a single picture or to create an identikit image from chosen elements of each; to do so would suppose that what they offer are partial glimpses of the 'historical Marcion', which together, as if from independent witnesses, might create a reliable whole. Instead, it is their distinctive profiles that should attract our attention, shaped as they are by the lens of their separate authors' own concerns and perceptions of the Christian message. Identifying that lens does indeed make it possible to correct some of the distortion it creates. Equally, examining the impact Marcion has made on them may illuminate each author's own sensitivities and fears. These 'constructed' Marcions are worthy of consideration in their own right. Indeed, they present their own lens through which the emergence within early Christianity of the idea of 'heresy' and how it should be addressed can be scrutinised; here, Marcion does become the model of the construction of 'the heretic'.

The second Marcion emerges when the most marked characteristics of the profiles that have been discovered are set within the currents of the second century. Here, the questions implied and the answers ascribed to him can be compared with those already being asked or being given by others among his predecessors or his peers. Marcion could not have made the impact he undoubtedly did if his questions and his answers had not resonated among his hearers; neither would he have made that impact if he had had nothing more to offer than did many others. Hence, similarity and difference are to be expected. Discovering this Marcion draws on those profiles already sketched and yet inevitably entails a further level of selection and discrimination.

The metaphor of crossroads – and not necessarily of only one of these – is a reminder that the second century was a period of intersecting paths moving in different directions, with as yet no obvious main road or right direction. It also points to a number of recurring questions: What were the influences on Marcion – from within and from outside of the 'Christian' topography? Where had his journey started? From philosophy or from biblical (or Pauline) theology? And to where was it directed? How far did he react to existing currents? How far did he initiate new ones? Was his path a solitary one, or does it enable us to observe the tracks of others who followed it? Indeed, does his particular crossroads belong in the centre of the map through which all had to pass or is it a side road, the exploration of which demands a potentially interesting but unnecessary detour? These questions return to the more specific ones asked earlier in this introduction. The more impatient may be tempted to proceed directly to the final chapter in the hope of finding at least some answers, but to revert instead to the metaphor of a laboratory, it is the stages in the experiments that may most deserve consideration and scrutiny.

PART I

THE POLEMICAL MAKING OF MARCION THE HERETIC

2

The beginnings of the construction of a heretic: Justin Martyr

> Then a certain Marcion of Pontus (*Ponticus*), who is even now teaching those who are persuaded to acknowledge another God greater than the creator (demiurge: δημιουργός). In every race of humanity through the agency of demons he has caused many to utter blasphemies and to deny the maker (ποιητής) of all as God and to confess some other as being greater to have made greater things than him.
>
> Justin Martyr, *Apol.*, 26.5[1]

Justin Martyr not only represents the various strands of the conventional ecclesiastical representation of Marcion, but in many ways, he was probably their fountainhead. Although he appears to have been a contemporary of Marcion, Justin already presents the difficulties of recovery and interpretation that will characterise all subsequent constructions of Marcion.

THE MAN

Already in this, the earliest reference to Marcion (and apparently while still active[2]), he is being 'mythologised' – reconstructed to serve the interests of his portrayer, on whose description any subsequent account must rely.

1 See Eusebius, *HE* IV. 11.9, who, alongside other minor variants, omits the second 'greater things'; for this to make sense, 'to have made' would also need to be omitted – unless the translation 'he made them deny' is adopted: see Denis Minns and Paul Parvis, ed., with an introduction, translation, and commentary on the text, *Justin, Philosopher and Martyr: Apologies* (OECT; Oxford: Oxford University Press, 2009), 150–1, who also propose reading 'another greater than the demiurge God' (see n. 26 below). See also p. 336 below.

2 The stress on 'even now' marks a contrast to Simon, whom Justin dates to the reign of Claudius; there is no reason to conclude that Marcion had been active for a considerable period and was *still* teaching (as argued by R. Joseph Hoffmann, *Marcion: On the Restitution of Christianity* (AARAS, 46; Chico, CA: Scholars Press, 1984), 45; Harnack, *Marcion*, 27–8).

The context is provided by the demands of an apologetic: Justin is having to negotiate the similarities and the differences between pagan mythology and the claims Christians made about Jesus. The hostile and devious activities of wicked demons provide him with the single thread that will explain these and that will also absolve 'true' Christians from any discreditable charges brought against them (*Apol.* 5.2; 21.6; 23.3; 25.3). Here, Marcion comes third in the line of those who, after the ascension of Christ and propelled by demons, 'claimed themselves to be gods' and yet who avoided Roman persecution; preceding him are 'a certain Simon from Samaria' and 'a certain Menander, also from Samaria … who was a disciple of Simon', although, unlike them, Marcion is not accused of inviting divine honours or of engaging in magical practices to deceive his gullible adherents.

Later in his argument, Justin returns to the theme of the imitative work of the demons, again using Simon and Menander as his examples and claiming that the former was honoured in Rome itself as a god (56.1–4). It is, he asserts, these self-same demons who stir up the hatred which leads to Christians facing death, although the latter do this with steadfast hope. Presumably, it is these links that prompt him also to return to Marcion:

> As I have already said, the wicked demons put forward Marcion who came from Pontus, who even now teaches [people] to deny [as] God the maker of everything in heaven and earth and [as] his son the Christ proclaimed beforehand through the prophets, and announces a certain other alongside God the creator of all and similarly a different son. Many are persuaded by him as alone understanding the truth, and they mock us, although they have no proof for what they say, but irrationally, like sheep seized by a wolf, they are the prey of atheistic opinions and demons.
>
> (*Apol.* 58.1–2)

Justin presents us with Marcion the man, although already certain biographical 'facts', such as his Pontic (ποντικός) origin, are being put on the same plane as his demonic inspiration and his fulfilment of the well-rehearsed role of the ravaging wolf (cf. Matt. 7.15); soon he will become 'the Pontic wolf'.[3] This elision of neutral description and rhetorical image invites caution towards the emphasis on his success among 'every race of humanity': Simon was successful, according to Justin, mainly among his own country-people; Menander specifically in Antioch, although some followers were still to be found; Marcion's attraction was more extensive – perhaps, although Justin

[3] See Rhodon in Eusebius, *HE* V. 13.4.

does not make this explicit, because he was active in Rome where all peoples met. It would be over-credulous to assume from this that Marcion had already achieved a successful universal mission following a period of energetic preaching activity.[4]

'ALL HERESIES'

Marcion has also been placed here within a sequence that begins with Simon, who was probably already a legendary figure in Christian tradition, even if Justin was unaware of the specific form that takes in Acts 8. However, unlike Menander, Marcion is not said to be the disciple of his predecessor in the list; on the contrary, he is appended somewhat awkwardly to the earlier pair. Nonetheless, this model of a sequence will also have significant consequences in later thought; it overlaps with a further framework that Justin introduces. The first passage cited continues:

> All who stem from such, as we said, are called Christians, in the same way as those who do not share the same doctrines among[5] the philosophers share the common predicated label of philosophy. Whether they practice those discreditable myth-like acts, the overturning of a lamp and the unbridled mixing and consumption of human flesh, we do not know; but that they are not persecuted or put to death by you, at least for their doctrines, we are certain. We have a compilation against all the schools of thought ('heresies') that have come into being, which we shall give if you wish to have it.
>
> (*Apol.* 26.6–8)

Justin here picks up a discussion he had introduced earlier concerning those whose actions contradict their avowed principles, on which their claim to the name of 'philosophers' rested (*Apol.* 4.8–9; 7.1–5). This was a familiar contemporary philosophical topos, chosen no doubt as one that might be expected to appeal to an emperor whom he addressed as 'philosopher' (Marcus Aurelius). Particularly striking here is his concluding appeal to the 'compilation against all "schools" (σύνταγμα κατὰ πασῶν αἱρέσεων)' and the implication that Simon, Menander, and Marcion might be found among such. With this, Marcion is being brought into association with a vocabulary, 'heresy' (αἵρεσις), and with a sequence of 'doctrines' (δόγμα) in a way that will also be determinative for his future image.

[4] See n. 2 and pp. 293–98.

[5] Or 'with'; Minns and Parvis, *Justin*, 150, add ἐν to clarify.

The idea of such a compilation of doctrines is not new: Cicero's Epicurean contemporary, Philodemus, had composed an 'Ordering (σύνταξις) of the Philosophers', whose aim is widely agreed to have been to integrate Epicureanism in a markedly nonpolemical fashion within the conventional understanding of the history of Greek philosophy.[6] The language of '*hairesis*', which means 'choice', also belongs to the contemporary description of intellectual schools of thought – philosophical or medical; in such contexts, it is largely neutral with no negative overtones. Before Justin, the term had already been used by Philo, Acts, and Josephus to designate the chief schools of interpretation within the 'Jewish philosophy', without any sense of embarrassment of belonging to one such.[7] It may be still in this sense that, perhaps contemporaneous with Justin, Ptolemy refers to Judaism as 'the old *hairesis*' (Epiphanius, *Panarion* 33.5.7). The potential for criticising others for their 'choices' or because they unnecessarily multiplied options seems rarely to have been taken up, although Philo's dismissal of those 'school-belligerents' (αἱρεσιομάχοι) who refuse to examine the positions they hold hints at future developments (*De Vita Mosis* I. 5 [24]).[8] This was, however, to become the fundamental category for understanding and categorising variation in Christian belief and practice and αἵρεσις swiftly became a term of excoriation: 'heresy' – as already in Irenaeus' work *Against Heresies* (*AH*).[9] The creation of a succession of teachers also belongs to the model of the 'school'; although Justin does not use the technical language associated with this elsewhere and Marcion is not explicitly brought within that pattern, he subsequently would be.

Whether Justin's contribution to the Christian heresiological tradition was more than embryonic depends on the nature and extent of the 'Syntagma' to which he here refers. Although the expression 'we have' is somewhat imprecise, this work is widely identified with that from which Irenaeus

[6] The title is given by Diogenes Laertius, *Vitae Philosophorum*, X. 3. On this, see Diskin Clay, 'Philodemus on the Plain Speaking of the Other Philosophers', ed. John T. Fitzgerald, Dirk Obbink, Glenn S. Holland, *Philodemus and the New Testament World* (NovTSup., 109; Brill: Leiden, 2004), 54–71.

[7] Philo, *De Vita Contemp.*, 29; Acts 5.17; Josephus, *AJ* XIII. 5.9 [171]; *BJ* II. 8.14 [162].

[8] See also *Quaest.in Exod.*, frag 1 (ed. R. Marcus, *Philo Supplement II* [LCL; Cambridge, MA: Harvard, 1953], 258), where it is used alongside ἑτεροδοξία. On the development of *hairesis*, see David T. Runia, 'Philo of Alexandria and the Greek Hairesis-Model', *VC* 53 (1999), 117–47, who sets out the typology, emphasising the element of school *of thought* in contrast to any institutional form; he does argue that there are traces of a negative connotation developing in Philo (p. 127).

[9] On this and what follows, see Judith M. Lieu, 'Heresy and Scripture', ed. M. Lang, *Ein neues Geschlecht? Entwicklung des frühchristlichen Selbstbewusstseins* (Göttingen: Vandenhoeck & Ruprecht, 2013), 81–100.

quotes as 'Justin in the Syntagma to Marcion'; this more limited title, it is argued, would reflect the place of Marcion at the climax of Justin's account, which for Irenaeus no longer justified the title 'all heresies' (Irenaeus, *AH* IV. 6.2).[10] Much effort has gone into reconstructing Justin's 'Syntagma':[11] its contents have been deduced from later writers – the shadowy Hegesippus and in particular Irenaeus – who are assumed to have made heavy use of it, while its arguments have been discerned behind his other writings, particularly the *Dialogue With Trypho*, where purportedly it has been recycled to address new purposes. Those who are most confident of being able to reconstruct the shape and style of Justin's 'Syntagma' are most likely to credit him with the foundation of the Christian concept and delineation of 'heresy'.[12] On this account, it was Marcion who provided a provocation – if not *the* provocation – for the idea of heresy, the veritable 'arch-heretic', not as the progenitor of all others but as the one to undermine whom the language of heresy was construed.

Attractive, though, in its simplicity as such an account might be, there are considerable difficulties in reconstructing Justin's 'Syntagma' and in crediting him with so formative a role; even Irenaeus refers to Justin only twice. Justin's surviving works make little use of the vocabulary and themes, particularly of succession, which will be so characteristic of his supposed heirs. '*Hairesis*' itself does not reappear in the *Apology*, while in the *Dialogue*, it is largely limited to Jewish contexts, including in supposed Jewish reports about the apostolic mission, which go little beyond the conventional meaning (*Dial.* 17.1; 62.3; 108.2), as well as to dominical prophecies of what would happen before the parousia (35.3; 51.2). The closest that Justin comes to formulating a negative account of '*hairesis*' is when he finds himself driven to acknowledge differences even among Christians 'of pure and pious opinion' regarding the rebuilding of Jerusalem for Christ's earthly reign (*Dial.* 80). These he distinguishes from those who claim to be Christians

10 Eusebius, who only knows of the 'Syntagma' from the references in Justin and Irenaeus, repeats this quotation or the opening phrase of it: 'I would not have believed the Lord himself if he proclaimed another God than the demiurge' (*HE* IV. 18.9). It is difficult to determine in the lines that follow whether Irenaeus continues to quote from Justin or adds his own elaboration. A further quotation from Justin by Irenaeus in *AH* V. 26.3 (= Eusebius, *HE* IV. 18.9) may also come from the 'Syntagma'.

11 See p. 30, and n. 11. See Pierre Prigent, *Justin et l'Ancien Testament* (Ét.Bib.; Paris: Libraire Lecoffre, 1964), 332–36; Enrico Norelli, 'Que pouvons-nous reconstituer du *Syntagma* contre les hérésies de Justin?', *RThPh* 139 (2007), 167–81.

12 So, most influentially, Alain Le Boulluec, *La notion d'hérésie dans la littérature grecque, IIe-IIIe Siècles* (2 vols. Paris: Études Augustiniennes, 1985), I, 36–91.

but who 'are atheistic and impious partisans (αἱρεσιώτης)'.[13] In particular, if Trypho should encounter those who

> are called Christians but … dare to blaspheme the God of Abraham and the God of Isaac and the God of Jacob, and who say there is no resurrection of the dead, but that at death their souls are taken up into heaven he should not consider them to be Christians, just as no-one would acknowledge as being Jews, if one were to interpret correctly, Sadducees or similar sects (αἱρέσεις) of Genistai and Meristai and Galilaeans and Hellelians and Pharisee(s and) Baptists[14] who are called Jews and children of Abraham but honour God with their lips …
>
> (*Dial.* 80.4).

Yet, despite having acknowledged that some of 'pure and pious opinion (γνώμη)' might disagree, he closes by asserting that 'any Christians who are in every respect of right opinion (ὀρθογνώμων)'[15] share his own convictions. Justin is treading carefully among variations in belief that might or might not properly cause necessary division and he may have at least one eye on those readers who would find themselves among the 'pure and pious' but not the 'right-minded'. On the other hand, unlike some later writers,[16] Justin nowhere suggests that the Jewish 'sects' are the source of the 'partisans', whom he totally rejects.

Whereas in the *Apology* it was in the face of persecution that Justin found himself having to address apparently internal variety in belief and practice, in the *Dialogue*, a new context, clearly differentiating 'you' Jews from 'us' Christians, forced him to reconsider the question, sharply distinguishing between permissible variation from what was impermissible. When Justin asserts that the superiority of Christianity is demonstrated when converts from the Gentiles face death rather than either worship idols or eat food sacrificed to them, Trypho protests that many who confess Jesus and who are called Christian do claim the right to eat such food (*Dial.* 34.8); Justin's rapid defence is that these merely fulfil Jesus' own predictions of the coming of false Christs and that they in no way undermine the greater faithfulness

13 Compare Philo's negative use of '*hairesiomachoi*' (n. 8); cf. Runia, 'Greek Hairesis-Model', 125–6.

14 Textual emendation would produce two groups here and an overall total of seven.

15 Found only here in Justin and rare elsewhere.

16 So perhaps already Hegesippus (see p. 27 and n. 2); Hegesippus lists the 'different opinions among the circumcision among the sons of Israel against the tribe of Judah and the Christ, Essenes, Galileans, Hemerobaptists, Masbotheans, Samaritans, Sadducees, Pharisees' (Eusebius, *HE* IV. 22.7).

and steadfastness of those whom he calls 'us'. He illustrates this initially by a general reference to those who teach others to say and do godless and blasphemous things, and he then continues:

> Others in a different manner teach (people) to blaspheme the maker of all, and the Christ who was prophesied by him as to come and the God of Abraham, Isaac, and Jacob.[17] We have nothing in common with them, but recognise them as godless and impious, wicked and lawless, and that instead of worshipping Jesus they confess him in name alone. They say they are Christians, but in the same manner as those among the Gentiles who engrave the name of God on things made by human hands and who participate in lawless and godless mysteries. Among them are some called Marcians,[18] others Valentinians, others Basilidians, others Satornilians, and others by another name, each named from the founder of their opinion, in the same way as each of those who are considered to practice philosophy, as I said in the beginning, is said to bear the name of the philosophy which they exercise from the father of the argument.
>
> (*Dial.* 35.5–6)[19]

Although this may seem to parallel the appeal to philosophical schools that Justin had made in the *Apology*, his approach here is different. In the opening chapters of the *Dialogue*, describing his journey through the 'classic' schools, he had argued that there was an original truth, knowledge of which and the search for which later successors had lost; these groups, not only the Platonists and the Pythagoreans but also the Stoics and the Peripatetics, were not all named after 'the father of the argument' (*Dial.* 2.1–2). Here, by contrast, the groups he condemns do not have and have never had any claim to the truth and their real equivalents are pagan idolaters. Justin's primary purpose is to deny that any of them could claim Jesus Christ as founder or as father; he reinforces this point by the form their names take – not Christ*ians* but Marc*ians*, Valentin*ians*, Basilid*ians*, Satornil*ians* – undoubtedly his own invention because on his own account, they said they

[17] On the text, see n. 27. [18] On the text here, see nn. 19, 22.

[19] Attention is often drawn to the parallel with Hegesippus in Eusebius, *HE* IV. 22.5: 'From these Menandrianists and Marcianists and Carpocratians and Valentinians and Basilidians and Satornilians'. Hence, some editors add after 'Marcians' 'and Carpocratians': so Pierre Nautin, 'Patristique et Histoires des Dogmes: 1. Le Livre Justin Contre les Hérésies', *EPHE* V^{e}Section, 90 (1981–2), 335–7; Miroslav Marcovich, ed., *Iustini Martyris Dialogus cum Trypho* (PTS, 47; Berlin: de Gruyter, 1997), 129. On the relationship, see also Le Boulluec, *La notion*, 92–105; however, Justin does not refer to Simon and Menander here as does Hegesippus. See p. 27.

were 'Christians'. However, despite asserting that 'they are called by us by the name of men' (35.4), he fails to name these true founders.[20] The last three are easily identified, and it is widely assumed that the first of these would have been Marcion, whose danger in Justin's eyes would be underlined as the only one also to have featured in the *Apology*.[21] However, this should have produced 'Marcionianoi' or, better, 'Marcio(a)nistai', which has been proposed as an emendation here, although it would have undermined his schema.[22] Marcus and his followers would be an alternative possibility, although Epiphanius calls them 'Marcosioi' (Irenaeus, *AH* I. 13–16; Epiphanius, *Pan.* 34); in that case, Marcion would disappear, at least by name, from the *Dialogue* – as would part of the case for this list providing the source of all later hersiological catalogues.[23]

This need not cause any surprise; although Justin refers back to the *Apologies* and, indeed, specifically to Simon, the latter is now presented only as a '*magus*' who deceived people: Justin makes no reference either to demonic activity, to Simon's Christian pretensions, or to Menander, his follower, in the *Apology* (*Dial.* 120.6). Even though he often refers to those who 'utter blasphemies', he routinely leaves them anonymous. All this, together with his failure to make any further reference to his 'Syntagma', makes it unlikely that the latter lies behind extended portions of the *Dialogue*.[24] Therefore, what form the 'Syntagma' took and what sort of material and arguments it contained must remain in the field of speculation. At most, the passages from the *Dialogue* already discussed may suggest that for him, 'all "heresies"' would include Jewish schools of thought and also, perhaps, given the broader context of the reference in the *Apology*, Greek philosophical ones, although he does not use the term of these.[25]

20 For the term ἀρχηγέτης, see Philo on the Therapeutai (*De Vita Contemp.*, 29).

21 Contrast the absence of Valentinus, a Roman contemporary, from the *Apology*, which is sometimes taken as evidence that Justin saw in him less of a danger; see p. 305.

22 See Marcovich, *Iustini Martyris Dialogus*, 129, n. at *Dial.* 35.6; compare Hegesippus. (See n. 19.)

23 See nn. 11, 12.

24 At *Dial.* 80.3, Justin offers to draw up for Trypho a '*syntaxis*' of his arguments; Prigent, *Justin et l'Ancient Testament*, 67, takes this as a reference to a new section of the 'Syntagma', to be identified with the treatise *On the Resurrection*, which, contrary to the consensus, he holds to be authentic. Philippe Bobichon, ed., *Justin Martyr, Dialogue avec Tryphon* (Fribourg: Academic Press Fribourg, 2003) II, 787, identifies it as a reference to the 'Syntagma' stemming from Justin's earlier notes.

25 Even Joannes Kunze, *De Historiae Gnosticismi Fontibus: Novae Quaestiones Criticae* (Lipsiae: Dörffling & Francke, 1894), who minimises the influence of Justin's 'Syntagma', suggests that the latter probably included the Jewish sects together with the three of the *Apology* (pp. 36–8).

Nonetheless, what Justin does mark is a stage in which the label 'Christians', perhaps itself a term of reproach or mockery by outsiders, becomes the subject of internal contestation. Here, the rhetoric of labelling 'others', particularly where those involved may not have recognised their 'otherness', does not only serve to create boundaries against 'outsiders', but it may also address internal anxieties and divisions – perhaps seeking to enforce unity in the face of a perceived common danger, where previously diversity had posed no problems. Justin does not speak of 'orthodoxy', although he does represent a stage in the development of the idea and of its functions. How far it was Marcion who helped provoke him to do this is, however, far from clear.

TEACHING ANOTHER GOD

Justin's sketch in the *Apology* of Marcion as teaching a certain other (ἄλλος τις) ('God' is understood) 'greater than the maker'[26] and perhaps also a different Son alongside the one belonging to the creator will provide the secure hallmarks of Marcion in subsequent representations. In the passages quoted earlier from *Dialogue* 35, such teaching becomes more generally assigned to all these 'godless and impious, wicked and lawless' 'partisans'. That may serve Justin's rhetoric of differentiation, but a tendency to treat all 'deviants' as holding the same fundamental principles and to gloss over any actual differences will itself become a recurring feature of later polemic. In the *Dialogue*, however, the one whom they deride is further identified; unlike the *Apology*, they specifically 'blaspheme' 'the God of Abraham, Isaac, and Jacob'. Recalling the divine self-identification in Exodus 3.2–4, this might seem appropriate to the broader context of Justin's debate with Trypho. However, Justin's rhetorical strategy is more complex than this alone might suggest. Firstly, for Justin, these words from the burning bush were spoken not by God the Creator and Father but by the pre-existent Son (*Dial.* 59–60; cf. *Apol.* 63.11–17). On one level, Justin might be indicating that it was this pre-existent Son – and not, as usually claimed, 'the God of the "Old Testament"' – whom Marcion derided.[27] However, Justin's primary intention in his argument about the scriptural theophanies

[26] Minns and Parvis, *Justin*, 150–1, emend *Apol.* 26.5 to read 'another greater than the demiurge God', thus denying Marcion's 'certain other': the epithet 'God'. However, the quotation from Justin in Irenaeus, *AH* IV. 6.2, uses the phrase 'other God'.

[27] Marcovich, *Iustini Martyris Dialogus*, 128, emends the sequence at *Dial.* 35.5 to read 'the maker of all and the God of Abraham and Isaac and Jacob and the Christ who was prophesied by him as to come'. Bobichon, *Justin Martyr*, I, 270–1, and II, 678, is probably

is to win Trypho's agreement that the Scriptures themselves do identify as 'God' or as 'Lord' someone who is *other* (ἄλλος) than the maker of all – but in number, not in intention; indeed, that 'other' is called God *by* the maker of all[28] and proclaims that which the maker of all wills, for 'there is no other God above' the latter (*Dial.* 56.4, 11). Within this wider strategy, those whom Trypho might mistakenly take to be Christians are portrayed as contradicting the central plank in Justin's own defence to a Jewish audience of the Christian interpretation of the (Jewish) Scriptures; his dismissal of them and his defence against Trypho serve to reinforce each other.

This illustrates well the intersecting pathways taken by Justin's exegesis of the Scriptures. It would be over-simplistic to suggest that Justin is mechanically repeating an argument initially formulated against Marcion's 'other God', accepting the label but finding it only already testified in the Scriptures, and to be identified with the pre-existent Christ (*Dial.* 56–60).[29] It would be equally wrong to conclude that the *Dialogue* is in reality directed against Marcion and others like him.[30] Justin, like his opponents on various fronts, were all wrestling with the same Scriptures and the exegetical challenges they posed. Justin's own tendency to repetition and his reuse of a variety of earlier sources provide a better explanation of the prolixity and inconsistencies in the *Dialogue* than a somewhat tortuous reuse of an earlier more coherent treatise.[31] Yet, he may also have been rightly alert to the most crucial, and hence, potentially vulnerable points in his attempt to forge a Christian reading of the Scriptures within the intellectual world of his time. Inevitably, then, threats to these would appear to be making common cause against him, as when he blames the Jews for making it possible for 'those without understanding' to assert that God 'did not always teach the same things as righteous' (30.1).[32] Unsurprisingly, he would also return repeatedly to the same passages and arguments; just as his debates with 'the Jew

right to reject the emendation, although taking 'the God of Abraham etc.' in apposition to 'the Christ …' remains awkward.

[28] Marcovich, *Iustini Martyris Dialogus*, 161, reads 'alongside' (παρά) instead of 'by' (ὑπό) at *Dial.* 56.4, but the manuscript reading ('by') can stand.

[29] For the argument that these chapters are drawn from the 'Syntagma', see Oskar Skarsaune, *The Proofs From Prophecy: A Study in Justin Martyr's Proof-Text Tradition, Text-Type, Provenance, Theological Profile* (NovTSup., 56; Leiden: Brill, 1987), 208–13.

[30] So Charles H. Cosgrove, 'Justin Martyr and the Emerging Christian Canon: Observations on the Purpose and Destination of the Dialogue with Trypho', *VC* 36 (1982), 209–32.

[31] While supporting much of Prigent's analysis, Pierre Nautin, 'Histoire des Dogmes et des Sacrements Chrétiens', *EPHE V*[e], 25 (1967–8), 162–7, argues that Justin is working with the (also lost) 'Dialogue of Jason and Papiscus'.

[32] This is identified as against Marcion by Prigent, *Justin et l'Ancient Testament*, 34–5.

Trypho' demanded that he revisit some that he had worked with in the *Apology*, they may have also taken him back to others he had debated against Marcion. More profitable than trying to discern these without the clues to do so will be to recognise what the issues were that Justin felt most threatened and most in need of protection – in whichever direction he faced.

JUSTIN'S MARCION

Although Justin does not label Marcion 'the heretic', he undoubtedly sows the seeds for the future; this is true not only of what he says about him but also of the way he positions him within the battles over the label and, hence, over the idea of being 'Christian'. He offers the advantages and the disadvantages of the contemporary; his starting point perhaps has to serve as the starting point for any attempt to understand Marcion's own thought and intentions and why they were so vehemently rejected. On the other hand, Justin will not have noted what he did not recognise as disturbing, and it does not follow that all subsequent accounts increase in imaginative power as they move further from his time. Certainly, what is true of him will be equally if not more true of his successors; excavating through the layers of polemical rhetoric and real or imagined enemies in the hope of finding 'the real Marcion' is doomed to failure. However, where Justin can offer more than his successors will be in offering a glimpse of the debates and concerns that engaged all parties that shaped Marcion – just as they shaped him.

3

Irenaeus and the shaping of a heretic

Contrary to recent reconstructions of the second century as a period of fluid boundaries and of experimentation, this is not how it appeared to Eusebius in his retrospective account; for him, it was the time when the devil marshalled a new weapon against the Church – deceivers claiming the label 'Christian' but seeking to undermine it from within. He takes for granted the pattern of a succession of 'schools of impious heresy (θεομισῶν αἱρέσεων διδασκαλεῖα)' – a mimicry, as it were, of the true Church (*HE* IV. 7.1–3). Although some would trace this model back to Justin's 'Syntagma', Eusebius himself identifies among those who used written demonstrations 'against the godless heresies' in the first place Hegesippus, a Jewish Christian,[1] who purportedly came to Rome in the time of Soter (c. 166–74 CE; *HE* IV. 8.1; 22). According to Eusebius, it was also Hegesippus who established what would become central weapons in the discourse of 'heresy' – namely, the appeal to conformity of belief among the bishops of different churches, although only Corinth and Rome are specifically named, and, at least at Rome, the idea of a succession of named individuals who could guarantee maintenance of the truth: 'While I was in Rome I formed a succession (διαδοχή) until Anicetus, whose deacon was Eleutherus, and Soter succeeded Anicetus after whom was Eleutherus. In each succession and each city the situation is as the law proclaims and the prophets and the Lord' (*HE* IV. 22.3).

In Hegesippus' account, it was at Jerusalem, or at least when Theboutis was not appointed bishop there, that 'the corruption' of 'the virgin church' began

[1] Eusebius assumes that he was a convert 'from among the Hebrews' because he reported what Eusebius identifies as unwritten Jewish traditions and Hebrew and Syriac works.

> from the seven sects (αἵρεσις), to which he belonged, in the people (λάος), from [or 'of'] which Simon, whence the Simonians, and Cleobius, whence Cleobienes, and Dositheus, whence Dosithians, and Gorthaius, whence Gorathenes and Masbothei. From these Menandrianists and Marcianists and Carpocratians and Valentinians and Basilidians and Satornilians introduced their own doctrine, each distinctively and differently.
>
> (*HE* IV. 22.5)

There is much that is uncertain about Hegesippus' original meaning in this excerpt, including whether those ('the people') among whom the 'seven sects' were to be found were non-Christian Jews or 'Jewish Christians' and what the relationship was between Jerusalem and the situation in Rome.[2] Despite the notable overlaps with the would-be but spurious Christians whom Justin lists in the *Dialogue* (35.6: 'Marcians, Valentinians, Basilidians, Satornilians'), there are also significant differences in content and particularly in framework, and these caution against the suggestion that Hegesippus drew directly from Justin's 'Syntagma'.[3] Yet, whether independently or from a common tradition, Hegesippus also testifies to the beginnings of the theme of the emergence of error and of a succession of its proponents, with Marcion included. Alongside this way of conceiving the problem of differing views, there is also developing a distinctive vocabulary and method of response – namely, as is also reflected in Justin, the construction of what will come to be designated 'heresy'.

However, these steps are but embryonic, and it is only with Irenaeus that they lead into a sustained statement of description and of refutation. Only then does Marcion appear not simply as a name in a list or as the exemplary proponent of a generalised set of principles in an exercise in self-justification, but instead as an iconic figure in the past characterised by a distinctive profile, although not one that is as yet systematically sustained; perhaps more importantly, he also then emerges as directly opposing the most fundamental tenets of assumed Christian truth.

2 Eusebius' own bias can be seen when he subsequently prefaces Hegesippus' account of seven 'different opinions (γνώμαι διάφοραι) in the circumcision among the sons of Israel' as 'the sects (αἱρέσεις) that had arisen formerly among the Jews' (*HE* IV. 22.7); among these are the Masbothei, who also appear in the list cited earlier; neither confusion by Eusebius nor textual corruption can be excluded.

3 See above, p. 20 and n. 19. It is striking that Justin, with reference to his 'Syntagma', and Eusebius, describing Hegesippus' account of the 'Jewish sects', use the phrase αἱ γεγενημέναι αἱρέσεις.

IRENAEUS AND THE BATTLE 'AGAINST HERESIES'

Irenaeus is rightly identified as a founding figure in the development of heresiology – the delineation and the refutation of 'deviant' teaching. Yet his great five-volume work *Against Heresies* is diffuse and often meandering; indeed, it fails to offer any single consistent theory of its theme. Nonetheless, it manages to produce an edifice which, while making limited use of the language of 'heresy' and still less that of 'orthodoxy', leaves readers in little doubt as to what might constitute each and why there can be no engagement between them. The conventional name *Against Heresies* is in fact misleading – not only because Irenaeus is more inclined to label 'heretics' (*haereticus*), albeit in a comprehensive or generalising sense, than he is to speak of 'heresy' (*haeresis*), a term that appears only eight times,[4] but, in addition, his avowed intention and the original title of the work were 'the conviction and refutation of falsely named knowledge (γνώσις)' (cf. 1 Tim. 6.20); this ensured the introduction of another key term into the debate: 'gnosis' or, in modern discussion, 'Gnosticism'.[5]

Irenaeus does not direct his work to those against whom he writes but to fellow believers;[6] his preface describes a situation in which many, particularly the more simple, have been seduced too easily by the subtleties of the false teachers. His task is to expose what might otherwise not be obvious and to bring into the open their teachings 'which until now have been hidden'. Irenaeus employs a rich variety of strategies to describe and explain 'error' as he perceives it and to demonstrate that which for him is the incontrovertible truth. Forming the central axis of these strategies is his assertion that 'the church, spread through the whole world even to the ends of the earth, received the faith from the apostles and their disciples' (*AH* I. 10). This faith, which the Church has preserved and handed down in a demonstrable unity through time and place, can be expressed in a rule or a set of proclaimed truths. At every point, error contradicts these principles of authentic apostolic tradition, of unity, and of proclamation.

Yet what Irenaeus implies is that, if indeed the differences were hitherto easily overlooked, all this may have been less self-evident both to the proponents of 'error' and to those persuaded by it. The former, he admits,

[4] 'Haereticus' appears 52 times; see A. Benoit, 'Irénée et l'hérésie: Les conceptions hérésiologiques de l'évêque de Lyon', *Augustinianum* 20 (1980), 55–67.

[5] For the title, see Eusebius, *HE* V. 7.1. On the use of the term, see Michael A. Williams, *Rethinking "Gnosticism": An Argument for Dismantling a Dubious Category* (Princeton, NJ: Princeton University Press, 1999).

[6] *AH* I. Praef. 'You (sing.) and those with you'.

say that they believe in God, and they claim the label 'Christians', failing to name their real teachers in order to deceive their hearers (I. 27.3; II. 28.4). Therefore, Irenaeus must take upon himself the task not only of setting out what he considers to be authentic Christian belief but also of describing – often in elaborate detail – his own account of the teaching of those whom he rejects. Although he hopes the extravagant myths he relates will thereby stand self-condemned, he also has to engage in more subtle discussion of the implications of his opponents' views about God, Christ, and salvation, and of their interpretation of the shared authorities of Scripture. 'From the outside indeed sheep, they appear to be like us externally because they use the same vocabulary as do we, and to say the same things as us, but within they are wolves' (III. 16.8). From time to time, he adopts the guise of addressing his opponents directly, even imagining their responses to his arguments;[7] whether this ever represents echoes of genuine debate or is nothing more than a rhetorical artifice cannot easily be decided. However, in so doing, he betrays that the issues under debate were far closer to the heart of Christian thought and practice than he could ever acknowledge. Irenaeus' construction of his opponents, Marcion included, is no less a construction of the parameters and bulwarks of a distinctive Christian identity.[8]

At the beginning of his second volume, Irenaeus looks back on his argument up to that point, in which he has set out the elaborate and self-contradictory details of the systems of Valentinus and of Marcus; he continues:

> and we have set out the teaching of their progenitor, the Samaritan Simon Magus and of all those who succeeded him. We have also spoken of the crowd of those who after him are Gnostics, and we have delineated their differences and doctrines and successions, and we have exposed all the heresies which were established from them. And we have shown that all the heretics who took their origin from Simon introduced impious and irreligious teachings into this life.
>
> (*AH* II. praef.)

This schema of a succession of heresies with their ultimate origin in the arch-heretic Simon was to prove enduring in the history of 'heresy', with its

[7] See herein p. 40.

[8] On Irenaeus' idea of 'heresy', see Le Boulluec, *La notion*, I, 113–88; also Ysabel de Andía, 'L'hérésie et sa refutation selon Irénée de Lyon', *Augustinianum* 25 (1985), 609–44.

echoes even in the present.[9] However, it had been established not at the beginning of Irenaeus' work but only towards the end of Book I, within what is an apparently self-contained section cataloguing the views, in varying detail, of individuals and groups who purportedly 'are the disciples and successors of Simon Magus the Samaritan' (*AH* I. 23–7). When he introduced this section, Irenaeus interrupted his own stated intention, on which he had made a start – namely, to deal with the teaching of Valentinus and his school, most notably Ptolemaeus (I. praef. 2). These figures now disappear from view until Irenaeus somewhat clumsily takes up the thread again by claiming that Valentinus and his school are born from such 'mothers and fathers and ancestors', presumably those who have been described in the intervening catalogue (I. 30.14; 31.2). There is good reason to suspect that in this section, Irenaeus is drawing on earlier material that loosely adopted the model of a succession of error and in which Valentinus did not feature. Although such a model might seem to offer a fitting counter to his own emphasis on the succession of truth from the apostles, handed down through bishops in the churches (III. 2–3), Irenaeus elsewhere only occasionally exploits the idea of a succession of false teachers, and he prefers to treat them as individuals who can be combined or contrasted to suit his argument.[10] However, there is insufficient internal coherence and too many indications of Irenaeus' own hand within *AH* I. 23–7 to claim that it constitutes an independent unitary source; in particular, there are no grounds to trace it directly to Justin's 'Syntagma' or to any of Irenaeus' known predecessors.[11]

9 See Stephen Haar, *Simon Magus: The First Gnostic?* (BZNW, 119; Berlin: de Gruyter, 2003).

10 Outside the passages cited, Simon is identified as the origin of the Gnostics only at *AH* III. 12.12; IV. 33.3, whereas at III. 4.3, Menander fills this role. Joel Kalvesmaki, 'The Original Sequence of Irenaeus, *Against Heresies* 1: Another Suggestion', *JECS*, 15 (2007), 407–17, dubs this section 'On Simon' and argues that Irenaeus added it, with various editorial interventions, after completing Book I in order to explain the origins of Marcion, whose importance for his argument he had now realised. Pheme Perkins, 'Irenaeus and the Gnostics: Rhetoric and Composition in Adversus Haereses Book One', *VC* 30 (1976), 193–200, had already established that I. 29–30 (on the 'Gnostic' adherents of Barbelo and the Ophites) use different techniques and did not belong with I. 23–7.

11 So already, rightly, Joannes Kunze, *De Historiae Gnosticismi*, 40; Frederick Wisse, 'The Nag Hammadi Library and the Heresiologists', *VC*, 25 (1971), 205–23, 213–5, sees it as an interim source between Justin and Irenaeus. K. Beyschlag, *Simon Magus und die christliche Gnosis* (WUNT 16; Tübingen: Mohr Siebeck, 1974), 16–8, traces the core of Irenaeus' information about Simon Magus to Justin's 'Syntagma', although some of the stylistic characteristics he notes are found widely throughout *AH*. There are no grounds for identifying the material as drawing on Polycarp as has been argued by Charles E. Hill, *From the Lost Teaching of Polycarp. Identifying Irenaues' Apostolic Presbyter and the Author of* Ad Diognetum (WUNT 186; Tübingen: Mohr Siebeck, 2006), 30–1.

MARCION AND IRENAEUS

This section of the *Against Heresies*, however, and the questions it raises are of particular importance because the final figure in the catalogue is Marcion; thereafter – and far more than any other – Marcion proves to be almost as important in Irenaeus' 'Refutation' as is Valentinus, whom he had initially identified as his target. The succession it sets out begins with Simon, 'from whom all heresies were established', and continues with Menander, another Samarian; from these come Saturninus in Antioch and Basilides in Alexandria. Next in the list, although not identified by the language of succession, is Carpocrates and then, 'belonging to this doctrine', Marcellina 'who came to Rome under Anicetus' (*AH* I. 25). The three who follow next fit somewhat uncomfortably here: Cerinthus, the Ebionites, and the Nicolaitans (cf. Rev. 2.6, 14–15), whose stated descent from Nicolaus (Acts 6.5) would appear to contradict any origin from Simon.[12] The account then returns to its original theme:

1. Then a certain Cerdo, taking the initiative from Simon and his associates,[13] settled in Rome under Hyginus, who held the office of bishop in ninth place by succession from the apostles, and he taught that the one who was preached as God by the law and prophets was not the Father of our Lord Jesus Christ. The former is known, the latter not known; the former just, but the latter is good.
2. Succeeding him Marcion of Pontus developed his teaching, *(i)* blaspheming without shame the one who was announced as God by the law and prophets, saying that he was the maker of evils and desirous of wars, and also inconsistent in precept, and self-contradictory. *(ii)* Jesus, however, coming from that Father who is above God, the creator of the world, *(iii)* into Judaea in the time of Pontius Pilate the governor, who was procurator of Tiberius Caesar, was manifest in human form to those were in Judaea; *(iv)* he dissolved the prophets and law and all the works of that God who made the world, whom he also calls Cosmocrator (Ruler of the world). *(v)* In addition to this, he mutilates the Gospel according to Luke, doing away with everything that is written about the birth[14] of the Lord, and removing much

[12] *AH* I. 26. These three are also absent from the lists of Justin and Hegesippus. Even without these, it is striking that the core figures of Saturninus [*sic*], Basilides, Carporcrates, and Marcion appear in the reverse order in Irenaeus from Justin (as reconstructed) and Hegesippus.

[13] So the Greek; the Latin reads 'from those who were the products (*erga*) of Simon'.

[14] Latin, *generatio*.

about the teaching of the words of the Lord in which the Lord is described as openly acknowledging the builder of this universe as his own father; so he persuaded his disciples that he himself was more to be trusted than those apostles who handed down the Gospel, handing down himself not the Gospel but a piece of Gospel. Similarly he cut away at the letters of Paul the apostle, removing whatever was explicitly said by the apostle about that God who made the world, that he is Father of our Lord Jesus Christ, and whatever the apostle taught making use of the prophetic announcements of the coming of the Lord.

3. *(vi)* Salvation will only be of those souls who have learned his teaching, while it is impossible for the body, in as much as it is taken from the earth, to participate in salvation. *(vii)* In addition to the blasphemy against God, he also adds this, certainly taking on the mouth of the devil and saying everything opposite to the truth: For Cain and those like him, and the inhabitants of Sodom and of Egypt, and those like them, and indeed all the gentiles who lived in every combination of wickedness were saved by the Lord, when he descended to Hades and they rushed to him, and he received them into his kingdom; Abel, however, and Enoch and Noah and the rest of the righteous, and those patriarchs who followed Abraham,[15] with all the prophets and those who pleased God, did not participate in salvation – so the serpent who was in Marcion proclaimed. Since they were aware, he says, that their God was always testing them, and suspecting that he was testing then, they did not rush to Jesus nor did they believe his proclamation; and for this reason he said their souls remained in Hades.

4. But since he is the only one who has openly dared to mutilate the Scriptures and without shame to attack God more than everyone else, we shall speak against him separately, arguing from his own writings, and with God's aid we shall refute him from those teachings of the Lord and the apostle which are acknowledged by him and which he himself uses. For the moment it was necessary to mention him so you might know that all who in some way or other adulterate the truth and harm the proclamation of the Church are the disciples and successors of Simon Magus.

(*AH* I. 27)

[15] The Latin reads 'who were the works of Abraham', but see n. 13.

Here, in a nutshell, appear the most significant principles that will recur repeatedly, albeit with important differences, in subsequent accounts of Marcion's life and teaching. Here there is also that continuing tension between the desire to locate Marcion among other heretics and the recognition in him of a distinct endeavour that invited a detailed and different sort of attack. Irenaeus, it would appear, never fulfilled his concluding promise to write a separate work against Marcion, although others would do so;[16] in practice, he proceeds throughout the subsequent books of the *Against Heresies* to attack Marcion repeatedly and at length – often in close association with Valentinus and others. In these later attacks, he adds substantially to the picture sketched here, changing the balance, expanding some elements at length, and drawing connections not made here. He undoubtedly had access to additional sources of information on which he drew, but his own strategies and theological concerns were the primary influence as he constructed his picture of Marcion. Although some of his more general polemic might also have had Marcion in view, the picture that follows will draw on those occasions where he specifically names him.

Cerdo

Irenaeus evidently knew very little about Cerdo; the teaching he attributes to him is formulaic – just enough to justify the supposed connection with Marcion, combining language soon used of the latter with conventional oppositions from elsewhere.[17] Cerdo's usefulness for Irenaeus is that he provides the necessary link with Simon, albeit a loose one; Cerdo does not succeed one of Simon's own successors but merely took his starting point from this group. Yet it is unlikely that Irenaeus has invented him for this purpose, for he easily could have made the same generalisation about Marcion himself. More probably, Irenaeus inherited the tradition that Marcion had a teacher named Cerdo, but it proved somewhat perplexing for his purposes. Later, when he wants to contrast the unbroken succession from the apostles within the Church, he asserts: 'Before Valentinus there were none who stemmed from

16 He repeats the intention at *AH* III. 12.12.

17 This is much more likely than the suggestion that teaching properly attributable to Cerdo has been transferred to Marcion; in Marcion, it belongs to a largely coherent system (see herein p. 344). On Cerdo, see David W. Deakle, 'Harnack and Cerdo: A Reexamination of the Patristic Evidence for Marcion's Mentor', ed. Gerhard May and Katharina Greschat, with Martin Meiser, *Marcion und seine kirchengeschichtliche Wirkung / Marcion and His Impact on Church History*: Vorträge der Internationalen Fachkonferenz zu Marcion gehalten vom 15.–18. August 2001 in Mainz (TU 150; Berlin: de Gruyter, 2002), 177–90.

him, and before Marcion there were none who come from him'; however, he immediately follows this claim by an account of how 'Cerdo, who was before Marcion ...', wavered between confession in the church at Rome and continuing his secret teaching (*AH* III. 4.2). Although Irenaeus is in no doubt that this prevarication must have led to official reproof and to at least temporary exclusion, it is more likely that his sources only identified Cerdo as present in Rome in the time of Hyginus and as Marcion's teacher.

It is in this later passage that Irenaeus dates Marcion's main activity to the time of Anicetus, after similarly describing Valentinus as arriving in Rome under Hyginus and continuing until Anicetus. Although the origins of Irenaeus' Roman bishop list and the precise status of those whom he names are much debated,[18] this precise dating is undoubtedly tied to his account of the visit that Polycarp made to Rome 'under Anicetus', when he, so Irenaeus claims, 'converted to the Church of God many of those heretics of whom we have spoken' (III. 3.4).[19] Irenaeus also adds at this point the story of Polycarp's encounter with Marcion himself, which, although this is not explicit, he may have assumed took place in Rome.[20] He intentionally presents this encounter as paralleling a similar meeting between John and Cerinthus, explicitly located in Ephesus; in so doing, he neatly reinforces Polycarp's apostolic credentials and Marcion's heretical ones. By Irenaeus' calculations, however, Polycarp was a direct auditor of the apostles, while Marcion, like Valentinus and Cerdo, was contemporary with Roman bishops who were several generations later than the original apostles, thus being further disqualified.

The strong focus in Irenaeus' polemic and argument on Rome, where his other main polemical targets were centred, does suggest that he had good reason for locating Marcion there. His account would have been far less effective had he known of any tradition of Marcion's 'excommunication' by the authoritative representatives of the Roman church; indeed, their failure to act as firmly as had the visitor Polycarp provided one more thread in his overarching purpose.[21] Irenaeus himself apparently visited Rome less than thirty years after Polycarp had done so,[22] and perhaps he had heard

[18] Although Hegesippus claims to have drawn up a succession as far as Anicetus, he does not identify it as institutional or episcopal (see herein p. 26). Irenaeus is inconsistent in his numbering of Hyginus (cf. *AH* III. 3.3; 4.3).

[19] Irenaeus also referred to this visit in his letter to Victor (Eusebius, *HE* V. 24.16).

[20] Jerome, *De Vir.Illust.*, 17, makes the Roman setting explicit. See pp. 295–6.

[21] See Daniel Wanke, 'Irenäus und die Häretiker in Rom: Thesen zur geschichtlichen Situation von Adversus Haereses', *ZAC* 3 (1999), 202–40.

[22] Eusebius, *HE* V. 4; cf. also Irenaeus, *AH* III. 3.3, when Irenaeus refers to Eleutherus as 'bishop now'.

there of the shadowy Cerdo; but beyond this, his efforts at dating Marcion probably rest upon little more than a web of supposition and deduction. Of Marcion's own biography, he knew little more than did Justin – namely, that he came from Pontus.

Marcion's teaching

Irenaeus' initial account of Marcion's teaching, by contrast, betrays more confident detail. It comprises seven key elements as identified in the translation given above: (i) the denigration of the God of the law and prophets; (ii) Jesus as sent from a Father who is above the Creator; (iii) that Jesus came to Judaea in the time of Pontius Pilate; (iv) that Jesus' task was the abolition of the works of the Creator, including the law and the prophets; (v) the selective use of an edited Gospel of Luke and Pauline letter corpus; (vi) that only souls are able to experience salvation; and (vii) that at Jesus' postmortem descent to Hades, Cain and those usually considered exemplars of unrepentant iniquity did accept salvation, while the righteous before and after Abraham rejected it. Whereas most of this account takes the form of reported speech, perhaps betraying an earlier source, the fifth and seventh items – marked by a telltale 'in addition' – disrupt the pattern; these are, it seems, expansions of that original nucleus – whether by Irenaeus or at an earlier stage of the source.[23] This does not, of course, mean that they are less historically reliable; different details would carry different significance to different opponents and in different contexts.

(i) 'Blasphemy' (or 'calumny') against God is a regular charge in polemic against those who differ, including against those deemed 'heretics', and it is already so used by Justin, but it is also one of Irenaeus' favourite terms. In Justin, the one who is so denigrated or even denied is 'the Maker of all' (*Apol.* 26.5; *Dial.* 35.5), and this is how Irenaeus describes him in subsequent clauses: *fabricator mundi*, another much-used epithet. Clearly, this is not the denial of the existence of the Creator but of his supremacy and hence of his meriting worship. At this earlier point, however, Irenaeus specifies blasphemy instead of 'the one who was announced (*annunciatus*) by the law and the prophets'. This particular formula is Irenaeus' own [cf. *AH* IV. 9.3] and it was therefore probably he who also described Cerdo's denial in the same terms. Justin's account was not dissimilar, but strikingly, whereas Justin had referred 'the one proclaimed in advance by the prophets' to Christ and had also

23 So also May, 'Markion in seiner Zeit', 3, who combines (2)–(4), so the additional items are numbered (3) and (5).

identified the object of Marcion's calumny as 'the God of Abraham, Isaac, and Jacob', for Irenaeus, the reference is unequivocally to the God of the scriptural account.[24] Hence, the charge that this God was the maker of evils, war-minded, and self-contradictory presupposes an appeal to and considerable disquiet about the stories of the biblical God. However, Irenaeus does not suggest that Marcion gave this God any other label, such as 'God of the Jews' or, still less, Yaldabaoth or Sabaoth – names he ascribes to the Ophites.[25] Instead, he gives the simple qualification 'whom he also calls Cosmocrator': This epithet originates in Ephesians 6. 12 – there applied to the 'rulers of the darkness of this world' – and it may well have been adopted by Marcion;[26] however, Irenaeus had already described the Valentinians as applying the same epithet to the devil and the comment may be one of his characteristic attempts at assimilating different groups to each other (*AH* I. 5.4).

Irenaeus does not expand here on examples of the failings of the Creator, although elsewhere, without reference to Marcion, he does address some of the scriptural passages that could be and sometimes were interpreted as evidence of God's weakness: 'For God, who gave aid to man and restored him to his liberty, is neither weak nor unjust' (*AH* III. 23.2–4).[27] Subsequently, in Book III, however, he describes Marcionite teaching in terms that suggest a more principled or philosophical foundation:

> Indeed those who stem from Marcion's line blaspheme the Maker, saying that he is the maker of evils, and, adopting a more acceptable[28] view of his beginning, say that there are by nature two Gods, distant from each other, one indeed good, but the other evil.
>
> (*AH* III. 12.12)

> Again, in order to remove the admonitory and judicial from the Father, thinking it unworthy of God, and supposing that they have found a God without anger and good, they say that one indeed judges (*judicare*) and the other saves, without realising that they are removing reason and justice

24 See p. 23 for Justin's references.

25 'God of the Jews' is used by Irenaeus only in his accounts of Saturninus and of Basilides (*AH* II. 24.2, 4); see p. 357. For 'Yaldabaoth' or 'Sabaoth', see *AH* I. 30.4.

26 According to Tertullian, Marcion identified the Creator with 'the rulers of this world' (2 Cor. 4.4), although Irenaeus does not attribute this exegesis specifically to Marcion; see p. 00 and Judith M. Lieu, '"As Much My Apostle as Christ Is Mine": The Dispute Over Paul Between Tertullian and Marcion', *EC* 1 (2010), 41–59, 55.

27 The reference is to God's punishment of Adam and question to Cain; see pp. 360–4.

28 The Latin reads 'unacceptable' (*intolerabiliorem*), although most editors prefer '*tolerabiliorem*', to make a contrast with Valentinus, whose theory of the Pleroma is described as 'more blasphemous'.

> (*justitia*) from both ... Therefore Marcion himself divides God in two, saying that one is good, the other judicial (*judicialis*), and in so doing takes God away from both.
>
> (*AH* III. 25.2–3)

This rather different framework is the source of a far-reaching problem in the reconstruction of the 'historical Marcion' – namely, whether he held a dualistic view of the divine, perhaps on philosophical principles, or whether he started from a more biblical account of divine punishment.[29] The confusion appears to be already integral to Irenaeus' own model here; he immediately recognises that 'justice'/'just' and 'judicial'/'judgement' are not synonyms and that the relationship between them needs defending, but he then proceeds to elide them by appealing to Plato's superiority in having already acknowledged that God is necessarily 'both just and good' (*AH* III. 25.3–5).[30] It was probably in order to anticipate this fundamental concern that Irenaeus already ascribed to Cerdo the contrast between the 'just' and the 'good' God (*AH* I. 27.1).

The consistent element in these accounts of Marcion's 'two Gods' is that the superior one is 'good' (*bonus*). When Irenaeus begins his defence of the Creator God, he contrasts the latter with the (Valentinian) 'Father of all with their pleroma' and with 'the good God of Marcion' (*AH* II. 1.1). This latter has an almost formulaic ring – perhaps as an expansion of the simpler and more widespread 'God of Marcion' (II. 3.1).[31] Like Justin (*Apol.* 26.5: 'to confess another as being greater'), Irenaeus sees Marcion's innovation as the invention of this other God (*AH* II. 30. 9; IV. 2. 2) and not as the interposition of an inferior creator; the arguments he marshals are against the logical and conceptual possibility of there being any such other God. His assertion that the proofs from the idea of space which he levels against the concept of a Pleroma which is nonetheless not all-encompassing are equally effective against Marcion's two Gods (II. 1.4; 31.1) demonstrates that even while trying to assimilate them to each other, he is faced with the inextricable difference between Marcion and his 'gnostic' peers.

(ii) By contrast, in the initial résumé of Marcion's teaching, this superior God is introduced almost in passing as 'the Father who is above the Creator God'. 'Father' undoubtedly means 'of Christ', for Irenaeus goes on to accuse

29 See pp. 339–42. There is some merit in Kavelsmaki's argument, 'Original Sequence', that the fuller details of Marcion's system in Book II and III reflect Irenaeus' realisation of Marcion's importance, which led him to include the 'On Simon' section (n. 10).

30 The reference is probably to the *Timaeus* on the Demiurge; see below, p. 337.

31 See p. 324.

Marcion of suppressing any evidence that Jesus recognised the Creator as his father. His only explicit appeal to Justin's 'Syntagma' comes in the midst of a subsequent discussion about the much-debated verse 'No-one knows the son except the father and no-one knows the father except the son' (Luke 10.22).[32] Irenaeus continues:

> This is the Maker of heaven and earth, just as has been shown from his teaching, and not he who is invented as a false father by Marcion or by Valentinus, or by Basilides, or by Carpocrates, or by Simon, or the rest of the falsely named Gnostics. For none of them was son of God, but Christ Jesus our Lord was, against whom they practice a contrary discipline, daring to announce an unknown God
>
> (*AH* IV. 6.2).

The dominical saying was an obvious proof-text and Irenaeus had already claimed that the Marcosians appealed to it, but the assertion that Jesus revealed the 'Unknown Father' becomes something of a commonplace (*AH* I. 20.3; 24.1 [Saturninus]; 26.1 [Cerinthus]; 30.13 [Ophites]).[33] The Marcosians supposedly contrasted the 'Unknown Father' with the Creator who was known to all and it was perhaps in imitation of them that Irenaeus had ascribed the same 'known/unknown' opposition to Cerdo. A different interpretation is offered by Cerinthus, who, according to Irenaeus, declared that the 'Power' responsible for creation, being separated from the first God by a vast distance, was ignorant of the latter (I. 26.1). Such 'variations on the theme' may be the inevitable result of the interplay between exegesis and a quasi-philosophical position or of the transformation of single verses into a mythic narrative;[34] they may equally be the result of Irenaeus' delight in tracing continuity, imitation, and also disagreement among the 'heretics'. Marcion's first place in the list cited above (IV. 6.2), then, should not be overemphasised; in fact, it is the views of the Valentinians that Irenaeus proceeds to target. Marcion's own concept of 'his God' remains remarkably opaque from Irenaeus' perspective.

32 See p. 19, n. 10; the quotation of Justin reads: 'Justin speaks well in the *Syntagma* against Marcion, that I would not have believed the Lord himself if he proclaimed another God alongside the Demiurge' (Eusebius, *HE* IV. 18.9); the Latin of Irenaeus appears to represent a longer quotation, although some of the language is suspiciously Irenaean. On the text of Luke 10.22 used by Irenaeus and by Marcion, see pp. 223–4.

33 Irenaeus claims that the Marcosians also cited Luke 2.49, which Marcion was unlikely to have used.

34 On this, see pp. 327–8.

(iii) Except for this qualification as to the identity of 'the Father', Marcion's account of the coming of Jesus in the time of Pontius Pilate as one sent by God might at first seem non-controversial. The dating, however, belongs not to Jesus' birth but to the beginning of his ministry as introduced in Luke 3.1, which would also supply the otherwise unexpected reference to Judaea. However, it is only in light of the later accusation that Marcion excised the birth narratives from the Gospel that this gains significance. In the same framework, the potentially conventional 'was manifest in human form' may also carry other resonances; neither 'manifest' (*manifestatus*) nor 'form' (*forma*) need suggest something less than a real human presence, but the same formula clearly does indicate this in Irenaeus' account of Basilides, who said that the redeemed 'ought not to worship him who was crucified but him who came in human form and was thought to be crucified' (*AH* I. 24.4). The repeated terminology suggests that it should be attributed to Irenaeus or to his source rather than to their opponents, but the lack of further detail here regarding what is otherwise a regular but ever varied topos in this catalogue of heretical Christologies is striking.[35] Certainly, Irenaeus himself does understand Marcion to have undervalued Jesus' humanity, but he is not much more explicit about what he thinks Marcion did claim; in a series of challenges to different 'heretics', he imagines Marcion being asked:

> Why did he acknowledge himself as son of man if he did not undergo that birth which belongs to man … and how, when he was not flesh but when he appeared as if man, was he crucified, and from his pierced side blood and water flowed? What body did the buriers bury and what was that which arose from the dead?
>
> (*AH* IV. 33.2)

Part of the problem here was, perhaps, that all sides were claiming to uphold the same truths about Jesus and that it is Irenaeus who is endeavouring to detect the fissures between the various opinions; elsewhere, he admits that those whom he accused of dividing between 'Jesus' and 'Christ' said that they were united (III. 17.4).

Another aspect of 'the coming of the Lord' is also only raised in the context of Marcion's tampering with the Scriptures – in this case that he removed from Paul's letters any passages demonstrating that the prophets

[35] *AH* I. 23.3; 24.2; 25.1,5; 26.1; Beyschlag, *Simon*, 190–1, and n. 117 claims a similarity between the description of the docetism of Simon and that of Marcion, asking whether this is due to a historical link – perhaps through Cerdo – or is a literary topos. In fact, the differences are more striking, although perhaps of intentional rhetorical effect.

had predicted it. This was already basic to Justin's account of Marcion, and subsequently, it plays an important role in Irenaeus' own picture:

> For we say against all heretics, and particularly against those who follow Marcion and against those who are like them, who say the prophets are from another God, 'Read carefully the Gospel which comes from the apostles, and read carefully the prophets, and you will find that every action and every teaching, and the whole passion of our Lord have been spoken beforehand in them.'
>
> (*AH* IV. 33.15)

Here, Irenaeus makes the fundamental connections that lie at the heart of his interpretation of the heretical position and of his own constructive theology with which he opposes them. He underlines and expands his point by protesting that if the prophets were inspired 'by another God, being ignorant of the inexpressible father as *you* claim', they could hardly have prophesied not only everything Christ did and suffered but also the 'new covenant' (*novum testamentum*). This last, in turn, opens up his own response to the question that he has imagined his interlocutors ('you') might ask: 'what then did the Lord bring when he came that was new?' (IV. 34.1–3). It is difficult to decide whether 'you' here are still the followers of Marcion in particular, who in lively debate made precisely this objection, or whether they are only a rhetorical aid to Irenaeus' own evolving argument. Certainly, the theme of the different dispensations in God's dealings with humankind is fundamental for Irenaeus' thought, and in a passage quoted earlier referring to Marcion, he asserts that the denigration of the Creator common to all the heretics arises out of their ignorance about 'the scriptures and the disposition (*dispositio*) of God' which makes them ask 'the reason for the differences between each covenant (*testamentum*)' (III. 12.12).

(iv) Marcion's own answer, according to the next clause, was not only that Jesus came from this other Father but that he actively brought to an end the Creator's establishment, embodied in 'the prophets and the law'. In Book IV, Irenaeus devotes a long section to demonstrating that Jesus did not abolish the law, but he obeyed it and extended and fulfilled it (*AH* IV. 8.2–13.4). He appeals to the Matthaean antitheses (Matt. 5.27–37) to argue 'All these do not contain what is contrary to and will abolish the past things, as those who belong to Marcion assert, but their fulfilment and extension' (*AH* IV. 13.1). It is unlikely that Marcion himself would have appealed to the Matthaean passage – his Gospel was Luke – but it is probably from here that Irenaeus has drawn the claim he attributes to Marcion that Jesus 'abolished (*dissolvo*) the prophets and law' (cf. Matt. 5.17). Irenaeus' own terminology and interpretive framework are also to be detected in his attack against 'all those of bad intent' – among whom he shortly includes Marcion – who 'think that the giving of the law is different from and contrary to the Gospel', echoing as it does his own positive assertion that 'two covenants (*testamenta*)' are 'without contradiction, the old which was the giving of the law in the past, the new which is a manner of life according to the Gospel' (*AH* III. 12.12; IV. 9.1).[36] Irenaeus' own interpretation of God's dispensation and covenants is indeed more complex than this; elsewhere, he will claim that just as there are four Gospels – or a tetraform Gospel – so also there are four covenants (III. 11.8).[37] It is this thoroughly biblical framework, together with the structures of Irenaeus' understanding of God's activity through history, that has determined the terms in which he frames his opponents' questions and attacks.

(v) Irenaeus has added to his underlying source the accusation that Marcion 'mutilated' the Gospel of Luke and Paul's letters; the charged terms he uses – 'does away with' and 'mutilates' (*aufero*; *circumcido*) – belong to his favoured vocabulary for accusing his opponents of casual misuse of Scripture and the truth, which is itself a standard polemical topos.[38] He inserts the charge here and not at the end of his account because the defence he will offer is integrally tied to the understanding of God he has just developed. Hence, the assertion that Marcion 'persuaded his disciples that he was more reliable than the apostles who handed down the Gospel' is not a quotation of any claim made by Marcion but betrays Irenaeus' own emphasis on the fourfold Gospel and on the apostolic tradition that authenticates it.[39] Thus, when he justifies on the basis of Rev. 4.6–8 that there can be neither more nor less than four 'faces' of the Gospel, Irenaeus again accuses Marcion in similar language to that used here of 'rejecting the whole Gospel, indeed cutting himself off from the Gospel while boasting that he has a share of the Gospel' (*AH* III. 11.9).[40] Marcion's use of a form of Luke is well

36 See pp. 402–03.

37 That is, those under Adam, Noah, Moses, and the fourth 'through the Gospel'.

38 See Gérard Vallée, *A Study in Anti-Gnostic Polemics: Irenaeus, Hippolytus, and Epiphanius* (SCJ 1; Waterloo, ON: Wilfrid Laurier University Press, 1981), 18 and n. 22; Lieu, 'Heresy and Scripture', 90–1. The use of 'the Apostle' (cf. also § 4) of Paul is also characteristic of Irenaeus but may be traced to Marcion; see Rolf Noormann, *Irenäus als Paulusinterpret: Zur Rezeption und Wirkung der paulinischen und deuteropaulinischen Briefe im Werk des Irenäus von Lyon* (WUNT 2.66; Tübingen: Mohr Siebeck, 1994), 39–41, who also compares the Presbyter of Irenaeus, *AH* IV. 27–32.

39 So also *AH* III. 12.12, directed to all heretics.

40 The same verb (*abscindo*) is used here as of Marcion's treatment of Paul's letters in *AH* I. 27.2. Irenaeus also attacks here those who do not accept 'the form' which is the Gospel

attested, but the terms and the framework within which that use will be understood are determined by Irenaeus' own conception of the written Gospels. Thus, it would also be wrong to assume that Marcion would have understood the charge that he and his followers were intent on 'dissecting *the scriptures*, not *recognising* some at all' and on claiming that only Luke and the Pauline letters were '*legitimate*' (III. 12.12); such language betrays Irenaeus' own perspective.

Irenaeus' own interpretation relies on a number of interlocking and reciprocally confirming threads. It is important to his argument that the Gospels represent the unified tradition held in common by all the apostles and disciples of the Lord; for such harmony in preaching from the very beginning, he appeals in detail to the Acts of the Apostles, 'when neither Valentinus nor Marcion were there' (*AH* III. 12.6). He rejects the possibility that the apostles in any way modified their preaching to accommodate the sensitivities of their hearers, perhaps suggesting that there were those who had argued this. To those 'who say that Paul alone knew the truth' – among whom he has already identified Marcion – he demonstrates that Paul himself supports the testimony of Acts and the witness of the other apostles, particularly in Galatians but also by confirming that Luke, whom Irenaeus assumes to be the author of Acts, was constantly present with him (*AH* III. 13.1–14.2).[41] Anyone who questions Luke's reliability – by implication in the Acts of the Apostles – 'will obviously reject the Gospel of which he claims to be a disciple'. Yet, Irenaeus continues, there is much peculiar to Luke's Gospel that is 'necessary for the Gospel', including much that 'both Marcion and Valentinus [*sic*][42] use'. 'Accept one, accept the other', he demands, 'and if indeed Marcion's followers do refute, they shall not have a Gospel; for indeed, as we said before, it is the one according to Luke, curtailing it, that they boast having as the Gospel' (III. 14.3–4). So governed is Irenaeus by his controlling theme that he lists in the events found only in Luke many of the details of the birth narratives without once taking the opportunity to repeat that Marcion had also removed these.

according to John and those who add a Gospel, such as the so-called Gospel of Truth. Again, Irenaeus does not take the opportunity to say that Marcion had been 'cut from' the Church, suggesting that he was unaware of this tradition.

41 See 2 Tim. 4.10–11; Col. 4.14. On Irenaeus' use of Acts and the question of its previous history, see Andrew Gregory, *The Reception of Luke and Acts in the Period Before Irenaeus: Looking for Luke in the Second Century* (WUNT 2.169; Tübingen: Mohr Siebeck, 2003); see pp. 430–2.

42 This despite the fact that he has previously said that the Valentinians favour John (*AH* III. 11.7).

This controlling theme is that what all the apostles, including Paul, are agreed on is precisely the preaching of the one God who created the world and who sent Jesus as his Son, as earlier prophesied. This is the theme that Irenaeus has laboriously traced through the early sermons of Acts, and it is therefore this that he accuses Marcion of removing from the Gospel and Pauline letters. The denial of that message is, for Irenaeus, fundamental to all heresy, encapsulated in 'the teaching of Simon Magus', and it necessarily entails the claim 'to have discovered something more than the apostles' and, indeed, 'to be more honest and wiser than the apostles' (*AH* III. 12.12). While Irenaeus recognises the different strategies of Marcion and others, including Valentinus, the outcome in his eyes is the same; whatever their own claims, the real choice is between them and the authenticated apostolic tradition.

Whether Irenaeus was sufficiently familiar with the detail of Marcion's Pauline text to support this claim about Marcion's excision is far from certain, and despite his own appeal to the Pastoral Letters, he shows no knowledge of their absence from Marcion's Pauline corpus. In addition, given his readiness to deride the spurious writings used by and penned by others, his silence about any other works by Marcion suggests that he knew of none. Similarly, he says little about Marcion's use of Scripture; the generalising assertion that those whom he denounces claim the right to interpret Scripture through their own revealed wisdom[43] – 'as if the truth were properly according to them, at one time in Valentinus, at another in Marcion, at another in Cerinthus, then indeed in Basilides' – mainly serves as a point of contrast to his own favourite theme of the one undivided tradition handed down from the apostles through the succession of elders in the Church (*AH* III. 2.1–2). He does, however, accuse 'the heretics generally' of failing to understand Paul and of asking inappropriate questions about his teaching (IV. 41.4). Although some of the passages he discusses to illustrate this are attributed to Marcion by later writers, such as the reading of 2 Corinthians 4.4 or the meaning of 1 Corinthians 15.50 (*AH* III. 7.1; V. 13.2), for Irenaeus, they only point to the underlying error shared by all heretics.[44]

(vi) Irenaeus also works into this overall interpretive framework the next element in his source. On its own, the exclusion of bodies, being 'earthly', from a salvation that was therefore reserved for the soul might have occasioned little surprise to many at the time. However, for Irenaeus, it is a common mark of all heresies that 'they reject that which God has formed, so denying their own salvation'; it here that 1 Corinthians 15.50 ('flesh and

[43] Irenaeus implies that they all appeal to 1 Cor. 2.6.
[44] See pp. 258, 265; it is probable that these passages were widely debated.

blood are not able to inherit the Kingdom of God') came into play, appealed to by all sides (*AH* I. 22.1; V. 13.2, 5). Irenaeus, however, understood the opposing position as the inevitable consequence of the rejection of the Creator and his works: 'for of all the things all heretics say with utmost gravity, the fullest extent of their deviancy is this, that they blaspheme the creator and deny the salvation of what God has formed, namely flesh' (IV. praef.). On the other hand, in contrast to Valentinian doctrine (I. 5.5–6; 7.3, 5), Irenaeus nowhere suggests that Marcion held that the soul or certain individuals because of their soul-like or spiritual nature had a particular affinity with the higher God. This idiosyncrasy, however, can still serve a polemical jibe: How can Marcion justify as good someone who 'removes people who belong to someone else away from the one who made them and summon them into his own realm'? (IV. 33.2).

Irenaeus, of course, can only conceive of salvation in his own terms; thus, he also asks Marcion: 'How can he (the unknown God) forgive us the sins which we owe our creator and God?' Likewise, 'How can the Lord, if he belonged to another father, justly take bread which belongs to our created order, and acknowledge it as his body and affirm the mixed cup as his blood?' (*AH* IV. 33.2). From here will follow naturally the questions about Jesus' own experience of human birth and participation in human flesh quoted earlier, for these are not isolated items of belief but are interrelated aspects of the understanding of God's activity. Therefore, Irenaeus subsequently generalises these arguments also, making plain their ultimate source: 'Vain indeed are those who deride the whole disposition of God, and deny the salvation of the flesh … if indeed this flesh is not saved, neither did the Lord redeem us by his blood, nor is the eucharistic cup a participation in his blood. … Blood is nothing else than what comes from veins and flesh and from the rest of human substance, in which the Word of God was truly made. …' (V. 2.1). Irenaeus is concerned only to demonstrate that Marcion – indeed, all the heretics – undermine the whole structure of salvation as properly understood and experienced in the Church – or rather to show that conformity with this understanding and practice is what defines the boundary between truth and error. He has no interest in investigating how Marcion and his followers themselves understood salvation or how that understanding was expressed in their worship and communal practice.

One way in which this was expressed would seem to have been through ascetic practice. Irenaeus supplements the source that he has been reworking with a summary of 'the many shoots of many heresies that have been produced by those described' (*AH* I. 28.1). First among these are the Encratites and Tatian; both are accused of rejecting marriage and of being inspired to this by Marcion and by Saturninus. He had already reported the rejection of marriage and procreation by Saturninus but not that this was also Marcion's view (I. 24.2). Irenaeus knows that Tatian had been a disciple of Justin, so he has to assume that he fell into 'error' only after the latter's death; 'encratite' simply means 'continent' or 'chaste' and, as shall be seen, had long been a term of honour.[45] It is Irenaeus who wishes to draw the boundary that will exclude all such practice, and to do so, he asserts that those who took this position were 'frustrating the original creation of God, *secretly* accusing the one who made male and female for the procreation of humankind'. By tracing their position to Saturninus and to Marcion, he further reinforces their exclusion, but doing so also reinforces the degree to which Irenaeus' superficially authoritative account is an exercise in constructing two mutually exclusive and coherent worlds out of the variety with which he was surely faced.

(vii) Irenaeus' final addition to the source is clearly intended as a climax to this construction, reinforced by a twofold reference to the inspiration of the devil; this conclusively demonstrates that Marcion 'speaks everything that is contrary to the truth'. Jesus' descent into Hades was a widespread belief in the second century; Justin even gives it scriptural warrant when he declares that the Jews have excised from Jeremiah the words 'The Lord God of Israel remembered his dead who slept in the earth of a grave, and he descended to them to preach to them his salvation' (Justin, *Dial.* 72.4).[46] However, Justin himself did believe that Noah, Enoch, and other righteous would be saved on the basis of their obedience to God (*Dial.* 45). Marcion is, therefore, represented as holding the same belief but of inverting its effect; the intended recipients, suspecting a trick, did not accept the message of salvation, while those who were bywords of obduracy responded with enthusiasm.

Nonetheless, this item in Marcion's system remains somewhat awkward; Irenaeus does not refer to it again nor does he observe that it might sit uncomfortably with anything that was less than real suffering and death. It does not appear to be repeated in this form by most later polemicists.[47]

45 See pp. 388–92.

46 There is no evidence of the words ever having been part of Jeremiah; see pp. 370, 383.

47 Contra Hill, *Lost Teaching of Polycarp*, who claims that Tertullian refers to this tenet in *AM* III. 24.1; IV. 14 (p. 30) and traces it to Polycarp (*AH* IV. 27.2 [p. 42]). Origen ascribes to Marcion Celsus' objection that the Saviour offered salvation to those condemned by the Creator (*C.Cels.* VI. 53), while Epiphanius only reports that Christ descended to save Cain and others who did not know 'the God of the Jews', leaving those – Abel and the rest – who had acknowledged the Creator God (*Pan.* 42, 4.3–4). It is repeated in Theodoret of Cyr's *Compendium Against Heresies*, I, 24 (PG 83: 372–6).

Instead, Irenaeus elsewhere implies that heretics are more likely to identify 'the depths' (*inferos*) to which Christ descended with this world and that the 'inner being' ascends to heaven, leaving the body here (*AH* V. 31.2). On the other hand, the idea that the Creator God tested the people, taken from the accounts of the wilderness wanderings, would easily belong to the catalogue of accusations that Marcion levelled against him; equally, Jesus' welcome of the responsive wicked into his kingdom (cf. *AH* IV. 33.2) might echo the Lukan account of his conversation with Zacchaeus.[48] Irenaeus does, moreover, describe Marcion and his followers as 'casting Abraham out from the inheritance', arguably reflecting a debate about the text and meaning of Galatians 4.30–1 (*AH* IV. 8.1). The fate of those who trusted the Creator God was bound to arise in debate if not in Marcion's first account of his ideas and one of the questions Irenaeus levels against him is 'Why was his goodness incomplete, since he did not save everyone?' (IV. 33.2).

Yet the suspicion remains that Irenaeus has phrased this final tenet of Marcion's teaching within terms that were important to himself. Similar inversions of values are a standard charge levelled against 'heretics'; Irenaeus subsequently asserts that some heretics claim that Cain came from the highest power and that Esau, Korah, the people of Sodom, and all such were his confrères (*AH* I. 31.1). The terminology used in this clause of his account of Marcion is Irenaeus' own.[49] He himself cites more than once the Jeremiah apocryphon to which Justin had appealed earlier (*AH* III. 20.4 [attributed to Isaiah]; 33.12; IV. 22.2; V. 31.1; cf. *Dem.* 78), and for him Christ's descent to Hades was a crucial step in the pattern of recapitulation, for by it he brought salvation to the patriarchs and to the righteous dead (*AH* III. 22.4; IV. 27.2; 33.1).[50] A 'myth-like' narrative – whether or not originally referring to the descent to Hades – has here become for Irenaeus the crowning demonstration that Marcion's scheme undermines the whole panorama or 'economy' of God's saving activity.

IRENAEUS' MARCION

Irenaeus almost certainly inherited key elements in his picture of Marcion, and he almost certainly also drew on his own direct experience as he added

[48] Or with the penitent thief if part of this were in Marcion's 'Gospel'; see, however, p. 217.

[49] 'Participate in salvation', cf. (vi) and also *AH* IV. 14.1; 33.5; V. 6.2; 19.2; 'run to him', cf. IV. 2.8; see also Perkins, 'Irenaeus and the Gnostics'.

[50] For its importance for Irenaeus, see Antonio Orbe, 'El "Decensus ad inferos" y san Ireneo', *Gregorianum* 58 (1977), 523–55; see also Tertullian, *De Anima*, 55. For the Jeremiah apocryphon, see p. 370.

to these; the dominant role that Marcion, alongside Valentinus, occupies in the work as a whole suggests that he represented for Irenaeus a very serious threat. Yet it is impossible to recover either Irenaeus' earlier sources or that experience with any confidence, for both are mediated through his own construction of the Christian faith, which is at the same time a construction of that which opposes its very principles. All his efforts are directed to this purpose, so even when he addresses Marcion or his followers directly, he does this more for rhetorical effect than from actual memory.

Irenaeus was not the first to set Marcion within a line of succession of heretics. For him, however, the particular usefulness of the model is to suggest a genetic affinity between the various positions he attacks; he repeatedly assumes that arguments against one are valid against another (e.g. *AH* II. 28.6; III. 4.3). He slips from one to another or he uses generalisations assumed to encompass all – a pattern that will be continued by his successors. It also means that Irenaeus does not have to explain how or why each reached the position they took, although he does imply that error arises from asking inappropriate questions of the Scriptures (II. 28.1–4). Certainly, there is no hint of the account that Tertullian will give that Marcion was originally a member of the Roman church. The philosophical setting of the idea of 'heresy' also determines that the focus is on what each teaches; only occasionally are practices referred to and then primarily to hint at debauchery or inconsistency. Yet, despite the exposition of the different elements in that teaching, it can for Irenaeus be reduced to a single principle that has its source in the very beginning of 'heresy' and its representative – Simon Magus – and which can then be predicated of 'all heretics':[51]

Hence, Marcion's thought is constrained within the parameters which for Irenaeus are fundamental to all heresy:[52]

- For whatever of utmost seriousness *all the heretics* say, at the end they all deviate in this way, that they blaspheme the Creator. …
- and deny the salvation of what God has formed, which is the flesh (IV. praef. 3).
- This is the maker of heaven and earth, as is shown by his own words, and not he who is invented as a false Father by Marcion or by Valentinus, or by Basilides, or by Carpocrates, or by Simon, or by the other falsely named Gnostics (IV. 6.4).

[51] This formula comes twenty-one times in the 'Against Heresies'.
[52] On these, see André Benoit, 'Irénée et l'hérésie'.

- According to no tenet of *the heretics* was the Word made flesh; if anyone were to read the affirmations of them all he would find that the Word of God and the Christ from above is represented by *all of them* as without flesh and impassable (III. 11.3).
- Vain and foolish are they *all*, and indeed shameless, who set aside the form of the Gospel, and introduce either more of fewer expressions of Gospels,[53] some so they may appear to have discovered more of the truth, others so they may set aside the dispensations of God (III. 11.9).

It should cause no surprise that the account of Marcion's teaching follows this same outline. Only on occasion does Irenaeus admit any real difference – the two Gods of Marcion as opposed to the aeons of Valentinus; Marcion's mutilation of the Scriptures as opposed to Valentinus additional traditions (*AH* I. 27.4; III. 12.12; 25.3). Even these differences he often blurs, asserting that the arguments against one are equally valid against the other (II. 1.1–4; 3.1; 31.1). Yet such differences are clearly more important than he will admit, and it is precisely these that may prove to be most significant for determining Marcion's own position.

However, these principles that he attributes to 'all heretics' are determined not by their own systems but by his; he projects upon those whom he opposes the negation of what were for him the key components of the 'rule of truth'. Whether or not his opponents were operating within the same overall but mirrored framework is for him of no interest; thus, it has not been possible to discover how Marcion himself would have understood salvation or eschatology, except where these fail to echo Irenaeus' own convictions. There may indeed be a hidden dialogue in process; the way that Irenaeus expresses his understanding of the divine 'economy' was not shaped in abstract or prior to any engagement with alternative ideas but in the exercise of excluding them. For example, despite his exegetical justification for the fourfold Gospel, it is difficult to imagine that he came to such a position entirely independently of those who advocated some other pattern of Gospel authority. Supporting the concealment of any such dialogue stands Irenaeus' concept of the Church in possession of the truth, unchanging and unanimous in a demonstrable succession. Here, the conflicts in which he was engaged – for example, over the celebration of Easter (cf. Eusebius,

[53] The contrast is between *species* (ἰδέα) and *personae* (πρόσωπα) and refers back to the argument for the necessity of the fourfold Gospel.

HE V. 23–4) – are passed over in silence, as is anything that might indicate anything other than peremptory and decisive encounters between those whom he opposes and representatives of his own authoritative tradition. To locate Marcion within the second century will require uncovering those more extensive hidden dialogues.

4

Marcion through Tertullian's eyes

WRITING *AGAINST MARCION*

The Marcion who has had the most impact on modern perceptions is undoubtedly the Marcion who emerges from Tertullian's lengthy polemics against him, particularly the five books comprising *Against Marcion* (*AM*). This 'magnum opus' makes up an estimated twenty per cent of the surviving total work of this prolific and erudite writer, who himself made such a major contribution to the development of Latin Christian literature. The clear and deliberate overall structure of the treatise also contributes to the impression that it provides a comprehensive account of Marcion's principles: firstly, the separate treatments of the superior God and of the Creator proposed by Marcion (Books I and II), then an extended rebuttal of Marcion's docetism and a detailed defence of the prophetic anticipation of Jesus' ministry and Passion (Book III), and finally a careful analysis of Marcion's text and interpretation of Luke's Gospel and of the ten Pauline letters (Books IV and V). It is this that has earned *Against Marcion* the descriptions of it as the 'first extended work of Christian argument' and the first systematic engagement with scriptural exegesis.[1] Such sobriquets are a reminder, however, that Tertullian saw his task not as the dispassionate record and discussion of his opponent's views, but as the argued demonstration of the coherence and integrity of the Christian truth. He had already established the contours of this task in his earlier *On the Prescription of Heretics* (*PrH*), and against Marcion he had 'only' to work out the foundational principles he had there established: 'For us there is no room for curiosity after Jesus Christ, nor for inquisitorialness after the Gospel';

[1] Eric Osborn, *Tertullian, First Theologian of the West* (Cambridge: Cambridge University Press, 1997), 90, 115.

'the primacy of truth, the lateness of the lie'; 'if they are heretics, they cannot be Christians' (*PrH* 7.12; 31.1; 37.2).

Tertullian was a combative writer who saw opposition and error on many fronts, outside as well as ostensibly within the Church. The principles he defends and the dangers to which he is alert, therefore, are the result of his extensive and intensive engagement with a far broader range of pastoral and polemical concerns than undertaken by any of his predecessors. It is within this framework that Tertullian develops a very strong consciousness of 'heresy' and also of the decisive role of the normative 'discipline' of the Church.[2] His much-celebrated antipathy towards philosophy and its sophistical arguments belongs here, but, despite it, he marshals to his own aid a panoply of philosophical and rhetorical skills that have led some to suppose that he was educated as a rhetor or as a jurist.[3] The consequences of all this will be greater if, as is likely, a number of his key writings were produced within a relatively short time period, one when he was also having to defend his own position against other significant Church leaders.[4] Tertullian composed *Against Marcion* during the period when he himself was openly advocating the cause of the 'New Prophecy' (Montanism), to which he does make passing reference (*AM* V. 16.4). This itself presented a challenge when attacking a message that itself emphasised the radical newness of God's revelation of doing so from a position where he too wanted to be free to defend 'newness' and the possibility of new revelations even beyond the time of the earthly Jesus.[5] Yet these particular commitments may have only exacerbated those characteristics that he already shared with Marcion – namely, an ascetic rigorism, a pessimism about the human condition, and a negative evaluation of how far a true understanding of God was evinced by, or possible to, those before Christ, as well as a love of antithesis and of apparent contradiction.[6] At every point, Tertullian's Marcion cannot be understood independently of Tertullian himself.

2 See Charles Munier, 'Les conceptions hérésiologiques de Tertullien', *Augustinianum* 20 (1980), 257–66.

3 See Timothy D. Barnes, *Tertullian: A Historical and Literary Study* (Oxford: Clarendon Press, 1971), 22–9; Robert D. Sider, *Ancient Rhetoric and the Art of Tertullian* (Oxford Theological Monographs; London: Oxford University Press, 1971), 11–20; Osborn, *Tertullian*, 6–11, gives a nuanced picture.

4 See Barnes, *Tertullian*, 30–56, and herein, p. 81.

5 For example, *De Ieun.* 1.3; 15.1–2, and p. 84 herein.

6 Harnack, *Der Moderne Glaübige*, 63, already compared and contrasted the 'überspannten Excentricität' of Marcion and Tertullian. See also, n. 90.

Marcion himself was long dead, perhaps even by the time of Tertullian's birth;[7] moreover, the former worked in a Greek-speaking context, the latter, although bilingual, wrote in Latin for an audience who in north Africa were presumably more at home in that language.[8] However, Tertullian's comment that 'Just as wasps make nests, so Marcionites makes churches', although typical hyperbole, probably does reflect something of the influence of the movement in the region (*AM* IV. 5.3). Even so, it would appear that Tertullian did not begin with a very full knowledge of the distinctive teaching of Marcion, at least before he engaged in detail in this enterprise.[9] Previous to that, Tertullian had made a number of charges against Marcion in the *Prescription of Heretics*, which is usually dated to somewhere around 203 CE. In that work he was more concerned to establish firm principles against heresy; to this end he brings together Valentinus and Marcion, along with Apelles, to form a representative triumvirate, and he pays less attention to identifying their distinctive ideas except where it suits his purpose, although, even so, his knowledge of Marcion's views appears sketchy (*PrH* 7.3; 10.7–8; 30, etc.).[10]

On Tertullian's own account there was a number of stages in the composition of *Against Marcion*, leading to the final structure of the argument across its five books: He explains that his preliminary attempt proved inadequate and that his second version was stolen and released to his discredit, before he produced the full work in its final form (*AM* I. 1). It was, however, a literary topos for an author to claim that he had been forced to publish by the illegitimate earlier release of a draft; in some cases, so doing served as a justification for producing for a wider public material that originated in argument and debate among a more limited circle. Here it would also allow Tertullian to contrast his own concern for accuracy with Marcion's destructive treatment of his texts.[11] It is, therefore, difficult to determine the precise period over which it was composed, including that of the final publication; a reference in Book I sets the date as 207–8 CE (*AM* I. 15.1), but there is no firm indication of the

7 Often dated to c. 150 CE, but Barnes, *Tertullian*, 57–9, argues for a date closer to 170 CE.

8 On the question of whether Tertullian read Marcion's works in Greek or in Latin translation, see herein, p. 193.

9 See herein, pp. 53, 57, 235.

10 See, generally, Dietrich Schleyer, transl. and introd., *Tertullian de Praescriptione Haereticorum. Vom Prinzipiellen Einspruch gegen die Häreticker* (FC 42; Turnhout: Brepols, 2002).

11 For the practice, see Jaap Mansfeld, *Prolegomena: Questions to be Settled Before the Study of an Author or Text* (Ph.Ant. 56; Leiden: Brill, 1994), 118; on Tertullian's use of it, Sider, *Ancient Rhetoric*, 29–30.

completion of the whole.[12] During the same period as he was producing *Against Marcion*, Tertullian was also writing targeted defences of the real fleshliness of Christ (*De Carne Christi*) and of the bodily resurrection (*De Resurrectione Carnis*), both of which included Marcion and Valentinus among their chief opponents.[13] Yet even with these it is difficult to gain a confident picture of the development of Tertullian's direct knowledge of Marcionite teaching. It is widely agreed that Books IV and V of *Against Marcion* were written only for the final version of the work, as a result of Tertullian having acquired direct access to 'the actual Scriptures which Marcion uses', something that is only in prospect in Book I (*AM* I. 15.1; 16.2; 29.9). On the other hand, although already in Book I he appealed to Marcion's 'Antitheses', 'that is the contradictory oppositions which attempt to establish the disagreement between Gospel and Law in order to argue for the difference of Gods from the difference of ideas in each document' (I. 19.4; cf. IV. 4.3), it is, as shall be seen, far from certain how much he knew of these, and when.[14]

In addition to such Marcionite texts as he may at various times have been able to consult,[15] Tertullian also drew on several earlier sources; although some are identifiable, others probably included works against Marcion now lost, most notably that of Theophilus of Antioch (Eusebius, *HE* IV. 24).[16] On occasion, Tertullian also directed against Marcion arguments that originally had some other target – for example, he makes more precise the generalised refutations 'against the heretics' by Irenaeus, and he even reuses his own arguments from different contexts.[17] A particular problem is posed by the close, often verbal, similarities between parts of

12 See Barnes, *Tertullian*, 255–6, who thinks the composition could have taken a matter of months rather than years, and suggests 207–8 CE; René Braun, introduction, texte critique, traduction et notes, *Tertullien: Contre Marcion*, Tome I (SC 365; Paris: Éditions du Cerf, 1990), 11–19, who also discusses the relationship to Tertullian's associated writings, suggests 211–12 CE.

13 He refers to *On the Resurrection* in *AM* V. 10.1, while *On the Flesh* refers to *AM* IV (*De Carne* 7.1) and is itself referred to by *De Res.* 2.5. Untangling these cross-references is made more complicated by the possibility that there were also initial drafts of these works. Jean-Pierre Mahé, introd., texte critique, traduction et commentaire, *Tertullien. La Chair du Christ* (2 vols.; SC 216–17; Paris: Éditions du Cerf, 1975), 1, 15–26, 86–92, argues that *On the Flesh* was written before Tertullian gained a precise knowledge of Marcion's system.

14 See further herein, pp. 273–6.

15 Most notably Marcion's purported letter (*AM* I. 1.6; IV. 4.3–4), on which see herein, p. 272, and Jean-Pierre Mahé, 'Tertullien et l'epistula Marcionis', *RSR*, 45 (1971), 358–71.

16 See herein p. 9. On his sources see Gilles Quispel, *De Bronnen van Tertullianus' Adversus Marcionem* (Burgersdijk & Niemans, 1943).

17 See, for example, the exegesis of 2 Cor. 4.4 (above, p. 44) and also the arguments crafted against Hermogenes (herein, p. 352).

Book III of *Against Marcion* and the later chapters of the *Against the Jews* (*AJ*) attributed to him.[18] There is a growing consensus that *Against the Jews* is a genuine and earlier work by Tertullian, which perhaps was never completed or properly published, although it seems likely that there also may have been some reverse influence from *Against Marcion* on its later transmission.[19] The fact that arguments 'against the Jews' (whether literally or as a genre) concerning the scriptural prophecies would be reused against Marcion, and vice versa, belongs to the reception history as well as to the construction history of the image of both protagonists. Thus, *Against Marcion* presents the reader with layers of polemic, both those of Tertullian himself and those of his sources; not only may his arguments not be his own, but even the views he credits to Marcion and his followers, especially when these are easily overturned, may not be theirs but may be inventions by earlier detractors, if not by Tertullian himself.

It is possible that Tertullian had been involved in oral disputes with Marcionites, and there may be traces of such in his polemic. However, his regular adoption of direct address, 'you say', owes most to the rhetorical conventions of diatribe; indeed, when, as often, the plural interchanges with the singular, this is for effect and not because Tertullian wants to distinguish between the master and his followers. In practice, his intended audience was not the committed Marcionites of his own day but members of his own community;[20] he closes by directly inviting his reader (singular) to study the arguments and to acknowledge their force (*AM* V. 21.2). Of course, such an assessment, 'not ... but', may be over-sympathetic to the position that Tertullian wishes to reinforce, that the 'churches' built by the Marcionites, and the ideas that they represented, were entirely separate from those of Tertullian, his readers, and those whom he includes among 'us'. The vigour of his polemic may suggest that this was not so readily taken for granted by all. It will not be very easy to determine how many people within the communities that Tertullian intended to address expressly identified themselves with the ideas taught by Marcion and his followers; however,

18 See especially Geoffrey D. Dunn, *Tertullian's* Adversus Iudaeos: *A Rhetorical Analysis* (NAPSMS 19; Washington, DC: Catholic University of America Press, 2008), 5–30; Hermann Tränkle, ed., *Q.S.F. Tertulliani Adversus Iudaeos: mit Einleting und kritischen Kommentar* (Weisbaden: Steiner, 1964), lxvii–lxxiv; Barnes, *Tertullian*, 53, 106–7, accepts *AJ* as genuine, and dates it to 197 CE, but suggests that he did not intend its publication.

19 See, for example, below, p. 66.

20 On this see Volker Lukas, *Rhetorik und literarischer 'Kampf': Tertullians Streitschrift gegen Marcion als Paradigma der Selbstvergewisserung der Orthodoxie gegenüber der Häresie. Eine philologisch-theologische Analyse* (EH. 23, Theologie 859; Frankfurt im Main: P. Lang, 2008).

as will become evident, at many points key theological language and principles as well as practices held on both sides could appear uncomfortably close to each other – as was already the case for Tertullian himself. Contrary to the rhetoric of self-evident incompatibility, Tertullian often has to demonstrate difference where not all would have recognised it; he also has to explore for the first time the consequences of such a demonstration.

Even so, the direct address and the responses that Tertullian imaginatively puts on the mouth of his opponent have encouraged readers to imagine the two protagonists in face-to-face conflict. Some even find it hard to suppress a sense that Marcion on occasion emerges the victor: 'two uneven opponents: the sharp-witted and yet somewhat less original Tertullian, and Marcion, far superior in profundity and originality'.[21] Such responses are partly a result of dissatisfaction with Tertullian's answers to some of the theological dilemmas that Marcion raises.[22] To the modern reader the argument may also often seem tortuous and repetitious – and not just to the modern, as Tertullian is well aware as he comes to a close: 'If you study the whole of this little work, you will condemn neither redundancy here nor hesitation previously' (*AM* V. 21.1). Moreover, modern self-conscious immunity to his rhetorical strategies may lead to a certain scepticism towards some of his arguments, forgetting their probable effectiveness by the standards of his own time; yet such a bias may also hide an over-hasty susceptibility to his account of Marcionite beliefs, interpretation, and textual readings. Tertullian's Marcion can only be reached through the strategies of Tertullian's arguments and the principles of Christian faith he wishes to defend.

TECHNIQUES OF PERSUASION

However Tertullian may present the genesis of *Against Marcion*, he consciously controls the structure of the argument at every level. Thus, despite his conventional admission of potential redundancy and hesitation, both the types of argument that he deploys and the overall structure of each book can be shown to conform to the recognised norms of forensic rhetoric.[23] So also, across the work as a whole, the separation between a

21 Meijering, *Tertullian contra Marcion*, ix; similarly, Osborn, *Tertullian*, 103, 113.

22 So, especially, Osborn, *Tertullian*, 101–3, 158.

23 In general see Sider, *Ancient Rhetoric*, 49–60; alternatively, Meijering, *Tertullian contra Marcion* presents this pattern as philosophically shaped. For the structure of individual books see the analysis in the introduction to each volume by Braun, *Contre Marcion*.

relentless philosophical exposure of the irrationality of Marcion's ditheism as he presents it in the initial books and the more exegetical analysis in the later ones is fully deliberate.[24] The conclusions that Tertullian has reached in the former exercise determine the way he presents both Marcion's reading of their shared scriptural texts and his response to that in the latter. Together these self-conscious choices already impose a shape that may well be alien to the structure and logic of Marcion's own system. However, it is the latter, the separation of modes, that does most to mould the reader's picture of Marcion and of the untenability of his position.

Marcion the man: vilification and association

Before he even appears on the page Marcion is doomed from his very origins; presupposing without comment the established tradition of Marcion's background, Tertullian opens with a sustained diatribe against the conventional – and mythical – characteristics of 'barbarian' Pontus. Ignoring the probable Greek parentage of his 'barbarian heretic', he repeatedly alludes to this Pontic inheritance: The people are inhospitable, nomadic, given to cannibalism, even of their parents' bodies, and promiscuous, with unrestrained women 'who prefer war to marriage', while the climate knows only extremes (*AM* I. 1.3–5; 10.3). Marcion himself outdoes not only the inhabitants but even its native wild animals, the beaver and stoat, whose proverbial characteristics anticipate his destructive treatment of both marriage and the Gospels.[25] He even compares unfavourably with the Cynic – in Greek, 'doglike' – Diogenes, who also came from the Pontic region.[26] Uncompromising denunciation of the character and lifestyle exhibited by philosophical opponents, particularly of those who might be associated with Diogenes, was an existing, and obvious, weapon in philosophical debate.[27] This fortuitous connection combines with an established tradition of excoriation to provide Tertullian with regular ammunition: 'O dogs, whom the apostle expels outside' (*AM* II. 5.1, cf. Rev. 22.15; Phil. 3.2). Similarly, Tertullian repeatedly alludes to Marcion's occupation as a 'sea-captain' (*nauclerus*) to draw every possible negative

[24] For the separation see Meijering, *Tertullian contra Marcion*, 51; for the repetition see René Braun, introd. traduction et commentaire, *Tertullien: Contre Marcion* Tome IV (texte critique by Claudio Moreschini; SC 456; Paris: Éditions du Cerf, 2001), 44–6.

[25] See Braun, *Contre Marcion*, I, 104, n. 1 for the castration of the beaver and ferocity of the stoat (or Pontic rat).

[26] Diogenes came from Sinope, which is later, although not by Tertullian, identified as Marcion's home; see below, p. 101.

[27] As in Philodemus' *On the Stoics*; see Clay, 'Philodemus on the Plain Speaking', 60–4.

association of a business easily open to dubious reputation: false accounting, smuggling, ship-wrecking rocks (*AM* I. 2.1; 7.7; 18.4; V. 1.2).[28] Such vilification by association is a conventional feature in the *exordium* or introduction to a speech,[29] and it prepares for the regular ejaculations that follow, 'totally impudent'; 'ignorant rustic' (I. 13.1; II. 4.2).

In practice Tertullian knows little about Marcion's early biography prior to his emergence in Rome.[30] He postpones any reference to that key event until it suits his argument, then emphasising the long delay since the ministry of Jesus: 'Indeed, in what year of the elder Antoninus [Pius] the pestilential[31] wind blew from Pontus I have not troubled to determine. In any case, it is agreed that he is an Antonine heretic, impious under Pius'. Tertullian then reinforces the point by contrasting his own lack of interest with the Marcionites' own very precise measurement, 115 years, six and a half months (*AM* I. 19.2; cf. IV. 4.5; V. 19.2 for Marcion as 'Antonine').[32] This is somewhat at odds with his earlier claim that both Valentinus and Marcion initially shared in 'the faith of the catholic Church when Eleutherus was bishop of the Roman church, but were ejected because of their restless curiosity' (*PrH* 30.2). Although this might be the result of the tendency to generalise from one to the other, and from the principle of the temporal priority of the truth, he still claims in *Against Marcion* that Marcion's own writings, apparently a letter, demonstrated that he was originally 'one of us', although here he does not state whether or not in Rome: 'Marcion lost the God whom he had found when the light of his faith was put out' (*AM* I. 1.5–6).[33] Later, he expands on this, here to demonstrate the priority of 'our' Gospel of Luke, in which 'Marcion himself had at one stage believed': After Marcion had fallen into heresy, the money he had given to the Church 'in the first heat of faith' was thrown out together with the man himself' (IV. 4.3). Surprisingly, he does not specify the amount here, as he had in his earlier account ('two hundred thousand sesterces', *PrH* 30.2), even though money and its abuses could easily provide further fodder for polemic. It would be hazardous, therefore, to use the earlier figure to estimate

28 On Marcion's occupation, see below, p. 318.

29 Sider, *Ancient Rhetoric*, 23–6.

30 See below, p. 296; it is difficult to think that Tertullian understands Marcion to have been active anywhere else than in Rome.

31 '*Canicularis*', a play on the 'dog', Diogenes (cf. *AM* I. 1.5, '*canicula*'); the translation is that of Ernest Evans, ed. and transl., *Tertullian, Adversus Marcionem* (2 vols.; OECT; Oxford: Clarendon Press, 1972).

32 On this date, see below, p. 296.

33 In explicit contrast with Diogenes who 'found men by carrying a lamp around in the middle of the day'. On the letter (*littera* in *AM* I. 1, and *epistula* in IV. 4, and *De Carne* 2.4–5) see above, n. 15, and below, pp. 272–3.

Marcion's social status, and the claim may simply reinforce a conventional association of almsgiving with doctrinal orthodoxy.[34] Neither does he repeat the claim made there that Marcion had repented but was only prevented from returning to the Church and reconciliation, together with those he had misled, by his death – itself an admonitory example.[35] The various purposes that these conflicting accounts serve warn against relying on them, still less harmonising them, to recover the 'historical Marcion'. Even the apparently precise time span, usually construed as 144 CE, does not specify which of these moments in Marcion's career it marks.[36] Silence may be more telling, in particular that Tertullian does not use another routine accusation, namely that of sexual impropriety or of giving women undue licence, this despite his barbed remarks about Pontic promiscuity – although such accusations would evolve in subsequent polemic.[37]

Other associations that Tertullian does make are equally routine and should not be taken as factually based: It is a standard topos to trace error to the influence of philosophers, 'by whose ingenuity every heresy is inspired', although Marcion treats the created order worse than they do (*AM* I. 13.3); he has acquired his God from the school of Epicurus, but even here he falls short (I. 25.3; II. 16.2; IV. 15.2) – although in his earlier treatment Tertullian had dubbed him 'learned in Stoicism' (*PrH* 30.1). Mocking the unheralded appearance of the Marcionite God, Tertullian suggests that perhaps he was constrained by some confluence of the stars: 'For Marcionites are particularly astrologers, unashamed to live themselves by the stars of the Creator' (*AM* I. 18.1) – a charge that has no other support than the routine association of heresy with magical practices (cf. *De Idol.* 9). On the contrary, even 'the popular superstition of the idolatry of the masses', when most positively understood, honours the creative achievements of God where Marcion fails to do so (*AM* I. 13.4).

More distinctive is Tertullian's association of Marcion with the Jews: 'Let the heretic give up borrowing poison from the Jew, the asp from the viper as the saying goes' (*AM* III. 8.1). The context for such association is for the most part the interpretation of the scriptural prophecies, particularly

34 See Richard Finn OP, *Almsgiving in the Later Roman Empire: Christian Promotion and Practice* (Oxford Classical Monographs; Oxford: Oxford University Press, 2006), who describes almsgiving in the Apocryphal Acts 'as a marker of the doctrinal orthodoxy recognised by their authors and redactors' and notes the interest in the texts in the size of donations (p. 130).

35 There may be an echo of Irenaeus' account of Cerdo as moving in and out of the Church (*AH* III. 4.3).

36 On the date see below, p. 296.

37 See below, pp. 101–2, 388.

those that Tertullian takes as messianic; in refusing this meaning Marcion is 'forced to ally himself with the Jewish error', although the Jews equally share in Marcion's error (III. 6.2; 7.1; 16.3). Most of such charges occur in Book III where Tertullian is reusing material from his own earlier work *Against the Jews*, and so they serve, perhaps, to justify his self-plagiarism:

AJ 9.21: Learn then the custom of your error: when Auses son of Nave was designated successor to Moses, he clearly gave up the first name and began to be called Jesus. "Clearly", you say. First we say this was a figure of what would come to be.	*AM* III. 16.3: Learn then this with those who share in your error, the Jews: when Auses son of Nave was designated successor to Moses, he clearly gave up the first name and began to be called Jesus. "Clearly", you say. First we say this was a figure of what would come to be.

Indeed, Tertullian most probably inherited a number of his arguments about scriptural prophecy and prefiguration from an earlier 'against the Jews' tradition; in this case, he is inviting his readers to transfer to Marcion the negative characterisation of Jewish unbelief that by now was common parlance: 'You are much to be pitied, you who, along with the people, do not recognise Christ prefigured in the person of Moses' (*AM* II. 26.4). In so doing he could also undermine any claims to 'newness' that Marcion may have made. Derivation from Jewish error is as rhetorically determined as is derivation from philosophical sophistry.[38] On the other hand, it is notable that Tertullian makes few attempts to discover 'pagan' roots for Marcion's ideas, although some of his own arguments are similarly drawn from existing apologetics against the 'pagan' failure to acknowledge the one God.

It is within that tradition that he accuses Marcion both of inconsistency and of ingratitude: 'You despise the earth ... and yet you extort from it its very marrow for your sustenance. You disapprove of the sea, but not so far as its riches, which you consider a more holy form of food ... Hypocrite, even if you were to prove yourself a Marcionite by self-starvation' (*AM* I. 14.4–5);[39] 'You, Marcion, also enjoy his [the Creator's] sun and showers, without gratitude' (IV. 17.7; cf. II. 18.2). Yet the argument from inconsistency betrays a total inability to appreciate the other's own integrity:

38 See further below, pp. 78–9.

39 Tertullian uses against Marcion, the Marcionite asceticism and vegetarianism, which presumably allowed the consumption of fish; see below, p. 394.

'Why then, if you do not fear God as one who is good, do you not abandon yourself to every pleasure, which is, I know, the highest joy for all who do not fear God? Why do you not frequent the regular delights of the frantic races, the savage arena, the lascivious theatre?' (I. 27.5). Tertullian knows that the answer will be a horrified 'Not that (*absit*)!', but all he can do with that is to mock it.

Even more creatively than does Irenaeus, Tertullian employs a whole lexicon of disparagement to describe Marcion's system: Marcion invents, creates, destroys, insinuates, and makes nothing but a chattering clamour; Marcion or his followers are audacious, stupid, and arrogant astrologers ... Like other heretics Marcion evaluates God according to the choice of his own mind (II. 2.1), just as he surrendered his initial faith and chose for himself one that did not previously exist – a 'chooser' being the very definition of 'heretic' (I. 1.5–6; cf. II. 2.7).[40] More specifically, Marcion is accused of an 'excess of curiosity', to be contrasted with the 'simplicity of the truth' (I. 2.2; II. 21.2). This, for Tertullian, is the most fundamental of errors, as in the celebrated contrast, 'What then have Athens and Jerusalem in common? What the academy and the church? What heretics and Christians? Our education is from the portico of Solomon who himself handed down that the Lord is to be sought in the simplicity of the heart' (*PrH* 7.9). Marcion fails to avoid the dangers of building on uncertainties and so of getting embroiled 'in those interminable questions which the apostle dislikes' (*AM* I. 9.7; cf. 1 Tim. 1.4). He misunderstands sayings that are really straightforward, although it is not to his credit that he appeals to those of 'uncultured minds' (*AM* I. 2.1; 9.1). In his exegesis he is 'extremely subtle' when the straightforward meaning of the words suffices, although in other cases he is to be castigated for paying attention only to the sound of the words and not to its true sense (V. 5.7; III. 12). Instead, 'like many people now, and especially the heretics', he becomes wearied by 'the question of evil' (I. 2.2): Although Tertullian will turn to that vexed question in detail (II. 5–11), the casual 'many people now' once again betrays the seriousness of a debate that was not limited to Marcion's own 'curiosity'.

Reason and logic

Such accusations reflect Tertullian's well-known ambivalence towards philosophy.[41] Interminable questions and the dismissal of the simple are

40 The Greek root of *hairesis* is the verb 'to choose', although Tertullian uses the Latin *eligere*.
41 See Osborn, *Tertullian*, 27–47.

the marks of those who rely on their own wisdom and reject the way of faith. That 'the power of truth is swift and loves brevity; many words will be necessary for falsehood', is presumably said without any note of self-mockery (*AM* II. 28.3). Yet this does not prevent Tertullian from deploying an arsenal of quasi-philosophical arguments or from betraying his own affinity for certain philosophical schemes.[42] This is certainly how Book I works, with few appeals to Scripture: 'since there is universal agreement on this – for no-one will deny that God is something entirely great … what then will be the character of that supremely great entity?' (I. 3.3). Here reason is not in conflict with faith: 'Whatever reasoning (*ratio*) does not allow the introduction of a number of supreme greatnesses, similarly does not allow two … Among us the strength of that reasoning does not allow belief in many gods because of the same limitation by which the rule (*regula* [i.e., of faith]) establishes one God, not two' (I. 5.2). Nonetheless, 'plurality of divinity ought to be established by the highest level of reason' (I. 5.4). Tertullian insists on arguing from first principles, not from hindsight: 'it was right and proper (*oportebat*) that God should be known. This is both good and reasonable (*rationale*). It was right and proper that there should be something worthy of knowing God. What could be considered worthy other than the image and likeness of God? This indeed is without doubt both good and reasonable' (II. 6.2–3).

Such language was familiar in philosophical debate and Tertullian continually calls upon it: What is proper, worthy, reasonable, befits God. That there might be any alternative logic is simply ruled out of court. Suppose God did act in some other way, for example, by overruling human freedom of will, 'would not Marcion call out, "Oh what a foolish lord, unstable, unfaithful, retracting that which he established!"?' (II. 7.3). So, when Tertullian introduces alternative viewpoints, they may be no more than devices to advance his own position: '"One way or the other", you say, "the substance of the Creator is shown to be capable of sin"'; 'But if you transfer the charge of evil from man to the devil' (II. 9.1; 10.1). No doubt there were those who could and did propose such possibilities, but they should not be taken as the genuine voice of Tertullian's opponent – he only allows those alternatives that he is able to dismiss. Fictive debates serve the same purpose: 'Undoubtedly you will admit that the Creator is a God? "Undoubtedly", you say. Why then do you think there is something human in God, and not everything divine?' (II. 16.3).

42 See Meijering, *Tertullian contra Marcion*, 1–3.

Just as Marcion was accused of inconsistency, so too are his arguments: 'But if you say, "Human opinion may think what it wants", then you are honouring your God with a title based on trickery' (III. 11.5). Most insistently, Marcion's logical inconsistency is displayed by the inconsistency of his God: 'So far it is enough to have demonstrated that [their] God is extremely inconsistent even in that celebration of his singular goodness, in which they refuse to ascribe to him those types of emotion of mind of which they disapprove in the Creator'; 'Now I can say that when Marcion's God disapproves of marriage as an evil and as dealing in unchastity, he acts against that very sanctity which he is supposed to encourage' (I. 26.1; 29.5). In due course Marcion's Christ will be accused of the same inconsistency (IV. 10.8–16). Repeatedly, this accusation is driven home by the withering irony that characterises much of Tertullian's polemic: So, then, Marcion's God 'came forward into notice when he wanted, when he was able to, when the destined hour approached' (I. 18.1). The bottom line for Tertullian is that 'Reason without goodness is not reason, but neither is goodness without reason goodness – unless perchance for the God of Marcion who is irrationally good, as I have shown' (II. 6.2). Once again, where Tertullian does allow his opponent to voice counter-protests, these serve his own rhetorical purpose, not the interests of open debate. Tertullian admits that many do indeed believe in Marcion's God, but their belief is devoid of reason for they have no pledge, namely the deeds worthy of God (I. 12.3). It is Tertullian's logic that determines this conclusion, not evidence that Marcion and his followers were moved by the convictions of their emotions alone.[43]

Nonetheless, Tertullian does work with certain fundamental principles, some of which belong to an analysis of his constructive argument. Best known, perhaps, is his 'rule concerning novelty' (*praescriptio novitatis*): 'For to the same extent as that which is introduced later is to be considered heresy, so too truth is recognised as that which was handed down earlier and from the beginning' (I. 1.6). This was a widely recognised norm, and novelty was a charge that had regularly been brought against Christianity itself.[44] Tertullian ignores this, although elsewhere the 'newness' of Jesus would have to be tackled. Instead he turns it also against Marcion's God: 'For when I hear of a new God, unknown and unheard of in an old world and in an old age and under an old God, one whom in so many ages in the past was no-one … I am thankful for this boast of theirs because especially with its help will I prove this confession of, if you want, a new deity to be heresy'.

[43] So Harnack, *Marcion*, 95. [44] See further below, pp. 406–08.

Of course, 'I know that the sense in which they declare him new is in general knowledge of him. But it is this very understanding of novelty, which deeply impresses simple minds, and this natural attractiveness of novelty that I want to press back, and so now to mount a challenge regarding this unknown God' (I. 8.1; 9.1). The reference to 'simple minds' may be another barb, but it may also hint again at an area of real vulnerability. At the same time it is obvious that the epithet 'unknown' is an important one for Tertullian's polemic.

Another principle with which Tertullian has some difficulty is the argument from analogy. When others make it he rejects it: 'This is how the heretics reach the assumption that if a God is angry or jealous or proud or embittered, then he is liable to corruption, then indeed he will die … How very foolish, those who make judgements about things divine from human circumstances'; but this does not prevent him from using similar anthropomorphic analogy to accuse Marcion's God of theft for stealing those who in effect were the possessions of another (II. 16.3–4; I. 23.8). Any language about God must remember that what God experiences God experiences in a manner appropriate to God alone, just as do human beings, but since 'we have been instructed about God from the prophets and from Christ, not from philosophers nor from Epicurus' (II. 16.7, 2), there must always be an element of subjectivity in just what language can be used.

BASIC PRINCIPLES

It is perhaps inevitable that detecting actual claims and counterclaims through the forest of rhetoric will be burdened by a strong degree of subjectivity. Even allowing for the sometimes wearisome repetition, any attempt to summarise Tertullian's argument against Marcion would demand a separate study of its own. Moreover, that argument is inseparable from the understanding of the work of God that Tertullian himself constructs and defends. The discussion that follows shall explore, particularly from the initial Books, the main principles that Tertullian presents as shaping Marcion's error, and as central to the right faith in God.

The principle and indeed therefore the entire matter of discussion is one of number, whether it is permissible to introduce two Gods (AM *I. 3.1*)

As Tertullian shifts to and fro to identify his own starting point, so too does the Marcion he constructs, thus earning the charge of inconsistency or of circular argument. At one point Marcion's downfall is the problem of evil;

later his separation between 'Law and Gospel' is the source of his error about the oneness of God (I. 19.4);[45] in the passage quoted, the issue is quite simple: 'The Pontic introduces two Gods' (I. 2.1). This is a philosophical assertion and it is as simply addressed, philosophically: At the heart of the notion of God-ness is that of the supreme greatness (*summum magnum*), a definition that Tertullian assumes to be universally accepted.[46] The superlative excludes any but a single God (I. 3–5). Yet Tertullian knows that the position he has projected is not the one that Marcion himself holds: The latter's two Gods are not equal; yet, the same philosophical tenet will disprove this, too. Again, his demonstration that 'newness' is equally incompatible with divinity has to be tempered with an acknowledgement that Marcionites do not mean newness in being but in knowledge by people; this, too, does not rescue them from the same philosophical exposure (I. 8–9).

Tertullian may be seeking to demonstrate a philosophical superiority to his adversary, but there is also a sense that he is struggling, and failing, to find the ground on which to meet him: At any rate, this does not seem to be Marcion's primary territory, even if he was inspired by philosophical notions of transcendence. Tertullian feels that Marcion would have done better with an 'entirely static and insensitive' deity of an Epicurean type (I. 25.3) than with one who is good and who intervenes for human benefit; but this, too, betrays a certain perplexity about, or a lack of interest in, Marcion's own rationale for his position. Indeed, Tertullian all but complains that Marcion fails to start from the very principle with which he himself began – 'You ought first to have established that there was one God of light, another of darkness' (IV. 1.11); a genuine dualism, he thinks, would have been a more logical position. Moreover, Tertullian also conducts the debate closer to home, if not with himself: The mere use of the name 'God', even in the plural as in Psalm 81.1, 6, is, he protests, no counter-argument – although it is unlikely that Marcion himself would have made this objection (*AM* I. 7.1–5).

Instead, Tertullian finds a more successful objection to be that the God whom Marcion proposes is one without guarantees, lacking the curriculum vitae that would establish divine credentials (I. 12.3, cited above). He concedes that this deity may have his own created order and world, but the status of these is uncertain; as Tertullian picks up Irenaeus' earlier arguments against a hierarchy of deities and of their concomitant spaces or even against

[45] See below, p. 71. [46] See Meijering, *Tertullian contra Marcion*, 16–21.

pre-existent matter, he again begins to lose sight of his target within the internal dynamics of his logic (I. 15). Such arguments had previously been made in debate over Greek philosophical ideas, and Tertullian gives only half-hearted support to crediting them all to Marcion.[47] Once over this, the real issues come into clearer focus. For Tertullian, what Marcion proclaims is 'a new God, a new Christ, the bringer to light of a new and great religion', and this is a proposition that can be disqualified both by the epithet itself and then by every evidence of any continuity with the past (IV. 17.13). The categories of 'new' and 'unknown' will appear repeatedly throughout the argument: Antiquity is superior to novelty; what is known is more trustworthy than what is not; and so, faith lays hold of what is proven. Yet, his opponents' answer was simple, albeit to Tertullian's mind incoherent: 'Our God has been revealed, indeed not from the beginning nor through creation, but by his very own self in Christ Jesus' (I. 19.1). To believe in this God is, presumably, to be convinced of his unheralded, self-determined, intervention, but Tertullian can scarcely comprehend such a possibility.

Tertullian knows that Marcion attributes to this deity the supreme quality of goodness (*bonitas*). This, too, provokes a litany of dissent, not least the objection that goodness is only imaginary if it does not exhibit anger and retribution against that which disobeys its precepts (I. 27). Chiefly, Tertullian cannot reconcile such an attribute precisely with the claimed 'newness', since that entails the long negligence of human need exhibited by this God. Again, the charge was one that could readily be laid not only against the Christian doctrine of Christ, but even against the scriptural account, and Tertullian's exposure of it has to be interwoven with his own apologetic: 'Even if Moses, he who appears to have been the first to consecrate the God of the world in the temple of his writings, is somewhat later, the birth of knowledge is not to be counted from the Pentateuch' (I. 10.1; cf. I. 22–3; IV. 19.5; 33.7). What Tertullian cannot give serious credence to is the suggestion that the mildness and goodness of Marcion's God did not token an inability to intervene, either before Christ or in judgement, but were expressed by a deliberate withdrawal (*cedere*) or self-restraint (I. 22.6–7).[48] Similarly, for Tertullian's opponents this intervention, inasmuch as it was directed to a world and to a situation that were not that God's responsibility, was exemplary in that it put others first: Not so, protests Tertullian; rather, it was

[47] Evans, *Adversus Marcionem*, 1, xi and 41, n. doubts whether the doctrine of preexistent matter was held by Marcion. See below, pp. 350–5.

[48] So also Enrico Norelli, 'Paix, justice, intégrité de la creation: Irenée de Lyon et ses adversaires', *Irenikon*, 64 (1991), 5–43, 30–1.

irrational or unjust, and if one then the other as well (I. 23). Both protagonists, therefore, and not just Marcion, have to deal with 'the interval between creation and the cross', and to do so not just as a historical sequence, as through Tertullian's appeal to prophecy, prefigurement, and preparation, but as testimony to the actual being and intentions of God.[49]

If God is good and prescient of the future and capable of turning aside evil, why...? (AM *II. 5.1)*

It would have been possible to build a movement around the salvific intervention of a newly proclaimed deity, and to dismiss the relevance of the God described in the Scriptures shared by Jews and other Christians. This was not Marcion's perspective; alongside the 'solely kind and supremely good' God there is also another one whom, according to Tertullian, Marcion insists on also calling 'God', presumably because so did his source, the Scriptures. This deity is most persistently 'the Creator'; he is 'a judge, fierce and warlike (*iudex, ferus, bellipotents*)' (I. 6).[50] More than this, he is proven to lack goodness, prescience, and omnipotence, and even to be actively responsible for evil, to be inconsistent and unreliable in his demands, and to be forever changing his mind (II. 5.2; 21; 23–4). Tertullian treats the initial set of characteristics as having been generated by a dualist opposition accompanied by an attempt to distance transcendence from the creation of the world, or even by an active devaluing of the latter. In response to this he endeavours to demonstrate that goodness and justice are not antithetical qualities but that they demand each other, and that neither Marcion's Jesus nor his followers live entirely independent of the Creator's creation (I. 23; 24–7).

Tertullian probably owes the term *Creator* to Marcion, and his persistent use of it betrays his awareness that it encapsulates the conflict between them.[51] However, as he turns to the defence of the Creator in Book II, it becomes evident that the battle is to be fought not on abstract definitions

49 Osborn, *Tertullian*, 102, concludes that Marcion wins here, 'because Tertullian's jealous God who smites and heals ... does not reflect the love of the cross, which is, for Tertullian, the world's sole hope'.

50 For *bellipotens* (also at *AM* III. 14.7; 21.3 of Christ) compare Irenaeus, *AH* I. 27.2, *bellorum concupiscens*. Braun, *Contre Marcion*, I, 125, n. 3, asks whether this may reflect the Latin of Marcion; if so, this would be a case where the same term in the parallel in the *Against the Jews* has been back-influenced by the *Against Marcion* (*AJ* 9.20/*AM* III. 14.7).

51 Braun, *Deus Christianorum: Recherches sur le vocabulaire doctrinal de Tertullien* (EAA 70; Paris: Études augustiniennes, 1977), 372–6 (374–5), notes that 763 of the 800 occurrences of *creator* in Tertullian are found in *Against Marcion*.

or on metaphysical questions but around the scriptural account of God. Initially this focuses on the story from Genesis 1–3, as to why humankind was created so as both to be capable of doing wrong and to do it, and as to why, in consequence, the God who so created humankind then punished them. Tertullian even suggests that according to Marcion the human capacity for sin must be retrojected on to the Creator who breathed into man, although he may be creating an opportunity to address issues about the soul that occupied him elsewhere (*AM* II. 9.1; cf. Gen. 2.7).[52] More generally, the problem of evil, on whose fascination Tertullian had blamed Marcion's heresy, here appears as a problem of the sovereignty of God, and if of sovereignty then also of consistency in will and in action. It is this that provides the context for the argument over God as judge which will be one of the most central themes: Having attributed human sin to their divinely given free choice Tertullian apparently concedes some ground: 'This is why God up to the point of human sinning was from the beginning only good, but thereafter was judge and severe and, as the Marcionites would have it, cruel … Thus, the goodness of God is prior in accordance with his nature, severity subsequent in accordance with a reason for it' (*AM* II. 11.1, 2). However, he swiftly modifies if not retracts this, appealing to Genesis 1 to see goodness and justice as coeval: 'His goodness created the world, justice moderated it'; but he also doubts whether expectation of one quality without the other would ever inculcate right behaviour in people. Hence, he does after all acknowledge a certain duality in God, 'a Creator always contrary to himself' (IV. 1.10): 'Father in clemency, Lord in discipline; Father in mild power, Lord in severe; Father to be loved from affection, Lord to be feared of necessity' (II. 12.1; 13.5).[53] To some extent, what separates the two protagonists here and elsewhere is how they handle such duality: 'take away Marcion's title (i.e., 'Antitheses') and the intention and thesis of his work, and it will present nothing other than a demonstration of God himself, supreme and judge, because these two [conceptions] come together in God alone' (II. 29.2).[54] Tertullian's Marcion is, unknown to himself, a witness to the true state of affairs; he offers Tertullian the pretext for expanding on his own conception of God, one who indeed is rightly to be feared (cf. IV. 8.7).

52 René Braun, texte critique, traduction et notes, *Tertullien: Contre Marcion*, Tome II (SC 368; Paris: Éditions du Cerf, 1991), 64, n.1 suggests that it is Tertullian who puts the proposal on Marcion's mouth.

53 See below, pp. 345–6, and note the association of 'Lord' with judgement.

54 See below, p. 278; on the importance of paradox in Tertullian, see Osborn, *Tertullian*, 48–64.

Here, too, belongs one element of the question of 'Law', which will later occupy Tertullian so much.[55] For Tertullian, the necessary balance between goodness and justice presupposes divine Law: Goodness without judgement leads to a 'discipline that is a phantasm' – like, a sensitive reader would realise, Marcion's Christ (I. 27).[56] Without law with its concomitant rewards and punishment, why would anyone not choose the path of self-indulgence? Tertullian cannot really comprehend a position where people will do good willingly and not out of fear. Even Marcion's God must have some requirements for human behaviour; but, 'Perhaps you may say these are determined by human laws'. If this were a genuine response it would suggest a very different understanding of human society, but Tertullian is quick with a reply drawn from a long tradition of Jewish and Christian apologetics: 'Moses and God precede all the Lycurguses and Solons; everything that comes later borrows from what precedes it' (II. 17.3).

The debate is not restricted to the opening chapters of Genesis. Tertullian has to counter an appeal to Isaiah 45.7, 'It is I who create evil things', by distinguishing moral evil, of which God is innocent, from justly merited penalties that humans experience as evil; to this end he has to explain why Pharaoh, whose heart God had hardened, and the children who mocked Elisha (2 Kings 2.23), merited their punishment, apparently examples cited by Marcion (*AM* II. 14).[57] This sets the pattern for the bulk of the argument over the Creator, whether over his stated requirements, such as the familiar example of the *lex talionis*, or over his behaviour, such as questions implying ignorance, changes of mind, apparent approval of what he himself disapproves, such as Israel's 'theft' of the Egyptians' goods (Exod. 12.35–6). Similarly, Tertullian uses Marcion's disparagement of a God who described himself as 'jealous', to assert that God's intention to save humanity necessarily involves his rivalry, and even anger or hatred, against all that might thwart that intention (*AM* I. 25.6).[58] Yet the disagreement extends to how God can be spoken of, and the status of language about the divine. Tertullian complains that Marcion can only interpret emotions as a human attribute or as one that is less than divine, failing to recognise that in his perfection God can experience even anger in his own way, that is 'auspiciously' (*feliciter*) (II. 17). In much of this there is little new either in the objections or in the response; some finds its echoes even in Jewish–non-Jewish debate, some in

[55] See herein, pp. 71–5, 403–5. [56] See below, pp. 81–2.

[57] On this and what follows, see below, pp. 285–8.

[58] See Braun, *Deus Christianorum*, 117–19, who suggests that Tertullian may have taken up *zelotes*, which is particularly prominent in *Against Marcion*, from Marcion.

the debates that surrounded the emergence of Christianity from its Jewish roots and then in Christian apologetics.[59] How far either side was consciously drawing on such sources is unclear, and it is even possible that once in his stride down this route Tertullian attributes to his opponents objections that they never voiced.

When Tertullian turns his attention more persistently to the Scriptures it will become evident that the Creator is responsible not only for the Law but also for the prophets. He does, so Tertullian deduces, therefore have a particular relationship with the Jews: 'How is the Creator alien to the Pharisees if he is properly God of the Jewish people?' (IV. 33.4); however, this epithet, like the more precise 'God of the Jews', appears to be Tertullian's coinage rather than one used by Marcion.[60] Tertullian does, however, exploit what he sees as the lack of logic in that the Jews should be condemned, especially by Jesus or by Paul, for failing to obey the prophets, if the latter, on Marcion's account, represented a God who was rightly to be discredited. Marcion's purported response, namely that 'they did not even act piously with their own prophets', sounds a hollow note (*AM* IV. 15.2; cf. V. 14.7–9; 15.1). Tertullian is yet more troubled that the Jews could hardly be blamed for disobeying their prophets and failing to acknowledge Christ as the promised one, and that, if they were blameless, then Marcion's God must be responsible for the destruction that awaits them (II. 15.3; 28.3). Such concerns about Jewish responsibility and merited punishment are evidently of central importance for Tertullian and for his whole reading of Scripture; Marcion represents the undermining of that whole scheme – but whether the place of the Jews was a genuine concern of Marcion himself or is projected upon him by Tertullian is far from obvious.

Nevertheless, from all this it is evident that both Tertullian and his opponent are reading the Scriptures, that both assume that these are the only source of knowledge about the God of whom they speak, and that, for the most part, they are reliable and mean precisely what they say. Marcion thus embodies both a warning that Tertullian had made earlier, and the solution to it: 'Therefore appeal is not to be made to the Scriptures, nor is the contest to be fought in those things in which there is no or uncertain victory, or one that is to some degree uncertain ... Where there

59 See further below, pp. 337–49.

60 Against Harnack, *Marcion*, 263*. Contra Braun, *Contre Marcion*, I, 146 n. 2 and p. 262, there are no grounds for ascribing 'God of the Jews' at *AM* I. 10.3 to Marcion; similarly at V. 13.6; 20.6 Tertullian's use of the phrase does not suggest that he is quoting Marcion.

is seen to be the truth of Christian discipline and faith there will be the truth of the Scriptures and of their exposition and of all Christian traditions' (*PrH* 19).[61] It is within this framework that he can hint at more satisfying figurative meanings, although he cannot rely on these for they would undermine his own defence of 'the simplicity of the truth, not curiosity' (*AM* II. 21.2; cf. 19.1). However, it is this that provides him with a further card to play, and it is one that again contains hints of a concession to Marcion's anxieties. Yes, it is true that 'the Father was visible to no-one' (Luke 10.22; Exod. 33.20): 'Whatever aspects you interpret as worthy of God are to be found in the Father, invisible and inapproachable and peaceable and, as I might say, the God of the philosophers; but whatever you reprove as unworthy are to be attributed to the Son who was seen, heard, and approached' (*AM* II. 27.6).

Here, then, is that other figure on the stage, but in the initial stages of the argument, it would seem, deliberately kept in the shadows by Tertullian. Challenging the 'antitheses' for which he criticises Marcion, he offers his own: 'Our God (i.e., the Creator) demands an eye for an eye, but yours by prohibiting retaliation makes more likely the repetition of the affront. For surely the person who is not hit back will hit again. Our God does not know the quality of those whom he chooses. Well then, neither does yours. He would not have chosen the traitor Judas if he had foreknowledge' (*AM* II. 28.2). Tertullian has, of course, at this point no intention of addressing the exegetical challenges that his own irony has provoked; however, he implies that for his opponent the point of comparison for the God of the Scriptures is Marcion's God, and Marcion's God is characterised by the teaching and expectations of the story of Jesus. Tertullian deliberately postpones any serious discussion of Marcion's 'Gospel', and by so doing he has driven a wedge through the substructure of Marcion's position. Yet he does so only after first using it to solve his own dilemmas, namely by appealing to the descent of the Son in order to explain the anthropomorphic theophanies of the Scriptures: 'Since you yourselves are already convinced that God dwelt in the form and the other circumstances of the human condition, you will not require to be persuaded at any great length that God made himself conform to humanity: you have been defeated by your own beliefs' (II. 27.2).

[61] See Geoffrey D. Dunn, 'Tertullian's Scriptural Exegesis in the *de praescriptione haereticorum*', *JECS*, 14 (2006), 141–55.

The separation of Law and Gospel is the characteristic and chief task of Marcion (AM *I. 19.4)*

Having mounted his attack against Marcion from primary philosophical principles and not from the Scriptures, Tertullian unexpectedly asserts that Marcion's antitheses or 'oppositions' were designed to prove the diversity of Gods on the basis of that between each *instrumentum* or document.[62] Introducing two key terms, he now claims that it is the separation between 'Law and Gospel' that produces the separation between Gods, one responsible for each, rather than the latter opposition, which has occupied him so far, resulting in the former. His refusal to allow Marcion's followers to disagree may suggest that they would have done so, at least in his terms. The claim is in any case shaped to add further support to his mockery of the late appearance of Marcion's God, now dated not to the reign of Tiberius – a date dangerously close to that upheld in the 'rule of faith'[63] – but to Marcion's own promulgation of his message under Antoninus (I. 19.4–5). This he does expect them to challenge, by claiming that Marcion did not innovate but restored a 'rule' (I. 20.1); although he dismisses this challenge as equally vulnerable to unseemly delay, he does address it, by proceeding to discuss not the preaching of Jesus but Paul's relationship with Peter, an issue evidently more widely debated, and one already defended by Irenaeus (*AH* III. 12.9–13.3; cf. Tertullian, *PrH* 23–4). It is striking that the almost talismanic 'separation of Law and Gospel' is absent both from Irenaeus' treatment of the incident and from Tertullian's own earlier discussion of it;[64] although reiterating it here (*AM* I. 21.5), Tertullian then largely ignores the theme until it resurfaces to dominate his interpretation of the Gospel and Pauline letters in Books IV and V. At that point he repeats that Marcion, distancing the Christ who came in the time of Tiberius from the promised Christ of Jewish hope, 'sets up between them as great and complete an opposition as between just and good, as between Law and Gospel, as between Judaism and Christianity (*christianismus*)' (IV. 6.3).[65]

The rhetorical climax he has reached here suits Tertullian's own style, and it anticipates the fact that he himself is not uncomfortable with these oppositions: 'therefore both the destruction of the Law and the building up of the Gospel serve my cause in this letter [Galatians] also' (V. 2.2).

62 On Tertullian's use of *instrumentum* see herein, p. 403.

63 See below, p. 414.

64 *PrH* 23.9 refers instead to the 'separation of the Gospel' between Peter and Paul (cf. Gal. 2.7–8).

65 Compare *AM* IV. 1.1, cited below, p. 73.

He himself will describe the apostles as 'turning aside from Judaism, when they exchanged the obligations and burdens of the law for the liberty of the Gospel' (III. 22.3). It is not the polarity itself that troubles him but its practical as well as its theological consequences: firstly, 'whether the Law of the Creator should be excluded from the Gospel in the Creator's Christ', and, secondly, whether the acknowledged difference points to a difference of deities (V. 2.2, 3). Tertullian's own answer is that the divinity preached is the same, but the discipline is different. The concentration of the language of 'Law and Gospel' in the *Against Marcion* among Tertullian's writings certainly suggests that Marcion raised the issues for him in a particularly focused way, but they were far from alien to his thought already. Writing on prayer, he himself had used the parables of wineskins and garments – reportedly key texts for Marcion – to point to 'a new form of prayer for new disciples of a new covenant [or 'testament']'; the Law is supplemented, prophecy fulfilled, and the Gospel added on (*De Orat.* 1.1).[66] Defending the insights of the 'New Prophecy', perhaps contemporaneously with his polemic against Marcion, he even traced a progression in justice, from the nursery stage of nature, to the Law and prophets in infancy, to the Gospel in youth, and finally to the Paraclete in maturity (*De Virg. Vel.* 1.10). In this last passage, an apologetic addition, 'yet the same God of justice and creation', betrays the unavoidable vulnerability of his attempts to separate between (evolving) 'discipline' and (unified) 'doctrine', and between the (changing) 'disposition' and (unified) identity of God.[67]

Tertullian, it would appear, is reading Marcion through spectacles that both share the same focus and are – perhaps as a consequence – profoundly sensitive to the distortions effected by a common set of tools. In light of his own efforts to understand the place of Law within a scheme patent of new demands and even of new revelation, he may have identified the polarity of 'Law and Gospel' as the vulnerable point both of his own system and of that of his opponent. On the other hand, he perhaps also found in it a language to articulate his own sense of newness and difference: Whereas in *AJ* 9.18 the 'divine word doubly sharp' refers to 'the two testaments of the Old Law and the New Law', against Marcion it becomes 'the two testaments of Law and Gospel' (*AM* III. 14.3; cf. Rev. 1.16).[68] Such passages demonstrate

66 He also contrasts the newness of the Gospel with what is old (*De Corona* 11.1; *De Pudic.* 12.1).

67 See Gerald L. Bray, *Holiness and the Will of God: Perspectives on the Theology of Tertullian* (London: Marshall, Morgan & Scott, 1979), 111–23.

68 The same change appears between *AJ* 9.22 and *AM* III. 16.4, which also add a contrast between 'discipline' and 'grace'.

the fluidity of Tertullian's own understanding of 'Law and Gospel', embracing articulation of discipline, covenant/testament, and also 'document' (*instrumentum*) – the last his own preferred term. When he says that Marcion's task was directed towards 'the separation of Law and Gospel, from this dividing two different Gods, one belonging to each document, or, as is more commonly said, testament', he is again undoubtedly reading his opponent through his own eyes, giving the opposition a textual form that it may not have had for the latter (IV. 1.1).[69] It must be far from certain whether Marcion himself spoke of a 'new testament', or, if he did, whether that would have had any reference to a body of literature.[70]

Although Tertullian had had to discuss the place of the Law in his defence of the justice of the Creator God, it is in Books IV and V that he engages most intensely with its relationship to the Gospel. The issues were not defined abstractly or as ultimate principles, but exegetically; equally, it was not only a matter of the reasonableness of the scriptural ordinances, including the familiar interpretation of the food and purity laws, but also of the accounts of the behaviour of Jesus and then of Paul. Tertullian makes much of Jesus' command to the healed leper to 'offer the gift which Moses commanded': 'In vain did he come down as one who would destroy the Law when he made concessions to those who followed the Law'; 'destroyer' may have been Marcion's epithet, and similarly 'enemy of the Law' (*AM* IV. 9.13; cf. Luke 5.14; *AM* IV. 20.14; 35.8). Likewise, Tertullian imagines his opponent commenting on Jesus' prohibition of divorce, 'Do you see the difference of Law and Gospel, Moses and Christ?' (Luke 16.18; *AM* IV. 34.1). Tertullian's response that a prohibition of divorce hardly sounds like the work of one committed to the destruction of Moses' 'constitution' is a deliberate imposition on Marcion of his own reading of 'Law' as command.[71] Marcion's imagined riposte, however, makes sense in its own terms: Moses and Christ are two authorities, Law and Gospel are the patterns of life they represent and demand.

69 See *Adv.Herm.* 20.4; 22.3, where he describes 'the Gospel' as the supplement to the 'old *instrumentum*' or even to Scripture.

70 Both Evans, *Adversus Marcionem*, 2, 275, and Braun, *Contre Marcion*, IV, 89, provide capitals in their translation at *AM* IV. 6.1; on the term see Wolfram Kinzig, 'Καινὴ διαθήκη: The Title of the New Testament in the Second and Third Centuries', *JTS* 45 (1994), 519–44, who does ascribe the new formulation to Marcion (p. 534). See further pp. 406–08 below.

71 See Philip Lyndon Reynolds, *Marriage in the Western Church: The Christianization of Marriage During the Patristic and Medieval Periods* (VCSup. 24; Leiden: Brill, 1994), 189–200, who shares Tertullian's sense of the incongruity of Marcion's position.

Tertullian himself is forced to a very careful defence of Jesus' own bearing towards the Law and of the Law's pedagogic and moral function as well as of its prophetic role; yet here, too, he is struggling at times, and he cannot avoid describing Gentile converts as those who 'turning aside from Judaism exchanged the obligations and burdens of the Law for the freedom of the Gospel' (III. 22.3; cf. V. 4.1). Although the themes of upholding the Law are stronger in Book IV, when interpreting Paul's letters he is more confident of speaking himself of 'the destruction of the Law and the building of the Gospel', and that 'the Gospel of Christ must summon them from Law to grace', even while insisting that this is not 'from Creator to another God' (V. 2.2, 4). Again, how is duality to be sustained? 'I have already defended the twofold power of the Creator, both as judge and as good, by the letter killing through the Law, by the spirit bringing to life through the Gospel' (V. 11.4).[72]

The opposition between 'Judaism and Christianity' also belongs to the common ground that the two protagonists share, even if the conclusions they draw are different: 'As if we also did not acknowledge that John established a form of boundary between old and new, at which Judaism ceased and from which Christianity began, but not as if the cessation of law and prophets and the initiation of Gospel, in which is the reign of God, Christ himself, were made by another power' (*AM* IV. 33.8, on Luke 16.16; cf. *AM* IV. 6.3 cited above). Tertullian undoubtedly found this contrast more straightforward: He had no interest in preserving in any form the continuing relevance of 'Judaism', nor did he find traces of 'Christianism' in the Scriptures. Although both terms are rare elsewhere in his writings, against Marcion he readily uses them in his own argument as well as when supposedly citing, or summarising, his opponent.[73] Indeed, it is this that makes it difficult at times to determine whose voice we are hearing. Marcion would have found 'Judaism' in his core text, Galatians 1.14, but how he understood it is less certain: Tertullian's assertion that Marcion held that it was 'the upholders of Judaism' within the Church who falsified even the Gospel of Luke and whom Paul opposed, if true, suggests that he identified it among the other apostles and their champions (*AM* IV. 4.4; V. 3.1).[74] Tertullian

[72] See Lieu '"As much my apostle as Christ is mine"', 48–50.

[73] Iudaismus: *AJ* 9.3; *De Pud.* 17; *De Res.* 50.2 (where he claims that some people interpret 'flesh and blood' in 1 Cor. 15.50 as 'Judaism', although he does not refer to this in *AM* V. 10 when discussing this verse); *AM* I. 20.3; III. 6.10; 22.3; IV. 4.4; 6.3; 11.1; 33.8; V. 1.8; 2.1; 3.1, 5; 4.8; 5.1; 6.10; 17.9; *christianismus*: *PrH* 7.11; *AM* IV. 6.3; 33.8; V. 4.8; 6.10. See below, pp. 408–10.

[74] Tertullian says that Jesus' contemporaries viewed him as 'a perverter and destroyer of Judaism' (*AM* III. 6.10), but this may be to align Marcion with them.

himself is much clearer about what both 'Judaism' and 'Christianism' stand for – the synagogue of the Jews and the holy Church (V. 4.8).[75] It is possible that, at least on occasion Tertullian has credited Marcion with a formulation that he himself felt least ambiguous about and so could reconstruct in his own terms.

We admit this separation by reformation, by expansion, by progress (AM IV. 11.11)

Thus, Tertullian agrees to diversity and agrees to separation; he even agrees to antitheses, except that these antitheses are the constant means of the operation of the same God's works and qualities, and even of the divine mysteries (i.e., of salvation, *sacramenta*) (IV. 1.9). For all his impatience with Marcion's 'new' God and 'new' religion, Tertullian cannot surrender the epithet 'new', which had such a central place in Christian self-understanding, not least as rooted in the prophecy of a 'new covenant (*testamentum*)' of Jeremiah 31.31 (*AM* I. 20.4).[76] Indeed, the language of 'newness' is more prominent in Tertullian's own treatment of the Scriptures than it is in any of his predecessors.[77] As has been seen, his own commitment to the 'new prophecy' only heightened the resultant tensions. The figure of Marcion thus provides him with a framework for tackling these tensions. On one level this meant finding a vocabulary to describe the connection between the pattern of relationship with God offered by Jesus and that which pertained before him, and also the relationship between the multifarious requirements set down in the Scriptures and those expected of believers in a Church that took for granted its Gentile character. Such a vocabulary had to emphasise continuity but not at the cost of obscuring such newness; it had to emphasise not just discontinuity but superiority, but not at the cost of allowing total rejection of the past. The former Tertullian achieves by the language of renewal, reformation, extension; the latter by that of abolition. An imagined Marcionite interlocutor allows Tertullian to maintain the balance: '"Clearly Christ teaches a new patience, prohibiting the reprisal for injury permitted by the Creator when he exacted an eye for an eye and a tooth for a tooth; instead he orders the offer of the other cheek, and in addition to the tunic the surrender

[75] See below, pp. 251–2.

[76] See Wolfram Kinzig, *Novitas Christiana: Die Idee des Fortschritts in der Alten Kirche bis Eusebius* (FKD 58; Göttingen: Vandenhoeck und Reuprecht, 1994), 258–62.

[77] See Jean Claude Fredouille, *Tertullien et la conversion de la culture antique* (Paris: Études augustiniennes, 1972), 266.

also of the cloak". Clearly Christ did add these things, but as supplements compatible with the discipline of the Creator' (IV. 16.2). Tertullian appears to be forever searching for new terms and forever refining them, afraid of sharing Marcion's ground, but sometimes coming close to doing so. Marcion here represents a static, unequivocal position, against which Tertullian can prove his more subtle nuances.

On another and more significant level, the question was what effect the separation and even antithesis that Tertullian admits had on the fundamental tenet of the unity of the one God which Christians had inherited from their Jewish past. For Tertullian, the conjunction of oppositions is what best conveys the nature of a God, 'whose antitheses the world itself makes known, regulated out of contrary elements by the highest reason' (II. 29.4). Such a dialectic was part of Tertullian's inherited Stoic loyalties – despite his avowed dismissal of any who would promote a 'Stoic and Platonic and dialectic Christianity' (*PrH* 7.11). Arguments of this kind, it would appear, were completely alien to Marcion. Behind the polemic, the question that he posed, and that Tertullian recognised, was evidently more specific; how does the story of the human experience of God given in the Scriptures relate to the very being of God – especially when that story is understood both in terms of progress and as within history?[78] Here it is insufficient merely to see old and new as necessarily balancing oppositions. Tertullian has a ready answer: It is 'a distinction of arrangements (*dispositiones*) not of Gods' (*AM* V. 13.8). Again, Marcion provides him with the language that he will concede: 'So, I also acknowledge that one order unfolded in the old disposition with the Creator, and another in the new with Christ. I do not deny that the lessons of the word, the precepts of virtue, the disciplines of law, are different from each other, so long as the entire diversity is contained in one and the same God, namely he by whom it is agreed that that diversity was ordained just as it was predicted' (IV. 1.3). There is indeed 'diversity in time', a diversity that is due both to events, such as human response, but also to the divine plan, but so understood it demonstrates the single action of one God.

Tertullian deploys a number of arguments to support his position. It is most easily done where he can show that the Creator God exhibits qualities of kindness, and that Marcion's God cannot avoid judging; that as perpetrator of the same deeds the Creator God acts fairly, whereas Marcion's God appears answerable to no one (II. 28). The argument from prophecy

[78] See Kinzig, *Novitas*, 261.

and typology plays a central role in sustaining this position, occupying much of Book III and assumed throughout. Conversely, Tertullian also reads Christ pre-existently, finding him present in the scriptural theophanies, thus providing evidence both of a consistency in divine behaviour and an answer to any supposedly inappropriate interaction with the human sphere on the part of the transcendent God (II. 27).[79] On the other hand, he picks up and develops an earlier tradition of polemic 'against the Jews' as he blames Israel's intransigence not only for the more recent loss of God's earlier grace but already for those laws, such as the food laws, of which Christians had no need (II. 18; III. 23).

Thus, what Marcion represents for Tertullian is not a failure to read the Scriptures but the failure to read them correctly. Tertullian's Marcion does not reject the 'old Law' or 'old document', so much as interpret it without reference to its proper role as a 'figure' whose true meaning has become manifest in Christ.

The Christ had come who had never previously been announced (AM *III. 6.1)*

Tertullian claims that having established the necessary unity of God there is no need to deal with the Christ, although he will nonetheless do so (III. 1.1); in fact, it has become evident that the story and interpretation of Christ's mission lay at the heart of the conflict between the two protagonists. Tertullian, like Justin before him, suggests that Marcion introduces 'another God and … another Christ' (III. 1.1; cf. Justin, *Apol.* 58.1 'a different son'), but the issue is really how the Jesus whose ministry is described in the Gospel – for Marcion a 'perversion' of Luke's Gospel – is to be understood as God's revelation. Tertullian knows what he has to do: 'I claim Christ for myself; I maintain Jesus for myself' (*AM* III. 16.7). The basic principle is that for Marcion Christ is self-authenticating, for Tertullian this would establish a most abnormal (*monstruosissima*) faith: 'Nothing from God is sudden because nothing from God is not preordained' (III. 3.1; 4.1; 2.3).

Tertullian confirms that Marcion read the Gospel as starting dramatically in the time of Tiberius with Jesus' 'descent' to Capernaum (*AM* IV. 7.1; Luke 3.1; 4.31). Although he mocks the credit that Marcion's God has thus given to Tiberius 'that in his reign divine goodness was set down on earth', the contemporaneity of the Christian message with the Roman Empire was

[79] See p. 70 above.

already an established theme of Christian apologetic (*AM* I. 22.10; cf. Melito in Eusebius, *HE* IV. 26.7). The mockery of a 'God … since Tiberius' is reinforced by Tertullian's modalist language; 'Your God … came down and preached and having suffered rose' (*AM* I. 11.8; 22.10). It may, however, also reflect the fluidity with which Marcion spoke both of God's son and of God's own manifestation: 'You yourselves have already believed that God was lodged in the form and rest of the structure of the human condition … I do not know whether you honestly believe that God was crucified' (II. 27.2, 7).

Tertullian also mocked 'the long age in which [Marcion's] God most patiently … delayed both his revelation and his intervention' (III. 4.2), although such a charge could inevitably be no less laid against even his own claim for the newness and decisiveness of the Christ event. This is why the argument from fulfilment of Scripture is so important for him: 'so great a work … required that it should be prepared for in order to be believed' (III. 2.4). For Tertullian's predecessors, the fulfilment of Scripture established that the one who came was the promised deliverer; for him the reverse is equally true: The deliverer's fulfilment of past prophecy authenticates the latter and the God responsible for it. In addition, the convergence between prophecy and Christ's actual ministry as described in the Gospel means that he cannot be anyone other than the one who was foretold (III. 2.3; 20.1).

The Christ who was prophesied was therefore 'the Creator's Christ'; the one proclaimed by Marcion had nothing to do with the Creator. For Tertullian, this further opposition between two 'Christs' is fundamental and is to be driven like a bulldozer through Marcion's own claims to the Christ of the Gospel narrative. Marcion's Christ has no right to the name 'Jesus', for it is prefigured already in the name of Joshua; Marcion cannot argue that Jesus' miracles were sufficient to establish his divine origin, for these also conform to prophetic expectation; Marcion's Christ must in no way match the one prophesied in Scripture (III. 3; 16.3, 7).

Tertullian also suggests that Marcion made the reverse argument, denying that Christ did indeed fulfil the scriptural prophecies, for example, those of Isaiah (III. 12.1; Isa. 7.14; 8.4, 8); on the other hand, he also denied that what happened to Christ, in particular the crucifixion, was itself prophesied in Scripture (*AM* III. 18.1). It is this double denial that leads Tertullian to tar Marcion with the same brush as the Jew, 'the blind borrowing from the blind' (III. 6.1; 7.1). All he has to do is to reuse the established arguments of the 'against the Jews' tradition, for the Marcion he presents and opposes has alighted specifically on those passages that were already at the heart of Christian scriptural apologetic. Indeed, Tertullian simply recycles his own earlier account of Jewish objections and his response to them, altering the occasional 'the Jews say' into 'you say', and adding references to the Creator: 'Similarly they are induced by the sound of the name, when they understand the "power of Damascus and the spoils of Samaria and the king of the Assyrians" as if these refer to a warlike Christ' (*AJ* 9.4), easily becomes 'Similarly you shall be led by the sound of the names when you understand the "power of Damascus and the spoils of Samaria and the king of the Assyrians" as if these refer to a warlike Christ of the Creator', which at the same time fortuitously intersects with Marcion's dismissal of the 'warlike Creator' (*AM* III. 13.1).[80] It is certainly possible that Marcion himself or his followers had engaged with, and found wanting, existing Christian proof-texting, but it is hard to avoid the suspicion that it is Tertullian who has cast his opponent in a role that would allow him to develop the arguments that he himself already found most persuasive for the nature of the continuity between the two 'testaments'.

The association of Marcion with the Jews is entirely shaped to serve Tertullian's own polemical purposes and it is never seriously sustained; nonetheless, the rhetorical effect of guilt by association invites the intensification of vilification against each. Tertullian exploits any opportunities to tie Marcion's position to that of the discredited Jews; so, by demonstrating that the destruction of their land in punishment for their disbelief was itself foretold, he seeks at once to prove his point and to infer the inevitable rejection that awaits Marcion (III. 23). If any of Tertullian's readers were attracted by a Marcionite position precisely because it gave such a decisive answer to the question of the place of the Jews, as enthralled by the Creator God, Tertullian has effectively discomfited them.

The consequence is that Tertullian's Marcion apes the Jews, or, better, apes Tertullian's Jews, by agreeing that the passages are prophetic but holding that they must refer to a Christ who is yet to come; it follows that this future Christ must be a 'Judaic Christ' whose brief extends only to the people of Israel:

> Neither in order to distinguish between two Christs can you establish that idea of yours, as if a Jewish (*iudaicus*) Christ were destined by the Creator to restore the people alone from the dispersion, while yours indeed was directed by the supreme God to liberate the whole human race. For indeed the Christians of the Creator are found to be anterior to those of Marcion, since all peoples were called into his Kingdom from the time when God

80 See further pp. 54, 59 above for the relationship between the two writings.

> reigned from the tree [cf. Ps. 96.10], when neither Cerdo nor Marcion were yet around.
>
> (*AM* III. 21.1).

It is the exigencies of Tertullian's argument that have generated this multiplicity of 'Christs'. His goal is to affirm the 'Creator's Christ' of prophecy, denying that he is in any restricted sense a 'Judaic Christ', 'Judaic' routinely referring to the Jewish people alone. Instead he identifies the one who was so determined by prophecy with the Jesus of the Gospel story, even while reading those prophecies through the lens of the latter. Yet this is a Jesus whom to some extent he shares with Marcion who reads the same story. So, when Tertullian dismisses 'Marcion's Christ', what he is dismissing is the explanatory framework within which Marcion understands the same story, the same text. At times this leads to an argument so tortuous as to defy untangling, and certainly to defy taking soundings for echoes of Marcion's own voice. The complexities to which this gives rise are exacerbated in the analysis of that story, as recorded in Luke's Gospel, in Book IV, where Tertullian endeavours to demonstrate that Jesus' words and deeds prove beyond question, both by continuity and by fulfilment, that he belongs to the Creator, whereas when ascribed to Marcion's Christ, the same deeds and words become meaningless (IV. 10.1–5; 13, etc.).[81]

Marcion also allows Tertullian to address other issues close to his own heart. An established element of Christian scriptural apologetic was the doctrine of the two comings, one in humility, one in glory, which was used to explain the distinction between those prophecies that could be seen as fulfilled in the earthly ministry and death of Jesus, and those that implied a glorious and final triumph.[82] Explaining this gives Tertullian his first opportunity to ally Marcion with the Jews (III. 7). However, there remained the challenge that some of those yet-to-be-fulfilled prophecies implied a return to the land, much transformed and extended, and the glorious rebuilding of Jerusalem, while other traditions, especially of Christ's and of Paul's teaching, suggested a more celestial and eternal promise. Marcion, Tertullian claims, expected 'an eternal kingdom of God and heavenly possession' while 'your Christ promises the Jews their previous state by restitution of the land and after the end of life rest below in the embrace of Abraham' (*AM* III. 24.1). Although most editors take 'your Christ' as Marcion's

[81] See the note by Evans, *Adversus Marcionem*, 2, 293 on *AM* IV.9.2 suggesting that Tertullian has become embroiled in his own arguments.

[82] See already Justin, *Dial.* 31–34.

description of 'the Creator's Christ' as championed by Tertullian, such a formulation would be anomalous and the logic is ambiguous; it may be that this is Tertullian's report of the concession that Marcion's Christ offers the Jews.[83] Tertullian uses his response to explain and to defend his own expectation of a thousand-year reign in a Jerusalem descended from heaven before the transformation of believers into the eternal Kingdom. By Tertullian's time such beliefs were less normative than they had been, and he may have felt the need to defend them against internal opposition; certainly, he obviously does have an internal audience in mind when in support of such a belief he proceeds to appeal to another work of his own, now lost, *On the Hope of the Faithful*, and also to recent Montanist prophecies, and even to an apparition certified by 'pagan witnesses' (*AM* III. 24.2, 4). Once again, he is able to use a polemic against 'Marcion' to address current contentious debates and to dismiss those positions at variance with his own.

He was not what he seemed, and what he was he falsified, flesh and not flesh, man and not man (AM *II. 8.2*)

Tertullian closes Book III and his celebration of the tangibility of his Christian hope, castigating Marcion whose 'Christ promised a heavenly reign but did not have a heaven, just as he presented himself as human while not having flesh. What a total phantasm! What juggler's illusions even of so great a promise!' (III. 24.13). The mockery here picks up his earlier dismissal of Marcion's 'juggler's tricks in regard to Jesus' putative bodiliness' (III. 11.1), just as he has described Marcion's God, his goodness and discipline, as imaginary and phantasmic (I. 22.1; 27.1). The same characteristics run like a thread through Marcion's whole system; the corporeity attributed to Jesus is a lie, fallacious, and so must also be all the claims made for him; Marcion's 'Gospel' is similarly 'false', derivative from the primordial truth, it promulgates lies (III. 8; IV. 5.7; 7.3, 7). The epithets are, of course, Tertullian's own, not those of his opponent. He paraphrases the beginning of Marcion's 'Gospel': 'In the fifteenth year of Tiberius Christ Jesus consented to flow down from heaven, a saving spirit (*spiritus salutaris*)' (I. 19.2); although the language serves as a channel for Tertullian's own biting ironical contrast

83 The question is complicated by the following exclamation, 'O supreme God who, once placated, returns what he had taken away when angered'; René Braun, introd., texte critique, trad., notes et index des livres I-III, *Tertullien: Contre Marcion*, Tome III (SC 399; Paris: Éditions du Cerf, 1994), 263–4, ascribes these words to Tertullian, against other editors who ascribe them to Marcion. This difficulty is solved if 'Your Christ' is also spoken by Tertullian.

with the 'pestilential wind from Pontus', it is probable that Marcion did speak of Jesus as in some sense 'spirit'.[84] However, Tertullian evidently found Marcion's position perplexing and, in his own terms, inconsistent, 'juggler's tricks'; he considers the more extreme position of Apelles more logical: 'I wish that you yourself would set out the intention of your God when he displayed his Christ not in the reality of flesh' (III. 10.1; 11.1–2).[85] Questioning whether Jesus' touching and being touched, and most of all his death, could then be anything but imaginary and so a lie, he acknowledges that Marcion did ascribe such actions to Jesus, and at one point he even says that Marcion has taught 'that that flesh was real' (III. 11.6; but contrast I. 8, 'false flesh').[86] What particularly perplexes Tertullian is that according to Marcion Christ did die on the cross – as already seen, he only denied that this fulfilled any earlier prophecy: 'if Christ genuinely did suffer those things, he was at least born. If he suffered as a lie, as a phantasm, he could have been born as a lie' (III. 11.8; 18–19). This perplexity may be why he often resorts to associating Marcion with the views of other heretics regarding the reality of Jesus' flesh: Marcion, he says, defends Jesus as a phantasm, 'although this opinion will have other originators, in some sense premature and abortive Marcionites [quoting 1 John 4.2]'. Similarly, when he anticipates that Marcion may appeal to angelophanies (e.g. Gen. 18) for a flesh that is adopted but is not real, he admits that his response is simply to 'the heretics' (*AM* III. 8.1; 9.7).[87]

Tertullian assumes that Marcion's God has rejected real flesh because of his avoidance of the work of the Creator, and, even more, because of an abhorrence of flesh as 'stuffed with dung'; betraying an awareness that his opponent's emphasis was that Christ's flesh had not experienced normal birth, he invites him to 'call the womb a sewer … to attack the unclean and shameful torments of child-bearing' (III. 10.1; 11.7). Tertullian makes the same invitation, in far more extensive and graphic detail, in *De Carne* 4, and in both cases it is difficult to determine how far the impression of 'pathological'[88] distaste is to be ascribed to Marcion himself, or how

84 See below, p. 371.

85 In *De Res.* 2.3 Tertullian states that Marcion and Basilides held that Jesus' flesh had no true existence, whereas Valentinus and Apelles held that it was of a distinctive quality.

86 Braun, *Contre Marcion*, III, 115 n.7 on *AM* III. 11.6, takes too easy a way out, saying that Tertullian must be referring to Apelles' teaching here, not to Marcion's.

87 In addition, the argument about angels is found in *De Carne* 6.9–11 against Apelles, where it may have been more pertinent: Mahé, *Chair du Christ*, 1, 86–92 argues that the replication of the argument against Marcion in *De Carne* 3 is secondary.

88 See the description by Norelli, 'Paix, justice', 25, of Marcion's almost pathological reaction to matter.

far to Tertullian's own rhetoric. Certainly, Tertullian does consider birth as meriting 'veneration of nature', but for him it is still a mark of Christ's gracious self-humiliation that he 'chose that human being who was coagulated in impurities in the womb, brought forth through organs of shame, and nourished through organs of ridicule' (ibid.; cf. *AM* IV. 21.11). It is beyond doubt that Marcion's 'Gospel' did not include the nativity stories or references to Jesus' parentage, and that Marcion himself denigrated marriage and procreation; however, once again, in practice, Tertullian's own position could appear uncomfortably close to that of his opponent, forcing him to create as vast a rhetorical difference between them as possible.

Tertullian's perplexity, as well as his anxieties, is grounded in his own convictions: 'for what is man other than flesh?' (I. 24.5). He does not thereby deny the soul, which is the image of God's spirit, but he insists that the body must participate, as in action and in sin, so also in salvation and in resurrection (II. 9; I. 24). He thus saw his writings on the incarnation and on the resurrection as a pair sharing a common goal (*De Res.* 2.11). He implies that the contrary position is the one adopted by Marcion: The created order is shameful (*indignus*); its Creator is not the source of salvation or the originator of the Saviour; flesh, through which people participate in the created order, is not the sphere of the Saviour or of the salvation he brings. Yet of necessity – for Tertullian utterly irrationally – 'the goodness of Marcion's God ... set out for the salvation of man who was alien to him (*hominis alieni*)' (*AM* I. 23.1). This of itself indicates that Marcion did not deduce any consubstantiality between the Saviour and those whom he saved, but how this played out in the fleshliness of Christ or in the anthropology of humanity Tertullian failed to understand.

We do not repudiate marriage but demote it; we do not demand chastity but encourage it (AM *I.29.2)*

Tertullian mocks the followers of Marcion whose lives in no way demonstrate their redemption from the power of the Creator; they still suffer from fever and the grief of the flesh. He finds it yet more inconsistent that they still not only are baptised but are also ready to be martyred, which he assumes implies some value for embodied experience (I. 14.5; 24.4, 6; 27.5). As has been seen, he cannot understand why, in the absence of any fear of a judgemental God, Marcionites do not indulge in every excess of behaviour, not least those popular spectacles of which Tertullian himself so vehemently disapproved (I. 27.2–3).[89] Yet perhaps where he stumbles most heavily is over the question, why does Marcion's God 'impose upon the flesh, excessively weak and shameful, so great a burden or glory, chastity … and why allow the honour of chastity to die with the flesh?' (I. 28.4). Tertullian's problem is, of course, that for him chastity is a glory and honour, and therefore it is the unequivocal imposition of it, expressed by the refusal of baptism to those who do not follow it, that he has to denounce, along with the inconsistency he detects in Marcion's position, as giving no place to the body while extolling 'bodily' practices. Similarly, when he himself defends the 'control of sexual intercourse' imposed by the restriction to a single marriage – namely, the denial of remarriage after the death of one partner – which on the surface no less appeared a contradiction of the Creator's summons to 'increase and multiply' (Gen. 1.28), he has to appeal to a higher authority, 'the spiritual reasoning on the authority of the Paraclete' (*AM* I. 29.4). The irony is that there were others who levelled against the 'new' manifestations of the Paraclete precisely the same objections against their novelty and lack of ecclesial heritage that Tertullian lays against Marcion (Eusebius, *HE* V. 16–19). Marcion, for his part, laid claim to no prophetic authority and so lost any justifiable right to innovation (*AM* I. 21.5; cf. IV. 4.5).

TERTULLIAN'S MARCION

Tertullian's argument, and the contrary position it implies, is necessarily far richer and more complex than the sketch given here can encompass. At every point Tertullian's own convictions and his construction of Marcion play off against each other like a light and the shadows it throws, the sound and its echo. At the same time, it is impossible to ignore the points at which their outlooks converge, for Tertullian too feels a certain alienation from the world as represented by contemporary society.[90] It is also likely that they may have appeared to other observers as being far closer to each other in the behaviour that they advocated – and many would have been swayed by that impression. Tertullian's Marcion emerges out of this complex of antithesis and attraction. Yet, although Tertullian's whole argument

[89] See Tertullian, *De Spectaculis*.

[90] See Barnes, *Tertullian*, 60–4, who sees such a sense of alienation as characteristic of African Christianity; cf. René Braun, 'Tertullien et l'éxégèse de 1 Cor. 7', ed. Jacques Fontaine and Charles Kannengiesser, *Epektasis: Mélanges patristiques offerts au Cardinal Jean Dianiélou* (Paris: Beauchesne, 1972), 21–8, who suggests that, whether consciously or not, Tertullian was marked by the Marcionite interpretation of 1 Cor. 7.

presupposes shared basic premises, there have been numerous hints that Tertullian's primary concerns may not have been equally important to Marcion. Although both arguably were wrestling essentially with the same sources and questions, the conscious principles that directed their responses were fundamentally different. The inconsistencies that Tertullian mocks in Marcion's God may often be the consequence of the tensions that he projected onto the construction of his opponent.

The picture painted here has concentrated on the initial stages of Tertullian's polemic as its own starting point. Evidently he had worked out much of the rebuttal as it appears in Books I, II, and III, before he had the opportunity to engage in any detail with that which above all they shared, Gospel and Pauline letters. It is not surprising that many of these arguments re-emerge when he turns to these; but it is also there that he betrays, at least through the lens of his own spectacles, rather more of Marcion's own starting point in these texts. Although in this earlier attack he could draw on his own and others' earlier work, as well as on his own ingenuity, in addressing the texts it is the latter that has to come to the fore. Tertullian's Marcion will only fully emerge from the shadows when his 'Gospel' and Pauline corpus have been fully investigated.

5

The heresiological tradition

The second century saw the beginnings of the transformation of the term '*hairesis*' from carrying a relatively neutral designation as a school of opinion, towards its acquisition within Christian discourse of a consistent negative tone applied to 'others' who by deception bore 'the same name as our doctrine' (Eusebius, *HE* IV. 7.2). This transformation cannot be traced to a single source nor did it take place speedily and decisively. While neither Justin himself, nor even Hegesippus in the surviving fragments, uses the term with sufficient consistency or regularity to claim that either of them established the new coinage, Irenaeus' preference for 'heretical', or for the plural or generalising 'every heresy', 'every heretic', cautions against speaking as yet of 'the concept of heresy' as such. On the other hand, there are intriguing consistencies, namely in the identification of supposedly distinct groups named after their purported founders, in the embryonic ideas of school succession, and in some of the actual members and sequence within the lists, consistencies that will be repeated in later authors.[1]

This broad coherence justifies speaking about a 'heresiological tradition', particularly subsequent to Irenaeus himself. By this is meant not merely the identification of different belief or practice as 'heresy', but the perhaps curious technique of creating a catalogue of such with the intention of demonstrating both common descent and iniquitous inspiration at the same time as the endless variation that is a demonstration of error. This undertaking continues alongside direct attacks against a single target, such as Tertullian's *Against Marcion*, although the two styles are by no means independent of each other, as Tertullian again demonstrates when he draws

[1] Justin, *Dial.* 35.6; Hegesippus in Eusebius, *HE* IV. 22.5; Irenaeus, *AH* I. 23–7: see above, pp. 26–7.

heavily on Irenaeus for his *Against the Valentinians*. At the same time, the variety of emphases that marks the earliest stages of this tradition continues to characterise it as it is adopted and adapted by different authors to suit their own purposes. The combination of derivation and innovation produces a genre, which, particularly in the wake of Epiphanius, its most creative exponent, almost acquires a life of its own extending across the centuries of Christian history.[2] Marcion is from the beginning a fixed component within this tradition.

THE *REFUTATION OF ALL HERESIES*

Irenaeus' most direct surviving heir in the construction of a comprehensive theory and rebuttal of 'heresy' is the *Refutation* (or *Conviction*) *(elenchus) of all Heresies*, discovered in its to-date most complete form in the mid-nineteenth century.[3] Towards its close the *Refutation* mounts a virulent attack against the apparently recently martyred Callistus, denouncing him for claiming episcopal authority in Rome while maintaining both lax penitential practice and monarchian theological views, and for establishing a 'school' around these (*Ref.* IX. 11–12).[4] On this basis, the anonymous work – the attribution to Origen in the title in part of the manuscript tradition is undoubtedly false[5] – was soon attributed to Hippolytus, to whom Eusebius ascribes a work *Against All Heresies* as well as one *Against Marcion* (Eusebius, *HE* VI. 22). In turn, this attribution led to biographical accounts of Hippolytus being enriched by the implications of the attack against Callistus, resulting in Hippolytus himself being described as the schismatic, reversing the charge that the *Refutation* brings against its opponent.[6] Curiously, Hippolytus himself appears to have been something of an elusive figure already by the time of Eusebius, who identifies him only as 'presiding over another church somewhere' (*HE* VI. 20.2), while the sources and value of reports given in later authors are far from certain, if indeed they all refer to the same person. The conflicting early traditions about 'Hippolytus'

2 See Averil Cameron, 'How to Read Heresiology', *JMEMS* 33 (2003), 471–92.

3 Miroslav Marcovich, ed., *Hippolytus. Refutatio Omnium Haeresium* (PTS 25; Berlin: de Gruyter, 1986), 1–8. Tertullian's *Concerning the Prescription of Heretics* is unsystematic and focuses on Valentinus, Marcion, and Apelles; except for passing references, it does not present a sustained model of succession (*PrH* 10.8; cf. 30.5–6 on Apelles and Marcion).

4 Initially αἵρεσις and then διδασκαλεῖον is used.

5 Book I, which was soon recognised to belong to the work, was already to be found among the works attributed to Origen.

6 Hippolytus has even been designated 'antipope' by those who anachronistically hold that the terminology of 'pope' is apposite for the second century.

are matched by the diverse theological positions and literary genres of the numerous writings that have been associated with him, and, despite the confidence of nineteenth-century scholars, doubts have grown stronger as to whether one man could generate them all.[7] Within all this, the authorship of the *Refutation* has again come under critical scrutiny, and it would be hazardous to conclude any more about the context of the author and his text than can be deduced from the work itself: In what follows, the text will be treated as anonymous, and there will be no assumption of common authorship with any other writings attributed to Hippolytus.

Although the *Refutation* is not only aware of Irenaeus' great work and even plagiarises it extensively in places, its overall principles of argument are very different. The author's stated aim is to demonstrate that the heresies have their origin not in the Scriptures but in Greek philosophies, mysteries, and astrology. To achieve this he first sets out a genealogy of these earlier systems, drawing attention to their weaknesses, misunderstandings, or corruption of their predecessors (Books I–IV), before he turns to the heresies themselves (Books V–IX).[8] However, although his stated intention is to pair each heretic with a philosopher, presenting the former as a plagiarist who misunderstands his source, in fact only four of his examples do this: Plato/Pythagoras and Valentinus, Aristotle and Basilides, Empedocles and Marcion, and Heraclitus and Callistus/Noetus. For the rest, he gives accounts of varying length of the various heretical systems, with occasional and inconsistent reference to their supposed parallels or sources.

The author presents his task as one of exposure, for these heretics do not acknowledge their true sources but adopt the language of secrecy and mystery, only fully initiating their followers when they have completely enthralled them (*Ref.* I. prol. 1–4). This charge was by now a well-established polemical topos, and one that had also been used by outsiders against the Christians. Indeed, such exposure is his main weapon, for he does not mount

[7] Most discussions refer back to Pierre Nautin, *Hippolyte et Josipe. Contribution a l'histoire de la littérature chrétienne de troisième siècle* (Études et texts pour l'histoire du dogme de la Trinité 1; Paris: Éditions du Cerf, 1947), and idem, *Hippolyte Contre les Hérésies. Fragment* (Études et textes pour l'histoire du dogme de la Trinité 2; Paris: Éditions du Cerf, 1949), 15–70. See further J. A. Cerrato, *Hippolytus Between East and West: The Commentaries and the Provenance of the Corpus* (OTM; Oxford: Oxford University Press, 2002); Allen Brent, *Hippolytus and the Roman Church in the Third Century: Communities in Tension Before the Emergence of a Monarch-Bishop* (VCSup. 31; Leiden: Brill, 1995); Aline Pourkier, *L'Hérésiologie chez Épiphane de Salamie* (Christianisme antique 4; Paris: Beauchesne, 1992), who follows Nautin in calling the author of the *Refutation* 'Josipus'. Marcovich, *Refutatio* accepts the attribution to Hippolytus.

[8] Books II, III, and part of IV are missing, but the method is clear from Book I.

a sustained intellectual argument against the opposing positions. Instead, his method is to intersperse quotations and his own interpretive comments, on the assumption that statement and juxtaposition are enough to prove the point; these quotations are taken both from the philosophers and from heretical tenets, and, in some cases, first-hand, from 'gnostic' texts that he appears to have discovered, with the result that, as a recent editor has noted, 'the Gnostic texts described in the *Elenchos* could not be proven as plagiarizing, while its author could'.[9] Although he claims that much detailed research had been required for these purposes, this is a familiar literary topos, and it is likely that at least some of his sources were available on the popular book market.[10] Nonetheless, the overall method has made the *Refutation* a much-examined source for early Greek philosophy as well as for these gnostic texts. On the other hand, as will become evident, the author does not only present the heresies in such a way as to match their philosophical models, but he also sometimes ensures that the philosophies more closely anticipate their gnostic offspring, and in addition he also freely copies elements of one system into another.[11]

As already noted, the author's further goals are to present Callistus, his opponent, as the apex of a long heretical tradition, and also at the same time to establish his own faith as unquestionably authentic, simply by the very vigour of his championing of it against 'all heresies'. That means that his own contemporary concerns, apparently belonging to the Roman context, are never very far away, and that these concerns were not necessarily dominated by the 'gnostic' groups to whom he pays so much attention. For example, while he expounds at length a number of scurrilous tales about Callistus, he is much more restrained about Marcion. These features create something of a tension with the value to be attributed to such material as is not derived from Irenaeus.[12]

9 Marcovich, *Refutatio*, 36. For the value of the philosophical sources, see Catherine Osborne, *Rethinking Early Greek Philosophy: Hippolytus of Rome and the Presocratics* (London: Duckworth, 1987); Jaap Mansfeld, *Heresiography in Context: Hippolytus' Elenchos as a Source for Greek Philosophy* (Ph.Ant. 56; Leiden: Brill, 1992); Ian Mueller, 'Hippolytus *Retractus*: A Discussion of Catherine Osborne, *Rethinking Early Greek Philosophy*', ed. Julia Annas, *Oxford Studies in Ancient Philosophy VII 1989* (Oxford: Clarendon Press, 1989), 233–51.

10 So Klaus Koschorke, *Hippolyt's Ketzerbekämpfung und Polemik gegen die Gnostiker: Eine tendenzkritische Untersuchung seiner "Refutatio omnium Haeresium"* (GO 6.4; Wiesbaden: Harrassowitz, 1975), 31–2.

11 Contra Marcovich, *Refutatio*, 45–50, who thinks any sharing of ideas can be traced to the actual gnostic systems themselves.

12 The new material relates particularly to the Naassenes, Peratae, Sethians, and Justin's *Baruch*, the *Apophasis Megale* of Simon, Basilides, the Docetists, and Monoimus. On this see Koschorke, *Hippolyt's Ketzerbekämpfung*, 82–5, 95–101, and on the internal context,

The Marcionites were not among the groups for which the author claimed discovery of any new sources; yet, as will become evident, in his description of Marcion's views (*Ref.* VII. 29–31) he appears largely to have ignored the account of Irenaeus, on whom elsewhere he is heavily dependent. This may be because the latter offered little that would have served his overriding theory of derivation and decline from a Greek philosophical position; nonetheless, although there is little to suggest that the *Refutation* draws on any substantial independent knowledge, its account cannot be entirely dismissed. This issue is made more complicated by the Epitome of the opinions of the heresiarchs, which the author offers before coming to his own summary of the truth in Book X; at least in the cases of Marcion and of Cerdo this bears little relationship to the earlier detailed account. Marcovich's comment that, 'it is not difficult to see why Hippolytus was not happy with his rather poor report on Marcion in VII.30, thus deciding to write a new report in X.19; then X.19 seems to presuppose the emptiness of VII.30', is a statement of the problem, but it does not provide its solution.[13]

Marcion and Empedocles

The Marcion of the main argument of the *Refutation* (VII. 29–31) is parasitic upon the fifth-century BCE philosopher Empedocles, who is here treated as a follower of Pythagoras. As is characteristic of the author's style and method, Empedocles' system is set out in far more detail, much of it unnecessary for the purpose, than is Marcion's: The intention of this excess of scholarship is presumably to impress and to persuade any readers. Empedocles, as the author presents him, proposed two governing principles, Friendship/Love (φιλία) and Discord (νεῖκος);[14] correspondingly, Marcion ('the Pontic': ὁ ποντικός) proposed 'the good and the evil' – perhaps, but not certainly, implying 'Gods'.[15] In a very detailed analysis, Jaap Mansfeld has shown that at the same time as Marcion is presented in Empedoclean terms,

pp. 87–92, although Koschorke may be over-optimistic in suggesting that in Rome in the third century there were few active gnostic groups (pp. 69–73); also Vallée, *Study in Anti-Gnostic Polemics*, 41–62.

13 Marcovich, *Refutatio*, 34; earlier he suggests (p. 33) that the author used a source for the chapter in the Epitome.

14 See Mansfeld, *Heresiography*, 208–29, who notes that this is an Aristotelian interpretation of Empedocles.

15 ἀγαθός, πονηρός: The adjectives are masculine whereas the Greek word 'principle' (ἀρχή) is feminine, supporting Marcovich's addition of 'God' (*Refutatio*, 304); later (VII. 30.3) 'good God' is used. However, Marcion's teaching is also represented in terms of 'principles' by Rhodon in Eusebius, *HE* V. 13.2–4. See also below n. 27 on Prepon.

so also Empedocles is 'marcionized': Thus, whereas other sources indicate that for Empedocles Love and Discord actually operated in balance with each other, here it is only the latter that becomes the Demiurge, and thus anticipates Marcion's evil Creator.

A similarly cross-fertilisation of attributes appears when the author ascribes to Empedocles the prohibition both of meat-eating and of sexual intercourse ('with a woman'), before subsequently accusing Marcion of imitating him with the same prohibitions (*Ref.* VII. 29.14–15, 21–22; cf. 30.3–4).[16] While the prohibition of sexual intercourse, which is widely attested for Marcion, is unsupported and improbable for Empedocles, the rejection of meat-eating, a standard feature of the Pythagorean tradition, is not explicitly attributed to Marcion in the earlier tradition.[17] The reason that is adduced here for Marcion's prohibition, 'that they may not eat any body that is a remnant of a soul that has been punished by the creator', consciously echoes that attributed earlier to Empedocles, and indeed it would be more at home in the latter's system of metempsychosis. The author may also have in mind the avoidance not only of marriage but also of 'what is living' ('ensouled', ἔμψυχος, the term attributed to Empedocles), which he had ascribed to the followers of Satornilus and to the Encratites, there copied from Irenaeus (*Ref.* VII. 28.7; VIII. 20.1; cf. Irenaeus, *AH* I. 24.1–2; 28.1). On another level for the alert reader, he couches Marcion's practice in an unmarked citation of 1 Timothy 4.3, supplementing 'forbidding marrying' with 'child-bearing'.[18] Yet, despite this cross-fertilisation, Empedocles' system is presented both as intrinsically more coherent and as offering a more unified conception of the entire cosmos; Marcion, by contrast, appears as someone who by selective misappropriation has constructed a 'crude dualism'.[19]

This dualism of good versus evil (here κακός) is presented as 'the first and purest heresy of Marcion', and as 'obviously belonging to Empedocles' (*Ref.* VII. 30.2). However, the next chapter of the *Refutation* introduces a recent disciple, Prepon, who in debate with Bardaisan innovated by introducing a third mediating principle, the just (δίκαιος; VII. 31.1–2).[20]

[16] Mansfeld, *Heresiography*, 214–16, 219–21; however, Osborne, *Rethinking*, 123, argues that a prohibition of intercourse would not be illogical for Empedocles.

[17] It is, however, possibly hinted by Tertullian, and is repeated by Epiphanius, *Pan.* 42.11.17, R24b; see herein p. 109.

[18] The passage is cited in full against the Encratites at *Ref.* VIII. 20.

[19] See Osborne, *Rethinking*, 128.

[20] According to Eusebius, Rhodon ascribed the introduction of a third principle to Syneros (Eusebius, *HE* V. 13.4); see further, p. 318. Again, the masculine adjective is used alongside the feminine noun 'principle', but here it would be difficult to add 'God'.

This principle, likewise, the author traces, with a suitable quotation, to Empedocles, who summoned to his aid the Muse, or 'just reason' (δίκαιος λόγος). Yet here too, according to the author, Marcion (!) betrays his plagiarism when he asserted that 'reason (ὁ λόγος) strove in support of Love, namely the good, and without begetting came down from above … being between evil (κακός) and good' (VII. 31.5).[21] It is, according to the author, in this framework that Marcion's denial of 'the begetting (γένεσις) of our saviour' is to be explained: It would be inappropriate for reason to come into being under something made by 'destructive Discord'. Here the author introduces a new term into the debate: 'Jesus descended unbegotten (ἀγεν<ν>ήτος)'.

In this the author of the *Refutation* again betrays his knowledge of standard accounts of Marcion, perhaps including the latter's exclusion of Luke 1–2. At this point he puts in Marcion's mouth the familiar combined introduction from Luke 3.1 and 4.31, 'in the fifteenth year of the governorship of Tiberius Caesar he came down from above', adding, 'to teach in the synagogues' (cf. Luke 4.15, not otherwise attested for Marcion's 'Gospel').[22] To demonstrate that Jesus transformed (ἀπαλλάσσω) both evil and good, Marcion, according to the author, cited Paul, 'that he might be a mediator' (cf. Gal. 3.19–20), as well as 'his' (Jesus') rejection of the title 'good' (cf. Luke 18.19).[23] Although the author does not make the connection, the reader is probably expected to read these references in the light of the charge which introduces the account of Marcion, namely that he had hoped it would escape detection that he had taken the whole structure of his heresy, down to its very terminology, from Empedocles, and transferred it 'into the Gospel (εὐαγγελικός) words' (*Ref.* VII. 30.1). The author evidently betrays, and expects from his readers, more knowledge of the structure of Marcion's thought than he admits.

Marcion without Empedocles

Despite this, the true extent of the author's interest in, if not familiarity with, earlier accounts remains ambiguous. It is the way in which Marcion reads 'the Gospel words', ('transferring', μεταφέρειν), that he attacks, not that he has edited or removed material from them.[24] There may be an echo of

21 On the argument and its sources, see Mansfeld, *Heresiography*, 221–6.

22 The omission of 'their', as in Luke 4.15, is striking, see below, p. 214.

23 *Ref.* VII. 31.6. Gal. 3.20 is often treated as absent from Marcion's 'Apostolikon'; see herein p. 254. For Luke 18.19 and the textual question, see pp. 207–08.

24 Marcovich, *Refutatio*, 304, finds a reference by inserting 'Scriptures' (γραφῶν) at *Ref.* VII. 29.1: 'Marcion … passing over the many things of the majority [*of the Scriptures*]';

Marcion's preference for Paul both in the quotation already cited and when the author denies that even Paul proclaimed 'such things', but surprisingly he couples Paul in this denial not with Luke but with [the Gospel according to] Mark (*Ref.* VII. 30.1).[25] Similarly, although 'such things' here refers to Marcion's introduction of 'arguments from the opposition (ἀντιπαραθέσις) of good and evil', the absence of any reference to 'the Law and the prophets' in his account makes it difficult to find here a reference to the 'Antitheses' of which Tertullian speaks. The same striking omission appears in the statement that Marcion ('you') says that, 'the good is the God who [or 'the good God is the one who'] destroys the works of the Demiurge', especially when compared with Irenaeus' claim that according to Marcion *Jesus* 'dissolved *the prophets and Law and* all the works of that God who made the world' (*Ref.* VII. 30.3; cf. Irenaeus, *AH* I. 27.2).[26] The Marcion of the *Refutation* certainly does consider 'the Demiurge and all his works as evil' (*Ref.* VII. 31.6), but there is nothing to suggest that he identified this Demiurge with the God 'of the law and the prophets'.

This feature becomes yet more marked when set alongside the description of Cerdo, which, surprisingly, is postponed until six chapters after that of Marcion (*Ref.* VII. 37). Here, the author does follow Irenaeus closely: Hence it is Cerdo who distinguishes between the *just* God preached by Moses and the prophets, who is known, and the Father of Christ who is good and unknown (cf. Irenaeus, *AH* I. 27.1). Surprisingly, still mindful of Irenaeus but avoiding the language of succession, a laconic remark adds, 'Marcion reinforced this man's doctrine, setting out the oppositions and whatever occurred to him to denigrate the Creator of all. His disciple Lucianus did the same' (*Ref.* VII. 37.2).

In naming Luc[i]anus and Prepon, absent from Irenaeus, the author evidently has access to other sources.[27] This is confirmed by the much more extensive account of Apelles, another disciple, that follows; the detail here, some but not all of which parallels that in other reports of Apelles, carries a much stronger note of immediacy, including the description of

there is little in the context to support what would still remain a very oblique allusion, and the phrase 'the many of the majority' probably contrasts Marcion with the elaborate system of Satornilus that has just been described.

25 The epithet 'stumpy-fingered' attached to Mark excludes any textual error.

26 On this in Irenaeus, see herein p. 31.

27 For Lucianus, or more usually Lucanus, see Tertullian, *De Res.* 2; Origen, *C.Cels.* II. 27; Ps. Tertullian, *Adv.Omn.Haer.* 6; Philastrius, *De Haer.* 46; Epiphanius, *Pan.* 43. Although not otherwise known, the identification of Prepon as an 'Assyrian', and that he should debate with Bardaisan, a known opponent of Marcion, are fully credible (see p. 147).

the God who spoke to Moses as 'fire-like', and the formation of Jesus' body from four elements (*Ref.* VII. 38).[28] However, in accordance with what has already been noted, 'Marcion also proposed' only the identification of a 'good God', while it is Apelles who is credited with denigrating the Law and the prophets and who 'chooses what suits him from the Gospels and apostle'. Unlike other heresiologists, there is nothing to suggest that the author of the *Refutation* wants here to stress the inconsistencies even among members of the same 'school'. Rather, he is determined to let nothing detract from his picture of Marcion as essentially parroting the philosopher, Empedocles. How far, in so doing, he deliberately suppresses his other sources, how far he is responsive to their more distinctively nuanced portrayals, remains somewhat obscure.

Marcion in the Epitome (Ref. X)

These peculiarities of the *Refutation*'s account of Marcion are, as has been anticipated, exacerbated by that in the Epitome (Book X), which not only summarises 'all the philosophies (and) heresies' of the previous books but also both selects from them and puts them into a different sequence. One consequence of this process is that the Docetae, Monoimus, and Tatian, who were previously described after Marcion (*Ref.* VIII. 1–16), are now introduced before him; this renders somewhat perplexing the comment that Tatian 'scarcely differs from Marcion in blasphemy and legislation concerning marriage', since the latter has yet to be described (X. 18).[29] The section that follows (X. 19) opens by combining 'Marcion from Pontus and Cerdo his teacher', although an unmarked switch from plural to singular verbs mid-sentence halfway through the account betrays either the elision of sources or the author's hand. Here their starting point is presented not as a philosophical dualism but as the familiar cosmological debate about originating principles: They propose three such principles, good, just, and matter (ἀγαθός, δίκαιος, ὕλη), while some of their disciples add to these

[28] Apelles here holds four principles, the good God, the just Creator, the fiery God who spoke to Moses, and a fourth, the cause of evils (κακός); in the Epitome the fourth is himself wicked (πονηρός: *Ref.* X. 20). Other accounts of Apelles include those by Rhodon in Eusebius, *H.E.* V.13, who represents him as a monist, and Epiphanius, *Pan.* 44. See K. Greschat, *Apelles und Hermogenes: Zwei theologische Lehrer des zweitens Jahrhunderts* (VCSup. 48; Leiden: Brill, 2000).

[29] Marcovich, *Refutatio*, 398, adds 'against begetting' after 'blasphemy', but the earlier chapter on Tatian only refers to his rejection of marriage (*Ref.* VIII. 16).

'wicked' (πονηρός) (X. 19.1–3).[30] It is the just one – or, according to some, the wicked one[31] – who is responsible for creation out of the substrate, matter, a creation that is therefore not pleasing (καλῶς) but irrational (ἀλόγως). This, they claim, is the meaning of the 'gospel parables' about the trees and their fruits (Luke 6.43), a parable widely associated in other sources with Marcion.

Secondly, 'he' (sing.: Marcion) identifies the Christ as the son of the good one, sent by him 'for the salvation of souls', calling him 'inner man' (ἔσω ἄνθρωπος).[32] The term is Pauline (Rom. 7.22; 2 Cor. 4.16; Eph. 3.16), although it takes considerable – albeit possible – exegetical dexterity to apply it to Christ. Indeed, it apparently had a wide currency within the Valentinian tradition, chiefly, however, with reference to the spiritual component of the human being which is redeemed through knowledge, a reference sometimes supported through an intertextual exegesis of Genesis 2.7.[33] This might suggest that the author has misread a source that attached the epithet to the 'souls' rather than to the Christ. However, an alternative origin for the author's use might be the dense and somewhat obscure passage in the *Refutation* where the term is apparently applied by Basilides to the redeemer when originally conceived in the divine fullness (*Ref.* VII. 27.5–6). Whatever its origin, the author ascribes to Marcion a distinctive Christological exegesis of the phrase: 'saying he appeared as man, not being man, and as enfleshed, not (being) enfleshed (ἔνσαρκος), having appeared in semblance (δοκήσις), not having undergone begetting or suffering except as it seemed' (X. 19.3). The structure of balanced formulae is striking, and is characteristic of second-century Christological affirmations, which may suggest that it draws on an earlier source.[34]

It is, however, the established heresiological tradition which supplies the end of the account: A laconic 'he does not want flesh to rise', the description

30 Marcovich, *Refutatio*, 398 adds 'fourth' in conformity with what follows in *Ref.* X. 20, although here and in the following sentence, which he also edits, it is unclear whether the evil is separate from or is a further qualification of the righteous.

31 The text is ambiguous and is emended by Marcovich, *Refutatio*; it might mean that the one responsible for creation is, according to some 'the just' and according to others 'the evil', or that some thought both were involved, or that some named the Creator 'just' and others 'just and evil'.

32 Marcovich, *Refutatio*, 399, adds 'the'. On 'inner man' see Theo K. Heckel, *Der Innere Mensch: Die paulinische Verarbeitung eines platonischen Motivs* (WUNT 2, 53; Tübingen: Mohr Siebeck, 1993). See below, p. 266 on 2 Cor. 4.16.

33 Irenaeus, *AH* I. 5.2–5 (cf. also the Marcosians in I. 21.4); Ps.Hippolytus, *Ref.* VI. 34.4–6; X. 13.3 (and *Ref.* V. 7.36 in a Naassene homily); cf. Clement of Alexandria, *Exc.Theod.* 50–1.

34 Compare Ignatius, *Eph.* 7.2: 'There is one doctor, fleshly and spiritual, begotten and unbegotten, in man God'; see further p. 378.

of marriage as 'corruption', and Marcion's direction of his disciples towards a 'somewhat Cynic style of life' – an association the author had already applied not only to Marcion but also to the Encratites and to Tatian[35] – in order to distress the Creator 'by avoiding things he had made or ordained'. Yet even here there may be clues that the author is suppressing a richer account: If 'ordained (ὁρίζω)' there refers to marriage it may perhaps provide a hint of the law-giver God of the Scriptures who is otherwise still notably absent.

It is very evident that in Book X the author is not summarising his earlier account of Marcion, as he does, for example, when he proceeds to turn to Apelles (*Ref.* X. 20). Neither is he adapting his earlier material on Marcion's followers, for the three principles attributed here to Marcion and Cerdo bear little relationship to those taught by Prepon according to the account in Book VII. It is possible that the account of Marcion in Book X is all that remains of the 'more moderate (μετρίως)' exposition of heretical doctrines which the author says he had initially composed (*Ref.* I. prol. 1); finding it unhelpful for a comparison with Greek philosophy, he may have simply jettisoned it. Where he has no such agenda, for example, in his description of Apelles and in his identification of Prepon as an Assyrian who addressed Bardaisan, he may be drawing more faithfully on his sources. This means that the Marcion of the *Refutation* is a composite, and even a contradictory, figure, being the product both of the author's own personal agenda, but also of other traditions and agendas, including but not limited to those of Irenaeus. From the work as a whole, it is evident that such inconsistencies were of no concern at all to an author who has, after all, been described as lacking 'the intellectual strength of an Origen or Clement' and of exhibiting 'apparent sloppiness'.[36]

EPIPHANIUS, *PANARION*

It is remarkable that there is little trace of sustained heresiological discourse for a century after Hippolytus. A new stage is marked by the *Panarion* or 'medicine chest against all heresies', composed c. 374–8 CE by Epiphanius, bishop of Salamis, which sets a pattern and style that cast a long shadow into the future.[37] Here, the artifice and the ideology of the exercise become

35 *Ref.* VII. 29.2; VIII. 20.1; X. 18. Tertullian enmeshed the Cynic association with Marcion's Pontic origin (*AM* I. 1.5; II. 5.1; cf. herein p. 56).

36 Mueller, 'Hippolytus *Retractus*', 251.

37 On the significance of Epiphanius, see Cameron, 'How to Read'; J. Rebecca Lyman, 'Ascetics and Bishops: Epiphanius on Orthodoxy', ed. Susanna Elm, Éric Rebilard,

immediately transparent – the number of heresies, eighty, is identified with that of Solomon's 'extra-marital' concubines (Song of Songs 6.8–9), while his apparently novel concept of four original or 'mother' heresies, Barbarism, Scythism, Hellenism, and Judaism, is drawn from Colossians 3.11.[38] The latter marks a major change from the traditional tracing of heresy to Simon, which Epiphanius nonetheless retains by dint of distinguishing twenty heresies 'before Christ', from those that follow (*Pan.* 21). The comprehensive account now becomes a device for setting Christianity on the world stage, asserting its embodiment of universal truth against 'pagan' and Jewish culture.

At the same time, Epiphanius was heavily involved in doctrinal controversy throughout his life, and his list of heresies continues up to his own day, with particular emphasis on those positions that had personal implications for him, most notably those of Origen and Arius. The work is directed towards a statement of the faith held by 'the apostolic church', the *De Fide*; by contrast, a 'heresy' is for him a 'sect', a group holding false views, and each such group is given its own label, in many cases devised by himself. Epiphanius develops to a high degree the familiar weapons of vituperation and slander, and yet he is also concerned to let the detail of each position lead to its refutation, for a medicine chest must include the antidote to the ills it diagnoses. To that purpose he had ferreted out a variety of sources alongside the investigations he had made himself; for his own period he is himself a valuable source, for the more distant past he relies on other authors, some known to us. It is the intersection between the demands of his overall scheme, his methods, and his intentions that makes any analysis of his material, particularly for historical information, so difficult.

Antonella Romano, *Orthodoxie, Christianisme, Histoire/Orthodoxy, Christianity, History* (Coll. de l'École française de Rome 270; Paris : École française de Rome, 2000), 149–61, who emphasises the change from philosophical 'choice' to a medical model, which recognises heresy as internal. On the periodisation of heresiology see Hervé Inglebert, *Interpretatio Christiana: Les mutations des savoirs (cosmographie, géographie, ethnographie, histoire) dans l'Antiquité chrétienne (30–630 après J.-C.)* (Coll. des études augustiniennes, Série Antiquité 166; Paris: Institut d'études augustiniennes, 2001), 395–412.

38 Whether Samartianism is a fifth 'mother' or is derivative from Hellenism is obscure. On this and what follows see Vallée, *Study in Anti-Gnostic Polemic*, 63–91; Frank Williams, transl. *The Panarion of Epiphanius of Salamis* (2nd revised edn; 2 vols. NHMS 63, 79; Leiden, Brill, 2009, 2013) I, xx–xxxiii; Frances M. Young, 'Did Epiphanius Know What He Meant by Heresy?', ed. Elizabeth A. Livingstone, *Studia Patristica* 17.3 (Oxford: Pergamon Press, 1982), 199–205.

Sources and heirs

Given his tendency to extrapolate and to give rein to his imagination, the question of Epiphanius' sources is an important one, albeit difficult to unravel. He himself acknowledges in his refutation of Valentinus that 'others have laboured, namely Clement, Irenaeus, Hippolytus, and many more' (*Pan.* 31.33.3), and this will apply equally to his refutation of the Marcionites. With regard to 'Hipploytus', there is no evidence that Epiphanius made use of the *Refutation*; however, he almost certainly did know the 'Syntagma against thirty-two heresies starting from Dositheus and continuing until Noetus and the Noetians', which Photius reports that Hippolytus drew up on the basis of Irenaeus' oral teaching (Photius, *Bibl.* 121). Although this work is lost, it is widely accepted that the (Latin) treatise *Against All Heresies*, erroneously attributed to Tertullian and often printed with his *Prescription of Heresies*, derives from it, for this too consists of a list of thirty-two heresies beginning with Dositheus, while the last figure, named 'Praxeas', seems to model the monarchianism associated with Noetus.

Three further debates have complicated the picture. Firstly, R. A. Lipsius argued that along with Ps.Tertullian, not just Epiphanius but also Philastrius, *On Heresies*, written between 383 and 391 CE, independently drew on the lost 'Syntagma' of Hippolytus.[39] He concluded that the 'Syntagma' could be reconstructed through a process of comparison and deduction from these extant writings: Information found in any two of them, or arguably in just one, might be attributable to Hippolytus. This position was made more complex by the subsequent hypothesis that Ps.Tertullian (and perhaps Philastrius) represents only a summary or Epitome of Hippolytus' 'Syntagma', while Epiphanius reflects its full form. Although this hypothesis is still often repeated, it is by no means secure, not least because it has become evident that Philastrius frequently drew directly on Epiphanius, so that agreement between these two cannot be used to trace a tradition back to the mid-third century.[40]

[39] Richard A. Lipsius *Zur Quellenkritik des Epiphanios* (Wien: Wilhelm Braumüller, 1865); subsequently he modified his views; see idem, *Die Quellen der ältesten Ketzergeschichte* (Leipzig: Barth, 1875).

[40] So already F. Heylen, *Philastrius. Diversarum hereson liber* (CCSL 9; Turnholt: Brepols, 1957), 210, following H. Koch, 'Philastrius', *PW* 38 (1938), 2125–2131, 2130. See also Brent, *Hippolytus*, 119–27, and Sebastian Moll, 'Three Against Tertullian: The Second Tradition About Marcion's Life', *JTS* 59 (2008), 169–80, who, however, does not seem to be aware that these doubts had been raised earlier. Stanley J. Isser, *The Dositheans: A Samaritan Sect in Late Antiquity* (SJLA 17; Leiden: Brill, 1976), 33–5, 57–63, defends the merits of the older view. Stanley F. Jones, 'Marcionism in the Pseudo-Clementines', ed. Albert Frey and Rémi

Secondly, a short treatise, *Against Noetus* (*Contra Noetum*), which survives in a single manuscript in which it is attributed to Hippolytus, has been identified by one editor, Pierre Nautin, as the concluding part of the latter's 'Syntagma' as it is described by Photius.[41] This treatise is also unmistakeably a source for Epiphanius' own refutation of Noetus in the *Panarion*, although he does not acknowledge its origin (Epiphanius, *Pan.* 57). The identification of the *Against Noetus* with part of the 'Syntagma' is still debated; but, evidently, if accepted, this will have consequences for any conclusions regarding both the likely character and the extent of that latter work.

Thirdly, and perhaps most intractable, is the question of how the (Ps.Hippolytus) *Refutation of All Heresies* relates to this hypothetical or reconstructed Hippolytan 'Syntagma'. As has been noted already, the author of the former does refer in the preface to an earlier, somewhat more 'moderate', effort (*Ref.* I. prol. 1). However, there is little expressly to support identifying this also-lost work with the 'Syntagma' in the form described by Photius. The *Refutation* here is of no help – if indeed it maintained anything of the shape of the earlier discarded work: Although it does mount an attack on Noetus, the *Refutation* as a whole operates on entirely different principles and with a different sequence from anything that might be reconstructed as the antecedent of Ps.Tertullian, *Against All Heresies*, and Epiphanius, *Panarion*. Indeed, Nautin has argued that the *Against Noetus* – in his view the final part of the 'Syntagma' – was derived from the *Refutation* rather than the reverse, and that it therefore has no relationship with the latter's 'more moderate' predecessor.[42] In any case, given the unresolved debates surrounding the authorship of the *Refutation* discussed earlier, it would be self-evidently mistaken to determine the potential contents of the 'Syntagma' of Hippolytus on the grounds of the known contents of the *Refutation*. In what follows, Epiphanius will provide the starting point for analysis, and other sources, particularly Ps.Tertullian (*Adv.Omn.Haer.* 6) and Philastrius (*De Haer.* 45), will be drawn on as seems appropriate; even so, only with

Gounelle, *Poussières de christianisme et de judaïsme antiques. Études réunies en l'honneur de Jean-Daniel Kaestli et Éric Junod* (PIRSB 5; Lausanne: Éditions du Zèbre, 2007), 225–44, 232–4, argues that the 'Basic Writing' behind the Pseudo-Clementines is also dependent on Hippolytus' 'Syntagma'.

41 Nautin, *Hippolyte Contre les Hérésies*; Nautin is followed by Pourkier, *L'Hérésiologie*. See also Brent, *Hippolytus*, 116–27.

42 Nautin, *Hippolyte et Josipe*, 63–88; on the basis of Photius, *Bibl.* 48, Nautin ascribes the *Refutation* to an earlier author whom he names Josipus.

extreme caution will it be possible to suggest where any of their themes might be traced back to the time of Hippolytus.

Epiphanius, the focus here, is not a mere collector of sources and traditions. The findings of Aline Pourkier's detailed comparison of his account of Noetus compared with that in Hippolytus, *Contra Noetum*, are more generally applicable; she concludes that Epiphanius is inspired by his source, following its plan and arguments, but that he is 'far from following servilely: He adds details, introduces where it seems opportune passages of his own, and above all he adapts to the theology of his own time that which he read in Hippolytus'.[43] In addition, as shall be seen, he frequently repeats details from one heresy in his account of another, or transfers material from his sources; this allows him to drive home his own arguments by multiple repetition, but also enables him to paint a picture in which the heresies both are tarred by a common brush and yet are forever in disagreement with each other. He also loves to pile up a number of alternative implications of a supposed 'heretical' argument, offering them and then refuting them, manufacturing a hypothetical system for his adversaries that existed only in his own imagination, while parading the rhetorical claim to comprehensive demonstration.

Sect 42: The Marcionites

Within Epiphanius' extended panoply the Marcionites come in as forty-second overall, and twenty-second since Christ. As was by now traditional, they immediately follow Cerdo, although Epiphanius knows little of the latter beyond what he could have found in Irenaeus or extrapolated from his supposed successor Marcion. By contrast, he could claim some knowledge of contemporary Marcionites for he had previously acquired access to their 'Gospel' and 'Apostolikon', and he had even made his own collation of excerpts from these and a rebuttal of them (*Pan.* 42.10.1).[44] Whether he had first-hand knowledge of 'the other accounts [Marcion] drew up for those deceived by him' is uncertain, but his recollection of a particular exegetical debate with 'some Marcionite or other' is not unlikely (42.9.3; 11.17, R60).[45] Despite his characteristic tendency to exaggeration, he therefore presumably had grounds for asserting the continuing spread of the sect's influence, particularly in the eastern regions with which he was familiar: 'Even now the heresy is to be found in Rome and in Italy, in Egypt and in Palestine, in

[43] Pourkier, *L'Hérésiologie*, 146. [44] See herein pp. 193–6.
[45] The refutation to Scholion 60 on the Gospel.

Arabia and in Syria, in Cyprus and in the Thebaid, and indeed in Persia and in other places' (42.1.1). Yet, despite this, his detailed knowledge of Marcionite teaching proves to be relatively limited, and at those points where he goes beyond earlier sources, both regarding this and regarding Marcion's life and later Marcionite practice, he needs to be treated with considerable scepticism.

Marcion's biography

Epiphanius begins with the established tradition that Marcion was from Pontus, the one consistently repeated fact since Justin, but he qualifies it: 'I mean Helenopontus, from the city of Sinope'. The former is merely a precision determined by the division of the earlier province by Constantine in c. 333–7 CE; the latter is perhaps his own suggestion, for it is not found in Ps.Tertullian, although Philastrius repeats it. If so it was a reasonable guess, for Sinope was the major port of the region and other sources had identified Marcion as a shipowner or seaman, even though Epiphanius himself does not do so, nor indeed do Ps.Tertullian or Philastrius.[46] In addition, Tertullian had already compared Marcion to the cynic Diogenes (Tertullian, *AM* I. 1.5), who himself came from Sinope, and this may be only a further development in that assimilation. In either case it has no independent historical value.

Epiphanius continues to weave a narrative out of earlier hints, standard accusations, and his own imagination, but he does so with an eye not only to entertainment and denigration but also to drawing morals that suited his own concerns. Marcion was, he asserts, the son of a bishop, and initially a celibate ascetic, but when he 'corrupted a certain virgin' he was excluded from the church because 'he had cheated the virgin of her hope'. Some form of this charge predates Epiphanius, for Ps.Tertullian offers a more succinct and geographically less precise version: 'Pontic by race, son of a bishop, driven from the common life of the church on account of sexual misdemeanour (*stuprum*) with a certain virgin' (*Adv.Omn.Haer.* 6.2). An earlier source, perhaps Hippolytus, is not excluded despite the absence of the story from Philastrius, who tends to be more focused, albeit often confused, but the story is clearly drawn from familiar stereotypes. Tertullian had made a similar charge against Apelles, Marcion's disciple, that he 'fell in relation to a woman, deserting Marcion's continence'; in

46 See above p. 56.

Apelles' case his well-attested association with the prophetess Philumene lent itself to heresiological misrepresentation of this kind (Tertullian, *PrH* 30; cf. *De Carne* 6). However, the charge of sexual misdemeanour is a widespread polemical theme; in addition, it also becomes a standard metaphor used against those who 'corrupt' the pure virgin Church: Hegesippus introduces his account of the roots of heresies, 'For this reason they used to call the church a virgin, for it was not yet defiled by vain reports' (Eusebius, *HE* IV. 22.4).[47] Marcion, it appears, has become the victim of the historicisation of such a metaphor, even though it contradicts the otherwise firm tradition of his strict sexual probity – allowing Epiphanius subtly to undermine the latter.

The description of Marcion's father as bishop is less easy to explain, and it has no obvious precedent other than in Ps.Tertullian. It is in any case anachronistic, for although Pliny testifies to the presence of Christian communities in the Pontic region at the beginning of the second century (Pliny, *Epist.* X. 96), the pattern of monarchical bishops was still in its infancy.[48] Epiphanius himself exploits the detail to his own ends, emphasising both the refusal by Marcion's father to grant his son absolution and the subsequent refusal by the Roman elders to undermine this, which together serve as models of proper episcopal behaviour and unity. These had long been pressing concerns, although this does not of itself explain the underlying tradition as also found in Ps.Tertullian.

The issue here is more than one of the degree of credulity to be permitted to a stereotypical slander against an apostate; the story implies that Marcion had already broken with a local church before he came to Rome, even if not for doctrinal reasons. This is very different from the claim made with such emphasis by Tertullian that initially Marcion was a faithful member of the Roman church.[49] The discrepancy has prompted the debate whether, contrary to Tertullian's claim, Marcion had already begun to develop his distinctive teaching before he came to Rome, and, if so, where else traces of this might be found. However, on closer investigation the support that has been claimed for such a tradition proves insubstantial. Although the curious closing comment by Philastrius, 'When he [Marcion] was defeated and put to flight by John the evangelist and by the elders from the city of Ephesus he

[47] See above, p. 26; Judith M. Lieu, *Christian Identity in the Jewish and Graeco-Roman World* (Oxford: Oxford University Press, 2004), 207–9.

[48] The identification of Marcion's father with Philologos (Rom. 16.15), first bishop of Sinope according to later Byzantine lists, seems to be a modern invention.

[49] See above, p. 57.

disseminated this heresy at Rome', might at first seem to support earlier 'heretical' activity by Marcion, it is best explained as a textual error, displaced from an account of some other early heretic, Nicolaus, Cerinthus, or Ebion, about whom similar stories are told (Philastrius, *De Haer.* 45).[50]

A more complex tradition is the one reported by the so-called Antimarcionite Prologue to John that describes Marcion's expulsion by John, and which adds the comment, 'He had brought to him writings or letters sent from the brethren who were faithful to Christ Jesus our Lord in Pontus'.[51] Curiously, this claim would suggest that Marcion had left Pontus in good standing, and it would therefore provide no reason for John's rebuff, in contrast to the account of Philastrius which places the incident after the statement of Marcion's error. The Antimarcionite Prologue, which is frequently dated to the fourth century but may have been written at least a century later, inspires no greater confidence in its transmission of earlier traditions: The account just given follows a claim that Papias wrote the Fourth Gospel at the Evangelist's dictation, and that this fact was attested by Papias himself. Evidently, all this is the result of the confusion of earlier sources of uncertain provenance, perhaps including the not dissimilar story told by Irenaeus of Marcion's encounter with Polycarp, purportedly a disciple of John, which follows a similar account of John's rejection of Cerinthus (Irenaeus, *AH* III. 3.4).[52] Various explanations of these overlapping traditions are possible: Papias and Polycarp may have been elided with each other in transmission, and then have been absorbed by their 'teacher' John; the story of one individual, heretic and/or hero, may have been transferred to another, as may also have happened in the case of Marcion/Apelles and the woman; it may even be the case that Tertullian's reference to Marcion's 'letter', and his interpretation of 1 John 2.18; 4.2, as proleptically refuting the latter's Christology, generated this new narrative.[53] The earliest

50 Heylen, *Philastrius*, 236n; for such traditions see below.

51 '*Verum Marcion hereticus, cum ab eo fuisset reprobatus eo quod contaria sentiret, proiectus est a Iohanne. Hic vero scripta vel epistulas ad eum pertulerat a fratribus missas, qui in Ponto errant fideles in Christo Iesu domino nostro*': see Jürgen Regul, *Die Antimarcionitischen Evangelienprologe* (VL. AGLB 6; Freiburg: Herder, 1969), 34–5 (text), 99–104. Ulrich Schmid, *Marcion und sein Apostolos: Rekonstruktion und historische Einordnung der marcionitischen Paulusbriefausgabe* (ANTF 25; Berlin: de Gruyter, 1995), 305–8, abandons his characteristic caution and uses this story as the basis of his own reconstruction.

52 See above, p. 34; compare John's rejection of Ebion in Epiphanius, *Pan.* 30.24.1.

53 On Tertullian see above p. 82. On these see also the critique by Benjamin W. Bacon, 'Marcion, Papias, and "the Elders"', *JTS* 23 (1922), 134–60; idem, 'The Anti-Marcionite Prologue to John', *JBL* 49 (1930), 43–54. The reference by Philastrius to 'elders' would then be a secondary duplication from the Roman expulsion.

form and date of the tradition is impossible to determine, but there are few grounds for according it much value for historical reconstruction.

Instead, it becomes apparent that the traditions that Epiphanius received about Marcion's experience in Rome were far more ambiguous than suited him. It is telling that at the end of the whole account the representatives of the church there refuse to accept him, not because of his teaching, which they have been examining, but on the grounds that the confession that 'there is one faith and one harmony' prevents them from opposing their 'most excellent fellow-minister', his episcopal father (*Pan.* 42.2.7). This rationale undoubtedly serves Epiphanius' own agenda, but it also highlights how the events that he describes in the interim are woven out of disparate traditions, again coloured with the compiler's own concerns.

The first of these intervening episodes has Marcion fleeing disrepute in Pontus and arriving in Rome after the death of Hyginus (*Pan.* 42.1.7); Epiphanius could have deduced this dating from Irenaeus' somewhat imprecise references, but from his own perspective the suggestion of an interregnum would also explain why Marcion's various encounters were only with 'elders', suggesting that these probably were a fixed component in the traditions.[54] Initially these are described as 'the elders who were still then alive (τοῖς ἔτι πρεσβύταις περιοῦσι)' – perhaps unlike Hyginus – 'and who began from the disciples of the apostles';[55] this is the language of succession although it is oddly expressed. Equally abstruse is the allusive account that follows, which describes how Marcion requested to be included but was rejected by them; it does, however, seem probable that Epiphanius is attempting to couch a tradition that he did not fully understand in terms that he could exploit. One thing he is clear about: It is resentment at this rejection, and at not attaining 'presidency or entrance to the church', that drives Marcion to join Cerdo's sect. Such resentment too, however, is simply another familiar topos, facilitated by Epiphanius' supposition of the death of Hyginus: Hegesippus had traced the beginning of heresy to a similar disappointment by a certain Thebouthis, Tertullian had made a parallel claim about Valentinus, and, perhaps most significantly, Epiphanius had given the same reason for Dositheus' desertion to the Samaritans and his decision to found his own sect (Eusebius, *HE* IV. 22.5; Tertullian, *Adv. Val.* 4.1; Epiphanius, *Pan.* 12.1.3).

54 Irenaeus dates Cerdo to the time of Hyginus and says that Marcion prospered under his successor, Anicetus; see above, p. 34.

55 There is no need to translate 'had been taught by', as does Williams, *Panarion*, 1, 295.

Notwithstanding this, a second encounter ensues, this time with 'the elders (πρεσβυτέροι) at that time' (*Pan.* 42.2). Again, the terminology probably comes from the tradition, although Epiphanius imposes on it his own understanding of church structure, subsequently calling them 'the meek and all-holy elders and [or 'who were'] teachers of the holy church of God'.[56] This meeting takes the form of an inquiry (ζήτημα) about the meaning of a scriptural passage, a common device used in polemic as well as in genuine debate throughout the period.[57] The passage under scrutiny is the double parable of the wineskins and of the patch on a garment (Luke 5.36–39);[58] although surprisingly absent from Epiphanius' subsequent conspectus of Marcion's 'Gospel', these verses are elsewhere reported as foundational to Marcion's exegesis, and this may explain why Epiphanius describes the question as 'as it were from the very beginning and as if from the entrance to questions'.

This encounter, like its predecessor, is absent from Ps.Tertullian, although the latter does report Marcion's appeal to the parable of the trees and their fruit (Luke 6.43); Philastrius demonstrates that he is derivative through an allusive reference to the debate in which he combines both the garment/wine and the tree/fruit passages.[59] More significant is the similar account given by Hippolytus of the break between Noetus and his own church of Smyrna, in which Epiphanius closely follows him: Here the 'blessed elders' summon Noetus and examine him; at the end they convict him and exclude him from the church, at which he is 'moved by such pride as to establish a school (διδασκαλεῖον)' (Hippolytus, *C.Noet.* 1. 4–8; Epiphanius, *Pan.* 57).[60] The parallel is suggestive, but it may not be close enough to demonstrate conclusively that Epiphanius has simply copied the story of Noetus into that of Marcion.[61]

56 On this see Gerhard May, 'Markions Bruch mit der römischen Gemeinde', ed. Greschat and Meiser, *Gerhard May: Markion*, 75–83, who suggests that there may be elements of historical value in the account although they need recovery by careful investigation.

57 See herein p. 308.

58 On the text, including the sequence 'wine skins – garment', see herein pp. 231–2.

59 Ps.Tertullian, *Adv.Omn.Haer.* 6.2; Philastrius, *De Haer.* 45.

60 There is a probable scribal corruption in the MSS tradition where Epiphanius (*Pan.* 57) describes Noetus as from Ephesus, whereas Hippolytus had said Smyrna.

61 If Nautin (*Hippolyte Contre les Hérésies*, 234) is right to interpret Noetus' denial that he is 'considering principles' or 'rulerships' (τὰς ἀρχὰς φρονεῖν) as referring to 'first places', a further link might be found, were it not that Epiphanius omits this. Certainly, Callistus in Ps.Hippolytus, *Ref.* IX. 11, is accused of ambition; Nautin (*Hippolyte Contre les Hérésies*, 121–34) argues that the story in *Against Noetus* 1 has been created by Hippolytus on the basis of *Ref.* IX. 11; so also Pourkier, *L'Hérésiologie*, 117.

An alternative explanation would be that in both cases a looser tradition of conflict over specific issues or passages has become enshrined in a stereotypical narrative whose origin is impossible to determine with confidence. Such exegetical debates were undoubtedly a regular feature of the encounters between different groups, particularly but not only in the earlier period when boundaries were more loosely inscribed. The elders' answer to Marcion, that the wineskins represent 'the hearts of the Pharisees and scribes' and that the garment represents Judas, is undoubtedly a piece of Epiphanius' own exegesis; he avoids describing Marcion's alternative interpretation, not because he did not know what at least contemporary followers would say about the passage, but because he did not want his readers to know. Although there may be an echo of older tradition in the identification of Marcion's opponents as 'elders', there are no grounds for tracing behind this account any genuine report of a formal process leading to his exclusion.[62] Indeed, Philastrius merely states that Marcion did not submit to the truth (*non adquiescebat veriti*), while Epiphanius cuts the debate short and concludes with the elders' repeated refusal to accept a man who had been excluded elsewhere; he then ascribes the determination to create a 'split' (σχίσμα) to Marcion's own resentful reaction.

Again, this outcome is not simply an imaginative expansion of earlier tradition; rather, Epiphanius is deliberately playing on the language of the Lukan parable (Luke 5.36). He drives the point home, commenting that it is Marcion and his followers who suffer from 'splitting' (σχίζω), whereas the (true) Church cannot be divided. This develops the exegesis he has just attributed to the elders, where Judas too suffers a 'split' because of his failure to 'agree' (συμφωνεῖν, Luke 6.36) with his heavenly calling, despite being tied to (συνάπτειν) the eleven apostles. Not only does this interpretation ally Marcion with Judas, but the play on words explains Epiphanius' – as noted, slightly strained – own choice of vocabulary in his account of Marcion's first failure to achieve his ends: There Marcion *meets* (συμβάλλειν) with the elders, asks to be *included* (συνάγειν), but no one *permits* (συγχωρεῖν) this. The heavy concentration of 'συν-' (with-) compounds underlines the elders' refusal to gainsay a 'fellow-minister' (συλλειτουργός) in the final episode. Woven through the account is an evocation of the

[62] Contrast those who see here an early Roman 'synod'. Brent, *Hippolytus*, 429, accepts the account of Marcion's meeting as reflecting the situation of the Roman church in the second century, and perhaps implies that the *Against Noetus* is modelled on it. See also p. 297 below.

unity of the Church and of the self-inflicted damage of those who found sects or who join them.

The elders' refusal to repeal Marcion's exclusion from the church by his father obviously reflects anxieties of a later period than that of Marcion himself.[63] Contrasting attitudes to the forgiveness of penitents was a major cause of conflict, at least from the third century. The author of the *Refutation* is particularly incensed by the offer of welcome and forgiveness made by Callistus (d. 222 CE) to those who had sinned, perhaps members of other congregations within a context of coexisting communities at Rome (*Ref.* IX. 12. 20–6).[64] Such debates were then compounded by differing responses to those who had lapsed during persecution, and by the conflict between Cyprian of Carthage and Stephen of Rome as to whether 'baptised' heretics wishing to join the church should or could be baptised again (Cyprian, *Epist.* 74). As shall be seen, Epiphanius continues to evoke this issue in his account of the practice of Marcion and his followers. The polemical account of Marcion's early history, whether or not it has any roots before Epiphanius, has been used as a weapon in a very different conflict.[65] The Marcion who emerges is consequently a very different character from the one who might be reconstructed from Tertullian.

Both Epiphanius and Philastrius, arguably supported by Ps.Tertullian, claim that it was as a result of these prior disagreements that Marcion turned to, and developed further, the heretical teaching of Cerdo in Rome. This is an important variation on the basic description of Marcion as a disciple of, or successor to, Cerdo as is implied by Irenaeus, Tertullian, and the *Refutation*. It should not, however, be used in an attempt to distinguish Marcion's 'original' views from their development under the influence of Cerdo;[66] rather than being based on independent sources, this is probably the result of the attempt to combine different evolving traditions into a coherent narrative.

63 Contrast the account in Tertullian, *PrH* 30 (but not repeated in *Against Marcion*), where Marcion repents of his schism but is preempted by death from returning to the Church with those he had misled, above, p. 58.

64 So Brent, *Hippolytus*, 291–2, 423–8. Compare also Tertullian's anger at the offer in *The Shepherd of Hermas* of a second repentance, which leads him to call the text 'adulterer' (Tertullian, *De Pud.* 10.12–13).

65 For Epiphanius' representation of the heretic as 'unholy man', a contrary picture to the contemporary accounts of the 'holy man', see Young Richard Kim, 'Reading the *Panarion* as Collective Biography: The Heresiarch as Unholy Man', *VC* 64 (2010), 382–413.

66 See above, pp. 93, 104.

Marcionite practice

Other echoes of more recent concerns can be heard in Epiphanius' account of the moral or ecclesial practice of Marcion and of his followers; here the silence of Ps.Tertullian and of Philastrius means that Epiphanius' sources are uncertain and perhaps drawn from hearsay at best: 'as I have heard from many' (*Pan.* 42.3.6). It is, therefore, most likely Epiphanius' own instincts that provoke the somewhat curt and yet positive comment, 'Marcion himself also preaches celibacy (παρθενία)', in place of the conventional emphasis on his hatred of marriage and procreation found in other polemicists, something that Epiphanius ignores. Instead he ascribes this to Luc(i)an, Marcion's disciple, who 'denies marriage and practices asceticism beyond the teaching of his master', not for asceticism's own sake but because child-bearing serves the interests of the Demiurge (42.3.3; 43.1.5). In the late fourth century questions about celibacy needed more careful handling,[67] and it may be no accident that Epiphanius subsequently makes no reference to Marcion's text and interpretation of 1 Corinthians 7. At the same time it serves his own ends that Marcion should forever be tarnished by that initial 'seduction of a virgin', and he recalls this offence twice more when he asserts that Marcionites allow up to 'three baths, that is three baptisms for the forgiveness of sins', a practice purportedly devised by Marcion himself to deal with his own transgression. This claim is hard to reconcile with other accounts of Marcion's rigorism, and it is not otherwise attested.[68] However, it may have arisen by a number of possible routes: Firstly, Epiphanius had already copied from Irenaeus the Marcosian doctrine of an initial baptism for repentance, modelled on that of John the Baptist, along with a second cleansing for perfection, purportedly justified by the words of Jesus in Luke 12.50, a proof-text that he also attributes to Marcion at this point (*Pan.* 34.19.3–6; Irenaeus, *AH* I. 21.2).[69] Secondly, the manipulation of charges about baptism is a

[67] Epiphanius describes Marcion's earlier asceticism as μοναζών, evoking his own calling.

[68] Except by Eznik, *De Deo* 432 (see pp. 176–8), who depends on Epiphanius. Although the concept of 'three baptisms' is found in gnostic sources, these have little to do with the current context: e.g., *Book of Jeu* II. 43, 45 (ed. Carl Schmidt and Violet MacDermot, *The Books of Jeu and the Untitled Text in the Bruce Codex* [NHS 13; Leiden: Brill, 1978] 102, 105) (baptisms in water, fire, and Holy Spirit); in *Pistis Sophia* III. 122 (ed. Carl Schmidt, trsl. and notes by Violet MacDermot, *Pistis Sophia* [NHS 9; Leiden: Brill, 1978]) a woman does come to Jesus who has been baptised three times and still needs repentance, but it is difficult to relate this text to Marcion.

[69] Epiphanius says that Marcion (but not Marcus) appealed to Mark 10.38 as well as to Luke 12.50; he makes no reference to Luke 12.50 in his conspectus of Marcion's 'Gospel', and neither does Tertullian.

concern that appears elsewhere in earlier polemics: Although the primary attack of Ps.Hippolytus, *Refutation* against Callistus is for offering forgiveness for post-baptismal sin, it does make a passing allusion to 'a second baptism'; the author of the *Refutation* had anticipated this in his own redaction of Irenaeus' account of Marcus, and he follows it in his account of how a certain Alcibiades arrived in Rome bringing a book of the revelations given to a certain Elchasai, who in the third year of Trajan had preached a new forgiveness of sins and had defined a second baptism even for those who engaged in forbidden sexual relations (*Ref.* VI. 41.2; IX. 12.26; 13.4; 15.1–6).[70] Epiphanius himself shows no knowledge of Alcibiades, and he apparently has a different source for his information about Elchasai: He presents him as Jewish in origin, and as having vigorously rejected celibacy and affirmed marriage, with no recorded teaching on baptism. Nonetheless, Epiphanius does have a pronounced antipathy towards groups that practice multiple 'baths', in particular the Ebionites.[71] It would seem that Marcion – who similarly emerged with a new 'Gospel' in the early second century – has again become the recipient of these other polemics, although whether this is entirely to be attributed to Epiphanius' strategy or is inspired by earlier traditions cannot be determined.

The remaining elements in Epiphanius' account of Marcionite practice are a mixture of convention, of assimilation to other groups, and of deduction. For example, he asserts that they use only water in the sacrament, a practice that is also ascribed to the Ebionites, and later to Tatian: Although Tertullian does refer to their use of bread in the sacrament in challenge to their hatred of the Creator, this is hardly unequivocal support for what Epiphanius says (*Pan.* 30.16.1; 46.2.3; Tertullian, *AM* I. 14.3). Also shared with the Ebionites is their rejection of meat, which Epiphanius reports later (*Pan.* 42.11.17, R24b; cf. 30.15.3); as noted earlier, although the *Refutation* makes the same claim, there it is in imitation of Empedocles.[72] On the other hand, Epiphanius' explanation that Marcion preached fasting on the Sabbath 'in order that we might do nothing that befits the God of the Jews' may have been his own extrapolation from previous polemic, particularly since the epithet 'God of the Jews' is his own (*Pan.* 42.3.3–4).[73] Tertullian had argued that to have

70 See Koschorke, *Hippolyt's Ketzerbekämpfung*, 65–66.

71 Epiphanius, *Pan.* 9.3.6; 17; 30.2.3–5; 15.3; 16.1; 21.1–2. For Elchasai, see *Pan.* 19.

72 Ps.Hippolytus, *Ref.* VII. 30.4; see above, p. 91. Irenaeus, *AH* I. 28.1 traces Tatian's rejection of marriage to Saturninus and Marcion, but he is less clear as to whether his rejection of animal foods is also derivative, although he had ascribed the same to Saturninus (*AH* I. 24.2; cf. Epiphanius, *Pan.* 23.2.5).

73 See further, p. 113.

shown himself to be against the *Creator* Jesus ought to have enjoined fasting on the Sabbath rather than have defended his disciples; although this could be read as a subtle challenge to Marcionite practice, it is perhaps more likely that Epiphanius has simply 'mirror-read' such a polemic (Tertullian, *AM* IV. 12; Luke 6.1–12).

Finally, as further evidence of Marcionite 'laxity', Epiphanius claims that they celebrate the mysteries in sight of the catechumens and that they allow women to administer baptism. The former concession is also attested by Jerome, purportedly based on Marcionite exegesis of Galatians 6.6, but both assertions had been made by Tertullian as an attack against heresies in general: 'In sum it is unclear who is a catechumen, who the faithful; they approach together, they hear together, they pray together ... the catechumens are as perfect as are the learned. As for the heretical women, how audacious! They who dare to teach, to dispute, to perform exorcisms, to promise healing, perhaps even to baptise!' (*PrH* 41).[74] Epiphanius would not have felt that he needed any explicit evidence to attribute such behaviour to the Marcionites, whether or not he had any further grounds for so doing.

Marcion's teaching

When it comes to Marcion's teaching, Epiphanius is at his most blithely inconsistent; he creates two Marcions and he almost entirely ignores that he is doing so. One is the 'exegetical Marcion', the man responsible for selecting, falsifying, and wilfully ignoring the inevitable implications of Luke's Gospel and ten Pauline Epistles. This Marcion emerges from Epiphanius' reproduction of what he claims to be a compilation of passages that he had drawn up previously 'from the aforesaid two books', and in particular from his own interpretation of these against the views that he claims Marcion held (*Pan.* 42.9–12). Although Epiphanius asserts that his original intention was to investigate Marcion's false claims and despicable teaching, the undertaking, a catalogue of 'scholia' with accompanying comments, sounds something like a conventional school exercise in the analysis of texts, perhaps in preparation for exegetical debate. Detailed examination of this compilation belongs to the study of Marcion's 'Gospel' and 'Apostolikon', but the internal inconsistencies and contradictions in Epiphanius' description of this earlier work, and in its reproduction in the *Panarion*, counsel caution against over-confidence in his investigative rigour and in his claim that he himself had carefully

[74] See further, below, p. 397.

worked from Marcionite copies (42.10.2–8; 11.16). He gives two lists of the scholia, the second accompanied by 'refutations', albeit with textual variation between these lists in the manuscript tradition, but he is inconsistent as to whether his original primary criterion for their selection had been to record 'the altered sayings that have been deceptively inserted', or to demonstrate that 'what is common to him and to us' supported his own position on the unity of God; in addition, he also finds symbolic significance in their total number, 118, as representing the sum of the name of Jesus and 'Amen' (42.11.13–15; 13.2–3).[75] Certainly, Epiphanius recognises that for the second apologetic task to succeed additional 'explanations' were needed, and it seems likely that he provided these for the second iteration of the list only when he came to write the *Panarion*, perhaps when he was already uncertain as to the meaning of his original transcription and notes.[76] This gives something of a 'scatter-gun' effect to his responses, which also variously addresses contemporary debates, such as that Jesus' brothers were sons of Joseph by another wife, or display encyclopaedic knowledge, such as the age of Aqiba, or defend the use of Hebrew alongside Greek (42.11.17, R11c, R26c; 12.3, R21). However, whether or not these issues were part of his original concern, the key principles that Epiphanius is now determined to defend against Marcion's denial of the same are, 'that the one and the same is maker of all and demiurge and lawgiver of old and new covenant, a good God and just and lord of all' (42.12.3, R15i), that Jesus was born, lived and died in flesh and not 'in appearance only', and that the body is raised and not the soul alone.

Marcion's counter-principles as implied by these are not alien to the second Marcion projected by Epiphanius, but they are of subordinate weight; this second Marcion is the Marcion of philosophical principle and myth, and he emerges from the doxographical sections which introduce and close Epiphanius' account, thus framing the exegetical part, but which are largely ignored by it (*Pan.* 42.3.1–8.6; 14.1–16.14). This second Marcion starts from the two contrasting principles held by Cerdo, a higher, unseen, good God, and the visible Creator and Demiurge, but he adds to them a

[75] 'Jesus'(ιη = 18) plus ἀμήν (=99) make 117, but to these is probably to be added the 'excerpt' from 'Laodiceans'; see below, p. 195.

[76] So Theodor Zahn, *Geschichte des neutestamentlichen Kanons. Volume II: Urkunden und Belege zum Ersten und Dritten Band, Part 2* (Erlangen and Leipzig: A. Deichert, 1892), 409–12; Karl Holl, ed. *Epiphanius II: Panarion haer. 34–64* (2nd revised edn; ed. Jürgen Drummer; GCS; Berlin: Akademie Verlag, 1980), 106 n., considers this an overstatement and attributes variations between the lists of scholia to textual corruption, but this is probably overly sanguine. It is possible that the list from the 'Apostolikon', which has additional difficulties, had a separate origin, see p. 236 below.

mediating figure, the devil (42.3.1–2). The visible God, Epiphanius adds, is 'of the Jews', an important clarification of earlier tradition, and is also 'judge (κριτής)', an epithet that becomes central, assuming that to be judge means to be just; further, as Epiphanius develops his own argument the third principle swiftly becomes 'the wicked God (φαῦλος/πονηρός)'.

Epiphanius' defence against Marcion's 'principles' in practice repeats many of the arguments shaped by earlier polemicists against a more binary system, sometimes clumsily adapted to accommodate this third principle: that it is unfitting for the good to invade the territory of another, or to act other than by the measures of justice; that both the Creator and the evil God can logically be shown to be more powerful than the other or than the good God; that the idea of circumscribed space by which each is bounded undermines the very concept of 'God', and invites a higher principle to adjudicate between them. There is indeed evidence that the Marcionite system, at least as reported by its adversaries, at some stage found the need to distinguish between the principles of justice and evil, and a third principle is attributed to some of his successors; thus, Epiphanius may well have encountered differing views on this.[77] At the same time, the separation of justice from evil suits his polemical agenda; the identification of one principle or God as both just and evil would not only be logically incoherent but would also be incompatible with the tradition of defence that proves the unity of the two dispensations or Gods: Epiphanius himself is clear that goodness and justice are inseparable from each other, whereas evil is not eternal, but has both beginning and end (42.12.3, R11). Hence, it is difficult to know whether his subsequent report of disagreement among Marcionites is genuine or is an attempt to discredit them and to cover his own inconsistency: Some, he says, acknowledge that Christ was not initially the son of the good God, but that he was sent by him as the adversary of 'his own natural father, whether that be the God who spoke in the law or the God of evil who is aligned alongside them as third principle' (*Pan.* 42.14.3–4). Similarly, whether the idiosyncratic identification of the third principle as the devil is independent or has been assimilated to Christian conceptions in order to serve Epiphanius' own polemical needs, must be a matter for conjecture.

Just as Epiphanius makes almost no effort to acknowledge the idea of a third principle in his challenge to 'the exegetical Marcion',[78] the brief charge, 'he rejects both the law and all the prophets' (42.4.1) is largely

[77] See above, pp. 94–6. (Ps.Hippolytus, *Ref.* VII. 31.1; Eusebius, *HE* V. 13.1–4)

[78] See only *Pan.* 42.11.15, R33, 'since approval is one and not at variance there are not two principles or three. For in fact God is one, who made all things, making well and not to the

ignored in his detailed refutation of 'the doxographical Marcion'. Instead it is subsumed under his description of the Creator God as 'of the Jews' (42.3.1). This epithet is repeated five more times in the following paragraphs, but not thereafter: Marcion instigated the Sabbath fast in deliberate defiance of 'the God of the Jews'; he taught that Christ came to convict 'the God of the Jews and law and prophets and such like'; and Christ's descent to Hades was to separate those who acknowledged the God of the Jews from those who did not (42.3.4; 4.2–4). This identification is undoubtedly an innovation by Epiphanius, and it is part of his general tendency to assimilate different heretical positions to each other. He has developed it from Irenaeus, who ascribed only to Saturninus and Basilides the identification of 'the God of the Jews', in their case with the chief of the angels who created the world; to these Epiphanius had already added the Ophites and the Archontikes as identifying Yaldabaoth and Sabaoth, respectively, also with 'the God of the Jews'.[79] Conversely, his assertion that Marcion 'rejects the law and all the prophets, saying that such things were prophesied from the ruler (ἄρχων) who made the world', recalls the angelic creator archons of Saturninus' system in his account (42.4.1).[80] Yet Epiphanius is also reflecting contemporary usage, for the term 'God of the Jews' was also becoming a commonplace in the fourth century, even in nonpolemical contexts.[81]

Both the 'exegetical' and the 'doxographical' Marcions, however, share the one theme that touched Epiphanius' own polemical anxieties most deeply, namely the resurrection of the body. This question recurs repeatedly in his interpretation of Marcion's scriptural texts, while in the doxographical

contrary'; compare also 43.1.4 where he says that Apelles does not say that 'there are three principles or two as Lucianus and Marcion thought'.

79 Irenaeus, *AH* I. 24.2 (= Ps.Hippolytus, *Ref.* VII. 28.5), 4; Epiphanius, *Pan.* 23.3, 6; 24; 24.2.4; 37.3.6; 40.5.1. Pourkier, *L'Hérésiologie*, 185–6, argues that Epiphanius intensifies the hostility of Satornilus (= Saturninus) towards the 'God of the Jews'.

80 Irenaeus had already claimed that Tatian's denunciation of marriage was kin to that of Marcion and Saturninus (*AH* I. 28.1 [Ps.Hippolytus, *Ref.* VIII. 16 drops the reference to Saturninus]); it might be thought that Epiphanius is merely extrapolating from the implied kinship of the latter two except that he does not repeat it.

81 The term is ascribed to Basilides and Cerinthus in Ps.Tertullian, *Adv.Omn.Haer.* 1, 3, and to Cerinthus only in Philatsrius, *De Haer.* 36. It emerges more widely in the third century (Tertullian, *Apol.* 21; 26; Origen, *C.Cels.*, VI. 7; 27 etc.), and is common in the fourth. See also below on the *Dialogue of Adamantius* which uses the term 'the God', 'the one', or 'the demiurge of the Jews' on three occasions (*Dial.* 4.26–6.6 [1.3]; 18.19–21 [1.9]; 20.27 [1.10]). On its absence from earlier reports of Marcion, see above p. 69, where it is argued that Tertullian, *AM* I. 10.3; IV. 33.4; V. 13.7 do not reflect Marcionite usage (ctr. Harnack, *Marcion*, 263*).

section he twice charges Marcion with holding a resurrection of the soul only, on the second occasion adding, 'and likewise he says there are reincarnations of souls and transmigrations from bodies to bodies' (42.4.6; cf. 3.5). Betraying just how much this matters to him, he even introduces this, for him repugnant, concept into his refutation of Marcion's text of the parable of the friend at midnight (42.11.17, R24; Luke 11.5–13). Such beliefs are for him anathema, traced back to the 'Hellenism' of the Stoics, Platonists, and Pythagoreans, and then repeated by the Gnostics and later by the Manichaeans (*Pan.* 5.1.1; 5.2.4; 6.1.1; 7.1.1; 26.9.4–5; 66.28.1); they are, however, most dangerously threatening in what he believes to be the denial of the resurrection of the body by Origen, whose condemnation he did so much to bring about (64.4.10; 63.1–72.9).[82] Here, as always, to listen to Epiphanius without one ear tuned to the concerns of his own day is to be deceived.

Epiphanius' 'doxographical' Marcion does interpret Scripture and even 'distorts' it: The example that Epiphanius gives is the interpretation of Galatians 3.13 as demonstrating that 'he came into a world belonging to someone else as purchaser to redeem us who did not belong to him' (*Pan.* 42.8.1–8). This exegetical argument is found elsewhere, but Epiphanius seems unaware that Marcion's interpretation had a textual foundation;[83] strikingly, he does not include the passage in his conspectus of Marcion's Galatians, providing further evidence of the haphazard character of that work.[84] Yet his discussion does betray that he is aware of a rather more elaborate soteriological narrative of the descent of Christ into the territory of the Demiurge, itself perhaps already under the sway of the evil principle. In his view such a narrative is 'a staged battle and tragedy', while his own account is 'pious argument and reasonable demonstration' (42.8.8). Such a judgement cannot obscure the fact that both interpreters are treating the language and imagery of Scripture as a vehicle for philosophical conceptions of the divine and human which are alien to their original context.

It would be natural to conclude that the 'exegetical Marcion' and the 'doxographical Marcion', as well as the initial more biographical accounts,

[82] On the importance of the issue of resurrection for Epiphanius' attack against Origen see Elizabeth A. Clark, *The Origenist Controversy: The Cultural Construction of an Early Christian Debate* (Princeton: Princeton University Press, 1992), 86–94; on the debate about metensomatosis in Origen see U. Bianchi, 'Origen's Treatment of the Soul in the Debate over Metensomatosis', ed. Lothar Lies, *Origeniana Quarta: Die Referate des 4. Internationalen Origeneskongresses (Innsbruck, 1–6 September 1985* (Innsbrucker theologischer Studien 19; Innsbruck/Wien: Tyrolia, 1987), 270–81.

[83] See pp. 261–2.

[84] Cf. also pp. 105, 108 above on Luke 5.36–9 and 12.50 (Pan. 42.2 and 42.3.10), which are not listed in the scholia.

represent different types of source material to which Epiphanius had access. This does not mean that they can be accorded different degrees of historical value, for to some extent they have simply evolved from different rhetorical strategies. Epiphanius' failure to integrate them may underline that, despite his claims as to the extent of contemporary Marcionite influence, there is little sense of direct immediacy in his challenge to the latter. The space he devotes to Marcion, and particularly to his scriptural text, need not undermine this assessment. Certainly the latter, and the extended biographical narrative, combine to create the illusion of a somewhat more rounded character than emerges from many of Epiphanius' profiles of other 'heretics', but the counter-arguments he offers are largely conventional except where they use Marcion to address concerns closer to Epiphanius' own heart. Both the heresiological tradition within which he stood and his pressing desire to progress to the more recent and controversial debates imposed considerable restraints on him, and consequently also on any chance for Marcion's authentic voice to be heard.

THE *DIALOGUE OF ADAMANTIUS*

Of a very different character to Epiphanius' work is a perhaps slightly earlier treatise, which traditionally, but clearly wrongly, was ascribed to his bête noir, Origen.[85] Its original title is lost, but in the Greek manuscript tradition it is headed 'Against the Marcionites' or 'Concerning the right (ὀρθός) faith in God', while in the Latin translation made by Rufinus towards the end of the fourth century, in which the ascription to Origen is explicit, it is described as 'against heretics'.[86] What is distinctive about this work within the heresiological tradition, however, is that it takes the form of a dialogue in which a representative of the Catholic church, Adamantius, engages successively with two followers of Marcion, Megethius and Marcus, with a follower of Bardesanes (Bardaisan), Marinus, and with two followers of Valentinus, Droserius

85 The date is difficult to determine because there are conflicting statements as to whether persecution belongs to the past or is still a present reality, both within the Greek text and between the Greek and Latin (*Adam.* 40.12–26 [1.21]). Robert A. Pretty, transl. with commentary, *Adamantius. Dialogue on the True Faith in God* (ed. for publication by Garry W. Trompf; Leuven: Peeters, 1997), 16–17, suggests 290–300 CE; on the basis of the post-Nicene terminology, Kenji Tsutsui, *Die Auseinandersetzung mit den Markioniten im Adamantios-Dialog: Ein Kommentar zu den Büchern I–II* (PTS 55: Berlin: de Gruyter, 2004), 105–08 argues for a date between 350 and 360 or 378 CE.

86 See Pretty, *Adamantius*, 1–2; W. H. van de Sande Bakhuyzen, *Der Dialog des Adamantius* (GCS; Leipzig, 1901); Vinzenz Buchheit, introd., ed., and comm., *Tyrannii Rufini Adamantii Origenis adversus haereticos interpretatio* (Studia et testimonia antiqua 1; Munich: Fink, 1966).

and Valens. Of itself the dialogue form is not new within Christian polemic, but in this case the antagonists are allowed far more space than is, for example, Trypho in Justin's *Dialogue*. This structure might seem to justify acclaiming, in contrast to the methods of Irenaeus or of Epiphanius, 'the literary "act of charity", in at least allowing "other voices to speak" (rather than engaging in open polemic)'.[87] However, on closer reading this assessment appears overly generous, and the 'dialogue' has none of the open-endedness of the Platonic or Ciceronian models. Instead it is shaped to serve the interests not of the named protagonists but of the outline of the 'true faith' that will triumph at the end, a true faith that betrays itself at various points to be that of Nicaea. This determines the structure of the work, so that the main theme of the first part with the two Marcionites (sometimes divided into two subsections following the Latin version) is that of the ultimate principles – of which Megethius says there are three, Marcus, two;[88] the second part (or three further subsections) addresses the origins of evil, the nature of Christ's body, and bodily resurrection. On the other hand, the opponents are manipulated so that they personify both an undifferentiated representation of what 'the impious heretics think' (*Adam.* 240.8 [5.28]),[89] and, at the same time, the discord and division that are a recurring feature in all antiheretical polemics. Hence, the protagonists are not confined to their section of the *Dialogue* but intervene in or even take over other parts, while at the same time, the two 'Marcionites', Megethius and Marcus, disagree with each other as do also the two 'Valentinians', Droserius and Valens.

Thus, the *Dialogue* is a literary device, designed to mimic the arguments, clarifications, and concessions of a real debate, when in reality such concessions will only be made on one side, and the author's controlling hand ensures that it all serves his own purpose. So, for example, Marcus initially claims that 'the Good one is good to all, the Creator promises to save those who trust in him', but when he is challenged as to whether the 'all' includes murderers and adulterers he qualifies it as, 'the Good one saves those who believed in him, but does not condemn those who are disobedient to him, the Creator saves those who believed in him, but judges and punishes sinners' (*Adam.* 64.28–66.1 [2.4]). Such a fundamental change in position, which then leads into a discussion of judgement as the necessary corollary of approval, is

[87] Garry A. Trompf, 'Series Editor's Preamble', in Pretty, *Adamantius*, XVI–XXI, XIX.

[88] See further below pp. 122–3.

[89] The text is cited following Tsutsui, *Auseinandersetzung* and, for part 5, Bakhuyzen, *Dialog des Adamantius*.

engineered by the author and in no way warrants citing either view as certain Marcionite doctrine.

A further distinctive characteristic of the *Dialogue* is that it is adjudicated by a, supposedly neutral, non-Christian, Eutropius. In practice Eutropius soon shows himself to be far from neutral, quickly persuaded by and repeating the position of Adamantius, and, by the end, declaring that 'although a stranger I wish to become a child of the catholic church' (238 [5.28]). The presence of an adjudicator is, it would appear, an innovative device in the dialogue-genre, but it was perhaps particularly apposite in the fourth century where imperial power adjudicated ecclesiastical conflict. However, the inconsistent internal indications of the date of the *Dialogue* make it impossible to relate this device to any specific scenario in the relations between imperial authorities and ecclesiastical positions in the fourth century.

Marcion, Bardaisan, and Valentinus formed a familiar triumvirate in the polemical tradition, particularly in the East, where the *Dialogue* is probably to be situated, perhaps in eastern Asia Minor or in the region of Antioch on the Orontes.[90] However, unlike Tertullian or Epiphanius, the *Dialogue* gives no personal details about these heresiarchs and makes no personal attacks against them; this suggests that they serve chiefly as ciphers for the errors to be combatted, even though followers, at least of the first two, continued to be active in the region in the fourth century. Interpretation is made more complicated by the fact that the *Dialogue* makes undoubted use of the writings of Methodius of Olympus (d. c. 311 CE), who was well-known for his attack against Origen. 'Adamantius' was a nickname given to Origen and this identification is made explicit in the Latin manuscript tradition, although the extent to which anti-Origenism should be understood as supplying one of the themes of the *Dialogue* is disputed.[91] In any case, this does not appear to be an issue within the Marcionite sections.

Marcionite identity and sources

Despite the stylised function of the protagonists and the evident fourth-century colouring of the *Dialogue*, vigorous arguments have been mounted

90 Pretty, *Adamantius*, 17–18, suggests southern Asia Minor or Syria, while Tsutsui, *Auseinandersetzung*, 105–9, favours Syrian Antioch while not excluding Asia Minor.

91 Clark, *Origenist Controversy*, 168–70, argues that Marinus is ascribed something close to the position of the historical Origen whereas Adamantius (a rehabilitated Origen) adopts that of Methodius; she considers that Rufinus' translation was specifically part of his defence of Origen. Tsutsui, *Auseinandersetzung*, 63, finds no explicit interest in anti-Origenism; see also Pretty, *Adamantius*, 13–14, 21.

that the sections dealing with the Marcionite positions do reflect earlier traditions, whether written sources or memory. More than once in the debate it is asserted that the Marcionite text of the 'Apostolikon' and 'Gospel' is being cited, and on some occasions this does seem to be the case.[92] At the core of the argument made by Megethius, supplemented by Marcus, is a series of succinct contrasts (or *kephalaia*) demonstrating that the Demiurge and Christ have nothing to do with each other (*Adam.* 22.1–40.3 [1.10–20]); the content of a number of these can be paralleled in earlier sources, especially in Tertullian, and their form has encouraged their identification with Marcion's own 'Antitheses'.[93] Further, there are, as already noted, a number of internal inconsistencies, in particular, different explanations of the number and character of the opposing 'first principles' in Marcionite teaching; it has been suggested that these are the result of the use of one or more earlier anti-Marcionite source(s), not necessarily themselves in dialogue form, and this is certainly possible although not demonstrable.[94] However, whatever their origin, they have been carefully used to contribute to the effect of the *Dialogue* itself, and it is on this level that the representation of the Marcionite position will be explored in what follows.

This combination of earlier motifs and immediate textual rhetoric is evident from the start. The *Dialogue* opens without any setting of the scene, and also without any identification of the allegiance of the participants. Adamantius invites Megethius to a discussion (λόγος), and the latter responds by addressing him as 'brother' and by concurring that 'faith and the right opinion towards God' are indeed pre-eminent, albeit disputed; however, Megethius then immediately accuses Adamantius – or his party ('you' pl.) – of 'blaspheming rather than glorifying God' (2.11–19 [1.1]). Within the rhetoric of the text this charge would provoke the attention of a reader who knows that it is one usually made *against* Marcionites and others; yet in the narrative world of the text the opening gambit suggests two parties, each equally committed to proclaiming the truth. Subsequently, once Megethius has introduced his three principles (see below), he identifies them as 'of the Christians, of the Jews, and of the Gentiles (ἐθνικοί)'; the model of 'three races' is one that does have roots in the second century, although the adoption of ἐθνικοί for non-Christian Gentiles reflects latter usage.[95] More remarkably, the initial implicit assumption held by Megethius that

[92] See below, pp. 124, 234. [93] See below p. 289.

[94] So Tsutsui, *Auseinandersetzung*, 78–91, who argues for the use of a source which itself incorporates an earlier second- or third-century anti-Marcionite writing.

[95] Although it first appears in Matt. 5.47; 18.17; 3 John 7; see *PGL* s.v.

he, as well, presumably, as Adamantius, are of necessity 'Christians' goes unchallenged (4.26–7 [1.3]). It is only considerably later that Adamantius denies him that label and says that he is instead 'a Marcionite', the first time that this has been made explicit within the narrative of the *Dialogue* (16.9–15 [1.8]). At this point Megethius rejects the opposition 'Marcionite *versus* Christian' that is implied, and offers instead 'catholic (καθολική) *versus* Christian': 'you say you belong to the catholic [fem. = church]; so you yourselves are not Christians'. This altercation leaves the readers with the opposition between 'Marcionite' and 'Catholic', each vying over the coveted label 'Christian'. As the scene develops, Adamantius continues to force upon Megethius the label 'Marcionite', while the latter consistently resists this, refusing, when invited, to rank Marcion higher than Paul, and conceding only that 'Marcion was my bishop'. This for Adamantius is admission enough, introducing a succession (διαδοχή) not of bishops but of 'false bishops', going back to the 'artificer of schism (ὁ σχισματοποιός), Marcion' (16.16–18.2 [1.8]). Self-evidently it would be mistaken to draw a historical conclusion from this, namely that Marcion himself instituted a parallel church order; rather, the polemical strategy that originates with Irenaeus of asserting unbroken tradition has been clothed in the institutional form of contemporary politics in a new context.[96] In this way the opposition between the two sides develops before the reader's eyes, becoming increasingly non-negotiable; although it is not impossible that this stems from a source reflecting a situation where differentiation was still in process, its rhetorical effectiveness is what dominates.

Within the logic of the *Dialogue* this increasingly sharp differentiation is specifically provoked by an extended debate concerning the scriptural authorities to which appeal may be made (8.23–16.5 [1.5–8]). This then becomes one of the key defining marks of each side and of what separates them; the dialogue thereafter is conducted through an extensive use of the Scriptures, regularly identified as 'ours' or as 'yours': 'that is not written in our Gospel; you know that you promised to give proof from our Gospel' (36.17–18 [1.17]).[97] Although such appeals have often been used to identify Marcion's own text, what is at stake is presented in terms that are clearly long subsequent to Irenaeus and Tertullian. On the one side stand the

96 Against Pretty, *Adamantius*, 48n, who claims 'this is an important statement'; on the succession of bishops in Irenaeus, see above p. 30. Tsutsui, *Auseinandersetzung*, 168, notes that two objections are combined, those of being named after a human person, and the spurious bishop list.

97 So Tsutsui, *Auseinandersetzung*, 179, against Pretty, *Adamantius*, 60, who follows Zahn, *Geschichte*, II.2, 421, in attributing the second clause to Adamantius.

Church's Gospels, which Megethius abruptly claims are demonstrably false (φάλσα) (8.23 [1.5]);[98] he denies that Mark and Luke were disciples of Jesus, claims that Paul speaks of one Gospel and not four, and protests that the Gospels disagree amongst each other. In reply Adamantius contends that Mark and Luke were among the seventy-two 'apostles' as well as co-evangelists with Paul; that Paul did indeed acknowledge a plural proclamation of the Gospel (Gal. 1.8); and that the four Gospels, which speak of one Christ, 'are no longer four but one', while the supposed differences are not contradictory, especially if it is recognised – as Megethius does not – that they are to be interpreted spiritually (noetically).

On the other side stands the 'one' Gospel that Megethius claims to have been written by Christ, although, when he is challenged that this would entail Christ recording his own death and resurrection, he concedes that this Gospel was supplemented by Paul (*Adam.* 16.1–5 [1.8]). This theme is taken up and developed by Marcus in the second section of the *Dialogue* (82.1–86.8 [2.12–14]):[99] he insists that Matthew and John, although sent out by Christ to proclaim the good news, did so orally, 'without writing' or 'unrecorded', while Paul by implication did so 'in writing'.

Nowhere in this confrontation is there any suggestion that the Gospel was one that both parties to some extent shared even if claiming that the other had corrupted it. By contrast, there is only a passing reference to Paul's letters in the first section when Adamantius agrees to use Megethius' 'Apostolikon' rather than his own, which the latter similarly dubs 'false' (10.17–33 [1.5]). In the second section, however, Adamantius introduces an extended debate about Paul's teaching by charging Marcion with perverting it: 'The wicked Marcion treated the apostle's writing casually, and did not abandon it entirely, and these people even now take away whatever does not accord with their own opinion' (96.6–9 [2.18]).[100] Despite this, the structure of the argument allows Adamantius both to introduce passages his Marcionite opponents will veto, and then to agree supposedly to resort to their texts, repeatedly trumping them from the latter, their 'home territory'.

It is difficult to be confident how far all this reflects the attitudes to their Scriptures by each party in the time of the *Dialogue* or even of its purported sources. Certainly, some of the issues raised were probably debated more

[98] Tsutsui, *Auseinandersetzung*, 128, suggests that Megethius' use of the Latin loanword '*falsa*', where in reply Adamantius uses the normal πλαστά, 'probably goes back to the source...The author wants in this way to make the Marcionites appear linguistically foreign'.

[99] See Tsutsui, *Auseinandersetzung*, 241–9.

[100] Pretty, *Adamantius*, 98–9, is overly influenced by Tertullian's vocabulary when he translates the verbs: 'corrupted ... did not completely erase ... remove'.

widely: The objection voiced by Eutropius that those who were witnesses should have been the ones to do so in writing, 'since what is said orally disappears quickly and does not serve as proof', seems likely to address long-running disputes about the value of oral tradition and about the authorship claimed for the Gospels or other writings. Adamantius' vigorous rebuttal of the claim by Marcus that 'Not Peter but Christ wrote the Gospel', on the grounds that this would entail Christ's self-testimony, perhaps betrays some vulnerability to external attacks that were based on the absence of any direct testimony by Jesus to his own claims and self-understanding. Moreover, debates about the plurality of the Gospels already emerged in the second century, and were vigorously pursued by Origen, for an internal audience as well as for an external one (Origen, *C.Cels.* II. 27).[101] However, even though these concerns may lie in the background, the stark opposition that is projected between the Church's four Gospels and Marcion's one reflects the developing attitudes to text and canon current in the fourth century; it is in this context that Marcus rejects 'the Acts of the Apostles', while Eutropius is primed to ask 'From which apostles do the Acts and Epistles [presumably the Catholic Epistles] come?' (*Adam.* 80.6–33 [2.12]).

Marcionite beliefs

One of the most striking aspects of the *Dialogue* is the predominately exegetical character of the debate between Adamantius and his two Marcionite opponents, in contrast to that with Marinus or with the two Valentinians, despite a nominal acknowledgement there that scriptural hermeneutics is central to all. The exegetical debate is not only centred on the interpretation of the Gospel and of Paul; Megethius' efforts to distinguish the Demiurge from Christ or his Father involve detailed discussion of relevant Old Testament passages. Admittedly, when Megethius cites Psalm 2 and Daniel 2.34–5 to demonstrate that 'the Christ through the law and prophets has not yet come', these were familiar enough for Adamantius to have a ready answer to hand (*Adam.* 46.1–50.8 [1.24–1.25]). However, other examples are more novel: When Adamantius explains the oft-quoted verse, 'no-one knows the father except the son …' in terms of Israel's earlier

101 See Oscar Cullmann, 'The Plurality of the Gospels as a Theological Problem in Antiquity', *The Early Church* (ed. A. J. B. Higgins; London: SCM, 1956), 39–54; S. Laechuli, 'The Polarity of the Gospels in the Exegesis of Origen', *ChHist.* 21 (1952), 215–24; Helmut Merkel, *Die Widersprüche zwischen den Evangelien: Ihre polemische und apologetische Behandlung in der Alten Kirhe bis zu Augustin* (WUNT 13; Tübingen: Mohr Siebeck, 1971).

obduracy and refusal to acknowledge the God whom they should have known, Megethius, the Marcionite, retorts, 'Why then does it say in Ezekiel, "I was known to your fathers in the wilderness"?' (44.1–10 [1.23]; cf. Ezek. 20.5). Adamantius certainly always has a ready answer, and to that extent the debate is manipulated by the author, but it remains very possible that it does nonetheless reflect precisely the exegetical sparring that characterised real-life encounters. If so it demonstrates that Marcion's followers did not simply discard the 'Old Testament' but continued to build their arguments around a detailed knowledge of it. The conflict between Marcus and Adamantius is over 'acknowledging' or 'obeying' (ὑπακούειν, δέχεσθαι) law and prophets' (76.11; 80.6 [2.10, 12]).

As elsewhere this scriptural awareness entails that the two Marcionites both deny that the Jesus who came was prophesied by law and prophets, and assert that both Christ and Paul abolished the latter (84.20–86.10 [2.14]). Marcus even reverses the verbs of Matthew 5.17, claiming Christ said, 'I did not come to fulfil the Law but to destroy it', and that the 'Judaisers' (ἰουδαισταί) were responsible for the Church's text, although who these Judaisers were he does not explain and there does not appear to be any specific polemic over the role of Peter (88.31–3 [2.15]).[102]

Despite the pervasively scriptural character of much of the debate, its starting point is, as already noted, apparently more doctrinal: Megethius responds to Adamantius' opening credal gambit with the assertion that there are 'three principles, God, the father of Christ, who is good, and another being the Creator, and another the Evil one. The Good one is not the creator of evils nor was he born from a woman, nor is this world created from him, for he is alien to all evil and every created thing' (4.16–20 [1.2]). Although, as discussed above, the three principles are assimilated to the conventional 'three races', this symmetry is not sustained even by Megethius himself: Firstly, there is but one Creator of all three races, namely 'the one of the Jews' – an epithet which functions very differently from 'the God of the Jews' in Epiphanius.[103] Secondly, the Good is strong*er* (a comparative, implying two) than the other two, whose relationship with each other is left opaque; thirdly, Megethius subsequently appeals to Luke 6.43 to demonstrate 'two natures, two laws' (56.14–17

[102] Instead, Marcus appears to cite Peter's confession at Caesarea Philippi to support his own position that Jesus was not John the Baptist, Elijah or one of the prophets (*Adam.* 84.1–6 [2.13]).

[103] However, on one occasion Marcus does refer to 'the law and prophets' as 'Jewish utterances' (*Adam.*76.7–8 [2.10]). See herein p. 113.

[1.28]). Even before this he identifies the Creator as 'the God of the law', and proceeds to differentiate him from Christ by the laws each establishes, thus working with a primarily bipartite pattern (6.1–5; 8.2–22; 18.7–18 [1.3, 4, 9]). Within the exegetical debate that follows it is, surprisingly, Adamantius who introduces the question of 'just (δίκαιος)' into the discussion about the character of the Creator, and who seems to prompt Megethius to then adopt that epithet for him.[104] On the other hand, as well as setting Gospel against Law, Megethius also identifies this opponent to the Good God as 'the 'God of begetting' or 'becoming' (ὁ θεὸς τῆς γενέσεως) – a translation that seems better than 'God of creation' or 'of the created order'.[105]

This inconsistency over a tripartite or bipartite pattern in Megethius' position is further exacerbated by the appearance at this point of Marcus, who is explicitly identified as 'a Marcionite': 'I declare that there are not three principles but two, evil and good' (60.12 [2.1]). This assertion provokes Megethius to reaffirm his tripartite position, now, however, moderated with the Creator as mediating (μέσος) and so able to ameliorate some of the dilemmas provoked by the dualism of Marcus (68.12–17 [2.6]). Conversely, Marcus proposes a threefold anthropology, body, soul, and spirit, which itself ameliorates the contradictions exposed in Megethius' argument that both body and soul originate with the Creator but that only the soul is saved (72.17–74.23 [2.8–9]). In the interchange that follows, the two Marcionites are shown to undermine each other's position, spurred on by the interjections of Adamantius, and so contribute to Eutropius' final adjudication that they are equally foolish (114.5–20 [2.21]).

Certainly the disagreements, inconsistencies, and failures in coherence between the two Marcionites serve the initial postulate of the *Dialogue* that the 'foundation of all virtues is the harmonious conception and faith in God'; even so, they cannot be attributed to the rhetorical skill of the author alone. Both make statements that are recognisable from other polemics against Marcion: Megethius appeals to the parable of the two trees, while Marcus cites those of wine and wineskins, patch and garment (Luke 5.36; *Adam.* 90.5–10 [2.16]). Both rely on their understanding of Paul and the Gospel, and Marcus cites such well-attested passages as the beginning of the Gospel 'under Tiberius Caesar' and the exegetical significance of the parable of Lazarus and the rich man. The status of law and prophets is also a major

104 *Adam.* 24.12–13; 34.10–36.2; 38.20–9 [1.10, 16, 19]. On the oppositions see p. 288.

105 *Adam.* 22.1; 24.24; 28.20 [1.10, 11,13], etc.; Contrast Tsutsui, *Auseinandersetzung*, 153, who decides for 'of the created world'. The epithet is not used by Marcus.

concern in both sections. Indeed, concern regarding the conceptual relationship between being Creator and being evil appears to be restricted to the devaluation of the world (76.3–8; 106.12; 110.20–6 [2.10, 19, 21]). While some details appear less probable – as when Marcus identifies the 'newness' of patch or wine with the Johannine Jesus' gift of a 'new commandment' (John 13.34) – others are more intriguing. Although, despite an appeal to 1 Corinthians 5.5, Marcus' view that the spirit alone is given and saved, is closer to the theories ascribed elsewhere to Saturninus, his claim that the spirit 'comes at the thanksgiving' (or 'eucharist', εὐχαριστία) is sufficiently idiosyncratic to counsel against its immediate rejection. Megethius and Marcus certainly embody what is a consistent theme of earlier polemics, namely that Marcion's followers developed conflicting views specifically regarding the number of original principles. Yet the sources available to the author may well have aided him in demonstrating this, and so may reflect earlier polemical traditions.

On the other hand, while a number of the points debated, both exegetical and metaphysical, can be paralleled in earlier accounts of Marcion,[106] other silences are striking. It is surprising that there is only limited discussion with the Marcionites of the nature of Christ's humanity (*Adam.* 102.3–8 [2.19]), which instead occupies a major section of the debate with the Valentinian Marinus; the same is true of the resurrection of the body, although an explicit appeal to Megethius' 'Apostolikon' and to his presence in that Valentinian debate probably acknowledges this was an issue in anti-Marcionite polemic also (222.10–13 [5.22]). Moreover, echoing the reserve that was also shown by Epiphanius, nothing is said about Marcion's attitude to marriage or to diet: These questions perhaps were too sensitive in the world and time of the *Dialogue*. Thus, in the end, as marked most blatantly by the final paean to Nicene faith and to the loyal bishops, the commitments of the unknown author control the whole.

THE CONTINUING TRADITION

As the heresiological tradition developed, Marcion continued to occupy the role of a major threat to be feared and demolished. Those who appealed to his authority and who claimed to reproduce his teaching and his Scriptures undoubtedly continued to be a recognisable part of the landscape. Thus, the continuing tradition is not an exercise in mere antiquarianism,

[106] Note also the theme of the Good God and Creator having their own heavens, *Adam.* 100.14–102.1 [2.19].

a growing encyclopaedia of past error, even if it does betray all the characteristics of copying and reinvention typical of an encyclopaedic style. Yet, it is not the contemporary proponents of a Marcionite theology who dominate the anxieties of the antiheretical authors. They have their own, often unnamed, more immediate enemies to be foiled, who represent debates that perhaps had yet to be decisively resolved, and where every weapon available was to be summoned for use. Perhaps most pressing, however, is their need to display their own authenticity, the incontrovertible authenticity of their expression of faith, their patterns of church practice and discipline, their participation in a network of other right-thinking holders of a faith they held was no less that of the earliest preachers of the Gospel. The Marcion with whom they did battle did, therefore, have to appear as the antithesis of all this; his priorities had to be theirs; his framework the mirror of their own, but fatally flawed.

6

Theology and exegesis against Marcion

In its various forms, starting already with Irenaeus, if not earlier in Justin's lost 'Syntagma', the discourse of 'heresy' serves to support the exposition of Christian truth through systematic exposure and rejection of its supposed opponents, in particular Marcion. However, the evolving conventions of the 'Against the Heresies' literature constitute only one way in which this is achieved, and a picture of Marcion is constructed. Elsewhere Marcion becomes a more malleable figure, to be summoned in the service of a constructive argument whose goal apparently lies elsewhere. This is what is found in Clement of Alexandria (c. 175–212 CE) and in Origen (c. 185–253 CE). Both of these worked within the tradition of teachers of Christian thought and practice rather than in that of figures within the ecclesiastical structure, both represented the distinctive intellectual tradition of Alexandria with its overt Platonic heritage, and both played a key role in the formation of a distinctive Christian educational formation or *paideia*; for both Marcion is a recurring figure to be combated. However, despite the sense of immediacy in some of their polemics, the Marcion who emerges from their engagement fits so neatly the mould demanded by the immediate argument, that it becomes particularly difficult to uncover any independent and coherent voice.

CLEMENT OF ALEXANDRIA

There is no certain evidence how and when followers of Jesus first established groups in Alexandria and its environs. The pattern elsewhere and the survival of Philo through Christian transmission would suggest some connection with the substantial Jewish communities there which suffered such devastation following the Trajanic revolt of 115–17 CE. Some support for this has been found in the reference to Apollos in Acts 18.24, and in attempts to associate some early texts, such as Hebrews or *Barnabas* with Alexandria. This has been set against arguments that the earliest clearly identifiable representatives of Christianity were those later condemned as 'gnostic heretics', including Valentinus and Basilides, and therefore that a gnosticising Christianity may have preceded anything that might be called 'proto-orthodoxy' in Egypt.[1] Within this framework, it has also been argued that the vigour with which Marcion is combated by Clement and Origen indicates that Marcionites also were a force to be reckoned with in Alexandria by the last quarter of the second century. This scenario, with its clear delineation of gnostic' *versus* 'proto-orthodox', has been largely abandoned in recent study. Nonetheless, although in different contexts Clement identifies a range of false positions to be addressed, Marcion joins Valentinus and Basilides as the lead players, forming a standard trio, to be combined indiscriminately or to be distinguished as best serves Clement's immediate argument.

However, whereas Clement undoubtedly displays direct knowledge of original writings by both Valentinus and Basilides, there is little trace of close, first-hand familiarity with Marcion's writings or with direct traditions about him.[2] At best, he does on occasion appeal to what 'they say', and he even suggests that they quote 'the Lord's words to Philip (*sic*), "Let the dead bury their dead"' (Luke 9.60), although that the last passage continues in a form which is closer to the Matthean parallel (Matt. 8.22), suggests that his information is derivative.[3] Indeed, Clement has little interest in any biographical information about Marcion, repeating only the standard epithet 'Pontic' (*Strom.* III. 4.25). There is one exception to this, which does provide something of an enigma, but which is hardly enough to contradict the general sense of disinterest in personal details. This is when, in his final reference to Marcion, Clement takes up the familiar heresiological assertion that 'the human assemblies' of the false teachers are self-evidently much later than 'the catholic church': Whereas the coming of the Lord dates from the time of Augustus, those who invented heresies began only with Hadrian,

[1] On the early history of Christianity in Alexandria, see Birger A. Pearson, 'Egypt', ed. Margaret M. Mitchell and Frances M. Young, *The Cambridge History of Christianity I: Origins to Constantine* (Cambridge University Press: Cambridge, 2006), 331–50.

[2] On Clement as a source for Valentinus and for Basilides, see Christoph Markschies, *Valentinus Gnosticus? Untersuchungen zur valentinianischen Gnosis mit einem Kommentar zu den Fragmenten Valentins* (WUNT 65; Tübingen: Mohr, 1992); Winrich A. Löhr, *Basilides und seine Schule: Eine Studie zur Theologie- und Kirchengeschichte des zweiten Jahrhunderts* (WUNT 83; Tübingen: Mohr, 1996).

[3] Clement, *Strom.* III. 4.25. Tertullian, *AM* IV. 23.10 implies the Lukan form.

continuing until the time of Antoninus. This, he insists, is the case regardless of what they may assert: 'so', he continues, 'Basilides, even if he claims as teacher Glaucias, as they boast, the interpreter of Peter. Similarly they hold that Valentinus heard Theudas, who himself was an associate of Paul. For Marcion, who belonged to the same age as them, associated as an old man with those younger.[4] After whom Simon briefly heard (*or* obeyed) Peter preaching'. Unexpectedly, Clement does not dismiss these claims, but repeats that 'if these things are so' they demonstrate how much later these heresies were than 'the most ancient and true church' (*Strom.* VII. 17.106–8). It is likely that even here Clement is combining disparate traditions: Unlike the other two, that about Marcion neither offers a report ('they boast'; 'they hold') nor makes any claim to an apostolic pedigree, while the dating of Simon, in whom Clement otherwise has little interest, is blatantly self-contradictory. It may be that Clement is consciously allowing his opponents to undermine themselves, although behind these statements there still may lie traces of what in practice were more evenly balanced conflicts over claims to authoritative tradition. Even so, it would be a mistake to rely on this for an attempt to date any of the triumvirate, or to determine their relationship with each other.

It is only in the *Miscellanies* (or *Stromata*), the final of Clement's three major linked works, following the *Exhortation* (*Protrepticus*) and the *Instructor* (*Paedagogus*), that Marcion or his followers are referred to by name. In this last volume Clement attempts to draw together the elements of an advanced Christian philosophical teaching, and it is therefore no surprise that Marcion is presented almost entirely within a philosophical framework. If Clement's anticipated 'On Principles', where he promises he will treat Marcion's views, does not refer to another section of the *Stromata*, the name itself and the explicit comparison with the philosophers shows that this, if available, would not change the picture (*Strom.* III. 3.13, 21). However, Rudolf Riedinger has argued that substantial traces of Clement's anti-Marcionite polemic are also preserved in letters attributed to Isidore of Pelusium, and has given supporting examples that almost entirely deal with scriptural exegesis and with the relationship between Old and New Testaments.[5] If this hypothesis were demonstrable, it would certainly

4 Μαρκίων γὰρ κατὰ αὐτὴν αὐτοῖς ἡλικίαν γενόμενος ὡς πρεσβύτης νεωτέροις συνέγενετο. See Löhr, *Basilides*, 21–3, on the implied claim to authority.

5 Rudolf Riedinger, 'Zur antimarkionitischen Polemik des Klemens von Alexandrien', *VC* 29 (1975), 15–32; Riedinger's suggestion (p. 27) that more examples would be found if Harnack's synthesis and source collection were systematically compared with Isidore's Letters betrays the problem, since it presupposes that Harnack offers an infallible guide.

change the balance in Clement's response to Marcion, but, although some of those examples can be paralleled in refutations of Marcion elsewhere, they were hardly restricted to these, and his case must be judged as far from proven.[6]

For Clement the fundamental principle that is at stake is a proper understanding of God, articulated certainly in the language of philosophy but witnessed to by the Scriptures when these are correctly understood. 'Since there is but one first cause', those like Basilides and Valentinus who read Scripture in some other way are, he protests, shown to be inventors of 'chirpings and warblings'; they and others, 'especially the followers of Marcion', stand condemned by Scripture itself (*Strom.* II. 8.37, 39). However, Clement is less concerned to refute their arguments, except by brief irony, than he is to use their positions to develop his own: 'God has no natural relation to us, as the creators of heresies have it,' ... but acted totally out of his inherent goodness (*Strom.* II. 16.74) – although this is a position that Marcion himself surely would have found far more congenial. Even when they are named separately, they serve Clement's own rhetorical goals in the exposition of his philosophy: 'For if a person knows God by nature, as Basilides thinks ... if one is saved by nature as Valentinus thinks, or someone is faithful and elect by nature as Basilides thinks ... for if one dared to say, following Marcion, that the Demiurge saves the one who trusted in him ... then from what we have demonstrated all the unbelievers are shown to be foolish' (*Strom.* V. 1.3–5).

Whereas Clement upholds the harmony of faith and knowledge towards God, Valentinus, Basilides, and Marcion are united by a common disposition, namely one of hostility and of opposition: The verb 'oppose' (ἀντιτάσσω) is used as a leitmotif throughout Clement's tirade, regardless of detail. Marcion's followers 'oppose their maker', and in particular 'they forbid the use of what belongs to the earth out of opposition to the Demiurge'. However, a little later the same charge is laid against those who reject any commandments, and who apparently adopt a lifestyle that Marcion himself would have also excoriated: 'You oppositioners ought not to engage in any sexual intercourse' (as they do to excess) since God enjoined 'be fruitful and increase' (*Strom.* III. 3.12; 4.25, 37). Clearly, those of whom Clement declares, 'We call "oppositioners" (ἀντιτάκται)', who

[6] See also Annewies van den Hoek, *Clement of Alexandria and His Use of Philo in the Stromateis: An Early Christian Reshaping of a Jewish Model* (Leiden: Brill, 1988), 71, who argues that Clement's demonstration of the unity of Old and New Testaments in *Strom.* II. 18.78–19.100, is targeted against Marcion.

assert that 'the God of the universe is our father by nature', equally cannot refer to the followers of Marcion (*Strom.* III. 4.34).[7] Such opposition, from wherever or whomsoever it comes, is not merely hostility to the Creator but is, for Clement, fundamentally out of tune with the overall harmony in the universe and in divine activity which he is determined to demonstrate (*Strom.* IV. 6.40). It is with this ultimate harmony in mind – although he postpones further discussion for the promised 'On Principles' – that he can complain that 'those contradictions of which the philosophers speak in riddles, the followers of Marcion turn into dogma': Far from being a reference to Marcion's 'Antitheses' as a literary document, this is a metaphysical principle.[8]

This assertion comes at the heart of the way that Clement tackles Marcion: Marcion is characterised by his hatred of 'begetting', and although in this he may seem to echo the sentiments of Greek philosophy, in fact he fundamentally misunderstands them. This in turn is a subset of Clement's primary concern with a proper understanding of God as Creator. The earlier chapters of Book III had been dedicated to a denunciation of the libertine theories and practice of Carpocrates, which he also saw as stimulated by hostility to the Creator God; to illustrate that polemic he had drawn on actual literature written by or used by Carpocrates and his son Epiphanius, challenging it with Scripture. Here, however, he presupposes that Marcion 'took the pretexts for his strange doctrines in an ungrateful and ignorant way (ἀχαρίστως τε καὶ ἀμαθῶς) from Plato', and that he is to be undermined by the demonstration of his misappropriation of these through extensive quotation of Plato himself (*Strom.* III. 3.21).

'Strangeness' and 'ingratitude' are two established themes in polemics against Marcion, and both are taken up by Clement. For Clement, ingratitude serves to define Marcion's differentness precisely at the point where he seems most to be like others. He commences his most extended critique by recognising that the followers of Marcion are but latecomers in regarding *genesis* (γένεσις), which is probably best translated as 'originating', 'birth', or 'procreation', as evil, for Plato and Pythagoras had already done so long before (*Strom.* III. 3.12–4.25).[9] However, for them such hostility was

7 Against André Méhat, *Étude sur les 'Stromates' de Clément d'Alexandrie* (Patristica Sorbonensia; Paris: Éditions du Cerf, 1966), 400. See Le Boulluec, *La notion*, II, 340.

8 *Strom.* III. 3.21: τὰς ἐνατιότητας ἅς οἵ τε φιλόσοφοι αἰνίσσονται οἵ τε περὶ Μαρκίωνα δογματίζουσιν.

9 See Gerhard May, 'Marcion in Contemporary Views: Results and Open Question', ed. Greschat and Meiser, *Gerhard May: Marcion*, 13–33 (= *Second Century* 6 (1987/88), 129–51), 24; contrast Dietmar Wyrwa, *Die christliche Platonaneigung in den Stromateis des*

grounded in the conviction that while entombed in the body the soul undergoes punishment and longs for liberation; even so, Plato, indeed, treated the world with reverence, 'having obtained good things from the one who set all things in order' (cf. Plato, *Polit.* 273B-C). By contrast, Marcion's followers consider 'nature (φύσις) to be evil, as made from evil matter and from a just Creator' (*Strom.* III. 3.12); thus, they avoid marriage so as not to fill the world created by the Demiurge, even though they eat the food and breathe the air provided by the latter, and so they fail in the gratitude they owe to him. In so doing, they have taken over the Greek sense of the inconveniences of procreation, but have done so in an essentially godless way; indeed, Clement even suggests that the Pythagoreans, contrary to popular misconceptions, valued the procreation of children and reserved abstinence for later life. On the other hand, the continence, 'ἐγκράτεια', of the Marcionites is driven by hatred for their maker and not by the exercise of free will; consequently it is without any value – 'if indeed it is to be called continence' – and as such it has nothing in common with the Christian virtue of the same.[10]

Presenting Marcion, or his disciples, as derivative from and yet as misunderstanding Plato clearly serves Clement's polemical purposes. In part he had prepared for this strategy by contrasting the communism of women advocated by Carpocrates with Plato's ideas of the same, despite the initial apparent similarity between them; his pointed comment that Marcion did not share this Platonic principle is therefore potentially double-edged (Plato, *Rep.* 457D-461E; Clement, *Strom.* III. 2.10; 3.12). To establish his argument he adduces a cento of passages both from Plato and from other poets and writers; this is only loosely adapted to suit his own argument, and in all likelihood it stems from existing school discussions on the topic, and so reflects the importance of debates over the right reading of Plato in the second and third centuries. There is little here to suggest that Clement actually believed that Marcion or his followers explicitly appealed to Plato, or that, if he did so believe, he was right.[11] The effect is to place in centre

Clemens von Alexandrien (Arbeiten zur Kirchengeschichte 53; Berlin: de Gruyter, 1983), 205, who argues that the parallel 'nature as evil' (see below) implies a translation, 'gewordene Welt, Schöpfung'.

10 *Strom.* III. 4.25; see also III. 7.60, where the charge is extended to other 'heretics'.

11 Against May, 'Marcion in Contemporary Views', 24–5; May had adopted a more cautious position in Gerhard May, 'Platon und die Auseinandersetzungen mit den Häresien bei Klemens von Alexandrinus', ed. Horst-Dieter Blume and Friedhelm Mann, *Platonismus und Christentum. Festschrift für Heinrich Dörrie* (JbAC 10; Münster: Aschendorff, 1983), 123–32.

stage Marcion's hostility to the natural world and processes and to their Creator, without acknowledging that there might be any alternative rationale for his beliefs and practice.[12] Similarly, without supplying any real justification Clement claims that a hatred of begetting led Cassian to adopt docetism and Valentinus to teach that Christ had a 'psychic body' (*Strom.* III. 17.102).[13] Yet it seems certain that it was the existing ambiguities in Christian attitudes to the body, and its own tradition of continence, that drove him. Clement also admits the place of Scripture in such ambiguities; he acknowledges that 'the oppositioners among the heterodox' think that Paul confronted the Creator in passages such as Romans 7.18, and he warns against anyone adopting a Marcionite 'ungrateful' exegesis of Paul's sentiments in Romans 8.7–30 as evidence of demiurgic evil (ἡ δημιουργία κακή), but he undoubtedly struggles with these passages in his own exegesis (*Strom.* III. 11.76; IV. 7.45).[14]

This ambivalence in Clement's position is even clearer regarding the epithet 'strange' (ξένος). In the passage cited earlier Clement may be hinting that despite their superficial similarity Marcion's doctrines are foreign also to Plato. However, he also suggests that the term was one that they vaunted: The followers of Marcion '"received the good news of the strange knowledge", as they say' (*Strom.* III. 3.12). Again, he makes a deft transition to those who, on the supposed grounds that 'they have come into a world foreign to them', feel free to live without sexual constraint: 'Does a stranger insult the citizens and do them harm?', he asks; 'Does he not as a temporary visitor make use of what is necessary and live alongside the citizens without offence?' (*Strom.* III. 4.31). Such language picks up a well-established topos in Christian discourse of the alienation of believers from the world (cf. Heb. 13.11), and Clement has to negotiate this with considerable care, both affirming it and subsequently distancing his own position from a more extreme asceticism: No one is by nature alien to the world, but the elect does live as a stranger (*Strom.* III. 14.95; IV. 26.165).

This attempt to reduce sharply contrasting alternative lifestyles to a shared single premise makes it easy to overlook the repeated abrupt changes of target; the historian seeking to describe a profile of the various groups has to mark such changes and to identify differences that Clement himself was at

12 See Le Boulluec, *La notion*, II, 290–7, who sees this as a distortion of Marcion.

13 He gives no evidence of Cassian's docetism, and elsewhere he claims that Valentinus did support marriage (*Strom.* III. 1.1).

14 Le Boulluec, *La notion*, II, 341, denies that this is necessarily a Marcionite exegesis, although Clement may be anticipating a potential one.

pains to obscure. His task was rendered yet more difficult by the fact that the language, principles, and even aspects of the lifestyle, adopted variously by these groups could sound and look not unlike his own. Particularly telling in this respect is where he describes those, 'not ours, only sharing the name', who hasten to surrender themselves (as martyrs) but do so out of hatred for the Creator. Whether or not these are Marcionites, as several scholars have concluded, there is here a remarkable admission that they were not readily distinguished from other Christians, and so of the problem he faced; his response is to insist that they die 'without martyrdom' (ἀμαρτύρως; *Strom.* IV. 4.17).[15]

All this indicates that, despite the stereotyping and instability in the identification of those being attacked, their views and their practice were elements in a very real debate. It is a debate where the issues are clear-cut in Clement's eyes, but where the protagonists or those whom they might persuade are not always distinct or at a safe distance. Similarly, he berates those who collect excerpts from the prophets, patching them together and interpreting literally what should be understood allegorically, along with those who when they read the Scriptures use their tone of voice or change of accents and punctuation to suit their own lustful purposes (*Strom.* III. 5.38–9). Judging tone of voice, correct punctuation, or even how a text *should* be interpreted demands authoritative guidance; yet despite his own assured tone, the context and extent of Clement's own authority within the church in Alexandria remains uncertain, and the *Stromateis* in particular hardly address the 'ordinary Christian'.[16]

Even so, it is difficult to determine the extent of any immediate knowledge that Clement might have of Marcionites. He balances their rejection of their Creator by their 'hastening to the Good one who has called, and not to the God, as they say, in another mode'; the epithet 'who has called' is striking, recalling Irenaeus' account of those in Hades running to him, as well as evoking a broader Gnostic theme of the divine summons.[17] Similarly, while their claim that they 'have received the good news of a strange knowledge' reflects his own interest in 'knowledge' (γνῶσις), the specific verb 'receive the good news' (εὐαγγελίζεσθαι) perhaps betrays the influence of Luke 16.16. Clement shows relatively little interest in their scriptural texts,

15 Anniewies van den Hoek, ed., *Clément d'Alexandrie: Les Stromates* IV, transl. Claude Mondésert (SC 463; Paris: Éd. du Cerf, 2001), 85, accepts the identification with Marcionites; see also below, p. 397.

16 See Henry F. Hägg, *Clement of Alexandria and the Beginnings of Christian Apophaticism* (OECS; Oxford: Oxford University Press, 2006), 51–70.

17 *Strom.* III. 3.12; cf. Irenaeus, *AH* I. 27.3.

although, he acknowledges their interpretation of Paul.[18] If indeed those who welcomed martyrdom as noted earlier are to be identified as followers of Marcion, then it is possible they are also those who rearrange (μετατίθεναι) the Gospels, reading, 'Blessed are those who are persecuted for the sake of righteousness because they shall be perfect; and blessed are those who are persecuted for my sake because they shall have a place where they shall not be persecuted' (*Strom.* IV. 6.41; cf. Luke 6.22).

It is also difficult to determine how far the references to Marcion's system arise from his own arguments, how far from knowledge of contemporary Marcionite ideas. For example, the description of nature as 'evil' because it was created 'from evil matter and from a just Creator', leaves unexplored both the status and origin of matter, and the relationship between 'evil' and 'just'.[19] As for the 'just Creator', earlier, in an exegesis of Proverbs 1.7, Clement understands the Law and prophets as God's preparatory discipline, and he tackles 'those others and particularly Marcion's followers' who, he claims, 'do not say that the Law is evil but just, separating the good from the just' (*Strom.* II. 8.39). Later, he attributes specifically to Marcion the view that the Creator 'saved the person who believed in him', before the coming of the Lord, although he objects that this would subject the 'power of the Good one' to the charge of appearing somewhat tardily, and he follows with further objections, familiar also from Tertullian, against the probity and geographical feasibility of the 'Good' saving what belonged to another (*Strom.* V. 1.4).[20]

To acknowledge the way in which Clement has 'Platonised' the polemical debate does not undermine his recognition that the positions represented by Marcion, Valentinus, Basilides, or others, implied crucial presuppositions and consequences that reached to the heart of any intellectual and philosophical engagement with the Christian understanding of God. The extent to which the instigators of those positions had themselves consciously articulated them is less evident, for Clement is not concerned to engage with them in an open debate. Clement's Marcion is fundamentally a

[18] See also above, p. 132; at *Strom.* IV. 8.66, Clement cites Col. 3.12–15 against Marcion, but he does not suggest that the latter had his own interpretation of the passage.

[19] φύσιν κακὴν ἔκ τε ὕλης κακῆς καὶ ἐκ δικαίου γενομένην δημιουργοῦ: *Strom.* III. 3.12; cf. III. 3.19, where he asserts that Marcion could not have taken from Plato the idea of evil matter.

[20] Alain Le Boulluec, ed., *Clément d'Alexandrie: Les Stromates* V (SC 279; Paris: Éd. du Cerf, 1981), 31 suggests that the objection, 'why so late' is taken over from pagan anti-Christian polemic.

philosophical Marcion because Clement recognised that this was the territory on which the Christian message would survive for the future.

ORIGEN

Origen continues this trajectory of locating Marcion within the attempt to achieve a proper philosophical articulation of the Christian faith; however, the range and variety of his writings, despite their incomplete and often indirect survival, mean that Marcion plays a more diverse and also a less sustained role. From this it is not easy to determine the extent of Origen's close knowledge of Marcion's teachings, or how serious a challenge Marcionite teaching posed within the settings, particularly in Alexandria and in Caesarea, in which he worked.[21] On the one hand, it has been argued that the provocation of addressing a Marcionite position played a key role in Origen's own intellectual development – although this need not entail direct encounter with Marcionites;[22] on the other hand, Origen evinces little interest in the details of Marcion's position, nor in whether or how it holds together as a system – although in this he is hardly unusual. Certainly, in his hands Marcion loses specificity, becoming a cipher for views contrary to a proper understanding of the Scriptures and of the teaching of the Church.[23]

It would be possible to distinguish the different contexts in which Marcion appears: Writing against Celsus, Origen has to refute an external critic who both knew of the distinctive teaching of Marcion and his disciples, and who used it as a weapon against Christian coherence (*C.Cels.* V. 62; VI. 74). Here, Origen takes little pleasure in the critical assessment of Marcion's teaching that Celsus makes, knowing that he fails to address the real and serious doctrinal debates involved; instead, Origen is content to dismiss the validity of any confusion by appealing to the familiar argument that true philosophy is hardly to be condemned for the erroneous views held by some such as the Epicureans (*C.Cels.* II. 27). But his restraint here is untypical: In the *On Principles*, Marcion, alongside Valentinus in particular, plays a key but not always distinct role – and one that in the scholarship is disputed; against this Origen can explore more systematically the nature and

21 Ruth Clements, 'Origen's Readings of Romans in *Peri Archon*: (Re)Constructing Paul', ed. Kathy L. Gaca and Larry L. Welborn, *Early Patristic Readings of Romans* (New York: T&T Clark, 2005), 159–79, 160, suggests that Origen encountered Marcionite textual criticism on his visit to Rome in c. 215 CE.

22 So Joseph W. Trigg, *Origen: The Bible and Philosophy in the Third-Century Church* (Atlanta, GA: John Knox, 1983), 46–50; see also below, pp. 140–1.

23 See Le Boulluec, *La notion*, II, 506–13.

activity of God. In the exegetical works, many of which were written after his move to Caesarea, he sharply challenges Marcionite exegesis in expected as well as in unexpected contexts, but he also uses Marcion as a general negative example, in particular of a fundamental misunderstanding of the right way to read Scripture. However, in what follows, space will not allow any attempt to identify the different constructions of Marcion in Origen's writings, or to trace a development between them.

In the *On Principles* and elsewhere in Origen's exegetical writings, Marcion belongs, as he does in Clement, to a regular triumvirate of archetypical heretics, along with Basilides and Valentinus; as such they are equally the subject of homiletic warnings – they speak the wisdom of the wise, use Scripture like the devil, or represent the wide gate through which many go (*Frag.in 1 Cor.* §8; *Hom. in Luke* 31; *Comm. in Matt.* 12. 12). At times, he distinguishes between them, reducing each to a single error: Marcion with his impious blasphemies against the Creator of the world, Valentinus with his fables of male and female aeons, and Basilides who denigrates those who die for their faith (*Comm. ser. in Matt.* 38). In other contexts he ignores any differences between them: For example, he cites as one of the objections brought by the triumvirate against divine justice that God created different souls with different natures that would ensure them different futures (*De Princip.* II. 9.5); there is little other independent evidence that Marcion himself denied free will or held that the fate of souls is predetermined, and Origen's reference to 'Marcion and all those who by varying fictions introduce different natures of souls' should be viewed with considerable scepticism (*Comm. in Rom.* II. 7, 89).[24] As in this last example, Origen sometimes generalises outwards, 'Marcion and all those who…'; on other occasions he hides behind a more general term: Marcion must surely be among those who are described only as 'those who say', 'our opponents', or 'the heretics', and who distinguish between the Father of Jesus Christ and the God of the Law, whose actions in the Old Testament they find to be so unworthy (*De Princip.* II. 4–5; *Comm. in Rom.* II. 9, 463–75).[25] These different

[24] Henri Crouzel and Manlio Simonetti, trans., *Origen. Traité des Principes. Introduction, texte critique de la Philocalie et de la version de Rufin* (4 vols.; SC 252, 253, 268, 269; Paris: Éd. du Cerf, 1978–80) II, 217, suggest that Marcion's followers may have developed this more 'gnostic' view. On the broader issue see Enrico Norelli, 'Marcione e gli gnostici sul libero arbitrio e la polemica di Origene', ed. Lorenzo Perrone, *Il cuore indurito del Faraone: Origene e il problema del libero arbitrio* (Genova: Marietti, 1992), 1–30.

[25] Those who emphasise the importance of anti-Marcionism for Origen's thought see Marcion as the prime target of the second 'cycle' of the *De Principiis* (II. 4–IV. 3); see Josep Rius-Camps, 'Origenes y Marcion: Carácter Preferentemente Antimarcionita del Prefacio y del Segundo ciclo del Peri Archôn', ed. Henri Crouzel, Gennaro Lomiento,

techniques result in a blurring of the boundaries, which should not be taken as evidence of an actual merging of views between these groups; it is a consequence of Origen's deliberate strategies, as well, perhaps, as of his dependence on earlier polemic. Consequently, when he ascribes to the heretics in general an appeal to 'that celebrated (*famosissima*) question' of the good tree producing good fruit, or to Jesus' words, 'None is good but ...', both passages that certainly were significant for Marcion, it is difficult to know whether such testimonia were by then, if not from the beginning, in wider currency in the debate, or whether Origen is again indebted to existing anti-gnostic polemic (*De Princip.* II. 5.4).[26]

Despite these tendencies, Origen does not engage in the heightened vituperation typical of the heresiologists; even so, he may sometimes allow his imagination some free rein, as is likely the case when he gives as an example of misplaced love that some say 'to sit at my right and left was said about Paul and Marcion' – although the dominical saying is not found in Marcion's 'Gospel' nor in canonical Luke (*Hom. in Luke* 25.5; cf. Mark 10.35–40; Matt. 20.21–3). On the other hand, Marcion and the other heretics do not simply play a purely symbolic role in a literary polemic that he has inherited from earlier tradition. Origen's vehement assertion that, in order to be able to defend the simple in faith from their influence, he *hears* what Marcion, Valentinus, or other detractors of the Creator, say, but that he does not *receive* it, undoubtedly serves his homiletic purpose, but it is still probably true that their teaching was part of his intellectual environment, perhaps closer to hand than he would want to admit (*Hom.in Exod.* III. 2.70). When it suits him, Origen recognises important differences, for example, when he distinguishes the views of the triumvirate from those who think the Creator is actually malignant; so too, he also admits that these heretics acknowledge the sacred Scriptures, whereas Apelles, although a disciple of Marcion, 'invented another heresy' when he denied that the Scriptures of Moses contain any divine wisdom (*De Princip.* III. 1.9, 16; *Hom.in Gen.* II. 2.3).[27] Although this does not constitute a major theme,

Josep Rius-Camps, *Origeniana: premier colloque international des etudes origéniennes. Montserrat 21 septembre 1973* (Istituto di letteratura Cristiana antica: Università de Bari, 1975), 297–312; Charles Kannengiesser, 'Origen, Systematician in De Principiis', ed. Robert J. Daly, *Origeniana Quinta. Papers of the Fifth International Origen Congress*, Boston College 14–18 August 1989 (BETL 105; Leuven: Leuven University Press/Peeters, 1992), 395–405. Alain Le Boulluec, 'Le place de la Polémique antignostique dans le Peri Archôn', ed. Crouzel, Lomiento, Rius-Camps, *Origeniana*, 47–61, is less specific.

26 See pp. 207, 340 for these passages; Le Boulluec, 'Le Place', emphasises Origen's indebtedness to earlier polemic.

27 See also *Comm. ser. in Matt.* 46 for the separate treatment of Apelles.

Origen also addresses Marcion's 'interpolation' of the 'evangelical and apostolic Scripture', both in his discussion of the instability of Romans 16.25–7 and, as shall be seen, in his defence of the fourfold Gospel.[28] Whether he actually had available copies of Marcion's scriptural texts is uncertain, although it seems likely that they would have suited the textual interests of the library established at Caesarea, and he does make some scattered references to particular readings in the Marcionite text.[29] Similarly, he knows that 'the divine volumes are read among them', even while he denies them the right to be entrusted with the oracles of God (Rom. 3.2; *Comm. in Rom.* II. 10,116–22).[30] Yet in a revealing admission, Origen also acknowledges that there are those within the Church who, while they maintain the unity of the Creator as the one God, still ascribe to that God savage and cruel behaviour (*De Princip.* IV. 1.8). Such admissions betray a setting where texts, ideas, and individuals crossed or undermined the boundaries that the language of 'heresy' and the naming of individuals were intended to reinforce.

This broad sketch highlights the difficulties in separating within Origen's writings independent traditions about the teaching of Marcion or his followers from the image left by its impact on his own intellectual development. As already noted, he undoubtedly did recognise in the schemes of Marcion and others a fundamental challenge to the conceptual heart of Christian theology, and it is this rather than any sustained attempt to explain Marcion that shapes the picture of the latter that he projects. Foremost here is the exposition of the unity and singleness of God; for Origen the ramifications of any rejection of this unity spread wide and far, something he already explores in his early and foundational work, the *On Principles* – a title and genre that had been anticipated by Clement.[31] Here, the heretics, Marcion included, represent one of the two extremes to be avoided, the other being a naïve understanding of unity.[32] The issue is

28 *Comm. in Rom.* X. 43, 7–18 (in Caroline P. Hammond Bammel, *Der Römerbriefkommentar des Origenes. Kritische Ausgabe der Übersetzung Rufins* Buch 7–10 [ed. H. J. Frede and H. Stanjek; VL 34; Freiburg: Herder, 1998]); see p. 241.

29 See n. 28 and also *Hom.in Luke* frag. 70, 75 on Luke 10.27 and 11.3 (Henri Crouzel, François Fournier, Pierre Périchon, introd., trad, et notes, *Origène. Homélies sur S. Luc. Texte Latin et Fragments Grec* [SC 87; Paris: Éd. du Cerf, 1962]). There may have been further references in lost commentaries on the Pauline Epistles: For example, Tijtze Baarda argues that Jerome's report that Marcion omitted 'and from God the Father' at Gal. 1.1 is taken from Origen's commentary on the epistle; see Tjitze Baarda, 'Marcion's Text of Gal. 1:1: Concerning the Reconstruction of the First Verse of the Marcionite Corpus Paulinum', *VC* 42 (1988), 236–56, 240–2, and below, p. 243.

30 From Caroline P. Hammond Bammel, *Der Römerbriefkommentar des Origenes. Kritische Aufgabe der Übersetzung Rufins* Buch 1–3 (VL.AGLB 16; Freiburg: Herder, 1990).

31 See above, p. 130.

32 So Le Boulluec, 'Le Place'.

not one of abstract philosophical principle or of the widely debated issue of the freedom of the will alone; it also embraces questions posed by the diversity among rational creatures and the hierarchy of fortunes that they experience without apparent justification.

At the heart of all such concerns lies the question of the justice of God, and whether such justice is compatible with divine goodness. The interpretation of Scripture is central on both sides, with 'the heretics' supposedly appealing to such familiar topoi as the punishment of Pharaoh whose heart God had already hardened, and to other examples of the severity of the Creator (*De Princip.* III. 1.9). Even though when he identifies alternative views Origen is more likely at most to generalise rather than to name individual 'heretics', many interpreters have found in the *On Principles* a fundamentally anti-Marcionite thrust, whether or not alongside one against Valentinus, whose association with Alexandria seems likely.[33] The same fundamental concerns also extend to Origen's exegetical engagement with Scripture: He appeals to Romans 5.10–11 to show that there is no substance that is naturally hostile to God, as is supposed by Marcion and Valentinus, and he imagines the heretics asking, 'How can God sometimes be good, sometimes be just?', while a defence of God in these same terms is a recurring theme, and one that is specifically directed against Marcion in his *Commentary on Romans* (*Hom. in Luke* 18.5; *Comm. in Rom.* I. 21, 15–34; IV. 10, 44–48; 12, 5–9).

The challenge is already articulated in terms of the Law in the *On Principles*, where 'the heretics' are described as purportedly using the epithet 'God of the Law' (*De Princip.* II. 5.1; III. 1.9). Unsurprisingly, it is this, rather than the language of 'the Creator', that provides a dominant framework in the exegetical polemic: The heretics say, 'Look at the God of the Law and the prophets; see what he is like' (*Hom. in Luke* 16.4). Inevitably, this is also a pervasive theme in the *Commentary on Romans*. Marcion epigrammatically is the person 'who says the God of the Law is other than the Father of Christ'; extended, this can mean that he 'treats the God of the Law with derision', that he 'rejects the Old Testament', and that he is presumably among the heretics 'who separate the Law from the Gospel(s)'. The first of these charges allows them to be aligned with the Gentiles, 'as if in a federation of detractors', and the last indirectly also with the Jews, who, in characteristic polemic, no less fail to properly understand their own Scriptures.[34] On the other hand, in differentiating between 'the God of the Law and the God of the Gospel(s)', the heretics 'wish the God of

[33] Markschies, *Valentinus Gnosticus*, 314–36.

[34] *Comm. in Rom.* II. 9, 460–6; 10, 116–22; III. 8, 16–17. On the plural 'Gospels' see below, p. 403.

the Jews to be other than God of the Gentiles' (*Comm. in Rom.* III. 7, 3–5). All these formulations would appear to be Origen's own creation, not theirs – and in at least some instances they may actually reflect the greater precision of his later translators'.[35] Origen had already appealed to Paul as an authority for the unity of Scripture in the *On Principles*, there using Marcion as his representative foil.[36] This he develops for a more sustained exegetical reading of the apostle: 'it is not I but the heretics who accuse the God of the Law, "the law is the evil root and ignorance of the law, which came through it, the evil tree"'. Marcion and the other heretics 'accuse the law as if the law were given so that sin might abound', and as if sin did not exist before the law; on the contrary, according to Origen, by 'law' here Paul refers to the natural law (Rom. 3.20–2; 5.20–1; cf. Luke 6.43).[37]

All this has profound hermeneutical consequences. Jews, heretics, and 'the simple' are united in the way in which they read Scripture in its literal sense, whether this leads to a refusal to recognise Jesus as prophesied in the past, or to ascribing to the Demiurge 'such things as would not be believed of the most savage and unjust of people' (*De Princip.* IV. 2.2). The heretics fail to read Scripture in the light of Christ, and so they read it like Israel according to the flesh. It is not the text nor what it describes that is at fault, but the appropriate perception of the interpreter: unless 'those physical wars acted as a figure of spiritual wars', Christians would not read books such as Joshua in the churches (*Hom. in Jos.* 14.1; 15.1). Properly understood, Jesus/Joshua's command to kill their enemies is not a lesson in cruelty 'as the heretics think', but points to the future; in the light of passages such as Romans 6.19 and Luke 10.19, such a command is a mark, rather, of kindness (*Hom. in Jos.* 11.6). This signals a leitmotif in Origen's understanding of Scripture, part of his emphasis on the necessity of recognising the different levels of meaning therein, from bodily to psychic and to spiritual, and on the possibility of

35 For example, Jerome's Commentary on Ephesians, which is derived from Origen, refers to the heretics who proclaimed one God of the Law and another of the Gospel, where the catenae of Origen have 'those who dissect the deity and think that the prophets belong to one God and the apostles to another' (on Eph. 2.19; cf. also on 5.9): Ronald E. Heine, *The Commentaries of Origen and Jerome on St Paul's Epistle to the Ephesians* (OECS; Oxford: Oxford University Press, 2002), 139; 219. However, Richard A. Layton, 'Recovering Origen's Pauline Exegesis: Exegesis and Eschatology in the *Commentary on Ephesians*', *JECS* 8 (2000), 373–411, 390–2, argues that parallels with the *Commentary on Romans* establish the basic argument as going back to Origen.

36 See Clements, 'Origen's Readings', 161.

37 Cf. Rom. 4.15; 5.21; see *Comm. in Rom.* III. 3, 133–7; IV. 2, 231–49; V. 1, 28–49; see Riemer Roukema, 'Jews and Gentiles in Origen's Commentary on Romans III 19–22', ed. Lies, *Origeniana Quarta*, 21–5.

progression from one to the next.[38] It is within this framework that the charge that Marcion and other heretics reject allegory belongs: Origen takes it for granted that Marcion could not reasonably understand the request for God's bread without recourse to allegory; yet in this case he would have to interpret it in the same way as 'we have rendered it' (Luke 11.3).[39] Although in theory an allegorical reading would open up multiple possibilities of meaning, for Origen the charge of rejecting allegory means that the heretics do not rightly understand the meaning of Scripture *as we understand it*. With this, Origen undermines any claim by his opponents to a deeper or more authentic reading of Scripture; at the same time he uses the interpretation of Scripture to draw the line that separates 'us' from 'them'.

One broader consequence of Origen's hermeneutical approach is that the Jews become disinherited, identified only by their literalist reading of Scripture; the fact that this argument was already made in the *On Principles* demonstrates that it was driven more by Origen's opposition to Marcionite and Valentinian claims to offer interpretations than by any specific knowledge of Jewish exegesis.[40] Yet more is at stake than this alone: When Origen attributes to Marcion's dislike of allegory his inability to understand why Paul should say that circumcision is of value (Rom. 3.1–2), he aligns him not with the Jews but with the Gentiles in their opposition to the law of God (*Comm. in Rom.* II. 9, 460–6). What is at stake for him is a total pattern not just of reading Scripture but of reading the world.

For Origen this acquires a particular focus in his understanding of the four Gospels. Marcion's followers have, he claims, misunderstood Romans 2.16 to indicate that Paul recognised only his one Gospel, and 'so they reject the Gospels' (*Comm. in Joh.* V. 7.1).[41] Like other polemicists, Origen's answer is that there is but 'one Gospel through four'. Yet he will neither deny the very real differences between these nor will he surrender them to detractors from outside; when Celsus accuses the Christians of altering the text of the Gospel three or four times over, arguably a reference to the different Gospels, Origen concludes that any such charge can only apply to the followers of Marcion or of Valentinus (*C.Cels.* II. 27).[42] The very

38 See Karen R. Tørjesen, *Hermeneutical Procedure and Theological Method in Origen's Exegesis* (PTS 28; Berlin: de Gruyter, 1986); Clements, 'Origen's Readings', 162–3.

39 *Hom.in Luke* frag. 75 (ed. Crouzel, Fournier, Périchon); Marcion apparently read 'your bread' rather than 'our', see above, p. 138, n.29.

40 So Clements, 'Origen's Readings', 167–9.

41 Origen read Rom. 2.16 as 'according to my Gospel in Christ Jesus'; see further p. 244 below.

42 Alternatively, the reference was throughout to the variations between manuscripts, of which Origen was well aware, even in copies not tampered with by 'heretics'.

disagreements between the Gospels are but an example of the apparent disagreements within Scripture as a whole, and it is these that prove that Scripture has to be interpreted spiritually. It is in this context that Origen accuses Marcion of denying the birth of Jesus through Mary and of deleting the relevant passages: In so doing Marcion mishandled 'the health-giving words', because he failed to understand how Jesus could be from David and not from David, human and not human (*Comm. in Joh.* X. 6.24). It is because Marcion says that allegorising is not allowed that he concludes that passages such as Matthew 19.12 'were not spoken by the Saviour' (*Comm. in Matt.* XV. 3).[43] The art of reading Scripture is the art of recognising how and whether the material and the spiritual can be read together or apart; even so, the material, the body, can never be left behind.

A similar approach also characterises Origen's defence of Christian marriage and chastity, which is more measured than that of Tertullian. Like others, Origen endeavours to interpret 1 Corinthians 7 in terms of second marriages. Indeed, the fact that Marcionites also practice asceticism is for him evidence that marriage or its avoidance is an adiaphoron, like circumcision or slavery (1 Cor. 7.18–22): 'they also practice celibacy and purity, but not like those of the Church (ἐκκλησιαστικοί); the latter do so to please the God who created the world, the former so that they may not co-operate with the God of the world' (*Frag. in 1 Cor.* 37). The rhetorical antithesis between the heretics and the Church is absolute, but it is evident that the social reality remains less so. It is the challenge that this presents that shapes much of Origen's representation of Marcion.

As with Clement, so for Origen, Marcion provides a useful foil for the development of his own theology and exegesis. To that extent Marcion could be the proverbial 'straw man'. Yet he is more than this, for clearly not only are there those who explicitly cite his authority for their own doctrine or challenges to that of the Church, but the positions they represent are also to be found closer to home, in internal questions and in perplexities at Scripture, while many of those same challenges and perplexities might be voiced from casual observers outside. The need continually to identify objections directly with 'Marcion', almost a century after his time, attests not so much to his significance as to the power of the image he has come to inhabit.

43 Applied to a passage found only in Matthew, this either is a stock charge against Marcion, perhaps as a cover for more widespread concerns about it, or is one that has been reapplied from elsewhere to this setting.

7

Marcion in Syriac dress

Marcion and Marcionism achieved a particularly long-lasting success in the Roman Near East, perhaps most vividly symbolised by the claim made by Theodoret of Cyrrhus, as late as the fifth century, that on one occasion he had converted eight villages full of Marcionites, and on another he had rescued more than a thousand souls of Marcionites and others.[1] That success is again almost entirely reflected through the eyes of opponents, and it is expressed in a variety of literary genres, and to serve a range of their own purposes – which in Theodoret's case was in an attempt to establish his own 'orthodoxy'. With the spread of Christianity beyond the boundaries of the Roman Empire, this picture of the Marcionite threat reached into the Sassanian Empire and eventually also entered the Arabic heresiological tradition under Islam.[2] However, in the midst of the debates inspired by such polemic as to whether the descriptions given are any more than formulaic stands the solitary witness by the community of self-styled Marcionites (συναγωγη Μαρκιωνιστων) in the village of Lebaba, southeast of Damascus, in the form of the stone marking their building, dedicated in 318 CE.[3] Some of the details are undoubtedly tantalising, for example,

[1] See below, p. 179.

[2] See Jean Maurice Fiey, 'Les Marcionites dans les Textes Historiques de l'Église Perse', *Le Muséon* 83 (1970), 183–7; Robert P. Casey, 'The Armenian Marcionites and the Diatessaron', *JBL* 57 (1938), 185–94; George Vajda, 'Le Témoinage d' Al-Maturidi sur la Doctrine des Manichéens, des Daysanites et des Marcionites', *Arabica* 13 (1966), 1–38; Wilfred Madelung, 'Abu 'Isa al Warraq über die Bardesaniten, Marcioniten und Kantäer', ed. Hans R. Roemer and Albrecht Noth, *Studien zur Geschichte und Kultur des Vorderen Orients: Festschrift für Bertold Spuler zum siebzigsten Geburtstag* (Leiden: Brill, 1981), 210–24.

[3] 'συναγωγη Μαρκιωνιστων κωμ(ης) Λεβαβων του κ(υριο)υ και σ(ωτη)ρ(ος) Ιη(σου) Χρηστου προνοια Παυλου πρεσβ(υτερου) του λχ'ἐτους'; Philippe Le Bas, *Voyage Archéologique en Grèce et en Asie Mineur. Inscriptions III i* (Paris: Firmin Didot Frères, 1870) no. 2558, pp. 582–4 = *OGIS* 608; see below, p. 387.

the name of the 'elder' responsible, 'Paul', and the spelling 'Chrestos'; in any other context the latter might be taken as a well-attested variant of 'Christos', but here it has been seen as a deliberate avoidance of the latter ostensibly more 'Jewish' form.[4] On the other hand, the term 'synagogue' is unexpected, while the use of abbreviations ('nomina sacra') is striking. Such questions about what a Marcionite community may have looked like at the beginning of the fourth century CE, and how far they may have maintained the beliefs of their founder, are reinforced by the distinctive character of the polemical accounts of Marcionism from the East, in comparison with those explored so far from further west.

Here, the key figure is Ephraem (c. 306–73 CE). However, neither Ephraem, nor Marcionism in the region, can be understood without some consideration of their context. In this case 'context' means not only Ephraem's own historical and cultural context but also how that context is itself to be located within a number of scholarly debates.

SETTING THE CONTEXT

Conventionally, for these purposes the region has been labelled 'Syria', smoothing over the changing internal and external political boundaries, and, often deliberately, suggesting a distinctive cultural homogeneity, implicitly contrasted with the Graeco-Roman dominance further west.[5] Equally conventionally, the history of Marcionism in 'Syria' has been viewed as symptomatic of that of Christianity in the region more generally, marked by diversity as well as by shared values, in particular by ascetic or encratic tendencies. However, despite the insights that accrue from such an approach, considerable caution is advisable. Antioch, Edessa, and Nisibis, to name but three cities that will feature in this chapter, had widely differing political histories within and outside the Roman Empire. Antioch had been the basis of Roman activity within the province of Syria since the beginning of the Empire; further east, however, although within the sphere of Roman influence earlier, it was only under Verus that such control became more securely established, and it was not until 212/213 CE that the hitherto independent Kingdom of Edessa became incorporated into the surrounding Roman province of Osrhoene. It was in this period also that Nisibis was

[4] Harnack, *Marcion*, 341*–45*.

[5] See David Bundy, 'Marcion and the Marcionites in Early Syriac Apologetics', *Le Muséon* 101 (1988), 21–32; Han J. W. Drijvers, 'Marcionism in Syria: Principles, Problems, Polemics', *Second Century* 6 (1987/88), 153–72.

secured by the Roman armies and incorporated into the province of Mesopotamia; it, however, continued to be much more vulnerable to Rome's eastern neighbours – in the 220s the Sassanians replaced the Parthians – and, following Julian's disastrous campaign and death, it was finally ceded to them by Jovian in 363 CE. This history meant that Nisibis and Edessa in particular were cultural meeting points between 'East and West', as indeed they had been since the Hellenistic period. For Edessa this has been more thoroughly mapped with the aid of archaeological remains, but it defies a monochrome epithet, 'Syriac', and what was true of an important urban centre with the eventual status of a *colonia* cannot necessarily be predicated of the surrounding countryside.[6]

Consequently, there continues to be an active debate both about the cultural allegiances and the linguistic practices throughout the region, and about how uniform they were.[7] The inscription from Lebaba, although identified as 'a village', is, like most others, written in Greek, albeit adopting the Seleucid dating. Ephraem, whose polemics are of most importance here, wrote in Syriac; he undoubtedly betrays the influence of 'Greek' philosophical concepts, but that he had any serious level of competence in the Greek language is far from certain. He spent most of his life in Nisibis, in the Roman province of Mesopotamia, but some of his works are to be associated with Edessa, in the province of Osrhoene, where he moved for the last decade of his life following the loss of Nisibis in 363 CE. Conversely, Theodoret of Cyrrhus wrote exclusively in Greek, so that the implications of identifying him as 'Syrian' remain highly contentious.[8] A sizeable body of pseudo-Ephraemic material also survives in Greek, whereas a number of other writings regularly treated as representative of the region were transmitted both in Greek and in Syriac, in some cases rendering uncertain the original language. For example, the *Odes of Solomon* are often presented as characteristic of Syriac piety, and yet not only their date but also their original language, and hence their location, remain matters of dispute.[9]

6 See Steven K. Ross, *Roman Edessa: Politics and Culture on the Eastern Fringes of the Roman Empire* (London and New York: Routledge, 2001), especially 117–38.

7 See Fergus Millar, *The Roman Near East 31 BC – AD 337* (Cambridge, MA: Harvard University Press, 1993); Kevin Butcher, *Roman Syria and the Near East* (London: British Museum Press, 2003). On these questions specifically in relation to Ephraem, Theodoret, and the *Odes of Solomon* see the discussion later in this chapter.

8 See Fergus Millar, 'Theodoret of Cyrrhus: A Syrian in Greek Dress?', ed. Hagit Amirav and Bas ter Haar Romney, *From Rome to Constantinople: Studies in Honour of Averil Cameron* (Leuven: Peeters, 2007), 105–25.

9 See Michael Lattke, *The Odes of Solomon. A Commentary* (trsl. Marianne Ehrhardt; ed. Harold Attridge; Hermeneia; Minneapolis; Fortress, 2009), 5–14; and below, p. 148.

This uncertainty, as will be seen, also extends to whether they harbour an implicit anti-Marcionite polemic.

Similar problems surround any attempt to map the origins and history of Christianity throughout the region. The New Testament gives a precise account of the origins of the Christian community at Antioch, and in particular of tensions recorded between believers of Jewish and of Gentile extraction (Acts 11.19–30; Gal. 2.11–14); some have argued that these tensions continued in other writings putatively associated with Antioch, such as the Gospel of Matthew, and that they were even sustained four centuries later in the polemics of John Chrysostom, bishop of that city, which were directed against members of his congregation who appeared unconcerned about dividing their loyalty between church and synagogue.[10] How Christianity reached Edessa is, however, lost in legend: Eusebius provides such a legend – the sending of the apostle Thaddai by Jesus at the request of the ruler Abgar (Eusebius, *HE* I. 13). The c. fifth-century *Doctrine of Addai* expands the story, providing a succession to Thaddai/Addai, although, curiously, when Addai's co-worker and successor Aggai dies suddenly, Palut, supposedly another co-worker, succeeds him and receives ordination from Serapion of Antioch, who in fact belongs to the end of the second century. No less striking, the *Chronicle of Edessa*, written in the sixth century but drawing on older traditions and documents, is silent about the Addai legend. The key dates that the *Chronicle* does mention after the birth of Jesus are Marcion's leaving 'the Catholic church' (137/138), the birth of Bardaisan (154), and the birth of Mani (239/40);[11] these three individuals are central to Ephraem's polemics and they continue in later tradition as arch-heretics, although they are not so characterised in the *Chronicle*. However, that there were also other groups who identified themselves as followers of Jesus prior to that date is evident; in the vivid account of the flood of 202 CE which opens the sequence, one of the casualties is the 'temple of the church of the Christians', although it is only with Bishop Qona, who 'laid the foundation of the church in Edessa' in 312/313 CE, that any details are given.

The fragmentary evidence about Christianity in Edessa fails to give a clear answer to a further hotly debated question, namely whether it was from the start expressed in Greek, perhaps stemming from Antioch, or whether, as implied by the legend of its foundation, it retained a 'Semitic' form, closer to

10 See Raymond E. Brown and John P. Meier, *Antioch and Rome: New Testament Cradles of Catholic Christianity* (London: Chapman, 1983), 12–86; Robert Wilken, *John Chrysostom and the Jews* (Berkeley, CA: University of California Press, 1983).

11 The last is in fact the date of Mani's first preaching rather than his birth.

the language of Jesus and/or more closely allied with the Jewish communities of the area.[12] Necessarily even more opaque are the origins and character of Christianity in Nisibis. The picture is made yet more complex by the equal uncertainty regarding the patterns of relationship between Christian and Jewish communities, and their effect. It has frequently been emphasised that the boundaries between these communities were porous, with ready movement between them of individuals, ideas, and exegesis, as can be traced in different ways in the writings of Chrysostom for Antioch, of Ephraem for Edessa and Nisibis, and of Aphraat in the Sassanian Empire further east.[13] In addition it remains a matter of considerable debate as to how far Judaism itself in the region was influenced from the West, how far from the Babylonian rabbinic communities of the East.[14]

Co-existence even between the 'Christian' communities need not have meant co-operation: According to Eusebius, Bardaisan wrote polemics against Marcion, while a Syrian ('Assyrian') Marcionite Prepon reportedly wrote against Bardaisan 'most recently, in our own times' (Eusebius, *HE* IV. 30; Ps.Hippolytus, *Ref.* VII. 31.1).[15] None of Bardaisan's own works survive, although he does appear as the protagonist in a dialogue on the balance between fate and human freewill by a disciple of his in the *Book of the Laws of the Countries* which was written in Syriac; on the other hand, Prepon's distinctive ideas – of three originating principles, good, just, and evil – were presumably known to the author of the *Refutation* in Greek.[16] Such patterns demonstrate the speed with which Marcion's ideas and debates about them must have criss-crossed linguistic boundaries even before the end of the second century.

A similar pattern of polemical relationships can be traced more extensively when the region is defined more broadly. In the second century, Ignatius of Antioch attacks vehemently those who, as he sees it, fail to

12 For the problem see Millar, *Roman Near East*, 463. For a 'Jewish' solution see Robert Murray, *Symbols of Church and Kingdom: A Study in Early Syriac Tradition* (2nd edn; London: T&T Clark, 2006).

13 See R. Wilken, *Chrysostom and the Jews;* Christine Shepardson, *Anti-Judaism and Christian Orthodoxy: Ephraem's Hymns in Fourth Century Syria* (NAPSPMS 20; Washington, DC; Catholic University of America Press, 2008); Adam Becker, *Fear of God and the Beginning of Wisdom. The School of Nisibis and Christian Scholastic Culture in Late Antique Mesopotamia* (Philadelphia, PA: University of Pennsylvania Press, 2006).

14 Han J. W. Drijvers, 'Edessa und das jüdische Christentum', *VC* 24 (1970), 4–33, accepts the importance of Judaism but denies that it was of a rabbinic type.

15 For 'Assyrian' see Tatian's description of himself, *Orat.* 42. At Ps.Hippolytus, *Ref.* VII. 31.1, Bardaisan is described as an Armenian; the usual view is that he wrote entirely in Syriac and may not have known Greek. On Bardaisan, see below, n. 25.

16 See above, p. 93.

submit to the bishop, elders and deacons, and those who question that Jesus 'really' suffered, died, and rose again. Justin already claims that Menander achieved considerable success in Antioch, while Irenaeus associates Saturninus with the same city (Justin, *Apol.* 26.4; Irenaeus, *AH* I. 24.1). Much has also been made of the association of Cerdo, Marcion's teacher in some traditions, with Syria, although this first appears in Epiphanius (*Pan.* 41.1.1). Moreover, a number of writings either popular in 'Syria' or originating there appear to oppose a form of docetic dualism that is often associated with the name of Simon (*3 Corinthians*; *Didascalia*);[17] on the other hand, so-called gnostic texts exhibiting similar tendencies have also been traced to this setting, albeit with varying degrees of confidence, including, in particular, texts associated with Thomas, such as the *Gospel of Thomas*, and *Acts of Judas Thomas*.[18] Drawing on these texts it has been argued that a distinctive form of 'gnostic' dualism was characteristic of the region, in contrast to that regularly associated with Egypt.[19] It is this range of material that has secured the continuing popularity of Walter Bauer's argument that even in Edessa the 'orthodox' did not gain any real power until the fourth century and were probably dependent on Bardaisan for the Diatessaron and on Marcion for a Pauline corpus;[20] for others it provides the evidence that renders the language of orthodoxy-heresy or epithets such as 'gnostic' entirely inappropriate. Syriac Christianity, according to this latter view, has to be understood and described in its own terms, perhaps at an early stage best exemplified by the *Odes of Solomon*, supposing that they do come from somewhere in this region. It is indeed the case that the *Odes* embody a number of the characteristics which appear to be echoed widely in the other literature already mentioned: They both invite and defy the label 'gnostic' as also that of 'judaic'; they are couched in language that is deeply symbolic, rich in images whose religio-historical sources cannot be readily tied down; they celebrate 'singleness', which is expressed, among other ways, through an ascetic ethos.[21] Similar in some ways is the *Ascension of Isaiah*, which has

[17] See Bundy, 'Marcion and the Marcionites', who also finds implicit polemic in the *Acts of Peter and John*.

[18] See Barbara Ehlers, 'Kann das Thomasevangelium aus Edessa stamen? Ein Beitrag zur Frühgeschichte des Christentums in Edessa', *NovT* 12 (1970), 284–317.

[19] See John J. Gunther, 'Syrian Christian Dualism', *VC* 25 (1971), 81–93.

[20] Bauer, *Orthodoxy and Heresy*, 1–43. For an opposing view see, however, Murray, *Symbols*, 5–7.

[21] See further Lattke, *The Odes of Solomon*, 12–14, and n. 26 below. For 'singleness' see Sydney H. Griffith, 'Asceticism in the Church of Syria: The Hermeneutics of Early Syrian Monasticism', ed. Vincent L. Wimbush and Richard Valantasis, *Asceticism* (New York: Oxford University Press, 1998), 220–45, 223–9.

some parallels with the *Odes of Solomon* and with ideas associated with Satornilus, perhaps suggesting a Syrian origin.[22]

The 'fluidity' of ideas and practices reflected in all these writings equally resists conventional models of clear boundaries between 'Christianity', 'Judaism', and also 'paganism', and also explains the emergence of new religious movements whose origins are equally difficult to determine. According to Ps.Hippolytus, *Refutation*, Alcibiades came from Apamea in Syria with a book of Elchasai purportedly received from 'the Syrians of Parthia' (*Ref.* IX. 13.1); the reliability of this tradition, and indeed the existence as well as the religious character either of an individual 'Elchasai' or of his book remain contentious issues in debates about the origins of Manichaeism, but the religious context implied remains suggestive.[23] Moreover, Apamea was also the city of the second-century Platonist Numenius, whose own philosophical system has been seen as including an unusual openness to 'eastern' religious ideas, including Jewish ones.[24] Bardaisan himself would seem to represent the impossibility of untangling the cultural and religious complexity of Edessa, in that he provokes radically contrasting interpretations of the balance between the philosophical and the religio-mythical frameworks of his thought.[25]

It is within this complex setting that both the spread of Marcionism, and the polemics against it, are to be plotted. Implicit polemic has been found widely, but a degree of circular argument is difficult to avoid. For example, although the *Odes of Solomon* deny that God is jealous, it is far from self-evident that this is necessarily directed against a specifically Marcionite

22 See Enrico Norelli, ed., *Ascensio Isaiae: Commentarius* (CCSA 8; Turnhout: Brepols, 1995), 53–64.

23 On Alcibiades and Elchasai see further p. 109 above.

24 On Apamea see Polymnia Athanassiadi, *La Lutte pour Orthodoxie dans le Platonisme Tardif de Numénius à Damascius* (Paris: Les Belles Lettres, 2006), 47–89; on Numenius, see further, below, pp. 313–15, etc.

25 See above at p. 147; just how far the *Books of the Laws* can be used for an account of Bardaisan's teaching is disputed: Barbara Ehlers, 'Bardaisan von Edessa: ein syrischer Gnostiker', *ZKG* 81 (1970), 334–51 (reprinted in Aland, *Was ist Gnosis?*, 355–74) relies mainly on Ephraem, against Han W. J. Drijvers, *The Book of the Laws of the Countries: Dialogue on Fate of Bardaisan of Edeassa* (Assen: Van Gorcum, 1964). See also, Edmund Beck, 'Bardaisan und seine Schule bei Ephräm', *Le Muséon* 91 (1978), 271–333; Thomas Kremer, 'Ephräm versus Bardaisan: Das Ringen der syrischen Christenheit mit dem Erbe parthischer Kosmologie', ed. Jürgen Dummer and Meinolf Vielberg, *Leitbilder im Spannungsfeld von Orthodoxie und Heterodoxie* (Altertumswissenschaftliches Kolloquium 19; Stuttgart: Steiner, 2008), 119–55; Ute Possekel, 'Bardaisan of Edessa on the Resurrection: Early Syriac Eschatology in its Religious-Historical Context', *OrChr* 88 (2004), 1–28 relates Bardaisan to a middle-Platonic context.

view of the Creator as has been argued.[26] As already noted, Bardaisan himself opposed Marcion, but the *Book of the Laws of the Countries*, if representative of his teaching, can be understood as addressing Marcion's views of the Creator only indirectly at best. No less problematic is the Pseudo-Clementine literature, which may include Bardaisan among its sources. Here Simon is represented as the prime antagonist to Peter, a role that has been interpreted widely as a cover for that of Paul, perhaps (also) as represented by Marcion.[27] A number of themes in the Pseudo-Clementines are also susceptible to an anti-Marcionite interpretation: for example, the explanation of difficult passages in the Scriptures through the concept of there being true and false pericopes.[28] However, it remains a matter of scholarly dispute whether such polemic belongs to one (or more) of their underlying sources or only to their fourth-century redaction.[29]

Certainly polemic does become much more explicit in the fourth century. Epiphanius listed 'Syria' as one of the areas in which Marcionism flourished in his own time. In the hagiographical *Life of Abercius*, probably to be dated to the fourth century, the eponymous hero travels through Syria attacking the 'heresy of the Marcionites': He even engages with an appropriately named 'Euxeinianos', a play on the Greek name of the Black Sea (Euxeinos), the region from which Marcion came. Even if the *Life* reflects more about the contemporary concerns of its place of writing, perhaps in Phrygia rather than in Syria, it may betray the conventional association of Marcionism with

[26] See *Odes Sol.* 3.6; 11.6; 20.7; 23.4; 7.3; 15.6. An anti-Marcionite purpose is argued by Han J. W. Drijvers, who dates the *Odes* to c. 200 CE ('Die Oden Salomos und die Polemik mit den Markioniten im syrischen Christentum', *Symposium Syriacum 1976* [OCA 205; Rome: Pont. Inst. Orientalium Studium, 1978] 39–55). Michael Lattke, *Oden Salomos. Text, Übersetzung, Kommentar* (3 vols.; NTOA 41/1–3; Fribourg: Academic Press/Göttingen: Vandenhoeck & Ruprecht, 1999–2005), 1, 17–18, suggests instead that it is an early Christian version of a Platonic commonplace. See below, p. 338.

[27] Han J. W. Drijvers argues that some of the polemic in the Grundschrift or material common to the Pseudo-Clementine *Homilies* and *Recognitions* draws on Bardaisan ('Adam and the True Prophet in the Pseudo-Clementines', ed. Christoph Elsas and Hans G. Kippenberg, *Loyalitätskonflikte in der Religionsgeschichte. Festschrift für Carsten Colpe* [Würzburg: Königshausen & Neumann, 1990] 314–23). A. Salles, 'Simon le Magicien or Marcion', *VC* 12 (1958), 197–224, argued that an earlier polemic against Simon had been recrafted against Marcionism by the editors of the *Homilies* and *Recognitions*.

[28] So Drijvers, 'Adam and the True Prophet'.

[29] See Jones, 'Marcionism in the Pseudo-Clementines', who finds polemic against both Marcionism and Apelleanism in the so-called Basic Writing, and argues that while some is drawn from the (lost) 'Syntagma' of Hippolytus, some reflects contemporary polemics. Nicole Kelley, 'Problems of Knowledge and Authority in the Pseudo-Clementine Romance of Recognitions', *JECS* 13 (2005), 315–48, argues that the fourth-century context of the *Recognitions* remains one of competing religious systems including those claiming the names of Paul, Marcion, and Bardaisan.

the latter; it does also, of course, draw on the second-third-century inscription of Abercius in which the author claims that he had travelled as far east as Nisibis – although ironically the assertion by the epigraphic Abercius that he had 'Paul as a companion' has been taken to suggest that he had 'marcionite tendencies'.[30] The *Dialogue of Adamantius* has, as has been seen, also been associated by some with the area around Antioch, although clear supporting evidence is lacking.[31] Another writing from the region directed against Marcion is the anonymous exegesis of eleven Lukan parables, which is often included among the writings attributed to Ephraem.[32]

EPHRAEM AGAINST MARCION

Ephraem's writings demand close attention for the (re-)construction of Marcion for two reasons: Firstly, he provides a firm anchor point in these swirling debates regarding the nature of Christian groups in the Roman Near East, and of Marcionism among them. Secondly, it is Ephraem's polemic against Marcion and his followers that has provided most evidence for the portrayal of Marcion not just as a biblical theologian or as a radical Paulinist but as arguing from (quasi)-philosophical grounds and even as constructing a 'gnostic-type' myth and system.[33] This picture of Marcion cannot be ascribed entirely to the development of Marcionism during the sixty years subsequent to Tertullian's work, for within it casual or fragmentary details in the earlier polemics suddenly find a persuasive context. Nonetheless,

30 David Bundy, 'The *Life of Abercius*: Its Significance for Early Syriac Christianity', *Second Century* 7 (1989/90), 163–76, argues for a Phrygian origin of the *Life*, and is dubious about its historical value. For the Abercius inscription see Margaret M. Mitchell, 'Looking for Abercius: Reimagining Contexts of Interpretation of the "Earliest Christian Inscription"', ed. Laurie Brink and Deborah Green, *Commemorating the Dead. Texts and Artifacts in Context. Studies of Roman, Jewish, and Christian Burials* (Berlin and New York: de Gruyter, 2008), 304–35.

31 See above, p. 117.

32 Bundy, 'Marcion and the Marcionites'; also idem, 'The Anti-Marcionite Commentary on the Lucan Parables (*Pseudo-Ephrem A*): Images in Tension', *Le Muséon* 103 (1990), 111–23. The recent editor, George A. Egan, *Saint Ephrem: An Exposition of the Gospel* (CSCO 291–2, Script.Arm. 5–6; Louvain: Sec. CSCO, 1968), accepts the writing as genuine and denies any Marcionite influence. On the prologue to this, which has sometimes been attributed to Marcion's 'Antitheses', see below, p. 000. The argument of René Roux, 'Antimarcionitica in the Syriac *Liber Graduum*: A Few Remarks', *Augustinianum* 33 (2013), 91–104, turns on the efforts in the *Liber Graduum* to explain difficulties in interpreting the Old Testament, which may not be adequate to prove his case.

33 So especially Drijvers, 'Marcionism in Syria'; also Jouko Martikainen, *Gerechtigkeit und Güte Gottes: Studien zur Theologie von Ephraem dem Syrer und Philoxenos von Mabbug* (GO: Wiesbaden: Harrassowitz, 1981), 39–40.

Ephraem's Marcion is as much, but no more, a construction of his own concerns as is Tertullian's.

To enter into the world of Ephraem's writings is to move into a very different one from that of Tertullian or even that of the theologians from further west closer to his own time. Ephraem does not construct his theology or his polemic through sustained discursive reasoning or through the development of precise definition so much as through imagery and symbol, and through the evocative power of paradox and poetry. On these grounds some have enthusiastically championed his distance from the philosophically grounded theological method of the western European tradition; however, alongside such differences of argumentative style must be placed an undoubted affinity with Greek philosophical concepts.[34] Similarly, Ephraem consciously aligns himself with contemporary Greek (Nicene) theological positions, and in so doing he undoubtedly helped to secure the eventual dominance of the form of Christianity that he represented.[35] In his writings he fights on a number of fronts at once, and it is sometimes difficult to determine whether a more historic enemy is providing cover for a more recent one. The contemporary conflict with 'Arianism' was evidently a driving force, and Ephraem was perhaps using his vigorous attacks against older recognised enemies to gain credit in this more contested field – a strategy that also shaped his vigorous polemics against the Jews.[36] Even so, the situation is unlikely to have been uniform: For the purposes of this analysis, there is considerable uncertainty as to whether his polemics against Marcion, invariably in association with Bardaisan and Mani, were composed in Nisibis or in Edessa, and so might reflect a particular place and time.

34 For the difference of approach see Sebastian Brock, *The Luminous Eye: The Spiritual World Vision of Saint Ephraem* (Cistercian Studies 124; Kalamazoo, MI: Cistercian Publications, 1992); Ute Possekel, *Evidence of Greek Philosophical Concepts in the Writings of Ephrem the Syrian* (CSCO Subsidia 102; Leuven: Peeters, 1999), emphasises parallels between Ephraem's thought and that of Greek philosophy, but acknowledges that they might have a number of sources including within diaspora Judaism.

35 So already Arthur Vööbus, *Literary-Critical and Historical Studies in Ephrem the Syrian* (Papers of ETSE 10; Stockholm: ETSE, 1958), 55–6; Sydney Griffith, 'Setting Right the Church of Syria: Saint Ephraem's *Hymns Against Heresies*', ed. William E. Klingshirn and Mark Vessey, *The Limits of Ancient Christianity: Essays on Late Antique Thought and Culture in Honor of R. A. Markus* (Ann Arbor, MI: University of Michigan, 1999), 97–114, 108–9, offers a more positive picture for Ephraem's own time (so also, idem, 'The Marks of the "True Church" according to Ephraem's *Hymns Against Heresies*', ed. Gerrit J. Reinink and Alexander C. Klugkist, *After Bardaisan: Studies on Continuity and Change in Syriac Christianity in Honour of Professor Han J. W. Drijvers* [OLA 89; Leuven: Peeters, 1999] 125–40).

36 See Griffith, 'Setting Right'. For Ephraem's anti-Jewish polemics see Shepardson, *Anti-Judaism and Christian Orthodoxy.*

The primary sources for these polemics are the *Prose Refutations* (*PR*) and the *Hymns Against Heresies* (*CH*). In their current form the *PR* comprise a set of twelve discourses: Five of these take the form of letters ('To Hypatius'), which are primarily targeted against Mani, with polemic against Marcion playing a minor role; of the remaining seven, three are explicitly directed against Marcion.[37] There is strong evidence that this shape is the result of editorial work after Ephraem's death, and that they were not initially conceived of as unitary works.[38] Similarly, the *CH* range widely in their targeted opponents and are also probably the result of subsequent collection and editorial work.[39] This renders it difficult to attempt to locate both sets of writings within a chronology of Ephraem's life and works, and strong arguments have been made both for Edessa and for Nisibis as their place of composition.[40]

It is the '*madraše*', for which the translation 'Hymns' can be misleading, which represent Ephraem's most distinctive and skilled teaching mode, although it seems likely that he was anticipated by Bardaisan in this strategy.[41] Designed for performance by soloist and responsive choir in a liturgical context, they are an effective means of shaping the response and the self-understanding of his audience. They are particularly suited for Ephraem to exploit his love of symbolism and contrast, allowing shifting images, comparison, antitheses, and paradox to be explored without needing final resolution. Sometimes addressed to God, sometimes to those attacked, and sometimes self-reflective, they create a world that combines spirituality, worship, and a call to commitment and steadfastness.[42] They are, of course,

37 C. W. Mitchell, *S. Ephraim's Prose Refutations of Mani, Marcion, and Bardaisan* (2 vols.; London: Williams and Norgate, 1912, 1921), cited by volume, page, and line number of the Syriac text.

38 See Chiemi Nakano, 'Des Rapports entre les Marcionites et les Manichéens dans un corpus Éphrémien: *S. Ephrem's Prose Refutations of Mani, Marcion, Bardaisan*', ed. Mohammed Ali Amir-Moezzi, Jean-Daniel Dubois, Christelle Jullien, and Florence Jullien, *Pensée Grecque et Sagesse d'Orient: Hommage à Michel Tardieu* (Bibliothèque de L' École des Hautes Études Sciences Religeuses 142; Brepols: Turnhout, 2009), 441–53.

39 Edmund Beck, ed., *Des heiligen Ephraem des Syrers. Hymnen contra Haereses* (CSCO 169–70, Script.Syr. 76–7; Louvain: Sec. CSCO, 1957), cited by Hymn number, stanza, and line numbers. See Griffith, 'Setting Right'.

40 In favour of Edessa: Christian Lange, *The Portrayal of Christ in the Syriac Commentary on the Diatessaron* (CSCO Subsidia 118; Leuven: Peeters, 2005), 19; in favour of Nisibis: Robert Murray, 'Ephraem Syrus', *TRE* 9 (1982), 755–62; Shepardson, *Anti-Judaism and Christian Orthodoxy*, 113–14, argues that they extend over a period of time.

41 Kathleen E. McVey, 'Were the Earliest *Madrase* Songs or Recitations?', ed. Reinink and Klugkist, *After Bardaisan*, 185–99.

42 It has not been possible to retain the poetry in the translations that follow, but as a reminder of it the sub-headings have been taken from the Responses.

directed to Ephraem's own congregations, and not to outsiders. It may even be that many among the audience are here meeting these alternative dogmatic positions for the first time, and that they are being told all they need to know about them, but also that others are being warned to make sharper distinctions between them than they were currently doing.[43] The consequence is that Ephraem has limited interest in the internal problematic of the systems he attacks. Although he does occasionally voice the imagined objections of his opponents, these often reiterate conventional positions and not the logic of their own scheme.

The argument of the *PR* is necessarily more systematic, alluding to the narrative myths of his opponents in order to demonstrate their lack of logic, and answering the objections they purportedly offer. For the former, Ephraem sometimes offers a direct rebuttal, and at other times he explores various possible consequences and options, 'if …', 'perhaps …'. As well as speaking to his peers, he also looks outward with direct address – 'O Marcion', 'if you say …'; with real or imagined responses – 'If the associates of Marcion come … and say'; and even with invitations to other partners – 'Let us ask the Jews', 'if the Jews say …'.[44] Such devices may give the feel of lively interchange, but their purpose is to ensure that he emerges as the victor. How far these imagined responses would find their counterpart in actual debate, oral or literary, remains unknown; if the situation was, as is often suggested, one where boundaries were not always sharply drawn, they would have been particularly effective.[45]

In any case, as has been noted, Ephraem was shaping his argument against a backcloth where the different forms of Syriac Christianity shared a number of practical values, particularly an emphasis on an ascetic lifestyle and a concern for sexual austerity.[46] This does not soften, but rather hardens the intensity of his polemic; he manipulates a wealth of strategies in order to keep the alternatives at a distance even when not all may have experienced them as such. Antithesis, binary patterns, and paradox are among his favourite rhetorical tools; yet he also constantly reiterates the centrality of the principles from which belief was articulated.[47] In formulating these and in his more discursive defences Ephraem may have drawn on earlier sources. Certainly some of his counter-arguments are already familiar from Irenaeus

[43] See Griffith, 'Setting Right'.

[44] *PR* 2. 56,45–6; 57,26–7, 42–5; 62,24–5; 92,3, etc. (See n. 37).

[45] Bundy, 'Marcion and Marcionites', 31.

[46] David Bundy, 'Criteria for Being *in Communione* in the Early Syrian Church', *Augustinianum* 25 (1985), 597–608.

[47] On his method see Shepardson, *Anti-Judaism and Christian Orthodoxy*, especially 21–68.

or from Tertullian, for example, that for someone (a God) to take away the possessions of another is theft, not goodness, or that mercy can only be shown towards those who have transgressed the laws of that same God (*PR* 2. 131,7–22; 132,30 – 133,16). However, Ephraem shows no evidence of direct knowledge of Tertullian's defence of Paul, or of Irenaeus' ideas of structure and hierarchy;[48] it is, however, possible that there would be some influence, perhaps indirect, from Theophilus of Antioch, whose work against Marcion is lost.

Defining opponents

To you be praise from those who are true

(*CH* 23 resp.)

Despite the conventional name of the hymns as 'Against Heresies', Ephraem does not share the concept of 'heresy' in the form developed by Irenaeus and Tertullian. What he opposes is often labelled simply 'teachings' (*ywlpn'*), a term that can also have positive content; these are promulgated by 'fraudulent' (*z'pn'*) teachers, 'deceivers' (*ṭ'y'*) who both go astray and lead others astray, or, especially in the *Hymns Against Heresies*, by 'those who deny' (*kpwr'*), a term that is shared with unbelievers of various kinds (*PR* 1. 40,4–6; *CH* 1. 1,1; 24. 5,1; 7,1). The fundamental contrast is simply that between 'error' (*ṭw'yy*) or deceit and 'the truth' (*qwšt'*, *šryr'*); it is a matter of principle and of definition that 'those who are true' are to be found only within his own church – 'the offspring of truth', 'the faithful' (*bny-qwšt'*, *šryr'*: *CH* 40. 4; 23 resp.). This unapologetic antithesis still does demand that Ephraem expound what he understands to be the authentic understanding of God and its origin: 'the issue revolved around the sources for knowledge and the philosophical structures acceptable for the articulation of Christian beliefs'.[49] On the other hand, Marcion, like other false teachers, has fallen into the trap of seeking to investigate God, searching into what cannot be known, and engaging in disputation (e.g. *CH* 39. 2,2–3, quoted below). This disavowal of 'investigating' is a pervasive theme in Ephraem's writing; it does

[48] Murray, *Symbols*, 306, suggests that Irenaeus had been translated into Syriac by the early fourth century, but he remains cautious as to Ephraem's knowledge of him (337, 344). Possekel, *Evidence*, 38–9, 195–6, suggests that Tertullian would have been useful to Ephraem and finds some similarities in their use of Stoic ideas, but this is insufficient to demonstrate any literary debts.

[49] Bundy, 'Criteria', 598.

not mean that he eschews all investigation, but rather that he thinks it has its proper limits: 'when we know we cannot know we cease to investigate'.[50]

However, this does not lead Ephraem's polemic to be any more reasoned than that of the Greek and Latin heresiologists further west. It is over-optimistic to claim that 'Ephraem provides us with a coherent picture of his opponent's views which are not misrepresented on purpose'.[51] He employs a rich range of vituperatives against his opponent: 'Disciple of madness, and master of faithlessness, teacher of strangeness, yes, preacher of impiety, who raves and denies and, yes, insults the Lord of all, the common Lord' (*CH* 37. 6,1–6). Marcion's activity is inspired by Satan, who is now seeking a new means of attack after earlier defeats: 'He [the evil one] greatly polished Marcion (*lmrqywn mrq*) so that he might make him tarnished' (*CH* 1. 9–18; 2. 1,4; 41. 5–6). The latter is a fine example of Ephraem's personal delight in wordplays: 'To one polluted teaching they give the name of the unclean dog, and raving they are not ashamed to be named with the name of a dog, just as neither are the Audians ashamed by the name "owl" (*'wd'*) nor the Arians ...';[52] although the initial reference here is most obviously to the Cynics it recalls earlier polemics against Marcion and it merges with a catalogue of other familiar epithets: 'rabid', dogs, wolves (*CH* 24. 16–17; cf. 52. 2–3; 56. 4,4). Ephraem piles up synonyms to show how his opponents find fault, blame, scoff, and attack (*CH* 38. 11–13). Some of the epithets he employs are equally targeted against the Jews, and his polemic against Marcion and other 'teachers' undoubtedly gives occasion for anti-Jewish polemic.[53] However, only rarely and allusively does he accuse Marcion of falling into the same error as them: 'The evil one turned the hearts of the Hebrews in the same way' (*CH* 35. 7–8; cf. 3. 10; 25. 6,12). Certainly, nothing suggests that he saw any substantive relationship between them.

Ephraem only once presents a catalogue that is at all redolent of those in the West. Here Marcion comes first as the one who 'increased error', followed by Valentinus, the Quqite, Bardaisan, and Mani, and subsequently the Arians, Paulinians, Sabellians, and other closer contemporaries (*CH* 22. 2–4).[54] Generally, however, Ephraem's standard scheme is the

50 From the 'First Discourse to Hypatius', Mitchell, *Ephraim's Prose Refutations*, 1, ET, xvi. Cf. Shepardson, *Anti-Judaism and Christian Orthodoxy*, 136–41.

51 Drijvers, 'Marcionism in Syria', 158.

52 Implied is the term 'lions' (*'ry'*).

53 Shepardson, *Anti-Judaism and Christian Orthodoxy*, 70–2.

54 On the 'Quqite' compare *CH* 24. 16,6 and see Han W. J. Drijvers, 'Quq and the Quqites; An Unknown Sect in Edessa in the Second Century', *Numen* 14 (1967), 100–29. Cf. *PR* 1. 125,1–5, where Mani's teaching comes 'from the house of Marcion and Valentinus and Bardaisan'. In *CH* 24. 20,7 Simon is named as the first.

triumvirate of Marcion, Bardaisan, and Mani: Marcion was 'the first blasphemer' or 'thorn, the first born of the thicket of sin'; Mani cannot claim the privilege of first born because before him was Bardaisan, and before him Marcion, Mani's 'two elder brothers' (*CH* 22. 17; 24. 11,1; *PR* 1. 140,21–3). Ephraem is aware that these three do not represent a simple succession – Bardaisan opposed Marcion even if he went astray in so doing (*CH* 3. 4); he is only concerned to de-legitimate each of them by denying them either originality or antiquity. Hence, it would be mistaken to accept uncritically his description of Bardaisan as 'Mani's teacher', or that of Mani as choosing a middle way between the other two (*PR* 1. 8,4–5; 140,19–37). When it suits him he will distinguish their positions: 'If only all of them bore witness to the scriptures of each other!' (*PR* 1. 52,37–9); on other occasions they form a single front: 'all the sons of error are united in that they have taken from the Greeks the hated concept *hyle* (matter)' (*CH* 14. 7,1–3).[55] Throughout, it is the rhetorical needs of his argument that drive Ephraem, not any desire to portray accurately the precise relationship between their positions. Indeed, this makes it particularly difficult to use the 'Discourses to Hypatius' in any detail, for in these polemic against one opponent merges into that against another, and it is the systems of Mani and Bardaisan that are probably more important for him than that of Marcion. As has been seen, Bardaisan appears to have been a product of the Edessene context, and the tendency for him to become a lens through which Marcion is viewed obscures the distinctive form that Marcionism may have taken in Edessa; similarly, it remains a matter of vigorous debate whether the similarities in or merging of Ephraem's portraits of Marcion and Mani reflect genuine continuities between the two systems or are a product of his polemic.[56]

Ephraem does on occasion appeal to the earliest stages of the Church and to the practice of the apostles, although this strategy plays a considerably lesser central role than it did for Irenaeus. In *Hymns* 22–4 Ephraem looks back to the time of the apostles when there were no 'tares' (Matt. 13), and when, with the prophets, they taught and baptised only in one name.

[55] Ephraem claims that this concept is not found in the 'Scriptures of the church' but that it is found in the writings of *all* the false teachers (*PR* 1. 141,3–7). On this claim, see below, p. 162.

[56] See Nils Arne Pedersen, 'Some Comments on the Relationship Between Marcionism and Manichaeism', ed. Bilde, Nielsen, and Søvensen, *Apocryphon Severini*, 166–79; on the reference to 'the God of Marcion' in a Manichaean context, see François C. de Blois, 'Review of *Iranian Turfan Texts in Early Publications [1904–1914]*: Photo edn; edited by Werner Sundermann (Corpus Inscriptionum Iranicarum. Supplementary Series, Vol. III. London: School of Oriental and African Studies, 1996)', *JRAS*, 3, 8 (1998), 481–85.

The name the first churches bore is, he assumes, the same as that which 'we bear', while, coming later, Marcion, Bardaisan, and others, deliberately gave their name to their followers, a practice condemned both by Jesus and by Paul (Matt. 23.8; 1 Cor. 1.12): 'You choose, O hearer, which is great and glorious, that you be called Christian (*mšiḥi'*) or nicknamed Marcionite?' For Ephraem, a name partook in the reality to which it applied (*CH* 24.11,9).[57] However, the actual situation was, it would seem, less straightforward: Despite the Lebaba inscription, it is by no means certain that the 'Marcionites' regularly so styled themselves any more than would the 'Arians' have done so, still less that they were so recognised by outsiders. Conversely, Ephraem admits that 'they in turn name us Palutians', a practice that he says Palut himself, as disciple of 'the apostle' (Paul), rejected – although, Palut is perhaps to be dated to the end of the second century.[58] Such nicknames belong to the internal battles for differentiation. Here Ephraem faces a twofold task: first to claim both continuity and priority for the community that he represents, and, second, to locate Marcion and those who came after him firmly later as the thief who stole the sheep from the true Church: 'the church of the nations was already in existence as the temple of the people was ravaged; and as the temple of the people was pulled down there the church was built; Marcion did not serve in it and there was as yet no mention of him at all' (*CH* 24. 21,1–6).

From Ephraem's perspective the followers of Marcion, like those of Bardaisan and Mani, are outsiders, in contrast to the contemporary Arians who are found within (*CH* 3. 9,5–6).[59] However, he can still say, 'For their works are like our works, and their fast like our fast, but their faith is not like our faith'; indeed Marcion is 'partly within and partly without' (*PR* 1. 184,29–34; 2. 125,26–8). The same term, 'church' ('*edt*') describes their assembly as it does his own, even if the latter alone is the 'church of truth' (*CH* 2. 17,6; 18,1).[60] On more than one occasion he assumes that the Marcionite eucharist bears witness to the body of Jesus, although at one point he identifies some, arguably Marcionites, who bring milk and honey (*CH* 47.6). Perhaps a particularly low point in his argument comes when he acknowledges that they fast but denies that they can sustain it, and admits the persistence of their prayer but denies that it is answered (*PR* 2. 67,37–68,43). He accuses them of having 'stolen from the church' ordinances or the milestones that marked the true way, namely trinity, oil,

[57] See below, n. 65. [58] See p. 146 above.

[59] See Beck, *Hymnen Contra Haereses*, 14; Griffith, 'Setting Right'.

[60] On the developing use of this term in place of *knwšt'* see Murray, *Symbols*, 17–18.

and baptism and eucharist (*CH* 22. 21,5; 27. 2–3). Yet this apparent similarity is the source of the danger they pose: Satan 'clothed Marcion in sack-cloth to bring injury to the children of light' (*CH* 1. 12,2).

Such affinities, therefore, sharpen rather than soften Ephraem's polemic. Yet there are surprising moments: The familiar charge that Marcionites are persistently ungrateful in the face of God's continuing kindness to them is accompanied by the suggestion that 'perhaps they are not blameworthy for him, for the Lord of goodness, because love for him has caused them to be at strife against him' (*CH* 35. 11,1–2). He acknowledges their readiness to suffer, and, like his predecessors, he sees their fasting as a form of self-martyrdom, although it is not obvious that he admires this (*CH* 38. 9–10). He even urges his readers, 'Let us pray for them that they may repent, for they are members who have been taken captive from us. See their fetters in their books and their bonds in their writings.' Perhaps this more conciliatory tone was particularly directed towards those within who had yet to make a firm decision (*CH* 47. 4,9–10).

For Ephraem it is axiomatic that the false teachers separate the 'testaments': 'the book they read lacks a beginning, and how can they form a body if there is no head?' (*CH* 36. 8,1; 2. 20,1–2). On the other hand, as shall be seen, he takes it for granted that they read, only to scoff at, accounts of God not only in the Torah but also in the historical books (David and Solomon) and writings (Psalms) (*CH* 39). He says somewhat less about their treatment of the text of Paul and of the Gospel(s), although, again, conflicting exegesis of key passages is central to his polemic. He cites Ephesians as 'written for them and for us', and he accuses 'their deception of stealing beauty from the apostle'; his identification of Palut as a disciple of Paul was, no doubt, polemically motivated (*CH* 36. 7,1; 40. 3,1–2). Although they have 'taken and blotted out the words which are written concerning the justice of the son since he is the son of the good one', they will be unable to do this thoroughly without being left with nothing, 'for the words which remain seek their companions which they blotted out' (*CH* 38. 7).

Ephraem himself was working from a context still relying on a Diatessaron rather than from four separate Gospels, and the form of the Gospel used by his opponents is somewhat unclear.[61] His charge that they not only

[61] Although there is evidence that the four Gospels were being translated into Syriac during his lifetime: see Christian Lange, 'Ephrem, his school, and the *YAWNAYA*: Some Remarks on the Early Syriac Versions of the New Testament', ed. Bas ter Haar Romney, *The Peshitta: Its Use in Literature and Liturgy. Papers Read at the Third Peshitta Symposium* (Monographs of the Peshitta Institute Leiden 15; Leiden: Brill, 2006), 159–75. Theodoret of Cyr, *Haereticarum Fabularum Compendium* (*PG* 83, 335–556), 371–2, describes how he found

mutilate the Testaments but also take and paste to form books may indicate some awareness that they have a different textual form from him (*CH* 2. 19,1–3). But Ephraem also uses textual differentiation as a polemical tool which both separates the Church from 'heresy' and gives it the clear advantage: 'to the true writings of the church all the teachings bear witness that they are true, but as for the writings among the teachings, only the teachings bear witness' (*PR* 2. 50,1–9). The sentiment can immediately be adapted to suit a particular target: 'Our writings which are among the Marcionites they bear witness to us [?] but to the blasphemies of Marcion only those of the Marcionites bear witness.'[62] Nonetheless, it is likely that Ephraem did know of Marcionite texts, perhaps exegetical: Marcion 'slanders the pure and holy one in his readings (*qryn*)' (*CH* 50. 7,1–2). Yet his assertions that 'their writings are written in the names of mere mortals' so that instead of 'so speaks the Lord Sabaoth' they read 'so speaks Marcion the raving one, or Mani and Bardaisan' is self-evidently born more from the necessities of polemic than from any real knowledge (*CH* 56. 4).[63]

The unity of God

Glory to the One Being who has no other alongside him

(*CH* 54 resp.)

For Ephraem, what unites Marcion, Bardaisan, and Mani is that they deny the necessary singularity and unity of God. At the same time, in teaching division they themselves are divided; each espouses a different construction of the divine, and Bardaisan explicitly denies Marcion's position. While Bardaisan, followed by Mani, spoke of multiple divine beings or essences (*'yty'* – a term which for Ephraem, but not for Bardaisan, could only apply to God), 'Marcion counts two Gods' (*'lh'*: *CH* 3. 6,4).[64]

and destroyed more than two hundred copies of the Diatessaron in use among 'orthodox' Christians.

62 *PR* 2. 54,6–13, following the reconstruction of the text suggested by Mitchell, *Ephraim's Prose Refutations*, 2, p. xxv.

63 On the importance of names for Ephraem see above p. 158 and below n. 65.

64 For Ephraem, in the light of the divine name in Exod. 3.14, '[self-existing] being' (*'yty'*) can refer only to God (*CH* 3), but Bardaisan, following earlier practice, distinguished the concepts; cf. Beck, 'Bardaisan und seine Schule', 275–83. Ephraem's concept of 'being' has been much discussed, see Jouko Martikainen, *Das Böse und der Teufel in der Theologie Ephraems des Syrers: Eine systematisch-theologische Untersuchung* (Publications of the Research Institute of the Åbo Akademi Foundation 32; Åbo, 1978), 21–30; Lange, *Portrayal*, 120–4.

Marcion's deities are routinely identified as the Stranger (*nwkry'*) and the Maker or Creator (*'bwd'*; *brwy'*). Although it is difficult to argue that Ephraem uses 'strange/Stranger' exclusively with reference to Marcion's system, these terms are undoubtedly most characteristic of it; Marcion is the one who introduced 'strangeness' (*CH* 22. 22,7; cf. *PR* 2. 53,47–8). This 'strange God had no name', which within Ephraem's metaphysic meant that he was a God without existence, since names partake in the reality that they represent (*CH* 41. 6).[65] Ephraem employs the epithet extensively, without further qualification and in parody and scorn: 'If, my Lord, you had not created us, the Stranger would also be obsolete' (*CH* 37. 1,1–2).[66] As generally in the polemical tradition against Marcion, this is the deity to be attacked, even on one occasion dubbed 'the God of Marcion' – a description, not a proper name (*CH* 40. 12,6).

Although the 'Stranger' is frequently alluded to in the *Hymns*, it is the *PR*, particularly the 'Third Discourse to Hypatius' and 'First Discourse Against Marcion', that provide the most systematic accounts. The Stranger has his own domain, or heavens, above and firmly separated from that of the Creator; at a particular moment he descended, unseen, into the latter's domain to rescue 'the sons of the Maker' (*PR* 1. 44,18–52,29). Taking such a narrative at face value, Ephraem finds it incompatible with his own understanding of the divine being. If the Stranger descended into where previously he had not been present, and then retreated again, he must be spatially bound; leaving behind his own space he is by definition less than that space, for space is itself unlimited while limiting other things. For Ephraem God, and God alone, is coterminous with space: God must be 'congruent with space ... is his own space' (*CH* 35. 1–5).[67] Ephraem imagines them appealing as an analogy to the sun's rays or to a flower's scent, which are able to extend far beyond the confines of their source; this he rejects, for in his metaphysic the sun has genuine substance but is delimited, the rays or scent, although diffused, lack any substance (*PR* 1. 50,45–52,29).

Although Ephraem accuses the Marcionites of 'hating our Creator', and of claiming that 'the Stranger did not create anything' (*CH* 33. 2,1; 37. 3,1–2), the real debate is centred around the Scriptures. As shall be seen, many of

65 So also *Hymni de Virginitate* 28. 13. On Ephraem's theory of names see Brock, *Luminous Eye*, 60–6; P. Tanios Bou Mansour, *La Pensée symbolique de saint Ephrem le Syrien* (Bibliothèque de l'Université Saint-Esprit; Kaslik, Lebanon: Université Saint-Esprit, 1988), 131, 160–87.

66 Drijvers, 'Oden Salomos', 49, notes 'Stranger' in *Odes Sol.* 3.6; Lattke, *Oden Salomos*, 1, 17 points out the wider currency of the term.

67 Possekel, *Evidence*, 127–54 (130); see also Martikainen, *Das Böse*, 33

the passages cited are familiar from the earlier polemical tradition – the affirmation 'I am God and there is none besides me', expressions of divine regret or repentance, God's judgement against those whom he had created and nurtured – while others develop them further.[68] The repeated charge that they scoff implies the same context, as too does the epithet 'the Just One (*k'n'*)': 'They find fault with the Just One because he delights in punishment' (*CH* 38. 11,1). By contrast, the higher God is 'the Good (*ṭb'*)'. However, these epithets do not play the primary role in the antithesis between the Gods, because, as will become clear, the polarity between goodness and justice is very important in Ephraem's own thought (*PR* 1. 46,39–40; 2. 54,16; see below). Yet behind the scriptural debate do lie more fundamental questions: He pictures his opponents laughing at Psalm 136.15, 'Pharaoh sank in the sea … his mercies are for ever': '"Where are those (mercies)?" they ask …; seeking an argument, they question, "From where does evil (*byšt'*) come?"' (*CH* 39. 1,3–2,3)

The answer that they would have given is less clear; in the *Hymns on Virginity* 28. 12,6, Marcion is said to have given the names 'Just and Good and Evil', but a simple tripartite system is not supported elsewhere in Ephraem's polemic.[69] However, having said that Marcion counted 'two Gods', he does then add that 'Marcion also named three roots (*'qr*)' (*CH* 3. 6,4; 7,5). The third 'root' or principle is evidently Matter (*hwl'* = *hyle*), which, according to Ephraem, Marcion himself introduced (*CH* 48. 1,4; *PR* 1. 142,11–14). Ephraem's concern here is more to assert that this most unscriptural of concepts is common to all those who deny the truth: 'all the sons of error have taken the one hated name of vile matter from the Greeks; Moses did not write of it in the law, nor did the prophets set it down, nor did the apostles write it.' For Ephraem a 'root' or 'principle', if self-existing and ungenerated, must be supposed to partake of that 'being' or essence that he sees as exclusively proper to the one God alone: Hence he concludes this stanza with an antithetical, 'All the sons of truth proclaim one Being (*'yty'*)' (*CH* 14. 7,5–6).[70]

Ephraem is far less explicit as to the precise status of 'Matter' for Marcion himself, and this prompts the question whether he is again reading Marcion through the lens of Bardaisan and Mani. He does hint, however, that even for Marcion, Matter was not passive and insentient, the substratum, as it were, of creation; instead it maintained an active but ambivalent relationship

[68] E.g. *PR*. 2. 59,20–4; *CH* 20. 5–7; see below, pp. 340–3.
[69] For this see also the catalogue of Bishop Maruta of Maipherkat (below, p. 178).
[70] See above, p. 160, for Bardaisan's understanding of *'yty'*.

with the Creator – 'the Maker tricked Hyle': 'from whom have you learned of the agreement between Hyle and the Maker and that each betrayed the other so that the agreement was broken?' (*PR* 1. 141,34–5; *CH* 48. 1,6–9). It is difficult to make much of this, although it seems to relate to the idea that body came from Matter and the soul from the Creator. Ephraem, however, is deliberately evasive: 'Marcion said concerning the holy one[?] that he saw a certain image; and we shall not speak of these other things that follow' (*PR* 1. 69, 45–70,2).[71] The implication seems to be that there are far more disturbing details of Marcion's system that are best left unspoken. As shall be seen, later Syriac polemics imply sexual imagery in the relationship between Matter and the Creator, but it may be over-interpreting to assume that Ephraem knew this; he may only be attempting to attribute to Marcion the sort of graphic myth, and even visual representation, that were usually associated with other Gnostics.[72] In the two passages just cited from the *PR* he is associating Marcion, Bardaisan, and Mani as closely as possible together, but does he have grounds for so doing? Those scholars who conclude that Marcion himself did indeed consider Hyle an uncreated, eternal principle may well be over susceptible to Ephraem's rhetoric, although to ascribe such a belief only to a later Marcionite sect may equally be guilty of seeking harmony between the church writers at all costs.[73]

The paradox of the divine

Blessed be the one who took all appearances to give us life;

Blessed be the one who approved and rejected sacrifices

(*CH* 30 resp.)

From Ephraem's perspective, Marcion's attack against the Creator was founded on a thorough misunderstanding of two foundational dialectical

[71] The meaning is far from clear; see Mitchell, *Ephraim's Prose Refutations*, 1, lxii–lxiii. Nakano, 'Des Rapports', reads 'beginning' instead of 'holy one' and compares Gnostic myths of origins.

[72] A more elaborate myth is ascribed to Marcion in Eznik of Kolb, *On God* 358; see below.

[73] Those who accept that Hyle was a third principle for Marcion include P. Tanios Bou Mansour, 'La défense Éphrémienne de la liberté contre les doctrines Marcionite, bardesanite et manichéenne', *OCP* 50 (1984), 331–46, 341, 344; Nabil El-Khoury, *Die Interpretation der Welt bei Ephraem dem Syrer. Beitrag zur Geistesgeschichte* (Tübinger Theologische Studien. Mainz: Grünewald, 1976), 65–81, 71. E. Beck, 'Die Hyle bei Markion nach Ephräm', *OCP* 44 (1978), 5–30, ascribes the development of a third principle, evil, to later Marcionites, and the further identification of this with a personified Hyle to a particular Marcionite sect separate from 'the Marcionite great church' (28).

truths concerning the nature of God. The first of these is the necessary consequence of the vast chasm between Creator and creation. Only God can bridge this chasm, and God therefore takes on images or appearances so that humanity might be able to come to some understanding of him.[74] God 'dissembles, that he has eaten when he does not eat the sacrifices which the fire consumes; he dissembles in human appearance although he is concealed from all in his Being; he dissembles in the regret that is not in him, so that he may arouse it in the race who are his' (*CH* 30. 1,3–8). It is this strategy that Marcion has crudely failed to appreciate, failing to see beyond the guise that God has adopted: 'The people of the Hebrews who grew sick with paganism; the means and fruits which the healer of all devised, Marcion made a pretext for his malady' (*CH* 31. 1,1–3). However God himself has made it entirely clear that there is no duplicity or division (*plg*) within himself: God has made it known that he does not eat sacrifice, and that, despite apparently living in the Temple, the heavens are full of him (*CH* 30. 2; cf. Ps. 50.13; Isa. 6.1). Marcion's criticisms can therefore be set to serve Ephraem's own agenda; he does not have to deny them but rather he celebrates them as divine pedagogy. In the divine nature (*kyn'*) God is always the same, but in his mercy he clothes himself in all forms; he becomes small by his will but not in his nature (*CH* 32. 13,7–8; 36. 6).

Such voluntary self-abasement by God is entirely for the sake of humanity. But if God did all this in the past in semblances (*dmwt'*), he did it in reality by sending his Son (*CH* 33. 6). In the face of this, Marcion fails on all grounds. Even according to their account the Stranger had taken on a form, and necessarily a human form or likeness; but such a form, while appropriate to its Creator, is, when taken by the Stranger, nothing less than theft (*CH* 30. 8). Scoffing at the accounts in the Old Testament, the Marcionites take the description of Jesus as a 'sacrifice for God' (Eph. 5.2) as an image, not reality; yet, when they reject the images taken by the Creator but trust those taken by the Stranger, they expose the lack of consistent logic in their position (*CH* 36. 7–9). The same flaw underlies their docetic Christology: 'As for our Lord who died and lived, his death they have considered a semblance (*dmwt'*), and as for our Creator who diminished himself in a semblance, his diminishing they have considered as reality' (*CH* 36. 11,5–8). For Ephraem God so acts in order to preserve human freedom – a fundamental theme in his theology, and one also important in Bardaisan's thought. Ironically this equally gives Marcion the freedom to respond:

[74] See Lange, *Portrayal*, 120–4; Bou Mansour, *Pensée*, 23–71, esp. 41–3.

'He leaves no means undone of helping the untrammelled freewill, so that the fault-finder may demonstrate his frenzy and the Compassionate One may demonstrate his goodness' (*CH* 33. 5,5–8).

Glory be to your goodness; glory be to your justice
(*CH* 39 resp.; 49 resp.)

Secondly, Marcion misunderstands the necessary dialectical unity between goodness (*ṭbwt'*) and justice (*k'nwt'*): 'Indeed, such justice without goodness is lacking, in the same way as goodness itself also needs justice. So may the deniers go and read in the writings of that Stranger' (*CH* 37. 9,1–6). Ephraem is adroit at turning their own arguments against his opponents: The brevity of the healing ministry of the Stranger when 'today life is full of pain' is an affront to his supposed goodness; Ephraem's own answer to this dilemma is that, whereas goodness cannot be restricted by time, it is appropriate that justice be so, for it may be determined by prestated commitments or by an overarching plan. He continues, 'Consider now the world, consider also the Scriptures, and understand that there is One who rules over all. Creation testifies concerning his goodness, Scripture trumpets concerning his justice' (*CH* 38. 1; 4). The former is demonstrated by the much-used example of God's gift of rain even upon the ungrateful, not least upon the followers of Marcion (*CH* 35. 10; 45. 5; *PR* 2. 55,28–56,3). But even that is too simple: God could have come in all his might; in love he came in our form (*CH* 34. 2).

This multilayered unity of potential opposites is fundamental to all Ephraem's thought, and it has not been adopted only to oppose Marcion's dualism. Ephraem is, however, very aware of the counter-claims made by the Marcionites and of their scriptural base. Against their appeal to the death sentence threatened by God in Genesis 2.16, he sets God's failure to impose it and cites Adam's long life (Gen. 5.5) as proof that 'God turned in [?...?] of goodness and moderated the fervour of justice' (*PR* 2. 60,23–26). If they suggest that God created humanity disorderly out of jealousy (*ḥsm*), then they both undermine their own label 'the Just', but are also disproved by God's readiness to restrain justice and to display his goodness so that they may be shamed into penitence (*CH* 15. 8–9).[75] Once both scriptural and personal history are understood as the field where God's goodness and God's justice co-operate and yet where the former always has pre-eminence,

[75] Cf. *CH* 33.4, 2, 'He made known that his love was without jealousy by giving us glory'; for the jealousy of the Creator as a Marcionite theme see pp. 337–40.

Marcion's whole foundation is undermined: 'He created and sustained us, he judged and had pity on us, and he chastised and gained us, he redeemed and purified us; his judgement is justice, his mercy is goodness. So where then is the Stranger?' (*CH* 50. 1).

The Marcionite question of evil can therefore in part be subsumed under that of justice but also under that of goodness. Pharaoh was engulfed in the sea only after he had repeatedly experienced and rejected God's mercy (Ps. 136.15, see above).[76] All suffering ultimately helps all, and comes from the one who is good to all. Even the uprooting of God's people is intended so that they might finally share in eternal life, and, even more, it is the means for the salvation of the Gentiles (*CH* 39. 8–11). Moreover, evil originates in the choices made by the human will whose freedom has been given by God (*CH* 28. 3).[77] Ephraem also appears to assume that even Marcionites are included among the 'all [who] preach the judgement to come' (*CH* 39. 3,3), but his own sights are set more firmly on God's ultimate salvation-historical goal. The followers of Marcion, he asserts, have no explanation for present suffering, whereas he can show that it is modelled on the prophets and scriptural prophecy, and that it is a sign of maturity and of God's grace (*PR* 2. 56,17– 57,41). Although elsewhere Ephraem was compelled to address both natural and man-made disasters,[78] natural evil does not feature large in his polemic against Marcion.

Within this framework it is evident that nature and the Scriptures are for Ephraem the two sources of knowledge of God, held together in a symbiotic polarity. Consequently, Marcion's disparagement of the natural created sphere sits comfortably alongside his rejection of the scriptural witness to God. This means that from Ephraem's perspective it is the unity of Law and natural creation that Marcion undermines, rather than separating Law from Gospel. For the Marcionites, the 'Stranger' abrogated the old laws and introduced new ones, and so established his alienation from the Creator (*PR* 2. 123,5–125,1).[79] Ephraem does not deny the premise but he does the conclusion. Firstly, repeated with delightful detail, is the fact that when Jesus healed the maimed he returned them to their proper created form: If he were alien to the Creator surely he would have changed creation; in the same way as he gave added interpretations to the law, so he should have supplied

[76] See Martikainen, *Gerechtigkeit und Güte*, 122–5.

[77] See Martikainen, *Das Böse*, 38–40, 47–50.

[78] Namely, the siege and capture of Nisibis, and the earthquake at Nicomedia: see Martikainen, *Gerechtigkeit und Güte*, 127–42.

[79] See Martikainen, *Gerechitgkeit und Güte*, 60–3.

additional organs (ibid.). Ephraem imagines the answer that the Marcionites would, or did, give, namely that this was a strategic choice designed in order not to alienate Jesus' contemporaries: 'In his law our Lord was a stranger, in his action he was of the household' (*PR* 2. 123,21–5; 125,21–4).[80] Yet he is immediately able to show that this is unsustainable, and its importance will be reiterated in their conflicting attitudes to the body. The second element in Ephraem's answer addresses the function of law: God 'created creatures according to his perfection, but he gave many laws because of our imperfection' (*PR* 2. 127,48–128,4). Humankind only needs laws because of their failure to obey the law written on the heart. Just as a doctor changes the medicine to match the particular problem so laws continually need to be changed to suit the situation in which they are applied; a lawgiver does not contradict himself when he makes such changes (*CH* 20. 4). This means that for Ephraem Jewish law to some extent takes its place alongside other systems as a cultural phenomenon; on the other hand, law in principle retains its significance as the God-given means of moderating the exercise of human free will, itself given by God (*CH* 45. 10–11).[81] Marcion does not only misread Scripture, but he misunderstands both human nature and God's dealings with humanity.

The unity of Scripture

Blessed be your image which is in the alphabet

(*CH* 22 resp.)

For Ephraem, therefore, the right understanding of God's unity is inseparable from a right understanding of the scriptural record; Marcion, failing in the latter, has failed in the former. Just as the alphabet is like a body, complete with all its members so that nothing can be added or removed, 'so also is the truth written in the holy gospel with the signs of the alphabet, a complete whole which admits neither loss nor addition' – a point reinforced by the acrostic form of this Hymn (*CH* 22. 1,5–9). The introduction of Marcion in the second stanza indicates that he is in mind here, not only for his 'removal' of parts of the Gospel, to which Ephraem makes little explicit reference, but also for his attitude to the 'Old Testament'.

Ephraem does not address the latter in the sustained way that he does Marcion's cosmology, but this should not overshadow his sensitivity towards

80 Mitchell, *Ephraim's Prose Refutations*, 2, lvii takes the latter as a quotation.

81 See Bou Mansour, 'La défense', 338.

it. Their criticism of 'the Just one' clearly takes its ammunition from the Scriptures: 'If the Creator is one and knew that Adam would sin against him why then did the Creator create?' (*PR* 2. 57,42–58,4) He turns their mockery of the idea of divine regret to his own advantage (Gen. 6.6) – regret is a sign of care, for God shows no regret over a lion whose wickedness stems from its nature, whereas humankind can be changed. If they say 'how hard he is' at God's punishment of the rebellious, they should know that only so is redemption possible (*CH* 20. 1, 5, 7). He has little trouble in meeting the objections that he chooses to repeat: They laugh at the description of God waking as from sleep (Ps. 78.65), forgetting how Jesus himself slept; 'they scoff that he gave the possession of the land of milk and honey to them as to the innocent; they scoff that still he sent them into captivity away from the land as wicked', failing to understand the nature of God's gifts and the response that God rightly expects (*CH* 33. 1; 38. 13,1–4).[82] For the most part their error is a misreading of the way in which God is bound to behave in response to human weakness. Marcion is not, it would appear, touching a raw nerve here.

Only occasionally are there suggestions that Marcion, or Ephraem himself, identified the question of the Old Testament with that of the place of the Jews. In an allusive and textually uncertain passage 'Marcion cried out continually[?] concerning [...] of the Maker and concerning his treachery and concerning his people' (*PR* 2. 54,1–6).[83] Although he tackles Marcion's concept of two Messiahs and asks, 'Does the Messiah come to save Israel or to torment her?', he draws no connection with Jewish messianic beliefs (*PR* 2. 111,40–4). For his part, Ephraem is confident that the Jews 'have been able to overcome the many teachings by their true Scriptures', although this does not mean that he was aware of any Jewish anti-Marcionite polemic: These are 'the Jews' as constructed by him. Similarly, he regularly rhetorically appeals to Jewish experience and response, even though he has no doubt that they themselves 'have succumbed to the church...' (*PR* 2. 53,20–6; cf. 56,45–57, 5; 61,16–21). Although he does denounce the Jews for failing to investigate the true nature of the law and for taking on the words without discovering the true force (*ḥyl*) of what is written, he does not tie this to his refutation of Marcion (*CH* 50. 4).

For Ephraem what is at stake is still the unity of the Testaments: 'The two Testaments (*dytq'*) which the deniers separate are together one with the

[82] Compare their mockery of Solomon's changing fortunes, *CH* 40. 5,1–2.

[83] On the text and translation see Mitchell, *Ephraim's Prose Refutations*, 2, xxv, although there appears to be a typographical error in the translation 'preaching' instead of 'treachery'.

other, sealed in harmony. For the Old Testament was in the form of a type and mould, which was fashioned on account of that which abides, and it served it and passed away. The New Testament was received in the types of its companion and was made complete' (*CH* 36. 8). Ephraem addresses this, however, not so much by appealing to the fulfilment of prophecy, as by demonstrating congruity between the behaviour and demands made in each: Jesus himself replicates the sufferings of the prophets as does the experience of true believers, so the followers of Marcion cannot claim that 'sufferings have been proclaimed only recently' (*PR* 2. 56,41–5; cf. 2. 67,5–12); as the people stood in awe at Mt. Sinai so did the disciples at the transfiguration; John the disciple was a virgin but so was Joshua (*PR* 2. 75,36–76,45). In sum, 'the two Gods ... are both angry at the same thing and approve the same thing' (*PR* 2. 75,1–7). God's sending of his son in human form is in harmony with his self-revelation in the past in 'likenesses'; Jesus' making of clay (John 9.6) is a sign of the Maker, and his healing of the sick and his provision of bread shows that he is the son of the Creator and the Provider; (*CH* 32. 9; 37. 3; 7).

There are two key incidents in the Gospel account to which Ephraem appeals at length as fundamental to his own sense of a single scriptural narrative, John the Baptist's message from prison (cf. Luke 7.18–35), and the appearance of Moses and Elijah at the transfiguration (cf. Luke 9.28–36). Since Jesus does not rebuff John's question, its premise – that Jesus was the fulfilment of prophetic and contemporary hope – is obviously correct; since Moses and Elijah supposedly belong to the Maker, their presence disproves any suggestion of conflict between the latter and Jesus. As shall be seen, the Marcionites evidently had an answer to these arguments, and Ephraem imagines a whole series of alternative explanations of Jesus' reply to John's messengers (*PR* 2. 66,29–67,36; 84,46–87,15).[84] He also alludes to a 'nonsensical story of Marcion, this matter agreed between Moses with the Stranger on the mountain' (*PR* 2. 91,16–20), and what follows implies a deal by which the Stranger purchased the souls of those to be saved from the Maker.[85] While not revealing any detailed counter-positions, the extended exploration of interpretive possibilities clearly indicates that these narratives were particularly contested exegetically.

84 The John the Baptist incident is discussed at *PR* 2. 62–67; 81–87; 106–8; *CH* 25. 4–5; in *CH* 22. 19, John the Baptist is the link in the tradition of laying on of hands that begins with Moses and continues 'to our church'

85 The Transfiguration is discussed at *PR* 2. 87–95; *CH* 48. 8–9. See further below, p. 173.

The redemption

Blessed be the exalted one who humbled himself in order to lift us up;

Blessed be the one who descended and ransomed us by his abasement
(*CH* 34 resp.)

From Ephraem's attack against it, it would appear that Marcion's story of the Stranger could be told on two levels or from two perspectives. One was the story of the Stranger, who 'crossed [the boundary] and descended to us, as they say', with the eventual result that 'the souls tore it apart and ascended, as they deceive' (*PR* 1. 46,10–15). The other was the story of Isu, the son of the Stranger (*PR* 2. 80,2–5). This distinctive spelling of his name (*yšw*), representing the Greek ἰησους, is found only in the *PR* – the *Hymns* use the familiar *yšw*ʿ; that the former represents Marcionite usage is possible, but that it reflects a deliberate rejection of the more semitic or 'Jewish' form is hardly demonstrable.[86] The Marcionites may not have seen a clear distinction between these two levels or narratives, and the contrast between them may be partly the effect of Ephraem's own polemical interests. To some extent the first is more at home in the 'Discourses to Hypatius', which bring Marcion into a close relationship with Bardaisan and Mani and their elaborate cosmology, while the second dominates the Discourses directly aimed at Marcion.

Both narratives afford ample opportunity for Ephraem's sarcasm. On the one hand, if taken literally, their description is illogical given the vast difference and distance between the realm of the Stranger and that of the Creator which had to be travelled: 'Even if they say something that is not likely, "The Stranger like a mighty one (*ḥyltn'*) was able to come"', then the souls he rescued, being weak, could hardly traverse the same distance back (*PR* 1. 47,30–4).[87] On the other hand, Ephraem mocks the picture of the Stranger who had to project his acknowledgement of his Son to the witnesses of the Transfiguration through the lower sphere of the Creator without the latter protesting, and without first ensuring that no one thought it was the Maker speaking (*PR* 2. 94,14–95,39; *CH* 48. 10). Moreover, since on their

86 This is argued by Michel Tardieu, 'Marcion depuis Harnack', in Adolf von Harnack, *Marcion. L'évangile du Dieu étranger. Une monographie sur l'histoire de la fondation de l'Eglise catholique.* Traduit par Bernard Lauret et suivit de contributions de Barnard Lauret, Guy Monnot et Émile Poulat avec un essai de Michel Tardieu MARCION DEPUIS HARNACK (Patrimoines christianisme; Paris: Éditions du Cerf, 2003), 419–561, 448.

87 Here and elsewhere the particle *lm* identifies a quotation.

own account Isu's coming and death involved a degree of humbling, how can they claim that he mirrors the Stranger who was not humbled rather than the Maker who, according to them, was (*PR* 2. 80,2–81,37)?

Ephraem focuses on four aspects of their interpretation of Jesus, elements of which have already been discussed. The first was his relationship, or the absence of any such relationship, with all that had gone before. For Ephraem, Jesus' reply to John the Baptist establishes him as 'the Messiah who is in the law' (*PR* 2. 83,6–7), for Marcion, presumably, the opposite. Just how Marcion did interpret Jesus' response to John is submerged in Ephraem's tortuous exploration of possibilities – 'if you say …' – which is designed to persuade his readers that his own reading is the only serious one. Probably Marcion presented John as heralding a future coming of 'that Just One and the greater of the (two) Messiahs', by implication as the Saviour of the Jews.[88] As so often, Ephraem refutes this by a reductio ad absurdum: that 'Just and Upright One' must either punish those who rejected John, and so prove to be 'the destroyer of the Jews and not their Saviour', or will fail to do so and so prove not to be just (*PR* 2. 112,20–113,10). His own solution is that the coming judgement of which John spoke is to be fulfilled in the second coming of the one Messiah, and in that context he has no hesitation in expecting him to 'execute vengeance on all these tribes who do not believe in John'.[89] On the other hand, Ephraem is willing to adopt Marcion's language and to ascribe to John a certain 'strangeness' in relation to the past, particularly in his baptism, a strangeness that 'Our Lord' also shares: 'Old Testament and New Testament (meet) in the new baptism of John' (*PR* 2. 116,20–3).

Secondly, Jesus' miracles of healing and over nature establish him as Son of the Creator, whose good work he restores. Marcion and Ephraem seem to have agreed that Jesus changed the laws and introduced new ones; they differ on how this is to be interpreted (*CH* 48. 12). For Marcion it established Jesus as alien to the Creator, the author of the laws; for Ephraem it was the appropriate response to new conditions by the original lawgiver. Ephraem makes only passing reference to Jesus' breaking of the Sabbath (*CH* 37. 3,10–12; cf. John 9.14), and he sees no need to defend Jesus' attitude to the Law. Instead he implies that the Stranger's laws add nothing new (or strange), other than the mistaken prohibition of marriage, which undermines the true intention of law to support freedom of the will (*CH* 45;

88 *PR* 2. 110,22–24 as read by Mitchell, *Ephraim's Prose Refutations*, 2, l. On the debate see Tertullian, *AM* IV. 18. See above, p. 69.

89 He explains to Marcion that Jesus can be son of David and yet not son of David (Luke 20.41–4) through the two natures (*PR* 2. 104,18–105,36).

cf. below). Here Marcion appears not at all the champion of law-free grace but rather as one who has lost sight of the nature of God's goodness.

Thirdly, Ephraem knows that for them Jesus' humanity lacked substantial reality: 'As for our Lord, who put on garments and limbs, they affirmed that these were likenesses, feigned … our Lord who in reality both ate and drank, (to them) he ate and did not eat, drank and did not drink'; (*CH* 36. 12,1–2; 13,1–2). How they did interpret Jesus' humanity is of no real interest to him, and he may not have fully understood the nuances of their position; disparagement serves most to inscribe more deeply a separation between the practice and spirituality of his listeners and those of the Marcionites. In fact, Ephraem himself also favours the language of Jesus 'putting on', and he uses it in ways that might at first appear to allow for 'a change that is not of the essence, in the way one puts on a garment and takes it off without a transformation affecting the being'.[90] This would only make it more imperative for him to deny that he and they genuinely shared what were apparently common creedal affirmations: 'If you say that Isu was indeed crucified you say it in semblance and not reality, and if you add that he descended to Sheol and ascended, you say it without it being true for you' (*PR* 2. 81,16–24).[91] For Ephraem this exposes their crass ingratitude and disqualifies every aspect of their religious experience: 'he was born and crucified for those who slander his birth and death'; how can they think that they have his blood in their (chalice) cloths when they deny the body of Jesus? (*CH* 33. 7,5–6; 47. 1,5–8).

These three aspects find their focus once again in the 'myth' of the Stranger's descent. His task was to 'give life to the sons of the Maker', but to their souls only and not to their bodies (*PR* 1. 141,25–28; *CH* 42. 3). Yet according to them the soul, just as the body, came from the Maker; there is no natural affinity between Stranger and the souls of the saved that would justify its selection (*PR* 2. 99,36–100,31). This remains the case even where the body is attributed to Matter (*hwl'* = ὕλη), and the soul to the Creator, if this view can be ascribed to Marcion (*CH* 48. 1–6).[92] Indeed, Ephraem suggests that they claimed that the Stranger was manifested to

90 On Ephraem's own language of 'putting on' see Brock, *Luminous Eye*, 85–97; Bou Mansour, *Pensée*, 226–35 (227), although he denies that this reading survives closer analysis.

91 Cf. *Hymni de Virginitate* 37. 9,1–2, 'The body (*pgr'*) which was from Maria reproves him who says that the heavenly dwelt in her with another body (*gwšm'*)'; l. 5 refers to a 'body from on high'. The editor suggests this may be directed against Marcion (Edmund Beck, ed., *Des heiligen Ephraem des Syrers Hymnen de Virginitate* [CSCO 223–4, Script.Syr. 94–5; Louvain: Sec. du CSCO, 1962] 117); cf. Lange, *Portrayal*, 131.

92 See above, pp. 162–3.

sinners, unlike the Maker who appeared only to the righteous (*PR* 2. 80,45–8). Their explanation would be that salvation took the form of purchase: 'Explain to us then what is the ransom (*zbn*) that the Stranger paid and from whom did he ransom it and with what did he ransom it?' (*PR* 2. 96,28–32; cf. 2. 90,27–44). Ephraem subjects all this to an extensive and characteristic *reductio ad absurdum*, debating the value of the price paid, whether it was something created, and whether the Stranger could retain his superiority over the Creator in such an arrangement. In his eyes the propriety of what they envisaged was only made worse by their further embellishment of their account with the use of war imagery.[93]

It would seem that they found in the Gospel narrative of the Transfiguration a mythic justification for their account; this gives Ephraem yet further grounds for mockery as he imaginatively reconstructs the negotiations that might have taken place, not losing the opportunity to point out that Jesus (or the Stranger) was trespassing on the Creator's territory (*PR* 2. 88,38–93,5). Yet they also drew on more Pauline imagery: 'He paid our debt (*pr'h lḥwbtn*) by his death', and, rejecting 'the term "plunder (*ḥtwpwṭ'*)", they have named it "ransom of humility (*zbynt' dmkykwt'*)"' (*PR* 2. 131,22–4; 132,30–6). Ephraem's contemptuous dismissal of these models offers no room for exploring any shared concepts and biblical resources (for example, the echoes of 1 Cor. 6.20; Phil. 2.6–8). Yet certainly he was aware of them: Admitting that they may 'have heard only the expression "ransom" and from it have named "strangeness"', he directs them to Isaiah 52.3, 'You were sold without payment', but he denies that this would offer any support for their cause (*PR* 2. 135,36–136,6). Instead he re-describes their model as 'the theft of slaves who belong to another', its perpetrator to be condemned (*CH* 34.9–10).

While the Stranger rescued the souls of the saved, the bodies are consigned to the realm of Matter, perhaps because this was their originating source. Again Ephraem alludes to the mythic dimensions of this and challenges its logic. Yet where he finds the greatest inconsistency is in the consequences that follow for the understanding of the soul and its relationship with the body: If the soul required transformation, why could the body not also be transformed? If the soul already possessed the potentiality of life, how and when was such potentiality achieved? If the soul as much as the body was the artefact of the Creator, how could the Stranger alter it?

93 *PR* 1. 47,30–4; 2. 93,10–96,19. See further, Han J. W. Drijvers, 'Christ as Warrior and Merchant: Aspects of Marcion's Christology', ed. Elizabeth A. Livingstone, *Studia Patristica*, 21 (Leuven: Peeters, 1989), 73–85.

Yet even here he detects inconsistency. He takes it for granted that the Marcionites are characterised by commitment to fasting and to prayer, but he finds it irrational that the Stranger should consign to death in *hyle* the bodies he has transformed by such practices (*PR* 1. 141,36–46; cf. 2. 68,32–4). As at length Ephraem proposes and then disposes of the various possibilities, it is difficult to discern any authentic echo of a dissenting voice, beyond, perhaps, 'And why then do they blame the body, saying, "that it causes the soul to sin"?' (*PR* 2. 121,14–16).

The unity of body and soul

> *You, O Lord, have raised to honour the feeble body with freewill over all creatures*
>
> (*CH* 11 resp.)

For Ephraem what unites the false teachers – and where he eschews any fine differences between them – is that they 'call the body filth that is thrown away' (*CH* 19. 1,1). Belief about future resurrection here combines with present practice. It is this that justifies his charge that Marcion 'attacked his Creator and slandered the one who made him', even though Marcion himself, or his contemporary followers, supposedly thought that the body itself came from *hyle*, and only the soul from the Creator (*CH* 1. 9,4–5; 48. 3–7). For Ephraem such views imply that the body is fixed in its nature, incapable of good or of transformation, rendering futile both free will and the Law. Ephraem himself propounds the total interdependence of body and soul, without which there can be neither freely willed action nor responsibility. Alongside the more general argument that the question of responsibility for sin excludes separating the soul from the body, Ephraem presupposes the view that the senses, usually sourced in the soul, are inseparable from the organs of the body, sight from eyes, hearing from ears: If the former are necessary to respond to the Saviour so too are the latter. God does not consider either the physical organs or the senses defiled but only their abuse, when they are used to perceive evil (*CH* 45. 8).

More specifically, the false teachers attack the Creator not only for his supposed inconsistencies (in Scripture) but also because he loves birth and marriage, and, so claims Ephraem, 'they scoff at the marriage of Cana, "God forbid that our Lord should go to it"' (*CH* 38. 11; 47. 3,1–2).[94] For Ephraem this is the nadir of their calumnies, a failure to recognise that

[94] The episode would not have been in their Gospel if they had a version of Luke.

generation is no less a sense than is sight: 'For they consider marriage defiled and, as if they were drunk, they do not understand that the bodily members are siblings just as the senses are companions and kin, and if the use of one member is defiled then it is evident that all of the members are defiled, in the same way as if one of the members suffers all of them suffers, as is written' (*CH* 45. 7; cf. 1 Cor. 12.26).[95] Yet even here Ephraem also points out that his opponents undermine their own logic. They celebrate baptism and eucharist, yet these rely on the symbiosis of physical and spiritual, body and soul (*CH* 42. 6–9). Logically the Stranger should prohibit eating and drinking, seeing and sitting, but he does not do so (*CH* 45. 2).

Nonetheless, this is a point at which Ephraem is on potentially unstable ground, for his own tradition gave high value to personal asceticism and to strict sexual codes, offering the possibility of perfection; therefore, he inscribes a deep dividing line along the place of human freedom to choose: 'For the law is divided for us into three aspects. For he gave family commitment,[96] and holiness, and virginity; possession, and renunciation, and perfection. He restrains everyone equally from evil, and the good things in all their differences to everyone without pressure according to their will' (*CH* 45. 10). Any outward similarity between the praxis of his church and that of the Marcionites has to be exposed as utterly inimical; to fail to make the right distinction here would be to clothe oneself in depravity.

For Ephraem, Marcion does not hold a sequence of erroneous views or misreadings of Scripture to be corrected but rather projects an entirely distorted perception. At every point his story fractures Ephraem's unified vision of God and of God's purposes, and so puts him outside its promise of life restored: 'All the sons of error are considered dead to him, because they do not breathe in life from his laws, and they do not suckle the benefits of the two Testaments. Their interpretation testifies to their death because they have denied their resurrection and disinherited their bodies, and they have cut off their hope because they have repudiated their creator' (*CH* 15. 11). This can only be wilful blindness, deliberate hostility against a God who never ceases to respond in mercy; such crass ingratitude cannot be expected to exhibit any inner coherence or to claim any rational justification.

Just as Ephraem sees the inseparable co-operation of nature and Scripture in witness to God, so Marcion cannot be understood as violating only one or the other. His alienation from the created order and his separation of the

95 On this see Possekel, *Evidence*, 189–90, who notes the Stoic affinities of the idea that generation is one of the seven senses.

96 So Beck, *Hymnen Contra Haereses*, 160, n. 4.

Testaments are integrally related, so that one cannot be credited as the cause of the other; indeed both find their origin supremely in Marcion's misperception of the necessary but gracious self-communication of a God who is indeed almighty and who alone subsists in ungenerated being. From this nature of God stem the polarities that must always be maintained in harmonious tension, but that Marcion persistently tears apart. There is, then, a necessarily metaphysical dimension to Marcion's error in Ephraem's eyes. Nonetheless, Ephraem's perception of the intrinsic interconnection between the systems of Marcion, Bardaisan, and Mani heightens this dimension, and this makes it difficult to determine how far the first did share in the philosophical principles of the other two, either in its original form or among Ephraem's contemporaries. However, whereas Ephraem's targeted polemic against Bardaisan pays particular attention to the latter's docetic interpretation of the death of Jesus and to the relationship between Adam and Christ, the complex exegetical debates, the appeal to Jesus' healing miracles, and the debates about the place of the law, do appear to be distinctive to the argument against Marcion, and these confirm the importance for debate with his followers of the close reading of Scripture even in the time of Ephraem.

AFTER EPHRAEM

Eznik of Kolb

Although Eznik wrote in Armenian and owes much to earlier Greek writers, including Epiphanius and, perhaps, Irenaeus, the Marcionism against which he fought was seemingly imported from Syria. Moreover, his account of Marcionite 'mythology' may stem from a Syriac source, which some have dated as prior to Ephraem on whose polemics he also draws.[97] Eznik's primary goal in the *De Deo* was to defend the Christian conception of one God within the complex religious situation of his day. Yet, although Marcion probably represents for him heresy par excellence,[98] his polemic still betrays a context where in the eyes of many observers there was little to differentiate

[97] On the sources see Louis Mariès, *Le De Deo d'Eznik de Kolb connu sur le nom de "Contre les Sectes": Études de critique littéraire et textuelle* (Paris: Imprimerie Nationale, 1924), 59–91, who favours Eznik over Ephraem's lack of a coherent account. Chapter divisions follow the edition of Monica J. Blanchard and Robin Darling Young, ET, introd, and notes, *A Treatise on God written in Armenian by Eznik of Kolb (floruit c. 430–50)* (Eastern Christian texts in translation 2; CSCO; Leuven: Peeters, 1998).

[98] His account of Marcion himself is drawn from Epiphanius (*De Deo* 432).

the various adherents to the Gospel and Pauline message. Unlike Ephraem, Eznik tackles head-on the apparent similarity between the Marcionites, who reject meat (but not fish) and who avoid sexual intercourse, and the 'covenanters', celibate men and women, of his own church; yet, in so doing, he acknowledges that such shared practice undermined the rhetoric of differentiation, and that they too perhaps claimed the same distinctive terminology of 'covenant' (*De Deo* 407–16).[99] Similarly, he caps his detailed description of the Marcionite 'myth' with the assertion already found in Irenaeus that only a few know this esoteric teaching; with this he could disarm any who questioned the veracity of his report while charging his opponents by implication both of elitism and of masking the nefarious foundation of their exegesis and practice (*De Deo* 358).

Eznik gives an account of Marcion's teaching in the form of a cosmogonic story: Humankind is the result of a joint creative act by the God of the Law and by Matter, which is ultimately evil; they then become entranced by the latter and condemned by the former. It is from this state, their torture in hell, that the Good or Stranger God sends his son to rescue them, 'taking the likeness of a slave'. The cross becomes the means by which the son descends into hell to rescue the dead; the God of the Law, or 'of creatures', who reacts in fury, then swiftly finds himself hoist with his own petard, condemned by the Law for his own condemnation of one who was not only righteous but divine (*De Deo* 358). The myth itself draws on the Genesis accounts of creation, assimilating the 'dust of the ground' of Genesis 2.7 to Matter, on Isaiah 45.2, surprisingly directed by 'the God of the Law' against Matter, and on an interpretation of the miracles of Jesus as anticipating his giving of life; in addition, Paul is given a specific role, carried off by Jesus to preach the message 'that we are purchased with a purchase price'.

Some elements of this story echo that implied by Ephraem, including the exploitation of the Pauline language of 'being bought for a price', but because it is not embedded in a theological refutation the result, despite some aporiae, is one of a greater degree of narrative coherence. It is possible to conclude from this that the story ultimately goes back to a Marcionite source,[100] but its neatness, including the incorporation of Paul, may invite suspicion. In turn, Louis Mariès was so impressed by the vivacity of Eznik's refutation of this story (*De Deo* 364–431) that he suggested it might owe something either to Irenaeus' or to Justin's work against Marcion, although the lack of evidence that they knew any such myth renders this conclusion

99 For the 'covenanters' in Syrian asceticism, see Griffith, 'Asceticism', 229–34.

100 So Casey, 'Armenian Marcionites', 192–3.

unlikely.[101] Instead it may well be that the creativity lies with Eznik rather than with his opponents. Further evidence that the myth does not go back to Marcion himself is that the system as represented addresses problems that he probably failed to consider. Thus, evil becomes attributed to Matter, while the salvation of soul but not of the body is attributed to the fact that the former is the work of the God of the Law, the latter that of Matter (420–1). Nonetheless, as well as rehearsing the familiar objections regarding the goodness, power, and omniscience of the so-called Good God, and the justice of the Just one, the appeals to Scripture, and particularly to 2 Corinthians 12 (362–3; 379–80), betray that the battle was still to be fought not on philosophical grounds but on exegetical ones.[102]

The later tradition

References to Marcion and Marcionism continue in other churches who traced their origins to the Syrian regions. A generation after Ephraem, Maruta of Maipherqat (d. c. 420 CE) was sent to reorganise the Persian church, where it would appear Marcionites were still numerous in the fourth century.[103] Among the writings attributed to him is a catalogue of heresies (*hrsys*), which merits attention because of the curious details in the account of the Marcionites.[104] Here they take third place, following the Sabbatiens and the Simoniens. Marcion is said to have taught 'three Beings', 'good, evil at the bottom, and just in the middle'. In addition, alongside the familiar charge of interpolating and excising the Scriptures, is the specific assertion that they removed the Book of Acts and replaced it with a volume of their own 'that would be like their own opinion'. The name given this volume is *sk'*, which is perhaps best translated as 'summary' or 'summit', although an alternative tradition of the text has *sb'*, 'the old one'.[105] Much has been made

101 Mariès, *Le* De Deo *d'Eznik*, 80–4.

102 In a passing reference Eznik refers to Marcion as having stolen from the philosophers (*De Deo* 360). Casey, 'Armenian Marcionites', notes that the argument presupposes Marcionite use of the Diatessaron, another example of their assimilation to their neighbours.

103 See Fiey, 'Les Marcionites dans les Textes Historiques'.

104 See Oscar Braun, *De Sancta Nicaena Synodo: Syrische Texte des Maruta von Maipherkat nach einer Handschrift der Propaganda zu Rom* (Kirchengeschichtliche Studien 4.3; Münster: Schöningh, 1898); A. von Harnack, *Der Ketzer-Katalog des Bischofs Maruta von Maipherkat* (TU 4.3; Leipzig: Hinrichs'sche, 1899); Arthur Vööbus, *The Canons Ascribed to Maruta of Maipherqat* (CSCO 439, Script.Syr. 191–2; Louvain: Peeters, 1982).

105 See François Nau, ed., *La première Partie de l'histoire de Barhadbesabba 'Arabaïa* (*PO* 23.2; Paris: Firmin Didot, 1932), 189, who suggests that *sb'* is the earlier reading.

of the echo of Tertullian's description of Marcion's 'Antitheses' as 'the supreme document' (*in summo instrumento*), an echo reinforced by the German translation of *sk'* as 'summa'.[106] However, to equate the two as referring to the same work is probably to read far more into both authors than either can sustain, and agnosticism is probably the best solution as to the identity of this text. Since the Marcionites are also accused in the catalogue of replacing the Psalms with their own Hymns (*mdrš'*) it is as likely that the reference is to a local development presupposing later canonical practices. In addition his followers are said to hold Marcion rather than Peter as chief of the apostles, which may merely be a rhetorical way of enforcing their separation from the Church which Maruta represented.

Theodoret of Cyrrhus

As noted at the beginning of this chapter, Theodoret, bishop of Cyrrhus, repeatedly refers to the strenuous efforts he took against Marcionites in his region, converting not just individuals but whole villages to the truth. The tale he tells is of the power of his prayers against the magical arts they used against him.[107] Such claims have often been cited as evidence of the continuing strength of Marcionism in the region. Yet caution is needed; Theodoret was compelled to defend himself against charges of 'Nestorianism', and he needed to show that he was a valiant defender of the truth. Thus, he also refers to his similar success against villages of Eunomians and Arians.[108] More specifically, he describes his opponents as 'those who in our own time are renewing the heresy of Marcion, Valentinus, Mani, and other docetists', and he appeals to his own writings against the followers of Arius, Macedonius, Apolinarius, 'and against the madness of Marcion' (*Epist.* 82).[109] Such strange bedfellows suggest that Marcion serves as a traditional 'heretic' in some way reincarnated in the current disputes over the person of Christ.

Secondly, Theodoret did also compose a *Compendium of Heresies*. Although he adds a personal anecdotal touch, recalling a ninety-year-old man 'who would not take anything from the Creator', his account of

106 If this is the right translation, see pp. 273–4 below.

107 *History of the Monks of Syria* 21.15–18 (= Pierre Canivet and Alice Leroy-Molinghen, ed. *Théodoret de Cyr. Histoire des Moines de Syrie* [SC 257; Paris: Éd. du Cerf, 1979]); cf. *Epist.* 81 (=Yvan Azéma, ed., *Théodoret de Cyr. Correspondance* II [SC 98; Paris: Éd. du Cerf, 1964] 448) for the rescue of eight villages of Marcionites.

108 Ibid.; also *Epist.* 113 (=Yvan Azéma, ed., *Théodoret de Cyr. Correspondance* III [SC 111; Paris: Éd. du Cerf, 1964] 62).

109 Azéma, ed., *Correspondance* II, 200–1.

Marcion builds on his predecessors.[110] Although some details recall Irenaeus,[111] he also betrays the influence of the more elaborate myth also found in Eznik: Here Marcion intensifies Cerdo's straightforward opposition of 'the Just versus the Good', introducing 'four unbegotten beings', the good and unknown Father, the Righteous Demiurge whom he also named bad (πονηρός), Matter which was evil (κακός), completed by 'another evil'. Yet of greater interest for the development of the genre is the way that Theodoret rejects the genealogical model of his predecessors in order to arrange the heresies in a doctrinal structure, those that address the doctrine of God and then those that address the doctrine of Christ.[112] Here the heresies of the distant past could speak again to the present; and once again Marcion is given new life as a warning for all who might waver.

110 Theodoret of Cyr, *Haer.Comp.*, *PG* 83, 335–556. Cerdo and Marcion are no. 24 in Book I (*PG* 83, 372–6). However, he does claim that whereas most of the heresies have suffered the fate due to tares, there are still followers of Valentinus, Marcion and Mani (II. Praef [*PG* 83, 387–8]).

111 See above, p. 45, n. 47.

112 See Helen Sillett, 'Orthodoxy and Heresy in Theodoret of Cyrus' *Compendium of Heresies*', ed. Elm, Rebillard, Romano, *Orthodoxie, Christianisme, Histoire*, 261–73; Cameron, 'How to Read Heresiology', 477–8.

PART II

MARCION THROUGH HIS SCRIPTURES

8

Marcion as editor and interpreter I: Marcion's 'Gospel'

'He mutilates the Gospel according to Luke … and similarly cuts away at the letters of the apostle Paul': With this accusation Irenaeus introduces what becomes one of the consistent characteristics of the picture of Marcion (*AH* I. 27.2). For many of his opponents it was this that constituted both the threat that Marcion posed, for he was in this respect an 'insider', but at the same time his major weakness, for they had no doubt that these texts, properly understood, could only support their own interpretation of true doctrine, and prove his to be illegitimate. Ground that is apparently shared is in need of the most intensive patrolling, but might thereby produce the most effective border. The questioning of such borders and their patrols in modern scholarship has rendered these charges a renewed source of fascination and even attraction.[1]

TEXTS, INTERPRETATION, AND POLEMIC

For all its novelty, this charge against Marcion has a long genealogy. In early Christian tradition, as also in Jewish tradition, the conflict over right belief is also a conflict over authoritative texts. This can take a variety of forms, the chief elements in which target the transmission of shared Scriptures, the interpretation of the same, the rejection by one party of writings that are

1 See, for example, J. B. Tyson, *Marcion and Luke-Acts: A Defining Struggle* (Columbia, SC: University of South Carolina Press, 2006). For the various attempts to recover Marcion's 'Gospel' and to use it to reformulate the history of the early New Testament see nn. 12 and 45 below. Markus Vinzent, *Marcion and the Dating of the Synoptic Gospels* (Studia Patristica Supplement 2; Leuven: Peeters, 2014) reviews the sources in order to argue for the priority of Marcion's 'Gospel'; this work, which is more interested in the emergence of the Gospels than in Marcion's teaching, appeared too late and is too comprehensive a theory to be addressed here, although the present author is not persuaded.

revered by another, and the composition and/or the promulgation of writings peculiar, at least from their opponents' perspective, to one group. The last named regularly include writings ascribed to a figure whose authority would be widely acknowledged, usually one of the apostles or some other figure in the distant past, as well as writings ascribed to a more immediate luminary with a distinctive role in the history of the group.

The first two of these occasions for conflict already characterised intra-Jewish debate as well as Christian polemic against the Jews.[2] Justin Martyr accused the Jewish teachers of excising from the Scriptures key passages which in his view indubitably pointed to the coming of Christ, although it is evident that some of these supposed excisions were in fact accretions within Christian collections of scriptural testimonia (*Dial.* 72). Similarly, a substantial part of his argument in the *Dialogue with Trypho* is dedicated to denouncing what he claims to be their interpretation of the Scriptures, and to defending his own. For Justin both battles have the same goal, to establish that the Scriptures, in practice held in common, 'are ours not yours' (*Dial.* 29.2). By contrast, in his admittedly limited references to those so-called Christians, including Marcion, whose teaching he denounces as blasphemous, Justin makes no explicit mention of their use either of the Scriptures or of the words of Christ. Although some have found an implicit polemic in his defence of the pre-existent Christ as the subject of theophanies to Abraham or Moses, and in his denial of contradictions in Scripture (*Dial.* 30.1; 56), there is no good reason for identifying Marcion as his opponent here.[3]

However, with Irenaeus conflict over the Scriptures, and in particular over the authoritative witness of the apostles, becomes a major theme in the claim to authenticity and hence in the identification and refutation of 'heresy'. Alongside his elaborate accounts of his opponents' cosmologies and numerologies, Irenaeus also adduces the more sober accusation of 'attempting to reconfigure (μεταμορφάζω) the prophetic words' as well as of introducing 'an unspeakable number of apocryphal and poisonous writings they themselves have invented'; he charges some with 'correcting' (μεθαρμόζω) in the same direction things found 'in the Gospel', and others even of labelling an invention of their own, for example as 'the Gospel of Judas' (*AH* I. 18.1; 20.1–2 [Marcosians]; 31.1 [Ophites]). Irenaeus claims to have come across the records (ὑπομνημάτα) of those who called themselves disciples of Valentinus (*AH* I. praef.), and he accuses them of

[2] See Lieu, 'Heresy and Scripture', 83–4. [3] See above, pp. 23–4.

> seeking to adapt things that were said well to ideas wickedly conceived by themselves. Not only do they endeavour to make use of proofs from the Gospel and apostolic writings, perverting interpretations and corrupting exegeses, but they also take from the Law and prophets many things spoken in parables and as allegories which are susceptible in many cases to attract ambiguity through exegesis … .
>
> (*AH* I. 3.5)

Such polemic has to be understood also within the second-century contexts both of general interpretive practice and of evolving attitudes to, and identification of, authoritative texts.[4] Yet, it is striking that Irenaeus still marks out Marcion as the one who '*alone* has openly dared to mutilate Scriptures'. This, he realises, demands that he 'refute him by challenging him from his own writings and from those sayings both of the Lord and of the Apostle which are recognised (*observatus*) by him …', and equally makes that task possible – although this was an intention that Irenaeus apparently never fulfilled (*AH* I. 27.2–3). The pattern set here by Irenaeus remains widely constant in subsequent accounts of Marcion: Attention focuses on his distinctive version, or 'mutilation', of a Gospel that was identified by his opponents as that of Luke, and of a Pauline letter corpus, as well as on his interpretation of these; the focus on these is often accompanied by the confidence that Marcion can be refuted even from the texts that he retained. On the other hand, charges that Marcion produced new or secret writings supposedly authenticating his teaching are few and far between and also inconsistent, including the often overstated 'Antitheses'; consequently polemic rarely directly confronts these.[5]

This tension between Marcion as textual insider or as textual outsider is reflected in the language used: Irenaeus' formulation 'the sayings … recognised by him' is echoed by Tertullian (*AM* I. 29.9); subsequently Tertullian struggles to argue convincingly both that Marcion's 'Gospel' is a corruption specifically of Luke, and is therefore a witness to the Church's version, and that, at the same time, it has nothing in common with any of the Church's Gospels or with their common voice when it comes to the 'substance of faith' (*AM* IV. 2.2). Similarly, Epiphanius knows that Marcion has 'only the Gospel according to Luke' and 'ten letters of the holy apostle', but he labels these 'the Gospel as it is called by them and the apostolikon as they name it' (*Pan.* 42.10.2). Remarkably, although the *Dialogue of Adamantius* does refer to 'their Gospel', it fails to make clear its relationship with that in the

[4] See below, pp. 306–08. [5] See below, pp. 270–2.

Church's possession 'according to Luke'.[6] Moreover, the silence on the topic by someone like Eusebius, who is interested in the writings accepted in the Church, remains as a warning against assuming a monolithic view in the early Church.

However, what these authors do not do is to credit Marcion with holding his 'Gospel' and 'Apostolikon' together in the way that they themselves were doing with their authoritative counterparts, as a single 'New Testament'.[7] This contrasts with modern discussion, which often has concentrated on whether Marcion initiated the idea of a 'New Testament', namely the combination of new authoritative writings of different genres into a single, separate, corpus; that he did so has routinely been seen as the converse of his supposed 'rejection of the Old Testament'. However such models are too precise and introduce fixed concepts that are anachronistic both for Marcion and for his opponents. The initial charges against him were that he denigrated the creator or the one 'spoken about in the Law and the prophets'; the defence by his opponents of the essential harmony between 'Old Covenant' and 'New Covenant', and their complaint that Marcion sought to establish a division between these, go hand in hand. Hence, the model and the language are theirs, especially as increasingly these 'covenants' come to be conceptualised as documents.[8] The status and interpretation that Marcion himself accorded the 'Old Testament' belong to a separate discussion from those of his own seminal writings, while even the status of the latter must await a contextual historical analysis.

The determination of his opponents to refute Marcion from his own writings, together with their perception of the threat posed by his apparent choice and 'manipulation' of texts that they counted as their own authorities, arguably mean that it is here that Marcion's own voice has most chance of being heard, or at least his creative pen of being seen at work. However, it was not the intention of his opponents to report any justification that Marcion may have offered for his text. Moreover, the form of the text could not be separated from how it was interpreted, in whatever way such interpretation may have been presented; however, only rarely do his opponents suggest how Marcion or his followers might explain their text – although Ephraem certainly signals some of the important narratives. Even such hints as there are must be treated with due caution, since, following contemporary convention, often they may be imaginatively constructed in order to suit the

[6] On these, see pp. 119–21.

[7] Epiphanius had possession, probably temporarily, of 'two books' of Marcion (*Pan.* 42. 10.2).

[8] See below, pp. 402–08.

polemicist's purpose.[9] Accounts of his 'Gospel' and 'Apostolikon' may appear to offer a bridge between the Marcion of his opponents and the shadowy, 'real' Marcion of second-century Christianity, but imagination will still have to construct the indispensable edifices of how he understood those texts.

RECOVERING AND EXPOUNDING MARCION'S 'GOSPEL'

Irenaeus sets a pattern that will be followed unquestioningly by his successors, namely by listing Marcion's (mutilated) 'Gospel' before the Pauline letters in anticipation of the eventual canonical order. Regardless of Marcion's own preferred order, this retains a certain heuristic value; both for Marcion's opponents and for most modern interpreters the established pattern of placing Luke alongside Matthew and Mark, and also John, helps set the agenda for interpreting Marcion's 'Gospel', namely through the analysis of 'parallel passages' and of the evidence of what is seen as textual editorial work at a literary level. In what follows that 'Gospel' will be the main subject of investigation, although many of the questions raised will then apply to his 'Apostolikon'.

The primary resources for any reconstruction of Marcion's 'Gospel' are the efforts of Tertullian and Epiphanius; both dedicate the bulk of their own refutation to convicting Marcion from his own writings, working through his texts in purported systematic order. There can be little doubt that both had access to versions of the text used by followers of Marcion, but, as by implication did Irenaeus, they measured that text both against the form familiar to them and against its location within the fourfold Gospel in contemporary usage, avoiding any acknowledgement of the variations between manuscripts that were a feature from the start. Epiphanius confidently asserts, 'You, Marcion, are greatly put to shame since the standard of the truth has been preserved and the excision of your thefts is exposed by the authentic copy (ἀντίγραφος) of the Gospel according to Luke' (*Pan*. 42. 11.17, R28). Similarly, when Tertullian claims that the Marcionites 'reform their Gospel every day just as they are every day refuted by us', this is evidently not merely polemical exaggeration but is intended to contrast with the supposedly harmonious tradition of the true Church (*AM* IV. 5.7).

Other critiques of Marcion's text are found in more piecemeal fashion, particularly, from Origen onwards, in exegetical contexts. Yet how

9 So, for example, Tertullian, *AM* IV. 15.2, 'you say'. See above, p. 61.

widespread close acquaintance with Marcion's text was elsewhere is far from certain, and it seems that the idea of a distinctive falsified text is considerably more powerful than any detailed knowledge of it. The *Dialogue of Adamantius* makes a point of claiming to cite the Marcionite text: Even when in debate with Marinus, who is supposedly a follower of Bardaisan, the orthodox Adamantius prefaces a quotation of the story of Bartimaeus, 'Since Megethius and his party, who belong to the doctrine of Marcion, are present, let me read from their Gospel' (*Adam.* 200.21–30 [5.14]); yet the text he cites here (Luke 18.35–43) displays no significant variants.[10] Other writers frequently accuse Marcion of having deleted or emended passages that in practice occur only in other Gospels; for example, Origen complains that because Marcion is unwilling to use allegory he denies that Jesus spoke passages such as that about eunuchs, although this is peculiar to Matthew (Matt. 19.12: *Comm. in Matt.* XV. 3). However apparently confident they may seem, isolated claims about Marcion's text and exegesis need to be treated with extreme caution.[11] Such difficulties have not deterred the various attempts to reconstruct Marcion's 'Gospel'.[12]

Tertullian and Marcion's 'Gospel'

Early in his work Tertullian had stated his intention of arguing from the Scriptures that Marcion used, although there is little evidence that at that stage he had had the opportunity to study them closely (*AM* I. 29.9). By the time he came to fulfil this plan he had already laid out in Books I to III the main framework and most of the detail of his interpretation of Marcion and of his refutation of him.

Hence, in setting out his account of Marcion's scriptural texts Tertullian is clear as to the issue: 'I say my Gospel is true, Marcion his; I affirm Marcion's is corrupted (*adulteratus*), Marcion mine.' Yet his immediate goals are

10 See above, p. 119; it is difficult to know whether the omission of 'of Nazareth' in the text of Luke 18.37 is significant or is simply part of a tendency to abbreviate.

11 Contrary, for example, to Harnack, *Marcion*, 369*, who treats a comment of Isidore of Pelusium as 'precious information', and who is followed by Riedinger, 'Antimarkionitischen Polemik', 16–17; see above, p. 128.

12 Zahn, *Geschichte*, II.2, 455–94; Harnack, *Marcion*, 177*–240*; Kenji Tsutsui, 'Das Evangelium Marcions: Ein neuer Versuch der Textrekonstruktion', *AJBI* 18 (1992), 67–132. Couchoud, *Creation of Christ*, II, 317–423, set out 'The Gospel According to Marcion' in quasi-poetic form to demonstrate its higher religious value (see p. 4 above). For a recent English reconstruction see Jason BeDuhn, *The First New Testament: Marcion's Scriptural Canon* (Salem, OR: Polebridge, 2013), which appeared too late for detailed consideration here (pp. 65–200 on the Gospel).

simple: Firstly, to demonstrate that, as one who emends, Marcion testifies to the text that preceded him; secondly, to persuade his reader that the Christ who came, and whose story is told, was indeed the one who was foretold in the prophets, and not a representative of some other God (*AM* IV. 6). The first task demanded that he address the origins that Marcion claimed for his 'Gospel', which apparently were, as Tertullian suggests, explained in Marcion's 'Antitheses'; this latter work, however, he preferred not to address directly, perhaps for strategic reasons since to do so would not have the same demonstrative effect as focussing on the 'shared' Scriptures. Consequently, Tertullian's counter-argument is so marked by allusions, questions, and suppositions that it is particularly difficult to disentangle how far he is putting words into Marcion's mouth. Exploiting the ambivalences of Luke amongst the other evangelists, as apostolic but not an apostle, he hints that for Marcion the Gospel had been 'corrupted also as to the title', although it is more likely that Marcion's 'Gospel' bore no title and that this was an inference by Tertullian or a subsequent defence by Marcionites (IV. 2–3). Further, Tertullian suggests that Marcion identified the (Church's) 'Gospel according to Luke' with that 'which had been falsified by the defenders of Judaism in order to form a unity with the Law and the prophets', itself an extrapolation from his reconstruction of Paul's difficulties with the other apostles, although this too may be a secondary apologetic (Gal. 1.8; *AM* IV. 4.4).[13] Tertullian repeatedly returns to this idea, labelling the putative interpolators simply as 'our people' (*nostri*), either an echo of Marcion's charges, or in order to bring the challenge sharply into the present (IV. 25.18). He even extends this aetiology to the Pauline letters: 'perhaps our false apostles and Jewish evangelisers introduced this' (V. 19.5 on Col. 1.16). Certainly, this explanation suits Tertullian's purposes all too well; by correcting what precedes him Marcion is made to acknowledge his own posteriority, in Tertullian's scheme a fatal flaw (*AM* IV. 5).[14] Tertullian's preference for the language of falsification to describe Marcion's activity rather than that of cutting or excision used by Irenaeus thus suits his

13 See *AM* V. 3 and below, p. 415. The Latin '*interpolatum a protectoribus Iudaismi ad concorporationem legis et prophetarum*' is ambiguous, not least because '*concorporatio*' appears to have been coined by Tertullian. 'Form a unity with', 'incorporation of/with', or 'make a single body of' are possible, modelled on the Greek 'συσσωματοποιέω' or 'σωματαποιέω'. Contrast Christopher M. Hays, 'Marcion vs. Luke: A Response to the Plädoyer of Matthias Klinghardt', *ZNW* 99 (2008), 213–32, 218, who relies only on LS and suggests the translation 'falsified into a harmony'.

14 See p. 62 for the importance of this theme in Tertullian, and further below, pp. 414–17.

argument, but it may also reflect that adopted by Marcion.[15] Between the lines it may still be possible to catch glimpses of a more serious conflict over origins, in which Marcion could be presented as the restorer of the original true Gospel, patiently identifying and removing the corruptions and interpolations: 'they say that Marcion did not introduce new things into the "rule" ... so much as recover that which had subsequently been corrupted' (I. 20.1). Such an endeavour would have been congenial to second-century practices of textual analysis and of philosophical polemic.

Tertullian's second, more constructive goal is what really drives him; yet the context is the shadow or negative produced by Marcion's own claim to the same Gospel narrative and by his reading of it. Despite his antithesis between 'my Gospel' and 'Marcion's Gospel', and consequently between 'my (or 'the Creator's') Christ' and 'Marcion's Christ', Tertullian is bound by his own strategy to follow the route that Marcion had already set out.[16] To this end he works his way laboriously through what he claims to be Marcion's 'Gospel', choosing passages that will allow him to argue that both the narrative and the words of Jesus himself consistently undermine Marcion's doctrines as Tertullian had already presented and rejected them in the previous books, while they also permit him to present his own positive theological arguments. He pays particular attention to occasions that can be shown to indicate that Jesus is thoroughly human and that he upholds the Law in its essentials; he is at pains to demonstrate that Jesus acts in harmony with the deeds of Moses or of the prophets, and with the prophetic anticipation. Hence, Tertullian appeals repeatedly to scriptural passages, often to those that he had used in the previous books, setting them alongside the Gospel excerpts. Jesus, he argues, consistently upholds the work and principles of the Creator, and so can only be the 'Creator's Christ'. At the same time he argues that without the framework or rationale provided by the Scriptures, namely within the alternative framework of an unknown God offered by Marcion, Jesus' actions are incoherent or represent a God who is inconsistent or lacking in credibility. Interwoven with all this, as already noted, is Tertullian's own affirmation of the dramatic newness or renewal brought about by Jesus; forced to distance himself from Marcion's own reading of this narrative as a new revelation from a new God, Tertullian traces through the Gospel the twin themes of continuity and discontinuity, and the core interplay between 'Law' and 'Gospel'.[17]

15 See Lieu, 'Heresy and Scripture', 91–5.

16 See above, pp. 77–80.

17 See herein, pp. 71–3, and 403–05.

The procedure and strategy just described inevitably result in much repetition; perhaps not surprisingly, coverage becomes increasingly cursory as the chapters progress, most notably in those recounting Jesus' death and resurrection, just where most careful debate might be expected. Despite accusing Marcion of falsifying the Gospel, it was not Tertullian's primary purpose to catalogue examples; indeed, there is little evidence that he had conducted a sustained and systematic comparison between 'Marcion's Gospel' and the Luke read in the churches. Passages in the Church's Luke that were absent from that 'Gospel' would have served his purpose less well, and some that he does accord particular emphasis are in fact restricted to Matthew, whether or not he was aware of this (e.g., Matt. 5.17, 45; *AM* IV. 7.4; 17.6,13).[18] Even changes in the text required careful handling: Tertullian exegetes in his own favour Marcion's 'division' (*separatio* = διαμερισμός) at Luke 12.51 before adding, 'the text is actually sword, but Marcion emends it' – although 'sword' is the Matthean reading (IV. 29.14; Matt. 10.34). On other occasions, he bases his argument on what was presumably Marcion's text without commenting on its irregularity: He enthusiastically agrees with, and expounds, Marcion's reading, '"Heaven and earth may pass away more easily", as also Law and prophets, "than one macron of the words of the Lord"', apparently without noting the virtual reversal of the Lukan text (*AM* IV. 33.9; Luke 16.17, 'than one hook of the law'). On the other hand, Tertullian is throughout in charge of the text he quotes and of his argument; to this end he employs a mix of summary, paraphrase, and quotation, with few indicators as to which he is using or when he is moving from one to another. A perhaps deliberate consequence is that the confident identification, let alone reconstruction, of the text of Marcion's 'Gospel' is difficult.[19] Moreover, Tertullian's own citations of Scripture, here and elsewhere in his writings, are often marked by variation: Within the space of a few lines he cites in two different forms the words of Jesus at Luke 9.41 (*AM* IV. 23.1–2).[20]

18 See David S. Williams, 'On Tertullian's Text of Luke', *Second Century* 8 (1991), 193–99; on Matt. 5.17 in anti-Marcionite polemic see Tsutsui, *Auseinandersetzung*, 252–3. Dieter T. Roth, 'Matthean Texts and Tertullian's Accusations in *Adversus Marcionem*', *JTS* 59 (2008), 580–97, argues that Tertullian is not claiming (mistakenly) that Marcion has eliminated such verses from Luke, but that he has omitted what belongs to the 'true' Gospel, but this does not explain the following example.

19 Tsutsui, 'Das Evangelium', 70 considers the use of direct speech decisive, although in practice this means that most of his 'direct citations by Tertullian' are words of Jesus. See also David S. Williams, 'Reconsidering Marcion's Gospel', *JBL* 108 (1989), 477–96, and now, BeDuhn, *The First New Testament*, who provides an English text.

20 '*O genitura incredula, quousque ero apud vos? Quousque sustinebo vos?*'/'*O natio incredula, quamdiu ero vobiscum, quamdiu vos sustinebo*'. The omission of 'and perverse', which is

Whether deliberately or through faulty memory, he sometimes modifies his own scriptural text: It is he who has elaborated that David went into the temple at Shiloh *on the Sabbath* (IV. 12.5; ctr. Luke 6.3–4; 1 Sam. 21). Despite, or perhaps because of, the exigencies of his argument it is unlikely that he was any more careful in relation to Marcion's text, particularly when paraphrasing.[21]

When it suits him Tertullian also introduces the exegesis of his opponents, but always in order immediately to refute it: 'He has brought into his argument the tax collector called by the Lord, outside the law and profane to Judaism, as if called by an adversary to the law. Perhaps he has forgotten about Peter, a man of the law …' – a triumphant reference to Marcion's own purported estimation of Peter's weakness (*AM* IV. 11.1).[22] Frequently he does so in the form of imagined dialogue: '"Who is this who orders winds and sea?" [Luke 8.25] Surely, a new lord and owner of the elements of a Creator who is now subdued and driven out! Not so, but the fundamentals recognise their author, they who were also accustomed to obey his servants. Consider Exodus, Marcion …' (*AM* IV. 20.1). Yet that initial 'surely' (*nimirium*) is carefully ambiguous: Is this Marcion's confident answer, or Tertullian's own mocking voice, preparing the ground for an unassailable riposte? Is it Marcion or Tertullian who scours the Gospel for references to the discarded Creator exercising unwarranted severity or to the hitherto unknown Father? Sometimes it may well appear that Tertullian can, and does, 'out-Marcion Marcion', driving through a systematic logic that reflects his own argumentative skill as much as that of his opponent, while ensuring the fatal weakness he can then exploit. Even so, Tertullian's Marcion is not just an emender, or mutilator, of the Gospel text, but a persistent reader and interpreter of it.

possibly supported by the compressed citation at Epiphanius, *Pan.* 42. 11.17, S19, follows Mark 9.19, but is also witnessed by a, e at Luke 9.41: see Williams, 'Reconsidering', 489. There is little to support the claim of Harnack, *Marcion*, 203*, and by implication of A. B. John Higgins, 'The Latin Text of Luke in Marcion and Tertullian', *VC* 5 (1951), 1–42, 38, that the former wording (*genitura*) was Marcionite and the latter (*natio*) Tertullian's; however, Adolf Jülicher, *Itala. Das Neue Testament in altlateinischer Überlieferung* III *Lucas-Evangelium* (Berlin: de Gruyter, 1954), 109, only gives *generatio* for the old Latin here.

21 To conclude, for example, that Marcion excised Luke 9.23 and 25 on the grounds that Tertullian ignores them and quotes verses 24 and 26 without a connecting 'for' (γάρ), fails to make any allowance for the latter's techniques and own stylistic sensitivities (*AM* IV. 21.7–8; so Tsutsui, 'Das Evangelium', 92).

22 On this see Enrico Norelli, 'Marcion et les disciples de Jésus', *Apocrypha* 19 (2008), 9–42, 16–17, who points out that Tertullian himself also assumed that tax collectors (*publicani*) were Gentiles (see also below, p. 409, on 'Judaism' here).

Discovering that Marcion entails, for the modern interpreter, one further question, that of the linguistic history lying behind Tertullian's discussion: Conventionally this has been posed as whether he had access to Marcion's texts in Latin translation, whether or not alongside a Greek original version, or whether he made his own Latin translation directly as he worked through the latter.[23] Similar debates surround Tertullian's general access to and use of his church's Scriptures, both septuagintal and proto-'New Testament' in Latin and in Greek;[24] however, whereas there is strong evidence for Latin translations of the Scriptures in the time of Tertullian, regardless of whether he personally made heavy use of them, the assumption that Marcion's works had been translated into Latin by the turn of the third century, although significant if the case, has no independent support. Confident claims have been made for both solutions, and while the debate is far from over detailed linguistic analysis seems to be favouring the view that Tertullian made his own translation of Marcion's 'Gospel' and 'Apostolikon' from the Greek.[25] Certainly, he does on occasion use Greek terms: Referring to an argument from the 'Antitheses' as addressed to someone, 'a sharer in misery and in being hated', he cites first the Greek terms and then coins his own Latin translation; if this implies that he was familiar with a Greek 'Antitheses', why not with the 'Gospel' and 'Apostolikon'?[26] The issue is of obvious importance for any detailed reconstruction of Marcion's text, but a firm solution will not prove decisive in what follows.

Epiphanius and Marcion's 'Gospel'

Epiphanius presents and uses Marcion's scriptures in a very different manner. It has been shown above how he offers a partly traditional, partly

[23] Those arguing that Tertullian used an existing Latin translation of Marcion include Harnack, *Marcion*; Braun, *Contre Marcion*, IV, 28–30; idem, 'Chronica Tertullianea', *REAug* 42 (1996), 305–7. Among those arguing that Tertullian made his own translation from the Greek are Gilles Quispel, 'Marcion and the Text of the New Testament', *VC* 52 (1998), 349–60; Schmid, *Marcion und sein Apostolos* (on Paul).

[24] See Gerhard J. D. Aalders, 'Tertullian's Quotations from St. Luke', *Mnemosyne* 5 (1937), 241–82.

[25] For this in the case of the Gospel see Dieter T. Roth, 'Did Tertullian Possess a Greek Copy or Latin Translation of Marcion's Gospel?', *VC* 63 (2009), 429–67; for the Pauline corpus, Schmid, *Marcion und sein Apostolos*, whose methodology Roth follows. However, the attempt by Higgins, 'Latin Text', to differentiate Tertullian's own translation choices from those of his reports of Marcion's text have too narrow a base to be successful.

[26] *AM* IV. 9.3; the Greek terms are συνταλαιπορος and συμμισουμενος; Tertullian uses the Latin equivalents, evidently coined by himself, *commiseronis* and *coodobilis*, again later in IV. 36.5. See also the epithet of Christ as ὁ ἐπερχομενος (IV. 23.1; 25.70).

inventive account of Marcion's life and teaching broadly following the model that he adopts for the other heresies of his *Panarion*; in the middle of this he comes to 'the things written or rather manipulated (ἐρρᾳδιουργημένα) by him' and introduces a sequential collection of excerpts or scholia, seventy-eight from the Gospel and forty from the Pauline letters. Here Epiphanius has a double purpose: firstly, to illustrate Marcion's 'malicious and recklessly devious abuse' of these Scriptures; secondly, to demonstrate that Marcion's own text nonetheless establishes 'that the Old Testament agrees with the New … that Christ came in the flesh … as fully human', as well as buttressing Epiphanius' own recurring concern with the resurrection of the dead. According to his own account, he had some years earlier composed this collation, already chosen to refute their author, drawn directly from Marcionite copies of the 'Gospel' and, so he claims, of the Pauline letters (*Pan.* 42.10; 11. 7, 15–16).[27] For the *Panarion* he reused this collation, first as a list (*Pan.* 42. 11.6 and 8), and then repeating it along with a refutation (*elenchus*) of each scholion in turn (*Pan.* 42.11.17 and 12.3).[28]

A number of these scholia specifically charge Marcion with introducing a false alternative text or with omission;[29] in these cases Epiphanius often attempts to draw a link with his own understanding of Marcion's theology, or to refute the latter: For example, Marcion has omitted 'God clothes the grass' (Luke 12.28) because of his denial that God is Creator, cares for all, and was acknowledged by the Saviour; similarly, he counters Marcion's excision of Luke 13.1–5, 6–9, 'the thief engineered the removal of all these things, hiding the truth from himself, because the Lord agreed with Pilate who judged such people well, and that those in Siloam died appropriately since they were sinners and thus were punished by God' (*Pan.* 42.11.17, SR31, 38). At other times he finds little to say, and this suggests that he had forgotten the reasons for the original selection; for example, it is not obvious why he includes the omission of 'your' after 'father' at Luke 12.32, to which he only comments, 'you have here in no way harmed us'; yet he also finds himself near-silenced by the much more striking 'he cut out the whole parable of the

27 See below, p. 236 for the suggestion that the collation from the Pauline letters is secondary.

28 It seems probable that he added the refutations when writing the *Panarion*; see above, pp. 110–11. These are cited as 'S' (scholion) and 'R' (refutation), or SR where the combination of both is being referenced.

29 It is difficult to discern any difference between Epiphanius' use of παρακόπτω (Schol. 25, 38, 40, 41, 42, 47, 52, 53, 58, 59, 63, 64, 67, 72, 77 to the Gospel; Williams, *Panarion*, 'falsify') and of ἀποκόπτω (48, 55, 56; Williams, 'excise'); both verbs are regularly taken to refer to omissions, and in the majority of cases omission is supported by the silence of other witnesses, although at Schol. 77 to the Gospel 'falsify' introduces an alternative reading. Epiphanius sometimes states 'he did not have' (Schol. 12, 22, 25, 28, 29, 31, 57 to the Gospel).

two sons' (*Pan.* 42.11.17, SR34, 42). Some scholia even consist only of a quotation without comment.

Again, the forms of the scholia vary: Frequently Epiphanius tries to score a point from how Marcion has supposedly undermined his own case by what he has retained, particularly emphasising where passages infer the physical humanity of Jesus, or where Jesus refers positively to scriptural figures or texts, or his affirmation of earthly realities or of judgement against disobedience.[30] Occasionally Epiphanius infers that Marcion has some alternative explanation: To the unexplained quotation 'lest he condemn you[31] before the judge, and the judge hand you over to the chastiser' he comments, 'you say the judge is the demiurge and the chastiser each of his angels ... but if then what the good God detests, these same things the judge and demiurge detests, he is shown from the deed and from the single approval to be one and the same ' (42.11.17, SR37; Luke 12.58b). Epiphanius also takes opportunities for an appropriate excursus; the somewhat puzzling scholion 'He spoke with the soldiers as to how to arrest him', leads to the riposte, 'O the craziness of Marcion; who "spoke with" except Judas?', and this in turn prompts an account of a discussion that Epiphanius had held with 'a certain Marcionite of his disciples' about the humanity and weakness of Jesus (*Pan.* 42.11.17, SR60; Luke 22.4). On other occasions he is at a loss: Faced with Marcion's reading of 'the evening watch' instead of 'the second or third watch', the best that Epiphanius can do is to charge him with ignorance and malice (*Pan.* 42.11.17, SR35; Luke 12.38).[32]

Epiphanius makes no claim that his catalogue is comprehensive, but, in typical fashion, he provides a numerological justification of the total – 18 for the name of Jesus and 100 for 'Amen'.[33] Even so, it is remarkable that passages that in his initial account of Marcion he identified as important for the latter, such as the parables of wineskins and patches or Jesus' anticipation of a 'baptism', are not included in his subsequent list (Luke 5.36–38; 12.50; *Pan.* 42.2.1; 42.3.9–10). The uneven distribution of examples and the haphazard way of expressing them reinforce the sense of a degree of randomness. There are extensive sections of the Gospel from which no passages are cited, whereas elsewhere a cluster of scholia focuses

30 *Pan.* 42.11.17, SR10–12 [Luke 7.36–38, 44; 8.19–20]; 42.11.17, SR51, 61–62 [Luke 18.35–42; 22.8, 19f.].

31 *Pan.* 42.11.6, S37 reads 'drag', and Holl, *Epiphanius* II, 140, therefore corrects the manuscriptal 'condemn' to this at 42.11.17, 37; however, 'condemn' is read at Luke 12.58 by D it $sy^{s,c}$.

32 A composite reading attested for Luke by D c supports the antiquity of the reading attributed to Marcion.

33 *Pan.* 42.13.2–3; 'Amen' in fact adds up to 99.

on a smaller range of verses: In particular – and in contrast to the balance in Tertullian – nineteen scholia pertain to Luke 22–4. More generally, sometimes a single passage is cited, sometimes referred to in summary, whereas sometimes a selection of phrases or of verses apparently stands for the whole passage.[34] Although Epiphanius on occasion draws attention even to minor textual omissions or variants, elsewhere his own variation of citation practice effectively produces unmarked distinctive forms of the text; in some cases these echo the synoptic parallels or other variants in the textual tradition, but in other places they are idiosyncratic. There are also regular, occasionally noteworthy, manuscript variants between the initial list of scholia, their subsequent repetition, and the text presupposed by the refutation.[35] Other oddities include the misplacement of Luke 6.33 between Luke 9.44b and 10.21; the duplication – in two different textual forms – of the charge that Marcion excised Luke 20.37–8, which provokes Epiphanius to a valiant effort at justification; and the absence of a refutation to the scholion from Luke 21.18 that follows this (*Pan.* 42.11.17, SR20–2, 56–8). Some of these anomalies may be due to Epiphanius' reuse of his earlier collation, others to the textual transmission of his work, but they also reflect his own style of working and interests: His intention was not to provide a conspectus of Marcion's 'Gospel', but to establish his own guiding plan ('hypothesis') even from Marcion's dregs (42.12.1).

Marcion and his 'Gospel': behind his opponents

To the witness of Tertullian and Epiphanius could be added that of others, including the *Dialogue of Adamantius*, and these would need similar scrutiny for their habits and for their purposes. Clearly it would be a mistake to expect them all to speak with a common voice, equally so to attempt to bring them into a neat harmony – as has already proved the case in exploring their more general profiles of Marcion. It might be expected that the text of Marcion's 'Gospel' would have experienced the same fortunes as his teaching, and would have been subject to development, reconsideration, and even modification by his successors, even while maintaining the distinctive profile that accompanied claiming or ascribing the label 'Marcionite'; on the other

[34] *Pan.* 42.11.17, S44 reads simply 'Concerning the rich man and Lazarus the poor man. That he was taken by the angels to the bosom of Abraham', although the following two scholia cite specific verses (Luke 16.25b and 16.29, 31).

[35] The variants are often obscured by the attempts of Holl, *Epiphanius* II to harmonise the two lists.

hand, texts can be zealously preserved by those who consider the precise detail important, just as they can be victim to intentional or unintentional alteration, cross-influence, or 'correction'. The various reports about Marcion's 'Gospel' provide potential evidence for each of these possibilities. Convergence between different witnesses in minor details or in major elements may indicate important continuities; differences cannot always be measured against each other to identify an original or earlier reading, but have to be recognised as a standard feature of all textual transmission in the period.

Consensus is firmest that Marcion's 'Gospel' lacked the birth narratives and other opening events of canonical Luke, and that it commenced the story of Jesus with his 'descent to Capernaum'. In addition, the explicit description by Epiphanius of a number of passages as 'excised' is supported by Tertullian's more characteristic failure to mention them: the killing of the Galileans and the parable of the fig tree, the parables of the Two Sons (Prodigal Son) and of the Tenants, and the two swords and cutting off of the servant's ear (Luke 13.1–9; 15.11–26; 20.9–18; 22.35–7, 49–51). Other cases demand a level of deduction: Epiphanius only specifies the omission of the Prodigal Son from Luke 15, but Tertullian makes no reference alongside this to the Parable of the Lost Sheep, despite elsewhere referring to its interpretation by Marcion's disciple, Apelles.[36] Yet, there is also a number of significant passages that are passed over in silence by all the extant sources, including the responses by the crowds to Jesus and John the Baptist, the interpretation of the Sower, the healing of Jairus' daughter, the parable of the Good Samaritan,[37] Jesus' visit to Martha and Mary, the healing of the man with dropsy, and the cost of discipleship (Luke 7.29–35; 8.11–15, 40–2, 49–56; 10.29–42; 14.1–11, 25–35). Each of these, if present in Marcion's 'Gospel', could have offered the sort of opportunities for attack which his opponents take up elsewhere, yet, equally, each, if absent, might be expected to have excited comment and condemnation.

On the other hand, there are some incidences where the witnesses are obscure or are contradictory; whereas Tertullian claims that Marcion omitted the division of Jesus garments, 'because of the prophecy of the psalm' (Luke 23.34b; *AM* IV. 42.4), Epiphanius explicitly mentions this in his characteristically compressed citation, 'And coming to the place named Skull they crucified him and divided his garments and the sun was darkened'

[36] According to *De Carne* 8, Apelles interpreted the lost sheep of the demiurgic angel.

[37] On this see Riemer Roukema, 'The Good Samaritan in Ancient Christianity', *VC* 58 (2004), 56–74, 57–8.

(cf. Luke 23.33a, 34b, 44).[38] Epiphanius then continues with the abrupt remark, 'he excised "Today you will be with me in Paradise"' (Luke 23.43), to which he adds the comment, 'You have taken away from yourself the entry into Paradise, for you will not enter neither will you allow those with you' (*Pan.* 42.11.17, SR72); however, whether that signals the absence of the whole of the preceding account of the penitent thief, which is also ignored by Tertullian, or only its climactic promise must remain obscure. It is not surprising that the various attempts since the nineteenth century to provide a list of contents of Marcion's 'Gospel' generally use three categories of verses, 'present', 'absent', and 'uncertain', even if there is less agreement as to what is included in each, especially the third.

For Marcion's opponents there was little difference between what they saw as his 'excision' of passages and his changes to the actual wording. The first example that Epiphanius gives of Marcion's 'mutilation' of the Gospel is in Jesus' instruction to the healed leper where he purportedly replaced 'as a witness to them' with 'in order that this might be a witness to you', a reading that is also assumed by Tertullian (Luke 5.14; Tertullian, *AM* IV. 9.10; Epiphanius, *Pan.* 42.11.6, S1; 11.17, R1).[39] Similarly, according to Epiphanius, '[Marcion] changes the truth even in the briefest phrase' when at Luke 12.8 he omitted 'the angels', reading only 'before God', a reading that Tertullian again supports without comment (Epiphanius, *Pan.* 42.11.17, S30; Tertullian, *AM* IV. 28.4).[40] So also, Epiphanius rebukes Marcion for not having 'his mother and his brothers but only "your mother and your brothers"', as if this would absolve the evangelist from having Jesus acknowledge his human family (Luke 8.19–21). Tertullian's more discursive account of the incident fails to reveal his reading of Marcion's text at this point; however, he does assume that Jesus' response was in the form of a question, 'Who is my mother and who are my brothers?' (ctr. Luke 8.21), and he suggests that not just Marcion but 'all the heretics' could take this as an implicit denial of any physical family; Epiphanius similarly warns Marcion against being led astray by that question. However, neither observes that the question is not found in Luke, at least in the extant textual tradition, although it is well-represented elsewhere.[41] Again, Epiphanius rails against Marcion because, 'instead of "you pass over the judgement (κρίσιν) of God"

38 Epiphanius, *Pan.* 42.11.17, S71; the text is closer to Matt. 27.33 than it is to Luke.

39 The canonical reading is omitted at *Pan.* 42.11.17, S1 but is presupposed by the refutation. 'To you' is also read in the textual tradition of Luke by D it.

40 The same omission is found here in the original hand of Sinaiticus.

41 Tertullian, *AM* IV. 19.6–12; Epiphanius, *Pan.* 42.11.17, SR12. Compare Matt. 12.48; Mark 3.33; the 'Gospel of the Ebionites' according to Epiphanius, *Pan.* 30.14. 5.

he has "you pass over the calling (κλῆσιν) of God"' (Luke 11.42); strikingly, Tertullian here actively assumes the latter wording in his own defence of Jesus' positive attitude to the Law: 'How can he be one who reviles (the Law) when he accuses them of passing over the more significant aspects of the Law, mercy and the calling and the love of God' (Epiphanius, *Pan.* 42.11.17, S26; Tertullian, *AM* IV. 27.6). Similarly, Epiphanius complains, 'He has excised what was said to Cleopas and the other, when he met them, namely, "O foolish and slow to believe everything the prophets spoke; was it not necessary he should suffer these things?" And instead of "which the prophets spoke" he formulated "which I spoke to you"' (Luke 24.25). Tertullian's rendering of the verse, 'O foolish and slow of heart by not believing all which was spoken to you', although ambiguous, probably suggests that he himself also took Jesus as the speaker, as is confirmed by his question, 'What things spoken? That he was of another God?', and by the parallel that he draws with Luke 24.6–7 (Epiphanius, *Pan.* 42.11.17, SR77; Tertullian, *AM* IV. 43.4–5).

As these examples also illustrate, in their accounts of the wording of Marcion's 'Gospel' Tertullian and Epiphanius on occasion exhibit a pattern of explicit or implicit mutually supportive witness. They also share some suggestive silences: Neither makes any reference to Jesus' prayer for forgiveness from the cross, an incident which is textually disputed (Luke 23.34a).[42] Yet, once again the picture is not uniform: According to Tertullian, Marcion permitted Moses and Elijah only to be 'standing with' Jesus on the Mount of Transfiguration, and not to be 'speaking with' him, whereas Epiphanius cites the verse, albeit in a form not otherwise attested, as 'And behold two men were speaking with him, Elijah and Moses in glory' (Luke 9.30, 32; Tertullian, *AM* IV. 22.16; Epiphanius, *Pan.* 42.11.17, S17).[43] Given the vagaries, already noted, of citation practice, textual transmission, and translation consistency, each of these also influenced by authorial or scribal familiarity with synoptic parallels, it is even more difficult to maintain confidence

[42] Although Ephraem cites the verse against the (Marcionite) claim that 'it was the father of an alien (God) who brought about the darkness', there is no suggestion that he is quoting the Marcionite Gospel (*Comm. in Diat.* 21.3 [Christian Lange, introd. and transl., *Ephraem der Syrer Kommentar zum Diatessaron* (FC 54,1–2; Turnhout: Brepols, 2008)]). Contrast Harnack, *Marcion*, 236*, who suggested that it was Marcion who introduced the verse into the textual tradition; although Tsutsui rejects this, he does accept the Ephraem reference and ascribes it to disciples of Marcion ('Das Evangelium', 125–6).

[43] However, earlier (*AM* IV. 22.2) Tertullian had given a summary in which they were in conversation with Jesus; the order in Epiphanius, with Elijah followed by Moses, is Markan (Mark 9.4).

about the text of Marcion's 'Gospel' than about its contents, but the effort should not be entirely surrendered.

Nonetheless, it is easy to see why Marcion's opponents found in his 'Gospel' sufficient evidence to persuade them that it was a bowdlerised form of that which they knew as the Gospel according to Luke. It shared the same overall distinctive shape and sequence, and a number of key episodes. What differentiated it was not an alternative order or additional elements but the absence of a number of other significant passages. The idea that Marcion's mutilation extended to the wording of the Gospel, already noted by Tertullian, becomes much more important in later writers as interest in the text itself develops, and as the assumption emerges of a normative canon and text, encouraged by exegetical practice as well as by the production of biblical codices.[44] From his opponents' viewpoint the shape and nature of Marcion's 'Gospel' were the result of his determination to make it reflect his prior theological position. However, there are numerous examples where they could not help but notice failures in his supposed procedure, namely inexplicable omissions as well as material retained which produced a potential or actual 'own goal'. Tertullian mocks Marcion's retention of the image of Jesus as bridegroom while rejecting marriage: 'Deny, then, Marcion, that you are a most demented person. Look, you attack the law of your own God' (Luke 5.34; *AM* IV. 11.8). For his opponents, such failures only underlined his cack-handed folly; for more recent analysts they have provoked questions as to whether those opponents were merely starting with mistaken assumptions. Whereas rhetorically they presupposed that the Gospel tradition was fixed and uncontested by those of right faith, and, indeed, whereas they used such consensus as a mark of right faith, contemporary study starts from the complex of unresolved literary and preliterary relationships between the canonical Gospels, from awareness of the continuing importance in the period of other 'Gospel-like' writings and traditions, and from an ever-expanding documentation of the textual variations that characterise the whole tradition from as early as can be traced and arguably even from its public emergence.

Thus, undoubtedly it is possible to measure the 'certain' or 'likely' absence of Lukan material from Marcion's 'Gospel' against his supposed theological predilections or aversions, although there is a danger of circular argumentation, accepting the identification of these latter theological inclinations when claimed by others precisely on the basis of the supposed textual choices. Some of the examples cited above highlight the evaluation of the 'Law and

[44] See Lieu, 'Heresy and Scripture', 95–100.

the prophets', the significance of Jerusalem, the physicality of Jesus, the exercise of judgement or justice, and the nature of God, all of which are often presented as cardinal features of Marcion's programme, although not only of his. Yet the study of the canonical Gospels themselves has also demonstrated that their authors and editors have selected and shaped their material to emphasise particular concerns, sometimes in (hypothetical) polemical contexts; in some cases such editorial revision was an extended process, as is most clearly evidenced by the endings to Mark's Gospel or by the composition-history of the Fourth Gospel. Hence, on a similar model, the phenomenon of 'Marcion's 'Gospel' *versus* canonical Luke' might be explained *in principle*, and independently of any analysis of dating, equally by the hypothesis that canonical Luke is the outcome of redactional additions to an earlier stratum; such potential additions might be subsequent to Marcion or to some hypothetical earlier Gospel also available to him. According to this proposal, whose roots go back to the nineteenth century, the character of what now appears as 'additional' ('Lukan') material is, at least in part, determined by its utility against views such as those adopted by Marcion, rather than by his distaste for it as in the conventional account.[45] A comment by John Knox, a pioneer in twentieth-century discussion of the question, regarding the birth narratives illustrates the issue well: 'Marcion would surely not have tolerated this highly "Jewish" section; but how wonderfully adapted it is to show the nature of Christianity as the true Judaism and thus to answer one of the major contentions of the Marcionites!'[46]

This latter solution, that canonical Luke is subsequent to Marcion's 'Gospel', can claim some support from the observation that a disproportionate percentage of 'Marcionite absences' represents material exclusive to Luke's Gospel (sometimes labelled 'L'), namely material additional to that common to Mark and Matthew, or to that shared only with Matthew.[47]

45 For the nineteenth-century debates, and their place within reconstructions of the development of the early Church, see Judith M. Lieu, 'Marcion and the Synoptic Problem', ed. P. Foster, A. Gregory, J. S. Kloppenborg, and J. Verheyden, *New Studies in the Synoptic Problem* (BETL 239; Leuven: Peeters, 2011), 731–51, 740–5; Dieter T. Roth, 'Marcion's Gospel and Luke: The History of Research in Current Debate', *JBL* 127 (2008), 513–27. For a thorough restatement see Matthias Klinghardt, '"Gesetz" bei Markion und Lukas', ed. Dieter Sänger und Matthias Konradt, *Das Gesetz im frühen Judentum und im Neuen Testament. Festschrift für Christoph Burchard zum 75. Geburtstag* (NTOA 57; Göttingen: Vandenhoek & Ruprecht, 2006), 99–128.

46 Knox, *Marcion and the New Testament*, 87.

47 See Knox, *Marcion and the New Testament*, 99–113, who estimates that of 1,148 verses in canonical Luke, 682, do seem to have been present in Marcion's 'Gospel' in some form, 283

For example, interpreters ancient and modern have struggled to explain why Marcion would have 'omitted' the Parables of the Prodigal Son or of the Good Samaritan, both of which are potentially exemplary of the gracious intervention by his loving, nonjudgemental, Father God, but both of which are also exclusive to Luke's Gospel among the Synoptics.[48] Also included here would be more 'neutral' incidents, such as Jesus' visit to Mary and Martha. The most extensive 'absence' in this category of 'characteristic Lukan' material is the infancy accounts of John the Baptist and of Jesus, which have long been identified as distinctive in style, and as largely self-contained, demonstrating little continuity with the narrative that follows, thus adding weight to Knox's comment just cited. Such distinctive material, it might be argued, is what gives the canonical Gospel of Luke its distinctive 'feel'. Marcion's 'Gospel', on this view, would then represent some form of 'pre-canonical Luke'.

However, attempts to go beyond this and to integrate Marcion's 'Gospel' directly into any of the conventional theories of the interrelationship and interdependency of the three Synoptic Gospels have proved unpersuasive – even at a time when such conventional theories are again becoming contentious.[49] Arguments from style and language have failed

absent, and 183 uncertain; he demonstrates that of those present 262.5 are exclusively Lukan and 419.5 have Synoptic parallels, whereas of the 'absences', 225.5, are exclusively Lukan and only 57.5 have synoptic parallels. 'Uncertain' verses are equally balanced (91 versus 92). The argument has been taken up by Matthias Klinghardt, 'The Marcionite Gospel and the Synoptic Problem: A New Suggestion', *NovT* 50 (2008), 1–27, and by Tyson, *Marcion and Luke-Acts*. For an early critique see L. Wilshire, 'Was Canonical Luke written in the Second Century? – A Continuing Discussion', *NTS* 20 (1974), 246–53.

48 The suggestion of Tsutsui, 'Das Evangelium', 110, that Marcion could not apply the parable of the Prodigal Son, whose omission is attested by Epiphanius (see above, p. 197), to internal ecclesial encouragement, as he did those of the lost sheep (if present) and coin, is hardly persuasive. See further, Lieu, 'Marcion and the Synoptic Problem', 739–41.

49 This is the fundamental flaw of the hypothesis of Matthias Klinghardt, 'Marcionite Gospel', particularly since he does not argue his case at the level of textual choices. His proposal takes as its starting point the so-called two-source synoptic theory, namely that Luke was dependent on Matthew rather than that both drew on a common, lost, source ('Q') alongside Mark; he suggests that 'the gospel which was used by Marcion and the Marcionites (hereafter Mcn)' (p. 5) stands between Mark and Luke, but that it also influenced Matthew who primarily drew on Mark. However, while this hypothesis, unsurprisingly, explains why Luke does not have certain distinctive Matthean additions to their common material, it does demand the additional direct influence of Mark on Luke, for example in Luke 20.9–18 (= Mark 12.1–12), which is omitted by Marcion (p. 25). The supportive evidence Klinghardt adduces is frequently more of a restatement of the theory; thus, he does not address Luke's acquisition of other omissions by Marcion from Mark (e.g., Luke 19.29–46), nor does he seriously consider the number of Matthew's omissions from Marcion – he gives a much abbreviated list of these and comments, 'These "omissions" underline that Matthew followed Mark closely and inserted additional material occasionally

singularly to determine whether 'absent' passages (i.e. not present in Marcion's 'Gospel') are best explained as omissions from or as additions to a prior form of Luke's Gospel, that is, whether they bear sufficient distinctive Lukan hallmarks not merely to be attributable to a final editorial polish.[50] In addition, Knox probably underplays the not-insignificant proportion of distinctive Lukan passages that are to be found in Marcion's 'Gospel', although so long as 'L' is not envisaged as a unitary block of material or source this is not a decisive objection; moreover, key incidents, such as the entry into Jerusalem and the cleansing of the Temple, absent according to Epiphanius, as well as the healing of Jairus' daughter, are all part of the three-source (triple) tradition.[51] Despite these ambiguities, there are good reasons to question whether the 'Gospel' that Marcion promoted was simply a heavily edited version of the Luke familiar to Tertullian and to Epiphanius, although that does not mean that he simply reproduced a text available to him. However the activities of the now-canonical Gospel authors and editors may be understood, redaction and 'correction' were widespread textual strategies in the second century, and there is no good reason for excluding Marcion from their exercise. Recovering the precise form and contents of the Gospel he encountered and took as his basis may prove unattainable, although that it was closely related to 'canonical' Luke is difficult to deny; similarly, it may not prove possible to determine with confidence all the changes he deliberately made.

This is even more the case when it comes to the textual details of Marcion's 'Gospel'. The probable absence, on the grounds of the silence of all the sources, from Marcion's 'Gospel' of Luke 5.39, a Lukan addition to Mark, proves a significant bridge; while the admission that 'the old' might appear 'more useful' would surely have been unattractive to Marcion, the verse is also absent from Codex Bezae (D) and from the old Latin tradition.[52]

only' (p. 23), which is not a judgement with which all would concur. More particularly, he does not undertake a close comparison of the textual relationships, which, as already noted, considerably exacerbate the problem. See now Vinzent, *Marcion and the Dating*.

50 Knox, *Marcion and the New Testament*, 88–99, against William Sanday, *The Gospels in the Second Century* (London: Macmillan, 1876), who nonetheless presents a remarkably cautious position.

51 It seems certain that this is what Epiphanius means by, 'He cut out the section concerning the ass and Bethphage and that concerning the city and the Temple, because it was written "My house shall be called a house of prayer and you make it a cave of thieves"', since the refutation asks how Jesus got from Jericho to speaking in the Temple (*Pan.* 42.11.17, SR53). The absence of the healing of Jairus' daughter is predicated on the failure of any source to mention it; see above, p. 197.

52 Harnack, *Marcion*, 190* attributes the D reading to Marcionite influence, see below.

Similarly, Tertullian's own interpretation apparently indicates that he, and perhaps also Marcion, read Luke 6.5 after Luke 6.10, that is at the end of the pair of Sabbath pericopes, a reading again found in Codex Bezae.[53] Indeed, it has long been recognised that many of the 'distinctive' readings or 'alterations' credited to Marcion are witnessed elsewhere in the textual tradition, particularly, but not exclusively or consistently, in the so-called Western text.[54] Kenji Tsutsui makes much of Marcion's reading at Luke 9.16, 'he gave a blessing *over* them (the loaves)' (εὐλογήσεν ἐπ 'αὐτοὺς), and suggests that this was a technical term from the Marcionite cultic meal which also avoided representing Jesus as directly blessing something from the created order; yet it might be enough to observe that the preposition 'over' (ἐπί) is also added by some 'western' witnesses (D it sy$^{(s)\ c}$).[55]

Apparent 'harmonisations' with another Gospel may also belong to this broader phenomenon: At Luke 17.1–2 Tertullian implies the addition of 'it would benefit him if he had not been born or a mill stone...', a phrase apparently taken from Matthew 26.24, but also found in parts of the old Latin tradition of Luke (*AM* IV. 35.1).[56] Of potentially greater significance, Tertullian implies that Marcion read Luke 12.14 as 'Who made me judge over you?', and apparently does not note the absence of 'or divider' (*AM* IV. 28.10); the omission is 'western' (D) and perhaps also diatessaronic (Ephraem, *Comm. in Diat.* 3.12).[57] This reading clearly would serve

[53] *AM* IV. 12.11; Epiphanius cites only this verse, but in a form closer to the Markan parallel (Mark 2.28), following a number of other Lukan manuscripts (*Pan.* 42.11.17, S3). Joël Delobel, 'Extra-Canonical Sayings of Jesus: Marcion and Some "Non-Received" Logia', ed. William L. Petersen, *Gospel Traditions in the Second Century: Origins, Recensions, Text, and Transmission* (Christianity and Judaism in Antiquity 3; Notre Dame, IN: University of Notre Dame Press, 1989), 105–16, ascribes the repetition of Luke 6.5 after 6.1–11 to Tertullian.

[54] See above p. 198 on Luke 5.14; conversely, quoting the Lukan 'concerning your cleansing as Moses commanded' here, Epiphanius also charges Marcion with excising 'the gift'; 'the gift' is found in Matthew 8.4 but also has minor western support (X b c) in Luke (and is read by Tertullian). See also nn. 31–2, 39.

[55] Tsutsui, 'Das Evangelium', 90–1.

[56] Other 'Mattheanisms' may be due to the reporter's greater familiarity with that Gospel; The Marcionite Megethius cites Luke 18.16 as 'for of such is the kingdom *of heaven*' (= Matt. 19.14; *Adam.* 32.26–28 [1.16]), but this is not attested elsewhere. The *Dialogue of Adamantius* gives a 'reading' of Luke 11.11 which is closer to Matt. 7.9 (*Adam.* 110.2–6 [2.20]), although this is not supported by Epiphanius (*Pan.* 42.11.17, S24). Harnack, *Marcion* 208*, follows the *Dialogue*, suggesting an oversight by Epiphanius, and claims a supporting allusion by Tertullian (*AM* IV. 26.10), but this is based on a misreading – the reference there is to the manna in the wilderness.

[57] On this and what follows see Tjitze Baarda, 'Luke 12, 13–14: Text and Transmission from Marcion to Augustine', ed. J. Neusner, *Christianity, Judaism and Other Greco-Roman Cults. Studies for Morton Smith at Sixty, I. New Testament* (SJLA 12; Leiden: Brill, 1975), 107–62. *Gospel of Thomas* 72 has a parallel anecdote where Jesus asks, 'Man, who made me a

Marcion's interests, allowing him, as Tertullian indicates, to demonstrate the rejection by Jesus of the role of judge, while perhaps accepting that Jesus was a cause of division. Yet, was Marcion the source of this reading or, as the text he knew, did it add fuel to his own understanding of Jesus?[58] Other contacts have been found between Marcion's 'Gospel' and the diatessaronic tradition, which may be unsurprising given that both Marcion and Tatian were active in Rome in the mid-second century.[59]

Other apparent examples of 'hamonising' prove to be more complex: A striking case is provided by the first part of the Sermon on the Plain (Luke 6.20–36; Tertullian, *AM* IV. 14.1–17.8). According to Tertullian, the first three Beatitudes were in the third person (as they are in Matthew), although those declared blessed, the poor, hungry, and those who weep, are Lukan, while the woes, which are exclusive to Luke, were in the second person plural. On the other hand, the citation of Luke 6.27–8, 'Love your enemies, and bless those who hate you, and pray for those who revile you', conforms to no extant text of Luke, or of the Matthean parallel (Matt. 5.44); in this case, however, it is evident that these maxims existed in a variety of forms, as is attested by the variant at Matthew 5.44, by Justin, *Apol.* 15.9, and by Theophilus of Antioch, *Ad Autol.* III. 14. Tertullian then continues by contrasting Luke 6.29 with the *lex talionis* (Exod. 21.21), as also does Megethius (*Adam.* 32.2–3 [1.15]); if this contrast were present in Marcion's text, it would suggest influence from Matthew 5.38, although it is possible that Tertullian is alluding to an interpretation, perhaps found in Marcion's 'Antitheses'.[60] Although somewhat of a paraphrase, the instruction not only not to hold back a shirt, but also to surrender the cloak (Luke 6.29; *tunica . . . pallium*), follows the Matthean order (Matt. 5.40), but does have some parallel in the old Latin of Luke.[61] If Tertullian's text in the remaining verses

divider?'; see the summary of debate in April D. DeConick, *The Original Gospel of Thomas in Translation: With a Commentary and New English Translation of the Complete Gospel* (Library of New Testament Studies. Early Christianity in context; 287; London and New York: T&T Clark, 2007), 228–30.

58 Baarda, 'Luke 12, 13–14', tentatively accepts a Marcionite origin, and also suggests that the variant reading δικαστήν, may also have been introduced by Marcion in antithesis to Exod. 2.14. Tertullian's *iudex* could translate either κρίτης or δικαστής.

59 So William L. Petersen, *Tatian's Diatessaron: Its Creation, Dissemination, Significance, and History in Scholarship* (VCSup. 25; Leiden: Brill, 1994), 11–12, 192–93.

60 Tsutsui, 'Das Evangelium', 83–4, accepts it as part of Marcion's text, against Harnack, *Marcion*, 193*. See further, below, p. 281.

61 Megethius, however, gives what becomes the standard textual order in Luke (*Adam.* 38.1–3 [1.18]). Again, Justin, *Apol.* 16.1, offers a different form of the saying.

is taken as a close quotation, then this uneven relationship with both the Lukan and the Matthean text continues at least to v. 36.[62]

A different situation is suggested by Marcion's version of the Lord's Prayer: Here Tertullian implies, but without criticism, that a petition for the coming of the holy spirit replaced that for the sanctification of God's name (*AM* IV. 26.3–4). There is no other textual support for this reading, but in the later textual tradition a similar petition does replace that for the coming of God's kingdom.[63]

All these examples, and others given elsewhere, admit of no single explanation: In many cases it is probable that Marcion was following the text already available to him; on the other hand, it would not be surprising if he did make textual changes or choices, for accidental or conscious changes are a widespread feature of scribal transmission in this period. It is not impossible that some readings original to Marcion subsequently made their way into the wider textual tradition – as was often argued in an older scholarship. Even so, it is easy to be over-confident in reading significance into the particular forms, terms, or silences of the reports by Marcion's opponents, second-guessing what may have been his intention. Such may be the case when, having argued from silence for the omission of Luke 9.23, 25, Kenji Tsutsui ascribes this to the reference to 'the whole world', whose loss would be no pain for a Marcionite, and adds the probable omission of 9.27, again from lack of attestation, on account of Marcion's hostility to the Twelve.[64] Identifying the text Marcion received as well as the deliberate choices or changes made by him will prove difficult if not impossible.

62 So Tsutsui, 'Das Evangelium', 84–5. Harnack concluded that Marcion was following 'a mixed text from Matthew and Luke' (*Marcion*, 193*), but this may be too simple a solution.

63 Here 'Marcion' appears to support P^{45} and B in the absence of a petition for the accomplishment of God's will, whose inclusion is attested by a number of manuscripts including D, which, however, also has a distinctive wording of that for the coming of God's kingdom. On this complex passage see Christian-Bernard Amphoux, 'La revision du "Notre Père" de Luc (11, 2–4), et sa place dans l'histoire du texte', ed. R. Gryson and P.-M. Bogaert, *Recherches sur l'Histoire de la Bible Latine* (Cahiers de la Revue Théologique de Louvain 19; Louvain-la Neuve: Faculté de Théologie, 1987), 105–21, critiqued by Tjitze Baarda, 'De korte tekst van het Onze Vader in Lucas 11:2–4: een Marcionitische corruptie?', *NTT* 44 (1990), 273–87. Joël Delobel, 'The Lord's Prayer in the Textual Tradition: A Critique of Recent Theories and Their Views on Marcion's Role', ed. Jean-Marie Sevrin, *The New Testament in Early Christianity: La reception des écrits neotestamentaires dans le Christianisme primitif* (BETL 86; Leuven: Peeters, 1989), 293–309, gives a useful overview.

64 Tsutsui, 'Das Evangelium', 92–3.

Exemplary of some of the issues to be addressed is Epiphanius' comment on Luke 18.18–19, an incident of undoubted importance in Marcion's interpretation:

> 'Someone said to him, "Good teacher, by doing what shall I inherit eternal life?" He (said), "Do not call me good; one is good, (God)". He [i.e., Marcion] added "the father", and instead of "You know the commandments" he says, "I know the commandments."
>
> (*Pan.* 42.11.17, S50)[65]

The second part of Jesus' reply here, 'one is good', is closer to Matthew 19.17, perhaps reflecting Epiphanius' own remembered text.[66] Tertullian identifies the significance of this response for Marcion, but it is unclear how far he is quoting him, and it is notable that he does not use the term 'father': 'But who is good (*optimus*) except, he says, the one God?'[67] On the other hand, in the *Dialogue of Adamantius* the Marcionite Megethius does support the reading 'Father', 'No-one is good except one, the Father' (*Adam.* 2.18–19 [1.1]).[68]

Secondly, Epiphanius elliptically claims that the purpose of the change from 'You' to 'I know' was so as 'not to point to the commands written beforehand'. On the mouth of Jesus this statement presumably would imply a reference instead to his own teaching, about to be given, but it might make better sense on the mouth of the questioner, who will therefore shortly be corrected; Megethius, in fact, explicitly put the retort on the questioner's lips, but in the second person form, 'You know', although this again produces poor logic (*Adam.* 92.27 [2.17]).[69] By contrast, Tertullian has Jesus pose it as a question, 'Do you know the commandments?', although here too this might have had the intention of avoiding their recitation by Jesus (*AM* IV. 36.4). It is certainly not impossible that Marcion emphasised a particular wording

[65] 'God' is omitted at the initial list of scholia in *Pan* 42.11.6, S50. See further, Lieu, 'Marcion and the Synoptic Problem', 735–39.

[66] At Matt. 19.17 'God' is added by parts of the Latin and Syriac tradition; 'Father' is added here by e and also at Luke 18.19 by d.

[67] Tertullian, *AM* IV. 36.3; because the question ('But who is good?') is not attested in the textual tradition Braun, *Contre Marcion*, IV, 446–7, only identifies 'except one God' as a quotation. Tertullian introduces this saying before recounting the encounter with the questioner, but this is probably in the interests of his own argument rather than following Marcion's order.

[68] At *Adam.* 92.25–32 (2.17) Adamantius cites the passage in the Lukan form, 'No-one is good except one, God'.

[69] 'You know' (*nosti*) is also read by Rufinus' Latin translation; Backhuyzen, *Dialog des Adamantius*, 93, corrects to 'I know', citing Epiphanius; this certainly reads more fluently but it is rejected by Tsutsui, *Auseinandersetzung*. See further Harnack, *Marcion*, 225*–6*.

of this incident, although precision is impossible: Hence Kenji Tsutsui may again go too far in seeing the absence of 'still' (ἔτι) from Luke 18.22 as quoted by Tertullian (*AM* IV. 36.4) and by the *Dialogue of Adamantius* (*Adam.* 92.31 [2.17]), as a deliberate attempt by Marcion to avoid having Jesus give some, if insufficient, value to obedience to the commands.[70]

An additional factor is that this exchange was more widely repeated in the second century, arguably independently of the Synoptic tradition, and particularly in polemical contexts.[71] A number of these accounts, including that by Irenaeus, identify without prejudice the God who is good as 'Father'.[72] Justin gives it with two different forms of Jesus' answer, that in the *Dialogue* as 'one is good, my Father who is in heaven' (*Dial.* 101.2; cf. *Apol.* 16.7). A further expansion is found in a reported reading from the 'Gospel of the Naassenes', 'Why do you call me good; one is good, my father in the heavens, who sends his sun on the righteous and unrighteous and rains on the holy and the sinners' (Ps.Hippolytus, *Ref.* V. 7.26). Strikingly, Tertullian also cites at this point this last clause, which canonically is restricted to Matthew 5.45, as evidence of the single and universal goodness of God, while elsewhere he accuses Marcion of having deleted it (*AM* IV. 17.6; 36.3). At the very least, Jesus' emphatic identification of the only one who is good as his heavenly father, was widespread in the tradition, and may even have strong support as one of the earliest recoverable forms of the exchange.[73] Undoubtedly, traditions of Jesus' words circulated in the second century in forms that did not eventually survive in the witnesses to the canonical text.[74] At the same time, there were what, from a later standpoint, look like harmonising tendencies of and between the written texts.

Thus, both at the macro- and at the micro-level any solution to the origins of Marcion's 'Gospel' – or indeed of all Gospel relationships – that

[70] Tsutsui, 'Das Evangelium', 116.

[71] See Markschies, *Valentinus Gnosticus*, 55–64.

[72] Irenaeus, *AH* I. 20.2; Ps.Clem. *Hom* XVIII. 3.4; Tatian [Ephraem, *Comm.Diat.* 15.9]; cf. William L. Petersen, 'What Text Can New Testament Textual Criticism Ultimately Reach', ed. Barbara Aland and Joël Delobel, *New Testament Textual Criticism, Exegesis and Church History: A Discussion of Methods* (CBET 7; Kampen: Kok, 1994), 136–51, 141–4; A. J. Bellinzoni, *The Saying of Jesus in the Writings of Justin Martyr* (NovTSup. 17; Leiden: Brill, 1967), 17–20.

[73] So Petersen, 'What Text?', 141–4, who argues that this version would have been suppressed because of its subordinationist nature. These witnesses, like those to Marcion's text, mostly agree also in ignoring the identification of the one posing the question as 'a ruler'.

[74] See Gilles Quispel, 'Review of *Tertullien contre Marcion, Tome IV* by René Braun; Claudio Moreschini', *VC* 56 (2002), 202–7, who argues that the reading 'have the key of knowledge' at Luke 11. 52, implied by Tertullian (*AM* IV. 27. 9; 28. 2), and also witnessed by Justin, *Dial.* 17.4, goes back to Jewish-Christian traditions that were less critical of the Jewish teachers.

presupposes relatively fixed and stable written texts, edited through a careful process of comparison, excision, or addition, and reorganisation, seems doomed to become mired in a tangle of lines of direct or indirect dependency, which are increasingly difficult to envisage in practice. Marcion's 'Gospel' is to be located in the midst of these multiple trends.

At the end of these investigations it remains certain that the Gospel that Marcion used as his core text followed the same structure and sequence of textual units as canonical Luke, but that it may have lacked some of the passages and verses now part of the latter. In what follows, as conventionally, it will be cited by the canonical chapter and verse. On the one hand, Marcion did edit the version of the written Gospel that he received, although arguably not to such an extent as his opponents believed, and as might appear from a comparison between a reconstruction of his 'Gospel' and canonical Luke. A consequence, but one that cannot be further tested here, must be that canonical Luke is itself the result of redactional development subsequent to the form known by Marcion, both on the level of textual variants and probably also of more extensive passages; however, that any such development was specifically directed against Marcion, although a matter for investigation, would be difficult to demonstrate. Indeed, if there is any substance to the claims that Basilides not only commented on Luke but also sought to produce his own 'Gospel', any reconstruction would needs be much more nuanced.[75] Yet Marcion's 'Gospel' also has to be set against a wider backcloth of the transmission of Jesus traditions in the second century, both orally and in written form. Finally, despite the uncertainties in any reconstruction, analysis must consider both contents and textual detail.

TEXT AND INTERPRETATION

Particularly once Marcion's own editorial work is minimised, it becomes evident that his 'Gospel' is in many ways neutral: It can only have served to inspire and support his system to the extent that he interpreted it; his opponents are able to cite it to their own advantage because they largely ignore such interpretation. Precisely how Marcion presented his text and expressed its interpretation remains an enigma. Clearly his 'Antitheses' were crucial, particularly if Tertullian's description of these as '*in summo instrumento*' indicates their position as an introduction to the 'Gospel'

[75] See Löhr, *Basilides*, 30–4; James A. Kelhoffer, 'Basilides's Gospel and *Exegetica* (*Treatises*)', *VC* 59 (2005), 115–34.

(*AM* I. 19.4).[76] However, while the 'Antitheses' may have indicated general principles, and even some examples, it is unlikely that they were the only source of Marcion's interpretation, particularly if, as seems to be the case, the 'Gospel' circulated without them, on its own or only with the 'Apostolikon'. Although much of the evidence for Marcion's text from the *Dialogue of Adamantius* comes in the section where the Marcionite Megethius is presenting a series of oppositions between Jesus and the Demiurge, arguably a form of the 'Antitheses', these do not follow the sequential order of the Gospel and are unlikely to come from it.[77]

Tertullian decided to counteract the 'Antitheses' not as a separate exercise but in the course of his discussion of the 'Gospel' (*AM* IV. 1.2), and he did this through a series of references to contrasts that Marcion had made, such as those between Jesus' healing of lepers and Elisha's healing of Naaman, between Jesus' love of children and Elisha's revengeful distaste, and between the instructions to the Seventy and those to Israel in the wilderness.[78] This procedure obscures whether it was Tertullian who made the connections between these oppositions and his sequential reading of the Gospel, or whether he was following some form of textual markers. On rare occasions it is possible that Marcion introduced or heightened an antithetical interpretation in his text itself: Arguably he transferred or repeated the reference to Elisha's healing of Naaman in Luke 4.27 as a comment by Jesus on the healing of the Ten Lepers (Luke 17.12–18); as already noted, he may have incorporated a reference to Exodus 21.21 at Luke 6.27–8.[79] If indeed Marcion did highlight Jesus' refusal to reign down fire on the unwelcoming Samaritan village, 'as did the Creator on that false prophet at Elijah's request', that contrast may already have been made in the text he inherited, for the words 'as did Elijah' are added to the disciples' request in a wide range of manuscripts (Luke 9.53–6; cf. 2 Kings 1.10).[80]

Tertullian does also refer to Marcionite interpretations of the text: 'You (sing.) say (*inquis*)' that Jesus' condemnation of the murder of the

[76] See Braun's note, *Contre Marcion*, I, 305–7, and below, pp. 273–6.

[77] *Adam.* 20.27–40.11 [1.10–1.20]; see Tsutsui, *Auseinandersetzung*, 148–52.

[78] *AM* IV. 9.6 (Luke 5.12–14; 2 Kings 5.9–19); 23.4; 35.6 (Luke 9.46–8; 17.11–19; 2 Kings 2.23–4); 24.2 (Luke 10.1–4; Exod. 12.34–6); see below, pp. 278–81.

[79] Tertullian, *AM* IV. 35.6; Epiphanius, *Pan.* 42.11.17, S48; on Luke 6.27–8 see above, p. 205.

[80] It is unclear whether the words are Marcion's or Tertullian's (*AM* IV. 23.7). They are read at Luke 9.54 by A C D and several others. Harnack, *Marcion*, 204*, and Braun, *Contre Marcion*, IV, 298–9, accept the reading as Marcion's although the latter denies that it constituted one of the 'Antitheses' and even suggests that Tertullian may have commented on the contrast because it was also in his text; Tsutsui, 'Das Evangelium', 94, and Delobel, 'Extra-Canonical Sayings', 112–16, are more cautious.

prophets did not indicate his support of them so much as his demonstration of the Jews' utter wickedness, 'because they did not even behave piously towards their own prophets'; Jesus commanded Peter to silence 'because he did not understand aright and so (Jesus) did not wish a lie to be spread around' (*AM* IV. 15.2 [Luke 6.23]; 21.7 [Luke 9.20–1]). Whether such interpretations are genuine or are invented by Tertullian as a step in the development of his own argument is difficult to determine; some may seem more probable than others. For example, Tertullian spends much effort in undermining the idea that 'Mammon' (Luke 16.1–13) might represent the Creator, not least because 'Mammon of injustice' (Luke 16.9) contradicts Marcion's 'just' Creator, but that Marcion ever made this identification is never actually stated, and it is perhaps entirely Tertullian's own invention (*AM* IV. 33.1–2). On the other hand, Tertullian and the *Dialogue of Adamantius* are agreed that in Marcionite interpretation both the rich man and Lazarus, along with Abraham, were located in Hades, albeit separated by a deep ditch: Hades was the Creator's place of reward and punishment for those who followed the Law and prophets (Luke 16.19–31; *AM* IV. 34.11–14; *Adam.* 76.14–80.6 [2.10–11]). This evidently had significant consequences for Marcion's overall scheme, as does its refutation for Tertullian and the *Dialogue*, although each offers a different explanation.[81] Since Tertullian denies that the parable establishes a 'distance between divinities', it is possible that Marcion's interpretation came from the 'Antitheses', but it is perhaps more likely that it was a separate proof-text for his teaching (*AM* IV. 34.17). However, it seems improbable that the 'Antitheses' would have included alternative explanations, such as those of Jesus' 'Woe' (Luke 6.24): Tertullian indicates that some interpreted them as 'admonition, not cursing', others as an expression of the fate of the rich at the Creator's hands (*AM* IV. 15.3–4). At other key moments Tertullian confesses himself bewildered as to how Marcion may have understood verses such as Luke 24.38–9, which would surely have demanded some explanation (*AM* IV. 43.6–8). This may be a diplomatic silence – it was not his intention to allow Marcion his own voice or to engage in detailed exegetical debate, but only to use Marcion's 'Gospel' to undermine Marcion's teaching as he himself had already represented it. Yet, on many such occasions his puzzlement may be genuine. Marcion's opponents do not describe him as writing other works about the scriptural text, although they readily refer to the literary endeavours of other 'heretics'.

[81] Tertullian takes 'Abraham's bosom' as an interim place, while for Adamantius it indicates heaven. Epiphanius refers to the parable but not to any Marcionite interpretation (*Pan.* 42.11.17, SR44–46).

Presumably Marcion's followers were taught his interpretation of their texts orally, as too were those of Tertullian's church; perhaps marginal notes were added to the text of the 'Gospel', although, if so, more awareness of these by his opponents might have been expected. Even then, quite how that tradition of interpretation was established and transmitted remains a further gap in our knowledge.

Despite all these uncertainties there are a number of points of entry into Marcion's 'Gospel' and its interpretation, from the shared perspectives of his opponents, from known key texts in the debate, or from places where the text intersects with core aspects of his teaching. It is among these that both his opponents' frustrations and even echoes of his voice are most easily overheard.

Title

Tertullian contrasts the Church's Gospels, whose names bespeak their authority 'from apostles [or] apostolic men', with that of Marcion which bore no authorial title; mere anonymity, he mocks, is itself a sign of shame. In principle this would be enough to establish its illegitimacy, but he takes upon himself first to identify it with Luke, and then to use that identification against Marcion's claims for it (*AM* IV. 2–3). Although he assumes that Marcion would consider the Church's 'Luke' 'falsified as to title also', there is nothing to suggest that Marcion himself in fact knew his core Gospel by that name, still less that he deleted any title. This in itself gives credence to the suggestion that this was the only Gospel Marcion knew: Titles may only have become normative once more than one circulated together.[82] Tertullian does also claim that Marcion appealed to Galatians 1.7; 2.4, 'in order to demolish the status of Gospels of those works which belong to and are published under the name of apostles or apostolic men'; this apparently insinuates that Marcion treated Luke on the same terms as he did Matthew, John, and Mark, but it reflects an estimation of all four that postdates Marcion since it makes the false assumption that he knew all four when 'making his choice'. It is Tertullian who concludes that the Gospel 'falsified according to Marcion by the proponents of Judaism' was identifiably that of Luke; undoubtedly Marcion's reading of Paul did presuppose a narrative of the corruption of Jesus' Gospel in part through the misunderstanding of the original disciples and in part through deliberate 'infection', but it is less certain that he tied

[82] See Silke Petersen, 'Die Evangelienüberschriften und die Enstehung des neutestamentlichen Kanons', *ZNW* 97 (2006), 250–74.

this 'corruption' quite so specifically to the minutiae of the written text of Luke. In any case, the tradition of the authorship of the third Gospel by a disciple of Paul does not seem to have played any role in Marcion's choice, and he was probably unaware of it. Equally, he evidently did not supply his 'Gospel' with an authorial title, neither 'of Marcion', nor 'of Paul', nor 'of Christ', despite the later claim by Megethius that Christ wrote the Gospel, with a supplement by Paul.[83] Whether it bore any other label, perhaps simply 'the Gospel', cannot be known.

Beginning

Epiphanius' charge that Marcion truncated not only the beginning but also much of the end and of the middle, is presumably designed to indicate that he left nothing untouched (*Pan.* 42.9.2). Nonetheless, it is with the beginning of the 'Gospel' that any discussion should start, for in the canonical Gospels also this determines the nature of Jesus' earthly ministry and its relation to God's self-manifestation.

Whether or not as the result of a deliberate act of excision, Marcion's 'Gospel' did not begin with Jesus' birth. Already Irenaeus accuses Marcion of have excluding anything to do with the 'generation' or 'birth of Christ (*generatione Christi*)', although it is possible that this refers more specifically to the genealogy that establishes Jesus' royal Jewish ancestry than to the full birth narratives (*AH* I. 27.2).[84] Even Tertullian in his response does little more than acknowledge that the birth narratives belong to 'our Gospel', and he discusses Marcion's treatment of Jesus' family in other settings: It is Jesus' 'tribe, people, and home', certified by the census, of which 'the Roman archives keep a most faithful testimony', that Tertullian defends (*AM* IV. 7.7, 11; 19.10; cf. *De Carne* 2.3). Certainly, Tertullian relishes Marcion's distaste for the birth process, particularly as applied to Jesus, but it is unlikely that the latter expressed this in any justifying commentary on the opening of his 'Gospel'.[85]

83 See above, p. 120.

84 W. Wigan Harvey, ed., *Sancti Irenaei Episcopi Lugdunensis Libros quinque adversus Haereses* (2 vols.; Cambridge, 1857), 1, 216, n.3. Theodoret, *Haer. Compend.* (*PG* 83, 372) only refers to Marcion's excision of the genealogy and most of that which established Jesus as born of the seed of David; similarly, he had accused Tatian of omitting the genealogies, although this seems improbable (see David Pastorelli, 'The Genealogies of Jesus in Tatian's *Diatessaron*. The Question of their Absence or Presence', ed. Claire Clivaz, Andreas Dettwiler, Luc Devillers, Enrico Norelli, with the assistance of Benjamin Bertho, *Infancy Gospels: Stories and Identities* [WUNT 281; Tübingen: Mohr Siebeck, 2011] 216–30).

85 See herein, pp. 82–3.

Instead Marcion's Christ was a 'sudden Christ', appearing without preliminaries 'in the fifteenth year of Tiberius Caesar' at Capernaum. From the agreement of several witnesses it is apparent that Marcion's 'Gospel' combined Luke 3.1 and 4.31, and that Marcion interpreted the verb 'descended' (κατῆλθεν) in the latter, whether or not through explicit textual emendation or annotation, as 'from heaven', further glossing it as 'appeared' (*AM* IV. 7.1–2).[86] Tertullian repeatedly mocks the long gap that Marcion thus acknowledges between his own time and the appearance of 'his' Christ, but such precise correlation of Jesus' life with the Empire was widespread. Comparison with canonical Luke emphasises the absence in Marcion's 'Gospel' of Jewish (or Judean) elements in the chronology and the connection made there with John the Baptist's activity, but Marcion can only be charged with omitting these if he knew them.

It may be that Marcion's 'Gospel' then followed the brief reference to Jesus' preaching at Capernaum (Luke 4.31–2) with the fuller, albeit abbreviated, story at Nazareth (4.16–30), postponing the healing of the demoniac (4.33–7).[87] Since Tertullian mocks Marcion for retaining Capernaum and Nazareth, and as there is possible evidence that later Marcionites emended these, Marcion himself presumably set limited store by any incoherence in the geographical locations. There is some attraction in Harnack's view that Marcion followed the text represented by D and the Old Latin (it) in omitting the description of Nazareth as 'where he was brought up' (4.16), although there is only Tertullian's silence, and the possibility that Marcion omitted the identification of Jesus as 'of Nazareth' at Luke 18.37, to support this.[88]

This sequence would reinforce that Jesus' initial activity was preaching, although in Tertullian's account there is no indication of what the content of that preaching was, merely that in his own view it was nothing new and that Jesus was cast out just for one proverb, usually identified as Luke 4.23, 'Doctor, heal yourself'.[89] It is unlikely that in Marcion's 'Gospel' this retort was provoked by any identification of Jesus as the son of Joseph (Luke 4.22b): Tertullian rarely misses an opportunity to assert that Jesus'

86 See below, pp. 371–2.

87 So Braun, *Contre Marcion*, IV, 103; although Tertullian treats Luke 4.33–7 immediately after 31–2 he does say he has 'anticipated this setting' (*AM* IV. 7.13).

88 It is omitted from Luke 18.37 at *Adam.* 200.25 (5.14). Less certain is Luke 4.34: Tertullian's explanation of the term '*Nazaraeus*' at *AM* IV. 8.1 may refer to this verse (although both the Greek and Latin have 'Nazarene') or to the sermon at Nazareth, which immediately follows in his discussion.

89 *AM* IV. 8.2.

peers must have known of his origins, and he has just had to make the rather less convincing claim that Jesus would not have been allowed in their synagogue if the records of the census did not confirm what they knew of his genealogy (*AM* IV. 7.7). In his defence of the incarnation Tertullian explicitly claims that 'the heresies have taken away from the Gospel' statements where Jesus' hearers identify his family (*De Carne* 7); yet, as 'the heresies' indicates, Marcion was not alone in such 'omissions', and therefore not necessarily directly responsible for them in his Gospel text. An alternative would be that 'proverb' referred to Jesus' riposte that a prophet has no honour in their own country (Luke 4.24), although it is difficult to see what Marcion would have made of this. Although commentators often assume that Marcion's Jesus, implicitly or explicitly, preached about 'another God', this may be over-interpreting Tertullian's routine argument that the admiring response of the people demonstrated that Jesus did *not* speak against the Law and the prophets. Tertullian also neither comments on whether Marcion's 'Gospel' contained the Isaianic quotation nor does he refer to the possible displacement of Luke 4.27 to the story of the Ten Lepers; instead he is more interested in countering any docetic interpretation of Jesus' escape.

He does, however, pay particular attention to the healing of the demoniac and to the latter's recognition of Jesus as Son of God (Luke 4.33–7). For Tertullian this can only refer to the Creator God since on Marcion's own account the demons could have no knowledge of any other deity. Yet he anticipates that Marcion will in turn emphasise Jesus' rebuke to them and his command to silence (*AM* IV. 7.8–11; cf. IV. 8.5–8). This version of what might be called 'the messianic secret' becomes a repeated theme: Are the demons right or wrong? Why does Jesus respond as he does to Peter's confession?[90] Is there a correct way to understand Jesus, but also a way which appears correct but is in fact not so? Does Jesus, or does he not, match prior expectations?

The passage as a whole well illustrates the difficulties in reconstructing Marcion's source Gospel as well as that which he produced, and even that with which Tertullian was familiar, together with Marcion's method of interpreting the text. The extent of reconfiguration of the text compared with canonical Luke is notable, and has few parallels elsewhere in Marcion's supposed redactional activity. This gives some weight to the argument that his source Gospel was markedly different in its opening from the canonical

[90] On this see *AM* IV. 21.6–8 and Norelli, 'Marcion et les disciples', 23–5.

Gospel, even allowing for uncertainty regarding the infancy narratives and genealogy. It need not necessarily follow from this that the opening chapters of canonical Luke, including the programmatic shape and contents of the sermon at Nazareth, were composed specifically against Marcion. Rather, the openings of the Gospels in particular may have been prone to textual instability and development. It is striking that Epiphanius similarly accuses the Ebionites of corrupting and mutilating what he identifies as the Gospel of Matthew, including the excision of birth narratives and genealogy; in his account their Gospel opened, 'It came to pass in the days of Herod, King of Judea, in the high-priesthood of Caiaphas, a certain man, John by name…', an odd correlation but one that might have some relation to Luke 3.1–2 (*Pan.* 30.13.6; 14.3).[91]

Death and resurrection

Even more elusive than its beginning is the ending of Marcion's 'Gospel' and Marcion's interpretation of it. By this stage Tertullian is becoming increasingly summary, spending fewer than 150 lines in Braun's edition on Luke 23–4 compared with 570 lines on Luke 4–5.[92] Given the importance of Jesus' death and resurrection in the debate this may seem surprising, although Tertullian had already addressed his main concern in Book III, namely establishing the fulfilment of prophecy in Jesus' crucifixion, something that he claims was denied by Marcion (*AM* III. 18–19, especially 18.1; 19.6). By contrast, ten of Epiphanius' scholia cover the last two chapters of the Gospel, but just two, with an additional comment on its opening, address Luke 4–5 (Epiphanius, *Pan.* 42.11.17, SR1–2, 69–78).

As already noted, Tertullian and Epiphanius give apparently contradictory reports about Marcion's account of the crucifixion. Whereas Tertullian identifies only the absence of the division of Jesus' garments (Luke 23.34b; *AM* IV. 42.4), Epiphanius includes that verse and charges Marcion with the excision only of Jesus' promise to the thief (Luke 23.43; *Pan.* 42.11.17, S72). Both sentences could pose difficulties for Marcion, but, equally, either could have been already absent without disrupting the stylistic and narrative flow.[93] On the other hand, nothing in Tertullian further contradicts the

[91] Herod, King of Judea, was long dead by the time of Caiaphas and of John the Baptist's ministry, but this could be a not unusual elision of that Herod with the tetrarch of Galilee, Antipas, whom Luke 3.2 identifies only as 'Herod'.

[92] Braun, *Contre Marcion*, IV, 92–152, 510–28.

[93] The two halves of v. 34 do not flow naturally although this might be explained either by 34a being an interpolation (see below), or by 34b being a subsequent addition influenced by the

possibility that Epiphanius' highly abbreviated summary of the crucifixion, division of garments, and darkening of the sun catalogues all that was included in his copy of Marcion's crucifixion narrative (*Pan.* 42. 11.17, S71: Luke 23.33a, 34b, 44).[94] This would entail the absence in addition not only of Jesus' prayer for forgiveness, which is textually uncertain, but also of the mockery of Jesus by the rulers (or in D by the people) and soldiers, and of the superscription, as well as all of the distinctively Lukan narrative of the two thieves (Luke 23.34a, 35–43). Arguably, Marcion may have felt uncomfortable with any suggestion that Jesus was crucified as 'King of the Jews' or as the Jewish Messiah; on Tertullian's account Pilate had asked him whether he was the Christ, not whether he was King of the Jews, while according to Epiphanius Marcion replaced the charge against Jesus of 'saying he was Christ a King', with 'and destroying the Law and prophets' (Luke 23.2–3); similarly, Epiphanius had already claimed that Marcion omitted the detailed passion prediction at Luke 18.31–3, which includes the mockery and abuse.[95]

The effect of such omissions would be for the crucifixion to be marked primarily by the dramatic darkness; for Tertullian this makes no sense – surely creation should rejoice at the death of the opponent of the Creator – but Marcion could no doubt offer a more congenial interpretation, perhaps that it was a sign of the defeat of the Creator's powers. Unlike Epiphanius, Tertullian also refers to the splitting of the Temple veil, caused, he says, by the violent exit of the angel deserting 'the daughter of Zion' (*AM* IV. 42.5). It is uncertain whether this represents his own interpretation or something that was in the text before him; such a tradition is found in a variety of forms in the second and third century, in some cases signifying the departure of God's presence or spirit from the Temple.[96] This takes a distinctive form in

parallels in Matthew and Mark, or both. In the *Gospel of Peter* one thief rebukes those who revile Jesus, but Jesus himself says nothing.

94 See above, pp. 197–8, and Judith M. Lieu, 'Marcion and the New Testament', ed. Andrew B. McGowan and Kent Harold Richards, *Method and Meaning. Essays on New Testament Interpretation in Honor of Harold W. Attridge* (SBL Resources for Biblical Study 67; Atlanta, GA: SBL, 2011), 399–416, 411–15; the form 'the sun was darkened' is widely attested.

95 Tertullian, *AM* IV. 42.1; Epiphanius, *Pan.* 42.11.17, S52, 69; Tertullian makes no reference to the whole of Luke 18.23–34. Less certain is Marcion's 'Gospel at Luke 24.7', which both Tertullian and Epiphanius cite without the words 'to the hands of sinful people', an omission that has some support from the old Latin. See further below, p. 219.

96 See Tertullian, *AJ* 13.5; Melito, *Peri Pascha* §98 l. 727, 'the people did not tear their clothes, the angel tore his'; *Test.Benj.* 9.4, and the discussion by W. Harm Hollander and Marinus de Jonge, ed., *The Testaments of the Twelve Patriarchs: A Commentary* (SVTP 8; Leiden: Brill, 1985), 79–81. Ephraem, *Comm. in Diat.* 21.4, gives as an interpretation of the torn veil that the Spirit had gone forth from it.

Eznik of Kolb's account of Marcion, where the Creator darkens the sun and tears 'his robe and the curtain of his Temple' in anger at the trick played on him (*De Deo* 358).[97] It seems likely that there is a link between these traditions, but whether it was an exegetical one, or was reflected in Marcion's text or glosses is impossible to judge.

Finally, neither Tertullian nor Epiphanius cite the words of the cry of Jesus from the cross (Luke 23.46), even though the former does acknowledge that Jesus fulfilled Psalm 31; instead both of them focus their attention on the statement that he 'expired' or 'ex-spirited' (ἐξέπνευσεν), and they use this against Marcion's supposed docetism.[98]

Thus, Tertullian's and Epiphanius' silences may point to a truncated crucifixion account that would be congenial to Marcion's position. Yet even if this were the account to be found in Marcion's 'Gospel', it need not follow that it was entirely the result of his own intentional editorial activity. The Lukan Passion narrative is distinctive both because of the degree of independent source traditions incorporated and/or of editorial reworking compared with Matthew and Mark, and also because of the number of textual variations in the manuscript tradition effecting both wording and details of the narrative. From a textual perspective it has been claimed that there is 'incontrovertible evidence that the text of these chapters was not fixed, and indeed continued to grow for centuries after its composition';[99] once again, this is the setting within which Marcion is to be located.

The situation appears to be rather different with the burial and resurrection narratives. Tertullian and Epiphanius both attest that Marcion's 'Gospel' had accounts of the burial by Joseph, the visit of the women and the appearance of shining figures, the encounter of the two disciples with Jesus on the road to Emmaus, and the final appearance of Jesus to the disciples, although evidence for the details of these narratives is largely lacking; silence may, however, suggest the absence of the visit of Peter to the tomb, a verse also missing in D it (Luke 24.12).[100] As already noted, it is highly likely that according to Marcion Jesus recalled Cleopas and his companion to his own earlier words rather than to those of the prophets

[97] For Eznik's account see above, p. 177.

[98] Jesus' words are cited by *Adam.* 198.8–12 (5.12), but this part of the *Dialogue* has less claim to be following the Marcionite 'Gospel'.

[99] David C. Parker, *The Living Text of the Gospels* (Cambridge: Cambridge University Press, 1997), 172; Parker also notes that Marcion's activity 'had an unsettling influence on the text' (p. 148).

[100] Tertullian, *AM* IV. 43: Tertullian identifies the 'shining figures' as angels (ctr. Luke 24.4) but this may be his own paraphrase; Epiphanius, *Pan.* 42.11.17, S72–8.

(Luke 24.25).[101] The first person 'I spoke', attested by Epiphanius and by the *Dialogue of Adamantius*, effectively means that Jesus has already 'blown his cover', which, as the former points out, renders void the need of the breaking of the bread – retained in Marcion's 'Gospel' – to prompt their recognition of him. In this form, the reading is paralleled by the first person in Luke 24.44, while Tertullian's third person singular matches the words addressed to the women, 'Remember what he spoke to you' (Luke 24.7), something to which Tertullian himself draws attention with approval.[102] These parallels could explain the origin of Marcion's reading of the first person at 24.25, or indeed could support its authenticity; on the other hand, as a deliberate change it would both remove any reference to prophecy and would also reinforce Jesus' self-revelation by his word. In addition it would sustain the pervasive theme of the disciples' persistent failure to understand Jesus' teaching.

A more striking conundrum is represented by Jesus' response to the fear of his disciples at his sudden appearance (Luke 24.37–40). Tertullian and Epiphanius agree that Jesus reassured them, '... see my hands and feet, (that it is I myself [Tertullian only]) because a spirit does not have bones, as you see me have'.[103] Both are perplexed by Marcion's failure to delete these words, which to them provide the most effective refutation of his explicit 'docetism'. Surprisingly, neither remarks on the absence, also attested by the *Dialogue of Adamantius*, of the Lukan Jesus' invitation to them to 'touch and see', or on the simple 'bones' against the 'flesh and bones' of the Lukan manuscript tradition.[104] Although in the *On the Flesh of Christ* Tertullian claims ignorance as to how Marcion interpreted this response, here he

101 Tertullian, *AM* IV. 43 4–5; Epiphanius, *Pan.* 42.11.17, S77; so also *Adam.* 198.6 (5.12); see above, p. 199. In contrast to the *Dialogue of Adamantius*, Tertullian makes no reference to the words that follow (Luke 24.26), 'must not the Christ suffer...?', while it is unclear whether Epiphanius charges Marcion with any further omission. This implies the absence of v. 27 and perhaps of v. 26 also.

102 The parallelism is reinforced by Tertullian's translation at both points '*quae*'; it seems likely that Marcion's 'Gospel' read 'ὅσα' at 24. 7 with D it, rather than 'ὡς' ('how'). Tsutsui, 'Das Evangelium', 128–9, follows Harnack, *Marcion*, 238*–9* in taking the first person singular reading as a later Marcionite modification of the third-person singular.

103 Tertullian, *AM* IV. 43.6: '*Quid turbati estis? Et quid cogitationes subeunt in corda vestra? Videte manus meas et pedes, quia ipse ego [ego ipse] sum, quoniam spiritus ossa non habet, sicut me habentem videtis [videtis habere]*'; cf. *De Carne* 5.53–4; Epiphanius, *Pan.* 42.11.17, S78: τί τεταραγμένοι ἐστέ; ἴδετε τὰς χεῖράς [μου] καὶ τοὺς πόδας [μου], ὅτι πνεῦμα ὀστᾶ οὐκ ἔχει, καθὼς ἐμὲ θεωρεῖτε ἔχοντα.

104 *Adam.* 198.18–21 (5.12) does read 'flesh (pl.) and bones', while Epiphanius concludes his refutation to the scholion (n. 103), 'The Saviour was clearly teaching that even after the resurrection he had bones and flesh, as he himself witnessed, "as you see (ὁρᾶτε) me having"'.

proposes that Marcion twisted the syntax so as to imply a positive comparison between a 'boneless' spirit and Jesus: 'A spirit does not have bones, which is how you see me having', that is, 'not having'. Undoubtedly, the differences between Marcion's and Tertullian's interpretation of key texts were sometimes based on different grammatical analyses, yet the latter's proposal here is remarkably tortuous – as he himself admits in a characteristic neologism (*tortuositas*). It may be doubted whether he had such a Marcionite interpretation before him, although that does not answer what guidance readers might have had in order to make sense of such an oblique statement.

Tertullian's focus on grammar may have been misplaced. It is notable that he describes the disciples as initially believing that they were seeing 'a phantasm' (Luke 24.37: *phantasma*); presumably this, rather than 'spirit', was the word read by Marcion, as it also is by Codex Bezae.[105] It is also the term that Tertullian consistently uses to describe Marcion's Christ. This may suggest that Marcion saw some significance in the difference between 'phantasm' in v. 37 and 'spirit' in v. 39, and perhaps also that he was more comfortable with such a being having 'bones' than having 'flesh' – whose absence, as noted, goes unremarked by his opponents.[106]

Again, such niceties may not have been entirely due to Marcion's creative reading of the Lukan tradition. Indeed, although 'flesh' is well attested in Luke 24.39, the textual variants there of the formula may suggest that scribes felt the need to clarify the relationship between the two. In addition, there is considerable evidence that this saying was also transmitted outside the Lukan tradition in various forms. In confirmation of his own conviction that Jesus was 'in flesh' (ἐν σαρκί or σαρκικός) after the resurrection Ignatius reports a tradition wherein Jesus 'came to Peter and his companions and said to them, "Take, touch me and see, that I am not a bodiless demon (δαιμόνιον ἀσώματον)"' (Ignatius, *Smyrn.* 3.1–2). A similar tradition occurs more widely, although its origin and transmission have been extensively debated; Origen associates it with 'the teaching of Peter' and Jerome with the 'Gospel of the Hebrews' or with another Jewish Gospel.[107] Some connection with the Lukan narrative seems probable, not least because Ignatius

105 In support is '*phantasia*' in the *Dialogue of Adamantius*, 'δοκοῦσιν αὐτὸν φαντασίαν εἶναι', although this is not attested in the Lukan manuscript tradition.

106 Surprisingly Ephraem quotes against Bardaisan's docetism, 'A spirit has no bones' (*PR* 2. 147,1–2; see Mitchell, *Prose Refutations*, 2, clvii, who describes it as 'an allusion merely, and in 7-syllable metre'.

107 See Origen, *De Princip.* I, praef. 8., '*non sum daemonium incorporeum*', although Origen goes on to distinguish ἀσωμάτος from the philosophical notion of '*incorporea natura*'.

continues with a statement that 'after the resurrection he ate and drank with them' (cf. Luke 24.41–3), although a literary relationship seems unlikely and an explicit challenge to a Marcionite position even less so.[108] Indeed, Ignatius' own somewhat ambiguous continuation that the disciples 'touched him and believed, being mingled with his flesh and spirit', and that while 'fleshly he was nonetheless spiritually united to the father' (*Smyrn.* 3. 2–3), indicate something of the flexibility that 'fleshly' or 'not bodiless' might encompass. Evidently, Marcion's understanding of Jesus' physical substance was far from as straightforward as his opponents suggest; indeed, he may well have seen in this incident a crucial evidence for that understanding, as shall be seen when it is further explored.[109]

It is likely that Marcion's 'Gospel' ended, as does Tertullian's account, with Jesus 'sending the disciples to the nations of the world' (Luke 24.47; *AM* IV. 43.9), avoiding any reference to his departure and to the disciples' return to Jerusalem. Once again, it is difficult to determine whether Marcion would have been producing a new text here, or whether this ending too might reflect the fluidity of the textual traditions in the second century. Endings are particularly susceptible to such fluidity, as evidenced by both Mark and John, and both the composition of Acts and its separation from the 'first volume' (Acts 1.1) may have had some impact. As so often, it is difficult to distinguish Marcionite exploitation of a distinctive text, his conscious editing of it, and his deliberate interpretive emphasis, however conveyed.

Jesus

As the account of Jesus' resurrection appearance to his disciples indicates, Marcion's opponents exploit every possible opportunity to demonstrate that his 'Gospel' contradicts his own interpretation of who Jesus was, at least as they

Petersen, 'What Text?' even suggests that 'bodiless demon' may represent the earliest recoverable form of the Lukan text, although he appears to imply that φάντασμα is read by D d in verse 39, as part of Jesus' reply, helping provide the crucial connection. See also Michael Wade Martin, 'Defending the Western Non-Interpolations: The case for an antiseparationist *Tendenz* in the longer Alexandrian Readings', *JBL* 124 (2005), 269–94, who argues that Luke 24 was the centre of Chrisological debates in the second century. See below, p. 378.

108 See further the discussion by Gregory, *Reception of Luke and Acts*, 70–5. See also Markus Vinzent, '"Ich bin kein körperloses Geistwesen": Zum Verhältnis von κήρυγμα Πέτρου, "Doctrina Petri", διδασκαλία Πέτρου und IgnSm 3', in Reinhold M. Hübner, *Der Paradox Eine: Antignostischer Monarchianismus in zweiten Jahrhundert* (mit einem Beitrag von Markus Vinzent; VCSup. 50: Leiden: Brill, 1999), 241–86, 257–73; see further below, p. 376.

109 See pp. 376–80.

understand it: for example, repeatedly they point to occasions when he touched and was touched by others.[110] However, as the previous discussion has shown, they may have misunderstood the nuances of his Christology, which in any case was probably formulated independently of the Gospel, whose narrative details may have occupied his attention less than they expected. This makes it particularly hazardous to make assumptions about what Marcion must have omitted where the only evidence is silence. A prime example is the appearance of the angel ministering to Jesus' agonised sweat of blood at the Mount of Olives (Luke 22.43–4). Epiphanius cites only Luke 22.41 and 22.47, in both cases arguing that one who could fall on his knees and be kissed could hardly be a phantasm (*Pan.* 42.11.17, SR45, 46); certainly one might have expected Jesus' bloody sweat, if attested, to offer a more telling proof, but Epiphanius regularly passes over the obvious to draw on apparently more recondite evidences. For his part, Tertullian is so summary at this point, and concerned only to address Jesus' foreknowledge of his betrayer, that little can be concluded of what he read between Luke 22.22 and 22.48 (*AM* IV. 41.1–2). This has not prevented interpreters from assuming that Marcion omitted the incident – which was known already in some form by his contemporary Justin (*Dial.* 103.8) – and that he perhaps even influenced the Alexandrian text where the omission is widely attested.[111] The variant is yet another example of the instability of the final chapters of Luke, within which Marcion's own readings must be located, and a firm decision in the face of silence is not possible: Marcion's 'Gospel' undoubtedly did contain passages that might seem to contradict the standard representation of his views.

In some similar cases, Tertullian suggests that Marcion interpreted words or actions of Jesus that were potentially inimical to his own understanding as being conciliatory or permissive, to make allowances for people's expectations or from an unwillingness to cause too much confusion: Jesus instructs the leper to make the due offering at the Temple out of kindness and leniency, not out of any support of the Law; it is out of patience that he does not correct the blind beggar's error in hailing him as 'Son of David' (Luke 5.14; 18.38; Tertullian, *AM* IV. 9.10–15; 36.9–10). Although elsewhere Tertullian himself concedes that God of necessity must accommodate divine revelation to the human capacity to receive it, he responds to these excuses with derision.

[110] Tertullian, *AM* IV. 9.5; 18.9; 20.13–14; Epiphanius, *Pan.* 42.11.17, S10, 14.

[111] So Harnack, *Marcion*, 234*; Christian-Bernard Amphoux, 'Les Premières Éditions de Luc. II. L'Histoire de Texte au IIe Siècle', *EThL* 68 (1992), 38–48, 39; see Claire Clivaz, 'The Angel and the Sweat like "Drops of Blood" (Luke 22:43–44): P69 and f13', *HTR* 98 (2005), 419–40, who suggests that P^{69}, which omits Luke 22.42–45a, might be a Marcionite-influenced text.

There were other passages that Marcion evidently read as explicitly supporting his own position, whether or not in a distinctive textual form. Jesus' response to his putative family was a particularly significant passage (Luke 8.[19]20–1). The incident apparently began only with the report to Jesus that his mother and brothers were there (v. 20).[112] Tertullian anticipates the 'the customary response from the other side' that the report was an attempt to catch Jesus out, and not evidence that the family origins of Jesus were well-known – as he himself claims, appealing to the census records; while not inconceivable, Tertullian takes such delight in pillaring the suggestion that it may be a rhetorical ploy that he had invented himself. More persuasive is that Marcion was able to take Jesus' question, 'Who is my mother and who are my brothers?' as a denial that he had any, although Tertullian dismisses this as reading *simpliciter*;[113] this would then prepare for Jesus' positive definition of his family as 'those who hear *my* words and do them' – apparently rather than canonical Luke's 'the word of God'.[114] Marcion was not alone in finding in this passage a clear expression of Jesus' own testimony concerning his family. Tertullian himself admits that 'this most persistent argument of all those who bring the nativity of the Lord into controversy' is made by 'heretics' and not just by Marcion, and he also devotes a long chapter to it in the *On the Flesh of Christ* (*AM* IV.19.6; *De Carne* 7). Epiphanius reports that the Ebionites used the passage in a similar fashion, again only citing the announcement made to Jesus (*Pan.* 30.14.5). While it is not impossible that it was Marcion who omitted v. 19, it may not have been present in the Gospel he knew, nor in that known to the Ebionites.

Another key passage whose distinctive reading was not peculiar to Marcion is Luke 10.22, which Tertullian reports, without critical comment, as 'No-one knows who the father is except the son, and who the son is except

112 Tertullian, *AM* IV. 19.6–12 (cf. *De Carne* 7); Epiphanius, *Pan.* 42.11.17, S12. See above, p. 198. Tertullian implies 'standing outside seeking to see him', which follows the Latin, and in part D. The similarity here with Matt. 12.46 should not be taken as evidence that Matthew is here closer to Marcion's 'Gospel' (contra Klinghardt, 'Marcionite Gospel', 20); in fact there is some textual evidence for the omission of the report to Jesus in Matt. 12.47, although perhaps by homoioteleuton.

113 See above, p. 198, for the question form, which is found in Matt. 12.48 but not in canonical Luke. Although Tertullian reads the dative 'for me (*mihi*)' in place of 'my', it seems unlikely that Marcion's 'Gospel' merely denied that they had any significance for him.

114 In *De Carne* 7 Tertullian probably implies the reading 'word of God'. Epiphanius' refutation could be taken in support of either reading (*Pan.* 42.11.17, R12). Compare Luke 11.28 where Tertullian implies the reading 'who hear the word of God and do it'; although here the Greek MSS read 'observe', 'do' is supported by some Old Latin witnesses.

the father, and to whomsoever the son shall have revealed it'.[115] Particularly striking here in comparison with canonical Luke (and with the parallel in Matthew 11.27) is the reversal of son and father, which gives priority to the revelation by the son of the unknown father, but also gives to the son the task of revealing who *the son* is. This form of the saying is found elsewhere in the second century, in Justin Martyr, where it is a matter of 'knowing the father/son' as in Matthew (Justin, *Dial.* 100.1; cf. Irenaeus, *AH* IV. 6.2).[116] Also well attested within this form of the saying is a further significant variant which Tertullian himself elsewhere ascribes to their 'shared Gospel', namely with the first verb in the aorist ('knew') rather than present ('knows') (Tertullian, *AM* II. 27.4, again with the 'Matthean' simple direct object, 'the father'); Megethius also cites the saying with the past tense, in order to illustrate the contrast between the Creator God who was known to Adam, and the unknown Father revealed only by the son (*Adam.* 44.1–2 [1.23]). It is precisely because of this interpretation by the 'heretics' that Irenaeus objects to reading the past tense, even though elsewhere he himself uses it against there being prior internal relations within the pleroma (Irenaeus, *AH* I. 20.3; IV. 6.1; cf. II. 14.7); yet others found it completely apposite as a rebuttal by Jesus of Jewish claims to know God, as does Tertullian himself here (Justin, *Apol.* 63.3, 13; Tertullian, *AM* IV. 29.10). Each of these variants, and others, can be found in the textual tradition of the saying in both Luke and Matthew. Here most starkly Marcion belongs in the crossfire of interpretations of the so-called thunderbolt from a Johannine heaven. Yet, given this Johannine affinity, and that the saying immediately follows Jesus' affirmation, 'all things have been given to me by the father', it is easy to see why the order 'no-one knows the father but the son' might have seemed most natural.

The Father and the Creator

Given the importance for Marcion of this acknowledgement by Jesus of his Father, it is surprising that the sources agree that Jesus addressed its opening thanksgiving to God as 'Lord of heaven', without the Lukan 'Father'

[115] *AM* IV. 25.10; this involves following most modern editors in omitting a repetition of the first two clauses in a form close to that of Matt. 11.27; see Braun *Contre Marcion*, IV, 322. For Ephraem see next note.

[116] However, since Irenaeus has just cited the verse in the Matthean form ('son–father, father–son'; *AH* IV. 6.1), editors generally correct this to match that. For what follows see also the list of cross-references given by Marcovich, *Iustini Martyris Apologiae*, 121n. Ephraem reports the first clause only and in this form, *PR* 2. 72,1–3.

(Luke 10.21; Tertullian, *AM* IV. 25.1; Epiphanius, *Pan.* 42.11.17, S 22). Arguably this may be an example of an otherwise un-(or poorly) attested textual variant;[117] less surprising may be the contrast with the Lukan 'lord of heaven and of earth', although the absence of 'of earth' is also attested by P^{45} – the earth belonged to the Creator.[118] Tertullian continues by hinting that Marcion found a potential contrast in the rest of the verse between what the Creator hid and what the Father revealed, by reading, 'you have revealed ... what was hidden [passive]', and he then develops that potential further from the passives at Luke 12.2 ('what was veiled ... hidden'), although even then this may be his own creative imagination at work.[119]

For his part, Epiphanius finds evidence of Marcion's denial of God's responsibility for the earth as the one who created and cared for everything when he charges him with 'excising' God's concern for the sparrows and, later, God's clothing of the grass (Luke 12. 6, 28; *Pan.* 42.11.17, SR 29, 31).[120] It is difficult to see how this could have the intended effect unless the omissions from the passage were much more extensive. Tertullian is of little help here: He passes over Luke 12.6–7 in silence and he discusses Luke 12.22–31 through a mix of paraphrase and select quotation, although he too sees the salient issue as the respective roles and authority of Creator and Father (*AM* IV. 28.3–4; 29.1–5). Both identify the crux as Luke 12.30, 'Your father knows that you need these things'; strikingly, however, Epiphanius glosses this with 'namely fleshly things (σαρκικῶν)'. It seems likely that this gloss was already in the text that Epiphanius had before him;[121] if so, it would surely have to be read as an acknowledgement, albeit concessionary, that while in the flesh even followers of Marcion would need to make use of what was provided by the Creator without thereby betraying their trust in the Father.

117 The omission of 'father' is possibly supported by one old Latin manuscript, a (so Jülicher, *Lucas-Evangelium*, 120, and *The New Testament in Greek: The Gospel according to Luke*, Part 1: Chapters 1–12, edited by The American and British Committees of the International Greek New Testament Project [Oxford: Clarendon Press, 1984], 231).

118 Epiphanius draws attention to both 'omissions', whereas Tertullian reads the text without comment; he also prefaces 'I acknowledge' by 'I thank'. Tertullian's allusive discussion may suggest a similar absence of 'on earth' of the son's authority to forgive sins (Luke 5.24; *AM* IV. 10.5–13), although Epiphanius does read the phrase. (*Pan.* 42.11.17, S2).

119 Tertullian, *AM* IV. 28.2, 'some may think'; Braun, *Contre Marcion*, IV, 356, ascribes the suggestion to Tertullian. Neither passage is attested by Epiphanius.

120 The point is only made explicit in the second instance but would seem to also apply back to the first 'omission' (see below).

121 Epiphanius, *Pan.* 42.11.17, S32; so also Williams, 'Reconsidering', 489. It is not found in Tertullian.

Potentially more serious debates over the respective roles of Creator and Father come to the fore elsewhere in the interpretation of Luke 12. Both Tertullian and Epiphanius take as their starting point the identity of the one who, according to Jesus, is worthy of fear as 'having authority to cast into Gehenna'; however, they part ways in the way they themselves interpret the text (Luke 12.4–5). Tertullian accepts that the reference is to the Creator: He then proceeds to argue that such a fate befalls only those who deny Christ and who are therefore denied before God, whereas, while those who confess may be killed for this, they have nothing to fear from the same (one) God, who is nonetheless judge (Luke 12.8–9).[122] For his part, Epiphanius introduces a contrast between the killing of the body and the casting of the soul into Gehenna (cf. Matt. 10.28), and he denies that the reference can be to the Creator; if it were, who gave him that authority, why does the other, supposedly good, God fail to rescue the souls, or, if indeed he rescues some, does he not display an unseemly partiality (*Pan.* 42.11.17, SR9)? The last position, Epiphanius hints, was that taken by Marcion: 'in myth form … the God above saves some, taking what belonged to another'. This storyline and the objection to it are familiar, and it is likely that this passage, like the parable of the rich man and Lazarus, played a key role in Marcion's interpretation.[123]

A similar theme appears to have been provoked by the question of the Sadducees about resurrection (Luke 20.27–40). The Lukan version of Jesus' response differs notably from that in Mark and Matthew: 'The sons of this age marry and are married,[124] but those who are considered worthy to attain that age and the resurrection which is from the dead do not marry and are not married' (Luke 20.34–5). Tertullian, does not quibble at the active form 'those whom God considered worthy', but he does complain that '*they*' take 'that age' with 'God' – 'the God of that age' (*AM* IV. 38.5–8).[125] While this reading makes better sense in Latin than in a putative Greek original, the well-attested Marcionite appeal to 2 Corinthians 4.4, 'the god of this age', adds credence to it.[126] Surprisingly Tertullian does not query the final clause,

[122] Tertullian, *AM* IV. 28.3–7; at Luke 12.4 Tertullian reads the object of 'kill' as 'you', which suits his interpretation; since it is not supported by Epiphanius, no conclusion can be reached for Marcion. On the omission of 'angels' see above, p. 198.

[123] On the rich man and Lazarus see above, p. 211.

[124] D, with some Western support, reads 'are begotten and beget, marry …'

[125] This implies that in Marcion's text, accepted by Tertullian, the verb preceded its subject: '*Quos autem dignatus est deus illius aevi possessione et resurrectione*'. The confusion works in Latin since '*dignor*' is deponent, although a derivative active form, '*digno*', does exist. A further problem is the relationship between the Greek infinitive 'to attain', which does take a genitive, and the Latin noun 'possession'.

[126] See below, pp. 258–60.

'being made sons of the God of the resurrection', which would be open to being read in the same direction (Luke 20.36).[127] Whether or not the textual form preceded Marcion, it would seem evident that he understood 'sons of this age' not as a temporal indicator but as defining only those, 'the men of the Creator', who did engage in and perform marriage.

The Law of the Creator

Therefore the opposition between the Father and the Creator for Marcion was not simply metaphysical but it determined the behaviour of those who gave to each their allegiance. One aspect of this was Marcion's presentation of Jesus as consistently challenging the Law. Tertullian takes pleasure in pointing out that Marcion's conclusion that Jesus made such a challenge when he allowed the leper or the haemorrhaging woman to touch him could carry no weight if Jesus was not possessed of a body that could be touched and incur the supposed defilement – although it is not self-evident that his own solution, that as God Jesus could not be defiled, is a great improvement (*AM* IV. 9.4–5; 20.11–14). Elsewhere Tertullian engages in the technical language of judicial debate to determine whether the Creator's written Sabbath injunctions and Jesus' practice can actually be reconciled through the concept of intention, although whether Marcion used similar concepts is unclear (IV. 12.5–8).[128] As already noted, Tertullian does not question Marcion's assumption that as a tax collector Levi was a Gentile, but only how to interpret the fact.[129] In such cases both sides recognise the need to interpret the textual account, but it is not obvious in these instances that there are substantial disagreements about the content of that text. It is striking that Tertullian makes no comment when he reads Luke 16.17 as 'Heaven and earth shall pass away more easily than one detail of the words of the Lord', presumably presupposing 'my words' on Jesus' mouth; indeed it is probably he himself who glosses 'heaven and earth' by 'the law and the prophets' (cf. Luke 16.16; Tertullian, *AM* IV. 33.9). Even though the former

[127] So D *pc* it sy^{s} – i.e. with the omission of 'they are sons', which might otherwise be attributed to homoioteleuton (cf. also Justin, *Dial.* 81.4, 'Because they shall be like angels, being sons of God of the resurrection', although Marcovich, *Iustini Martyris Dialogus*, 212, here adds 'and'). However, Braun, *Contre Marcion*, IV, 468 punctuates Tertullian to read 'like angels of God, being made sons of the resurrection'.

[128] See F. H. Colson, 'Two Examples of Literary and Rhetorical Criticism in the Fathers (Dionysius of Alexandria on the Authorship of the Apocalypse, and Tertullian on Luke VI)', *JTS* 25 (1924), 364–77, 374–6.

[129] See above, p. 192 and n. 22.

substitution would suit Marcion it need not have originated as his deliberate change; it may even be the result of a, perhaps unintentional, harmonisation with Luke 21.33.[130]

What really engages Tertullian in this passage is the way that Marcion implicitly interpreted the verse by the stricture that Jesus immediately then issued against divorce, in apparent contradiction to the Deuteronomic injunction (Luke 16.18; Deut. 24.1), demonstrating from it the 'diversity of Law and Gospel, Moses and Christ' (*AM* IV. 34.1). Although the argument fits what might be expected in the 'Antitheses', it is tightly integrated into its broader exegetical setting within the Gospel. Tertullian himself is somewhat stretched to make reply, and takes recourse to the Matthean discussion, and even to the specific case of Herod's relationship with Herodias (IV. 34.2–9). Once again, the Gospel text itself is not in dispute – although Tertullian does chastise Marcion for not receiving the other Gospel 'of the same truth and the same Christ'; rather, both sides are seeking a context against which to interpret it.[131] How and where Marcion or his followers expressed such an interpretation remains unclear, but the issue was an important one with practical consequences, and Tertullian would have to return to it again (V. 7.6).

Alongside the rejection of the Law, Tertullian also implies that Marcion found evidence in the Gospel that Jesus deliberately refused to identify himself with the Jews and with their hopes. As in examples already discussed, his text may have avoided messianic epithets and appeals to prophetic fulfilment; he also interpreted Jesus' response to messianic acclamation as rejection or as temporary concession.[132] Both Tertullian and Epiphanius dispute Marcion's appeal to Jesus' words regarding the faith of the centurion, protesting that if he had not 'found such faith in Israel', then he had surely found some, not none at all (Luke 7.9; Tertullian, *AM* IV. 13.1; Epiphanius, *Pan.* 42.11.17, R7). Yet some examples seem rather to reflect a tendency to make the ethical and soteriological contrasts independent of the immediate Jewish context of Jesus' words. Apparently according to Marcion it was 'the just' who would be in the Kingdom, not 'Abraham, and Isaac, and Jacob, and all the prophets' (Luke 13.28); however, it is not difficult to see how such a more inclusive reading may have been prompted by Jesus' preceding

130 See above, pp. 191, 199.

131 It is therefore hazardous to press Tertullian in order to identify a distinctive Marcionite reading; thus NA[27] cite Marcion as evidence for the omission of 'everyone' of the divorced woman in the middle of the verse (with P^{75} B D) but ignore its absence at the beginning.

132 See above, pp. 215, 217.

rejection of 'all you workers of injustice', and need not have been restricted to Marcion or have been inspired specifically by any conscious 'anti-Jewish' sentiment (Tertullian, *AM* IV. 30.5; Epiphanius, *Pan.* 42.11.17, SR40).[133] A similar result would be achieved by the absence of the exceptive clause regarding Jonah in Jesus' response to the request for a sign, thus making his denial of a sign 'for this generation' absolute, particularly if the epithet 'evil' was also missing; the omission of the counter-examples of the people of Nineveh and Queen of Sheba would then follow naturally, particularly since they implied the possibility of repentance, even by non-Jews, under the Creator (Luke 11.29–32; Epiphanius, *Pan.* 42.11.17, S25; cf. Tertullian, *AM* IV. 27.1). However, the transmission history of the saying is undoubtedly complex, exacerbated by its apparently independent presence both in Mark and in the extra material common to Matthew and Luke, provoking numerous possibilities of cross-influence on a literary as well as on an oral level.[134]

Perhaps part of the same process would be the absence of Luke 11.49–51, the vengeance to be exacted for the murders of prophets from Abel to Zachariah, with its opening declaration by 'the wisdom of God' (Epiphanius, *Pan.* 42.11.17, SR28; cf. Tertullian, *AM* IV. 27.8). Clearly this omission was not due only to the references to prophets since, to the perplexity both of Tertullian and of Epiphanius, Luke 11.47–8 was part of Marcion's 'Gospel'; arguably it was because the passage firmly locates those prophets in the past under the Creator's regime, whereas in its absence Jesus' words become a potentially open-ended narrative of the opposition between the faithful (including 'prophets') and those who would kill them.[135] Although this can be only supposition, it coheres well with Marcion's undoubted conviction that just as Paul was attacked for his proclamation of the true Gospel of Jesus, so too those who upheld that proclamation would be attacked, not least those who like him were hated (*commiserones et coodibiles*).[136]

133 Epiphanius notes Marcion's 'retention' of 'daughter of Abraham' at Luke 13.16. See also, Justin, *Apol.* 16.11–12, 'And then I shall say to them, "Go away from me, workers of lawlessness" [cf. Luke 13.27; Matt. 7.23]. Then there shall be weeping and gnashing of teeth [cf. Luke 13.28; Matt. 8.12; 13.42], when the just shine like the sun and the unjust are sent into the eternal fire [cf. Matt. 13.43]'. Both Tertullian and Epiphanius indicate that Jesus continued '[you] kept out' rather than 'cast out'; Braun, *Contre Marcion*, IV, 386, sees this as more in keeping with Marcion's theology, but it may have been prompted by the preceding parable of those excluded by the householder who has locked his door.

134 Mark 8.11–12/Matt. 16.1–4; Matt. 12.38–42. See also Justin, *Dial.* 107.3–108.1. There are numerous variants in the Lukan passage, particularly in D.

135 Note how Jesus' encouragement a few verses later to his friends not to fear those who kill the body would follow neatly.

136 Tertullian, *AM* IV. 9.3; 36.5; see above, p. 193.

Key passages

It is evident, therefore, that Marcion did not systematically remove all references to 'Old Testament' figures; both Tertullian and Epiphanius deride him for retaining the appearance of Moses and Elijah at the Transfiguration, and the scene also played a significant role in Ephraem's polemic.[137] Here again, more important than divergent texts is where the emphasis is put on reading them. Marcion apparently read the incident as a displacement of the representatives of the Creator, probably emphasised by their 'separation' (διαχωρίζεσθαι) from Jesus (Luke 9.33). Hence, both Tertullian and Epiphanius emphasise that the two share Jesus' glory (Luke 9.31), although it is uncertain whether this means that Marcion was more interested in the emphatic '*his* glory' (9.32). For Marcion the divine words 'listen to him' carried as a corollary, 'and not to them'; the authority and origin of those words may have been reinforced by the heavenly voice coming not from the surrounding cloud (as in canonical Luke) but 'from heaven' (*de caelo*: *AM* IV. 22.1), recalling the origin of Jesus as well as his future coming elsewhere in Marcion's 'Gospel' (Luke 4.16; 21.27).[138] Certainly his opponents were quick to mock how the heavenly voice could be recognised as that of the Father, and not obstructed by the Creator. Echoing a theme that was pervasive in Marcion's estimation of the disciples, Tertullian also rejects any disparagement of Peter's interjection implied by the comment, '*but* (*sed*) not knowing what he said';[139] he retorts that in the absence of any pictorial representations Peter could only *know* the identity of Moses and Elijah 'in the spirit'. It is often assumed, largely from silence, that the subject of the three men's conversation (in Luke, 'his exodus') was absent from Marcion's 'Gospel'; at one point Tertullian suggests that Marcion excluded Moses from 'talking with him' (9.30), only permitting him to be 'standing' (9.32), although he contradicts this elsewhere.[140] It is significant that the episode is central to Ephraem's account where the scene is the occasion for a deal struck between the Creator and Jesus or the Father; there is little evidence

137 Luke 9.28–36; Tertullian, *AM* IV. 22.1–16; Epiphanius, *Pan.* 42.11.17, S17–18; Ephraem, *PR* 2. 87,16–95,39; *Comm.Diat.* 14. 9. See above, pp. 173, 199.

138 However, Tertullian subsequently mocks the Father for using the Creator's clouds (*AM* IV. 22.7). On Luke 4.16 see above, p. 214; Luke 21.27 appears to have read 'from heaven' (*de caelis*) rather than 'on the clouds' (*AM* IV. 39.10). There is some textual evidence for the addition of 'of heaven' to 'clouds'.

139 '*Sed*' may indicate an adversative in Marcion's text.

140 See above, p. 199. Tsutsui, 'Das Evangelium', 93–4, decides it is an oversight by Tertullian, against Harnack, *Marcion*, 202*–3*, who is followed by Norelli, 'Marcion et les disciples', 27–9.

that Tertullian was aware of this interpretation, but this may equally be because he avoids such 'mythologising', because it represents a different development, or because it was not found closely attached to the text of the Gospel.

Another significant passage regarding Jesus' relationship with all that had gone before was the message sent by John the Baptist and Jesus' response (Luke 7.18–23). Marcion's opponents are agreed that the contested verses were John's question and Jesus' assessment of his status (Luke 7.20, 28). The former could be read as indicating that Jesus did not match the Jewish expectations represented by John, particularly if, as implied by Ephraem, Marcion read this as, 'Have you come or are we awaiting another?' (*PR* 2. 62,14);[141] Tertullian similarly opens his discussion with an implied Marcionite exegesis, 'But John was offended when he heard of the great deeds of Christ, as belonging to another' (*AM* IV. 18.4). Epiphanius (followed by Ephraem) charges Marcion with having altered Jesus' words so as to make 'Blessed is he who is not offended at me' (Luke 7.23) be addressed to John himself (Epiphanius, *Pan.* 42.11.17, S8 [cf. Ephraem *PR* 2. 86,6, 24]).[142] It is not difficult to see how Marcion could have seen in Luke 7.28 a statement that the Kingdom of God announced by Jesus belonged to a different schema from that in which John might be honoured, and it is Tertullian's and Epiphanius' alternative explanations that are rather more strained. The same might be said of Luke 16.16 (which leads into the discussion of the Law noted above): Whether or not Tertullian's objection, 'As though we did not ourselves also recognise that John constitutes a certain boundary between the older and the new, at which Judaism gives way and from which Christianity begins' (*AM* IV. 33.8) echoes his opponent's own language, it does betray the extent to which all were reading the text within a similar framework.[143]

There can be little doubt that the language of 'old' and 'new' was fundamental for Marcion's interpretation, and the paired parable of patched garment and wineskins seems to have served as a central symbol of the contrast (Luke 5.33–9; Tertullian, *AM* III. 15.5; IV. 11.9–11). In Epiphanius' account it was the refusal of the Roman church authorities to accept

141 Mitchell, *Ephraim's Prose Refutations*, 2, clv, suggests that 'it is just possible that Ephraem may reproduce the wording of the Marcionite version'.

142 In his refutation Epiphanius implies that the alteration meant that some might be offended at *John*; this seems unlikely, especially in the light of Tertullian and Ephraem, and conceivably Epiphanius has misunderstood his own comment in his earlier compilation.

143 See also Tertullian, *AM* IV. 11.5 on Luke 5.33–5; Norelli, 'Marcion et les disciples', 19–21; below, pp. 408–10.

Marcion's interpretation of the parable that prompted him to break away, intending to create a split (σχίσμα) in the Church forever, which suggests that Marcion's exegesis was known independently of his 'Gospel' (Epiphanius, *Pan.* 42.2).[144] Again Tertullian agrees, perhaps echoing Marcion, that the parable indicates that Jesus was separating the 'newness of the Gospel from the oldness of the Law', and is concerned only to emphasise that old and new belong to the same person or God (*AM* IV. 11.10). Particularly striking is the reversed order in nearly all reports of Marcion's interpretation, with the wineskins preceding the patched garment;[145] however, since the same sequence is found in the *Gospel of Thomas* 47, albeit with a different content, it is possible that once again this reflects variant parallel traditions.[146]

Tertullian was aware of Marcion's use of this text before he encountered its distinctive form in his 'Gospel' (*AM* II. 15.5), and the same is true of another pivotal text, the two trees and their fruit (Luke 6.43; *AM* I. 2.1; II. 4.2; 24.3). The Marcionite Megethius succinctly caps this, 'Two masters (or lords) are demonstrated. Do you see two natures, two masters?' (*Adam.* 56.14–17; 58.11–13 [1. 28]); more strongly, Tertullian asserts that Marcion 'allegorizes' this of two Gods, whereas Jesus referred it to people, although in his discussion of the 'Gospel' he does not repeat the earlier association he made between the passage and the persistent heretical obsession with the origin of evil (*AM* I. 2.1; IV. 17.9). Yet his opponents do not go so far as to suggest that Marcion identified a 'bad tree' with a 'bad God', and they are surely right in this; Luke's adjective 'rotten' (σαπρός), applied to both tree and fruit (contrast Matt. 7.18), would not be conducive to such an application, whereas the (perhaps, Tertullian's) Latin 'bad' (*malus*) would.[147] In fact,

[144] Epiphanius does not include the verse in his list of scholia, confirming their selectivity; see above, p. 106.

[145] So also *Adam.* 90.6–10 [2.16]; contrast Tertullian, *AM* II. 15.5, perhaps before Tertullian had studied Marcion's 'Gospel'.

[146] Arguably the wine follows more naturally after the picture of fasting and a wedding; if in Marcion's 'Gospel' the patch was not from a 'new garment' as in Luke 5.36 but of 'unstretched cloth' (Mark 2.21/Matt. 9.16), as is suggested by Epiphanius and the *Dialogue of Adamantius*, the explicit old/new contrast of the wineskins may have seemed preferable. Luke 5.39, unattested for Marcion's 'Gospel', is also absent from D it; see above, p. 203.

[147] Megethius' quotation differs on each occasion. Harnack, *Marcion*, 195* over-interprets Origen, *De Princip.* II. 5.4, as indicating a Marcionite identification of the 'bad tree' with the 'Weltschöpfer'. Harnack's conclusion that Marcion read 'produce' rather than 'make' and thus shows Matthean influence is also over-confident; The *Dialogue of Adamantius* ('*fero*') may be influenced by Matthew, and Tertullian's '*proferre*' may be influenced by Luke 6.45. The variation between singular and plural 'fruit' is also found in the manuscript evidence.

Megethius rests his argument mainly on the two masters of Luke 16.13, whereas Tertullian bases his long discussion of this verse on the, arguably fictive, premise that Marcion explicitly identified Mammon with the Creator.[148]

Another point at which, according to Tertullian, Marcion identified the Creator and the superior God was the parable of the armed man defeated by one stronger than himself (Luke 11.21–2; *AM* IV. 26.12; V. 6.7).[149] The passage was an important one in early Christian polemic (cf. Irenaeus, *AH* V. 21.3), and in an allusive reference Origen describes how Marcion 'ridicules, introducing two divine sons, one of the Creator and another of Marcion's God; he describes their single combats …' (*C.Cels.* VI. 74). Ephraem also refers to the Marcionite account of the coming of the Stranger 'like a Mighty One' (*PR* 1. 47,30–4).[150] The image of conflict or of a battle, however conducted, is one of the principle metaphors of Marcion's soteriology.[151]

MARCION'S 'GOSPEL' STRATEGY

Examples could be multiplied and will be taken up again in the exploration of Marcion's teaching. What is evident is that while Marcion's text and interpretation of Luke as represented by his opponents allow some analysis of the strategies adopted on all sides, and of the layers of editing and transmission, his 'omissions', whether directly claimed or deduced from silence, are necessarily opaque. Certainly it is possible to suggest explanations in accordance with his known interests, but these are inevitably tentative and sit uncomfortably alongside Marcion's proven willingness to 'retain', to edit, or to 'reread' what might seem inimical to his outlook. Like all readers of the Gospel(s), Marcion both was inspired by it as he understood the mission of Jesus and found in it the justification of his theology and a powerful tool for promulgating that theology. The only way to deal with this hermeneutical circle is to leap into it.

148 See above, p. 211.

149 Harnack, *Marcion*, 283* identifies this as the origin of the epithet given Christ by Marcion 'ἐπερχόμενος [Greek]' (*AM* IV. 23.1; 25.7: see Braun, *Contre Marcion*, IV, ad loc., for the manuscript variations); this is not very satisfactory but there is no obvious alternative. Braun, *Contre Marcion*, IV, 293, who thinks the interpretation of Luke 11.21–2, is Tertullian's invention, tentatively traces the epithet to Luke 7.19.

150 See above, p. 170. 151 See below, pp. 381–4.

9

Marcion as editor and interpreter II: Marcion's 'Apostolikon'

Irenaeus already drew a close connection between Marcion's 'mutilation' of the Gospel according to Luke and his 'cutting away' at Paul's letters.[1] He sets this in clear contrast to his own developing 'canon consciousness': 'Marcion and his followers are committed to cutting up the scriptures, which in fact they do not acknowledge in their totality; instead, mutilating the Gospel according to Luke and the letters of Paul, they claim only those to be legitimate, which they themselves have abbreviated' (*AH* III. 12.12). The charge thereafter becomes a routine one, reinforced by Tertullian's devotion of a volume to exposing each, and by Epiphanius' continuous list of scholia. It is not surprising, therefore, that both the challenges of reconstructing Marcion's Pauline corpus or 'Apostolikon' and some of the results follow a similar pattern to those regarding his 'Gospel'. The primary sources are the same, chiefly Tertullian and Epiphanius, while the *Dialogue of Adamantius* claims that the debate is being carried out on the basis of the Marcionite 'Apostolikon' (*Adam.* 66.9–10 [2.5]), and additional support comes from Origen's commentaries on the Pauline Epistles insofar as these are recoverable, in part through Jerome.[2]

RECOVERING AND EXPOUNDING MARCION'S 'APOSTOLIKON'

There are, however, significant differences in the way that both Tertullian and Epiphanius handle the Pauline letters. Unsurprisingly, for Tertullian the Gospel has a certain precedence: His task is to show that 'the apostle is mine

[1] *AH* I. 27.2: *Circumcidens . . .auferens. . . similiter . . . abscidit . . . auferens.*

[2] For attempts at reconstruction see Zahn, *Geschichte*, II.2, 495–529; Harnack, *Marcion*, 67*–127*. Schmid, *Marcion und sein Apostolos*, I/315–44, lists the distinctive Marcionite readings. BeDuhn, *First New Testament*, 228–59, gives an English translation and adds notes.

just as Christ is mine', and that the apostle no more spoke of another God than did Christ, as he had already proved in the previous book; it is the model of 'the heretic's Gospel which must predetermine' that the Epistles of Paul have been mutilated (*AM* V. 1.8–9). Although in Books I to III he refers to Marcion's high evaluation of Paul and to his interpretation of the controversy in Galatians 1–2, it is unlikely that Tertullian had direct access to Marcion's 'Apostolikon' until he came to write Books IV and V of *Against Marcion*.[3] However, in the latter he draws attention to far more examples of Marcion's 'falsification' of the text of the Epistles than he had in the Gospel, noting both changes of single words, and extensive omissions such as the numerous 'ditches' for which Marcion was responsible, particularly in Romans;[4] 'I am not surprised that he suppresses syllables since he takes out most frequently whole pages', he declares, before accusing Marcion of omitting the preposition 'in' at Ephesians 3.9 (*AM* V. 18.1). Even so, it is still often necessary to rely on his silences, for example, to decide whether, as seems probable, Marcion's text omitted Romans 4. In some cases Tertullian has a clear explanation of Marcion's rationale, even while he mocks his inconsistency: The 'diligence of the heretic erased the reference to Abraham' (Gal. 3.6–9) but should be embarrassed by its subsequent retention (Gal. 4.22) (*AM* V. 3.11; 4.8). On the other hand, at times his own imagination may well be at work – for example, when he reads Romans 10.4 as Israel was ignorant *of God*, omitting the words 'righteousness of', and claims that the heretic might refer this to Israel's ignorance of the superior God (*AM* V. 14.6). No doubt, more generally he would rely on his blanket assertion that Marcion deleted ideas that contradicted his own views, retaining those that agreed with them, even while failing to succeed in both (IV. 6.2). Yet, he does not feel constrained to demonstrate this in detail: The absence of the Pastoral Epistles merely demonstrates Marcion's determination to falsify, 'even in regard to the number', while by holding the letter that the Church knows to be to the Ephesians to be to the Laodicaeans Marcion spuriously pretends the role of a 'most thorough investigator' (V. 1.9; 17.1; 21.1). With regard to the 'Gospel' Tertullian had implied that Marcion had identified it with the Gospel perverted by the false apostles (Gal. 1.7–9; 2.4; *AM* IV. 3.2–4.3); by contrast, despite his mocking suggestion that 'perhaps our false apostles and Jewish evangelists introduced' the list of all that was 'created in Christ'

3 In *AM* III. 5.4 Tertullian's argument follows the 'catholic' order, and he cites Ephesians without reference to Marcion's identification of it as to the Laodicaeans.

4 For example, *AM* V. 10.7, 10; 13.4.

(Col. 1.16), Tertullian provides no such rationalisation on behalf of Marcion's approach to the Pauline letters (*AM* V. 19.5).

Predominately, however, Tertullian focuses on those passages that support his own argument, although, as he admits as early as his discussion of Romans, his treatment becomes increasingly scanty as he progresses through the letters (V. 13.1). Nonetheless, as with his account of the 'Gospel', his characteristic rhetoric demands a hermeneutic of suspicion: It is difficult to judge whether the answer to his question, 'What will the heretic say? That the limbs of Christ will not rise because they are now not ours?' (1 Cor. 6.15, 19), carries more irony than genuine report since it serves so neatly his own priorities (*AM* V. 7.4). Certainly his vehement denials may betray his adversary's position, just as may his quick defence: 'We *also* (*quoque*) acknowledge that the principal letter against Judaism is that which instructs the Galatians' (V. 2.1). On the other hand, his very cursory treatment of 1 Corinthians 7 probably reflects his own discomfort in attempting to clearly distinguish his attitude to marriage from that of his opponent, and it need not mean that the chapter was correspondingly briefer in Marcion's text (*AM* V. 7.6–8).[5] Yet, even more than in the 'Gospel', his triumphant exposure of Marcion's lack of consistency or logic has to be resisted; Tertullian is only driven to pay close attention to unravelling the apostle's argument because this is what Marcion had already done. Indeed, at times he seems to be thinking on his feet, developing his argument as he goes along: 'In this way even as the arguments of the opposing party are destroyed, our own explanations are being built up' (V. 6.9).

Epiphanius, on the other hand, pays less detailed attention to Marcion's Pauline text. He cites just forty scholia from Paul's letters, and these are, as he himself describes, both highly selective and in a curiously random order; despite both his initial claim that his earlier compilation had been from both 'books' and his parallel procedure in their treatment, the Pauline section may be a subsequent addition to that from the Gospel, carried out with rather less consistent attention.[6] Although he lists Philippians, 1 and 2 Thessalonians, and Philemon among the ten letters that Marcion accepted,[7] he cites no scholia from them; he himself appears to have forgotten what principles

[5] See further below, pp. 390–1.

[6] This seems to be implied by the introductory paragraph, which is hopelessly textually corrupt (*Pan.* 42.11.7–8). The order given there contradicts both Epiphanius' later claim that he had originally followed the Church's order, and the Marcionite sequence that he adopts for his present purposes: see *Pan.* 42.12.1, and below.

[7] That is, excluding 1 and 2 Timothy, Titus, and Hebrews, as Epiphanius states according to the reconstructed text at *Pan.* 42.11.10–11.

were at work in their absence from his selection, and when he came to add the refutations he resorted to the somewhat dubious explanation of that silence as because 'everything of Marcion's version is distorted'. On the other hand, only on six occasions does he refer to Marcion's alterations to the text, describing just two of these as 'cutting out' (2 Cor. 4.13; Eph. 5.31: *Pan.* 42.12.3, S27; 38).[8] This in turn accords with his more moderate description of Marcion's treatment of the Epistles as 'curtailing (περιτέμνειν) some of them, changing some sections' (*Pan.* 42.9.2). Instead, Epiphanius uses these passages supposedly from Marcion's own scriptures to argue at length for the unity of the two Testaments and for the fleshliness of Christ, with the result that the whole discussion is not much shorter than that devoted to the seventy-eight Gospel scholia.

Epiphanius also draws specific attention to Marcion's distinctive ordering of the Pauline letters, and in particular to his placing at their head not Romans but Galatians.[9] Tertullian presupposes the same position but makes no comment on it, and both continue with 1 and 2 Corinthians, Romans, 1 and 2 Thessalonians, Ephesians, Colossians, followed in Tertullian by Philippians and Philemon while Epiphanius reverses that order. In addition, Epiphanius lists in final position a single scholion from a letter identified as to the Laodicaeans, 'One Lord, one faith, one baptism, one God and father of all, who is over all and through all and in all' (*Pan.* 42.11.8; 12.3, S40); from this he deduced that Marcion also had 'parts of the so-called letter to the Laodicaeans', later expanding this to claim that Marcion deliberately added it as an eleventh letter, while he ignored the fact that the same testimony could be found in Ephesians (*Pan.* 42.9.4; 13.1–8; cf. Eph. 4.5–6). No doubt this assertion is to be related to Tertullian's challenge to Marcion for identifying as to the Laodicaeans the letter that he himself knew as directed to the Ephesians (*AM* V. 11.13; 17.1). Tertullian's language, and his dismissal of the issue as largely immaterial, indicates that in his Marcionite text, and probably also in that familiar to him, no location was given at Ephesians 1.1, as is the case also in part of the manuscript tradition (P^{46} ℵ* B*); the question for both Tertullian and Marcion was of the superscription and hence one of interpretation, in the Marcionite case probably a conjecture based on Colossians 4.16.[10] It is possible that the displacement of one

8 The latter case depends on assuming that the 'cut out' (παρακόψες) in the refutation can be read back into the probably textually corrupt scholion, which reads only 'from' (παρά).

9 Epiphanius, *Pan.* 42.9.4; 12.1; at *Pan.* 42.12.3 (Philem.) he is less concerned about the variable position of Philemon in the church's list.

10 Against Schmid, *Marcion und sein Apostolos*, 111, who assumes that '*titulus*' refers to the opening greeting as at *AM* V. 5.1; however, at IV. 2.3 it is used of the superscription.

citation explicitly identified as directed to the Laodicaeans originated in Epiphanius' Marcionite source, but it may be due only to his somewhat chaotic compilation.

Reaching behind these polemics to reconstruct the character and origins of Marcion's Pauline corpus presents problems comparable to the recovery of his 'Gospel', as well as distinctive ones. There is, for example, in the Pauline letters no precise equivalent to the potential influence of the other Synoptic Gospels on the Lukan text of Marcion or of his opponents, or on the subsequent textual tradition of both. Nonetheless, as with the 'Gospel', detailed analysis has suggested that Marcion's Pauline text exhibits affinities with the Western tradition; Ulrich Schmid has argued more precisely that it presupposes an earlier text form from which the Western text and particularly the old-Syrian text known to Ephraem and Aphraat are also descended.[11] Indeed, on this basis Schmid limits the number of variants that can be attributed specifically to Marcion, and by emphasising the range of potential reasons for textual variation and scribal modification he reduces to a minimum those that demand a theological motivation. For example, although Tertullian explicitly states that Marcion has omitted Ephesians 6.2b, an omission not otherwise attested in the textual tradition, Schmid still prefers to explain this as due to the potential objection that the command to honour parents is not the first of the ten commandments, rather than to a specific Marcionite rejection of an appeal to the Old Testament;[12] similarly, he accepts as Marcionite the omission of 'not' in Galatians 4.8 – 'those who by/in nature are [om. 'not'] Gods' – but he explains this as a mechanical slip, thus dismissing by silence any attempt to find therein significant theological meaning.[13] Schmid even suggests that the apparent omission (or lack of attestation) of Galatians 3.15–25/26 might be due to homoioteleuton, the scribe's eye slipping from 'of faith'

11 Schmid, *Marcion und sein Apostolos*, 280–1, largely supported by Quispel, 'Marcion and the Text of the New Testament'.

12 Schmid, *Marcion und sein Apostolos*, 113, with reference to ancient commentary discussion, against Harnack, *Marcion*, 120*.

13 Schmid, *Marcion und sein Apostolos*, 116. On the text see René Braun, introd. trad. and comm., *Tertullien. Contre Marcion*, Tome V (texte critique by Claudio Moreschini; SC 483; Paris: Éditions du Cerf, 2004), 116, who also accepts the omission of 'not' against Evans, *Adversus Marcionem*, etc. For the interpretation of the verse see Emanuele S. Ludovic, 'Sull' interpretazione di Alcuni Testamenti della *Lettera ai Galati* in Marcione et in Tertulliano', *Aevum* 47 (1972), 371–401, 385 (accepting 'not'); Han J. W. Drijvers, 'Marcion's Reading of Gal 4,8: Philosophical background and influence on Manichaeism', ed. J. Duchesne-Guillemin, W. Sundermann, F. Vahman. *A Green Leaf: Essays in Honour of Jes P. Asmussen* (Acta Iranica 28; Leiden: Brill, 1988), 339–48.

(τῆς πίστεως) in 3.14 to the same phrase in 3.25 or 26.[14] At the same time he notes that there are other variants in the textual tradition that potentially would have suited Marcion's position but which are not to be attributed to his influence.[15]

Allied with the textual form is the particular question of the order of the letters, on which Tertullian and Epiphanius largely agree. Conventionally, this has been seen as Marcion's own work, reflecting the importance of Galatians in his interpretation of Paul.[16] However, a similar sequence is implied by what probably constitutes the original nucleus of the earliest prologues to the Pauline Epistles, which are preserved in a number of old Latin and Vulgate manuscripts and are traceable back to the fourth century.[17] The style of these prologues suggests that this original nucleus gave an account of the churches addressed rather than of the individual letters as such, with a single Prologue each regarding the church at Corinth and that at Thessalonica, and perhaps that they formed a single introduction to a corpus rather than being distributed among the letters as prefatory matter as they are in the surviving textual tradition.[18] Further, the Prologue to Colossians implies there has been a previous description of the Laodicaean church, while that to the Ephesians appears to be modelled on the Philippian Prologue and so may be secondary;[19] consequently, internal cross-references indicate the original sequence was Galatians, Corinthians, Romans, Thessalonians, Laodicaeans, Colossians, Philippians. There is no Prologue to Hebrews and those to the Pastoral Epistles are clearly also secondary.[20] A recurring theme in what probably formed the nucleus is that of how 'the apostle' recalled each church to the truth in face of the

[14] Schmid, *Marcion und sein Apostolos*, 248–9; see below, p. 250.

[15] Schmid, *Marcion und sein Apostolos*, 249–54.

[16] So still Braun, *Contre Marcion*, V, 81. Complicating the issue is the suggestion that Marcion inherited a collection that began with Ephesians, which he then displaced with Galatians: see John Knox, 'A Conjecture as to the Original Status of II Corinthians and II Thessalonians in the Pauline Corpus', *JBL* 55 (1936), 145–53.

[17] On these see Regul, *Antimarcionitischen Evangelienprologe*, 88–94; Eric W. Scherbenske, *Canonizing Paul: Ancient Editorial Practice and the Corpus Paulinum* (Oxford: Oxford University Press, 2013), 85–93, 237–42.

[18] The prologues to 2 Corinthians and 2 Thessalonians are secondary as perhaps is that to Philemon; see n. 20. Knox, 'A Conjecture', suggests that 1 and 2 Corinthians and 1 and 2 Thessalonians were originally counted as one each, the greeting to the second letter being a later addition.

[19] The Colossian Prologue opens, 'The Colossians are themselves also Asians like the Laodicaeans'.

[20] The Prologues to 2 Corinthians, 2 Thessalonians, 1 and 2 Timothy, Titus, and Philemon, take the form 'he wrote to' or equivalent, while the Prologues of the nucleus take the form 'The XX (people) are XX' as in n. 19.

activity of false apostles, a theme that echoes Marcion's reconstruction of Paul. These features have led to these Prologues conventionally being labelled 'Marcionite', although properly this would refer only to the original nucleus.[21] Against this identification of the Prologues, it has been shown that there is little else that is distinctively Marcionite in them, and that their brief references to the errors introduced by the false apostles might easily be drawn from the letters themselves. Although Marcionite influence might still seem attractive, whether by Marcion or a later disciple, it remains difficult to envisage how they would then have been later transferred into 'mainstream' church tradition. On the other hand, the alternative argument that they, and hence the collection and sequence that they presuppose, should be dated prior to Marcion, and therefore reflect the tradition on which he drew, is undermined by the absence of any clear traces of the Prologues in the early period.[22] Raising similar questions, and perhaps offering some support to the view that Marcion was not alone in his order of the letters, is a stichometry of the canonical books surviving in Syriac and contained within a list, ascribed to Irenaeus, of the seventy disciples. In this the Pauline letters follow the order Galatians, 1 and 2 Corinthians, Romans, followed by Hebrews, Colossians, Ephesians, Philippians (given twice), 1 and 2 Thessalonians, 2 Timothy, Titus, and Philemon.[23]

Evidently Marcion or his followers did treat his corpus as a collection, inviting the label 'Apostolikon' as ascribed by his opponents.[24] However, the important issue that underlies these debates is whether Marcion inherited such a collection of Pauline letters, whose order he may have adjusted,

21 See further Karl Th. Schäfer, 'Marcion und die ältesten Prologe zu den Paulusbriefen', ed. Patrick Granfeld and Josef A. Jungmann, *Kyriakon: Festschrift J. Quasten* (Munster: Aschendorff, 1970) I, 135–50, who suggests authorship by a disciple of Marcion in the Latin West.

22 Their pre-Marcionite date was argued by Nils A. Dahl, 'The Origin of the Earliest Prologues to the Pauline Letters', ed. W. Beardslee, *The Poetics of Faith: Essays offered to Amos Niven Wilder* (Semeia 12; Missoula, MT: SBL, 1978), 233–77 (reprinted in ed. David Hellholm, Vermund Blumkvist, Tord Fornberg, *Studies in Ephesians: Introductory Questions, Text- and Edition-critical Issues, Interpretation of Texts and Themes* [WUNT 131; Tübingen: Mohr, 2000] 179–209). Geoffrey M. Hahnemann, *The Muratorian Fragment and the Development of the Canon* (Oxford Theological Monographs; Oxford: Clarendon Press, 1992), 110–15, argues for a mid-second-century origin in Greek with a Latin translation a century later, and does not ascribe them to Marcion. For counter-arguments see also Regul, *Antimarcionitischen Evangelienprologe*, 88–94.

23 See Agnes Smith Lewis, *Catalogue of the Syriac MSS in the Convent of S. Catharine on Mount Sinai* (Studia Sinaitica I; London: C. J. Clay & Sons, 1894), 11–14. That this reflects a Marcionite sequence is accepted by Quispel, 'Marcion and the Text of the New Testament'.

24 See Epiphanius, *Pan.* 42.11.7; *Adam.* 10.19–20 [1.5], and Tsutsui, *Auseinandersetzung*, 130.

or whether he initiated this collection.[25] Certainly, there is evidence prior to Marcion of authors who know more than one Pauline letter, including *1 Clement* and Ignatius. Yet such references and allusions do not demonstrate a corpus of ten letters, such as Irenaeus probably presupposes for Marcion and as Tertullian claims. A mediating position could also be considered, namely that Marcion knew, or created, a smaller corpus, which had been extended probably by the time of Irenaeus and certainly by that of Tertullian in parallel to similar processes elsewhere in the Church.

Such a possibility is not strictly parallel to the debate considered earlier as to whether the Gospel to which Marcion had access was an earlier form of that which the Church subsequently received as 'according to Luke'. The closest analogy to the latter process would be the assertion made by Origen that Marcion not only 'completely removed' the doxology in Romans 16.25–7, but also dissected everything from 14.23 to the end (Origen, *Comm. in Rom.* X. 43, 7–18, on 16.25), a claim that is supported by the silence of the main polemicists regarding Romans 15–16. On the surface 'dissected' (*desecuit*) might mean that Marcion's text did retain parts of the last two chapters; however, there are considerable textual arguments for the early circulation of a fourteen-chapter (1–14) version of the letter, and these strengthen the assumption that this is all that Marcion himself knew.[26] To go beyond this in reconstructing a pre-Marcionite version of a Pauline corpus is difficult: While arguments from style and structure have been made for interpolations within Pauline letters, these are not easily co-ordinated with the evidence for Marcionite 'omissions'.[27] Conversely, 1 Corinthians 14.34–35, which is often viewed as a later interpolation, is attested for Marcion. On the other hand, the absence of any evidence for 2 Corinthians 7.2–11.1 in Marcion's text is most probably to be laid not at his door but at Tertullian's, and so is of no relevance to arguments for the later compilation or redaction of 2 Corinthians; the same is probably true with

25 For this and what follows see below, pp. 419–20. Harry Gamble, 'The Redaction of the Pauline Letters and the Formation of the Pauline Corpus', *JBL* 94 (1975), 403–18, 414–5 rejects the hypothesis of a single prototype collection.

26 That Marcion did retain parts of 15–16 is held by Zahn, *Geschichte*, II.2, 519–20, and by Thomas P. Scheck, *Origen: Commentary on the Epistle to the Romans* (2 vols. FOC 103–4; Washington, DC: Catholic University of America Press, 2001–2), 307, n. 350; for the omission of 15–16 see Schmid, *Marcion und sein Apostolos*, 289–94; Gamble, 'Redaction', 414–7, who thinks such a form predated Marcion.

27 See, however, William O. Walker, 'Romans 1.18–2.29: A Non-Pauline Interpolation?', *NTS* 45 (1999), 533–52, who does note the possible absence of Romans 1.19–2.1 from Marcion's text, following P. N. Harrison, *Paulines and Pastorals* (London: Villiers Publications, 1964), 79–85.

regard to Philippians despite its (pen-)ultimate position and the poor attestation of its last chapter in Marcion's list. Undoubtedly the formation of the Pauline collection is unlikely to have taken place at one moment as a single, unparalleled event; at the very least, it seems more probable that Marcion was unaware of the Pastoral Epistles, whose absence is noted by Tertullian, or of Hebrews, added by Epiphanius, than that he intentionally omitted them. Beyond this, the process of compilation and collection may well have left its mark on the text, contents, and shape even of individual letters, but to recover this must remain even more in the realm of conjecture than is the case with the Gospels; little progress can be made by attempting to explain Marcion by such conjectures or to substantiate them by reference to him.[28]

As with the 'Gospel', therefore, Marcion's reading of the Pauline text is best approached as a combination of textual choices and of interpretation. It is within this framework that the role played by a Pauline corpus, as opposed to a haphazard collection of disparate letters, must be considered. Although how his own exposition of the apostle's meaning was articulated and communicated is never evident from his opponents, it should be assumed that it was neither obviously naïve nor incomprehensible. Alongside taking such hints as one can from the opponents' polemic, comes the challenge to try to read Paul through Marcion's eyes, to discern therein an alternative logic to that self-evident to Tertullian. Enrico Norelli has endeavoured to demonstrate what such a disciplined reading of Romans might look like, recognising, and seeking to control by reference to other evidence, the necessarily hypothetical nature of the undertaking.[29] While a similar exercise cannot be undertaken here, his work will offer significant insights; in what follows, certain primary themes will be investigated that appear to emerge from the textual choices attributed to Marcion and from reactions to his interpretation.

MARCION AND HIS 'APOSTOLIKON'

Apostle extraordinary

For Marcion the letter to the Galatians established Paul's pre-eminent authority as an apostle, 'not from men nor through man but through Jesus

[28] For the principle, see William O. Walker, 'The Burden of Proof in Identifying Interpolations in the Pauline Letters', *NTS* 33 (1987), 610–18.

[29] E. Norelli, 'Marcione lettore dell' epistola ai Romani', *Cristianesimo nella storia* 15 (1994), 635–75.

Christ' (Gal. 1.1; *AM* V. 1.3).[30] Against him, Tertullian mocks the lack of prescience shown by a Christ who failed to avoid the need for a new apostle when he drew up the primary apostolic list recorded in the Gospel; he himself proposes the solution to the supposed dilemma to be its anticipation in Old Testament 'prediction', and hence its anticipation by the Creator (Gen. 49.27; 1 Sam. 24.18, 'Saul'). This sets the pattern for their conflicting interpretations of the first two chapters of the letter; for Marcion these establish Paul's reception of the Gospel truth and his resolute defence of it against its dereliction by the other apostles, but for Tertullian they demonstrate not merely the harmony between them all but Paul's readiness to make concessions to the others in order to maintain it. Whereas Irenaeus had argued the former, namely apostolic harmony, by eliding Galatians with the Acts of the Apostles, in part 'against those who say Paul alone knew the truth' (*AH* III. 13.1), Tertullian is driven further by the need to construct from Paul's own words a 'Paul who is mine as is also the Christ' (*AM* V. 1.8).

Tertullian surprisingly largely bypasses Paul's account of his conversion in Galatians 1.13–16; rather than reflect any lack of interest in it by Marcion, this may even suggest some embarrassment on Tertullian's own part. The same anxieties may be at play in his failure to fulfil an earlier promise to return in discussion of 'your apostle' to Marcion's interpretation that the 'third heaven' (2 Cor. 12.2) belonged to the Father and not to the Creator; at the requisite point he merely makes a cross-reference to another treatise 'On Paradise', unfortunately now lost (*AM* I. 15.1; V. 12.7[8]). The shared theme of 'revelation' in the two passages together with Tertullian's passing reference here to Paul's calling 'by the Lord *in the heavens*' (*AM* V. 1.2), not found in Galatians, suggests that Marcion understood 2 Corinthians 12.1–4 as reinforcing the exclusive character of Paul's calling as an apostle; in fact this interpretation is made explicit in Eznik, *De Deo* 379–84. It was from that same 'third heaven' that 'your lord, the superior God' had descended (Tertullian, *AM* I. 14.2). For Marcion this heavenly revelation would provide a forceful context for Paul's implacable denunciation of all other proclamations of the Gospel as incompatible with his own and therefore with Christ's Gospel (Gal. 1.6–9). Not only does Tertullian's defensive response

30 Marcion's text may have omitted 'and (through) God the Father'; this would have the consequence of making Jesus the subject of the following words, if present, 'who raised him (i.e., himself) from the dead'. This is made explicit by Jerome, *Ad Gal.* I. 1,1 ll.86–93 (Giacomo Raspanti, ed., *Commentarii in Epistulam Pauli Apostoli ad Galatas* [S. Hieronymi Presbyteri Opera Pars 1. Opera Exegetica 6; CCSL 77A; Turnhout: Brepols, 2006] 13); he is probably following Origen: see Baarda, 'Marcion's Text of Gal. 1:1'.

indicate such an exegesis, but the Marcionite Megethius also appeals to the passage from Galatians in the *Dialogue of Adamantius*, here reinforced by an intertextual interpolation from Romans 2.16: 'there is no other according to my Gospel'. The context of Megethius' appeal is a defence of a single Gospel rather than four Gospels, and Origen also attributes to the Marcionites a similar use of Romans 2.16.[31] Such an argument would be anachronistic for Marcion himself and it may well demonstrate how exegetic appeal could be modified or redirected in new settings. Tertullian himself renders Galatians 1.7 as 'which is *absolutely* [*omnino* = παντῶς] not other', but whether the additional emphasis belongs to his own rhetoric or to Marcion's text is uncertain; on the other hand, the probable omission of 'to you' after 'were to proclaim' in Galatians 1.8 (as also read by א* b g), an omission that reflects a wider textual tendency to universalise, would have allowed Marcion to see Paul's rejection of any other proclamation as absolute and as not restricted to the Galatian situation (*AM* V. 2.5–6).

The apparent absence of 'again' in Marcion's text of Galatians 2.1 with reference to Paul's visit to Jerusalem suggests that the earlier visit in Galatians 1.18–24 was also omitted, which is confirmed by the lack of any other evidence of Marcion's knowledge of this passage. The same absences, however, are found also in Irenaeus (*AH* III. 13.3), and they provoke no objection by Tertullian. This was, it would seem, a shared 'selective' reading of Paul's narrative: For Marcion it would have reinforced the identification of the problem and its perpetrators in Galatia (Gal. 1.6) with those encountered by Paul in Galatians 2; conversely, for Irenaeus and Tertullian it facilitated an identification of the Jerusalem visit in Galatians 2 with the story in Acts 15, thus adding a further layer to their argument for an agreement between Paul and the apostles, who were represented as responsible for the writing of Acts and not merely as the subjects of its narrative. Tertullian's defence here of the apostolic harmony demands that he engage in a somewhat convoluted exegesis, leading him to emphasise, firstly, that the issue under debate between them was not the identity of the God preached but circumcision, as demonstrated by the statement that Titus was not circumcised (Gal. 2.3); secondly, that Paul did have to respond to the danger posed by certain 'false brothers', who were inspired by commitment to the Law, but that even if they did 'pervert' (*perverto*) the Gospel, they did

[31] *Adam.* 12.5–21 [1.6]; Origen, *Comm. in Joh.* V.7 as cited by Tsutsui, *Auseinandersetzung*, 132–3. Enrico Norelli, 'La Funzione di Paolo nel Pensiero di Marcione', *Revista Biblica* 34 (1986), 534–97, 556, suggests that the preceding elision of Gal. 1.8 and 9 in *Adam.* 12.7–8 [1.6] may come from the 'Antitheses'.

not interpolate Scripture nor did they introduce some other Christ (Gal. 2.4). Thirdly, he concludes, that, in order to pre-empt any danger, Paul *did* 'for a moment yield to subjection' (Gal. 2.5), an action that he would not otherwise have done but that was governed by his stated policy of 'being all things to all people in order to gain all' (1 Cor. 9.20–2); this concession in turn was exemplified when – as recounted in Acts – Paul circumcised Timothy and when he brought those with shaved heads into the Temple (Acts 16.3; 21.24–6; *AM* V. 3.2–6).[32] For this third point Tertullian's interpretation relies on a text that omits both the relative pronoun ('to whom', οἷς) and the negative at the beginning of Galatians 2.5, so that Paul *did* yield, but it was not specifically to the 'false brothers'; the same double omission is attested by D and other Latin witnesses, while Irenaeus also presupposes the omission of the negative, although in his case he interprets the verse of Paul's acquiescence ('yielding') to the agreement in Acts 15 (Irenaeus, *AH* III. 13.3).

Marcion himself did read the negative in Galatians 2.5, in company with the majority of other witnesses; nonetheless, Tertullian expressly describes this as 'a violation of Scripture' indicating just how important the issue was. Counter-reading suggests that Marcion pointed to the whole episode as the occasion of Paul's resolute and perhaps solitary stand against those who themselves did interpolate or even violate Scripture.[33] Marcion evidently identified the false brothers of Galatians 2.4 as false apostles, an interpretation that Tertullian tacitly accepts.[34] He further understood Paul's charges against the troublemakers in Galatians 1.7 as further evidence of their 'perversion' of the Gospel, and then interpreted this far beyond the confines of the Galatian situation (Tertullian, *AM* IV. 3.2; 5.5). He apparently reached this conclusion by reading Galatians 1.6–9 with 2.4 and alongside 2 Corinthians 11.13–14, where Paul accuses those explicitly named 'false apostles' of deceit and of adopting the form of apostles of Christ. Arguably

32 It is not entirely clear how Tertullian (or Marcion's text) understood the relationship between vv. 3–5. Braun, *Contre Marcion*, V, 94 n. 2, concludes from the broader context that Tertullian read a full-stop at the end of v. 3, so that v. 4 provokes the 'yielding' in v. 5; Schmid, *Marcion und sein Apostolos*, 105–6, notes that Tertullian's actual citations imply the omission of 'but' (δέ) at the beginning of v. 4 in Marcion's text (as also in f and some Latin writers), thus linking vv. 3 and 4 – Titus was not circumcised despite the presence of the false brothers.

33 The absence of the relative 'to whom' in v. 5 in Marcion's text, at least according to Tertullian, does not appear to be shared with other witnesses who read the negative, but it does improve the syntax. Lodovici's contrary argument that Tertullian himself did read the relative so that the issue was submission to the twelve (= 'false brothers') is not persuasive ('Sull' interpretazione', 377).

34 See on this Lieu, 'Heresy and Scripture', 94–5.

Marcion also found a further cross-reference to the same situation in 2 Corinthians 12.2–7, where Paul's heavenly calling is followed by the pains inflicted by 'an angel of Satan'; this formula would recall the references to Satan transformed as an angel of light in 2 Corinthians 11.14, and to an angel from heaven, who, according to Galatians 1.8, might preach 'another Gospel'. At each of these three passages Tertullian rejects any association of the angel with the Creator, an indication that Marcion may have made precisely such an association (*AM* V. 2.6; 12.7, 8). However, for Marcion the key piece in this jigsaw of events was Paul's reported rebuke to Peter for failing to behave strictly according 'to the truth of the Gospel' – the location and the chronology of the events described were presumably of little interest to him (Gal. 2.14; *AM* V. 3.7; I. 20.2–4). This would have allied Peter with the false brothers *alias* perverters of the Gospel *alias* false apostles; it is noteworthy that Tertullian defends both Peter at Galatians 2.14 and the false apostles of 2 Corinthians 11.14 in the same way, namely, that they had failed only in behaviour (*conversatio*) and not in doctrine. Within this framework Paul's rebuke specifically of Peter could be extended to his fellow leading apostles, James and John, and this is presumably how Marcion understood Galatians 2.13, 'the rest of the Jews joined in his hypocrisy' (*AM* IV. 3.2–3).[35] This would have provided Marcion with a good reason to describe these apostles as 'too close to Judaism', a term supplied by Paul's own account (V. 3.1; Gal. 1. 4). If, as Tertullian implies, Marcion did indeed label Galatians 'the principal letter against Judaism', he presumably understood this as exemplified by the 'false apostles' who opposed Paul (*AM* V. 2.1).

Marcion's interpretation of these key events in Galatians 1–2 was not restricted to the text of the 'Apostolikon', as Tertullian's repeated reference to them indicates (*AM* I. 20.1–4; IV. 2.5; 3.2–5). Tertullian's own argument suggests that Marcion set it out in the 'Antitheses' as the justification for his own restoration of the Gospel following its perversion (IV. 4.4), but this would not have ruled out further commentary or explanation elsewhere, perhaps based on close textual citation and reasoning. Marcion evidently also interpreted other passages within this framework, and there may be

[35] Norelli, 'Funzione', 557 suggests that Marcion may not have read 'Jews' in Gal. 2.13 so that 'rest' (λοιποί) referred to James and John from 2.9; however, there is no explicit textual support for this reading, and it may not be necessary. Norelli also appeals to Harnack's reconstruction that Marcion read 'the rest' (λοιποί with P[46] DFGL etc.; Harnack, *Marcion* 66*) at 2 Cor. 2.17, referring it to the other apostles; although not impossible in principle the evidence for this is weak. Tertullian, apparently following Marcion, consistently reads 'Peter', not 'Kephas', and he places Peter at the head of the triumvirate, in both cases with considerable, especially western, textual support (Gal. 2.9, 11, 14).

further echoes of this. As already noted, in his own exegesis of Galatians 1–2 Tertullian himself had appealed to Paul's defence in 1 Corinthians 9 of his apostolic authority and behaviour, and the same chapter figures repeatedly elsewhere in his argument (*AM* II. 17.4; III. 5.4; IV. 21.1; V. 7.10–11). The enthusiasm with which he draws attention to Paul's own approval for 'another' (*alium*) to make use of the provisions of the Law for support may in turn suggest that Marcion saw here yet more evidence of the dangerous proximity to the Law exhibited by Peter (and 'the rest') in contrast to Paul's own refusal to obstruct the Gospel (1 Cor. 9.5–12).[36] Anyone alerted to the intra-textual echoes that link these passages might note that they extend to Galatians 5.7–10, and not only explicitly pick up the language of Galatians 1.6–7, but also connect with the key passages from 1 and 2 Corinthians.[37] According to Jerome, 'some', not explicitly identified as Marcionites, saw the warning as a covert attack against Peter.[38] It is difficult to know whether there is any deliberate irony when Epiphanius describes Marcion's own textual procedures with the very verb of Paul's exasperated cry, 'Would that those who are disturbing you would cut themselves away' (ἀποκόπτειν: Epiphanius, *Pan.* 42. 11.17, R1, S55; 12.3, R18k).

Evidently, the primary letters within Marcion's 'Apostolikon' also set out some of the key components of Paul's Gospel as Marcion understood it. Certainly it is Tertullian who sees Galatians as particularly addressing the question of Law and Gospel; however, his defence of the position of Peter and the 'brethren' indicates that he is genuinely responding to his opponent here, even if his own reading of Acts 15 alongside Galatians 2.1–7 refines the question in terms of 'obedience to the Law of Moses' (cf. Acts 15.5). Without the aid of Acts Marcion would have interpreted the same question in a different direction; the conclusion he drew was that by rejecting – as he saw it – such adherence Paul showed that he represented a deity other than the one who demanded it.

However, no less important was the narrative of Paul's vigilant defence of the truth of his Gospel against those, even apostles, who so readily

36 1 Cor. 9.5, 'The rest (λοιποί) of the apostles'; see n. 35 above.

37 'The one who called you' (Gal. 1.6; 5. 8); 'upset you (ταράσσειν)' (Gal. 1.7; 5. 10); '(pose) an obstacle (ἐνκόπτειν)' (1 Cor. 9.; Gal. 5.7); 'deceive (δολοῦν)' (2 Cor. 11.13; Gal. 5.9 in Marcion's text according to Epiphanius, *Pan.* 42. 12.3, S4, and also in D* lat). To these may be added 2 Cor. 2.17 and 4.2–4, where Paul denies that he, like some, peddles in or adulterates (καπηλεύειν, δολοῦν; in both cases Lat. '*adultero*') the word of God, immediately preceding a passage that Marcion interpreted of the activity of the Creator God (see below p. 258).

38 See Jerome, *Ad Gal.* II. 5,10b ll.2–6, and compare Harnack, *Marcion*, 77*. It is easy to see how the final words, 'whoever he may be' (Gal. 5.10), could lend themselves to such a reading.

compromised it. Tertullian recognised the problem and he resolved it by representing Paul as someone young in faith, anxious lest he had gone wrong and so seeking the approval of his seniors, gaining it, and ultimately working in complete agreement with them (1 Cor. 15.11); perhaps, Tertullian conceded, initially Paul had reacted in the somewhat over-heated manner of a new convert, but in due course he would learn the virtues of adaptability (1 Cor. 9; *AM* I. 20.1–4; V. 3.4). Marcion's picture could not be more different; although Tertullian represents the disagreements between Paul and the others as over behaviour not doctrine, for Marcion they are not so much over doctrine rather than behaviour as over the very truth of the Gospel.[39] For Marcion also Galatians presumably demonstrated that the conflict was not resolved – he read Galatians 6.7 as a statement, 'You are in error', and not as a warning (*AM* V. 4.14);[40] this then provoked the interpreter to continual alertness for its subsequent manifestations. He may have found such a manifestation even in the final letter of his collection, Philippians, which perhaps he, like the 'Marcionite' prologue, took as written from Rome. Tertullian goes to great pains to point out that what Paul here tackles is not the variety of doctrine or *rule* but only that of the human sentiments from which it is preached, and that the 'truth' Paul upholds refers to the faithfulness of the preaching, and does not distinguish a true rule from some other (Phil. 1.12–18). It was, on the contrary, precisely the authentic 'rule', adulterated by false preachers, which Marcion claimed to recover (*AM* V. 20.1–2; cf. I. 20.1).

Galatians 4.22–6

Analysis of a particular passage will again serve to highlight a number of aspects of the difficulties and possibilities in reconstructing Marcion's text and interpretation, as well as the strategy of his opponents. Tertullian discusses Galatians 4.22–6 immediately following Galatians 4.10.[41]

> For just as it happens to thieves that something falls from their booty which indicts them, so I think that Marcion has left behind the last reference to

[39] See Robert D. Sider, 'Literary Artifice and the Figure of Paul in the Writings of Tertullian', ed. Babcock, *Paul and the Legacies of Paul*, 99–120, who also notes that Tertullian's Paul is drawn more from the Corinthian letters than from Romans or Galatians.

[40] I.e without the negative of a prohibition, μή.

[41] Epiphanius combines Gal. 3.13b with 4.23b, possibly to bring the former under his scheme of redemptive prophecy and fulfilment, although he himself may have forgotten the principles guiding his original collection of excerpts (*Pan* 42.12.3, R2).

Abraham, although nothing more needed removing, even if he has changed it somewhat. If then – '**Abraham had two sons, one from the maidservant and the other from the free woman, but the one from the maidservant was born in fleshly manner, and the one from the free woman through promise,**[42] **which things are allegorical**, that is predictive (*portendentia*) of something; **for these**[43] **are two testaments** (*testamenta*), or two manifestations (*ostensiones*) as we find it interpreted; **one from mount Sinai** into the synagogue of the Jews according to the law **giving birth into servitude**, the other giving birth ***above every principality, power, domination, and every name that is named not only in this age but also in the future*, which is our mother**, into which we have (been) promised,[44] the holy church,' and therefore he adds, '**Therefore, brothers, we are not children of the maidservant but of the free**' – so then he has made clear that the nobility of Christianity locates its allegorical sign in the son of Abraham born from the free woman just as the legal servitude of Judaism does in the son of the maidservant, and therefore each disposition is from the same God, from whom we find the setting out of each disposition

(*AM* V. 4.8).

Tertullian's own habitual concerns are evident in this passage: He does not challenge Marcion's identification of two dispositions (*dispositio*), Judaism and Christianity, but he does deny that they are so antithetical as to come from different deities. As elsewhere, the fact that they are anticipated in Scripture proves for him their common source; it establishes that Christianity was part of God's plan and not a sudden innovation, and that this God is the God at work throughout the scriptural narrative. The text that Tertullian weaves into his own interpretation is that of Marcion, but he does not comment on its idiosyncrasies other than on the rendering of the Pauline covenants ('διαθῆκαι', v. 24). However, the force of his explanation at this point would differ according to whether he is working from the Greek text of Marcion's 'Apostolikon' or from one already translated into Latin. In the latter case, this Latin translation presumably offered '*ostensio*' where Tertullian would have preferred '*testamentum*'.[45] In the former case, Marcion's Greek text, which

42 Epiphanius *Pan* 42.11.8, S2, 'One from the promise through freedom'; 12.3, S2, '... through the free one'; Holl, *Epiphanius* II, 120, 156, reads 'free one' in both cases although one MS at 42.12.3, S2 also reads 'freedom'. Given the inversion of order and prepositions, 'freedom' makes better sense once the broader context of the allegory is ignored.

43 Neuter plural (*haec*) as also in the Latin tradition; the Greek is feminine plural, αὗται.

44 The text is debated; the manuscript tradition is 'we have promised'.

45 So Braun, *Contre Marcion*, V, 120–1, following Harnack, *Marcion*, 76*; however, Braun's appeal to '*ostendo, ostensio*' in *AM* V. 11.4 as evidence that this is a Marcionite term does not rule out the possibility that it translates a distinctive Greek word.

Tertullian is translating as he works, either replaced 'διαθῆκαι' or glossed it, in the text or in the margin, with another term which Tertullian renders as '*ostensio*', probably ἀπό-, ἐπί-, or ἔνδειξις.[46] The broader question cannot be decided on the basis of this passage alone; in either case, however, it would appear that Marcion favoured language suggesting manifestation or revelation over the potentially legal or documentary sense of 'testament'.

In Tertullian's Latin version, whether or not in any underlying Greek, the two 'testaments' refer not to the women (feminine plural) as in the Greek text of Galatians 4.24, but to two events or facts (neuter plural). This interpretation could have arisen from the preceding parenthetical comment 'which things (neuter) are allegorical', but it would also suit the way in which Marcion apparently understood Paul's claim that the Scriptures contained allegory.[47] A similar approach is evident in his treatment of 1 Corinthians 10.1–11, a passage that is well-attested for Marcion although the differences between Tertullian, Epiphanius, and the *Dialogue of Adamantius* obscure the precise form of his text; according to Tertullian 1 Corinthians 10.6 read 'these things happened as examples *for* us', rather than the genitive 'of us', enabling Marcion to take this, as also 1 Corinthians 10.11, not as positive typology but as a warning lesson of the consequences of following the Creator.[48] Hence, Tertullian's mockery of Marcion for failing to excise the reference to Abraham in Galatians 4.22 as apparently he had done in 3.14a, 15–25 misses the point; Marcion did not delete systematically all scriptural references and passages, for to the extent that they spoke of the Creator they offered a contrary model to the Gospel. It is not surprising, on the other hand, that the text of the passage as quoted by Tertullian does omit the somewhat obscure explanation of Hagar and Mt. Sinai as well as the references to Jerusalem, both present and above (Gal. 4.25, 26a), and may also have omitted vv. 27–8 and perhaps also vv. 29 and 30, for these would not have served that purpose.[49]

Equally striking are two additions; firstly, preceding 'which is our mother' (Gal. 4.26b), is an insertion (in bold italics above) apparently taken from

46 So, among others, Schmid, *Marcion und sein Apostolos*, 125–6.

47 Jerome, *Ad Gal.* II. 4.26 ll.48–58, notes that Marcion and Mani retain the allegory on the grounds that it shows 'against us' that the Law is to be understood other than as is written.

48 See Norelli, 'Funzione', 568–70. In *Adam.* 94.6–10 [2.17] the Marcionite Marcus protests that 1 Cor. 10.11 does not read 'as a type' (τύπος) but as a nontype (ἀτυπῶς); however, the word is not attested with this meaning and the claim may be an anti-Marcionite invention (see Schmid, *Marcion und sein Apostolos*, 224–5; Tsutsui, *Auseinandersetzung*, 264–5).

49 Stephen C. Carlson, '"For Sinai Is a Mountain in Arabia: A Note on the Text of Galatians 4,25', *ZNW* 105 (2014), 80–101, argues that the phrase (= v. 25a) is a marginal gloss incorporated into the text. It is impossible to tell whether Marcion read this.

Ephesians 1.21 and built around the repetition of 'giving birth'. The effect of this is to improve the internal parallelism of Paul's analogy, so that both testaments (not mothers, see above) give birth, but at the same time it serves to shift the weight of interest emphatically onto the second birth-giver, and to ensure that they do not in any way appear as commensurate, albeit different, dispensations. The second addition apparently provides a destination for each birth-giving, the first 'the synagogue of the Jews according to the law', the second the holy Church.[50] It would be easy to imagine that Marcion might make the first alteration, particularly since Ephesians 1.21 was a favourite testimony for the transcendence of the supreme God (see Irenaeus, *AH* IV. 19.2; 24.2); the second addition at first sight seems to make Marcion responsible for an unusually explicit 'anti-Jewish' interpretation.

However, a similar but briefer expansion of the Pauline passage is also found in Ephraem's commentary on Galatians: 'These (women) indeed were symbols of the two testaments, one of the people of the Jews according to the law giving birth in slavery to the likeness of the same, Hagar ... but the higher Jerusalem is free as is Sara and is high above all powers and principalities. This/she is our mother, the holy church, which we have confessed.'[51] Clearly Ephraem is not quoting a Marcionite text, and unintentional dependence on one seems improbable; it has been argued that both independently reflect an earlier form of the text, and even that Ephraem's version is more primitive.[52] This may be so, although the style of this commentary elides quotation of the text, paraphrase, and comment, so that it is not certain that Ephraem is working with a distinct text form. However, such a contrast between 'people' or 'the synagogue' and 'the holy church' can be traced back at least to the mid-second century. Justin Martyr provides a striking parallel in his interpretation of the two daughters of Laban for whom Jacob laboured, 'thus Leah is your people and synagogue, Rachel is

[50] This makes best sense although the word order is not fully clear; see Braun, *Contre Marcion*, V, 122–3.

[51] '*Hae vero fuerunt symbola duorum testamentorum. Una populi Judaeorum, secundum legem in servitude generans ad similitudinem ejusdem Agar. Agar enim ipsa est mons Sina in Arabia; est autem illa similitudo hujus Jerusalem, quia in subjection est, et una cum filiis suis servit Romanis. Superior autem Jerusalem libera est, sicut Sara; et eminet supra omnes potestates ac principatus. Ipsa est mater nostra, Ecclesia sancta, quam confessi sumus. Neque nos sumus hujus inventores, Isaias enim praeveniens discit de haec: Latare sterilis quae non pariebas: quia multi fuerint filii Ecclesiae sterilis quam filii populi virum habentis*'. *S. Ephraemi Syri in Epistolas D. Pauli nunc primum ex armenio in latinum sermonem a patribus Mekitharistis translati* (Venice: Sanctus Lazarus, 1893), 135.

[52] So Schmid, *Marcion und sein Apostolos*, 126–9.

our church. And Christ serves until now on behalf of these and of the enslaved in both' – although his final comment and what follows would better fit an application to believers of Jewish and of Gentile descent (*Dial.* 134.3). Likewise, the description of the church as mother, although a possible deduction from Galatians 4.26 so read, also fits in the second half of the second century (cf. Eusebius, *HE* V. 1.45).[53]

Detecting earlier parallels does not resolve all the problems posed by these expansions. While Ephraem's 'the holy church which we have confessed' makes good sense, this is not the meaning of the wording given by Tertullian; apart from the awkward word order, the verb *repromitto* clearly recalls the 'through promise' (*per repromissionem*) of Galatians 4.23, and this echo rules out any suggestion that there is a reference to *confession* of faith 'in the church'.[54] That the Church is in some sense the fulfilment of the promise is contextually more likely, although this demands reading the verb as a passive, 'we have been promised';[55] even so, it is not obvious how Marcion would understand that, unless perhaps that the promise awaited eschatological fulfilment, perhaps reinforced by the addition of Ephesians 1.21. Other aspects of Marcion's interpretation can only be guessed at; for example, in the context of what has preceded, it is possible that he referred 'the synagogue of the Jews' to the interpretation represented by the (false) apostles, and so to the Church which appealed to them.[56]

It can hardly be decided whether the more elaborate reworking of the Pauline text presupposed by Tertullian is to be attributed to Marcion himself or whether it had already evolved from the more basic source text represented by Ephraem. In either case this may be a developing process of marginal glosses being embedded in the text; the underlying interpretive model followed fits well in the second century, and it is not of itself distinctively 'Marcionite'. The effect of the intensified oppositional language may appear anti-Jewish,[57] but it does not follow that this was an intentional characteristic of Marcion's interpretive principles.

[53] Compare the Church as woman in the *Shepherd of Hermas*, and the feminine imagery of Church and heresy (pp. 101–02).

[54] So the translation by Evans, *Adversus Marcionem*, 2, 531. Thus, it is unlikely that it refers to initiation into the Marcionite church (so Norelli, 'Funzione', 575), and the speculation by Blackman, *Marcion and His Influence*, 8, as to the character of Marcion's creed and its relationship with that of the Catholic church is rendered void.

[55] So Braun, *Contre Marcion*, V, 122–3. [56] So Norelli, 'Funzione', 573–4.

[57] So Schmid, *Marcion und sein Apostolos*, 129.

Law, sin, grace, and faith

One element of this heightened opposition is the addition of 'according to the law' into the text of Galatians 4.24. This could be intended merely to clarify the connection of the analogy with Paul's concerns about the Law in the surrounding verses. Indeed, despite his identification of 'the opposition between Law and Gospel' as the central tenet of Marcion's 'Antitheses' (*AM* IV. 9.3), it is Tertullian himself who repeatedly identifies slavery with the Law, even supplying it where it is absent from Paul's argument (V. 4.9 on Gal. 5.1). Earlier he paraphrased the danger posed by the false brothers, 'lest they brought us into slavery', the wording also preserved by Marcion, as 'lest they brought it ('the Christian liberty') into slavery to Judaism' (*AM* V. 3.5 on Gal. 2.4). Tertullian's tendency to introduce the language of Law can be found elsewhere: Commenting on the 'new covenant' of 2 Corinthians 3.6, he asserts, 'We have already defended the double force of the Creator, both judge and good, killing by letter through the Law, giving life by the spirit through the Gospel'; neither 'Law' nor 'Gospel' are provided by the immediate Pauline context, but Tertullian continues, 'this coheres with my faith also by placing the Gospel above the Law ... indeed, mine more' (*AM* V. 11.4–5).[58] This exegetical tendency can make it difficult to untangle the voices of Tertullian and of his opponent: If it was Marcion who asserted that the false brothers acted through 'perseverance in the law, no doubt from a total faith in the Creator', Tertullian would have agreed, determined only to present it as a matter of 'behaviour not of religion, of discipline not of divinity' (*AM* V. 3.2; 2.4).

It is, therefore, Tertullian's interests that lead him to elide Galatians 2.16 with 3.11, once again paraphrasing Paul's formula as 'a person is justified by the freedom of faith, not by the servitude of law' (*AM* V. 3.8). How much of the intervening verses were retained in his text of Marcion is therefore obscure, and Jerome's question remains valid, 'Let us ask Marcion, who repudiates the prophets, how he interprets what follows?'[59] Yet evidently Marcion did include the quotation from Habakkuk 2.4 at Galatians 3.11, although Tertullian does not capitalise on this 'oversight'.[60] Indeed, ignoring the initial chapters of Galatians so important to Tertullian's defence,

58 See Lieu, '"As much my apostle as Christ is mine"', 59–60.

59 Jerome, *Ad Gal.* I. 3,1a ll.59–60; at I. 3,6 ll.2–5, he states that Marcion erased Gal. 3.6–9, and this is confirmed by Tertullian at *AM* V. 3.11. Tertullian alludes to Gal. 2.18, and the *Dialogue of Adamantius* (*Adam.* V.22 [222.13f]) cites Gal. 2.20.

60 It is less certain whether Marcion's text retained the quotation at Rom. 1.17.

Epiphanius chooses Galatians 3.11b/Habakkuk 2. 4 to open his first Pauline scholion, prefixed by an imperative 'learn' (μάθετε).[61] It is followed by Galatians. 3.10a in an idiosyncratic form, 'as many as are under the law are under a curse', and then by Galatians 3.12b (= Lev. 18.5), 'the one who does these things shall live by them' (*Pan.* 42.12.3, S1). The effect is perhaps to interpret the quotation from Leviticus in a positive sense, drawing on the shared verb 'shall live' in order to explicate 'the righteous'. It is unlikely that this selectivity is to be attributed to Epiphanius, who generally is more interested in emphasising the witness of Scripture and unity of the Testaments, but whether it can be traced to Marcion is less certain. Once again, it is easy to imagine how the initial imperative, 'learn', could have entered the text from a marginal comment or section heading, and also how easily a scribe or exegete might wish to make explicit the parallel between being *under* the law and *under* a curse.[62]

Yet Tertullian would not have challenged such an elision of law and curse; he agrees that 'in the law there is curse, in faith, indeed, blessing', but he denies that this is an opposition 'of authors' (*AM* V. 3.9; cf. Gal. 3.9a). Marcion apparently grounded his reading on the Creator's words spoken in the Law, 'Cursed be everyone who is hung on a tree'; this indubitably established his utter alienation from Christ, in contrast to 'the blessing (reading εὐλογία with P^{46} D* F G, etc. instead of 'promise') of the spirit [which] we receive through faith' (Gal. 3.13b, 14b; *AM* V. 3.9–11).[63] After this Tertullian continues his own explanation directly with Galatians 3.26 in the otherwise unattested form, 'For you are all sons of faith'. Presumably Galatians 3.15b–25 were missing from his copy of the 'Apostolikon', although he makes no comment on this; if Marcion had wanted to avoid references to Abraham he need only have omitted vv. 14a, 15–18.[64] On the other hand, the apparent omission 'of God through' in 3.26 would have served little purpose;

[61] This has the result that the introductory 'ὅτι' ('because') is now read as 'that'.

[62] See Schmid, *Marcion und sein Apostolos*, 190–1, who does not think Marcion's text had the verses in this order, although he notes that the form 'under the law' is found in Ephraem. Braun, *Contre Marcion*, V, 103, suggests that Tertullian's '…law, in which the doer (*operarius*) is not justified' (*AM* V.3. 8[9]) may refer to Gal. 3.10a, 'from deeds of the law', but an alternative would be that it refer to Gal. 3.12b.

[63] Curiously, Epiphanius combines Gal. 3.13b with an adaptation of 4.23b, 'the one from promise through the free woman/freedom' (*Pan* 42.12.3, S1). See above, n. 41.

[64] Schmid, *Marcion und sein Apostolos*, 249, suggests omission due to homoioteleuton, the scribe's eye jumping from 'of faith' in 3.14b to the same phrase in v.25 or 26. See ibid, 114–6 for a discussion of the text of v. 26. At this point Tertullian refers to 'the heretical diligence's' erasure of mention of Abraham, but alludes only to 3.6–9.

however, the effect, and perhaps the origin, of the section, whether or not by Marcion, is to heighten the contrast with being 'under the law'.

Although Paul's letter to the Romans took fourth place in Marcion's 'Apostolikon', it might be expected that it would provide the major context for him to wrestle with the relationship of law, sin, faith, and Gospel. Tertullian would agree with him that this letter 'appears most of all to exclude the Law', but his comment that there were more gaping holes here than in any other letter suggests that Marcion's 'Apostolikon' was marked by significant omissions (*AM* V. 13.1, 4). By now, however, Tertullian, explicitly wearying of over repetition, does not pretend to a detailed analysis of Marcion's text and interpretation, and this renders their recovery particularly difficult.[65] He starts by citing Romans 1.16–18, which he follows immediately with 2.2, and, after making a comment on Marcion's gaps, with references to 2.16a, 12, 14, 16b (*sic*: *AM* V. 13.2–5). By finding cross-references and equivalents within these verses Tertullian argues that judgement, wrath, law, nature, truth, Gospel, and Christ must all pertain to the same God, and he insinuates that for Marcion they did not do so. The sequence of verses, which entails the omission of Romans 1.19–2.1 as well as of 2.3–11, suits the structure of his own argument, but arguably he is also following Marcion's text here; if in his copy 1.19–2.1 had been present they would have provided useful proof that nature belonged to the same God.[66] Marcion, he implies, understood the God of 2.2 and 2.16, whose judgement is 'according to truth' or 'according to the Gospel',[67] to refer to the Father, the revelation of whose righteousness is central to the Gospel, leading away from faith in the Law to faith in the Gospel – something on which Tertullian and Marcion would agree. The revelation of wrath (1.18), however, could not pertain to the same God; indeed, it is possible that Marcion omitted the genitive 'of God' here, since it is absent from Tertullian's citation despite his subsequent question 'wrath of which God?'[68] How Marcion would have explained Romans 2.12–15 is difficult to determine: Norelli suggests that the 'hearers' of the Law would refer to the Jews or to those who rely on the Law for salvation, the 'doers' to those who according to vv. 14–15 observe the Law

65 For a detailed attempt to reconstruct Marcion's reading of Romans see Norelli, 'Marcione lettore'.

66 Against Schmid, *Marcion und sein Apostolos*, 85–7, who emphasises that the omission serves Tertullian's rhetoric.

67 Tertullian omits 'my', but it is not clear whether Marcion did so also; Tertullian, and probably Marcion, read the future, 'will judge' (with D^2 M latt).

68 At *AM* V. 17.9 on Eph. 2.3b, Tertullian anticipates that the heretic might call 'the Creator the Lord of wrath', but this is a clearly hypothetical suggestion.

out of ignorance, and therefore without seeking salvation from it; righteousness and unrighteousness, he further suggests, are defined for Marcion by response to the Gospel, so that judgement becomes a form of 'self-selection'.[69]

There are firmer grounds for concluding that Marcion understood Romans 2.21–22 as a deliberate attack against the Creator as the one who forbade theft even while instigating it, most notoriously in the instruction to the Jews to take with them the goods of the Egyptians (*AM* V. 13.6; cf. Exod. 12.35–6). This is a well-worn example, and Marcion was not the first to see it as undermining God's character, although crediting Paul himself with the critique probably was an innovation.[70] How far through the following verses Marcion traced a continuing indictment of the Creator is unclear; Norelli suggests cautiously that perhaps he could have so read the rest of the chapter.[71] Tertullian himself insinuates that Marcion understood 'the Jew in secret' (Rom. 2.29) as the one who responded to the proclamation of a previously secret God, although that Marcion would use the term 'Jew' in a positive sense is unexpected.[72] All this suggests that Marcion's complaint was not against the Law as such so much as against the inconsistencies of character displayed by its author, the Creator. Certainly it was fundamental for Marcion that 'the law is not from the God of Christ', which, according to Tertullian, he concluded from his reading of Philippians 3.9, 'now having a righteousness not his own which is from the law, but which is through that one (*ipsum*, presumably Christ) from God' (*AM* V. 20.6).[73] Within this framework, law and faith or grace belonged to two contrasting and to some extent consecutive orders: Marcion's text of Romans 3.21 read, 'Then the Law, now the righteousness of God through faith in Christ' (*AM* V. 13.8). More particularly, Marcion seems to have suggested that the Law was (but) a means by which the Creator deceived, an idea against which Tertullian protests: 'Therefore it is not the law that seduced but sin through the opportunity of the command; why do you impute to the God of the law what the Apostle does not venture to impute to his law?' (V. 13.14). Such a view would also explain Origen's claim that Marcion and those

[69] Norelli, 'Marcione lettore', 641–51 who speaks of 'Autogiudizio'.

[70] On the charge see Tertullian, *AM* II. 20; 28.2; IV. 24.5; Irenaeus, *AH* IV. 30.1, 3; 31.1; Philo, *De Vita Mosis* I. 141. See p. 361.

[71] Norelli, 'Marcione lettore', 654–55.

[72] *AM* V. 13.7; however, Braun's claim that Marcion himself called the Creator 'the God of the Jews' is not substantiated (*Contre Marcion*, V, 265).

[73] Tertullian does not comment on the omission of both references to faith, the first of which ('through *faith of* Christ') is essential to the argument.

like him condemned the Law for introducing sin, presupposing that prior to the giving of the Law there was no sin (Rom. 5.20).[74] Even so, it is difficult to understand how Marcion interpreted Romans 7.12, that the law is holy, and possibly 7.14, that it is spiritual, verses that apparently were in his text (*AM* V. 13.14–15).[75]

This, together with a more precise sense of how Marcion understood the relationship between the Law and sin, is obscured by Tertullian's own failure to discuss Romans 7.14b–25. Undoubtedly this passage was to be found in the 'Apostolikon', and Tertullian refers back to Romans 7.23 in his defence that Jesus' flesh was real, albeit not sinful (*AM* V. 14.1; Rom. 8.3). Even so, it is not difficult to imagine how the passage could be read in a way congenial to Marcion's position, with its view of the desperate condition of the human being, particularly as fleshly. More particularly, Romans 7.24, 'Wretched man (ταλαίπωρος) that I am', may have supplied Marcion with the self-description that Tertullian mocks, 'fellow wretch' (συνταλαίπορος, *commiseronis*; *AM* IV. 9.3).[76] By contrast, the concluding cry of gratitude to God, particularly if known to Marcion in the 'Western' form, 'the grace of God', would supply a fitting answer to the search for rescue from 'this body of death'.

The Creator

The Creator is not, however, defined only in terms of the Law. It is Tertullian who insists that the 'weak and impoverished elements' to which Paul accuses the Galatians of returning must refer to 'the initial aspects of the Law' (Gal. 4.8–10; *AM* V. 4.5–7).[77] Although he anticipates having to rebut Marcion's triumphant and ironical response, 'Did he [i.e., the Creator] remove what he himself established?', Tertullian is more concerned to challenge his interpretation of them as 'cosmic elements', and hence of Paul's words as derogatory of the one who created them. Similarly, he denies what is presumably Marcion's view, that 'the elements of the world' at Colossians 2.8 can refer to 'heaven and earth', insisting that they point to

74 *Comm .in Rom.* V. 6,4–8 (Caroline P. Hammond Bammel, *Der Römerbriefkommentar des Origenes. Kritische Aufgabe der Übersetzung Rufins* Buch 4–6 [ed. H. J. Frede and H. Stanjek; VL 33; Freiburg: Herder, 1997]).

75 Tertullian takes 'spiritual' to mean 'prophetic', but how Marcion would have understood it is unknown. Norelli, 'Marcione lettore', 661, against Barbara Aland, 'Marcion und die Marcioniten', *Was ist Gnosis?*, 318–40 (= *TRE* 22 [1992] 89–101), 327.

76 See above, p. 193.

77 Tertullian here appeals to the meaning of the Latin '*elementa*' among Romans, which might suggest that he is arguing from a Latin version of Galatians.

'human sophistry and especially that of philosophers' (*AM* V. 19.7). Somewhat more difficult to interpret is Tertullian's text of Galatians 4.8, 'If therefore you serve (or 'have served') those who are Gods *in* nature', where the Greek manuscript tradition of the verse reads, 'You served those who by nature are *not* Gods'. Although a number of editors have emended Tertullian's text to match the Greek,[78] the absence of the negative makes good sense of his argument that the error is of a 'physical, that is natural, superstition which puts the elements in place of God'. If Marcion did so read the text, it would have reinforced a close link between 'nature', 'elements of the universe', and a being named 'God'; although it is less certain in what sense he would have identified the elements *as* 'Gods', fundamental to the Creator is his responsibility for the created order.[79]

Although distinguishing Tertullian's rhetoric from actual Marcionite exegesis is often hazardous, it is in harmony with these examples that Marcion's interpretation of 'world' (*mundus*, κόσμος/αἰών) with reference to the Creator is a repeated topos. The classic location for this interpretation, and perhaps its primary inspiration, is 2 Corinthians 4.4 where Tertullian roundly rejects the translation, 'in whom the God of this age has blinded the minds of unbelievers', and insists that the genitive qualifies the final noun, 'unbelievers of this age'. Nonetheless, he suggests that even if Marcion's reading were accepted 'God of this age' would have to refer to the devil or else to those whom the Gentiles worshipped as God (cf. Eph. 2.12), and not to the Creator of whom they were ignorant (*AM* V. 11.9–13).[80] Tertullian is neither the first nor the last to offer the first of these alternatives, showing that Marcion was also not the only one to see the implications of the most natural reading of the Greek.[81] However, the conclusion that the Marcionite Marcus draws in the *Dialogue of*

78 Tertullian's text reads '*qui in natura sunt dei*', emended by several editors (including Evans, *Adversus Marcionem* 2, 528) to '*qui non natura sunt dei*'; some, including Braun, *Contre Marcion*, V, 116, also read the perfect '*servistis*' (following the Greek aorist) in place of the present '*servitis*'. There is no other manuscript evidence for the absence of the negative.

79 Drijvers, 'Marcion's Reading of Gal. 4,8', argues that Marcion believed that the Gentiles had worshipped nature deities, but he links the argument here with the Marcionite third principle of Hyle.

80 Contra Norbert Brox, '"Non huius aevi deus" (zu Tertullian, adv.Marc. V 11,10)', *ZNW* 59 (1968), 259–61, who proposes adding a negative to maintain Tertullian's consistency.

81 See Irenaeus, *AH* III. 7.1–2, and the note by Harvey, *Sancti Irenaei*, 2, 25; see also *AM* IV. 38.7–8 and above, p. 226, for a similar issue in Luke 20.34–6. See Lieu, '"As much my apostle as Christ is mine"', 54–5. Per Bilde, '2 Cor. 4,4: The View of Satan and the Created World in Paul', ed. Per Bilde, Helge Hjaer Nielsen, and Jørgen Podeman Søvensen, *Apocryphon Severini presented to Søren Giversen* (Aarhus: Aarhus University Press, 1993), 29–41, argues that Paul himself thought that the created world was under Satanic powers.

Adamantius, that the attempt to prohibit illumination proves that 'the God of the world' is evil, may go beyond what Marcion himself claimed (*Adam.* 110.20–6 [2.21]).

The same conflict of interpretation emerges at Ephesians 2.2–3, where Tertullian again asserts that 'Marcion cannot interpret here also ... (age of this) world' as 'God of the world'. Tertullian's primary objection on this occasion is that what is created cannot be identified with its Creator, but his more exegetical objection is that the appositional 'prince of the power of the air' would be an inadequate epithet for one who is the 'prince of the power of the ages', and that in any case the Creator would hardly put into effect the unbelief 'which he himself suffered from both Jews and Gentiles'. It must, he asserts, with a cross-reference to the disputed reading at 2 Corinthians 4.4 ('elsewhere'), refer to the devil; Paul's retrospective reference to the behaviour 'of us all' refers not to humankind under the Creator but to his own earlier persecution of the Church under the impulse of the devil (*AM* V. 17.7–9).[82]

However, as an extension of this, on occasion Marcion seems to have interpreted even the simple phrase 'the world' as indicating the Creator. So, at Galatians 6.14 Tertullian stresses that when Paul says that he is crucified to the world and the world to him he does not say, '(to) the God of the world', as was perhaps interpreted by Marcion; instead characteristically he explains that 'world' refers rather to 'its behaviour' (*AM* V. 4.15). Marcion's reading of 2 Corinthians 3.14 apparently followed the same pattern, namely that 'the minds of the world' (instead of 'their minds') are hardened, where he again interpreted 'world' as referring to the Creator: Tertullian makes the same objection to the interpretation but he does not question the reading, which although not otherwise attested may not have originated with Marcion.[83] At 1 Corinthians 1.21, 'the world did not know God through wisdom', Tertullian again tackles those whom he describes as 'the most subtle heretics (who) here particularly interpret "world" (*mundum*) through "Lord of the world"', and who from this argue the Creator's ignorance of the 'unknown' God. They would, he anticipates, defend their position against his own identification of 'the world' with 'the people in the world' by appealing to 1 Corinthians 4.9, 'a spectacle to

82 Tertullian is particularly exercised by the Pauline phrase, 'children of wrath by nature', which perhaps aided Marcion's own interpretation.

83 *AM* V. 11.5; Schmid, *Marcion und sein Apostolos*, 118, notes how the verse parallels 2 Cor. 4.4, and suggests that the reading 'world' may have originated as a pre-Marcionite scribal attempt to universalise the sentiment beyond the Jews who are intended in the context.

the world, angels, and men'; this for them represented three descending categories, whereas for him the last two are encompassed by the first (*AM* V. 5.7; 7.1).

Marcion's text of Ephesians 3.9 could have further supported his position: Omitting the preposition 'in' before 'God' (with ℵ*), it described 'the mystery that had been hidden from the beginning *from* God who created all things'.[84] Yet here caution may be merited: Tertullian's detailed exposé of the lack of any logic in such a position turns on the unresolved question whether the principalities and powers of the following verse belong to the Creator or to the superior God; as he imagines first one answer, then another, and then, finally, portrays the heretic as compelled to change his position, suspicion grows that the entire debate has been set up by Tertullian himself to discredit an opposition who may not have recognised their own position at any point (*AM* V. 18.1–4). Likewise, responding to 'Our fight is ... against world-rulers' (Eph. 6.12), Tertullian mocks, 'How many creator Gods!' (*AM* V. 18.12); it is possible that Marcion found a reference to the Creator in this verse, particularly since Irenaeus claims that Marcion called the Creator '*kosmokrator*', a term that comes only here in the New Testament, but it again may be Tertullian who is determined to find wherever possible a 'straw Creator' to knock down.

Tertullian's very determination to undermine any such interpretation undoubtedly indicates that there were points where at least some found it compelling. The themes of hiddenness and ignorance come together in a key way at 1 Corinthians 2.6–9. Although Tertullian passes over in silence his own, or his opponent's, interpretation of 'the rulers of this age who are coming to nought' (2.6), it seems highly probable that Marcion would have found here also a reference to the Creator.[85] This would prepare for the position that Tertullian's subsequent vehement denials project, namely that the God who hid wisdom before the ages was someone other than the Creator, and that the rulers of this age, being the representatives of the Creator and equally victims of that hiding, crucified 'the Lord of glory', Christ, out of ignorance (*AM* V. 6.1–9; cf. III. 23.5).[86] Initially Tertullian grants parts of Marcion's interpretation, but he identifies 'the rulers' with

84 The *Dialogue of Adamantius* reads the text with 'in' (*Adam.* 106.30–108.6 [2.20]) and uses it against the Marcionite position.

85 Epiphanius, *Pan.* 42.12.3, R11, uses the plural to refute Marcion's idea of three principles (see p. 112), and reports nothing about Marcion's own interpretation.

86 Tertullian adds a further layer to his exegesis by understanding 'our glory' as the object of 'determined in advance' in v. 7, and then identifying this with 'which' at the beginning of v. 8. It is unclear whether this follows Marcion's text.

'the apostate angels and the devil', erstwhile members of God's court but excluded from God's counsels; subsequently, however, he decides that even they knew what they were doing, and, once again blaming the need to find an alternative explanation on Marcion's second thoughts at calling the powers of the Creator 'rulers', he comes to the conclusion that the reference is rather to the Jewish people, their rulers, Herod, and even Pilate.

Although Tertullian passes over in silence 1 Corinthians 2.9, it is easy to see how Marcion could have understood this climax to the passage as supporting his own exegesis; indeed, the *Dialogue of Adamantius* may allude to this verse when Adamantius charges the Marcionite Marcus with saying, 'the Christ was a stranger and never entered the understanding of anyone'.[87] The saying, whose origin is unknown, is widely attested in early Christian literature as applied to the revelation brought by Jesus (cf. *Gosp.Thomas* 17).[88] A similar effect would be achieved by Marcion's retention of Romans 11.33–35, while, to Tertullian's disgust, omitting the preceding scriptural quotations; on their own these verses would become an acclamation of the inscrutable ways of the newly revealed God (*AM* V. 14.9).

Christ the revealer

Clearly for Marcion Paul's teaching established the incommensurability between the Creator and the Christ, revealer of another God. Another passage which would reinforce this was the curse from Deuteronomy 21.23 cited in Galatians 3.13: 'Why', asks Tertullian, 'is it not more appropriate (*competo*) for the Creator to have given up his own son to his own curse than for that God of yours to have submitted to a curse, and indeed on behalf of a person who does not belong to him?' (*AM* V. 3.10; cf. III. 18.1 where Tertullian promises to explain the curse later, but fails to do so). The almost 'modalist' identification of ('your') God with Christ suits Tertullian's rhetoric and should not be over-pressed; however, the 'inappropriate' purchase of what belonged to another was apparently precisely what Marcion did find in Paul. Although Tertullian makes no comment on the verb 'redeem' (ἐξαγοράζειν, Gal. 4.5; cf. 3.13), Epiphanius cites as his prime example of Marcion's distortion of Paul's words his explanation of Galatians 3.13: 'If we

87 *Adam.* 84.20–1 [2.14]; Tsutsui, *Auseinandersetzung*, 247, notes that Marcus nowhere does say this and suggests that it goes back the source used in places by the work. See also, below, p. 272.

88 See also Ps.Hippolytus, *Ref.* V.24.1 (Justin the Gnostic) where Marcovich, *Refutatio*, 199n lists other references; similarly DeConick, *Original Gospel*, 99–101.

did belong to him, he would not have purchased (ἀγοράζω) what belonged to him. He made the purchase and came into a world alien to him to redeem us who are not his. For we were the creation of another and for this reason he purchased us for his own life' (*Pan.* 42.8.1).[89] There is some evidence that at Galatians 2.20 Marcion read, 'the son of God who purchased me (in place of 'loved me') and gave himself for me'.[90] 1 Corinthians 6.20 (cf. 7.23) could be understood in the same way, particularly if Marcion's text did read 'you were bought for a *great* price'; Tertullian accepts the principle but is content to conclude that Jesus must have had something, namely a body, with which to make the purchase (*AM* V. 7.4–5).[91] At Galatians 5.1, however, he rejects the model and argues that 'manumission' can only be effected by the person who already owns the slaves. However, this interpretation becomes somewhat strained when the slavery to which they may return is that of the Law, and it is not difficult to imagine how others may have found an alternative solution (*AM* V. 4.9).

Thus, Christ's independence of the Creator and the created order is fundamental. Tertullian goes out of his way to draw attention to Marcion's omission of the identification of Christ with Abraham's seed (Gal. 3.16–18, *AM* V. 4.2). When it comes to 'born of a woman, born under the law' (Gal. 4.4), Tertullian's silence and a certain presumption that he would have cited it if available may be enough to indicate that it too was omitted; Jerome, perhaps following Origen, does claim that 'Marcion and the other heretics' want the text to read 'born through a woman' (*factum per mulierem*), but this generalisation is too common to establish Marcion's text.[92] Yet there can be no doubt that Marcion did find grounds in Paul for denying to Christ ordinary created flesh. Tertullian's detailed explanation that 'the likeness of flesh of sin' in which the son was sent

89 *Pan.* 42.8.1, although he does not cite this part of the verse in his list of scholia. So also *Adam.* 52.10–13 (1.27); at 104.20 (2.19) Marcus appeals to the notion of adoption in Gal. 4.5 as demonstrating that there was no prior relationship. See also Origen, *Hom.in Exod.* on Exod. 6.9, who refers this interpretation of 1 Cor. 7.23 to 'heretics'.

90 I.e. ἀγοράσαντος for ἀγαπήσαντος (loved); the reading is only attested by the Latin of *Adam.* 222.13–15 (5.22), but it is not easily explained; see Schmid, *Marcion und sein Apostolos*, 232. However, without obvious Marcionite influence a few MSS read 'redeemed' instead of 'set free' at Gal. 5.1, which may indicate a wider scribal tendency to maintain the same metaphor (see NA[27] and Schmid, *Marcion und sein Apostolos*, 252).

91 Eznik, *De Deo* 386 refers to 'that saying of Marcion, "We are the price of the blood of Jesus"'.

92 *Ad Gal.* II. 4,4–5 ll.4–7; see Schmid, *Marcion und sein Apostolos*, 241, and above p. 140 for this tendency in Jerome's use of Origen. The claim that Origen witnesses Marcion's omission of Rom. 1.3, 'born of the seed of David', misreads the text: so rightly Schmid, *Marcion und sein Apostolos*, 238 against Harnack, *Marcion*, 102*.

(Rom. 8.3) points not to a difference in substance but only in the matter of sin, and his denial that 'likeness' could encompass either the spirit or a phantasm, indicate that this is how he understood Marcion's own interpretation (*AM* V. 14.1–3). Yet it was, he asserts, particularly Philippians 2.6–8 that the Marcionites claimed in their support: '**being made in the form of God he did not think it theft to be made equal with God, but emptied himself, having taken on the form of a servant** – not in truth – and **in the likeness of man** – not in man – **being found in form man** – not in substance, that is not in flesh' (*AM* V. 20.3).[93] Whether it is Tertullian who has creatively supplied the glosses or whether they do reflect genuine Marcionite commentary, in the text, margins or in some other source, is unclear. The terminology of substance (*substantia*) is important for Tertullian's own philosophical position, but elsewhere he does conjure his opponents as explaining that 'he could only have dealings among men through the image (*imagino*) of human substance' (*AM* III. 10.2). In the present context Tertullian directs against them Paul's words 'even death on a cross' as ruling out any phantasmic cheating of death; elsewhere, however, he acknowledges that they also believed that 'he 'subjected himself to death even death on a cross' (Phil. 2.8; *AM* II. 27.2).[94]

Undoubtedly, 'flesh' was the crucial term and it may well be that, as Tertullian claims, Marcion read Ephesians 2.14 as, 'annulling the hostility in flesh', with the crucial omission of 'his' (*AM* V. 17.14). Commenting on Colossians 1.24, 'in flesh on behalf of his body which is the church', Tertullian denies that 'body' can be entirely divorced from any fleshly substance; in support he appeals to its susceptibility to death in Colossians 1.22, 'reconciled in his body through death', although he fails to remark on the apparent absence of 'of flesh' in his text here, and arguably also in that of Marcion.[95] Marcion, it would seem, did make precisely this distinction between body and flesh, as is evident from Tertullian's rebuttal on Romans 7.4, 'through the body of Christ' (*AM* V. 13.12). Whether Marcion appealed for further support to Colossians 1.18, which

93 Schmid, *Marcion und sein Apostolos*, 76, ascribes the apparent omission of 'as' before 'man' to the influence of a Latin translation known to Tertullian, rather than to a (unnecessary) tendentious omission by Marcion; an omission in Marcion's text seems a simpler solution.

94 See further, pp. 372–3.

95 Schmid, *Marcion und sein Apostolos*, 251–2, notes that there are other textual variants to this verse which conceivably could be read docetically and he raises the question whether the omissions at Eph. 2.14 and Col. 1.22 may already have been in the text Marcion received; although not impossible, Marcion would hardly have founded his 'docetism' on such omissions, and his responsibility for them is as likely as not.

might serve his cause, is again hidden by Tertullian's silence; but that silence is the more telling because Tertullian pays considerable attention to the rest of Colossians 1.15–20. He defensively asserts that 'we also' describe (the Creator) God as unseen, any visibility being the activity of the Logos, and he criticises Marcion for omitting vv. 15b–16, and perhaps 17b. It is here that he raises the possibility that Marcion might blame 'our false apostles and Jewish evangelists' for the introduction of the omitted verses, although the rarity of such a rationale in the 'Apostolikon' must provoke some scepticism (*AM* V. 19.3–6). Yet these verses do embed Christ into the created order, and their omission would complement Marcion's interpretation, as implied by Tertullian, of Colossians 1.19 as referring to 'his own God'.

Resurrection body

As all this indicates, where Marcion saw radical discontinuity, Tertullian saw continuity, something well conveyed by his defensive alternative to the conventional (and probably to Marcion's) reading of 2 Corinthians 5.17 – 'If then there is any new creation in Christ, the old things have passed away, behold all things have been made new' (cf. Isa. 43.18; *AM* V. 12.6). For Tertullian, continuity and fleshliness are integrally bound together, and the necessarily fleshly nature of body is nowhere so urgently to be defended as over the question of resurrection. 'Thus the whole work of God is made void. The whole weight and fruit of the Christian name, the death of Christ is denied, which the apostle stresses so strongly, indeed as true, setting it as the supreme foundation of the Gospel and of our salvation and his preaching, "For I handed on to you first ... [1 Cor. 15.3–4]"' (*AM* III. 8.5; cf. V. 9.1–10.16; 11.14–12.5). To this issue, as well as the long text-based discussions of 1 Corinthians 15 and 2 Corinthians 4.7–5.10, he also dedicated a free-standing work, the *On Resurrection*, which has Marcion as its chief opponent alongside Apelles, Basilides, and Valentinus. Perhaps surprisingly, he does not deal with the witnesses to the resurrection in 1 Corinthians 15.1–11;[96] instead, his focus is on Christ's fleshliness, in life, death, and also resurrection, as this intersects with the hope of believers. It is because of his own interest, reinforced by the attention given the chapter by Epiphanius and by the *Dialogue of Adamantius*, that Marcion's text of

[96] There are brief references in *De Carne* 4 and *De Res.* 48.

1 Corinthians 15 is particularly well attested, and it need not follow that it was equally at the centre of Marcion's own thought.[97]

The battle is fought mainly over interpretation, and only a few verses invite specific textual attention.[98] Of these perhaps the most significant are 1 Corinthians 15.45 and 47 where Tertullian derides 'the most foolish heretic' for reading 'Lord' in place of the second reference to 'Adam' and to 'man' respectively, a reading confirmed by the Marcionite Marcus (*AM* V. 10.7–9; *Adam.* 100.4–102.11 [2.19]): 'First man, Adam ... last Lord; ... first man ... second Lord'.[99] Tertullian objects that 'first' is meaningless without 'second' or 'last', and that it is enough to establish continuity; Marcion, whether he identified the 'second' with the resurrection or with the revelation of the 'Lord' (from heaven, v. 47), undoubtedly saw discontinuity.

Both, however, saw Christ's resurrection body as a prototype for his followers, something that had important moral consequences. For his part, Tertullian finds in 1 Corinthians 15.49, 'let us bear the image of the heavenly' (reading the subjunctive, with P^{46} ℵ A C D etc.), a summons to discipline in the present, and he denies a reference to the 'substance of resurrection', which perhaps was how Marcion took it, especially if he read the future verb (with B; NA^{27}). Similarly, Tertullian takes 1 Corinthians 15.50, where Marcion apparently also read the future (with F G lat), 'flesh and blood will not inherit the Kingdom of God', as referring to 'the deeds of flesh not its substance' (*AM* V. 10.11–13; 14.4 [on Rom. 8.9]). For Tertullian it follows that only through the resurrection of the flesh can the deeds done in the flesh be judged or rewarded: If God 'does not raise up this substance in which so much is endured for faith in him' then God is indeed 'ungrateful and unjust' – a sideswipe at Marcion's Creator; yet the 'life of Christ (to be) manifested in our body' cannot refer to the present but only to the future life (2 Cor. 4.14; *AM* V. 11.15).[100] Tertullian can permit no contrast between body

97 According to Schmid, *Marcion und sein Apostolos*, 242, 34 out of the 58 verses of 1 Cor. 15 are attested. Although Epiphanius only devotes one scholion to the chapter it incorporates verses from the whole (*Pan.* 42.12.3, S24).

98 Marcion may have omitted 'according to the scriptures' at 1 Cor. 15.3 (see Harnack, *Marcion*, 91*). Tertullian's explanation of Marcion's text at 1 Cor. 15.55 is difficult to follow, but probably Marcion followed the text of ℵ* B, and the variant is not significant for these purposes.

99 This provides strong evidence for the reading, although Tsutsui, *Auseinandersetzung*, 278, suggests the two authors may go back to a common source. Although Marcion is the only witness for 'Lord' in 1 Cor. 15.45 it is more broadly attested for 15.47, perhaps originating as an explanatory gloss (see Schmid, *Marcion und sein Apostolos*, 108); this makes it difficult to be certain whether the first variant is to be ascribed to Marcion himself, but it undoubtedly would assist his interpretation.

100 The substitution of 'Christ' for 'Jesus' is common and is probably Tertullian's own.

and spirit: At Romans 8.10–11, 'the spirit is life' is necessarily experienced in the body which was 'dead because of sin'; just as the future vivification of 'your mortal bodies' depends on Christ's resurrection from the dead, so it in turn confirms Christ's own 'bodily substance' in which he was also raised – Tertullian passes over 'through his indwelling spirit in you' in v. 11 (*AM* V. 14.4–5). Thus, for Tertullian, the circle is closed encompassing the fleshliness of Jesus shared with all humankind, his death and resurrection in that same flesh, along with the death, resurrection, and hope beyond judgement in flesh of believers. Beyond this he does concede that 'we do not defend the Kingdom of God for the flesh, but the resurrection for its substance, which is the door to the Kingdom and through which it is entered'. It is because resurrection precedes and so is separate from the Kingdom that those who are raised need flesh, so that it can then be transformed: 'what shall those who rise first do? Will they have nothing from which to be transformed?' (*AM* V. 20.7 on Phil. 3.21).[101]

Marcion presumably offered an alternative circle, although only glimpses of it can be caught. If, for him, the life of Christ manifested at 2 Corinthians 4.14 did refer to the present, then 'the destruction of the outer man' (2 Cor. 4.16) perhaps did, contrary to Tertullian's vehement denial, refer to the 'eternal dissolution after death' (*AM* V. 11.16). More clearly, Tertullian's emphasis that Paul's answer to the question, 'How are the dead raised? With what body do they come?', deals with different 'qualities' but not different 'substances' explicitly contradicts Marcion's interpretation of this as a matter of substance. It is likely, despite Tertullian's claim that he 'only acknowledges the salvation of the soul', that Marcion did not simply identify 'body' with 'flesh', and that he may have felt that it could equally be qualified by 'soul-ish' (or 'animal', ψυκικός) or by 'spiritual': 'you who deny the salvation of flesh, and, if body is named in this sense at all, you interpret it by I know not other way than the substance of flesh' (*AM* V. 10.3–6; 15.7–8 on 1 Thess. 5.23).[102] It is difficult to know whether this is compatible with the reading of 1 Corinthians 15.51 attested for Marcion only in the *Dialogue of Adamantius* (partly supported by P[46]): 'We shall not all sleep, and not all of us will be changed' – the first clause addressing those still alive at the parousia, the second the dead who will rise in soul(-substance) only

101 On Tertullian's understanding of the resurrection, in this case in contrast with gnostic readings, see Francis Watson, 'Resurrection and the Limits of Paulinism', ed. J. Ross Wagner, C. Kavin Rowe, and A. Katherine Grieb, *The Word Leaps the Gap: Essays on Scripture and Theology in Honor of Richard B. Hays* (Grand Rapids, MI: Eerdmans, 2008), 453–71.

102 See above, p. 263 on Rom. 7.4; also Norelli, 'Marcione lettore', 664 on Rom. 8.11.

(*Adam.* 226 [5.23]).[103] Tertullian does not cite this verse in the *Against Marcion*, and his text in *On Resurrection* does not make easy sense, even in his own terms.[104] Nonetheless, the common thread here is easily discernible, namely an overriding sense of the intrinsic wretchedness of human flesh (cf. Rom. 7.18, 24; see above).

Bodily discipline

'Now then how shall we honour, how are we to bear, God in a body destined to perish?' (1 Cor. 6.20; *AM* V. 7.5).[105] Tertullian's question highlights the moral consequences for him of the bodily resurrection of both Christ and believers. Yet the question is a serious one, for Tertullian nowhere suggests that Marcion adopted interpretations with libertine consequences. Indeed, the opposite; Tertullian's concern to emphasise that Paul prefers 'circumcision of the heart not of the flesh' may be to complete the parallelism with 'in spirit not in letter', but it may also suggest that Marcion interpreted Romans 2.29 as encouraging an ascetic ('fleshly') disposition (*AM* V. 13.7). If so, this would contradict Origen's claim that 'Marcion who is not prepared to understand through allegory' had no way of interpreting Romans 2.25 (Origen, *Comm. in Rom.* II. 9,460–2).[106] The text read at 2 Corinthians 7.1, 'cleanse yourselves from every pollution of flesh and *blood* (NA[27] "spirit")', perhaps reflected how for Marcion holiness could only be achieved by the avoidance of intrinsic bodily, or 'fleshly', activities (*AM* V. 12. 6).

The aspect of Marcion's asceticism with which Tertullian most struggled was his rejection of marriage. Tertullian agrees that 1 Thessalonians 4.3 defines holiness by avoidance, but he insists that it is avoidance of unchastity (*stuprum*) not of marriage; to treat one's 'container'[107] with honour means 'not in sexual excess (*libido*) like the Gentiles', which in turn refers not to

103 The text is debated; Bakhuyzen, *Dialog des Adamantius*, reads without the negative before 'changed', but notes that manuscripts do read 'not all'; see also Pretty, *Adamantius*, 182 n. 207, 185, n.226.

104 See P. Brandhuber, 'Die sekundären Lesarten bei 1 Kor 15,51. Ihre Verbreitung und Enstehung', *Biblica* 18 (1937), 303–33, 418–38, at 307–13, who defends this reading for Marcion. Brandhuber assumes that for Marcion the souls of the dead rise, but the other passages cited suggest rather a soul-body. On Tertullian, *De Res.* 42, 'We shall all indeed rise, but we shall not all be changed', see also Evans, *Adversus Marcionem*, 291–2.

105 'Are we to bear' (*tollemus*) presupposes a Greek ἄρατε, presumably a corruption of ἄρα γε (then) which is found as a variant here; whether this goes back to Marcion or Tertullian is unclear.

106 Braun, *Contre Marcion*, V, 264–5, suggests Marcion read the text as supporting encratism.

107 The ambiguity of the Greek σκεῦος is retained by the Latin *vas*, so it is unclear whether Marcion took the reference as to a wife or to one's own body.

marriage but to 'extreme and unnatural and monstrosities of luxury'. His problem here is that he himself still wishes to give a higher place to continence and virginity over marriage: 'It is the destroyers of the God of marriage I reject, not the adherents of chastity' (*AM* V. 15.3). The chapter that gave him most anxiety was, inevitably, 1 Corinthians 7, and it is probably this anxiety rather than any curtailment of the chapter by Marcion that explains the brevity of his treatment and its largely negative tone: Marcion, he objects, denies marital union (*concubitum*) to the faithful and orders repudiation before marriage, but Tertullian does not expand on how each of them interpreted the text before him.[108] His own admission ('*certe*') that Paul prescribes marriage 'only in the Lord' (1 Cor. 7.39) paired with his explanation that this refers to the prohibition of marriage with an unbeliever (*ethnicus*!), may suggest that Marcion interpreted the passage far more rigorously.

It is possible that Ephesians 5.25–33 also played some part in Marcion's exegesis. Marcion apparently read vv. 28–9 as 'He loves his own flesh who loves his wife, as Christ also the Church'. Without any allusion to v. 30 Tertullian follows with a distinctive form of v. 31: 'for the sake of this (fem.) a man will leave father and mother, and the two will become in one flesh' (*AM* V. 18.8–9). Here, with the omission, also explicitly attested by Epiphanius,[109] of the phrase, 'and will cleave to his wife', the quotation of Genesis 2.24 becomes a model of the renunciation demanded of members of the Church; the feminine 'this' then refers back to 'the church' of the preceding verse as attested (i.e. v. 29). It is in this framework that Harnack's suggestion that Marcion's version of vv. 28–9 would mean love 'sex-free' is quite attractive;[110] Tertullian's rebuttal, 'For so Christ loved the flesh too, as also the Church', would both echo and subvert Marcion's position. The textual evidence, however, indicates that Marcion was not the originator of this reading, although he may have

[108] See further, below, p. 390. Braun, 'Tertullien et l'exégèse de 1 Cor. 7', suggests that Marcion's influence helped move Tertullian to a more rigorist position.

[109] *Pan.* 42.12.3, S38: Although Epiphanius, in the refutation, only refers to the omission of 'wife', the verb would make no sense on its own; the scholion is even more incomplete. The phrase is also omitted by 6 1739* Origen and Cyprian; Schmid, *Marcion und sein Apostolos*, 184–5, prefers omission by homoioarcton, presumably already in Marcion's exemplar, to Marcionite influence on the tradition. However, Joseph Schäfers, *Eine altsyrische antimarkionitische Erklärung von Parabeln des Herrn und zwei andere altsyrische Abhandlungen zu Texten des Evangeliums: mit Beiträgen zu Tatians Diatessaron und Markions Neuem Testament* (Münster: Aschendorff, 1917), 213–4 argues that if the verb were retained 'the church' might be understood.

[110] Harnack, *Marcion*, 120*.

refined an existing one.[111] The omission of v. 30 is necessary for the smoothness of the reading, but it need not be attributed to Marcion although it could have served his assimilation of the bodies of believers to Christ's 'celestial body' (cf. 1 Cor. 6.15).[112]

Marcion did not ignore other ethical precepts. Tertullian raises the possibility that the perfect participle, 'the whole law has been fulfilled' (Gal. 5.14) might be taken to mean that it therefore no longer holds; but he immediately anticipates that his opponents will assert that the precept of love of neighbour is to be maintained.[113] Evidently Marcion also retained it at Romans 13.9, together with the moral exhortation of the previous chapter.

MARCION'S READING OF PAUL

Marcion's Paul was evidently not so much a mutilated Paul as an interpreted one, and like all interpretation it involved both choices and a framework. What is striking about Marcion's method here is as much the intertextual links made between the letters as the deletion of any particular passages. He was not the only person to approach Paul's letters as a coherent corpus in this fashion, but he is the first of whom there is any evidence. So, too, he appears to be the first to draw from them not isolated proof-texts for theological debate or admonition, but a narrative both about Paul and about the revealer. In this, Marcion may have done much to stimulate others, including both Irenaeus and Tertullian. His opponents may have refused to recognise Marcion's Paul, but they could not ignore him.

111 See the long discussion by Schmid, *Marcion und sein Apostolos*, 144–8, who notes that 'flesh' in the first clause rather than 'body' (Eph. 5.28 'bodies') is distinctive to the Marcionite version. Schmid (*Marcion und sein Apostolos*, 69–70) thinks the feminine pronoun ('this') in v. 31 most probably comes from Tertullian (cf. *De Virg.* 5.4) rather than Marcion. However, his atomised discussion of the variants enhances his minimalist approach and may underestimate the degree of distinctive Marcionite interpretation, if not emendation, of the passage.

112 In Ps.Ephraem, *Exposition of the Gospel*, v. 30, follows v. 25; although rejected by Egan, *Exposition of the Gospel*, 2, 46, this has some attraction (cf. Schäfers, *Eine altsyrische antimarkionitische Erklärung*,153–6), although relying on this source for Marcion's text is questionable. To this intriguing textual history must be added the 'western' addition at Eph. 5.30, 'of his flesh and of his bones', with its echo of Luke 24.39 (cf. Irenaeus, *AH* V. 2.3 and p. 219 above).

113 *AM* V.4.12–13; Marcion's text apparently read 'fulfilled *in you*' instead of 'in one word'; Schmid, *Marcion und sein Apostolos*, 130–1, persuasively argues that this does not reflect a Marcionite theological ideology, but results from an earlier error; D F G lat read 'in you in one word'.

10

Marcion's other writings

What distinguished Marcion's system was not some alternative account or revelation but his interpretation of the received texts. Yet, evidently, in due course if not from the beginning, that interpretation must have been expressed and disseminated in written form. It is therefore surprising that his opponents are agreed on his 'adulterated' 'Gospel' and 'Apostolikon', but that for the most part they betray little knowledge of or consistent interest in any other idiosyncratic writings by him. By contrast, they do refer to contemporary critical writings by others later deemed heretics, in particular the 'Problems' of Tatian and the 'Manifestations' and 'Syllogisms' of Marcion's erstwhile disciple, Apelles;[1] indeed, two hundred years later Ambrose is still able to attribute to Apelles a series of 'problems' regarding the Scriptures (Ambrose, *On Paradise* 5–8 [28–41]).

ECHOES AND ALLUSIONS

Epiphanius demonstrates the lack of any consistent tradition when he offers only the cursory statement that 'he (Marcion) drew up other compilations by him for those led astray by him', and this is probably an assumption rather than any indication that he knew of any such (*Pan.* 42.9. 3).[2] Similarly, Ephraem's reference to Marcion's 'readings', which in context perhaps refer to an interpretation of Exodus 19 or 33, reveals nothing about the literary form or setting of these (*CH* 50. 7).[3] Also from the Syriac setting is the charge in the heresy-catalogue attributed to Maruta, bishop of Maipherqat (late fourth/early fifth century), that the Marcionites replaced the Acts of the

1 Eusebius, *HE* V. 13.8; Tertullian, *PrH* 30; Ps.Tert. *Adv.Haer.* 6.
2 Epiphanius' term, συντάγματα, belongs to a root he uses regularly elsewhere.
3 See Beck, *Hymnen contra Haereses*, II, 173, nn. 9–10.

Apostles with a book of their own; yet little can be concluded from this, in particular as in the transmission and of the text and by later editors there are two different renderings of this book's title, one suggesting something old (*sb'*), the other a compendium (*sk'*).[4] The same account also claims that the Marcionites had their own 'hymns' (*madraše*) in place of the Psalms; certainly, such compositions were part of the missionary and catechetical strategies of the time, particularly in the East.[5] Curiously, the Muratorian canon also includes among the books which 'we do not receive' 'a new book of psalms of Marcion'; however, the Latin at this point is so obviously corrupt as to be beyond useful recovery.[6] Earlier in this 'canon' a list of the Pauline letters is followed by the explicit rejection of those 'to the Laodicaeans and to the Alexandrians invented in the name of Paul for the heresy of Marcion'.[7] It seems certain that the 'Letter to the Laodicaeans' which both Tertullian and Epiphanius credit to Marcion was that now known as 'Ephesians'. On the other hand, while a pseudo-Pauline letter to the Alexandrians is unknown, a letter to the Laodicaeans does survive in Latin; although there is no consensus as to its origins, attempts to associate it with Marcion are at best strained.[8] Whether the author of the Muratorian canon, or its sources, had direct knowledge of any of these writings or was repeating a, perhaps already confused, tradition is unclear; a complex history undoubtedly lies behind the text and behind its translation, and a more persuasive context for this might be the fourth century when references to supposed apocryphal writings become a frequent theme, with or without justification. That later Marcionites may have produced distinctive writings is possible but there is nothing here that can be identified with any confidence, still less traced back to Marcion himself.

Apparently more specific but equally intriguing is the mocking reference in an exposition of the Lukan parables attributed to Ephraem to what

4 See above, pp. 178–9, nn. 104–06; Braun, *De Sancta Nicaena Synodo* renders the Syriac *sk'* as '*summa*'; so also Vööbus, *The Canons Ascribed to Maruta of Maipherqat*; for *sb'*, translated as 'le veillard', see Nau, *Le première Partie*, 188–9.

5 As for example, by Bardaisan and Ephraem: see above, p. 153.

6 *Mur.Frag.* ll. 81–3. 'We accept nothing at all of Arsinous or Valentinus or Miltiades, who (pl.) wrote a new book of psalms for Marcion together with Basilides the Asian founder of the kataphrygians'. On the problems of this text see Hahnemann, *Muratorian Fragment*, who argues for a fourth-century date.

7 *Mur.Frag.* ll. 63–6, '*Fertur etiam ad Laudecenses alia ad alexandrinos Pauli nomine fincte ad heresem marcionis et alia plura quae In chatholicam eclesiam recepi non potest*'.

8 On the Epistle to the Laodiceans, see Paul A. Holloway, 'The Apocryphal *Epistle to the Laodiceans* and the Partitioning of Philippians', *HTR* 91 (1998), 321–5; Enrico Norelli, 'La Lettre aux Laodicéns: essai d'interpretation', *Archivum Bobiense* 23 (2001), 45–90.

Marcion wrote in a 'book they named Proevangelium (= προευαγγελιον)'; how, the author asks, can there be anything prior to the Gospel of the sudden appearance of Marcion's Christ?[9] Yet even here only the beginning of the work is cited, an acclamation:

> And it is written in the beginning of the book in this manner, 'O the exceeding greatness, the folly, the power (*better* "the wisdom of the power" [Codex B]), and the wonders for there is nothing to say about it, nor to think concerning it, and there is nothing to render like unto it'.[10]

The wording undoubtedly echoes key passages in Marcion's scriptures, identified by F. C. Burkitt as from Romans 11.33; 1 Corinthians 1.18, 23; and Luke 5.26, to which should be added 1 Corinthians 2.9.[11] However, this betrays nothing of the extent or character of the work that followed, and there are no further references to it. The form would fit a collection of 'hymns' or 'psalms' such as suggested by the catalogues just mentioned but there is nothing to confirm such a context.

THE 'ANTITHESES' IN TERTULLIAN

Given the allusiveness of such references it is not surprising that accounts of Marcion have relied heavily on Tertullian's explicit references to his writings, and that they even have used these as a major guide to understanding Marcion's thought. Tertullian ascribes to Marcion two significant writings: The first was a letter, which, so he asserts, proved that Marcion had been a member of the church before he 'rescinded' that faith (*AM* I. 1.6; IV. 4.3–4; *De Carne* 2).[12] On his second such reference in the *Against Marcion* (*AM* IV. 4.3–4) Tertullian admits that Marcion's followers might refuse to acknowledge this letter, although the ease with which he turns this statement to his own advantage undermines its credibility. Even so, he gives no hint of what

9 See Egan, *An Exposition*, who defends authorship by Ephraem against Schäfers, *Eine altsyrische antimarkionitische Erklärung*. Bundy, 'The Anti-Marcionite Commentary', defends the pseudonymous character and independence of the text, dating it to the early fourth century.

10 Egan, *An Exposition*, 2.1. Egan gives the text of A but prefers B as noted.

11 Francis C. Burkitt, 'The Exordium of Marcion's Antitheses', *JTS* 30 (1929), 279–80. Burkitt drew on Schäfers' edition (*Eine altsyrische antimarkionitische Erklärung*) to offer his own translation; a reference to Luke 5.26 seems least likely, while the following comment may echo 1 Cor. 2.9. See above, p. 261 for other references to 1 Cor. 2.9.

12 At *AM* I. 1.6 the text appears to state that it was the disciples who had previously been 'with us', but most editors emend to refer to Marcion. See above, p. 57.

this letter contained, to whom it was addressed, and why it was preserved; moreover, in his earlier account in the *On the Prescription of Heretics* he had already referred to Marcion's initial membership of a church, there specifically identified as at Rome, without any reference to such a document (*PrH* 30). Any conclusions about this letter, however attractive, for example, that it was an exercise in self-justification or in propaganda, raising some of Marcion's fundamental objections, can only be supposition.[13] Instead, most attention has focused on the writing that Tertullian labels the 'Antitheses'; indeed, echoing Tertullian's own claims, this has come to be seen as Marcion's definitive work, and even as modelling both his message and his method.

Tertullian himself appears to have been equally unaware of the 'Antitheses' when he gave his admittedly brief account of Marcion in the *Prescription*. Although he already ascribed to Marcion the separation of old from new Testament there, his charge that 'Marcion openly and plainly used the sword not the pen' points only to the manipulation of the text – in contrast to his reference to the *Manifestations* of Apelles (or of Philoumene) (*PrH* 30; 38). Even when he refers for the first time to the 'Antitheses' in the *Against Marcion* his language is somewhat indirect:

> The separation of the Law and Gospel is the distinctive and chief work of Marcion, and his disciples cannot deny that which *they hold in the supreme document (in summo instrumento habent)*, by which indeed they are initiated and inculcated into this heresy. Now these are the 'Antithesis' of Marcion, namely contrasting oppositions which attempt to establish the disagreement of the Gospel with the Law, in order that from the difference of tenets (*diversitas sententiarum*) of each document (*instrumentum*) they may argue a difference also of Gods.
>
> (*AM* I. 19.4)

Precisely what Tertullian is claiming here about the nature and status of the 'Antitheses' is disputed: '*in summo*' might indicate either position or evaluation, while '*instrumentum*' is a favourite term of his own, whose meaning ranges from 'canon' to a particular document. Adolf von Harnack's interpretation has, as elsewhere, been particularly influential; although he avoided translating, he asserted that Tertullian's wording indicates that this writing was evidently authoritative for Marcion's church, particularly for those at the point of joining, although it did not share the unqualified status

[13] Mahé, 'Tertullien et l'epistula Marcionis', suggests that it included Marcion's interpretation of the two trees (Luke 6.43) and his discussion of Isa. 45.7 (*AM* I. 2.1–2).

of his 'Gospel' and 'Apostolikon'. Harnack also claimed that this is the work referred to in the catalogue of Maruta, prompted in particular by the then-recent editor's rendering of the disputed '*saka*' by '*summa*'.[14] René Braun's translation of '*in summo instrumento habent*' as 'which constitutes for them the sovereign book', goes even further than Harnack.[15] However, given the more conventional use of '*instrumentum*' in the next sentence, it might be better to follow Ernest Evans' more equivocal rendering, 'which stands at the head of their document'.[16] Even so, Tertullian's language is surely hyperbolic and not to be over-pressed; despite what he says about 'initiation' (*quo initiantur et indurantur in hanc haeresim*), it is notable that he does not use terminology associated elsewhere with baptism or with creeds, and it would be wrong to gloss 'heresy' here as 'Marcion's church', as if assent to the 'Antitheses' was a mark of membership.[17]

In fact, there is little in the first three books of the *Against Marcion* to demand that Tertullian's initial account was based on close first-hand examination of these 'Antitheses', even when, in Book II, he turns to a detailed refutation of the 'difference of Gods'.[18] The characteristics of God to which he offers his own sardonic 'competing antitheses' there are largely formulaic – God is ignorant, the author of sin and death, susceptible to suffering, given to changing his mind and to regret, encouraging theft, demanding retribution, unaware of the character of those he chooses, and ready to practice deceit (*AM* II. 28–29). As if acknowledging the lack of precision, he then immediately defers any sustained attack against 'the Antithesis of Marcion', protesting that 'truth requires but few words, deceit a multitude'.[19] That excuse, together with his claim, 'take away Marcion's title [or 'the title "of Marcion"'] together with the intention and proposal of his work, and he has nothing to offer except the demonstration of one and the same God, good and judicial', does little more than suggest that

[14] Harnack, *Marcion*, 74–6. On the catalogue of Maruta see above, p. 270 and n. 4. The Latin translation of a parallel Arabic catalogue, which probably goes indirectly back to a Syriac original, reads '*Liber propositi finis*'; Harnack dismissed this as 'willkürlich', although Lat. '*finis*' and Syriac '*sk*'' do share a semantic range: see A. von Harnack, *Der Ketzer-Katalog des Bischofs Maruta von Maipherkat* (TU 19.1b; Leipzig: Hinrichs'sche, 1899), 6, 15, where he accepts that the 'Antitheses' may have been positioned between the Gospel and Acts.

[15] Braun, *Contre Marcion*, I, 305–7. [16] Evans, *Adversus Marcionem*, 1, 49.

[17] Contrast Harnack, *Marcion*, 76, who comments, 'it was Marcion's style to set everything in his Church on defined foundations'. This does not rule out the suggestion that the 'Antitheses' formed an initial guide to Marcion's reading of the Gospel and Paul: see Eric W. Scherbenske, 'Marcion's *Antitheses* and the Isagogic Genre', *VC* 64 (2010), 255–79.

[18] So Quispel, *Bronnen*, 81–4.

[19] So Braun, *Contre Marcion*, II, 170, who transfers this comment from the end of chapter 28.

Tertullian knew only the basic thrust and style of Marcion's conclusions regarding the character of God. Only when he comes to tackle Marcion's 'Gospel' in Book IV does Tertullian explicitly address the 'Antitheses', now almost as if he were introducing them for the first time:

> In order to build up confidence he has devised a sort of dowry for it [his 'Gospel'], a work which is called '*Antithesis*' because of the oppositions of contradictions and which is directed to the separation of Law and Gospel; by this [separation] he then disconnects two Gods as different, each of each document (*instrumentum*), or, as is more commonly said, 'testament', in order thus to offer patronage to a Gospel which is to be believed according to (the) Antithesis(es).
>
> (*AM* IV. 1.1)

Yet at this point again, in almost the same words as he had used in Book II, Tertullian steps back from the direct attack he could make, preferring to refute the 'Antitheses' through his reading of Marcion's 'Gospel' and by offering his own counter-antitheses.[20] Despite this, there are surprisingly few further references to the 'Antitheses' in Book IV;[21] of no less significance, there are no references in Book V, a silence that undermines the widespread supposition that Marcion's opposition of Law to Gospel was primarily built around his reading of Paul. Even so, the doubt expressed by Gerhard May whether Tertullian had ever actually held them 'in his hands' is not only over-pessimistic but is probably still based on a false premise.[22] It remains far from obvious that Tertullian's references can substantiate the initial assumption that the 'Antitheses' formed a substantial independent document, such as is routinely presupposed by editors' propensity to render the term in italics and capitalised. Rather, Tertullian's subordination of any discussion to his treatment of Marcion's 'falsified' Gospel indicates that as a 'dowry' (*dos*) the primary role of the 'Antitheses' was to be its preliminary prospectus. This is, as shall be seen, confirmed by the language he uses and

[20] *AM* II. 29.1 '*Ceterum per ipsas quoque antithesis Marcionis comminus cecidissem*...'; IV. 1.2 '*Sed et istas proprio congressu comminus, id est per singulas iniectiones Pontici, cecidissem*...'.

[21] *AM* IV. 1.1–2, 10–11; 2.1; 4.4; 6.1; 9.3; 23.4; 24.1, 4; 35.13; 36.12–13.

[22] May, 'Markion als der Begründer', 88 (dated 2000), expresses this doubt yet more strongly than he did in 'Markions Genesisauslegung und die "Antitheses"', Greschat and Meiser, ed., *Gerhard May: Markion*, 43–50 (= Dieter Wyrwa, Barbara Aland, Christoph Schaüblin, ed., *Die Weltlichkeit des Glaubens in der alten Kirche: Festchrift für Ulrich Wickert* [BZNW 85; Berlin: de Gruyter, 1997] 189–98), 47–8, while in 'Marcion in Contemporary Views', 23 (1989), he had accepted the importance of the 'Antitheses' for Tertullian.

by his subsequent claim that it is through the 'Antitheses' that Marcion argued for the falsification of the Gospel (IV. 4.4; 6.1).[23]

Contradiction and polemic

It follows that Harnack's argument, fundamental for his picture of Marcion, that the 'Antitheses' must have incorporated every distinctive feature of Marcion's teaching will not stand scrutiny.[24] Even he admitted that Tertullian was the only person to give the work its title, and that a long list of opponents had not seen it, including 'Adamantius', Jerome, Epiphanius, Maruta, and Eznik.[25] This list should be extended, and attempts to find references to the work elsewhere – including Harnack's own identification of references to it in Maruta and also in Pseudo-Ephraem – are simply extrapolations from the initial mistaken view that it must have constituted a foundational work.[26]

Undoubtedly, it does become a commonplace to identify Marcion with 'opposition(s)', but he is not the only culprit so accused, and the specific terminology and the implied model adopted in such charges vary, indicating the absence of any stable reference point.[27] Some of these project a philosophical model: Thus Clement of Alexandria describes the followers of Marcion as turning into dogma the 'oppositions (ἐναντιότης) which the philosophers use as riddles', while according to the *Refutation* attributed to Hippolytus Marcion 'presented words from the juxtaposition (παράθεσις) of good and evil'.[28] In both cases the concept belongs naturally among the presuppositions of philosophical discourse, and neither author clearly envisages a systematic or complex cohesive text.

23 *AM* IV. 4.4 is difficult to translate, as is shown by the difference between Evans' rendering, 'Certainly Marcion's *Antitheses* not only admit this, but even make a show (*praeferunt*) of it', and that of Braun, 'There are then certainly the *Antitheses*, which they not only admit to be Marcion's, but which they also place above everything'. At *AM* IV. 6.1 the verb is '*praestruo*'.

24 Harnack, *Marcion*, 77–84; Quispel, *Bronnen*, 80–103, argued this caution persuasively for Books I–III, and demonstrates how often Harnack attributes to Marcion ideas that are at best Tertullian's own.

25 Harnack, *Marcion*, 76–7; but Harnack did think that Maruta referred to it, see above, n. 14.

26 See already J. Rendel Harris, 'Marcion's Book of Contradictions'. *BJRL* 6 (1921/22), 289–309, who rejects the suggestion that the acclamation from the 'Proevangelium' in Pseudo-Ephraem belongs to the 'Antitheses'.

27 For example, the presbyter(s) cited by Irenaeus, *AH* II. 28.1, speak(s) of 'those who seek to introduce another Father, setting in opposition by contrast what the Lord did to save them … but being silent about his judgement'.

28 Clement, *Strom.* III. 3.21; contrast Tsutsui, *Auseinandersetzung*, 149. Ps.Hippolytus, *Ref.* VII. 30.1, 2; 37.2; contrast. *PGL* s.v. which identifies a reference to Marcion's 'Antitheses'. Ps. Hippolytus uses the term himself at *Ref.* VII. 14.6.

A different starting point is presupposed by Origen; he charges 'the leaders' of a heresy that he has identified only by its view of the Father as a different God, with 'collecting together when they find in the Scriptures of the Old Testament a story' of destruction, while 'from the New Testament they bring together words of compassion and piety' (*De Princip.* II. 5.1). That Marcion adopted such a tactic of identifying problematic passages is certain, although the contrast between 'Old' and 'New' Testaments understood in documentary terms, reflects Origen's perspective more than it does that of Marcion's time. As shall be seen, such a procedure was not limited to Marcion, and even Origen does not suggest that such 'collections' were either fixed or authoritative; it is more probable that they constituted a familiar but adaptable arsenal in polemic. Similarly, the anonymous *Song against the Marcionites* (*Carmen adversus Marcionitas*), probably to be dated to the fifth century, attacks the wickedness of seeking to prove that the 'two Testaments sound contrary to each other by the wide difference of principle (*sententia*)'.[29] Indeed, this particular technique is most succinctly developed in the series of proofs or 'headings' (κεφαλαία) that the Marcionite Megethius offers in order to demonstrate that the Christ overturns the things of the Creator, or that the Gospel opposes the Law (*Adam.* 18.13–18; 20.31 [1.9–10]). Here the examples are embedded in extended argument and counter-argument, which makes it difficult to detect an early kernel or subsequent expansion.[30] Like the earlier references, these may reveal aspects of the methods that Marcion adopted; more important, while they cannot be reduced to a single authoritative text, they do point to a developing 'genre' whose effects, as shall be seen, can be traced elsewhere.

The antithesis of 'morals, laws, and powers'

As already noted, although Tertullian subsequently repeats his charge that Marcion's aim in the 'Antitheses' is the separation of Law and Gospel, or even of old and new Testaments, these formulations are already found in the *Prescription* without reference to the 'Antitheses', and they undoubtedly reflect his own preferred language (*PrH.* 30; *AM* IV. 6.1; 9.3). Elsewhere, he himself is happy to describe the two edges of the sword of Rev. 1.16 as 'the

29 Karla Pollmann, *Das Carmen adversus Marcionitas: Einleitung, Text, Übersetzung und Kommentar* (Hypomnenata 96; Göttingen: Vandenhoeck & Ruprecht, 1991), 145–6, finds a reference to the 'Antitheses' here. Moll, *Arch-Heretic*, 21–4 proposes a third-century date for the *Carmen*, but with little justification.

30 See Tsutsui, *Auseinandersetzung*, 148–52; the term that is used, κεφάλαιον, merely identifies these as self-contained statements.

two testaments of Law and Gospel' (*AM* III. 14.3). However, other terms that Tertullian uses are more revealing of the character and function of Marcion's work. Having excused himself from a detailed refutation of the 'Antitheses' in *AM* II. 29.1, Tertullian acknowledges that they attempt to 'alienate Christ from the Creator' on the basis of the values of the 'morals, laws, or powers (*ingenia, leges, virtutes*)', whereas, so he claims, he has already demonstrated that the 'paradigms' (*exempla*) of goodness and justice are equally congruent of the one Creator God. This terminology, and in particular that of '*exemplum*', which is repeated throughout this paragraph (II. 29.1–4), appears again in the introduction to Book IV where Tertullian admits the differences in the 'precepts of power and disciplines of Law', but charges Marcion with twisting against the Creator 'the antitheses of paradigms', contrary to the exposition that he himself offers of how the 'deeds and morals operate through antithesis' in the one God (IV. 1.3, 10).

The appeal to *exempla*, and also to *sententiae* (epigrammatic sayings or tenets) as in *AM* I. 19.4 ('from the difference of tenets of each document'), is deeply rooted in classical philosophy and rhetoric; by the second century such appeals were a mainstay of rhetoric, both forensic and more generally. They regularly gained particular effect through the use of antithesis, whether an internal one, such as the contrast Tertullian himself made between the brevity required by truth, the long-windedness by deceit (a *sententia*, II. 29.1, above), or an external one, such as the widespread use of a contrast between principles and praxis, or between the behaviour of different individuals (*exempla*). Plutarch, for example, wrote on 'The Contradictions of the Stoics'.[31] This second model was a popular one, allowing for considerable development, and it provided a context where 'morals, laws and powers' would feature prominently.[32]

Subsequent direct or implicit references to the 'Antitheses' in Book IV fit this model precisely. The first such reference introduces the healing of the leper (Luke 5.12–14) where, so Tertullian implies, his opponent found a double contrast, namely between the healing by Elisha of *one foreigner* and the healing by Jesus of any *number* of lepers in *Israel*, and between the

[31] Plutarch, *Moralia* 1033A-1057B.

[32] See Kristoffel Demoen, 'A Paradigm for the Analysis of Paradigms: The Rhetorical *Exemplum* in Ancient and Imperial Greek Theory', *Rhetorica* 15 (1997), 125–55; Paul A. Holloway, 'Paul's Pointed Prose: The "Sententia" in Roman Rhetoric and Paul', *NovT* 40 (1998), 32–53. Winrich A. Löhr, 'Did Marcion Distinguish Between a Just God and a Good God?', ed. May and Greschat, with Meiser, *Marcion und seine kirchengeschichtliche Wirkung*, 131–46, 145, draws attention to the language of 'morals' (*ingenia* – ethos), but not to that of *exemplum*, *sententia*, and *antithesis*.

need for Naaman to *bathe seven* times while Jesus healed by *word alone* (2 Kings 5). Presumably the second 'antithesis' here would establish a contrast in 'powers' (*virtutes*), the former perhaps one in 'ethos' (*ingenia*), while Jesus' physical contact with the man might also establish one in 'Law'. In this case, Tertullian extends the confrontation to include Jesus' reason for sending the man to show himself to the priests – 'as a witness to them' – although this is a move that probably reflects a subsequent level of debate centred on the interpretation of the Lukan passage itself (*AM* IV. 8.9–11).[33] The primary contrast with the Syrian Naaman was already anticipated in the text of the Gospel itself familiar to both protagonists, as is betrayed by Tertullian's own interpretive phrase, '*Israelite* lepers' (compare Luke 4.27). There is some attraction in René Braun's suggestion that Marcion would have seen a parallel between Naaman who was cured by a foreign deity, and the Israelite lepers who were healed by a Christ foreign to them;[34] however, this would entail that the exercise was not simply one of contrast but could also allow some, at least superficial, similarity. Both the overall argument and the specific comparison are repeated in Tertullian's discussion of the healing of the ten lepers (Luke 17.12–19), suggesting to Harnack that a version of Luke 4.27 was to be found in Marcion's text there; this is not impossible, but it may be that the two narratives were already associated in the 'Antitheses' (*AM* IV. 35.4–11). This, then, arguably would have inspired Tertullian when, with reference to the pericope that follows (Luke 17.20–32), he speaks of 'our antitheses' (*AM* IV. 35.13).

It may be no coincidence that the next explicit reference also concerns Elisha: 'Yet Christ loves little ones, teaching that those who always wish to be greater should be as such, but the Creator sent bears against the boys, avenging Elisha the prophet when he suffered insults from them': This too is an antithesis in 'morals' or ethos (*AM* IV. 23.4; Luke 9.47–48; 2 Kings 2.23–24).[35] Tertullian's riposte to this 'impudent antithesis' may seem like special pleading if not eisegesis: He asserts that that those boys (*pueri*) were old enough to be responsible for their actions, although there is no obvious difference between the 'small child' (παιδίον) of Luke and the 'little child, child' (μικρόν παιδίον, παίς) of 2 Kings. Rhetorically, Tertullian is more successful when he continues with his own antithetical *sententia*, which again operates on a superficial similarity, that Pharoah (by killing them) did not allow children to be brought up, but Marcion (by prohibiting sexual intercourse) did not even allow them to be born.[36] The Marcionite

[33] See p. 198 above. [34] Braun, *Contre Marcion*, IV, 120.
[35] See also *AM* II. 14.4, and below, p. 359. [36] See also *AM* I. 29.8.

Megethius cites the same example of Elisha and the boys, although the contrast he draws is with Jesus' words in Matthew 19.14 (cf. Luke 18.16), while Adamantius responds with the justification that the boys approached Elisha with insults, while the children were seeking a blessing from Jesus (*Adam.* 32.24–34.12 [1.16], see further below).

Tertullian follows this discussion with a further implied quotation, 'The Creator causes a plague of fire on that false prophet at Elijah's request'; the point of contrast here is not expressed but presumably it is Jesus's refusal to do the same. Here the appeal to a precedent in Elijah's action is likely already to have been attributed to the disciples in Marcion's text of Luke 9.54, particularly since it also appears within the manuscript tradition there.[37] However, replacing as the victim the innocent captain and his cohorts of 2 Kings 1.9–13 with a false prophet would serve Tertullian's exegetical needs more than it would those of Marcion. It may be Tertullian who has formulated an 'antithesis' for his opponent, in order then to furnish himself with a finishing stroke: He caps it by turning to 1 Kings 19.12 for a counter-antithesis, 'For he said then also to Elijah, "The Lord is not in the fire but in the gentle spirit"' (*AM* IV. 23.7–8).[38] Yet even if Tertullian has again expanded the antithesis, underlying it may still may be one traceable to Marcion, for it would also have highlighted the disciples' misunderstanding and their self-alignment with Elisha and with the Creator, a familiar theme.[39]

Less ambiguous is the next explicit reference to an 'antithesis': 'the Creator led the expedition of the sons of Israel out of Egypt laden with those spoils of gold and silver vessels and clothes along with the dough in their containers, but Christ commanded his disciples not to take even a staff on the journey' (*AM* IV. 24.2; cf. Exod. 12.34–36; Luke 10.4; 9.3). Megethius makes the same contrast, also eliding the two Lukan mission instructions, although his wording is closer to that of the canonical text (*Adam.* 22.1–9 [1.10]).[40] Both respondents argue that the difference – for Tertullian, the *antithesis* – is one of circumstances (*causae*), not of 'powers';[41] for Tertullian these circumstances are the needs of a desert journey against those of an urban one, while for Adamantius they are those of a mission that will bring peace against one of flight from hostility and persecution.

37 So A C D, etc.; see p. 210. 38 So Braun, *Contre Marcion*, IV, 299 n. 6.

39 Tardieu, 'Marcion depuis Harnack', 444–6, suggests that the series may have reached a climax with the Transfiguration (Luke 10.1–11).

40 However, Adamantius associates this with the sending of the disciples 'into the world'; see below.

41 For the importance of '*causa*' see Quintillian, *Inst.Orat.* III. 5.17; 6.25–8.

The final example that Tertullian explicitly cites would appear to be a contrast between David who attacked the blind when they resisted his taking of Jerusalem and Jesus who helped the blind man when he welcomed him at Jericho (2 Sam 5.6–9; Luke 18.35–43; *AM* IV. 36.13).[42] Tertullian's account of this is deeply intertwined both with his own wordplay about the blind falling into an antithesis-ditch and with a debate as to whether Jesus is the Son of David. It is possible that any original antithesis that Marcion may have drawn was only one between the behaviour of David and that of Jesus; the further denial that Jesus was Son of David would then belong more naturally to a subsequent interpretation of the Lukan passage itself.

All these vignettes would count as *exempla*, but they could also be expressed succinctly in the form of a *sententia* or principle.[43] Without using the language of 'antithesis', Tertullian challenges the supposition that Jesus, who refuses to judge, manifests a 'different *exemplum*' from Moses' violent intervention (Luke 12.13–14; Exod. 2.13–14; *AM* IV. 28.9–10). Other antitheses may have taken the form of a contrast only between independent sayings or teaching. Again without explicitly labelling it an 'antithesis', Tertullian attributes to Marcion a contrast between the heavenly rest promised by Christ and the punishment or consolation 'below' (*apud inferos*), which is the Creator's reward for those who obey 'the law and the prophets', and, similarly, one between the hope of an eternal and heavenly Kingdom over against the earthly Kingdom promised to the Jews (IV. 34.11; III. 24.1).[44] It may be this that prompted him to respond in kind, citing Luke 17.20–1 and Deuteronomy 30.11–14 as 'according to our antitheses … a single *sententia*', namely the presence of the Kingdom in obedience to God's command (*AM* IV. 35.12–14). Tertullian also puts into the mouth of his opponent an opposition between Christ's prohibition of divorce and Moses' implied permission of it: 'Do you see the difference between Law and Gospel, Moses and Christ?' (IV. 34.1; Luke 16.18; Deut. 24.1). The contrast here between 'Law and Gospel' betrays Tertullian's own terminology, but that between Moses and Christ as contrasting teachers may be more original to Marcion: 'that Christ of yours who teaches contrary to Moses and the Creator' (*AM* IV. 34.3). Following the same pattern would be the opposition set between the *lex talionis* and the command by Jesus to offer a tunic alongside the stolen cloak (Exod. 21.24; Luke 6.29), an example that is also given by Megethius

42 Chrysostom, *Hom.in Matth.* 26, 6, claims that the Marcionites described David as a murderer and breaker of marriage; see Harnack, *Marcion* 282*.

43 See also the uses of *sententia* in *Carmen adv.Marc.* II. 15–22 (above p. 277).

44 Quispel, *Bronnen*, 84 sees *AM* III. 24.1 as containing a trace of the 'Antitheses'.

(*AM* IV. 16.2; *Adam.* 38.1–3, cf. 32.3–6 [1.17, 15]).[45] On the other hand, when Tertullian surmises that 'some might want to argue' that the Creator commanded giving to one's brethren, but Christ to all who seek, this may be an invention of his own;[46] it may incorporate an echo of Matthew 5.43, a verse that Megethius explicitly cites in antithesis to Matthew 5.44 (*AM* IV. 16.10; *Adam.* 26.18–22 [1.12]). Once established as a style, it was not difficult for 'antitheses' to be found and to be multiplied, both by friends and by foes.

Undoubtedly the language of *exemplum* is congenial to Tertullian himself, and he himself makes regular use of the trope throughout his writings.[47] It is therefore no surprise that he uses it to his own advantage against Marcion: On the one hand, he challenges Marcion to offer an *exemplum* of God's goodness rather than relying of faith, and yet, particularly with reference to the Old Testament, he contrasts *exemplum* with unmediated truth (*AM* III. 24.13; V. 4.1 ['is not *exemplum* but truth']). Yet, it is equally clear that he can do this because he read Marcion within the same framework: 'Do not only pay attention to the judge but turn also to the *exempla* of the Best (God); note when he takes revenge, when he is indulgent … come finally to a study of his doctrines, discipline, precepts and advice' (I. 17.2). Although Tertullian himself can use *sententia* in a nontechnical sense of ideas or judgements, frequently it does denote a single significant statement in the Law or in the teaching of Jesus (II. 15.3; IV. 9.15; 14.1, etc.). Indeed, when he accuses Marcion of deleting whatever contradicts his own *sententiae* and of preserving that which agrees with them, Tertullian is cleverly undermining Marcion's own claim to be appealing to the *sententiae* recorded in the texts (IV. 6.2). Whether Marcion used the same terminology (in Greek παράδειγμα, γνώμη) must be a matter of supposition, but it is not an unlikely one. Certainly the term 'Antithesis' is likely to have been Marcion's choice and not merely introduced by Tertullian; the latter does not use it elsewhere in his writings, and, indeed, it is notable that Quintillian translates the Greek ἀντίθετον as '*comparatio*', or '*contrapositum*'.[48] Yet, in

[45] See above, p. 205, on the text here.

[46] See also, for example, *AM* IV. 19.2 where Tertullian hypothesises a contrast between Isa. 6.9 and Luke 8.8, but does so only in order to dismiss it within his own argument.

[47] See Barnes, *Tertullian*, 213–4, 217–19; Hélène Pétré, *L'Exemplum chez Tertullien* (Dijon: Imprimerie Darantière, 1940), who rejects the suggestion that Tertullian drew on an existing catalogue.

[48] Quintillian, *Inst.Orat.* IX. 2.100-101; 3.81 (I am grateful to Dr. Gerald Downing for these references); at IX. 1.34; 3.90 Quintillian's term '*contrarii*' seems close to Marcion's (and Tertullian's) use of 'antithesis'.

using it, and in its application, Marcion would have been doing no more than adopting a conventional mode of argument.

A preface to the Gospel

What else may have been included in the 'Antitheses' is uncertain. Tertullian suggests that it incorporated something of an apology for Marcion's reading or editing of the Gospel: In his defence of the priority of the Church's version of Luke he adds the qualification, 'if indeed that Gospel which is ascribed to Luke among us – we shall see whether it is by Marcion – is the same one as Marcion through his Antitheses denounces as falsified by the protectors of Judaism in order to form a single unit of the Law and prophets, from which they might so construct Christ …' (*AM* IV. 4.4).[49] The comment is a surprising one, given that two chapters previously he had explicitly left aside the 'Antitheses' to turn his attention to the 'Gospel'. In the interim he had claimed that Marcion took his idea of the 'corrupted Gospel' from Paul's letter to the Galatians, although he is inconsistent as to whether Marcion then used that against 'the status of the Gospels' published under the name of the apostles or specifically against the Church's 'Luke', and, indeed, both possibilities are probably anachronistic for Marcion's own time (IV. 3.2; 4.1). While the exploitation of the conflict between Paul and Peter at Antioch certainly did play a focal role for Marcion, he was not the only person, and perhaps not the first, to draw attention to it; independently of his attack against Marcion, and certainly without reference to the latter's 'Antitheses', Tertullian had already in the *Prescription* dismissed those who appealed to the story (*PrH* 23). At this point in Book IV of the *Against Marcion* Tertullian himself only alludes to the incident, and he saves his more detailed analysis of that conflict for the continuous discussion of Galatians in Book V; Marcion may have treated it likewise with different detail or emphasis in the two contexts. Indeed, the story could be presented as another pair of contrasting *exempla*, setting Paul over against the other apostles. Such a context would account for the ambiguity that there seems to be in how negative a portrait Marcion gave of the other apostles: The structure of the 'Antitheses' would prompt a more negative picture than the continuous interpretation of the Gospel or Pauline text need do.[50]

From Tertullian's own account, therefore, the 'Antitheses' would appear to establish a set of premises and of examples for reading the 'Gospel'.

[49] See above, p. 189. [50] See above p. 280 on *AM* IV. 23.7.

The language he uses of them, 'dowry', 'preliminary plan' ('*praestruo*', *AM* IV. 6.1), even 'put first' (*praefero*, IV. 4.4), supports such a function. As such they could have been read on their own, perhaps in an initial catechetical context, establishing a foundation for further instruction.[51] Tertullian's oblique statement that Marcion paid detailed attention to the account of the healing of the leper 'as if in the presence of one who is his fellow in misery and hatred' may also suggest an address to actual or would-be insiders (IV. 9.3; cf. 36.5).[52] Tertullian himself was able to pick up specific 'antitheses' as he read through the Gospel, presumably either because something in his copy of the text prompted him to do so or because he was able to make his own connections; but conceivably some individuals or even communities might have had access only to the 'précis' version. Even so, other antitheses may well lie embedded in Tertullian's discussion, and it is not being claimed here that those explicitly identified constituted the sum total. Nonetheless, there is no evidence that the 'Antitheses' contained the whole of Marcion's system, and much, particularly regarding Marcion's cosmology, would have to be explained elsewhere. This would be similar to Ptolemy's *Letter to Flora*, which likewise focuses on the identity of the origin of the Law, and hints at deeper truths to be divulged later.[53] Understanding Marcion's enterprise will not be served by gathering under the heading of his 'Antitheses' every opposition he did exploit or that he may have done so.[54]

On the other hand, there is no reason to suppose that the 'Antitheses' was the only location that Marcion used for setting out such '*exempla*'. Tertullian himself had already appealed to the story of Elisha and the bears in his defence of the Creator as judge in Book II, there drawing the moralising conclusion, 'The precocity of an age which ought to show respect needed to be punished' (*AM* II. 14.4). He himself had independently appealed to the contrast between Pharaoh's 'more humane severity' and that of Marcion's denial of birth, which he then repeats later (I. 29.8, cf. IV. 23.5–7). He also returns more than once to the taking of the Egyptians' goods by the Israelites, without setting this against Jesus' instructions to his disciples

51 See above, p. 274, and also Scherbenske, 'Marcion's *Antitheses*', although his use of 'genre' is ambiguous, and he does not note the focus on the Gospel in the relevant passages.

52 See above, p. 193, on the use of the Greek with a Latin translation here.

53 See further, pp. 411–13.

54 Contrast Harnack, *Marcion*, 256*–96*, who lists 31 items, and then adds all the passages in Luke and the Pauline letters which provoke a Marcionite opinion (297*–313*); although more restrained, the 18 antitheses that Tsutsui, *Auseinendersetzung*, 148–52, finds in the arguments of Megethius and Marcus over-stretch the category (see nn. 67, 69, 71 below).

(II. 20; V. 13.6); instead, his defence that the Israelites were only taking what was their due for years of unpaid labour shows that he takes the problem to be that the God who forbade theft here commands an action that might be taken as theft. Certainly this could be taken as a self-contradiction on the part of the Creator, and as evidence of flawed 'morals', but Marcion need not have made such criticisms in the 'Antitheses' alone; these may have concentrated on oppositions between the *exempla* of the Creator and the *exempla* of Christ. Even if the 'Antitheses' set out models and a programme of oppositional analysis, the exercise could have been carried out wherever the text was cited.

Although the label 'Proevangelium' reported by Ps.Ephraem and discussed above might seem to suit the position of the 'Antitheses' as 'dowry' in Tertullian's account, there is nothing to determine whether they are the same work. As already noted, the language of the opening acclamation undoubtedly counts as 'keywords of Marcion's Bible', although these are predominately Pauline.[55] Certainly, the doxological style may have been a feature of some of Marcion's writing: Tertullian more than once ascribes to him perversions of such, 'O untrustworthy Lord, unstable, unfaithful, withdrawing that which he established...' (*AM* II. 7.3; cf. IV. 38.1). Yet it would be wrong to tie such language specifically to the 'Antitheses', particularly if the profile that has emerged so far is correct; contrary to the suggestion by Harnack, and to the more confident claim by others since, the opening acclamation cannot be directly located as the prologue of the 'Antitheses'.[56] Further, even if Marcion did open one of his writings with a declaration of praise, or if his disciples collecting notes on his teaching similarly did so, there are no grounds for finding here a glimpse into Marcion's own spiritual experience.[57]

The 'exempla of the Creator'

All this suggests that in the 'Antitheses' Marcion's focus was on the character of the Creator: Marcion, Tertullian claims, perverted the antithesis of *exempla* against the Creator (*AM* IV. 1.10), and he himself repeatedly refers to the 'examples of the Creator' (*exempla creatoris*). Albeit in mockery, he envisages another acclamation by Marcion, 'O best (*optimus*) God, O God

55 So Burkitt, 'The Exordium', and above, p. 272.

56 Harnack, *Marcion*, 256*: 'wahrscheinlich'; 356*: 'höchstwahrscheinlich'.

57 Harnack, *Marcion*, 87, describes this as 'the only extensive phrase that we have directly from Marcion's pen'.

different from the *exempla* of the Creator' (IV. 38.1). However, in practice the Creator could be represented by Moses, Elijah, and Elisha, and perhaps by others, for these are the narrative actors who enact the *exempla*: It is this that prompts Tertullian's defence, 'For Moses is an apostle just as the apostles are prophets' (IV. 24.8).

On the other side there would be room for some flexibility as to the contrasting partner. For the most part this seems to have been Christ: 'For that very exercise in opposing Christ to the Creator by those *exempla* actually points to unity' (II. 29.2).[58] Only secondarily, as implicit here, does that lead into a direct contrast between the Creator and the best, the unknown, God. This further step does not indicate that Marcion confused or elided Christ with God, but it was a consequence of his assumption that the narrative he upheld (about Christ) is the only and necessary source of knowledge of God. It is within this framework that a possible opposition between Christ (of the unknown God) and the as-yet-to-come 'Jewish Christ' has to be understood, if indeed such an opposition does belong to the 'Antitheses': 'So you cannot establish that insinuation of yours for the differentiation of the two Christs, as if the Judaic Christ was destined by the Creator for returning the people alone from the dispersion, but your one was devoted by the best God for liberating the whole human race' (III. 21.1).[59] Even here, the primary effect is to separate Christ from the Creator (cf. IV. 6.1), although, as shall be seen, it opens the door to new developments.

It follows that the 'Antitheses' do assume that the scriptural accounts offer an appropriate foundation for investigating the character of God. Difficulties in the Old Testament account of God were not detected first or only by Marcion. They were familiar topoi in both Jewish and Christian exegetical debate and were evidently also noted by other interested or hostile observers.[60] To this extent the 'Antitheses' must be seen as participating in an ongoing debate about the reading of the Jewish Scriptures as a record of the character and activities of God, a debate that took a distinctive and intense form within Christian circles. Marcion's contribution is to set them in an antithetical framework, which provides its own solution. However, this method echoes similar strategies elsewhere. Tatian, attacking Greek mythology, where 'Artemis is a sorceress, Apollo heals', concludes, 'How can they be respected among whom there is so much contradiction (ἐναντιότης) of doctrines' (Tatian, *Orat.* 8.2); by contrast, in his celebrated eulogy of Jewish harmony Josephus had claimed, 'Among us alone one will hear no

[58] Cf. *AM* IV. 6.1 quoted above, p. 284. [59] So Quispel, *Bronnen*, 84.
[60] See further below, pp. 358–66.

self-contradictory statements about God' (*C.Apion*. II. 19 [179]).[61] In conflicting apologetics the charge of contradiction is recognised by all as an effective weapon. As such it may be a persuasive tool for achieving a position reached on other grounds, although if indeed persuasive it will then invite further conclusions to be drawn.

Tertullian is well aware of this, which is why so much of his effort is expended in order to argue that the apparent contradictions are in fact oppositions that are necessarily resolved in that which holds them together: Only the one who creates can also destroy that which they have created. His counter-strategy, subsequently systematised by the *Dialogue of Adamantius*, follows the same pattern – to establish alternative consistencies between the Creator and Christ: 'Just as the Lord told them to speak peace to any house they entered, which comes from the same example (of Jesus' sending of his apostles), so also Elisha when he visited the Shunamite said to her, "Peace to you, peace to your son". These are our better antitheses which compare, not separate, Christ' (*AM* IV. 24.4, see above). Another response is to offer alternative contradictions which can then be easily explained: In contrast to Elisha's murderous bears Adamantius appeals to his giving life to the Shunamite's son, and adds the woe by Jesus against his betrayer who would better have not been born', each receiving their just deserts (*Adam*. 34.3–14 [1.16]).[62] The appearance of the same episodes in different contexts suggests an established repertoire of examples and counter-examples to be used as seemed most appropriate by different protagonists. Within all this, as Dungan rightly notes, the determination to read these narratives literally, eschewing any allegorical amelioration, is a strategic choice not a fixed hermeneutical principle.[63]

For Marcion the contradictions did not undermine the belief system as a totality, as they did for Celsus, who appealed to some of the same examples (Origen, *C.Cels*. VII. 18, 28). Rather they exposed an internal incompatibility that could only point in one direction. His focus was on the Creator, whom Tertullian accuses Marcion of insulting: The behaviour of the Creator is not simply contradicted by that of Christ but is thereby revealed to be unworthy of God. The 'Antitheses' do not, it appears, address the problem of creation itself – that Marcion would do elsewhere.[64] The character of the Creator is manifested by his representatives, by Moses, Elijah, and Elisha or by

[61] For these examples and the argument see David L. Dungan, 'Reactionary Trends in the Gospel Producing Activity of the Early Church: Marcion, Tatian, Mark', ed. M. Sabbe, *L'Évangile selon Marc: Tradition et redaction* (BETL 34; Leuven: Leuven University Press, 1974), 179–202, 182–93.

[62] See above, p. 204, for the text here.

[63] Dungan, 'Reactionary Trends', 194–8.

[64] See May, 'Markions Genesisauslegung'.

David – in other terms by the Law and the prophets, whether or not these terms were adopted by Marcion. Christ's behaviour necessarily points elsewhere, to another God and to a pattern and hope available to all.

It follows that the evidence in no way allows the conclusion that it was through the 'Antitheses' that Marcion's thought was articulated as fundamentally theologically antithetical. Equally misconceived is the question, 'What are the theses against which Marcion set himself?'[65] On the other hand, it would be wrong to describe the 'Antitheses' only as 'a philological, exegetical work'.[66] Even if Tertullian's lens of 'Law versus Gospel', 'Old versus New Testament', and even, 'Creator versus most high God' produces a significant degree of distortion, Marcion's 'Antitheses' both arose from and resulted in hermeneutical principles of profound consequence.

The growth of 'Antitheses'

Given the ubiquity of the antithetical mode of reasoning, and the ease of subsuming other arguments within it, it is hardly surprising that the list of '*exempla*' and '*sententiae*' should expand, and also develop in new directions. As has been seen, this process is already discernible in Tertullian himself, and it continues in later polemics.

For example, the differentiation between the Christ who came and the Christ of the Creator demanded both the denial that the Christ of the Gospel fits Old Testament prophecies, and also the further conclusion that these refer instead to the future Jewish Christ. Hence, Megethius adopts an antithetical form when he cites Psalm 2 to show that 'the Christ who came is other', and, similarly, appeals to Daniel 2.34–5 to prove that 'The Christ through the law and prophets has not yet come' (*Adam.* 46.1–11 [1.24]; 48.1–9 [1.25]).[67] The same technique could be used as a polemic against alternative readings of Scripture. Megethius contrasts Moses, who stretched out his hands to destroy many (Exod. 17.8–13), with Christ, who stretched out his hands to save (*Adam.* 24.24–9 [1.11]). Christian apologists had long seen in the Exodus account a prophetic anticipation of Jesus' death with outstretched arms (*Barn.* 12.2; Justin, *Dial.* 90.4); here Marcion or, more

65 W. Bienert, 'Marcion und der Antijudaismus', ed. May and Greschat with Meiser, *Marcion und seiner kirchengeschichtliche Wirkung*, 191–205, 198, who appears to assume that an 'Antithesis' presupposes a thesis, a philology which is not justified in either Greek nor in Latin.

66 May, 'Marcion in Contemporary Views', 23.

67 These are usually identified as the 13th and 14th 'antitheses' in the *Dialogue of Adamantius* (Tsutsui, *Auseinandersetzung*, 148); see also the fifteenth, *Adam.* 50.9–14 [1.26]: John the Baptist's question demonstrates that Christ is not the one prophesied.

probably, his followers may have seen a weakness to be exploited in their rejection of the appeal to prophecy.[68]

In another development, Megethius also appeals to Pauline texts in antithetical form, something, as already noted, that Tertullian markedly does not do: 'The prophet of the God of becoming, in order to destroy more of the enemy, made the sun stop so it would not set until he had finished destroying those who were fighting the people; the Lord, who is good, says, "Do not let the sun set on your anger"' (*Adam.* 28.20–3 [1.13]; Josh. 10.12–14; Eph. 4.26).[69] Similarly, he presents other aspects of Marcionite teaching in an antithetical form: 'The Creator did not know where Adam was, saying "where are you?"; the Christ knew the hearts of men' (*Adam.* 36.13–14 [1.17]; cf. Gen. 3.9).[70] The criticism of divine ignorance was a familiar one, and Tertullian had taken the offensive by appealing to Jesus' question, 'Who touched me?' (Luke 8.25; *AM* IV. 20.8); however, the generality of the antithetical example given by Megethius is probably evidence of its later date.[71] Similarly, Megethius' appeal to Isaac's blindness, which was not healed, while Jesus healed many who were blind, bears the marks of a secondary imitation of the model (*Adam.* 40.1–3 [1.20]). In this, as in other cases, the weakness of the example prompts the suspicion that it may have been invented by opponents for the sole purpose of then shooting it down.

This tendency for 'Antitheses' to multiply and to take new forms makes it difficult to argue back to Marcion from later catalogues and polemics, or to trace simple lines of continuity from him to subsequent users of the genre. This has already been seen within developing Marcionism itself, but it is no less true of Manichaean and anti-Manichaean polemics.[72] Marcion may be credited with the literary formalisation of a popular model, but his success in so doing is marked by the number and creativity of his imitators.

68 See Tsutsui, *Auseinandersetzung*, 161–2.

69 According to Tsutsui, *Auseinandersetzung*, 148, 167, this is the fourth antithesis. See also *Adam.* 38.16–19 [1.19] (Isa. 5.28 *versus* Eph. 6.13, 16); 52.10–13 [1.27], which cites Gal. 3.13 but not in an antithesis (see n. 71 below).

70 The seventh in the list by Tsutsui, *Auseinandersetzung*, 148.

71 The 16th, 17th, and 18th Antitheses as identified by Tsutsui, *Auseinandersetzung* would belong here: *Adam.* 52.10–13 (1.27: We were foreigners to the Christ who appeared, and who redeemed us [cf. Gal. 3.13]); 64.28–9 (2.4 by Marcus: The good God is good to all, while the demiurge promises to save those who trust him – no scriptural references are cited); 68.22–6 (2.6: The creator regretted creating humankind and wished to destroy them, the good one showed mercy to the human race).

72 See Jason BeDuhn, 'Biblical Antitheses, Adda, and the *Acts of Archelaus*', ed. Jason BeDuhn and Paul Mirecki, *Frontiers of Faith: The Christian Encounter with Manichaeism in the Acts of Archelaus* (NHMS 61; Leiden: Brill, 2007), 131–47, who is over-confident in tracing a line back to Marcion from later polemics.

PART III

THE SECOND-CENTURY SHAPING OF MARCION

11

Marcion in his second-century context

The Marcion portrayed by his opponents changes shape and form not only because of the distorting effect of the lenses through which they view him but also because of the uses to which they put him within their own rhetorical strategies. From the very earliest reference that survives in Justin Martyr, Marcion is contextualised within a broader framework of argument driven by apologetic and polemic. Moreover, the Marcion who is so contextualised, or recontextualised, by subsequent writers is one who, even if he does come to them through his contemporary adherents, does so much more through an inherited polemical tradition. It is in this way, accessible now only through the surviving written texts, that Marcion was 'made a heretic'. Any attempt to elicit from such multiple 'constructed Marcions' a plausible 'historical Marcion' is fraught with difficulty, and this remains true even with an optimistic assessment of the possible recovery of his own core texts.

Much recent study of Marcion has operated with a parallel antithetical model; although not always overtly polemical, it has continued to set him within a narrative of action and counter-action. Such approaches routinely take as their starting point a more or less precise typology of his views, and use this as the axis against which other writings and developments in early Christian thought and structure can be plotted.[1] A recurring theme in scholarship, and one that has received recent enthusiastic revival, has been the proposal that a number of Christian writings, for the most part earlier than Justin with whom the overt tradition starts, were targeted against Marcion, whether or not they themselves are explicitly polemical, namely the Pastoral Epistles, the Acts of the Apostles, perhaps together with the final

[1] So Markus Vinzent, *Christ's Resurrection in Early Christianity and the Making of the New Testament* (Farnham: Ashgate Publishing, Ltd., 2011).

redaction of Luke's Gospel, and Polycarp's *Letter to the Philippians*.[2] Similarly, the reaction against Marcion has been seen as responsible for various elements in the formation of a New Testament canon, whether for the insistence on four Gospels, for the inclusion of a letter collection associated with the 'pillar apostles', or, indeed, for the very idea of a *New* Testament expressed through a body of authoritative writings and modelled around the combination of narrative about Jesus and apostolic writings.[3] The formalisation of anti-Jewish argument around accusations of blindness to the true meaning of the Scriptures and of an inveterate hard-heartedness that demanded the divine imposition of the Law has likewise been traced to the defence of the Christian retention of the now-labelled 'Old Testament' in reaction against its rejection by Marcion.[4] In these scholarly accounts Marcion himself is not explained, perhaps in an unconscious echo of the implicit assumption of the heresiologists that the ideas and practices of heretics neither merit nor are capable of serious explanation, but he himself is credited with a far-reaching explanatory power. Those who deny any or all of these effects frequently subscribe to the same basic model, only rejecting either that these 'Christian' developments required an external provocation, or that Marcion provided such a one.[5]

It is here that the well-practised research into the so-called historical Jesus offers instructive insights. There, too, an earlier tendency had been to minimise any explanation of Jesus' ideas and to concentrate on their transformative effect, externally (on rabbinic Judaism) and internally. Attempts at redescribing Jesus also have to negotiate the challenge of relying almost

[2] See also p. 431. See Martin Rist, 'Pseudepigraphic Refutations of Marcionism', *JBL* 22 (1942), 39–62; the argument has been taken up by a number of writers recently: Vinzent, *Christ's Resurrection*, especially pp 84–110; Adele Yarbro Collins, 'The Female Body as Social Space in 1 Timothy', *NTS* 57 (2011), 155–75; Tyson, *Marcion and Luke-Acts*, 76–8, 121–31. A number of these (but not Vinzent) rely on the earlier dating posited for Marcion by R. J. Hoffmann, *Marcion*. See also pp. 102–3.

[3] See the summary by Christoph Markschies, *Kaiserzeitliche christliche Theologie und ihre Institutionen: Prolegomena zu einer Geschichte der antiken christlichen Theologie* (Tübingen: Mohr Siebeck, 2007), 245–7.

[4] So already David P. Efroymson, 'The Patristic Connection', ed. Alan Davies, *Antisemitism and the Foundations of Christianity* (New York: Paulist Press, 1979), 98–117; Hanns Christof Brennecke, 'Die Kirche als wahres Israel. Ein apologetischer Topos in der Auseinandersetzung mit Markion und der Gnosis', ed. Christoph Schubert and Annette von Stockhausen, *Ad veram religionem reformare. Frühchristliche Apologetik zwischen Anspruch und Wirklichkeit* (Erlanger Forschungen A.109; Erlangen: Universitätsbund Erlangen-Nürnberg, 2006), 47–69. See further, below, pp. 411–13.

[5] For example, the more restrained analysis by Blackman, *Marcion and His Influence*, who concludes 'but he was not altogether ineffectual' (p. 127); see also the review and assessment on the canon by Markschies, *Kaiserzeitliche christliche Theologie*, 245–7, 257–61.

entirely on texts predicated on commitment, albeit here positive, and so have to admit the more cautious goal of plausibility. Increasingly, such plausibility has been recognised as in part determined by the ability to present a persuasive historical and intellectual context that would allow for the continuities and discontinuities that characterise any seminal figure. More fruitful than an antagonistic model is a richly contextual one, which, nonetheless, does not seek to erase the creative potential of any individual. So, too, for Marcion: He belonged to the second century, and it is by reimagining the contours of that context that it becomes possible to trace the dynamics that shaped both him and the responses to him. This was a complex period, particularly for the movement initiated by Jesus of Nazareth as it consolidated its place within the towns of the Roman Empire, and as it gradually emerged from under the wing of the Jewish communities, and as in its own right it engaged directly with contemporary social and intellectual currents. However, various consistent elements in the polemical traditions about Marcion do suggest a coherent starting point.

TIME AND PLACE

Justin's repeated assertion in his *Apology* that Marcion is teaching 'even now' (καὶ νῦν) locates him firmly in the mid-second century, most probably in Rome.[6] However, it is Irenaeus who establishes the tradition that has continued as a basis for consensus. Although his initial account does nothing more than identify Marcion as a successor of Cerdo, who is described as coming to Rome under Hyginus (c. 136–40 CE), he subsequently elaborates, that 'Marcion succeeded him and flourished under Anicetus, who was tenth in line as bishop' (Irenaeus, *AH* I. 27.1; III. 4.3). Earlier he had described Polycarp's visit to Rome at the time of Anicetus (c. 155–66 CE), when he 'turned towards the Church of God many of the afore-mentioned heretics', by implication Valentinus, Marcion, and their followers; what is less clear is whether he thinks, or has any tradition, that the encounter that he describes between Polycarp and Marcion took place there (*AH* III. 3.4).[7] Epiphanius adopts and develops this tradition using it as the framework for an account of Marcion's rupture with the

[6] Justin, *Apol.* 26.5; 58.1–2; see above, pp. 16–17. That he was in Rome is not explicit, and there is no suggestion that Menander was there, but it would explain 'in every race of humanity'.

[7] Gerd Lüdemann, 'Zur Geschichte des ältesten Christentums in Rom', *ZNW* 70 (1989), 86–114, 89–90 argues that the tradition about the dating of Cerdo and Valentinus to the time of Hyginus may be older, but that Irenaeus has identified Marcion as the former's successor and constructed the story of the encounter with Polycarp.

Roman church, which he by implication fixes to the interregnum following the death of Hyginus (Epiphanius, *Pan.* 42.1.3).[8]

For Tertullian's argument it is important that Marcion was initially a believing member of the Roman church, even giving it a substantial donation (although the sum is not specified in the *Against Marcion*).[9] However, he prefers to locate him chronologically within a Roman imperial context: Marcion is 'Antonine', impious under 'Pius' (Tertullian, *AM* V. 19.2–3). This plays a key role in his mockery of the late appearance of Marcion's God and his long incompetence: He pleads ignorance as to the actual date under Antoninus when 'the pestilential breeze blew from Pontus', but claims that the gap between Tiberius (14–37 CE) and Antoninus (138–61 CE) is 'one hundred and fifteen and a half years and half a month' and that this is what the Marcionites themselves 'put between Christ and Marcion'. Much has been made of this, with most scholars using as a start point January 29 CE (the fifteenth year of Tiberius, Luke 3.1), thus reaching July 144 CE as the end point; however, what that end point marked is a matter of debate, with most deciding either for Marcion's arrival in Rome, or for his initial preaching, or for his break with the Roman church.[10] That the last of these could be quite so precisely dated presupposes the arguably anachronistic model of a decisive act of 'excommunication', while that either of the former two would be so remembered may seem unlikely. Indeed, it may be entirely mistaken to read 'that much time they put (*ponunt*) between Christ and Marcion' as evidence that the precise figure was one celebrated by Marcion's followers rather than the result of Tertullian's opaque computation of the gap between Tiberius and Antoninus, which is what he states. Even so, this is not so different from the date set by the Chronicle of Edessa for when Marcion left 'the catholic church', even if this is equally anachronistic (137/8 CE).[11]

8 This may be his deduction from a tradition that has Marcion in conflict not with a bishop but with elders: see above, pp. 104–06. A number of scholars accept that authority in the Roman church was still corporate until the time of Victor (189–99): see Peter Lampe, *From Paul to Valentinus: Christians at Rome in the First Two Centuries* (transl. Michael Steinhauser, ed. Marshall D. Johnson; London: T&T Clark, 2003), 397.

9 See above, p. 57. Those who rely on such a narrative often ignore the fact that Tertullian is more precise in the *Prescription* when he had little knowledge of Marcion's writings than in the *Against Marcion*.

10 See Braun, *Contre Marcion*, I, 186–7n.; Lampe, *Paul to Valentinus*, 244 (who attempts to relate this to a shipowner's calendar); Regul, *Antimarcionitischen Evangelienprologe*, 177–97.

11 See also above, p. 128 for Clement of Alexandria's account of Marcion's association with Basilides and Valentinus as 'an old man with those younger'. Although Marcion is routinely paired with Valentinus as 'arch-heretics', there is no consistent sequencing of them.

A further complication is the tradition in Ps.Tertullian, *Against All Heresies*, and in Epiphanius, that Marcion has already 'been excluded from the church' in Pontus before he came to Rome, although for a sexual misdemeanour.[12] Harnack accepted the exclusion but not the cause, and he also accepted the tradition from the 'Antimarcionite Prologue' to John that Marcion then went to Asia Minor, taking letters from the Christians of Pontus, but was again rebuffed, perhaps after the encounter with Polycarp; indeed, Harnack then follows this by Marcion's arrival in Rome, his initial acceptance by the church there, and his subsequent exclusion, with his money (Tertullian), after an exegetical debate, by 'the first Roman synod' (Epiphanius).[13] Such a harmonising of the various traditions to create a coherent narrative ignores the multiple influences that have shaped them, as well as the internal inconsistencies within them. Yet, without going so far, a number of scholars have argued that Marcion did have a period of teaching before his arrival in Rome, and that the best evidence of this is the 'anonymous' polemic against him discussed above; some have even attempted to trace a development in his thought in order to explain the conflicting accounts of the influence of Cerdo, of the description of the Creator as actively evil, or Justin's failure to mention Marcion's treatment of Gospel and Paul.[14]

It will not be possible to give an incontrovertible account of Marcion's life, not even of his life as a Christian (and as a 'heretic'); still less will it be possible to use such a life, including traditions such as his career as a sailor or ship owner, to explain the development of his teaching and his relationship with the broader Christian tradition. Nonetheless, it will be argued that there are overarching themes that run through the various polemical accounts of Marcion, and that belong securely in the second century; chief among these are the role of 'scriptural texts' and their interpretation, and, secondly, the philosophical questions regarding the nature of the divine and its relationship with the created order. Concern with these themes coheres well with the most stable tradition that associates Marcion with Rome, and it is with Rome that this exploration of a plausible context for Marcion will begin. Here again, just as Justin Martyr provided the starting point for tracing the polemical construction of

[12] See above, p. 101.

[13] Harnack, *Marcion*, 23–7. On the 'Antimarcionite Prologue', see above p. 103.

[14] Knox, *Marcion and the New Testament*, 14, suggests that Marcion developed his teaching based on a Pauline antithesis before he came to Rome, but acquired an intellectual framework from Cerdo at Rome.

Marcion the heretic, so he can also provide a starting point for exploring the intellectual and social worlds in which both men moved, and so can both inspire and discipline the imagination.

A PARALLEL LIFE

Of the various figures who populate the anecdotes and texts of emerging Christianity in the second century, probably the best known is Justin Martyr. He, too, was a teacher who grappled with questions of God and of Scripture, and who, coming from an Eastern province, eventually settled in Rome. Moreover, he treated Marcion as a contemporary, and he even, apparently, composed a sustained attack against him, and perhaps others. Tracing Justin's life and concerns provides something of a template against which to set the far more fragmentary and distorted echoes of Marcion's experience, and it suggests further avenues to explore.

Justin was 'a provincial', born in Flavia Neapolis, a Roman colony in what after 135 CE was designated by Hadrian the province of Syria Palestine, something that he is careful to explain in his *Apology* to Hadrian's successor, Antoninus Pius (Justin, *Apol.* 1.1). That means that he was, as he admits only in passing in the *Dialogue*, 'of the people of Samaria'; but he was not a 'Samaritan', and his writings do not explicitly demonstrate any particular familiarity with Samaritan religious practice or tradition (*Dial.* 120.6). Instead, in the *Apology* he presents himself as belonging to the Christian adherents 'from the Gentiles', who are far more numerous than those from 'Israel and Samaria'; in so doing he reiterates his conscious self-orientation towards the Empire, and ultimately towards its centre, Rome (*Apol.* 53.3–6). Conversely, he emphasises the inconspicuous origins of Simon Magus 'from a village called Gitta', itself in Samaria, and that it was among his own people that Simon had his initial success; similarly, Menander, a disciple, was 'also from Samaria' and from an equally obscure village; last in the list, 'the Pontic Marcion' is being put in his place in the same fashion (*Apol.* 26.1–4; 53.3–6; 56). Origins count for much in a polemic of respectability, but their actual cultural influence is more difficult to trace.

Justin had a Greek education; he traces his philosophical journey in pursuit of truth via the Stoics, the Peripatetics, the Pythagoreans, and finally Plato (*Dial.* 2); although this account is highly stylised, many young men of his background would have spent a period of time studying under various teachers. When he subsequently came to explain the various competing groups claiming the label 'Christian', it was to the model of philosophical 'schools' that he turned.[15] Just to what extent his conversion entailed a reversal of his earlier values may be a matter of perspective; in the *Dialogue* he attributes it to the discovery of the prophets and so of the one to whom they pointed, mediated by a mysterious encounter in a deserted spot, but in the context of his *Apology* he lays stress instead on the impact made on him by the fearlessness of the Christians in the face of death (*Dial.* 3; 2 *Apol.* 12). In either case there ensued strong continuities and discontinuities with his previous values and world view. To a degree unparalleled before him among Christian writers, he endeavours to find a place for the great searchers for truth in Greek thought, and he also continues to use the models and patterns of thinking provided by his philosophical education. Yet the sources on which he bases his arguments and which he repeatedly interprets and reinterprets are the (Jewish) Scriptures. He is not alone in this curious hybridity: Theophilus of Antioch and to some extent Aristides display something similar, although at the same time they are very different from him and from each other. However, it is only with Justin that we can attempt to locate this within a broader social and intellectual context and in his personal biography.[16]

It is this double allegiance and inheritance that makes Justin such an interesting person and that signals his importance both for the development of second-century Christian thought, and as a marker of the path that others would inevitably follow. It is striking that in the *Dialogue*, with its ostensibly Jewish audience, he presents his discovery of the prophets and of the words 'of the friends of Christ' as the discovery of the 'only safe and beneficial philosophy'; it is this that authenticates his self-designation as a philosopher and his wearing of a philosopher's robe, which first drew Trypho to him (*Dial.* 8.1–2). Whether or not he had already made the transition to the role of a teacher before his conversion, thereafter that apparently became his defining task. Evidently this role involved some degree of travelling. Neither the location of his conversion nor that of his encounter with Trypho is known; Eusebius locates the latter at Ephesus, although recently Syria Palestine has been proposed for both.[17] Eventually Rome became the main

15 See above, p. 17.

16 See Nicole Zeegers, 'Les trois cultures de Théophile d'Antioche', Bernard Pouderon and Joseph Doré, ed., *Les Apologistes Chrétiens et la Culture Grecque* (Théologie historique 105; Paris: Beauchesne, 1998), 135–76, who explores the inheritance of Theophilus in terms of its pagan, Christian, and Jewish nature and ends with the possibility that he may have been a proselyte.

17 Eusebius, *HE* IV. 18. 6; see Adalbert G. Hamman, 'Essai de chronologie de la vie et des oeuvres de Justin', *Augustinianum* 35 (1995), 231–9.

centre of his activities, but probably not the only one: In the account of his martyrdom, which is broadly plausible, he describes his current sojourn in Rome as his second visit (*Mart.Just.* 3). Not only did Rome attract many such temporary or permanent visitors, but the contacts and links established were essential to the development of early Christianity just as they were a core element of other social and intellectual networks.

Justin's account of Christian baptism, eucharist, and practice indicates his participation in the life of the worshipping community (*Apol.* 60), but he has little interest in ecclesiastical structures and he was apparently not part of any hierarchy. He gives no evidence of how the Christian community in Rome was organised or whether there was any overarching authority. His own chief role was as a teacher, and it is from the *Martyrdom* that the picture emerges of him living above the baths of Myrtinus,[18] where he willingly shared the 'words of the truth' with any who came seeking. He was not primarily an evangelist: Those who are arrested with him were already Christians before they came to listen to him even if they then became established disciples. He was not the only such teacher in Rome: He describes the arrest and martyrdom of a certain Ptolemaeus who had been the 'teacher of Christian doctrines' for a Roman woman, herself accused as a Christian.[19] Justin perhaps presented himself as one philosophical teacher among many: He himself at this point anticipated that he would be denounced by a Cynic philosopher, Crescens, with whom he had already had some lively debates (2 *Apol.* 2–3). As shall be seen, this was a pluralistic environment: Justin's knowledge of alternative exegeses by Jewish teachers arguably originated in similar encounters between rival teachers (*Dial.* 43.8; 60.2–3). On the other hand, he is also aware of other self-identified Christian teachers whose tenets he presents in terms of their view of God, for whom implicitly, although not explicitly, he reconfigures the category '*hairesis*' (*Apol.* 26).[20]

The actual content of Justin's public teaching can only be deduced from those writings that survive, the *Apologies* and the *Dialogue with Trypho*; he also wrote a work against heresies or sects, which may have had a more internal audience, although his offer to send it to the Emperor suggests it may also have had an apologetic function (*Apol.* 25.8). Eusebius lists further writings (*HE* IV. 18), now lost, and others came to be attributed to him.

18 The textual tradition of the name is corrupt, so the identity of this place is uncertain.

19 Whether this Ptolemaeus was the author of the 'Letter to Flora' is a matter of ongoing debate; see below, pp. 411–12.

20 On this see above, p. 18.

Given their distinctive literary genres, neither the *Apologies* nor the *Dialogue* can represent directly the style of his oral lectures; however, there is good reason to suppose that many of the points he makes, and even extended arguments, may be borrowed from earlier settings. In *Dial.* 98–106 he presents an extended exegesis of Psalm 22 whose overall unity of conception and whose inclusion of distinctive terms and principles would be well suited to an oral exposition.

Yet, despite his many innovations, Justin was the heir to earlier work and he had available a variety of sources; however, he may have accessed these. It has been shown that many of his short scriptural quotations, often combined together and accompanied by a distinctive Christological interpretation, probably go back to earlier written Christian collections or arguments.[21] One of the challenges that Justin then faced was how to reconcile these 'testimonia' with the different forms of the text to be found in the scriptural manuscripts preserved by his Jewish contemporaries, forms which from his lengthy citations appear to conform much more closely to the septuagintal tradition. One of his responses to this inconsistency was to charge his Jewish opponents with having corrupted the Scriptures in their possession (*Dial.* 72). At the same time some of his own exegetical choices, as well as those he claims for his opponents, can be traced in later Jewish sources, suggesting that real interactions lie behind his narrative. As shall be seen, concerns about the corruption of authoritative texts were a commonplace in the period; more specifically, the sensitivity that he shows to the possibility of contradictions in the Scriptures or to problems such as God's apparent ignorance reflects more widespread debates and is not simply part of his own anti-Marcionite polemics. In addition, Justin also alludes to, or quotes traditions of, Jesus' life and teaching, drawn, if not directly from Matthew, Mark, and Luke, then from a harmonising precursor or version of these, which may itself have been developed for catechetical purposes.[22] Further, while he never names Paul, he does mimic some of Paul's exegetical moves, particularly with regard to the interpretation of Deuteronomy 21.23 and its intersection with Deuteronomy 27.26 (*Dial.* 89–96).

Attempts at this point to measure and to define Justin's continuing indebtedness to Greek philosophical structures have reached differing conclusions, with much turning on the primary origins of his doctrine of the Logos, which for him serves both as a mediating principle and as the

[21] On this and what follows see Skarsaune, *The Proof from Prophecy*.

[22] See pp. 184, 429.

pre-existent principle of divine activity incarnated in Jesus Christ.[23] Certainly, the questions about God that Justin sought to answer resonated with the familiar questions of philosophical debate of his time. However much his understanding of God's activity may have been adapted to the witness of the Scriptures, his fundamental definition remains that God is 'That which always continues the same and in the same manner and is the cause of the existence of everything else', and 'the one who is not moved, being incapable of confinement in one place, even in the whole universe' (*Dial.* 3.5; 127.2). It is his philosophical principles that make it self-evident – that not even 'one with the smallest mind' would disagree – that 'the maker and father of everything [would not] leave the all that is above heaven to make an appearance on some small portion of earth'. This meant for him that if the scriptural accounts do describe one who can be called 'God' so appearing, for example in the Burning Bush or in conversation with Jacob or with Abraham, then clearly they must refer to some other who can still be so named (*Dial.* 60). Such conclusions might suggest that Justin was endeavouring to accommodate the recalcitrant Scriptures to normative philosophical principles, but his own account moves in the opposite direction, giving primacy to the Scriptures and letting them define the true nature of what philosophy has only dimly grasped. In this approach many have drawn a parallel with the first-century Jew, Philo of Alexandria, whose writings have sparked similar debates as to where his ultimate intellectual loyalty lay, with Scripture or with philosophy.[24] Both thinkers attest to the impact of, and to the possibilities afforded by, contemporary interpretations of Plato for an exploration of the biblical God amongst the intellectual circles of the early Empire.

Much more could be said about Justin's own thought and about the broader range of issues that he addressed. Enough can be seen from this brief sketch both of the sort of physical and intellectual journey that others also may have made in the second century, and of the social and conceptual contexts that provided the framework and the challenges of such journeys.

[23] See Mark Edwards, 'On the Platonic Schooling of Justin Martyr', *JTS* 42 (1991), 17–34. For the view that Justin remained constrained by his Greek philosophical heritage see Nils A. Dahl, 'Justin und die griechische Philosophie', ed. Claus Zintzen, *Der Mittelplatonismus* (WF 70; Darmstadt: Wissenschaftliche Buchgesellschaft, 1981), 369–96 (= *Philosophie und Christentum* [Acta Theologica Danica 9. Copenhagen: Munksgaard, 1966] 272–92).

[24] See David T. Runia, *Philo of Alexandria and the Timaeus of Plato* (Phil.Ant. 44; Leiden: Brill, 1986), 3–31.

Justin's social context

Justin was not the only Christian teacher in Rome in the middle of the second century; alongside Marcion, whom he explicitly describes as *teaching* – unlike Simon and Menander with whom he initially brackets him – and Ptolemaeus, other surviving names include Valentinus, Basilides, perhaps Heracleon, and later Tatian and Rhodon.[25] In what is known of their activities and style each of these fits well in the wider profile of Roman society in this period, in contrast to the very different profile that they exhibit from the wandering teachers or 'prophets' of the *Didache* 11–12, or even those in the *Shepherd of Hermas* (*Man.* 11).[26] Teachers of philosophy were a key feature of the cultural life of Rome, as of other major urban centres: More than forty are known by name from Rome in the second century, and among these those of Greek origin are dominant.[27] The patterns adopted by such teachers varied: Some were dependent on the patronage of a wealthy person; others practised in a more public setting, attracting young men to complete their intellectual formation or *paideia*.[28] Their audiences might include 'philosophical tourists', but some teachers also purported to offer for a circle of disciples a model of personal as well as of social improvement; this would lead to the close pattern of relationships between teacher and pupils such as is pictured in the *Martyrdom of Justin* between Justin, Chariton, Euelpistus, and Hierax. Not every would-be teacher was successful: According to Lucian, another contemporary of Justin, Proteus Peregrinus, was expelled from Rome for his intemperate abuse even of the Emperor, although a more sympathetic account might suggest that his problem was his inability to secure high-ranking protection (Lucian, *Peregr.* 18). Certainly it would be wrong to overplay the broader intellectual status of men such as Justin or Ptolemaeus, but undoubtedly they did fill something of a vacuum in the emergence of a Christian culture. They helped shape a framework for the development of a Christian intellectual

25 Löhr, *Basilides*; Markschies, *Valentinus Gnosticus?*; Ansgar Wucherpfennig, *Heracleon Philologus: Gnostische Johannesexegese im zweiten Jahrhundert* (WUNT 142; Tübingen: Mohr Siebeck, 2002).

26 On the earlier style of teachers see Peter Pilhofer, 'Von Jakobus zu Justin: Lernen in den Spätschriften des Neuen Testaments und bei den Apologeten', ed. Beate Ego and Helmut Merkel, *Religiöses Lernen in der biblischen, frühjüdischen und frühchristlichen Überlieferung* (WUNT 180; Tübingen: Mohr Siebeck, 2005), 253–69.

27 So Johannes Hahn, *Der Philosoph und die Gesellschaft: Selbstverständnis, öffentliches Auftreten und populäre Erwartungen in der hohen Kaiserzeit* (Weisbaden: Franz Steiner, 1989), 150–3.

28 This is a term Justin uses in *Apol.* 1.1; 2.2.

elite and for a pattern of a distinctive *paideia*, both of which would achieve a more public flowering in the Alexandria of the early third century.[29]

The relationship between such teachers and local organised worshipping communities with their own leadership must have varied. There are no grounds for finding in Rome a straightforward contrast between the more 'simple' theology of the established Christian community and the more intellectual ideas introduced by a variety of teachers from outside.[30] The ambivalence of Justin's position was, perhaps, typical; Valentinus apparently did produce sermons or homilies, which may point to a worship setting, but this is not how he is primarily represented (Clement of Alexandria, *Strom.* IV. 8.59; VI. 6.52).[31] However, in this period it is not clear what mechanisms there were, if any, to authorise people who might wish to teach within the church community, and it is easy to envisage that such absence of centralised control could become a cause of dissent. A clearer school pattern was to emerge in Alexandria; according to later tradition this originated in the second century, with a line from Pantaenus to Clement of Alexandria and thence to Origen, but it is more likely that only with Origen was a formal catechetical school established, and that the first two acted as independent teachers, attracting students but not operating within any formalised structures. In Rome there is little evidence for any centralised ecclesiastical structure uniting the various Christian communities throughout most of the second century, and much more to indicate divisions following social and geographical fault lines as well as theological inclination: In such circumstances there must have been even more room for variety and for lack of control over individual teachers.[32] Indeed, it may be no accident that Irenaeus could offer no report of any measures taken by the Roman community against those who came there and whom he

[29] See B. Pouderon, 'Refléxions sur la formation d'une elite intellectuelle chrétienne au IIe siècle', ed. Pouderon and Doré, *Les Apologistes Chrétiens et la Culture Grecque*, 237–69; Dietmar Wyrwa, 'Religiöses Lernen im zweiten Jahrhundert und die Anfänge der alexandrinischen Katechetenschule', in Ego and Merkel, *Religiöses Lernen*, 271–305. R. Klein, 'Christliche Glaube und heidnische Bildung', *Laverna* 1 (1990), 50–100, is more negative about the extent of such activity than is Pouderon who posits such schools in Rome, Alexandria, Athens, Antioch, and Carthage.

[30] This was suggested by Langerbeck, 'Zur Auseinandersetzung von Theologie und Gemeindeglauben'.

[31] See Markschies, *Valentinus Gnosticus?*, 123, 388–92. Tertullian, *De Carne* 17, refers to 'the psalms of Valentinus'.

[32] See Lampe, *From Paul to Valentinus*, 381–408, who dates the emergence of more coherent structures and the possibility of exclusion to the time of Victor in the past decade of the second century (Eusebius, *HE* V. 24). See above, p. 105, for attempts to locate Epiphanius' account of Marcion in this setting.

identifies as heretics.[33] Hence, although later tradition denounced Valentinus as a heretic, the earliest references suggest that he had a closer albeit independent relationship with the worshipping communities and with other schools. Justin Martyr's silence regarding Valentinus in his list of spurious teachers in the *Apology* may indicate that at that stage he saw no threat in his teaching; similarly, if the Ptolemaeus mentioned above, whose martyrdom is recounted in the *Second Apology*, is to be identified with the 'Valentinian' Ptolemaeus whose letter to Flora is preserved by Epiphanius, then again Justin saw him only as another teacher of Christian truth.[34] Things may already have been changing: By the time Justin wrote the *Dialogue* the Valentinans could appear in his list of those whose claim to the name 'Christian' is spurious, although how much he knew about any of these groups is unclear (*Dial.* 35.6).

As well as locating themselves to a greater or lesser degree in relation to the church communities, such teachers and their disciples also saw themselves, and surely would have been seen by others, in parallel to similar teachers with a Jewish or 'pagan' background. To this extent it is possible to speak of them as operating in or as a 'school', over against the somewhat more enclosed and self-sufficient 'church', although it would be wrong to represent these as entirely opposed to each other.[35] Within the framework of 'schools' there would be room for debate both within the particular traditions but also between them, 'Jewish', 'Christian', or other, and this would extend to the sharing of questions and of possible solutions.[36] Audiences may have been eclectic, self-selecting, and this would have encouraged the various attempts to compare authorities or to experiment with different models which, as shall be seen, were characteristic of the period. Such interactions were possible because all who were involved did not just share a style of activity and certain social structures, but they also had in common fundamental principles regarding their task; they would have shared a common educational formation, and all accorded a

33 So Einar Thomassen, 'Orthodoxy and Heresy in Second-Century Rome', *HTR* 97 (2004), 241–56, 243, who notes that it was left to Polycarp to do this when visiting Rome (*AH* III. 3.4). This is more persuasive than Wyrwa, 'Religiöses Lernen', who retains a distinction between Gnostic 'conventicles' and 'the great church'.

34 See Lüdemann, 'Zur Geschichte', 100–10.

35 See Ismo Dunderberg, 'Valentinian Teachers in Rome', ed. Jürgen Zangenberg and Michael Labahn, *Christians as a Religious Minority in a Multicultural City* (JSNTSup. 243; London: T&T Clark, 2004), 157–74, who argues for different positions among the different groups; see also Thomassen, 'Orthodoxy and Heresy'.

36 For Philo as functioning in a similar environment in Alexandria, see Gregory E. Sterling, '"The School of Sacred Laws": The Social Setting of Philo's Treatises', *VC* 53 (1999), 148–64.

central role to the interpretation of authoritative written texts. On the other hand, such pluralism could be marked by heated polemic between rival claims to different or to the same authorities, or to correctly elucidating their meaning.

Justin's literary context

The core texts to which each of these teachers appealed varied, but the questions that they were addressing were similar – the nature of the universe and its relationship with the transcendent God, and the meaning and goal of human existence. For Justin when writing the *Dialogue*, the prophets alone had access to the truth, but what matters is that 'their writings', like those of Moses, 'are still available … providing such things as a philosopher needs to know' (*Dial.* 7.1–3). Yet Justin is also able to cite Plato's *Timaeus*, noting points of comparison between them (*Apol.* 59–60; cf. *Dial.* 5). It need not follow that Justin had actually read 'Homer … and the teachings of the writers, Empedocles and Pythagoras, Plato and Socrates, and of those who said the same as these' (*Apol.* 18.5), for handbooks of their teaching and selections or chains of excerpts and earlier citation and interpretation were readily available; even his references to the *Timaeus*, one of the most widely invoked writings in the period, appear to be second-hand.[37] Claiming greater antiquity for one's progenitors, founding figures, or inventors, was a fundamental strategy in the competitive apologetics of the age, but Justin's trump card is that those to whom he appeals are older than all other *writers* (*Apol.* 23.1; 59.1). Yet what he presupposes, and what his peers of all traditions would have agreed with, is not only that these writers, or those championed by any individual, understood and conveyed the truth, but that the faithful recovery of that understanding demanded correct interpretation of what they wrote – with the consequent need to expose the flawed interpretations proposed by others. Obviously, the choice of particular texts, for most initially Homer but also the classical playwrights and philosophers, reflected and reinforced their authority and so contributed to the idea, albeit in loose terms, of a canon. The methods of such interpretative activity and its further literary shape would have varied among different teachers and settings. Recent scholarship has painted the picture of the teacher providing oral commentary on and interpretation of earlier authoritative texts or opinions; this was duly noted down by his disciples, perhaps to become

[37] This is suggested by the form of his citation; see below, p. 312.

the object of further comment and elucidation by the next generation.[38] Such notes were rarely published, but they could have circulated among groups of disciples; other works were published more widely, perhaps with a conscious distinction between those designed for pupils and those intended for a general audience.[39]

The problem underlying such activity was that these older texts contained obscurities and even apparent problems, giving rise to conflicting claims to rightly expound them. Philosophical texts may have failed to answer contemporary questions, or, rather, could only be shown through skilful exegesis to have answered them. Homer, which still occupied a foundational status, raised particular issues of apparent inconsistency or moral impropriety. What was 'fitting' was a core measure across behaviour and speech, and was an important tool in reading authoritative texts.[40] The fundamental presupposition was that the authoritative text cannot be flawed and that it carries an intended meaning; any failure in sense is not due to any incoherence by the author.[41] Writing on 'Homeric problems', Heraclitus (first century CE) declared that 'If he did not allegorise everything then he was totally impious'.[42] At fault must be either the corruption of the text in its transmission or inappropriate reading or some defect in understanding on the reader's part; the first invited the identification of interpolations or omissions, and the correction of mistakes, the second and third an explanation of a superior way of reading. In the second century, philosophers such as Plutarch began to view traditional religious practice and texts as potential sources of the ultimate truth, if only they too were properly interpreted. Inevitably, the Jewish Scriptures invited a similar approach; like Homer they too contained many potential obscurities or morally disturbing passages, but their claim to convey the truth about God was even more unequivocal. Hence, Jewish scholars, particularly in Alexandria, had already responded

38 David Sedley, 'Philosophical Allegiance in the Greco-Roman World', ed. Miriam Griffin and Jonathan Barnes, *Philosophia Togata I: Essays on Philosophy and Roman Society* (Oxford: Clarendon Press, 1989), 97–119.

39 See Mansfeld, *Prolegomena*, 110, 118–22; William A. Johnson, *Readers and Reading Culture in the High Roman Empire: A Study of Elite Communities* (Oxford: Oxford University Press, 2010), 85–8, on Galen. Similarly Philodemus' works were perhaps circulated among his disciples at the instigation of his patron, Piso, rather than formally published; see Dirk Obbink, 'Craft, Cult, and Canon in the Books from Herculaneum', ed. Fitzgerald, Obbink, Holland, *Philodemus and the New Testament World*, 73–84.

40 See Max Pohlenz, 'τὸ πρέπον. Ein Beitrag zur Geschichte der griechischen Geistes', *NGWGPh*, 1933, 53–92.

41 For this and what follows see Sedley, 'Philosophical Allegiance'.

42 Heraclitus, *Hom.Prob.* 1.1; see Donald A. Russell and David Konstan, ed. and transl., *Heraclitus, Homeric Problems* (Leiden: Brill, 2005).

to, or, in some cases, adopted, the methods of their peers.[43] As already noted, Justin accuses Jewish *teachers* both of corrupting and of misinterpreting the prophetic writings while he himself rejects emphatically any insinuation that he even contemplates the possibility of there being contradictions in Scripture (*Dial.* 48.3; 65.2).

Although Justin's surviving writings are not presented as 'school products', they do reflect some of the genres and techniques commonly adopted in that setting. Justin assumes that the debate over the Scriptures with Trypho can be settled by a series of questions or investigations (ζήτησις, ζήτημα) addressed to them; he charges his opponent with failing to recognise that the renaming of Joshua (= Jesus) by Moses demanded analysis and explanation, and with reopening issues that had already been extensively demonstrated and agreed (*Dial.* 68.3 [ἀνερωτάω]; 71.2; 113.1 [ζήτησις]; 123.7 [ἀπόδειξις]). Such language reflects the influential and long-lasting genre of 'Questions and Answers' (ἐρωτοαπόκρισεις) or 'Investigations and Solutions' (ζητήματα, λύσεις), which usually took the form of a series of questions concerning the text, provoking one or more possible solutions. The literary setting of such 'questions and answers' is frequently a social one where different participants are involved in dialogue or in analysis, and this may reflect a similar actual social context for such exercises, at least in origin.[44] Although rooted in the pedagogical relationship between teacher and pupil, this technique could easily become a means of articulating and reinforcing a 'correct' reading of the text. Again, Justin had Jewish precursors, whether or not he was aware of this: According to Eusebius Aristobulus addressed questions or 'investigations' to the Scriptures, particularly identifying the contrast between the natural and the allegorical meaning; Philo adopts, among other techniques, the question and answer style as well as the technical vocabulary of Graeco-Roman analysis, but he also attacks others within the Jewish community whose methods or conclusions he rejects.[45] Subsequently, Justin's disciple, Tatian, addressed difficulties in Scripture in a work entitled 'Problems', while his erstwhile disciple Rhodon

43 See Maren R. Niehoff, *Jewish Exegesis and Homeric Scholarship in Alexandria* (Cambridge: Cambridge University Press, 2011).

44 See Christian Jacob, 'Questions sur les questions: Archéologie d'une pratique intellectualle et d'une forme discursive', ed. Annelie Volgers and Claudio Zamagni, *Erotapokriseis: Early Christian Question and Answer Literature in Context* (CBET 37; Leuven: Peeters, 2004), 25–54.

45 Eusebius, *HE* VII. 32.17 ; PE VIII. 10.1; Philo, *QG*; *QE*. See Maren R. Niehoff, 'Homeric Scholarship and Bible Exegesis in Ancient Alexandria: Evidence from Philo's "Quarrelsome' Colleagues', *CQ* 57 (2007), 166–82; eadem, 'Questions and Answers in Philo and *Genesis Rabbah*', *JSJ* 39 (2008), 337–66; eadem, *Jewish Exegesis*, 133–85.

promised his own 'Solutions', titles that recall a chapter in Aristotle's discussion of Homer (Aristotle, *Poet.* 1460B) as well as the recent work of Heraclitus; later Ambrose discusses the questions that Apelles, the disciple of Marcion, had asked two centuries earlier, including a question regarding the two trees in the Garden (Gen. 2) 'in his thirty-eighth volume' (Ambrose, *De Parad.* 28). On the other hand, Tertullian's attack against the 'syllogisms' of the Valentinian Alexander suggests that these likewise took the form of questions pressing the logic of claims as to the flesh of Christ.[46]

Other literary products included commentaries and various handbooks, which, although having older roots, flourished in this period. Such commentaries are widely represented among the papyri, where they can take a variety of forms: lexica, texts with marginal comments, or lemmata, whether a single word, a phrase, or a few lines. Such variety resists any simple explanation of development, and it witnesses to the literary creativity at play. Alongside these were 'hypotheseis', narrative summaries of older works, and handbooks supplying information about myths, genealogies, and narratives.[47] Commentaries might sometimes cite earlier interpreters, often anonymously, either with approval or in order to refute them. Yet commentaries could frequently serve a polemical purpose, undermining previously held positions and offering a framework within which to develop alternative philosophical ideas.[48] Justin's own treatment of the Scriptures, and the testimonia on which he perhaps draws, belong more to the tradition of the messianic interpretation of prophetic proof-texts whose precursors lie in Jewish exegesis, including the Pesharim among the Dead Sea Scrolls. However, terms used for other contemporary works betray an awareness of the wider intellectual climate: the 'ὑπομνήματα' of Hegesippus, the five books of 'exegeses of the words of the Lord' by Papias, and Julius Cassianus' 'ἐξηγητικά' (Eusebius, *HE* III. 39.1; IV. 22.1; Clement of Alexandria, *Strom.* I. 21.101). Apparently more systematic and directed, and so more firmly within the category of a Commentary, are Heracleon's

46 Eusebius, *HE* V. 13.8; Tertullian, *De Carne* 15–17. On the genre in Christian tradition see the extensive survey by G. Bardy, 'La littérature patristique des "*Quaestiones et Responsiones*" sur L'Écriture Sainte', *RevBib* 41 (1932), 210–36, 341–69, 515–37; 42 (1933), 14–30, 211–29, 328–52.

47 See Guido Bastianini et al., ed., *Commentaria et Lexica Graeca in Papyris Reperta* (Leipzig/Munich: K. G. Saur, 2004); Monique van Rossum-Steenbeek, *Greek Readers Digests? Studies in a Selection of Subliterary Papyri* (Mnem.Sup. 175; Leiden: Brill, 1998).

48 Han Baltussen, 'From Polemic to Exegesis: The Ancient Philosophical Commentary', *Poetics Today* 28 (2007), 247–81; on the development of the style of Commentary see Craig A. Gibson, *Interpreting a Classic: Demosthenes and His Ancient Commentators* (Berkeley, CA/London: University of California Press, 2002), 13–32.

comments of the Fourth Gospel preserved by Origen, prompting the description of Heracleon as 'the first serious Christian philologian and exegete'.[49] To this perhaps should be added Basilides' 'twenty-four books on the Gospel', which, on the basis of fragments, it has been claimed probably combined exposition, text-criticism, and evaluation, from a contemporary philosophical perspective.[50] Both writers, it seems, although in different ways, were concerned to interpret the text so as to address problems within the framework of the Platonism of the time; both also were interpreting the distinctive Christian writings whose relative antiquity and authority were already sufficiently established to demand their interpretation. No doubt, not all these works of criticism were of the same intellectual standard and thoroughness, but they represent the extent to which early Christian writers were active participants in the literary and intellectual culture of their day.

It follows from this that Irenaeus' attempt to distance the Christian reading of Scripture from the 'questions' of the philosophers has to be treated with caution. Indeed, even he acknowledges that others did not make this distinction (Irenaeus, *AH* II. 27.1; III. 13.11). Similarly, Eusebius reports criticisms in the early third century against those who subordinate Scripture to syllogisms, and who engaged in close textual criticism and emendation; however, he himself carried out his own 'investigations and solutions' into the genealogy of the Saviour (*HE* V. 38.13–19; *DE* VII. 3.18).

A further aspect of Justin's literary context that anticipates his philosophical context is hinted at in his offer to send the Emperor a copy of his collation 'Against all the *haereseis* that have come into being' (*Apol.* 26. 8). As has been seen already, in his occasional use of the term 'αἵρεσις', Justin anticipates, if he does not generate, what will become a significant shift in its meaning. However, the novelty should not be over-stressed. From its root sense of a position or choice, 'αἵρεσις' had come to be used of the different philosophical schools or systems.[51] In part this is visible in the distinctive literary genre characteristic of Hellenistic philosophy 'Concerning Sects (περὶ αἱρέσεων)' with its comparison, whether informatively or defensively,

49 Wucherpfennig, *Heracleon Philologus*, 413; see also Christoph Markschies, 'Origenes und die Kommentierung des paulinischen Römerbriefs – einige Bermerkungen zur Rezeption von antiken Kommentar-techniken im Christentum des dritten Jahrhunderts und ihrer Vorgeschichte', ed. Glenn W. Most, *Commentaries – Kommentare* (Aporemata 4; Göttingen: Vandenhoeck and Ruprecht, 1999), 66–94.

50 Eusebius, *HE* IV. 7.7; Löhr, *Basilides*, 5–14; Kelhoffer, 'Basilides's Gospel'; above, p. 209.

51 See above, p. 18.

of the positions of the various schools.[52] Perhaps, Justin's volume was a deliberate parody of the genre, and an attack against the variety such comparisons documented.

Justin's philosophical context

Although heavily stylised, Justin's account of his philosophical quest in the opening chapters of the *Dialogue* illustrates the broader context within which second-century Christians would need to interpret their understanding of God and of the implications of their faith in Jesus Christ. The initial climax of that quest in Platonism (*Dial.* 2.6) reflects the importance of the latter in the second century, even if the fragmentary nature of the major sources continues to produce disagreement as to precisely how this is to be described.[53] Philosophical questions and debate were not restricted to limited circles of the intellectual elite that may have counted few Christians among their number: 'Platonism at this time was in the mouth of every wandering pedagogue, every sophist, every speculator of whatever professed allegiance.'[54] Handbooks and collections of key passages and doctrines of the authorities of the past were widely available alongside direct access to their writings, whose precise meaning, as has been seen, was the subject of heated discussion and regular reinterpretation. The period might be defined less by a focus on 'schools' defined by their interpretation of central philosophical ideas, and more through the conscious concern to rediscover the original teaching of those authorities.

The fundamental concern within this environment was how the ultimate reality, or for some the highest God, was to be described, if indeed that was possible; Christian apologists affirmed the problem even if they had their own solution to it. Justin appeals to the philosophers' truism, here ascribed to Socrates, that 'it is not easy to discover the father and creator

52 See Jaap Mansfeld, 'Sources', ed. Keimpe Algra, Jonathan Barnes, Jaap Mansfeld, and Malcolm Schofield, *The Cambridge History of Hellenistic Philosophy* (Cambridge: Cambridge University Press, 1999), 3–30, 19–23; Christopher Heil, 'Arius Didymus and Luke-Acts', *NovT* 42 (2000), 358–93, who (p. 373) criticises the view that this usage was a second-century development.

53 See George R. Boys-Stones, *Post-Hellenistic Philosophy: A Study of its Development from the Stoics to Origen* (Oxford: Oxford University Press, 2001), who rejects the epithet 'Middle Platonism', as also does Michael Frede, 'Numenius', *ANRW* II.36.2, 1034–75, 1040. See also John Whittaker, 'Plutarch, Platonism and Christianity', ed. H. J. Blumenthal and R. A. Markus, *Neoplatonism and Early Christian Thought. Essays in honour of A. H. Armstrong* (London: Variorum, 1981), 50–63.

54 Edwards, 'Platonic schooling', 21.

(δημιουργός) of all, nor, having found, safe to speak of him to all', but he then asserts that what was neither easy nor safe 'our Christ did through his own power'; that dual theme of God's otherness, and of Christ as sole revealer, runs throughout both the *Apologies* and the *Dialogue* (2 *Apol.* 10.6–7). Justin was not alone in citing Plato's dictum that 'to discover the maker (ποιητής) and father of all is a *task*, and having found him to speak to all *impossible*' (Plato, *Tim.* 28C), which was extensively quoted and modified in the philosophical tradition, including by Christian writers (Athenagoras, *Leg.* 6.2). Likewise, Justin was not alone in replacing Plato's 'Creator' with the distinctive 'Demiurge' drawn from surrounding sections of the *Timaeus.*[55] These echoes of other second-century formulations suggest that Justin's less dogmatic version, repeated by Tertullian in his *Apology* (46.9), may have been drawn not directly from a reading of Plato but from a handbook of some kind, and, like them, that it reflects broader debates about the precise meaning and implications of Plato's teaching and language.[56] The term *demiurge* is not found in the Greek Bible, although it first enters Christian vocabulary shortly prior to the Apologists, in the predicate 'artisan and craftsman' in Hebrews 11.10, and then in *1 Clement* and in the Apologists;[57] 'maker' is also absent from the Septuagint but is taken up by Jewish and Christian authors in this period, and this is Justin's preferred term in the *Dialogue*, where he also on occasion combines it with 'father' (Justin, *Dial.* 56.1, 10; 58.1, etc.).

As shall be seen, such broader debates necessarily focused on the nature of the transcendent reality and the possibility of interaction or mediation between it and the world of human experience, often summarised as between 'Being' and 'Becoming'. Plato's introduction, in the *Timaeus*, of the source of creation as the 'Demiurge', was taken up by many of his successors, but his failure to develop the relationship between it and the transcendent 'Being' or 'Good' of his other writings left much room for expansion and debate among his later interpreters.[58] Justin, like other Apologists, following a line already taken by Philo and Plutarch, identifies

55 Plato, *Tim*, 28A, 29A; Alcinous, *Didaskalikos* 7.3; 13.1; Plutarch, *De Anim. procr.* 1017A ('father and demiurge').

56 Compare Alcinous, *Didaskalikos* 27.1, 'To find the most valued and greatest good is not easy, nor safe for those who find it to convey to others'. See also Minucius Felix, *Octavius* 26.12; see below, pp. 000–00 and Jaroslav Pelikan, *What Has Athens to Do with Jerusalem? Timaeus and Genesis in Counterpoint* (Ann Arbor, MI: University of Michigan Press, 1997), 30–2, 72–4.

57 *1 Clement* 20.11; 26.1, etc.; Aristides, *Apol.* 15.3; Athenagoras, *Leg.* 6.2; 10.4 etc.; *Diog.* 7.2; 8.7. See Charles H. Dodd, *The Bible and the Greeks* (London: Hodder & Stoughton, 1935), 136–44.

58 See below, pp. 333–4.

the God who is beyond change with the Creator, and he uses the phrase 'Father and Maker' as did they, to express this (Justin, *Apol.* 8.2; 63.11; cf. Athenagoras, *Leg.* 13.2). However, as already noted, when it comes to the scriptural theophanies he recognises the impossibility that the Creator should leave the heavenly sphere, and so he identifies the one who says 'I am the one who is' in Exodus 3 as the pre-existent Son (Justin, *Apol.* 63). Other Christian writers took alternative routes: Justin's disciple Tatian describes the Logos as the Creator or 'Demiurge' both of the angels and of humankind, thus establishing a tensive distance from God, which could accommodate free will and responsibility (Tatian, *Orat.* 7); the *Letter to Diognetus* introduces (but does not sustain) a more nuanced arrangement by having 'the God who is truly almighty and all-creating and unseen' send 'the very craftsman and creator (τεχνίτης καὶ δημιουργός) of all, by whom the heavens were created', like a king sending his son (*Diog.* 7.2).[59]

Plato's authority is again summoned when Justin insists that 'we have been taught that he created every principle as good from formless matter (ἀμόρφος ὕλη) for the sake of man', although his more immediate authority is Genesis 1.1–3, which he claims to be Plato's source (*Apol.* 10.2; 59). Yet the question of the character of that out of which the world was created was to some extent generated by Plato's model of the craftsman. Once again Justin is participating in contemporary debates both about the underlying matter and about the nature of the creative process.

Of the Platonists of the first and second centuries it is Numenius who has most invited comparison with Justin. Numenius also came from the east, from Apamaea in Syria, and he may have spent time in Rome. Numenius was willing to find sources of the original truth in the wisdom of other peoples, including the Jews – to him was attributed the saying 'What is Plato but Moses talking Attic? (Eusebius, *PE* XI. 10.14 = *Frag.* 8).[60] According to Origen, Numenius interpreted Moses and the prophets allegorically, 'not unpersuasively'; indeed, he must have had some acquaintance with noncanonical Jewish traditions since he proposed an interpretation of Jannes and Jambres, and even, according to Origen, of an anonymous story about Jesus (Origen, *C.Cels.* I. 15; IV. 51; Numenius, *Frag.* 1b, c, 10a). In particular,

59 However, in the next chapter the author identifies God as 'master and creator (demiurge) of all' who sent his child (*Diog.* 8.7).

60 Numenius is cited according to the edition by Édouard des Places, ed., *Numénius Fragments* (Paris: Les Belles Lettres, 1973). On what follows see Myles F. Burnyeat, 'Platonism in the Bible: Numenius of Apamea on *Exodus* and Eternity', ed. Rocardo Salles, *Metaphysics, Soul, and Ethics in Ancient Thought. Themes from the work of Richard Sorabji* (Oxford: Clarendon Press, 2005), 143–69.

it seems that Numenius did identify the Creator of the Jews with the Demiurge as conceived by himself, namely as subordinate to the supreme God. As shall be seen, it is less certain whether he labelled this supreme deity not just 'that which is' (neuter), but as 'the one who is' (masculine), an echo of Exodus 3.14 and of the identification already made by Philo (Numenius, *Frag.* 8, 13); although Eusebius believed this to be so, many subsequent scholars have doubted it.[61]

Undoubtedly there are synergies between the thinking of Numenius and that of Justin: Both men might be said to share a spiritual quest, in Numenius often attributed to the 'Pythagoreanism' for which he was best known in the ancient world – their emphasis on the goal of contemplation or knowledge of the ultimate Being as the source of salvation.[62] Indeed, it is notable that both Justin and Numenius drew on the pseudonymous Second Letter of Plato (Justin, *Apol.* 60.7; Numenius, *Frag.* 21).[63] Although Justin would have rejected outright Numenius's 'demotion' of the Creator/ Demiurge, he would have agreed with the need to find a principle of mediation that would make it possible to encounter and to have knowledge of God. Mark Edwards has found significant parallels between Numenius's Second Intellect and Justin's 'spermatic logos', which is the channel for knowledge of the divine and of participation in it, not least in the disputed *Fragment* 13, 'the one who is a seed of every soul sows'.[64] The problems of

[61] Eusebius, *PE* XI. 10.12; 18.13; on the negative side, see Robbert M. van den Berg, 'God the Creator, God the Creation: Numenius' Interpretation of Genesis 1:2 (Frg. 30)', ed. George H. van Kooten, *The Creation of Heaven and Earth: Re-interpretations of Genesis I in the Context of Judaism, Ancient Philosophy, Christianity, and Modern Physics* (TBN 8; Leiden: Brill, 2005), 109–123; Mark Edwards, 'Atticizing Moses? Numenius, the Fathers and the Jews', *VC* 44 (1990), 64–75. Burnyeat, 'Platonism in the Bible', 146–9, makes a strong case in support of Eusebius. See also John Granger Cook, *The Interpretation of the Old Testament in Greco-Roman Paganism* (STAC 23; Tübingen: Mohr, 2004), 36–8; see n. 64 below.

[62] On Numenius' 'Pythagoreanism' see Michael Trapp, 'Neopythagoreanism', ed. Robert W. Sharples and Richard Sorabji, *Greek and Roman Philosophy 100 BC–200 AD* (BICS Sup. 94; London: University of London, ICS, 2007) II, 347–63. For an argument for links with 'gnosticism' see A. H. Armstrong, 'Gnosis and Greek Philosophy', ed. Barbara Aland, *Gnosis. Festschrift für Hans Jonas* (Göttingen: Vandenhoeck & Ruprecht, 1978), 87–124, 107–9, and compare Edwards, 'Atticizing Moses', who suggests that Numenius had access to 'Jewish adherents of a fanciful Zoroaster'.

[63] See Christoph Markschies, 'Platons König oder Vater Jesu Christi? Drei Beispiele für die Rezeption eines griechischen Gottesepithons bei den Christen in den ersten Jahrhunderten und deren Vorgeschichte', ed. Martin Hengel and Anna Maria Schwemer, *Königstorrschaft Gottes und himmlischer Kult im Judentum, Urchristentum und in den hellenistischen Welt* (WUNT 55; Tübingen: Mohr Siebeck, 1991), 385–439, 415–24.

[64] Edwards, 'Platonic schooling', 25–27; the translation is that of Edwards, 'Atticizing Moses', 65–66, who does not see a reference to Exod. 3.14 as in the alternative translation 'the one who is sows a seed of every soul'. See below, p. 356 and n. 106.

mediation that are inherent within the Platonic revival could be both exacerbated by and addressed within the Christian tradition by an understanding of the role of Christ. None of this establishes any direct relationship with Justin or any other Christian 'philosopher', not least because the precise dates of Numenius' life remain unknown;[65] yet it remains indicative of the shared worlds in which these men moved.

Justin himself appealed to such shared worlds, claiming Socrates as a Christian, and recalling the teaching of Plato about the punishment of the unrighteous and that of Menander about proper worship (*Apol.* 5.4; 8.4; 20.5; 24.1). Yet for him, any truth they glimpsed was but a preliminary expression of that fully articulated in Christ. More confrontational is his denigration of the gods of the Greeks as manifestations of wicked demons, unequivocally sweeping away all the attempts of contemporary philosophy to integrate them into an understanding of the ultimate truth (*Apol.* 5; 9). It may be right to see in Justin, as in his peers, how '[p]hilosophical monotheism acquired a religious dimension',[66] but that religious dimension is shaped by and founded on his Christian convictions with their Jewish-scriptural heritage.

Justin's Jewish context

From this it becomes evident that a simple polarity that would oppose Justin as a philosopher to Justin as a Christian theologian is mistaken; this is no less true of the opposition sometimes posited between the 'Greco-Roman philosophical' and the 'Jewish' shaping of himself or of other Christian thinkers, as if the philosophical marked a decisive step away from the early Christian world view rooted in its scriptural heritage. Jewish interpreters were already deeply engaged with the challenges of a philosophical presentation of a scriptural understanding of God and of negotiating which set of principles should be the primary driver. There were well-established Greek-speaking Jewish communities in Rome in the second century, and there is good reason to suppose that they too would have been part of the intellectual and cultural mix in which Justin moved.

Yet Justin himself is well aware that the status he claims for 'the prophets', and the dominant place that they have in his argument and search for the

[65] See Frede, 'Numenius', 1038–9; Edwards, 'Platonic schooling', 30–1.

[66] Peter van Nuffeln, 'Pagan Monotheism as a Religious Phenomenon', ed. Stephen Mitchell and Peter van Nuffeln, *One God: Pagan Monotheism in the Roman Empire* (Cambridge: Cambridge University Press, 2010), 16–33, 29.

truth would be contentious if not unacceptable to many of his interlocutors. He is no less aware that in making that claim he has to differentiate his position from that of the Jews, and to resist any attempt to relegate it purely to amongst their internal squabbles. It is this, together with his conscious direct engagement with an antagonistic Jewish response, which makes his relationship with 'Judaism' both markedly nuanced and pivotal in second century Christian thought. On the one hand, in his engagement with the Scriptures he can be compared with several of his contemporaries, including the *Letter of Barnabas* and Theophilus of Antioch, each of whose Jewish roots emerge in very different forms; yet the exegetical moves he makes and the system he constructs would prove to be more enduring than theirs.[67] Firstly, Justin's own indebtedness to Scripture and its interpretation not only owes much to earlier Christian interpretation but apparently also betrays awareness of contemporary Jewish exegesis. Although he vigorously claims exclusive ownership of the Scriptures against Jewish interpreters, in practice, and in the eyes of observers, there were conceptual continuities and probable intellectual exchange between them. Behind his polemic lies a degree of continuing dependency by Christian teachers on local synagogue communities; Justin himself is well aware of differences in the text of the Scriptures and, even while accusing Jewish leaders of excising key passages that support the Christian position, he feels compelled to argue from the text they accept, and perhaps had recourse to the synagogues to access it (Justin, *Dial.* 72–3).[68] He claims knowledge of Jewish restrictive measures against the Christians both within their liturgy and through prohibition of meeting and discussion (*Dial.* 38.1; 137.2). While the historical value of these charges is debated, what is evident is that the status and reactions of the Jewish community still hold a significant place in his mental world view. This is also true in his *Apology* where he is careful to distance the Christians from the Jews responsible for the recent revolt, even while claiming the antiquity of their shared Scriptures (*Apol.* 31). It is evident that Justin's Jewish context consists not merely of ideological or conceptual continuities and discontinuities but also of more hidden social relationships.

The second aspect to note is the way that Justin deliberately exploits the recent Bar Kochba revolt and its impact on the Jewish people; he draws attention to the Roman victory as incontrovertible proof of God's punishment of the people, and of their misinterpretation of circumcision as a sign

[67] See further below, pp. 411–12.

[68] Judith M. Lieu, *Image and Reality: The Jews in the World of the Christians in the Second Century* (Edinburgh: T&T Clark, 1996), 124–40.

of God's favour (*Dial.* 16.2–3; 92.2–3; *Apol.* 47). This response to the events of his own time is particularly striking in view of the sparsity of evidence for other contemporary reactions. Other Christian writers put most emphasis on the destruction of Jerusalem in 70 CE as demonstrating God's judgement for Jewish unbelief, coming, as it did, within a generation of Jesus' death. Some Jewish writings, such as 4 Ezra and 2 *Baruch*, do address the challenges to their understanding of God after 70 CE, but it is more difficult to track responses to the subsequent defeats, especially from the Diaspora; if there were many hellenistic Jewish writings in this period they have not survived. Jewish communities were an established feature of many cities in the Graeco-Roman world, and they had long experience of negotiating their relationship with their wider context, both socially and ideologically. Although the revolt of 132–5 CE under Bar Kochba could hardly have failed to affect attitudes to the Jews, compounding the impact of those of 70 CE in Judaea and of 115–17 CE in Cyprus, Cyrenaica, and Egypt, traces of this are more difficult to detect. Some interpreters have argued that the 'disempowering' of the Jewish God in Gnostic sources may have been one such response, from outside and perhaps from within the Jewish community, but it is difficult to see how this could be proven, or whether it explains much else that is characteristic of these writings.[69]

MARCION IN JUSTIN'S CONTEXT

These various aspects of the social and intellectual context for Justin's life and teaching provide a persuasive framework for considering Marcion. Although Tertullian exploits the well-established topos of the inhospitality and barbarity of Pontus, Pliny's letters from the beginning of the second century portray a well-established Roman province, even if less so than Bithynia, the home of Dio Chrysostom among others.[70] The cities will have been thoroughly Greek in character, and it is likely that Marcion belonged to the descendants of the Greek settlers and would have had a not-dissimilar

[69] This was classically argued by R. M. Grant, *Gnosticism and Early Christianity* (2nd edn; New York and London: Columbia University Press, 1966), 27–38; see Williams, *Rethinking Gnosticism*, 223–8.

[70] That Pliny's Pontus is just as much a construct as is that of Ovid's exilic laments is argued by Greg Woolf, 'Pliny's Province', ed. T. Bekker-Nielsen, *Rome and the Black Sea Region: Domination, Romanisation, Resistance* (Black Sea Studies 8; Aarhus: Aarhus University Press, 2006), 93–108. Jesper Majborn Madsen, *Eager to be Roman: Greek Response to Roman Rule in Pontus and Bithynia* (London: Duckworth, 2009) is more positive about the pro-Roman propensities and opportunities.

experience to Justin. He would not have been the only member of a local elite who went to Rome to pursue a career, although the various terms used to describe his nautical role make any assessment of his social status difficult.[71] His commercial activities need not have detracted from his access to a philosophical education, regardless of any decision as to whether he was more or less erudite than Justin.[72]

Eusebius illustrates well the parity between the two men in his account of their successors (*HE* V. 13). Rhodon, also from the provinces, from Asia, studied at Rome under Tatian, himself a disciple there of Justin. Among his various books Rhodon addressed 'the heresy of Marcion', a label perhaps coined by Eusebius rather than by Rhodon himself, describing its division into different opinions. Their disagreements lay in the number and nature of ultimate principles: Apelles, who Rhodon admitted to be respected for his manner of life as well as for his age, held there to be one principle (ἀρχή) while attributing prophecy to 'an opposing spirit'; others held there to be two, a position he also attributed to Marcion, while yet others supposed there to be three 'natures' (φύσις). Rhodon described debates with Apelles, perhaps in Rome, where the latter purportedly failed to demonstrate that he did in fact maintain one principle 'in the same way as our doctrine'. Yet, according to Eusebius, Rhodon's accusation was that Marcion's followers failed to examine arguments properly or to investigate the 'division (διαίρεσις) of things', a technical term for the Platonic mode of analysis and retrogression to first principles; he mocks Apelles for describing his convictions as 'inclination' rather than as 'knowledge', and so for being unable to establish what he taught.[73] Rhodon apparently also promised to provide his own solutions (ἐπίλυσις) to Tatian's 'Problems', which had set out 'what was unclear and hidden in the divine Scriptures'. Eusebius intends to present Rhodon as a champion against heresy, and as

[71] See Lampe, *From Paul to Valentinus*, 241–4, who attempts to understand Marcion within the context of his occupation. A more nuanced discussion is given by Gerhard May, 'Der "Schiffsreeder" Markion', ed. Greschat and Meiser, *Gerhard May: Markion*, 51–62 (= ed. Elizabeth A. Livingstone, *Papers presented to the Tenth International Conference on Patristic Studies held in Oxford, 1987: Studia Patristica* 21 [Leuven: Peeters, 1989] 142–53). On shipping and ship owning see Peter Temins, 'A Market Economy in the Early Roman Empire', *JRS* 91 (2001), 169–81.

[72] Markschies, *Kaiserzeitliche christliche Theologie*, 253, labels Marcion an intellectual dilettante, lacking the critical acumen of Alexandrian scholarship, but this is perhaps unfair for his time and place.

[73] See Katharina Greschat, '"Woher hast du den Beweis für deine Lehre?" Der altkirchliche Lehrer Rhodon und seine Auseinandersetzung mit den römischen Marcioniten', ed. M. F. Wiles, E. J. Yarnold, with the assistance of P. M. Parvis, *Studia Patristica* 34 (Leuven: Peeters, 2001), 82–7.

testifying to the inevitable collapse of a heretical position into irreconcilable internal conflict; it seems more likely, however, that he is a witness to, and a participant in, the sort of debates about philosophical principles and argument that were a feature of the age and particularly of intellectual life in Rome. Such disagreements were a normal characteristic of philosophical schools, where pupils refined the positions of their teachers or claimed to represent more accurately the original teaching of their founder. Both Rhodon and Apelles were, it would seem, modifying the positions of their teachers, proffering new models that might address objections and that might win wider support. On the other hand, when Celsus moves seamlessly from objections against a Marcionite position that sounds similar to those already levelled by Marcion's opponents to other objections that have a decidedly Marcionite tone, he may well have learned both from debates held between the two parties before an easily confused public (Origen, *C.Cels.* VI. 53).

Marcion's own literary output also conforms closely to the pattern of contemporary scholarly analysis. What his opponents denounce as his corruption of Luke and the Pauline letters matches the practice of textual emendation in the 'recovery' of an original text and meaning that was a regular aspect of contemporary scholarly activity. It is unclear from Tertullian's and Epiphanius' accounts whether the copies of Marcion's 'Gospel' and 'Apostolikon' that they knew included both text and some commentary or marginal notes. Parallels from this period would suggest the latter would be relatively brief – more extended scholia were a Byzantine development. In some instances this might be all that was needed, for example the comments 'not in truth … not in man' added to Philippians 2.6–7, or a gloss 'from heaven' qualifying the 'he descended' of Luke 4.16, but such limited expansions would hardly be adequate to explain the substructures of his position.[74] As has been seen, his 'Antitheses' appear to have belonged to the exposure and analysis of problems within an authoritative text: Marcion was by no means the first to draw attention to the problems in Scripture, although he may have done so more systematically than his predecessors.[75] However, many of the passages associated with his objections were, as shall be seen, already familiar topics of debate and explanation.

Evidently the way in which Marcion presented his position, and most probably the defining agenda for him, turned decisively on the reading of

[74] See pp. 214, 263. [75] So Bardy, 'Littérature patristique' (*Rev.Bib.* 41), 217–19.

Scripture; there is far less to determine how systematically he set out the philosophical principles that governed him, or that exercised his followers. In addition, there is little evidence that he was concerned to find a place for traditional Greek religion within his understanding of the ultimate truth. Even so, the debates and conceptual concerns that provide a framework for Justin's thought do the same for Marcion's.[76] Marcion's unknown God is thoroughly transcendent, and is also absolutely Good. Tertullian claims that Marcionites distinguish between the visible and invisible world, but his assumption that they believe that their higher God must have created his own sphere may be drawing conclusions they would not have done (Tertullian, *AM* I.15; 16.1). Although Tertullian is able to mock the consequences of a literal interpretation of the higher habitat of the supreme deity, both Justin and Alcinous, as has been seen, readily use such language. Nor would the idea that this higher God should be the goal of the human quest and the source of security be seen as contradictory to this radical otherness: Numenius can still say that 'in place of the movement inherent in the second God, the stability inherent in the first is an internal movement, from which comes both the order of the world and its eternal resting, and from which security (σωτηρία) extends to the whole' (Numenius, *Frag.* 15). Although the term 'Demiurge' is important for Justin himself, it is likely that when he describes Marcion as positing a God other than the 'Demiurge (of all)', he is also echoing Marcion's own language (Justin, *Apol.* 26.5; 58.1; cf. Eusebius, *HE* IV.18.9). Certainly the term was to become pre-eminently associated with the gnostic subsidiary creator power – Irenaeus speaks of 'the one whom you call the Demiurge' (Irenaeus, *AH* II. 28.4) – but in the broader second-century context it could be neutral if not actively good. Marcion explicitly denigrated 'becoming', in later sources represented by Plato's term '*genesis* (γένεσις)', and he evidently associated this with the Creator God. However, although Marcion might have agreed with Numenius in distinguishing between the supreme power, who can be called Father, and the Demiurge, he differed fundamentally from him by denying any relationship between them. Also distinctive is the absence from contemporary discussion of any real equivalent to Marcion's radical pessimism about the world; yet the notion of 'disorder' was to be found more widely, as was a recognition that however much creation was understood as the imposition of order, this is never entirely successful. This did leave open the possibility

[76] See May, 'Marcion in Contemporary Views', 26–8, for an attempt to set Marcion in a Platonic context, with brief reference also to Numenius.

of viewing matter as autonomous or of allowing for an evil principle. Marcion's opponents disagree as to the precise role 'matter' played within his system, and as to how far it could also be described as autonomous; Tertullian's more limited account that for Marcion matter was pre-existent but also was fundamentally evil would not be totally out of place, and would not justify the conclusion that matter thereby constituted a fourth deity (Tertullian, *AM* I. 14.4–5). If others elaborated further, it would not be surprising that contemporary debates should form the framework for either his opponents or his followers to interpret his thought: Neither Hippolytus nor Clement of Alexandria were totally misguided, while the reinterpretations by Apelles and others reflect precisely the issues most at issue in the period.

Most difficult to determine is the extent of any Jewish context for Marcion's thought, and an active Jewish influence or concern is difficult to demonstrate.[77] Certainly there were Jewish communities on the Black Sea coast; tradition associated Aquila, who translated the Scriptures into Greek in the second century, with Sinope, later also identified as Marcion's birthplace. In Rome, too, Marcion would have been as likely to be aware of the Jewish communities as was Justin. However, when Tertullian in particular portrays Marcion as an ally of the Jews, this association serves Tertullian's own polemical agenda: The Jew with whom Marcion allies himself is a rhetorical one. On the other hand, as will be seen, the difficulties that Marcion encountered in reading the Scriptures were also acknowledged by Jewish authors, although it is unlikely that he owed his questions directly to them. Some have argued that Marcion represents an extreme example of the early Christian distancing of itself from Judaism after the Bar Kochba revolt.[78] More broadly, it has been suggested that the harsh demotion of the 'Jewish God', including his characterisation as 'war-like', might be a reaction to the perceived defeat of that God in the three great revolts.[79] Yet such theories belong to the wider debate regarding the origins, perhaps within 'Judaism', of other demiurgical (or 'gnostic') movements that share that motif, and only then to Marcion's relation with such, a subject for separate discussion.[80]

[77] Against Harnack, *Marcion*, 21–2; *Neue Studien*, 15–16. Hoffmann, *Marcion*, goes further in trying to argue not only for the importance of the Jewish context (pp. 4–8, 26–8) but also for the 'pro-Jewish orientation of Marcion's theology (p. 227).

[78] Robert M. Grant, *Heresy and Criticism: The Search for Authenticity in Early Christian Literature* (Louisville, KY: Westminster/John Knox Press, 1993), 33–47, and above n. 69.

[79] See Lampe, *From Paul to Valentinus*, 248–9.

[80] See below, pp. 349, 365–6.

A context that brings Marcion not just over against Justin but also alongside him, as the founder of a school, if not the first of such,[81] may seem very different from the conventional, still 'heresiological', view of Marcion as more of an ecclesial figure, being ejected from, or breaking decisively from, 'the Roman church' and forming an independent church with its own structures and hierarchy. The framework presented here would still allow for heated polemic or denunciation from other teachers, although what ecclesial expression this might have is more difficult to determine. In what follows the context that has emerged here will provide an explanatory map for exploring the consistent and inconsistent recurring themes in the polemicists' constructions of Marcion.

81 Peter Gemeinhardt, *Das lateinische Christentum und die antike pagane Bildung* (STAC 41; Tübingen: Mohr Siebeck, 2007), 99, describes him as 'das erste römische Schulhaupt', an epithet that Harnack had expressly denied (*Marcion*, 160).

12

The principles of Marcion's thought and their context I: God

Like Justin Martyr, Marcion belongs within the intersection of philosophical ideas and questions with the attitudes to Scripture that were circulating in the second century. This is why it would be wrong to make him the sole catalyst or culprit wherever echoes are found of ideas conventionally associated with him. Rather, he represents one of the more visible points where, in the questions being asked and answered, and in the continuing debate taking place in different places, times, and ways, positions were explored, rejected, or reinforced. Yet the immediacy and the persistence of the polemics targeted against Marcion mean that he cannot simply be reduced to a cipher of the diversity of the second century. Undoubtedly he, or his followers claiming to represent his intentions, held a sufficiently coherent set of positions on a number of key issues to constitute a 'school', which continued over a considerable span of time and place.

Even where Marcion's opponents display some broad agreement regarding those positions or issues, they differ as to what the starting point or the inspiration for them was, and it is no wonder that subsequent scholarship has repeated those different conclusions. In the most general of terms, was Marcion driven primarily by 'philosophical questions' – God, the problem of evil, the nature of the human being?[1] Or was he a 'biblicist', whether this be taken as a critical reader of texts, namely as a 'philologian',[2] or as the avid, whether or not misguided, disciple of Paul.[3] Other approaches, for example, those that relegate him to a subcategory of 'Gnosticism', only postpone the question while failing to give sufficient credit to the distinctive features of his system. The determination to identify a single starting point may be just as mistaken, or at least as incapable of

1 So firmly Meijering, *Gotteslehre*, 166–8.

2 Markschies, *Kaiserzeitliche christliche Theologie*, 254–61.

3 Harnack, *Marcion*, 30–5.

satisfaction. Philosophical presuppositions and the reading of texts work in dialogue with each other; whatever might be said about Marcion himself, among those who responded to him and so who arguably were responsible for giving his views coherence and function, some may have been primarily enquirers after ideas, others were the readers of texts.[4]

In what follows, the primary persistent themes in Marcion's thought, as they have emerged from previous chapters, will provide a framework for exploring how they belong within contemporary debates, and within the intersection between philosophical positions and the reading of texts, without predetermining the extent to which he was a, or the, catalyst in these activities. Without prejudging whether this is the point at which he himself started, 'God' may seem a natural place to start, not least because of the way that opponents speak of 'the God of Marcion'.[5]

ANOTHER GOD

According to Justin Martyr, Marcion was responsible, firstly, for proclaiming 'another' God, 'greater' than the maker of all, and, secondly, for slandering ('blaspheming') and denying the Creator (or for persuading others to do so) (*Apol.* 26; 58). This remains the fundamental theme in later writers, and it appears to have priority over the further equation of the Creator with 'the God proclaimed by the law and the prophets'. However, once introduced by Irenaeus, that further equation then continues at the heart of all subsequent polemic, perhaps in part because of the extent to which it resonated with other early Christian debates (*AH* I. 27.2).[6] Other epithets or characterisations become attached to this 'greater' God; most significantly, Irenaeus already emphasises that this is 'the *good* God of Marcion' (*AH* II. 1.2), an epithet not only repeated by Clement of Alexandria, Tertullian, Ps.Hippolytus, *Refutation*, Ephraem, Epiphanius, and others, but one that is essential to the character of the arguments portrayed on both sides.[7] It is striking that it is this 'other God', soon dubbed 'Marcion's

[4] Compare Mark Edwards, 'Pauline Platonism: The Myth of Valentinus', ed. M. F. Wiles and E. J. Yarnold, with the assistance of P. M. Parsons, *Studia Patristica* 35 (Louvain: Peeters, 2001), 205–21, on the frameworks within which Valentinian 'myth' might be read.

[5] So already Irenaeus, *AH* II. 3.1. Note the use of the term still in a Manichaean Hymn from Turfan (M 28), 'Like what they did [to] that God of Marcion ...' (see above, p. 157 and de Blois, 'Review of *Iranian Turfan Texts*').

[6] On Justin's account, and the phrase 'the maker of all and the God of Abraham, Isaac and Jacob' (*Dial.* 35), see above, p. 21.

[7] See above, pp. 66, 90, 162 etc.

God', who is presented as appearing from nowhere, with no prior credentials, and who is the brunt of the polemicists' ire. Rather than accepting the status of this God and then defending his (*sic*) involvement in creation and intervention in history, they defend the Creator and his goodness together with his lack of any inferiority to some other being.

What makes this tactic surprising is that the transcendence of the supreme God was a common theme among thinkers of the second century, whatever their allegiance. The Apologists in particular appeal to this conviction in order to both show the consistent superiority of the Christian conception of God over the conception ascribed to 'the Greeks', which is usually characterised by the myths of the gods and by the way they were represented, and present their own understanding of God in terms that met the intellectual and philosophical expectations of the day: The *Preaching of Peter* is characteristic when it starts by defining the one God, 'unseen … uncontainable … ungraspable …', and continues, 'worship this God, not in the manner of the Greeks … nor of the Jews' (Clement of Alexandria, *Strom.* VI. 5.39–41).[8] In a similar vein, Aristides opens his *Apology* with a catalogue of what cannot be predicated of God: God is by definition uncreated, without beginning or end, without name, without form, without gender, and without emotion; in terms of his own nature God is unknowable (Aristides, *Apol.* 1). As Aristides proceeds to divide the human 'races' according to their grasp of the truth, he appeals to the principles of this essentially 'negative theology', although the consequences take him far beyond them. Certainly, this conception provoked the challenge of whether to, and how to, relate the biblical traditions about God, as well as the specifically Christian ones, to the Greek philosophical 'negative theology'.[9] Consequently, the Apologists have provoked different assessments of where their primary loyalty lay, whether in philosophy or with the biblical tradition. In practice, however, it is wrong simply to contrast the 'impersonal God' of contemporary Platonism with the 'personal' God of the Christian tradition.[10] All were part of an ongoing debate: On the one hand, there is a move in those Platonic sources for more personal language to be used, perhaps under the influence of ideas stemming from the Pythagorean

[8] Given the pervasiveness of this topos, there are no grounds for limiting it to a reaction against Marcion.

[9] See, for example, Darryl W. Palmer, 'Atheism, Apologetic and Negative Theology in the Greek Apologists of the Second Century', *VC* 37 (1983), 234–59.

[10] See Dahl, 'Justin und die griechische Philosophie', 384; Jan Hendrick Waszink, 'Bemerkungen zum Einfluß des Platonismus im frühen Christentum', ed. Zintzen, *Der Mittelplatonismus*, 413–48 (= *VC* 19 (1965), 129–62), 426.

tradition; on the other hand, when Christian writers do use more personal language, they do so with caution, carefully addressing the question of the status of such language.[11] So, even Justin is careful to explain that terms such as 'father' and 'lord' are not *names* of God, and that even 'Christ' has an element only of the 'unknown' to it. (2 *Apol.* 6.3).

Hence, the deep sense of the transcendence of the supreme being necessarily led to the question of whether, or how, knowledge of this God was possible. Justin Martyr has already illustrated how Plato's statement of the difficulty of discovering or speaking of 'the Maker and Father of everything' was taken up and paraphrased in the second century, with both Philo and Christian sources also turning it to their advantage (Plato, *Tim.* 28C; Plutarch, *Plat.Quaest.* 1000E; Philo, *De Opif.* 5 [21]; Justin, 2 *Apol.* 10.6; Athenagoras, *Leg.* 6.2; 27.2).[12] Numenius, who, as shall be seen, distinguished between the First Intellect and the Demiurge, claimed that Plato understood that the latter alone was known among humankind, while the former 'who is called "Self-existent" is totally not-known (ἀγνοούμενον)' (*Frag.* 17).

In such philosophical debate the issue was whether the transcendent *could* be known, whereas the specific epithet 'unknown' (ἄγνωστος) puts the emphasis on the supposedly evidential, and permits Tertullian's mockery of a deity who suddenly emerges, 'not from the beginning or through creation but through himself alone', as it were without credentials (*AM* I. 19.1; cf. 8.1; 10.4, *ignotus*).[13] On the other hand, 'unknown' is also routinely ascribed by the heresiologists to the deity espoused by a number of their opponents, including by Cerdo, Marcion's supposed teacher (Irenaeus, *AH* I. 27.1; IV. 6.4 [*incognitum*]; Ps.Hippolytus, *Ref.* VII. 37.1; cf. Ps.Ignatius, *Trall.* 6; *Smyrn.* 6).

However, there were other threads here, too. Irenaeus explains at length Jesus' words in Luke 10.22/Matthew 11.27 ('no-one knows [who] the son … the father [is]'), both so as to refute those, including Marcion, who took

[11] See Whittaker, 'Plutarch, Platonism and Christianity'.

[12] See above p. 312; see also the Armenian version of Aristides, *Apol.* in James Rendel Harris, ed. and transl. *The Apology of Aristides on Behalf of the Christians from a Syriac Ms. Preserved on Mount Sinai* with an appendix containing the main portion of the original Greek text by J. Armitage Robinson (Texts and Studies 1; Cambridge: Cambridge University Press, 1891), 26. At *De Opif.* 5 [21] Philo reverses Plato's dictum as 'Father and Maker of all', and this order becomes routine in Christian authors. Tertullian, *Apol.* 46.9, however, quotes the passage to contrast to what the 'Christian labourer' is able to do.

[13] Acts 17.23 (and perhaps also Justin, 2 *Apol.* 10.6) may be an attempt to elide two different concepts of a God who is not known; see Braun, *Contre Marcion*, I, 291–2. Similarly, Lucanus is said to have ascribed the Jerusalem Temple to 'a indistinct God' (see Numenius, *Frag.* 56).

them as evidence that God was unknown until the coming of Jesus, but at the same time so as to deny the claim ascribed to the Jews that they did indeed know God (Irenaeus, *AH* IV. 4–7).[14] Irenaeus achieves the first aim by appealing to the revelatory work of the 'Word' both in creation and through the law and the prophets, but in order to prove the second he emphasises the correlation of 'Father' with 'Son', even though he does not restrict 'the Son' to the period of the incarnation; God may necessarily be 'invisible and inexplicable to all that is made by him, but he is in no way unknown' (*AH* IV. 20.5). It is striking that when he comes to attack Marcion's 'new' God Tertullian appeals to God as known not only through revelation to Abraham and Moses, but even prior to that through the created order as well as in the instinctive apprehension of the soul, something demonstrated by the casual invocations made by ordinary people, even in Pontus (*AM* I. 8–10). According to Marcion, it was, rather, the Creator God of the law who was known, so Tertullian has to supplement his argument with the presupposition that what is known must have priority over the unknown. The Marcionites who say, as represented by Tertullian, 'Rather, our God was revealed not from the beginning and not though creation, but through himself in Christ Jesus', were, therefore, rejecting precisely this sort of solution (I. 19.1). It is possible that the primary factor was this temporal logic of revelation rather than the principled dualism ascribed to the Marcionites by Megethios in the *Dialogue of Adamantius*, 'The Creator was known to Adam and those at that time, as is evident in the Scriptures; the Father of Christ is unknown, as Christ himself said about him (Matt. 11.27; *Adam.* 42.29–44.1 [1.23]).[15]

An alternative widespread variation in the theme of 'the unknown' is that it was the Demiurge who was ignorant of the higher God.[16] Both Irenaeus and Tertullian ascribe such a view to Marcion;[17] yet the appeal to the supposedly self-deceiving and hubristic claim 'I am God and there is no other' (Isa. 45.5–6), which is widespread in the polemic of the heresiologists as well as in a range of so-called gnostic texts, is less well attested for Marcion.[18] The self-claimed exclusiveness of the God of the Jews was

[14] See above, p. 224, and Lieu, 'Marcion and the Synoptic Problem', 735–9.

[15] ἄγνωστος comes particularly frequently in the *Dialogue*; see Tsutsui, *Auseinandersetzung*, 188.

[16] See above, p. 38 for Irenaeus.

[17] On Irenaeus see above p. 39; Tertullian, *AM* I. 11.9; II. 28.1.

[18] For example, Irenaeus, *AH* I. 5.4; 30.5, where it is the Sethians who ascribe the claim to the Demiurge; *Apoc. John* [NH II. 1] 11.19–22; *Second Apocalypse of James* [NH V. 5] 55.27–57.1. Ephraem, *PR* 2. 95,40–96,12 [xliv] cites the passage but without implying that his

well-known: For Tacitus it is bound up with their proverbial 'hostile hatred' (Tacitus, *Hist.* V. 5), while, perhaps more neutrally, Numenius is said to have described their God as 'considering no-one worthy to share in his honour' (Numenius, *Frag.* 56). However, the particular elision between scriptural proof-texting and the more general theme of the 'unknown' transcendent deity is probably a secondary development. It readily lay itself open to further 'mythological' development, for example in 'gnostic'-style accounts of the descent of the redeemer escaping the notice of the Demiurge or his emissaries (*Asc.Isa.* 11.22–33; cf. 1 Cor. 2.8).

Likewise, the identification of God as 'good', or with 'the Good' (τὸ ἀγαθόν, cf. *bonus*), which in relation to Plato's thought has prompted considerable interpretive debate, becomes somewhat more axiomatic in the second century. Numenius, one of whose treatises was entitled 'Concerning the Good', argues that while the Demiurge is 'good' (ἀγαθός), the first God or Intellect alone can be 'the good' or 'good in himself' (τὸ ἀγαθόν, αὐτάγαθον) (*Frag.* 16; cf. 20).[19] Similarly, Athenagoras describes 'the good' as 'an attribute and co-existent with God as colour is with corporeal substance'; indeed it is this that ultimately distinguishes God from matter (*Leg.* 24.2). Such philosophical notions did not determine what the effect or the nature of 'the good' might be; Marcion, according to his opponents, glossed the epithet with such terms as 'mild', 'peaceful', 'compassionate', identifying its expression in God's salvific action on behalf of what was not his own, and in his refusal to judge.[20] These characteristics do not necessarily emerge from the philosophical debate but rather might have been supplied by antithesis, in contrast to the Creator God's retributive nature, as Tertullian suggests (*AM* IV. 15.5; 16.10 and see below), or they may have been drawn from a reading of the Pauline tradition. However, 'the good' does not of itself infer 'the evil' as its opposite; the polemical sources are much more consistent in characterising Marcion's opposing principle as 'the just' (δίκαιος, *iudicialis*), while, as shall be seen, the role of evil is more ambiguous.

It is less clear whether 'Marcion's' description of the supreme God as 'the stranger' belongs to this same semantic and philosophical field.

Marcionite opponents did so. See Hans-Martin Schenke, *Der Gott 'Mensch' in der Gnosis: Ein religionsgeschichtlicher Beitrag zur Diskussion über die paulinischer Anschauung von der Kirche als Leib Christi* (Göttingen: Vandenhoek & Ruprecht, 1962), 87–93, who, however, interprets this as the development of a myth out of allegorical exegesis of a single verse.

19 See Mark J. Edwards, 'Middle Platonism on the Beautiful and the Good', *Mnemosyne* 44 (1991), 161–7. Again, Philo had already anticipated this theme: see Peter Frick, *Divine Providence in Philo of Alexandria* (TSAJ 77; Tübingen: Mohr Siebeck, 1999), 61–8.

20 Tertullian, *AM* I. 17.1; 22–6; Ephraem, *PR* 2. 58,34–7; 137,1–44.

In Ephraem's writing the epithet (*nwkry'*) has acquired the same quasi-titular force as does the opposing 'the Creator': He describes 'the Stranger' as actively leaving his own realm and descending, but he also speaks of Jesus as the son of the Stranger (*CH* 34–36 etc.; *PR* 1. 44,20–49,3).[21] Behind this, however, the earliest contextualization of the epithet, repeated since Irenaeus, appears to be that the world is 'alien' to this God, who nonetheless intervenes within it – a cause for mockery by opponents, but for the Marcionite position evidence of gratuitous generosity, perhaps with an appeal to Luke 4.27 (Irenaeus, *AH* IV. 33.2; Tertullian, *AM* I. 17.1; 23.2; IV. 9.6). Thus, Marcion's God is strange just as he is unknown, because he had no natural affinity with humankind: Tertullian claims that Marcion's followers justified the fact that their God was 'unknown' to previous generations precisely because these were 'alien' (*extraneus*) to him (*AM* I. 11.1). This was a sufficiently familiar topos apparently to have been repeated by Celsus (Origen, *C.Cels.* VI. 52–3). Yet despite Origen's disavowal, the idea has deep roots, with a striking parallel offered by Ignatius: Emphasising the total incommensurability of the divine epiphany in Christ, like a star in the heavens which exceeds them immeasurably and is incomprehensible to them, 'his newness provoked strangeness ... there was perplexity about the origins of this newness, so dissimilar to them' (Ignatius, *Eph.* 19.1–3).

There are also scriptural sources for the idea: From the regularity with which it is cited, Ephesians 2.11–13, 'you were alienated from (ἀπαλλοτριόω) ... strangers to (ξένος)', appears to have played a particularly important role, although it is impossible to determine whether an appeal to the passage goes back to Marcion himself.[22] Tertullian may suggest a different trajectory: He implies that Marcion took the contrast in Luke 16.12 between 'faithfulness to what is another's' and 'to what is mine [*sic*]' as evidence that the Creator was 'other' or 'alien' (*alterius*) to Christ and his disciples, a reading which would have been reinforced by the pivotal reference to the impossibility of serving two masters that follows.[23]

21 Above, pp. 172–3.

22 Tertullian, *AM* V. 17.12–14 ('alienati ... peregrini [Vg. 'hospites']'); Epiphanius, *Pan.* 42.12.3, SR36; *Adam.* 96.27 (2.18).

23 Tertullian, *AM* IV. 33.4, which implies that Marcion read 'what is mine' (so also a few witnesses: 157 e i l); it is unclear whether or not Marcion identified 'unrighteous mammon' with the 'another' (ἀλλότριος) in this passage. Romans 14.4 might also be interpreted in similar vein, but there is no evidence of how Marcion took this verse. Similarly, the Creator God's assertion of sole power is accompanied by a rejection of any 'strange God' in Deut. 32.12, Isa. 43.12, and Ps. 81.9 (LXX 80.10), but again the sources give no support to reading these in Marcionite fashion.

On the other hand, there was a strong tradition, as exemplified in different ways by 1 Peter 1.17; 2.11, and Hebrews 11.13 (ξένος), of describing Christians as not 'at home' in society or in the world: 'they live in their own native countries, but as resident aliens; they share everything as citizens and endure everything as foreigners. Every foreign place is their native country, and every native country foreign' (*Epistle to Diognetus* 5.5). In these texts the balance between social experience and 'spiritual' allegiance within an eschatological tradition is a fine one. Perhaps this is why the metaphor could easily be taken up in new directions: 'He ransomed those who were strangers and made them his own' (*Gospel of Philip* [*NH* II.3] 53.3–4). Thus, it becomes difficult to determine whether Marcion's 'stranger' God is primarily a projection of his devotees' self-understanding within this tradition of alienation, or whether that self-understanding is an embodiment of their identification with an 'unknown' God.[24] On the other hand, from a polemical perspective the term had a long history in polemic against 'new religions', and so was readily recyclable in a new context.

The *Dialogue of Adamantius* exploits the subversive potential of the term 'foreign' (ξένος) when it attacks 'the foreign and unknown God proclaimed according to them'; here it is striking that 'foreign', although used repeatedly by the 'orthodox' participants in the *Dialogue*, is never found on the mouth of the Marcionite protagonists themselves (*Adam*. 98.2 [2.18]; 104.6 [2.19]).[25] Here, however, the primary theological focus appears to be whether or not Christ, or the God he proclaimed, is *alien* to the Creator or to the dispensation of the law and prophets.

In all, Marcion does seem to represent a distinctive, albeit recognisable, position amongst contemporary debates. He would agree with, but would be even more insistent on, the impossibility of any natural knowledge of the transcendent God, whom he identified as absolutely Good. It is, therefore, not necessary to trace his thought to the Epicurean denial that the gods had any interest in human affairs;[26] indeed Tertullian grudgingly admits that Marcion did not deny to his God all emotions (*AM* I. 25.3). Yet, despite the accusations that he promoted 'the God of the philosophers', and contrary to those who have traced his understanding of God exclusively to any

24 See Clement of Alexandria, above, p. 132.

25 *Adam*. 84.10, 20; 86.7, 8; 88.18–27; 90.19, 24, 29; 92.5–10, 21, 23; 94.2; [96.27]; 98. 1, 2, 5, 7; 104.6; 178.16; 240. 7 (2.13–19; 5.3, 28).

26 As argued by John G. Gager, 'Marcion and Philosophy', *VC* 26 (1972), 53–9; Antonio Orbe, 'Marcionitica', *Augustinianum* 31 (1991), 195–244, 205. Woltmann, 'Der Geschichtliche Hintergrund', 15–42, argues that Marcion may share a common route with the Epicureans, but he takes it to a very different goal.

particular philosophical school, there is little evidence that Marcion ever used the Platonic language of 'Intellect' or any other similar abstraction. Even if the term 'Father' resonates with Plato, for him, as for other Jewish and Christian apologists, it has been shaped within the biblical, or specifically the Jesus/Pauline, tradition.

God and space

Within the framework of the priority of the transcendent, Irenaeus' statement that Marcion's two Gods were 'separated by an infinite distance' from each other is entirely natural (*AH* IV. 33.2).[27] In Tertullian this takes a somewhat cruder form: Marcion's God must have 'his own creation, his own world, his own heaven'; the readiness with which Tertullian can subject such conceptions to his withering irony may render them suspect (*AM* I. 15). However, Epiphanius also attributes to Marcion's superior God his own circumscribed space as does Ephraem; here too the imagery is essential to the mocking pictures of the Father or his Son having to leave their own space and traverse that below, inhabited by the Demiurge.[28] Yet behind such language arguably lies a recurring problem in Greek thought, and one that was an evident preoccupation in the second century, namely whether for the divine to exist and to be intelligible it must also be bounded in some sense, not infinite.[29] Such ontological problems were readily articulated in terms of space: Philo identifies as one of the most difficult questions of philosophy, 'where the living God is, and whether he is in any place at all'; in the course of an exegesis of Jacob's experience at Bethel, he explains Jacob's sense of dread as because he knew that God 'surrounds everything, but in truth and reason is not surrounded by anything' (Philo, *De Somn.* 31–2 [182–7]; cf. *De Confus.* 27 [134–41]). Elsewhere Philo speaks of 'the invisible, shapeless, incorporeal world' where God is, and he draws a distinction between the intelligible world and the sense-perceptible world, a distinction that he also finds within Scripture, in the two creation narratives (*De Opif.* 44 [129–30]). Similarly, faced with the biblical theophanies,

27 It is unclear whether Justin's account should be read as already describing his 'greater' God as having 'made greater things', presumably his own universe as in Tertullian; see above, p. 15, and, on Irenaeus, p. 37.

28 Epiphanius, *Pan.* 42.7.3–6; Ephraem, *CH* 35. 4; *PR* 1. 46,8–50,41; 2. 94,23–40; see above, pp. 112, 161.

29 On this and what follows, see William R. Schoedel, 'Enclosing, Not Enclosed: The Early Christian Doctrine of God', ed. William R. Schoedel and Robert L. Wilken, *Early Christian Literature and the Classical Intellectual Tradition* (ThHist. 53; Paris: Beauchesne, 1979), 75–86.

Aristobulus had appealed to the huge numbers purportedly present at Sinai to assert that God's descent there was not limited to a single place (Eusebius, *PE* VIII. 10.12–15; cf. Exod. 12.37).

Christian Apologists addressed the same problem; Athenagoras engages in a lengthy argument as to why there can be no other deity than the God whom he identifies as the Creator. Since it is fundamental that 'the one who made the world is above all that came into being and surrounds that which he made and ordered', there is no place for any other God to occupy; that any other deity must be above or outside the sphere of the Creator renders such a deity unintelligible and so nonexistent (Athenagoras, *Leg.* 8). Like their Jewish forbears, these Apologists had to address not only the conceptual problem but also the scriptural accounts that used the language of spatial location of God; Theophilus of Antioch sees a contrast between the 'heaven' of Genesis 1.1 and that of 1.8 (*Ad Autol.* II. 13). Similarly, they have to explain the biblical accounts of theophanies. Justin, as has been seen, makes Christ the subject of the these: 'anyone, even someone with little understanding, will be ready to say the Maker of all and Father did not leave the all above the heaven and appear in a small segment of the earth'; Theophilus has a similar explanation of the one who walked in Paradise and spoke with Adam (Justin, *Dial.* 60.2; cf. 127.3; Theophilus, *Ad Autol.* II. 22). Tertullian draws on these philosophical debates in his polemic against Marcion, reworking precisely the sort of spatial arguments that Athenagoras had used against the existence of other gods. That such a God could have his own 'world' and place to belong receives short shrift, but Tertullian can make this argument only because he insists on reading such language literally and on ignoring the sort of distinctions made by earlier apologists (*AM* I. 16). Similarly, although Tertullian can explain the anthropomorphic language of the scriptural theophanic accounts to his own satisfaction, he still mocks Marcion for describing the distant Father as 'descending'.

God, Creator, and creation

Justin's accusation that Marcion denies 'the Maker of all' probably echoes, albeit indirectly, Plato's formula in the *Timaeus*, with which, as has been seen, he was familiar, 'Maker/Creator and Father of all'.[30] Its ubiquity as a routine epithet for God in the second century means that when found in Christian sources it need not carry any polemical overtones. Yet such

[30] See p. 312 above.

language hides a fundamental philosophical dilemma, namely that the created order and its origins are intrinsically marked by change, something utterly alien to the transcendent divine. Plato's own cosmogonic scheme was founded on a fundamental distinction between 'Being' and 'Becoming', and hence between the noetic or intelligible world and the sensible or aesthetic world. This opposition and its formulation are axiomatic for his followers: As Numenius explained, 'For he [Plato] denied that being (τὸ ὄν) has a becoming (γένεσις); for that would involve change: What is changed is not eternal' (Numenius, *Frag.* 7). In the *Timaeus* Plato addresses the problem by presenting the source of creation as the 'Demiurge' (δημιουργός). However, the relationship between the Demiurge and the transcendent 'Being' or 'Good' of his other writings is not worked out in any detail: The Demiurge 'gazes towards that which remains the same for ever', and so grasps the ideas that will provide the ultimate pattern for that which is created. At the same time, a degree of separation from the order of becoming is sustained by a distinction between the Demiurge's tasks of contemplation and of creating divine things and 'the becoming of mortal things', which is entrusted to the lesser gods he had created (Plato, *Tim.* 28A–29A; 69C).

Marcion, as represented by Justin, belongs in a context where Plato's successors in the first and second centuries CE were returning to this to answer contemporary concerns, often with recourse to Plato's term 'Demiurge'. Plutarch, on the one hand, seems to have had no hesitation in identifying 'God' and 'the Demiurge' with the authentic Being of Plato (*Plat.Quaest.* 1000E–1001B).[31] Others heirs of Plato, however, took a different line.[32] As already noted, Numenius understood Plato as teaching that the Demiurge could be known but that 'the First Intellect was entirely unknown to them', and, indeed, he distinguished between them precisely on the grounds of Plato's 'Father *and* Creator' (*Frag.* 12; 17); to the Demiurge belongs 'becoming', so that the relationship between Demiurge and First Intellect is parallel to that between 'becoming' and 'being', in each case a secondary one of imitation or image (*Frag.* 16).[33] With slightly less clarity,

31 See Franco Ferrari, 'Der Gott Plutarchs und der Gott Platons', ed. Rainer Hirsch-Luipold, *Gott und die Götter bei Plutarch: Götterbilder-Gottesbilder-Weltbilder* (Religionsgeschichtliche Versuche und Verarbeiten 54; Berlin: de Gruyter, 2005), 13–25. However, see below at n. 90.

32 See Jan Opsomer, 'Demiurges in Early Imperial Platonism', ed. Hirsch-Luipold, *Gott und die Götter*, 51–99, 52–5.

33 See John Dillon, 'Numenius: Some Ontological Questions', ed. Sharples and Sorabji, *Greek and Roman Philosophy*, II, 397–402; Frede, 'Numenius', 1056–70, notes the lack of clarity in how the first and second Gods relate to each other. On whether Numenius called his First God 'the one who is', see below.

the mid-second-century handbook often attributed to Alcinous appears to have made a distinction between the primal God and the heavenly intellect, which are described at one point respectively as 'the God above the heavens' and 'the God in the heavens': 'he (i.e., the former) is Father through being the cause of all things and bestowing order on the heavenly intellect (the latter) and the world soul in accordance with himself and his own thoughts' (*Didaskalikos* 10.3; cf. 28.2). In this both Alcinous and Numenius exhibit the impulses towards seeing the supreme God as utterly transcendent, beyond being, a move perhaps influenced by Pythagoreanism as then understood, and one that would become more clearly articulated in Neoplatonism.[34]

Inevitably such debates would impact on any philosophical reader of Scripture. Philo responds characteristically, even arguing that in Genesis Moses had already anticipated Plato, or, rather, that he was the source of the latter.[35] He routinely refers to God as 'Maker' (ποιητής) and 'Demiurge', despite the absence of both terms from the Septuagint. He is, however, unequivocal in his identification of the Creator with the God 'who is', even while he incorporates into his reading of Scripture Plato's noetic sphere: first of all, 'the world which existed in ideas … in the divine reason which made them' (Philo, *De Opif.* 5 [20]). Furthermore, deliberately echoing Plato's identification of the ultimate reality as 'Being' or 'that which [neut.] is' (οὐσία; τὸ ὄν), Philo identifies God the Creator and Demiurge with the God who in Scripture self-identified as 'the one who [masc.] is' (ὁ ὤν), and as the God of Abraham, Isaac, and Jacob who identified himself in the words 'I am your God' (Exod. 3.14–16; Gen. 17.1; *De Mut.Nom.* 2–4 [11–39]). In addition, Plato's formulation 'Maker and Father' (regularly reversed) enables Philo to understand the biblical designation of God as Father as signalling God's role as Creator, and the consequent providence of God (*De Confus.* 33 [170]; *De Opif.* 25 [77]).[36]

On the other hand, the first-person plural in Genesis 1.27, 'Let us make …', prompted Philo to address the philosophical problems of this position. He refers those words not to 'the most high God, the Father of the Universe', since no created thing could be made like the one who is above reason, but to 'the second God'.[37] Elsewhere, following a lengthy

[34] For 'Neopythagorean' influence see Trapp, 'Neopythagoreans', 357–63. Opsomer, 'Demiurges in Early Imperial Platonism', suggests also the influence of the Aristotelian 'unmoved mover' and of criticisms from Epicureans.

[35] So also Aristobulus in Eusebius, *PE* XIII. 12.

[36] Frick, *Divine Providence*, 49–50.

[37] In *De Spec.Leg.* I. 16 [81] Philo says that the world was created ('demiurged') through the Logos. Hans-Friedrich Weiss, *Untersuchungen zur Kosmologie des hellenistischen und*

consideration of alternatives, he concludes that it was appropriate for God to use assistants in creating a being capable of evil choices for which God could not be responsible (Philo, *De Provid.* I = Eusebius, *PE* VII. 21; *De Opif.* 24 [72–5]).[38] Philo was not alone in wrestling with the scriptural conundrum; elsewhere in Jewish thought this finds expression in ideas that attributed creation to a mediating power or agent of God. It seems likely that rabbinic references to those who taught 'two powers in heaven' belong here; *Genesis Rabbah* shows repeated concern that the Genesis narrative, including the first person plural of Genesis 1.26–7, might give room for an interpretation that said 'two powers created the world' (*Gen.R.* 1.7; 8.8–9). Justin himself attributes to his Jewish opponents a number of interpretations of the 'let us make', before asserting that God was speaking to the first created offspring (Justin, *Dial.* 62). Although it is difficult to date the 'two powers' traditions, and to identify with any precision the 'heretics' (*minim*) held responsible, the sources of such views have been traced back to the end of the Second Temple period, and perhaps to apocalyptic and other circles later deemed heterodox.[39]

Several of the Apologists follow a similar pattern: God is 'sole Demiurge of all' or 'Maker and Demiurge of the world' (Tatian, *Orat.* 5.3; Athenagoras, *Leg.* 10.5).[40] Again, the scriptural tradition provides the language of mediated agency: 'he made the beginning of all … by a word of his power'.[41] Athenagoras goes further, concluding that '[God is] one, unbegotten and eternal and invisible and impassible and incomprehensible and infinite, apprehended by the mind and reason alone, surrounded by light and beauty and spirit and inexpressible power', and continuing, 'by whom through the word from him there came about and was ordered and is held together everything'; on this basis he argues that human notions of the divine based

Palästinischen Judentums (TU 97; Berlin: Akademie-Verlag, 1966), notes the rarity of 'demiurge' elsewhere in Hellenistic Judaism.

38 See David T. Runia, *Philo: On the Creation of the Cosmos According to Moses. Introduction, Translation and Commentary* (Philo of Alexandria Commentary Series 1; Atlanta, GA: SBL, 2001).

39 On the two powers in heaven see Alan F. Segal, *Two Powers in Heaven: Early Rabbinic Reports about Christianity and Gnosticism* (Leiden: Brill, 1977). Adiel Schremer, 'Midrash, Theology and History: Two Powers in Heaven Revisited', *JSJ* 39 (2008), 230–54, is much more cautious about supposed references to an actual 'theology', especially in tannaitic sources. Although some have traced the gnostic demiurge to this tradition, Marcion in no way fits it.

40 Heb. 11.10; *1 Clement* 20.11; 26.1, etc.; Aristides, *Apol.* 15.3; Athenagoras, *Leg.* 6.3; etc.; *Diog.* 7.2; 8.7; Ptolemy, *Letter to Flora* (in Epiphanius, *Pan.* 33. 3); on Justin see above, p. 326.

41 *Ker. Petri* in Clement of Alexandria, *Strom.* VI. 5.39, where it is probably Clement who adds the comment, 'of the gnostic scripture (?) that is the son'.

on logic and mental apprehension are at best inadequate, and that a knowledge of God is only possible through the Son, 'in whose likeness and through whom all things came into being (compare John 1.3)', but also through the Spirit who inspired prophetic witness (Athenagoras, *Leg.* 10.1–4, citing Prov. 8.22).[42] For these authors there is a continuum between creation and revelation, whether the agent of such revelation is identified with the pre-existent Christ or with the Spirit; what is striking is that a number of them, notably Athenagoras, Theophilus of Antioch, and Tatian, make no appeal to the earthly Jesus as an agent of revelation. Addressing the same concern, the *Apocryphon of John* excludes creation from the process: Nonetheless, it also caps a sustained paean to the God who can scarcely be spoken of – 'He is not corporeal nor incorporeal. He is not great and not small. It is not possible to say, "What is his quantity", or "What is his quality"' – with the affirmation, 'We do not know … except from him who came forth from him' (*NH* II.1. 3.23–4.18).

For Marcion, it would appear, 'the Demiurge' was the primary signifier of the deity responsible for the created order, and this becomes almost a technical term in Tertullian (*creator*), while Ephraem uses both 'Maker' (*'bwd'*) and 'Creator' (*brwy'*).[43] When Justin claimed that Marcion denied 'the Maker' and 'acknowledged another as greater', what he meant was that Marcion rejected the dominant position of the Apologists and instead followed those who distinguished between Demiurge and transcendent deity. In the *Dialogue of Adamantius* the Demiurge is also identified as 'the God of becoming (or 'of the created order' or 'of birth': ὁ θεὸς τῆς γενέσως)' (*Adam.* 18.31–22.1 [1.10]).[44] Whether this epithet can also be traced with any certainty back to Marcion is difficult to establish; even so, it remains possible that he did identify a fundamental problem as that of 'becoming', γένεσις, a term that is rare in this sense among the Apologists.

Marcion apparently took the separation between supreme and Creator deities much further than any of his contemporaries might have envisaged,

[42] In *Leg.* 13.2 Athenagoras explicitly alludes to the Genesis narrative; he also cites a catena of prophetic passages, imagining the divine spirit playing on the prophets as a flautist on a flute (*Leg.* 9.1–2). On Athenagoras's epistemology, see David Rankin, *Athenagoras: Philosopher and Theologian* (Farnham: Ashgate, 2009), 73–99; see also above, p. 313 for *Diognetus*.

[43] Thus, *AM* III. 13.9 closely parallels *AJ* 9.13, except for the '*Creatori*' in the former and '*scripturis divinis*' in the latter. See also Cyprian, *Epist.* 73 and 74, where Marcion's fault is his failure to confess, or blasphemy against 'God the father and creator'. On Ephraem, see p. 161 above.

[44] Or 'of creation'; see above, p. 123, and Tsutsui, *Auseinandersetzung*, 156–8, who compares Clement of Alexandria, *Strom.* III. 12.1–25.4 (above, p. 130).

until it becomes an unfathomable gulf, a gulf that can only be conceptualised in spatial language. Others, the so-called gnostics, did something similar, but they qualified it by a cosmological myth that would ultimately derive the Demiurge back from the transcendent deity. Marcion did not follow this path nor apparently did he have any alternative myth of origins; either this was not the inspiration of his thought or, more probably, it was unnecessary for his explanatory or soteriological purposes. It is therefore difficult to decide whether Marcion was ultimately a Monist, as might be claimed for Valentinus and as is asserted by Hippolytus, or a dualist; in part this is because, as will be seen below, it is not philosophical principles but scriptural imagery that shapes his account of the Demiurge.[45]

THE CHARACTER OF THE DEMIURGE

While Justin's accusation that the Marcionites among others calumniate (or 'blaspheme') the Maker (*Dial.* 35) is ambiguous as to the nature of such denigration, subsequent polemicists are more precise in their claim that Marcion brought a series of uniformly negative charges against the Demiurge.[46] This would seem to bring him most into conflict not only with the mainstream Christian but also with the Platonic tradition. Within the latter, Plato's axiom was sustained that the Demiurge is good, and so is responsible for a world that is as beautiful as it could be: 'He was good and never harboured any jealousy (or envy: φθόνος) about anyone' (Plato, *Tim.* 29E–30A; Plutarch, *De Anim.* 1014A–B; Celsus in Origen, *C.Cels.* VIII. 21). Even those who drew a distinction between the Demiurge and First Intellect, such as Numenius, would affirm that both were good, the latter being intrinsically good, the former by derivation.

Plato's axiom was not simply an abstraction: Goodness, when defined as the absence of envy, meant the readiness to share what was good with others. This, perhaps deliberately, challenged what was already a theme of poetry

45 For Valentinus as a monist see David Dawson, *Allegorical Readers and Cultural Revision in Ancient Alexandria* (Berkeley, CA: University of California Press, 1992), 158, 177–8. Hanns Christof Brennecke, 'Marcion oder das philosophische Gottesbild in der Spannung zwischen Orthodoxie und Häresie', ed. Jürgen Dummer und Meinolf Vielberg, *Leitbilder im Spannungsfeld von Orthodoxie und Heterodoxie* (Altertumswissenschaftliches Kolloquium 19; Stuttgart: Steiner, 2008), 11–28, 23–4, asks whether Marcion in fact spoke of two strictly separate functions of the one God. Hippolytus, *C.Noetum* 11, combines Valentinus, Marcion, and Cerinthus as unwilling preachers of 'the One'.

46 On the more neutral wording of the *Apology* see above, p. 15; see Irenaeus and Origen for the repetition of the charge (pp. 35, 136 above).

and literature in fifth-century BCE Athens, namely that the ways of the gods and their intervention in human affairs were not only unpredictable and sometimes destructive of human happiness but also often motivated by envy.[47] While such jealousy could be portrayed as the appropriate defensive reaction of the gods to human pride or to overstepping of the proper limits, it often seems to be triggered by their resentment at human good-fortune – and fear of such resentment may have been a powerful force in popular sentiment.[48]

Characteristically, Philo finds in the Genesis account the ultimate authority for Plato's insight (Philo, *De Opif.* 5; 25 [21; 77]; cf. *De Cherub.* 35 [127]). He repeatedly emphasises that God's goodness is 'without envy' ('unstinting'; ἀφθον-), although it is difficult to determine whether this carries any additional polemical edge against those who supposed otherwise (*Leg.Alleg.* I. 26 [80]; III. 56; 72 [164; 203]; *Deus Immut.* 23 [108]). However, in view of what is to follow, it is notable that he avoids the striking biblical term 'j[z]ealous God' (θεὸς ζηλωτής; cf. Deut. 4.24). Moreover, he is sensitive to the suggestion that Genesis 3.22 might seem to suggest envy (φθόνος) on the part of God, and he is careful to explain that, on the contrary, it demonstrated the concern for humanity's well-being shown by a God who is 'without part in any evil' but who 'created the world as a benefactor' (*QG* I. 55).[49]

Both themes continue. The more general affirmation of God's abundant generosity or lack of jealousy (ἀφθον -) is a repeated theme in the *Odes of Solomon*: (11.6), without that necessarily carrying any polemical intent.[50] On the other hand, Theophilus of Antioch also discusses Genesis 3.22, and explicitly denies that God's prohibition of the tree of knowledge meant that 'God was jealous (φθονέω) towards him (Adam) as some suppose' (*Ad Autol.* II. 25). That 'some' did so indeed suppose is confirmed by charges such as, 'But of what sort is this God. First he envied Adam that he should eat from the tree of knowledge. And secondly he said, "Adam, where

47 See Fritz-Gregor Herrmann, 'φθόνος in the world of Plato's Timaeus', ed. David Konstan and N. Keith Rutter, *Envy, Spite and Jealousy: The Rivalrous Emotions in Ancient Greece* (Edinburgh Leventis Studies 2; Edinburgh: Edinburgh University Press, 2003), 53–83.

48 See Thomas Rakoczy, *Böser Blick, Macht des Auges und Neid der Götter: Eine Untersuchung zur Kraft des Blickes in der griechischen Literatur* (Classica Monacensia 13; Tübingen: Gunter Narr, 1996), 247–70; this double reference is difficult to nuance through the English terms 'envious', 'jealous'; see below.

49 See Frick, *Divine Providence*.

50 See *Odes of Solomon* 7.3; 15.6; 17.12; 20.7; 23.4; Lattke, *Oden Salomos* 1, 17–18, for this as a theme in the Odes. Drijvers, 'Oden Salomos' argues for an anti-Marcionite polemic and dates the *Odes* accordingly later. See further p. 148.

are you?"' (*Testimony of Truth* [NH IX.3] 47.14–29);[51] 'The rest of the powers became jealous (at the creation of the human being)'; 'The Father was not jealous' (*Apocryph.John* [NH II.1] 19.33–20.9; *Gospel of Truth* [NH I.3] 18.38–9). Some have seen in such exegetical assertions an inversion of the explanation, which was already found in Jewish interpreters, that the disaster in Eden was due to the envy felt by the serpent against Adam (Josephus, *AJ* I. 1.4 [41]; Wisd. 2.24).[52] But it would be wrong to look for only a single line of development: Irenaeus himself explained the enemy who sows tares (Matt. 13.25) as 'the apostate angel who was jealous of God's creature' (Irenaeus, *AH* IV. 11.3), while parallel charges are also to be found in 'pagan' criticisms of the Jewish and Christian God – Julian argued that the serpent was surely humankind's benefactor, whereas God was malignant in seeking to prevent their access to the tree of knowledge (*C.Galil.* 75B–94A). If these were fuelled by gnostic criticism of the 'catholic' Christian's God,[53] it would only be within a complex pattern of exegetical argument.

It is striking that Irenaeus cites Plato's aphorism about God's lack of jealousy immediately following his account of Marcion's 'judicial' God, although he recognizes that the charge against the Demiurge was made by others also (Irenaeus, *AH* III. 25.3–5; V. 4.1). Tertullian repeatedly alludes to Marcion's supposed mockery of the 'jealousy' of God, while making a spirited defence of God's behaviour.[54] However, although he does discuss Genesis 3.22 (Tertullian, *AM* II. 25.4), most of his attention is directed elsewhere. In particular he defends the epithet 'j[z]ealous God', transliterating the Greek as *deus zelotes*; from the way he addresses this it is evident that passages such as Exodus 20.5, where it is as 'θεὸς ζηλωτής' that God punishes children for the sins of their parents, were a particular source of contention (*AM* II. 15.1; IV. 27.8). Yet Tertullian is equally emphatic that a God who holds sole authority and who seeks to save must needs be 'jealous':

51 See Birger Pearson, 'Jewish Haggadic Tradition in *The Testimony of Truth* from Nag Hammadi (CG IX,3)', *HTR* 73 (1980), 311–19; more generally, Willem C. van Unnik, 'Der Neid in der Paradiesgeschichte nach einigen gnostischen Texten', ed. Martin Krause, *Essays on the Nag Hammadi Texts in Honour of Alexander Böhlig* (NHS 3; Leiden: Brill, 1972), 120–32.

52 Karlmann Beyschlag, *Clemens Romanus und der Frühkatholizismus: Untersuchungen zu 1 Clemens 1–7* (BHT 35; Tübingen: Mohr Siebeck, 1966), 57, suggests that that the 'gnostic Demiurge' is to be traced to the serpent/devil of the Adam legend, but this is over-simplistic.

53 So Klaus Koschorke, *Die Polemik der Gnostiker gegen das kirchliche Christentum* (NHS 12; Leiden: Brill, 1978), 148–52.

54 *AM* I. 28.1; II. 29.3; III. 23.7; IV. 21.10; 25.2–3; 27.8; 39.18; 42.2; V. 5.8; 7.13; 16.6; see above, p. 168.

'nothing takes its course without jealousy (rivalrous emulation: *aemulatio*) because there is nothing without opposition' (*AM* I. 25.6; cf. II. 29.4). Evidently also at stake were the biblical God's efforts to defend his authority, and his demands for sole allegiance, and whether this was compatible with unrestricted beneficence.[55]

It might be objected that ζῆλος ('jealousy'/'zeal') and φθόνος ('envy'/ 'jealousy') represent distinct theological and linguistic traditions: In the Septuagint the former and its derivatives are used not only of God in his response to human disloyalty and in the denial of the right of any other potential usurper but also both of those loyal to God, and of intra-human emotions, both positive and negative; φθόνος, by contrast, is rare. However, in early Christian moral rhetoric the two terms had become parallel: In *1 Clement* together they form a dark thread running from Cain (or the Serpent) through biblical and to more recent Christian history (*1 Clem.* 3–5). While, as already noted, Philo does not use 'θεὸς ζηλωτής', for Aristides it was ζῆλος that characterised and so disqualified the Greek gods (Aristides, *Apol.* 10.7; 11.1).[56] Alongside the linguistic elision is the fine line that separates proper defence of the perceived truth from self-interest, as well as legitimate tenure and defence of supreme power from the illegitimate aspiration to such. As felt by the Creator, such an emotion would have been in Marcion's eyes ignorant hubris.

Other evidence suggests a similar complex network of exegesis and tradition, while excluding simple lines of dependency. Marcion's complaint that the Demiurge was jealous was part of a catalogue of other charges: Tertullian initially states that Marcion was preoccupied by the problem of evil, 'as are most people, especially heretics', but he then suggests that Marcion's own understanding was inspired by combining the Creator's claim, 'I am the one who creates evils', with Jesus' parable of the fruits of the good and bad trees (Isa. 45.7; Luke 6.43; Tertullian, *AM* I. 2.2; cf. II. 14.1). Marcion's appeal to the parable is well-established, but that he combined it with the divine claim in Isaiah is not; even so, although the latter is important for Tertullian's own argument, this need not mean that he invented it (*AM* II. 24.4).[57] The issue is complicated by Tertullian's appeal

55 Ekkehard Muehlenberg, 'Marcion's Jealous God', ed. Donald F. Winslow, *Disciplina Nostra: Essays in Memory of Robert F. Evans* (PMS 6; Cambridge, MA: Philadelphia Patristic Foundation, 1979), 93–113, argues that for Marcion goodness excludes the obligation or self-assertion that lie behind 'jealousy' and the exercise of justice.

56 Both terms are surprisingly rare in the Apologists.

57 See Braun, *Contre Marcion*, I, 108–9, n. 3; on Marcion's use of these passages see above, pp. 232–3, 327.

to the similar passage in Deuteronomy 32.39, 'I kill and I make alive'; here, however, he implies that Marcion was more concerned with the Creator's apparent self-contradiction, although once again Tertullian's own delight in the passage as evidence of the 'antithesis' that is integral to the one God may suggest that he is supplying Marcion with arguments that would serve his own cause (*AM* I. 16.4; IV. 1.10; cf. II. 13.4; 14.1; III. 24.1; V. 11.4). Yet these scriptural passages readily provoked controversy: Within Jewish tradition the Deuteronomy passage was used in debates with those who held some version of a 'two powers in heaven' theology, and also, defensively, against those who denied the resurrection.[58] Again, the complex network of exegetical debate cannot be reduced to a single narrative; it would be difficult to accommodate Marcion into a simple linear trajectory, and arguably an appeal to these verses came at a second stage either in the polemical tradition or in the development of his thought by his followers.

Here already the philosophical question is mediated by the biblical tradition, but the latter inevitably turned the spotlight on to human responsibility and divine punishment. This is well illustrated by the primary charge against the Demiurge made by Marcion, or by his followers' ('you pl.'): In Tertullian's words, 'If God is good, has fore-knowledge of the future, and is able to avert evil, why did he allow man, who was indeed his image and likeness, even his substance as it were through the ownership of the spirit, to fall into death through disobedience to the law, outmanoeuvred by the devil' (*AM* II. 5.1).[59] The question of divine control and human responsibility in the face of evil was a widely discussed one, although the problem would be the greater where there is but one, omniscient and all-powerful, deity. Whereas the Epicureans famously denied that the gods were interested in or intervened in the world of human affairs, both the Stoics and Platonists affirmed the guiding force of the divine principle, albeit in different forms.

58 See *Sifre Deut.* 329; Segal, *Two Powers*, 241–3, who discusses the relationship with Marcion; idem, 'Dualism in Judaism, Christianity and Gnosticism: A Definitive Issue', in *The Other Judaisms of Late Antiquity* (BJS 127; Atlanta, GA: Scholars, 1987), 1–40; Schremer, 'Midrash, Theology and History', argues that this is one element in a more fundamental debate about the ability of God to defend his people. Jacques T. A. G. van Ruiten, 'The Use of Deuteronomy 32:39 in Monotheistic Controversies in Rabbinic Literature', ed. Florentino García Martinez, Anton Hilhorst, Jacques T. A. G. van Ruiten, and Adam S. van der Woude, *Studies in Deuteronomy: In Honour of C. J. Labuschagne on the Occasion of his 65th Birthday* (VTSup. 53; Leiden: Brill, 1994), 223–41, 234–40, argues that a number of alternative positions may have been in view in the tradition but that the main focus in *Sifre* is on the unity of God; see also Catrin H. Williams, *I Am He: The Interpretation of 'Anî Hû' in Jewish and Early Christian Literature* (WUNT 2.113; Tübingen: Mohr-Siebeck, 2000), 135–9.

59 See above, pp. 66–9.

Josephus nods in that direction when he uses the topos to differentiate the 'schools' among the Jews (Josephus, *BJ* II. 8.14 [162–5]). Philo addresses the same problem: After consciously echoing Plato's affirmation of the unstinting goodness of the Creator, he points to its expression in God's necessary accommodation to the limited capacities of the created order as the recipient of God's goodness; more generally, when he denies that God was a relentless tyrant who behaved with cruelty and violence he is not rebutting any who held such a view but is recognising the challenges that any doctrine of divine control or providence faces (Philo, *De Opif.* 5–6 [21–23]; *De Provid.* II. 2 = Eusebius, *PE* VIII. 14.2–6). Elsewhere, Philo had already recognised that scriptural language could mislead 'weaker members' into thinking that Moses taught that events were governed by fate (*Quis Haer.* 60 [300–1]). Similarly, Justin Martyr recognises that his own emphasis on the fulfilment of prophecy may suggest to the readers of his *Apology* that 'things happen of necessity through fate', and he immediately sets this question in the framework of human responsibility for their actions and of their liability for judgement, a concern he traces also in Plato, who himself derived it from Moses (Justin, *Apol.* 43–44).[60]

For many, the most troubling aspect of the question of human responsibility was that of the origin of their capacity for the wrong choices. Again, Plato's *Timaeus* offered a multilayered myth whose primary goal was to ensure that the Demiurge would be 'guiltless of any future evil in any of them' (Plato, *Tim.* 41D–44D, esp. 42D). In hellenistic Judaism both Wisdom literature and apocalyptic sought solutions that would also distance the Creator from responsibility for human as well as for angelic evil, and such ideas, particularly of heavenly rebellion, were readily adopted by the early Christians: Athenagoras is typical in appealing to the Enochic tradition of the giants, although his identification of one of them as 'the ruler of matter' (ὁ τῆς ὕλης ἄρχων) betrays a more platonising perspective (Athenagoras, *Leg.* 24–5; cf. *1 Enoch* 6).[61] Hence, when Irenaeus attributes to those who would thereby charge God with a lack of power or of knowledge, the specific suggestion that God *ought* (*oporteo*) not to have made angels and humans capable of disobedience, it is unlikely that he has Marcion alone in view (Irenaeus, *AH* IV. 37–8). Celsus makes the same

[60] This broader setting means that there are no grounds for supposing that Justin has taken this argument from his work against Marcion or other heresies; contra Norelli, 'Que pouvons-nous reconstituer du *Syntagme*', who associates the passages from Justin, Irenaeus, and Tertullian.

[61] Compare also Justin, *Apol.* 5.2; *2 Apol.* 5.4–5.

complaint, again probably drawing on more widespread debates about the Jewish-Christian narrative; in response Origen accuses him of confusing various 'sects' with each other, and of failing to recognise both the variety of opinions 'among the Greeks' and the need to differentiate different sorts of evil (Origen, *C.Cels.* VI. 53–4).

However, as represented by Tertullian in the passage cited above, the Marcionite position adds a distinctive element to this widespread concern, namely the congruity – image and likeness – between Creator and his human creation (Gen. 1.26–7; 2.7). As already noted, Marcion would not have been the first to recognise the difficulties posed by these verses within a Greek philosophical understanding of the divine. His concern, however, was not with the first person plural but that if humanity was created in the image of the Creator, then the Creator models human behaviour. Again, this was not an entirely novel approach to this verse: With a more optimistic understanding of human potential Philo had recognised this event as the moment at which the sense-perceptible human being is granted that which makes them capable of immortality (Philo, *De Opif.* 46 [134–5]). Tertullian's anxiety in response to distinguish between the breathe that God in-breathed and God's Spirit suggests that he was well aware of the potential sensitivities in a reading that was predicated on a more negative understanding of human nature (*AM* II. 5; 9).[62]

Goodness and justice

The 'calumnies' discussed so far fit comfortably within contemporary debates about the nature of the divine or of the gods in their interaction with humankind, in particular where Scripture was being read within a popular, platonising, philosophical framework. However, the polemical sources present an alternative framework for Marcion's system. Although absent from Justin's account and from Irenaeus' initial core passage, it thereafter quickly becomes established among his opponents that Marcion distinguished between the God who is 'good' (ἀγαθός), and the God who is 'just' (δίκαιος).[63] This is repeated by Ps.Hippolytus, *Refutation* (X. 19), by

62 However, it is possible that Tertullian has taken this argument from his dealings with Hermogenes: see Frédéric Chapot, 'L'hérésie d'Hermogène. Fragments et commentaire', *Rech.Aug.* 30 (1997), 3–111, 78.

63 See above, p. 37; in later accounts Marcion or some of his disciples made 'the just' a mediating figure between good and evil, but this is probably derivative from the tendency for either Marcionite ideas, or for their polemical description, to move towards a dualism (above, pp. 91–2, 177).

Clement of Alexandria and by Origen, while for Ephraem 'the Just One' is one of the routine epithets of 'the Maker'.[64] Irenaeus himself credited Cerdo with this distinction, with the epithet 'just' clearly tied to this God as 'proclaimed by the law and the prophets'; subsequently, however, he does claim that 'Marcion divides God into two, the one good, the other judicial' (*iudicialis*: only the Latin is extant here; *AH* I. 27.1; III. 25.3). Cerdo has become so overshadowed by Marcion in the heresiological tradition that it is nigh impossible to untangle where originality and where imitation or imitative attribution lies, and it is with Marcion that any discussion must start.[65]

That the primary association of Irenaeus' term 'judicial' is with the practice and enforcement of judgement is confirmed by Tertullian's description, 'judge, fierce, lover of war' (*iudicem, ferum, bellipotens*), and by his claim that the Marcionites have 'removed' from their God the 'exercise of severity and judicial acts', which for him is so necessary (*AM* I. 6.1; 25.3). Elsewhere, however, Tertullian tends to generalise the implications of 'just', while at the same time he embeds the 'diversity' between 'just' and 'good' within that between Law and Gospel; indeed he even presents these 'two different Gods' as a product of Marcion's separation between 'Law and Gospel', established through the 'Antitheses', and as each belonging to a different 'testament' (IV. 1.2). Later polemicists follow this pattern, and they then have no difficulty, either in principle or through biblical example, in demonstrating that justice must necessarily be good, and goodness just.[66] Yet this necessary interdependence is so much of a commonplace in both philosophical and scriptural tradition, that Marcion's own concern requires a more nuanced interpretation.

It is integral to the biblical understanding that God is both merciful and judge. Yet that there is a potential tension between these is already acknowledged within the scriptural account, and it surfaces more acutely subsequently, particularly after the destruction of the Temple (Gen. 18.22–33; Ps. 85; Bar. 2). Thus, the question is not only a philosophical one but is also rooted in the experience of God. Philo addresses the issue more systematically; he distinguishes God's creative power, associated with the divine name 'God' (θεός = *elohim*), from God's sovereign power, associated with the septuagintal 'Lord' (κύριος). The former, 'God', indicates God's goodness and mercy, the latter, 'Lord', God's action as law-giver and judge (Philo, *De Abr.* 24–5 [121–4]; *De Plant.* 20 [86–8];

64 See pp. 94–5, 134, 165.
65 See David W. Deakle, 'Harnack and Cerdo'.
66 See above, pp. 67, 166.

Leg.Alleg. III. 23 [73]).[67] Although at times the former has priority, being closer to the true nature of God, both are rooted in God's being as it is experienced by humankind; on the other hand, Philo can also say that God's benefits are received directly, whereas God's punishment is exercised by divine command through the agency of others (*De Fug.* 13–14; 18 [65–74; 97–9]; *De Abr.* 28 [145]). Matching this are the contrasting human responses to the divine, namely fear, which is inspired by God as judge, and love, which is inspired by God's benefits. However, whereas contemporary philosophy saw fear as inappropriate, at least for the wise, even if useful to instil obedience to the laws into the masses, for Philo, and later for Tertullian, each has its proper place. Yet, just as the philosophers explored these ideas of fear and love in relation to notions of the exercise of sovereignty by human as well as by divine rulers, so too does Philo.[68]

Philo uses a variety of terms to express the two modes of divine action: goodness, and graciousness, on the one side, and authority, law-giving, and even retribution, on the other. Yet there does seem to be a firm connection between his ideas and the more consistent rabbinic tradition which divides between the goodness and the retribution (*ṭb'wt', pwr'nwt'*), or, perhaps at a later date, between the mercy and the justice (*rḥmym, dyn*), of God; although in the dominant tradition the assignation of these to the divine names is the reverse of Philo's – so that *elohim* represents justice, the tetragrammaton mercy – the oldest pattern may have agreed with him.[69] Necessarily, throughout such discussions these are the two attributes of the one God. Yet, what for Philo is a unity in tension could become more fundamentally divisive. There may be hints that the tension could be aligned with the belief in two powers (*mBer.* 5.3; *Mek* on Exod. 15.3).[70] In the Targumic traditions Cain and Abel dispute whether the world is created through mercy and whether it is judged by standards of justice and/or of mercy; the positions

67 On this and what follows see Yehoshua Amir, 'Philons Erörterungen über Gottesfurcht und Gottesliebe in ihren Verhältnis zum palästinischen Midrasch', *Die hellenistische Gestalt des Judentums bei Philon von Alexandrien* (Forschungen zum jüdisch-christlichen Dialog 5; Neukirchen-Vluyn: Neukirchener, 1983), 164–85.

68 See Jutta Leonhardt, *Jewish Worship in Philo of Alexandria* (TSAJ 84; Tübingen: Mohr Siebeck, 2001), 106; Harry Wolfson, *Philo: Foundations of Religious Philosophy in Judaism, Christianity, and Islam* (Cambridge, MA: Harvard University Press, 1947), 1, 424–56.

69 So Arthur Marmorstein, 'Philo and the Names of God', *JQR* 22 (1932), 295–306. He finds a reaction against Marcionism in subsequent debates about the identification of *elohim* with judgement (300). See also Nils A. Dahl and Alan F. Segal, 'Philo and the Rabbis on the Name of God', *JSJ* 9 (1978), 1–28, who, however, reject any explicit reaction against Marcion.

70 So Dahl and Segal, 'Philo and the Rabbis', esp. 16–20; however, that this is so in *Mekhilta* is questioned by Catrin H. Williams, *I Am He*, 124.

ascribed to each protagonist vary, and it is not evident whether this is a matter of literary variation, of development, or of a change in implicit opponents.[71] However, a consistent theme is that Abel affirms that the world is judged according to justice, while Cain denies this;[72] the problem, then, is not the fact of judgement but the accountability of the judge. Despite the late date of the final form of the Targumim, other parallels suggest that such traditions go back at least to the second century CE. Originating in the same period, the *Apocryphon of John* probably echoes similar traditions when it identifies Yahve with Cain and Elohim with Abel; even here the different recensions of the text disagree as to whether it is Yahweh who is righteous and Elohijm who is unrighteous, or the reverse.[73]

These debates, which were evidently live ones in the second century, provide a possible framework for considering Marcion's antithesis, and particularly the ambiguity in the language of 'justice'. Tertullian's response that the good person must make judgement against what is wrong, and that the judge must be good, is so conventional as to entirely miss the point (*AM* II. 11–13). In his more sustained exploration Origen cites as his chief example the destruction of Sodom and Gomorrah (Gen. 18–19), and this perhaps suggests that the issue was not the exercise of evaluation itself but the nature of the punitive action taken by the judge (*De Princip.* II. 5). The Jewish explanation of the destruction of the city was perhaps well-known, and invited apologetics.[74] Philo had explained the confusion regarding the agents of the visitation as evidence of God's use of mediating powers to exercise judgement (*De Abr.* 28 [145]), while even Justin argues that the 'Lord' of Genesis 18. 1–3 could not be 'the Maker of all' but some other who could, however, be called God and Lord (Justin, *Dial.* 56). The fine line is marked by Ptolemy, who in his *Letter to Flora* rejects those who ascribe the creation of the world 'to a god who causes destruction', claiming it instead for 'one who is just and hates evil', who, however, is inferior 'to the single good God' (Epiphanius, *Pan.* 33.3, 7). Tertullian defends against Marcion, not only the punishment of Adam, but also that through the flood as well as the destruction of the two cities by fire; he denies that these are 'evils of injustice to be ascribed to malice', for, since they are just, they are not evil (*AM* II. 14.3–4).

[71] See J. Bassler, 'Cain and Abel in the Palestinian Targums', *JSJ* 17 (1986), 56–64.

[72] In the Palestinian fragmentary targum Cain simply asserts that it is judged by mercy, perhaps in context meaning without accountability.

[73] In *NH* IV.1. 38.4–6 it is Yahweh who is righteous, and in III.1. 31.15–16, Elohim is righteous.

[74] See Strabo, *Geog.* XVI. 2.44; Celsus apparently saw the story as copied from Greek myth (Origen, *C.Cels.* IV. 21).

The more extensive catalogue of charges that Marcion supposedly brought against the Creator follows on from these concerns: Tertullian itemises them throughout Book II – creator of evils, judicial, severe, ignorant, contradictory, capricious, inconsistent, petty, a lover of war. In scholarly study of other demiurgical (or 'gnostic') traditions it has been suggested that the destruction of the Temple, or the Bar Kochba defeat, may have triggered a radical reversal in trust in God's necessary justice, and in this context the epithet 'lover of war' might carry extra weight.[75] Such an explanation necessarily remains speculative, and such epithets could naturally arise simply from a reading of the biblical narrative. The underlying anxiety about what was appropriate to God was widely shared. Tertullian identifies the philosophical problem for the heretics: 'if God is angry and jealous and proud and angry, then evidently he is also subject to corruption, and indeed may even die' (*AM* II. 16.3). Yet, since God could not be so, those who represented him in such terms could also not be trusted. The Homeric and classical stories of the gods already lay themselves open to such charges, and these were taken up readily by Christian apologists. Tatian accuses Zeno of presenting God as 'maker of evils' or the Greeks of presenting Zeus as 'jealously plotting humankind's destruction' (Tatian, *Orat.* 3.2; 21.1), while Athenagoras mocks conceptions of the gods that ascribe to them anger or desire (Athenagoras, *Leg.* 21), and both do so with the implicit assumption that their supposed educated audience will fully concur. Theophilus mocks the accounts of 'Kronos the child-eater and Zeus who consumed his daughter Metis … the dance-loving Athena and the shameless Aphrodite' (Theophilus, *Ad Autol.* III. 3), although his primary target is the Greek authors, and especially the poets, who composed such things. However, although very different from these, the scriptural accounts could also provoke profound ambiguity as to the motivation of God's interventions, not least in a context where Jewish apologists were keen to denounce Greek polytheism and anthropomorphisms. In some ways Marcion gives the Scriptures the same attention as Theophilus gives the 'poets' with their accounts of the gods; but, whereas Theophilus concludes that the latter are perverse and thoroughly mistaken, Marcion takes seriously the Scriptures' claim to speak of 'God', albeit of the Creator. Indeed, what is striking here is that Marcion would seem to give the Scriptures far more attention than did many contemporary Apologists, Justin excepted; even here, different parts of the Scriptures formed his starting point than Justin's. Yet he sees the Creator as also

[75] For *bellipotens* see *AM* III. 14.7; 21.4.

depicted within his new authoritative texts, the 'Gospel' and 'Apostolikon', albeit by 'antithesis' and covertly in the figurative language of parables and metaphor, and in references to his creation, 'the world' or 'this age', of which he is 'god'.[76] Therefore further examination of Marcion's view of the Demiurge in particular must start from his reading of the Scriptures.

Such an account might seem to ignore those polemical traditions that claim that Marcion's Demiurge was not only the source of evils but was also essentially 'evil'. This would make of him a principled dualist, and hence as taking an even more radically different position than that of his philosophical contemporaries. At one point Tertullian already asserts this, but he grounds Marcion's position in the two trees of Luke 6.43 (*AM* I. 2.1–2; IV. 17.12).[77] Undoubtedly the verse was an important proof-text, although that of itself suggests that any language of 'bad' with reference to the Creator – and it is striking that Luke 6.43 uses σαπρός for both the tree and its fruit – referred more to the outcomes of his activities than to any qualitative essence.[78] Those accounts which ascribe to Marcion an opposition of principles appear to be secondary, and were perhaps driven by efforts to establish his 'true' philosophical inheritance: Hence Ps.Hippolytus, *Refutation* claims that his doctrine of two 'principles', good and evil, exposes him as a disciple of Empedocles (*Ref.* VII. 29; 30).[79] Although Ptolemaeus rejects those who ascribe the Law to the 'devil who brings destruction, and who ascribe to him the making of the world, saying he is Father and Maker', there is no reason to identify this specifically as a Marcionite position (Epiphanius, *Pan.* 33.3).[80] Undoubtedly this was a step that some of his followers did take, although others, as shall be seen, preferred to assign evil to the primordial matter on which the Demiurge worked.[81] The evident confusion most likely goes back to attempts to address Marcion's own avoidance of any explanation of evil in terms of 'principles'.[82]

76 See, for example, 2 Cor. 4.4 (pp. 211, 258–60, above).

77 Although at another point he denies it: see above, p. 64, and, for Irenaeus, pp. 36–7.

78 See above, p. 340. However, the word choice in Marcion's text of Luke is uncertain: Tertullian, *AM* IV. 7.1 uses *malus*, while *Adam.* 56.14 [1.28], follows the Matthaean wording (σαπρός ... κακός). Gerhard Rottenwöhrer, *Unde Malum? Herkunft und Gestalt des Bösen nach heterodoxer Lehre von Markion bis zu den Katharen* (Bad Honnef: Bock & Herchen, 1986), 31, suggests the possible influence also of Gal. 5.19–21.

79 However, Ps.Hippolytus, *Ref.* X. 19, ascribes to Marcion and Cerdo three principles, good, righteous, and matter, and only to some of his disciples a fourth, evil (see p. 94 above).

80 Moll, *Arch-Heretic*, 14–17, assumes this identification and then uses it as the basis of his reconstruction of Marcion; see further below, p. 412.

81 See above, p. 95 for this as an issue among Marcion's disciples according to Hippolytus.

82 Ctr. Moll. *Arch-Heretic*, 47–58; see Löhr, 'Did Marcion Distinguish?', who concludes that Marcion was not interested in speculation 'concerning principles'.

So far Marcion's understanding of the Creator has been explored largely independently of other 'demiurgical' traditions. Assigning creation to a subordinate deity is a consistent marker of what has been traditionally known as 'gnostic(ism)', and has led to the suggestion that it would better be known as 'biblical demiurgical'.[83] Yet applying a single label should not obscure the different ways in which the Creator is portrayed across these writings. Indeed, Irenaeus already assigns such a belief to Cerinthus, although the latter labels the Creator of the world only as 'a certain power' (*AH* I. 26); moreover, Cerinthus does not seem to have identified the Creator as evil.[84]

A linear model of influence or derivation among these writings or systems is not easy to demonstrate, still less one that incorporates Marcion. Elsewhere Origen's defence against Celsus suggests that Celsus himself switched, perhaps unaware, between statements made by those with 'gnostic' or Marcionite sympathies and polemical ripostes against these (*C.Cels.* VI. 52–3). What seems most likely is that all parties were drawing on a common stock of denigration which had multiple sources within polemic and debates between Jews, 'pagans', and Christians, and amongst the internal divisions within these. The appeal to Scripture in intramural debates could easily be picked up and inverted by outsiders, particularly where the Jewish Scriptures were denied the same right to be read allegorically as was assumed for Homer.

The created order

Tertullian parodies Marcion's denigration of the natural order; he envisages him pouring scorn on 'the minute creatures to which the great craftsman (*artifex*) deliberately gave extended skill or strength', and he retorts 'imitate if you can the house-building of the bee, the stabling of the ant ...' (*AM* I. 13–14). The real issue here, he suggests, is whether this order is 'worthy or not' (*dignus/indignus*) of a supreme God: That question, namely of what is 'fitting' or worthy of the divine was a familiar one in contemporary philosophical debate.[85] Even Tertullian responds by arguing that the

83 See Williams, *Rethinking "Gnosticism"*.

84 According to Ps.Tertullian, *Adv.Omn.Haer.* 3, Cerinthus said creation was 'by angels': The God of the Jews was not the lord but an angel. On this see Christoph Markschies, 'Kerinth: wer er war und was lehrte er?', *JbAC* 41 (1998), 48–76, 56–7, 72–3.

85 See Max Pohlenz, 'τὸ πρέπον. Ein Beitrag zur Geschichte des griechischen Geistes', 53–92. Isabelle Bochet, 'Transcendance divine et paradoxe de la foi chrétienne. La polémique de Tertullien contre Marcion', *RSciRel* 96 (2008), 255–94, 255–60.

'visible' is but one side of the diversity of what God has made, the other being the, surely greater, 'invisible things'; once again, it is this diversity that Marcion splits between his two Gods, attributing to each a world, one inferior and the other superior (*AM* I. 16). However, according to Tertullian, much more serious was Marcion's assertion that the Creator established the visible and inferior world out of matter (*materia*), which was for him neither created nor engendered. In Tertullian's uncompromising logic, matter, if uncreated, is eternal, and hence is itself a divine principle or 'God'; he pushes that logic yet further, asserting that it follows that 'place' as occupied by such matter is yet a further deity, and that if evil is attributed to matter, it too must be eternal and so serve as a fourth deity (*AM* I. 15).[86]

The attribution of evil to the primordial matter would seem to be an alternative option to making the Demiurge responsible for evil. That Marcion took this position is claimed by some of his opponents; Clement of Alexandria does so although his purpose is to deny Marcion any right to appeal to Plato, and if Clement's 'Antitactae' are Marcionites, they blamed evil on a rebellious angel (*Strom.* III. 3.19; 4.34).[87] Certainly such a position might have been more easily related to the biblical accounts, but it may be that such systematisation was the task rather of his later successors.[88] The ambiguities regarding Marcion's position do in any case make sufficient sense within the context of the period.

Certainly the status of the source of creation was a topic of intense contemporary debate, often with inconsistent conclusions. As underlined by the model of the craftsman, the process of creation was routinely understood as formation: In the *Timaeus* God sees 'the whole visible system not at peace, and moving in a way that is uncontrolled and disorderly' (Plato, *Tim.* 29E), and Philo, perhaps consciously, alludes to this passage when he appeals to 'one of the ancients', 'that the Father and Creator was good; on which account he did not grudge the substance a share of his own excellent nature, since it had nothing good of itself but was able to become everything' (Philo, *De Opif.* 5 [21]). When Justin similarly insists that

86 Tertullian goes on to argue that Marcion implied a parallel structure for the supreme being and so a further three 'substances of divinity' (excluding evil); adding to these Christ and the yet-to-come Creator's Christ would result in nine gods. However, according to his interpretation of the healing of the lepers, Marcion took 'by word alone' as a sign of his God's creative power (*AM* IV. 9.7).

87 See p. 129 above.

88 Ernst U. Schüle, 'Der Ursprung des Bösen bei Marcion', *ZRGG* 16 (1964), 23–42, 36 argues that Marcion was forced by a lack of biblically sanctioned alternative to attribute evil to matter. For the (inconsistent) development of three principles in later Marcionite tradition see, for example, pp. 94–6 above, and Rottenwöhrer, *Unde Malum?*, 38–47.

'we have been taught that he created every principle as good from formless matter (ἀμόρφος ὕλη) for the sake of man', he would have been in good company; he cites as his authority Genesis 1.1–3, and he claims that this is the source of Plato's own teaching of how God took shapeless matter to create the world (Justin, *Apol.* 10.2; 59). However, such language did not prevent debate as to the precise status of such 'matter', and in what sense that which is 'disordered' can be said to participate in 'being'.[89] For example, Plutarch insists that creation was from matter (ὕλη): It was not out of that 'which was not' but out of what was disordered; nonetheless, at times he does seem to hint at the presence of an evil principle that might be responsible for that which is disorderly, a position that does have the potential to move towards a dualism (Plutarch, *De Anim.* 1012; 1014).[90]

Among other contemporary exponents, Numenius' position is particularly obscure, although it does indicate how such potential might be developed. Although initially he appears to teach a First and a Second Intellect or God, the Second itself becomes a dyad and so can be described as a Second and a Third God; this is a consequence of its gazing both on the noetic and on matter, a split that is further reinforced because matter itself is dyadic (Numenius, *Frag.* 11).[91] Underlying this is a further opposition, namely that between the One, or a Monad, and the Dyad, an opposition which again may owe something to the contemporary revival of so-called Pythagoreanism. Unsurprisingly, this aspect of Numenius' teaching has provoked considerable debate, particularly since according to one Fragment he identified the three Gods as Father, Maker, and what is made: 'the world according to him is the third God' (*Frag.* 21). Even if this is in fact a later misunderstanding of Numenius' position, he undoubtedly does imply that matter is not derivative from the Monad but is in opposition to it, and to some extent is never fully brought into order by the Demiurge.[92] Although

89 See Numenius, *Frag.* 4b; Athenagoras, *Leg.* 4.2 identifies 'matter' as 'what has come into being' (γενητή), and with reference to God continues 'that which is does not come into being but that which is not'.

90 See John Dillon, 'Plutarch and God: Theodicy and Cosmogony in the Thought of Plutarch', ed. Dorothea Frede and André Laks, *Traditions of Theology: Studies in Hellenistic Theology, its Background and Aftermath* (Ph. Ant. 89; Leiden: Brill, 2002), 223–37, 225–32, who refers to Plutarch, *On the E* 393F–394A and the discussion of 'some other God or daemon' in relation to nature in decay and becoming.

91 See Frede, 'Numenius'.

92 See Dillon, 'Numenius', 401–2. Karin Alt, *Weltflucht und Weltbejahung. Zur Frage des Dualismus bei Plutarch, Numenios, Plotin* (Abhandlungen des Geistes- und Sozialwissenschaftlichen Klasse 8, 1993; Mainz: Akadamie der Wissenschaften und der Literatur; Stuttgart: Steiner, 1993), 27–30, ascribes Numenius' dualism to his Syrian/oriental origins, but denies any gnostic influence in Plutarch.

this would be a further step, it is easy to imagine how negative ideas about the world might bring the Demiurge down with them.[93]

Philo epitomises the problem as it emerges when philosophical terminology is brought together with biblical imagery: God, who could have no immediate contact with 'limitless and chaotic matter', necessarily had recourse to intermediaries in creation, and yet can also be described as the one who 'called things that are not into being, order out of disorder' (Philo, *De Spec.Leg.* I. 60 [327–9]; IV. 35 [187]). Athenagoras appears to accept that matter is that on which God works creatively, appealing to the model of a craftsman (τεχνίτης), even while describing it as 'perishable and corruptible' (Athenagoras, *Leg.* 15). Only clearly with Theophilus of Antioch is there a deliberate challenge to the Platonists who declared that both God and matter were uncreated; Theophilus asserts that God's power would be seen, not in making the world out of some substrate matter, but in making whatever he wished 'out of things that are not' and in endowing it with soul and movement (Theophilus, *Ad Autol.* II. 4). Yet such a view seems to be criticised by his contemporary, Galen: Galen, assuming that creation is a matter of the ordering (κοσμέω) of matter, lambasts Moses for attributing to God's will alone how God creates, preferring Plato's acknowledgement that some things were impossible by nature and so that God did the best from what was possible (Galen, *De Usu Part.* XI. 14).[94] Another prime opponent of Theophilus was Hermogenes, who denied *creatio ex nihilo*, not least, it would seem, because this would involve making God responsible for evil. It may be no accident that Tertullian's argument against Marcion partly echoes that which he also made against Hermogenes;[95] certainly, he, and perhaps Marcion's contemporary followers, were addressing this problem in a new intellectual context.

Thus, the problem of evil, which, as has been seen, hovers behind the character and activities ascribed to the Demiurge, also haunts debates over the nature and sources of any creative activity. On the one hand, there is the question of the character of 'matter' as the substrate of such activity; yet from this might follow the question whether that character continues, either

[93] Jaap Mansfeld, 'Bad World and Demiurge: A "Gnostic" Motif from Parmenides and Empedocles to Lucretius and Philo', ed. R. van den Broeck and Maarten J. Vermaseren, *Studies in Gnosticism and Hellenistic Religions: Presented to Gilles Quispel on the Occasion of His 65th Birthday* (EPROER 91; Leiden: Brill, 1981), 261–314, argues that the idea of an evil demiurge was a possibility in Greek philosophy even if never taken up as such.

[94] See David Sedley, *Creationism and Its Critics in Antiquity* (Sather Classical Lectures 66; Berkeley, CA: University of California Press, 2007), 241–3.

[95] See above p. 343, and Braun, Contre *Marcion*, I, 299–301.

because 'matter' continues or because its defects remain part of that which is created. Philo distinguished between that which God called 'good', and so which is worthy of praise, and 'souless' matter, which he had used for his creative activity, and which, Philo is clear, is 'of itself perishable' (Philo, *Quis Haer.* 32 [160]). When Athenagoras explains the origins of human evil in terms of heavenly rebellion and fall, he blames in particular 'the ruler of matter and the forms in it and others who belong to the first firmament' (Athenagoras, *Leg.* 24.5); similarly, in Tatian demons are a reflection of matter and of evil (Tatian, *Orat.* 15.4). In Marcion's later followers matter would indeed almost acquire a character of its own, as is most sharply illustrated by Eznik of Kolb.[96] However, Marcion's own language may have been more 'biblical', drawing rather on the language of 'this age' and 'the world', which he found in Paul (1 Cor. 2.6; Gal. 6.14) – a move that was also made by John and by Ignatius.[97]

Yet the traditional scriptural position brought its own dangers. Early Christian Apologists readily started from the ordering and justice of the universe to recognise God as the one who 'moves' and 'holds together' (Aristides, *Apol.* 1; Athenagoras, *Leg.* 4.2). On the other hand, a standard theme in the Apologists is a vigorous invective against the veneration of the natural order, such as of the sun or moon.[98] Athenagoras appeals to Plato who affirmed the beauty of 'the elements' (στοιχεῖα) but who also firmly asserted that they are subject to change and so cannot be the objects of worship; indeed for Athenagoras the failure to distinguish the created from the uncreated as proper objects of worship is replicated in the failure to distinguish between matter (ὕλη) and God, and is manifested in the worship of 'idols made from matter' (*Leg.* 15.1–16.4).

Such polemics have their roots in a long Jewish tradition 'against idolatry'; yet the Apologists turned these against the Jews themselves, creating a powerful rhetorical distance. Aristides acknowledges that the Jews have come closer to the truth than the other nations, when they say that 'the one God is creator of all and all-powerful, and that no-one is to be worshipped other than this God', but he then maintains that Christians alone actually sustain this conviction (Aristides, *Apol.* 14.3; 15.3). Even more

96 See p. 177, above.

97 See above, pp. 258–60; see also John 12.31; 14.30; 16.11; Ignatius, *Eph.* 17.1; 19.1. Alan F. Segal, 'Ruler of This World: Attitudes about Mediator Figures and the Importance of Sociology for Self-definition', ed. E. P. Sanders, *Jewish and Christian Self-Definition*, Vol. 2 (Philadelphia, PA: Fortress, 1981), 245–68, attempts to establish a link with the later rabbinic epithet for God.

98 See Palmer, 'Atheism, Apologetic and Negative Theology'.

sharply, for the 'Preaching of Peter' their purported worship of the created order, including of angels, demonstrates that Jews no more genuinely *know* God than do the Greeks, despite their claims to do so (*Ker.Pet.* in Clement of Alexandria, *Strom* V. 5.39–41).

Within a Pauline tradition this set of associations could be even more potent. According to Tertullian, Marcion read Galatians 3.15 with 4.3, interpreting the claim that 'when we were children we were subjected to the elements of the world in order to serve them' as in some way referring to the situation experienced by humankind; in Galatians 4.8–9 these same 'weak and impoverished elements' are, for Marcion, 'those who in nature are Gods' – all readily taken as being references to the Demiurge. Tertullian presumably was unaware of the risks that he was taking when he himself identified the 'elements' of Galatians 4.8 with the 'rudimentary aspects of the law', despite having taken those referred to in 4.3 as the sun and stars worshipped by 'the nations' (*AM* V. 4.1, 5).[99]

Later Marcionite exegesis may have taken a further step. In the account of Marcion's myth reported by Eznik of Kolb creation is the result of intercourse between the God of the Law and Matter, but Matter's resentment led to the seduction of the people through adultery (*De Deo* 358).[100] Such more elaborate myths are almost certainly secondary to the earlier traditions that ascribe the creation of body and soul to the Demiurge; moreover, they presuppose that matter is both evil and pre-existent, a view alien to that of the Jewish traditions. Nonetheless, there may be earlier roots to such speculation. Justin also refers to a Jewish interpretation of Genesis 1.26–7 that God was addressing the elements; in a long discussion of the verse in *Genesis Rabbah* 8.3 the suggestions that God consulted 'the works of heaven and earth' or that which had been made on the previous days, are posed only to be ignored. The scriptural text generated a number of lines of interpretation, which may have intersected, whether by chance or through cross-influence and -resistance.

99 See above, p. 258, and Edwards 'Pauline Platonism', 217. Athenagoras, *Leg.* 16.3–4 (cited above) echoes Gal. 4.9 in his description of the 'poor and weak' (heavenly) elements.

100 Drijvers, 'Marcion's Reading of Gal 4,8', argues that these ideas do go back to Marcion, who did have a cosmosgonic myth of creation; see also Menahem Kister, 'Some early Jewish and Christian exegetical Problems and the Dynamics of Monotheism', JSJ 37 (2006), 548–93, 570–2. For the later development, see Michel Tardieu, 'L'imitation du monde selon Marcion d'après les auteurs orientaux', ed. Philippe Gignoux, *Ressembler au Monde: Nouveaux documents sur la théme du macro-microcosme dans l'antiquité orientale* (Bibl. de l'École des Hautes Études: Section des Sciences Religeuses; Turnhout: Brepols: 1999), 41–53.

Marcion echoes his contemporaries, but goes much further than them, in denying that the natural order can witness to God. More fundamentally, however, he accepts as do they that the Scriptures speak of the Creator; however, the story he reads from these is a consistently negative one, of a God who repeatedly demonstrates himself to be weak, unreliable, self-contradictory, and given to irrational acts of anger and wanton cruelty. With this must be allied Marcion's extreme negative evaluation of creation, which will be discussed in what follows.

Creation and the Law

In scholarly accounts of Marcion his attitude to the Law has been routinely located within a tradition that went back to Paul and continued to his own context.[101] This is certainly important, but what is notable about Marcion's position is his association of Law with God as Creator. Tertullian's defence indicates that Marcion saw the command that the first-created beings not eat of the tree (Gen. 2.18) as exemplary of the Creator's operation by law (*AM* II. 4.5). He would not have been the first to do this. The status of law as mandated by the nature of creation, a natural law, is an important philosophical concept. Again in the *Timaeus* one of the first acts of the Demiurge is to establish his laws (Plato, *Tim.* 41E–42E). The same theme is found in Stoicism.[102] Yet Jewish sources also linked the order of the universe with the divine Law, and hence located human disobedience and merited judgement within the creative intentions and activity of God (*1 Enoch* 1–9). The biblical theme of the word of God as active harmoniously in creation and in the giving of the Law is an important apologetic topos.[103] For Philo the Jewish festivals point to the created order, and on an individual level obedience to the Law both signifies and effects a person's recognition of their place within the universe (Philo, *De Spec.Leg.* I. 49–50 [262–70]; II. 28 [150–8]; *De Opif.* 23 [143–4]): Moses wished to show that 'the Father and Maker of the cosmos was in truth the Lawgiver; further the person who would observe the laws will embrace following nature' (*Mos.* II. 8 [48]). Thus, world and Law are co-existent and interdependent.[104] This was an obvious apologetic topos: An anonymous synagogue sermon on Jonah describes God as 'the Lord of

101 See below, pp. 410–14.
102 See Woltmann, 'Der Geschichtliche Hintergrund', 32; Willem C. van Unnik, 'Is 1 Clement 20 Purely Stoic?', *VC* 4 (1950), 181–9.
103 So Aristobulus in Eusebius, *PE* XIII. 12.3–4.
104 See Wilfried Eisele, *Ein unerschütterliches Reich: Die mittelplatonische Umformung des Parusiegedankens im Hebräerbrief* (BZNW 116; Berlin: de Gruyter, 2003), 379.

the Law', clearly indicating the law visible from nature that all people should observe.[105] The influence of such apologetics may be detected when Numenius, in the so-called Exodus fragment, labels the Demiurge, without explanation, as 'the law giver' (νομοθέτης) (Numenius, *Frag.* 13), an association that is also made by Theophilus of Antioch (*Ad Autol.* III. 19.1).[106]

Both within this tradition and as a challenge to it, Paul already links the Jewish Law with the 'elements of the world', and hence as functioning in much the same way and so holding humankind in check.[107] The tensions that this would generate are self-evident: The *Letter of Ptolemy to Flora* separates those parts of the law that it ascribes to Moses and to the elders, from the first whose source, the 'one who established the law', it identifies as 'the demiurge and maker', different in 'being' from the supreme God, although by no means evil.[108] For Ptolemy it is this origin that similarly explains the composite character of this subdivision also: Part is allegorical, part is 'interwoven with inferiority and injustice', and so is destroyed by the Saviour, and part, 'properly called Law' yet 'pure but imperfect', is fulfilled by him. Law and the created order presumably evince the same lack of perfection, and so together reflect the character of their source. Even Tertullian, who is keen to associate Moses with the Law, recognises the presence of Law before Moses (*AJ* 2.9; *Apol.* 18.2–3).[109]

Certainly Marcion identified the Law laid down by the Demiurge with the Law as it was articulated in the Scriptures. The character of that Law and the character of the Demiurge are inseparable from each other, and as shall be seen, the contradictions of the Law expose the inconsistency and even deliberate deceit exercised by the Demiurge over those under his sway. For Marcion, it was this that constituted the story told by the Scriptures, although how far he therefore treated the miscreants of that story as heroes, to be saved by the Supreme God, as already suggested by Irenaeus' account

105 Ps.Philo, *On Jonah* 30 (115) in Folker Siegert and Jacques de Roulet, transl, notes and comm., with the assistance of Jean-Jacques Aubert and Nicolas Cochand, *Pseudon-Philon. Prédications Synagogales* (SC 435; Paris: Éditions du Cerf, 1999).

106 See above, p. 314, n. 61, and Burnyeat, 'Platonism in the Bible', 149–59, for the debate whether in this excerpt Numenius also refers to the First God as 'the one who is (ὁ ὤν)' (ὁ μὲν γε ὢν σπέρμα πάσης ψυχῆς σπείρει). See also Longinus, *On the Sublime* 9. 7–8 quoted below at p. 365.

107 See above, p. 354; George van Kooten, *Cosmic Christology in Paul and the Pauline School: Colossians and Ephesians in the Context of Graeco-Roman Cosmology with a New Synopsis* (WUNT 2.171; Tübingen: Mohr Siebeck, 2003), 59–79.

108 Epiphanius, *Pan.* 33.5–7; see above at p. 348.

109 See Claude Aziza, 'La figure de Moïse chez Tertullien', *Annales de la Faculté des Lettres et Sciences Humaines de Nice* 35 (1979), 275–95.

of the descent 'ad inferos' and of the salvation of Cain and others, is uncertain.[110] The Demiurge as author of the Law would indeed be identified as the Jewish God, but this was, in an important sense secondary: It is significant but not surprising that Marcion apparently did not use 'God of the Jews' as a title for the Demiurge, as, for example, did Satornilus who belonged to an Antiochene Christian tradition that did develop a sharp antithesis to the Jews.[111] It is only later polemicists who represent Marcion as identifying the Demiurge specifically as 'the God of the Jews'.[112]

SCRIPTURE AND EXEGESIS

Although many of the principles that underlie Marcion's cosmological concerns belong within the philosophical framework of his time, it has become apparent that they acquire a particular focus in relation to the scriptural account of the Creator. It was from Scripture that the Creator could be characterised as loving war, inconsistent, responsible for evil, and so on. In this sense, for Marcion Scripture – which Christians would come to call the Old Testament – was a primary evidential authority, although not a moral or a spiritual one. To this end, it would seem, he used it in different ways, with two applications being particularly notable. The first, which is primary, develops problems in Scripture to which others also had drawn attention. The second is a form of proof-texting, using Scripture to demonstrate the true character of the God of whom it speaks, such as the appeal to Isaiah 45.7 (*AM* II. 14.1), or the various 'paradigms' that contributed to his 'Antitheses'.[113] Obviously these two usages overlap, and the second may sometimes be a secondary development by Marcion's followers, or indeed by their opponents – as, for example, when Jerome claims that 'the Marcionites and Manichaeans' cite Micah 1.12 as evidence that 'the God of the law is the producer of evils' (Jerome, *In Michaeam* I. 1.10/15).

Marcion, according to Tertullian's picture, adopted the categories of a critical reading of authoritative texts that, as has been seen, were standard practice at the time: 'Now to all the Questions...' (*AM* II. 5.1; cf. I. 9.7; 21.3; III. 9.1; 11.5 etc.).[114] Initially those questions do cluster around the human capacity for evil, both as created by God and as infused with the divine

[110] See above, p. 46 on Irenaeus, *AH* I. 27.2.
[111] See Enrico Norelli, 'Situation des Apocryphes Pétriniens', *Apocrypha* 2 (1991), 31–83.
[112] See above, p. 113. Origen cites Celsus as referring to those who 'maintain that the God of the Jews is accursed', but this may be Celsus' wording (*C.Cels.* VI. 27).
[113] See above, pp. 285–8; so also Origen, p. 137 above. [114] See above, pp. 306–11.

breath; even casting blame on the devil does not absolve the Creator (II. 10.1). Tertullian's appeal to misunderstandings arising from the translation of Greek terms, for example, of πνοή at Genesis 2.7, acknowledges the 'philological' nature of the exercise (II. 9.2). As already noted, this framework extends to questions of justice and mercy, often prefigured scripturally in the persons of Cain and Abel.[115] Yet they also extend beyond this to examples that undermine what might be 'appropriate' of God, a further contemporary norm: the *lex talionis*, the food laws, the detailed sacrificial legislation (II. 19). What for Tertullian are yet further 'blasphemies' were in Marcion's eyes evidences from the scriptural narrative itself of the Creator's deficiencies: Of inconsistency in the injunctions to the Hebrews to steal from the Egyptians, to Joshua to march around Jericho for seven days thus contravening the Sabbath, and to Moses to make an 'image' of the serpent (II. 20–2); of a tendency to a change of mind, whether towards the choice of Saul or the condemnation of Nineveh (II. 23–4); of admissions of ignorance regarding Adam's whereabouts or Cain's criminality; and of weakness in the face of Moses' intercessions on behalf of a people destined for destruction (II. 25–7).

In principle, and in several specific instances, these are not new. Jewish apologetic literature had already addressed actual or potential criticisms of their Scriptures levelled by critical Hellenistic readers. Aristobulus (Eusebius, *PE* VIII. 10; XIII. 12), and Aristeas had given a full symbolic or allegorical reading of Jewish Law (*Aristeas* 144–67). Philo provides the richest store both of objections potentially levelled against the Scriptures and of attempts to address them, although this is a matter of the survival of his writings and not necessarily evidence that he was alone in so doing. His *Questions and Answers on Genesis* address many of the problems that others, including Marcion, pick up: 'Why did Moses say, "He brought the animals to Adam that he might see what he would call them", when God can never be in doubt?'; 'Why does God ask Adam, "Where are you?" when he knows everything?'; other questions appear less potentially contentious: 'Did the serpent speak with a human voice?' (*QG* I. 21; 45; 32). No doubt in some cases these questions belong to the normal activity of the school setting as well as to that of actual criticism from sceptics – and the two are not exclusive of each other. Objections may have come from within or without the Jewish community. Philo defends the story of the Tower of Babel against those who denigrate 'the ancestral way of life' through a sustained mockery of the

[115] See above, pp. 344–6.

Scriptures, yet whom he also imagines protesting, why did God deprive them of the benefits of a universal language (*De Confus.* 2–5 [2–15])? Although the identity and location of such objectors remain unclear, for them the self-evident pervasive presence of myth undermines any claim to represent a norm of truth. Philo himself attempts to tread a careful line between the literalism of some defenders and such sophistry through a careful allegorical reading.

Perhaps most familiar, and most easily dealt with, were those anthropomorphisms that presented God as possessing physical characteristics, such as references to the face, eyes, or feet of God, or to God as moving from one place to another.[116] The Christian narrative both exacerbated and offered a solution to such language: What might be impossible of a God conceived in Platonic terms, could be ascribed to a pre-incarnate Christ, and, even more, could invite reflection on the significance of the incarnate one (*AM* II. 16.3). However, it was the attribution to God of emotions, most notably of anger, that posed a particular problem. Tertullian indicates that Marcion made much of this, but Philo had already found himself negotiating a path between acknowledging that the attribution to the gods of anger, jealousy, and passion is a device used by the poets along with thunderbolts and whirlwind, and discerning a real pedagogical purpose in the use of such language of a God who had strict moral demands (Philo, *Deus Immut.* 13–15 [60–73]).

However, a careful reader who knew the Scriptures would readily find examples that challenged any easy explanation. Two striking examples attributed to Marcion that come not from Torah but from the prophetic narratives are those of Elisha's bears and Elijah's fire; these are presented not as 'problems' in themselves but as demonstrating for Marcion the true character of the Creator God by 'antithesis' (2 Kings 2.23–4; 1.10; *AM* IV. 23.4, 7–8). However, these passages, too, may also already have been the topic of contemporary concern: In the *Testament of Abraham* God rebukes Abraham for willing similar types of retribution on the various wrongdoers in the world, and for failing to acknowledge God's mercy, and the same pattern has been traced elsewhere (*Test.Abr.* 10).[117] Tertullian's response to the former of the two incidents, that these were not children but

[116] E.g. Gen. 4.16; 11.5; Philo, *De Post.* 1–9 [1–31]; *De Confus.* 27 [134–40]. Justin asserts that the Jewish teachers take verses such as Ps. 8.4 to mean that God really did have 'hands and feet and fingers and a soul', and hence could be the subject of epiphanies on earth (Justin, *Dial.* 114.3).

[117] See Dale C. Allison, 'Rejecting Violent Judgement: Luke 9:52–56 and its Relatives', *JBL* 121 (2002), 459–78, who notes that Num. 16 is also seen as problematic.

boys old enough for responsibility, is also echoed in Talmudic rabbinic debate where the Hebrew 'little boys' is taken, *i.a.*, as referring not to their chronological age but to their immature behaviour (*bSotah* 46b–47a).[118] On the other hand, Marcion's rejection of circumcision because of the pain it causes a child, as reported by Origen, takes up an established theme of internal Christian debate, with parallels in rabbinic sources, but it does so from a distinctive perspective (Origen, *Comm. in Rom.* II. 9,469–71).[119]

A number of the other charges that, according to Tertullian, were levelled by Marcion can be paralleled elsewhere. God's apparent display of ignorance in Genesis 3.9 is echoed by the *Testimony of Truth* (NH IX.3) 46.18–47.22, it is softened by the Targumic traditions which read it as 'How?' rather than 'Where?', and it is explained by Theophilus of Antioch as providing Adam the opportunity 'for repentance and confession' (*Ad Autol.* II. 26).[120] Accounts of God's regret or repentance could open the door to more serious charges of his moral culpability or incompetence. Philo considers Genesis 6.5 at length, rejecting any overhasty interpretation that would be in danger of undervaluing the seriousness of human wickedness; instead he concludes that the verse refers only to God's internal reflection, which was in no way inconsistent with divine foreknowledge (Philo, *Deus Immut.* 5–10 [20–50]; *QG* II. 54). Marcion's appeal to the same divine inconsistency towards Nineveh (Jon. 3.10; 4.2) had already been anticipated by an anonymous synagogue sermon 'On Jonah', which explains that God has sovereignty over Law and over judgement, and so can properly remove the sentence of death.[121] In the *Targum to Jonah* 3.9–10; 4.2, it is the people of Nineveh who repent, and only then does God 'restrain his *memra*': Here, the reference to God's '*memra*' or 'word' distances God's direct action in a similar way to Christian appeals to the Logos. More generally, the later targumic

118 The participants include an anonymous tanna' and other second century rabbis; the tradition is also reported that Elisha's sickness and death were, *i.a.*, a consequence of this incident.

119 See Maren R. Niehoff, 'Circumcision as a Marker of Identity: Philo, Origen and the Rabbis on Genesis 17:1–14', *JSQ* 10 (2003), 78–123, who notes the shared question in Justin (*Dial.* 19.4) and *Genesis Rabbah* 11.6 as to why circumcision was not given to Adam.

120 For the targumic traditions see Étan Levine, 'Some Characteristics of Pseudo-Jonathan Targum to Genesis', *Augustinianum* 11 (1971), 89–103, 96; idem, *The Aramaic Version of the Bible: Contents and Context* (BZAW 174; Berlin: de Gruyter, 1988), 47–56, notes the variety of responses to the problem of anthropomorphisms in the Targums.

121 Ps.Philo, *On Jonah* 30 (115) and 46 (182–6) (in Siegert and de Roulet, *Pseudon-Philon*). For the history of the debate provoked by Jonah see Elias J. Bickermann, 'Les deux erreurs du prophète Jonas', *RHPhR* 45 (1965), 232–64, who notes the similar debates in Graeco-Roman thought as to whether an oracle or other divine judgement could be averted.

tradition is careful to circumvent the problem of divine regret, and earlier parallels may support the antiquity of these efforts.[122]

Perhaps a closer reading of the Scriptures is indicated by accusations of apparent divine inconsistency, particularly between different commands given by God at different times. Tertullian expostulates particularly heatedly over the Marcionite appeal to the injunction that the Hebrews, fleeing from Egypt, take with them their masters' gold and silver, surely in clear contradiction to the law against stealing (Exod. 12.35–36; *AM* II. 20).[123] Again, Philo testifies to the currency of the debate, defending the action of the Hebrews against those who accuse them of avarice, and explaining it as no more than their claiming but a fraction of the payment due to them for their long enforced labour (Philo, *De Vita Mosis*, I. 25 [140–2]). The incident also sparked debate among the rabbis, particularly since the stolen goods included 'gods' (*Gen.R.* 61. 2; *bSan.* 91a). Tertullian's claim that the Hebrews 'even today' make this their own defence against the Marcionites may well have some truth in it, even if in fact this was part of a more general apologetic. That this was the case is supported by the sharp warning uttered by an anonymous predecessor of Irenaeus against those who used the story as a basis for harsh denigration of 'the people'; he reminds his Gentile audience, who have similarly 'gone out', of the goods which rightly belonged to their previous neighbours and oppressors, and from which they have benefitted, and he warns them against unwarranted feelings of superiority (Irenaeus, *AH* IV. 30). In this case these detractors would have been Christians, but they may also have been heirs to more extensive debates about these events.

122 See further Étan Levine, *The Aramaic Version of Jonah* (Jerusalem: Jerusalem Academic Press, 1975), 45, 88–92; Daniel J. Harrington and Anthony J. Saldarini, *Targum Jonathan to the Former Prophets: Introduction, Translation and Notes* (Aramaic Bible 10; Edinburgh: T&T Clark, 1987); Eveline van Staalduine-Sulman, *The Targum of Samuel* (Studies in the Aramaic Interpretation of Scripture 1; Leiden: Brill, 2002), 325–6, 335 on 1 Sam. 15.11, 35. Leivy Smolar and Moses Aberbach, *Studies in Targum Jonathan to the Prophets* (New York: KTAV, 1983), 134, list a number of passages where God's repentance is avoided, including those also used by Marcion. The earliest reference in Jewish discursive exegetical sources appears to be by Kimchi who made heavy use of Targum Jonathan; for this and for a contemporary response to 1 Sam. 15 see Yairah Amit, '"The Glory of Israel Does Not Deceive or Change His Mind": On the Reliability of Narrator and Speakers in Biblical Narrative', Proof-texts 12 (1992), 201–12.

123 Compare *AM* IV. 24.3, where this example is cited as an 'antithesis', in contrast to Jesus' injunction to his disciples in Luke 9.3; 10.4. At *AM* V. 13.6 Tertullian suggests that Marcion may have cited the story in his interpretation of Rom. 2.21 (so Braun, *Contre Marcion*, V, 263, n. 6). On this and what follows see Joel S. Allen, *The Despoliation of Egypt in Pre-Rabbinic, Rabbinic and Patristic Traditions* (VCSup. 92; Leiden: Brill, 2008).

Marcion's appeal to the making of the bronze serpent as contradicting the Creator's rejection of images (*AM* II. 22) also belongs within a continuing debate that predated him and continued long after.[124] According to Wisd. 16.5–8 the incident was in fact a reminder to the people of God's Law, and that God's word alone could heal; the Mishnah similarly sees it as directing the people to God, whereas Philo offers an allegorical interpretation of the event.[125] On the other hand, for Christian writers it quickly invited a Christological interpretation (John 3.14–15; *Barn.* 12); indeed, for Justin Martyr it is precisely the contradiction with the prohibition of images that establishes its proper prophetic purpose (Justin, *Dial.* 94).

Rather more recondite is the appeal to the seven-day circumvention of Jericho, in inevitable contravention of Sabbath observance. However, here too it is likely that Marcion was participating in current debates, although the evidence is more scattered. The statement that the city fell 'on the seventh day' (Josh. 6.4, 15) inevitably invited interpretation. Josephus himself circumvents the problem by tying the events to the days of Passover, and thus according them a festal character (Josephus, *AJ* V. 1.4–6 [20–7]). However, it did become a matter of debate as to whether the seventh day here was indeed the Sabbath, an assumption that forms the basis of further halakhic debate perhaps by the third century (*Gen.R.* 47.10; *jMoed Qatan* 2.4).[126] Although this evidence is later, Jewish avoidance of fighting on the Sabbath was a matter of debate both by outsiders and internally, and while Josephus does not connect the fall of Jericho with this concern, others may have done so.[127] In fact, Tertullian himself in the *Against the Jews* appeals both to this example and to the account of the Maccabees fighting on the Sabbath as evidence that the abolition of the Sabbath was no new thing (Tertullian, *AJ* 4.8–10). If that work is prior, then either Tertullian is providing Marcion with an objection that he himself had invented and dealt with previously, or Marcion was responding to current debate and even to Christian argument.[128] However, when it comes to countering him

124 See Marc Turnage, 'Is It the Serpent That Heals? An Ancient Jewish *Theologoumenon* and the Developing Faith in Jesus', ed. Kenneth E. Pomykala, *Israel in the Wilderness* (TBN 10; Leiden: Brill, 2008), 71–88.

125 *mRHS* 3.8; Philo, *Leg.Alleg.* II. 20 [79–81].

126 In both these cases this appeal is made in a discussion between R. Johannan ben Levi and Resh Lakish. See also *jSabb.* 1.7.

127 See Herold Weiss, 'The Sabbath in the Writings of Josephus', *JSJ* 29 (1998), 363–90, 370–80, on the issue of fighting on the Sabbath.

128 Victorinus of Pettau makes the same argument as Tertullian but adds that Joshua told them to circumvent Jericho on the Sabbath and to wage war against the foreigners (*De Fab.Mund.* 6). Aphrahat, who displays some knowledge of Jewish traditions, sees a positive

Tertullian takes a different tack: Parading the ark of God under God's orders was not human work but divine (*AM* II. 21.2). Tertullian's own appeal to Elisha's healing of the Shunamite woman's son as being on the Sabbath illustrates the creativity of the search for examples in debate (*AM* IV. 12.15, contrast 2 Kings 4.23); whereas his timing of the event is apparently without parallel, it is not surprising that this incident did become a key proof-text in arguments about the resurrection of the dead, perhaps also as part of a long interpretive tradition (*PRE* 32).[129]

Inconsistency was not only self-evidently 'inappropriate' for God; it might also suggest a lack of divine foreknowledge, something that Christian attitudes to the Sabbath or to sacrifice had had to counter already (Justin, *Dial.* 92.5). Thus, once again, there are glimpses here of a complex web of debates concerning the interpretation and the status of the Jewish Scriptures that could be taken up for different ends and in different contexts. It is no surprise that some are commonplaces among demiurgical texts that demote the Creator: The *Hypostasis of the Archons* rewrites the narrative of Genesis 3 to emphasise the envy and ignorance of the 'Chief Ruler': 'The Female Spiritual Principle came [in] the Snake… (and) said: "With death you shall not die, for it was out of jealousy that he said this to you"…Then the chief Ruler came; and he said, "Adam! Where are you?" – for he did not understand what had happened' (*NH* II.4. 89,31–90,21).[130] Yet the scattered evidence for the continuity of such objections, and for their emergence in such different settings and times, suggests that they were not only topics of concern in internal debate, but were also overheard or easily raised independently by outsiders.[131] When Theophilus of Antioch merely says, 'Someone will say, "Was man created mortal by nature?" Not at all. "Why, then, immortal?" That we do not say', it is impossible to identify that 'someone' with any certainty (Theophilus, *Ad Autol.* II. 27). More than a century after Philo, Celsus reiterates many of the earlier objections, for example, ridiculing the ascription to God of anger, threats, and other human

relationship between Joshua's destruction of Jericho on the Sabbath and the dissolution of the world on Jesus' seventh day (*Dem.* 21.11). The question of the contravention of the Sabbath does not appear to be raised in Jewish exegesis before David Kimchi.

129 See Jon D. Levinson, *The Death and Resurrection of the Beloved Son: The Transformation of Child Sacrifice in Judaism and Christianity* (New Haven, CT: Yale University Press, 1995), 224.

130 *Val.Exp.* (NH XI.2), 38.38, says that (the creator) God 'almost regretted' he had created the world.

131 See above, p. 339. See further, Woltmann, 'Geschichtliche Hintergrund', 34, and, more generally, Edmund Stein, *Alttestamentliche Bibelkritik in der Späthellenistischen Literatur* (Lwów: Związkowe Zakłady Graficzne, 1935).

emotions, protesting at divine acknowledgement of ignorance, and mocking the assigning of days and nights to creation even before the creation of sun and moon had taken place (Origen, *C.Cels.* IV. 71–3; VI. 58–64; cf. Philo, *Leg. Alleg.* I. 2–3 [2–7]).[132] This suggests that it would be mistaken to trace all echoes of such views, or of defences against them, to the explicit or covert influence of Marcion – as has been suggested even of rabbinic sources.[133] It would be better to view him as one of the many voices engaged in these debates, even if he was among the more systematic and insistent ones. One of his successors, Apelles, drew up a series of syllogisms that undoubtedly included many such objections, yet when Ambrose repeats them later it is presumably because they continue to cause trouble: Why does the tree of life have more power to give life than the power of God; why should Adam be condemned for disobedience if he does not have knowledge of good and evil? (Ambrose, *On Paradise* 5.28; 6.32). At the same time, new ones easily accrued to the list.[134] Similarly, many of the rabbinic discussions are in sources too late to provide an immediate context for Marcion; in some cases they may be responses to the fourth-century encounter between Christianity and Judaism.[135]

As was the case among contemporary readers of Homer, such 'problems' generated different strategies of interpretation, which could be equally hotly debated. Philo himself knew that some permitted such myths an educational purpose, at least for the masses, although it is not clear how far he himself subscribed to this.[136] Celsus certainly knew of those who interpreted the scriptural stories through similar allegorical techniques as were applied to the Greek myths, but he was determined to deny the validity of such a

132 Stein, *Alttestamentliche Bibelkritik*, 10, suggests that Celsus had read Philo. See also Peder Borgen, 'Philo of Alexandria as Exegete', ed. Alan J. Hauser and Duane F. Watson, *A History of Biblical Interpretation, Vol. 1: The Ancient Period* (Grand Rapids, MI: Eerdmans, 2003), 114–43, 127.

133 So Rosalie Gershenzon and Elieser Slomovic, 'A Second Century Jewish-Gnostic Debate: Rabbi Jose ben Halafta and the Matrona', *JSJ* 16 (1985), 1–41: Clemens Thoma, 'Rabbinische Reaktion gegen die Gnosis', *Judaica* 44 (1988), 2–14. Levine, 'Some Characteristics', 95–6, suggests that Cain represents a Marcionite position. Ithamar Gruenwald, 'The Problem of Anti-Gnostic Polemic in Rabbinic Literature', ed. van den Broeck and Vermaseren, *Studies in Gnosticism and Hellenistic Religions*, 171–89, is sceptical of there being such polemic.

134 See above, pp. 288–9 on the *Dialogue of Adamantius*.

135 So Maren Niehoff, '*Creatio ex Nihilo* Theology in *Genesis Rabbah* in Light of Christian Exegesis', *HTR* 99 (2006), 37–64; Rimon Kasher, 'The Palestinian Targum to Genesis 4:8: A New Approach to an Old Controversy', ed. Isaac Kalimi and Peter J. Haas, *Biblical Interpretation in Judaism and Christianity* (LHB/OTS 439; London: T&T Clark, 2006), 33–43, associates the debate between Cain and Abel with Christian debates over Pelagianism.

136 See Adam Kamesar, 'Philo, the Presence of "Paideutic" Myth in the Pentateuch, and the "Principles" or *Kephalaia* of Mosaic Discourse', *Stud.Phil.Ann.* 10 (1998), 34–65.

reading (Origen, C.Cels. IV. 48–50). If, as Origen states, Numenius did interpret the Scriptures allegorically he may have been going against a more widespread refusal to do so.[137] On the other hand, the author of *On the Sublime* contrasts 'the legislator of the Jews', whose account of creation by God's speech is worthy of the power of God, with the dubious exploits of the Homeric gods, 'which if they are not taken allegorically are utterly impious and violate our sense of what is fitting' (*On the Sublime* 9.7–8).[138]

According to his opponents, Marcion similarly resisted any allegorical interpretation. However, this claim cannot simply be taken at face value, for it is a routine polemical charge against someone who interprets differently. Justin asserts that the Jewish teachers take verses such as Psalm 8.4 to mean that God really did have 'hands and feet and fingers and a soul', and hence could be the subject of epiphanies on earth (Justin, *Dial.* 114.3), whereas Ambrose charges Philo with limiting his interpretation to the 'moral aspect' of Scripture because as a Jew he did not understand its spiritual import (Ambrose, *On Paradise* 4.25.8). This latter presumably means that he did not read *Christologically*, and the same may well have been Marcion's 'failing'.[139] Indeed, Tertullian implies as much when he identifies here an unholy alliance between the heretic and the Jew, and draws his polemic from his earlier work *Against the Jews* (Tertullian, *AM* III. 6–7).[140] However, the lines are by no means straightforward, since developing anti-Jewish polemic was itself fuelled by anxieties about Marcion.[141] Hence, Marcion was being charged with rejecting a strategy for retaining and reading the Scriptures that he himself, in part, had made necessary. In fact, it is evident from his retention of 1 Corinthians 10.1–6 and of Galatians 4.21–7 that Marcion did read 'symbolically' in some sense;[142] however, he does not seem to have applied this technique systematically to the scriptural narratives of God's behaviour. Conversely, he does not seem to have drawn the conclusion adopted by Celsus that the scriptural stories are therefore to be dismissed as fables; instead he took them seriously, as direct and reliable evidence of the Creator's character and behaviour. It is this conclusion, that the Creator

137 See Burnyeat, 'Platonism in the Bible', 146–8.

138 On Longinus's argument see Mark D. Usher, 'Theomachy, Creation, and the Poetics of Quotation in Longinus Chapter 9', *Class.Philol.* 102 (2007), 292–303.

139 See Dungan, 'Reactionary Trends', 193–7, on such accusations as part of a polemical strategy.

140 See above, pp. 59, 78–9.

141 See Stephen G. Wilson, *Related Strangers: Jews and Christians 70–170 C.E.* (Minneapolis, MN: Fortress Press, 1995), 219–21; Lieu, *Image and Reality*, 261–70.

142 Jerome acknowledges this (*Ad Gal.* II. 4,26 ll.48–58), but he rejects Marcion's (and Mani's) specific application of the allegory of Gal. 4.26–7 (see above, p. 250).

is morally distinct and inferior, that might seem to ally him with other demiurgical or 'gnostic' writings. Yet, on the other hand, he did not follow many of these in spinning out of this exegesis an elaborate myth; he did not give to the Demiurge names from the exegetical tradition, such as the frequently found 'Yaldabaoth', nor did he people his universe with other figures such as Wisdom/Sophia. Secondly, and concomitantly, whereas in many of these myths the Demiurge is, however distantly or distortedly, derived from the supreme God, Marcion apparently allowed for absolutely no relationship between them both, and indeed attributed to the supreme God no role or intention prior to the advent of Jesus.[143]

All this indicates that Marcion is not simply another hellenistic Bible critic; instead, his reading of Scripture as the reliable record of the Creator God of whom it speaks matches neatly his extreme distrust of that same God, which, as has been seen, belongs within a wider cosmological world view. While, on the one hand, the challenges he laid against the Scriptures and their God locate him securely within his second-century context, on the other hand, the availability of a variety of other solutions or ways of reading suggest that these problems did not constitute his primary starting point, so much as reinforce and help offer a rationale for a position held on other grounds.

143 See also Aland, 'Marcion', 303–6, 314–17, for the difference between Marcion and Gnostic principles.

13

The Principles of Marcion's thought and their context II: the Gospel

THE DESCENT OF CHRIST

For Marcion the story of Jesus began without preparation or announcement in the time of the Emperor Tiberius (14–37 CE); although apparently not noticed by Irenaeus, there can be little doubt that Marcion took this, and its precise dating to 'the fifteenth year', from his 'Gospel' (cf. Luke 3.1; 4.31).[1] This also supplied him with the description of Jesus as having 'descended', by implication from the supreme Father, and perhaps textually glossed as 'from heaven' or 'from above'; he likely also described Jesus as having 'appeared' or 'been manifested'.[2] Although his opponents, from Irenaeus on, accuse him of deleting any reference to Jesus' birth or genealogy, it is far from certain that they were ever present in his sources. Clement of Alexandria claims that the followers of Basilides celebrated the baptism of Jesus, taking 'the fifteenth year of Tiberius' as indicating the fifteenth (or eleventh) of the Egyptian month Tubi (*Strom.* I. 21.146), which might suggest that his 'Gospel' also began in terms similar to Luke 3.1.[3] More important, in starting with the adult Jesus, Marcion would not be alone; it is here that Mark identifies 'the beginning of the Gospel', without, of course, denying Jesus a human mother and family (Mark 1.1). According to Epiphanius the 'Gospel' used by the Ebionites, which he identifies as a truncated 'Matthew', began not with the genealogies but, 'in the days of

[1] See pp. 213–14 above; Irenaeus, *AH* I. 27.2 'Jesus ... coming into Judaea in the governorship of Pontius Pilate who was procurator of Tiberius Caesar'.

[2] Tertullian *AM* IV. 7.1; Ps.Hippolytus, *Refut.* VII. 31.5 adds 'from above'; at his first reference to the date Tertullian uses the verb 'was revealed' ('*revelatus sit*': *AM* I. 15.1; cf. 19.2).

[3] See Löhr, *Basilides*, 42–8; Ronald H. Bainton, 'Basilidian Chronology and New Testament Interpretation', *JBL* 42 (1923), 81–134, attempts to argue that Basilides and Marcion presuppose a prior celebration by the church of Epiphany as Jesus' baptism.

Herod king of Judaea, in the high-priesthood of Caiaphas, a certain John came, baptising…' (Epiphanius, *Anc.* 30.13.6; 14.3–4).

Indeed, the addition to the earlier narrative tradition about Jesus of detailed birth narratives that trace divine intervention to his conception creates tensions that are already evident in the Gospels, and that continue to be so subsequently – for example, in the uncertainty as to whether Jesus' divine sonship was to be traced to his conception, to his birth, or to his baptism. These tensions are well illustrated by Justin Martyr; the birth traditions are undoubtedly important for him, yet, immediately following an appeal to 'the records made under Quirinius, your first governor in Judaea', he continues to justify 'that he was to escape the attention of other people until he reached manhood' by an appeal to Scripture that is far from persuasive (*Apol.* 33; 34.2–35.1). By contrast, in the *Dialogue* Justin claims that 'when born he had his own power', but he is quick to add that Jesus followed the normal stages of human development; nonetheless, he immediately proceeds to explain the voice from heaven at his baptism, 'You are my son, this day I have begotten you', as indicating that 'his birth/becoming (γένεσις) took place for people from the moment when knowledge of him began' (*Dial.* 88.2, 8). This is a concession that Tertullian would later resist, appealing to Jesus' freedom of access to teach in the synagogue as evidence that he could not previously have been unknown (Tertullian, *AM* IV. 7.7).

Probably the earliest, and the most persistent, attempt to 'fix' Jesus in the global historical record was the dating of his suffering or crucifixion 'under Pontius Pilate'. The beginning of this point of reference is difficult to trace; the early sermons of Acts (3.13; 4.27; 13.29) are hardly independent of the Gospel narratives, but 1 Timothy 6.13 and Ignatius (*Smyrn.* 1.2; *Trall.* 9.1; cf. *Magn.* 11.1) perhaps show the formulaic beginnings of what would become a creedal norm. Only by extension would Jesus' prior ministry also be dated to Pilate, perhaps with the some influence from Lukan traditions (Justin, *Apol.* 46.1; 48.3).[4] Such precision served both theological and apologetic ends: Justin invites the Emperor to check the records of Pilate's period (*Apol.* 48.3), while Tertullian assumes that Tiberius, to whose reign he dates 'this way of life', protected the Christians on the grounds of Pilate's report to him (Tertullian, *Apol.* 5.1–2; 8.3). This dating by reference to Roman rulers, even or especially where Pilate was not directly implicated in Jesus' death, also served to locate Christianity on the stage of the Empire and to distance it

[4] In Justin, *Apol.* 13.3 Jesus' crucifixion under Pilate is glossed 'who was procurator in Judaea in the time of Tiberius Caesar'. Justin also adds references to Herod, suggesting influence from Lukan or similar traditions (*Apol.* 40.5; *Dial.* 103.4).

from its Jewish origins: Ignatius' appeal to his readers to be fully persuaded of Jesus' birth, death, and resurrection, which took place in the time of Pontius Pilate, immediately follows after his insistence that 'Judaism' has no place in 'Christianism' (Ignatius, *Magn.* 10–11).[5]

However, this concern to date Jesus within recoverable history also created further problems: Justin knows of those who asserted that the claim by Christians that the Christ 'was born 150 years ago under Quirinius and taught that which we say he did somewhat later under Pontius Pilate', left earlier generations free of responsibility or of guilt, a problem he solves by the pre-existence of the Logos (Justin, *Apol.* 46). Irenaeus, who has a similar solution, brings a parallel charge against the suggestion that 'Christ began at that moment when he exercised his coming as man and the Father is said to show concern for men from the times of Tiberius Caesar' (Irenaeus, *AH* IV. 6.1). Marcion, who is mentioned in the next paragraph, may well be in view, but the default fixing on the dating of Jesus' public ministry is probably equally natural to Irenaeus. Facing a different problem Tertullian has to go to some lengths to explain why Christianity, which is widely known to belong to the time of Tiberius, as is admitted by Christians, does nevertheless lay claim to 'the very ancient books of the Jews' (Tertullian, *Apol.* 21).

Within this framework, Marcion's chronological starting point was probably traditional, particularly for someone whose attention was so firmly directed towards the saving activity of Jesus. The manner of Jesus' appearance similarly resonates with other contemporary formulations. Once again Marcion's Scriptures provided an anchor: That Jesus 'descended' was, as already noted, provided, or at least confirmed, by Luke 4.31, while the gloss 'from heaven' or 'from above' could be supported by 1 Corinthians 15.47 where Marcion's text read 'the second Lord from heaven'.[6] It is striking that the close parallel in John 2.12, 'After this, he went down (καταβαίνειν) to Capernaum', was interpreted by another contemporary exegete, Heracleon, of the 'uttermost parts of the cosmos, the hylic to which he descended' (Origen, *In Joh.* X.9; XIII.59).[7] Although there is little evidence that Marcion systematically interpreted the characters or the geography of the Gospels allegorically or symbolically in a similar fashion, on occasion he may have

[5] This suggests that the creedal clause 'suffered under Pontius Pilate' did not only have an antidocetic intention.

[6] See above, p. 265.

[7] See Einar Thomassen, *The Spiritual Seed: The Church of the "Valentinians"* (NHMS 60; Leiden: Brill, 2006), 107–8. Subsequently Heracleon identified the royal officer of John 4.46–54 as the Demiurge.

done so, most notably the events on the Mount of Transfiguration, which also end with Jesus' descent (Luke 9.37).[8]

More generally, the characteristic Johannine 'he/the bread/I came down from heaven' (καταβαίνειν) may point to the wider currency of such language (John 3.13; 6.33–58). Certainly it is widespread in the second century; Aristides' account of the Christians offers independent witness to its development: 'God came down from heaven and from a Hebrew virgin took and clothed himself in flesh'. The Syriac here appears more primitive than the polished Greek, which reads, 'the son of God most high came down (καταβαίνειν) from heaven by the holy spirit for the salvation of humankind' (Aristides, *Apol.* 2 [Syr]; 15 [Gk.]). Here, the language of descent is combined with that of the virgin birth, as it is also by Irenaeus who speaks of the 'descent' of the Word into Mary (Irenaeus, *AH* III. 22.1). Similarly, and illustrating the 'unconscious' modalism which slips between God and Word or Son as subject, fragments of a homily which may go back to Melito of Sardis describe how 'the Word of the Father, loving mankind, descended because of man and lived with them', and asks 'Why did it concern God, descent to earth, and conception in the body from a virgin?'[9] However, behind such formulations lie different ways of conceptualising the coming of Jesus, together with some of the tensions generated; illustrating this, the *Ascension of Isaiah* juxtaposes two scenes: In one the Lord descends to the earth through the heavens, while in the second the pregnant Mary recovers her normal profile even as a tiny child suddenly appears in front of her and the startled Joseph (*Asc.Isa.* 10.16–31; 11.1–11).[10] Celsus deliberately pilloried such language, which he attributes both to Christians and (with future reference) to Jews: 'What is the purpose of such a descent on the part of God?' (Origen, *C.Cels.* IV. 2–5). If Marcion used similar language it may have been with little deliberate reflection.

Within the Gospel narratives it is the spirit that descends (καταβαίνειν), in the form of a dove, at Jesus' baptism, which, as just noted, marked the beginning of his public activity (Mark 1.10; cf. Matt. 3.16; Luke 3.22; John 1.32).

[8] κατέρχεσθαι is found in Luke only at 4.31 and 9.37. See pp. 382–3 and Tardieu, 'Marcion depuis Harnack', 441–50.

[9] *New Fragment* II, 1, 47–9; Stuart George Hall, text and transl., *Melito of Sardis.* On Pascha *and Fragments* (OECT; Oxford: Clarendon Press, 1979), 86–8.

[10] Particularly intriguing is the proof-text that Justin ascribes to Jeremiah, 'The holy Lord God remembered his dead from Israel who slept in the ground and went down to them to preach to them his salvation'. Irenaeus, who varies between ascribing the citation to Jeremiah and to Isaiah, applies it to the descent to Hades, and this may be Justin's understanding, but its original application is lost (Justin, *Dial.* 72.4; Irenaeus, *AH* III. 20.4; IV. 22.1, etc.).

Accounts of Marcion's 'Gospel' suggest the absence of any narrative of Jesus' baptism, but in this case the traditions of that event probably still contributed to his thought. Tertullian, in his first, highly ironical, reference to Marcion's understanding of Jesus, which was arguably based on knowledge of his teaching but not yet of his 'Gospel' text, says 'In the fifteenth year of Tiberius Christ Jesus deigned to flow down from heaven, a saving spirit (*spiritus salutaris*)'; he follows with a mocking comparison with the 'malignant ("bitchy", *canicularis*) breath from Pontus', which likely confirms that the former phrase is Marcion's own (Tertullian, *AM* I. 19.2).[11] Another echo may be provided by Celsus to whom Origen protests that 'we do not say that the Spirit of the Supreme God came among men on earth as to strangers' (Origen, *C.Cels.* VI. 52). The Christological use of 'spirit' language and categories is well attested in this period, and, as shall be seen, took a distinctive form in Marcion's thought.[12] However, Jesus' baptism at the hands of John the Baptist presented a number of ambiguities to many readers; it could give a narrative justification for a separation between the passible and impassible, or between the human and divine, within Jesus, by indicating that this was the moment when the divine ('Christ') descended upon the human Jesus (a view proposed by Cerinthus according to Irenaeus, *AH* I. 26.1). On the other hand, any suggestion that Jesus was dependent on, and therefore potentially subordinate to, John needed careful handling; canonical Luke's truncated and underplayed account already testifies to this sensitivity, as do the later attempts to explain the significance of John (Luke 3.21–2; 7.18–30; 16.16). Marcion was undoubtedly implicated in these various currents, and his opponents take him to task on his interpretation of these later passages.

It is Tertullian who is determined to see the imagery of 'descent' as fundamental to Marcion's cosmogonic theory; for Marcion himself it was supplied by Scripture and tradition, but perhaps was best understood with a gloss, 'he appeared'.[13] An echo of his preference for this formulation might be heard from Megethius, who in the *Dialogue of Adamantius* refers to Jesus as 'the having appeared Christ' (ὁ φανεὶς χριστός: *Adam.* 52.10–11 [1.27]).[14] This verb (φαίνειν [pass.]) also has strong credentials: Ignatius describes

[11] The sense seems clear even if the text is corrupt: see Braun, *Contre Marcion*, I, 271–2; '*canucularis*' may be a play on the cynic Diogenes of Pontus.

[12] On the Spirit in Marcion's thought see Orbe, 'Marcionitica', 216–32, who suggests an echo of Luke 3.6 in Marcion's *spiritus salutaris* (p. 223).

[13] So Tertullian, *AM* IV. 7.2; cf. I. 19.5, '*apparentia Christi*'.

[14] The *Dialogue of Adamantius* also uses the epithet 'the Christ who came' (ὁ ἐλθὼν Χριστός: *Adam.* 8.12 [1.2]; 46.10 [1.25]; 76.3 [2.10]); see above, p. 193, n. 26.

Jesus Christ as the one 'who was with the father before the ages and appeared at the end', words echoed also by the *Epistle to Diognetus*, 'for this reason he (God) sent the word to appear to the world ... he was from the beginning, appeared as new and was discovered as old, and is born always new in the hearts of the holy' (Ignatius, *Magn.* 6.1; *Diog.* 11.3–4). On the other hand, the verb did allow of some ambiguity: Justin regularly uses it of the pre-incarnational epiphanies of the Logos in contrast to when 'he was born' or 'became man', but also uses it of the resurrection appearances (Justin, *Apol.* 63.10, 16; 67.7; *Dial.* 61.1; 113.4; 138.1). If Tertullian's 'he appeared (*apparuit*)' represents the Greek φανερόω, this verb too is widely used of the resurrection appearances but also of the incarnation (1 John 1.2; 2.28; 3.2–8; lat. *apparuere*).

THE FLESH OF THE REDEEMER

As this demonstrates, the language of descent need not negate birth, although the circumstances of that 'birth' might be disputed. However the polemical tradition is all but unanimous that according to Marcion, Jesus did not undergo normal human birth: Only Justin makes no explicit reference.[15] This, it is reported, Marcion argued not only by the 'excision' of the narratives of birth but also by his exegesis of passages that might be understood as representing Jesus as challenging the assumption of his contemporaries that they knew his immediate family.[16] However, beyond this base Marcion's position created some perplexity among his opponents, as it does among modern interpreters; apparently he did not say what they expected him to say. Indeed, Irenaeus' initial account of Marcion had, without adverse comment, described Jesus as 'coming into Judaea ... (and) having been manifest in human form (*in hominis forma*)', despite the subsequent reference to the removal of 'everything to do with the *generatio* of the Lord' (Irenaeus, *AH* I. 27.2).[17] More explicitly, according to Tertullian Marcion insisted that Jesus had not experienced normal human birth, while apparently fully admitting his suffering and death: 'if Christ did truly suffer

15 It is unnecessary to limit the repeated emphasis in *Dial.* 98–105 that Jesus 'truly became passible/a man capable of suffering' to a refutation of Marcion, perhaps drawn from Justin's 'Syntagma'.

16 See p. 223, above.

17 Cf. *AH* IV. 33.2, 'Why is he confessed as Son of Man if he did not undergo that 'generation' which comes from man?' At *AH.* I. 28.1 the Latin *generatio* represents the Greek γένεσις. Later polemicists compare Marcion to those Christological positions that qualified the nature of Jesus birth: see Harvey, ed., *Sancti Irenaei*, I, 216–7.

those things, to have been born would have been a lesser matter' (Tertullian, *AM* III. 11.8; cf. II. 27.2).[18] Tertullian struggles to make sense of this, contradicting himself in quick succession: At one point he implies that Marcion declared that Jesus was 'flesh and not flesh, man and not man', and he asks, 'If his flesh is denied how can his death be affirmed?'; at another he complains that Marcion affirmed the reality of Jesus' flesh, 'You have rejected a spurious birth but you have taught that flesh was true', while, by contrast, elsewhere he contrasts Marcion's combined denial of nativity and flesh with the more nuanced positions taken by Apelles and Valentinus (*AM* III. 8.2–6; 11.6; *De Carne* 1; *De Res.* 2.15). Yet, again, he imagines Marcion defending Jesus' need of 'the likeness (*imago*) of human substance' in order to be able to interact with other human beings (*AM* III. 10.2).

One of the problems is undoubtedly that all participants in the debate were having to define what constituted 'flesh', and specifically the flesh of human beings. In addressing this, prepositions, qualifying adjectives or adverbs, and comparisons, played a key role, but one that was no less open to disagreement. For Tertullian, genuine birth, albeit the peculiar birth from a virgin, is essential. Elsewhere he rejects the position of Valentinus who allowed Jesus to be born 'through (*per*) but not from (*ex*) the virgin, in but not from the womb', for that could only result in an 'idiosyncratic' flesh. For him, the same outcome results from the position taken by Apelles that Christ was possessed of a genuine body, but one whose flesh was provided by the stars and so not acquired through birth (*De Carne* 6, 19–21; cf. *De Res.* 2.15, '*proprie qualitatis*').[19] Tertullian refuses to allow Apelles to appeal that the angels who visited Abraham and Lot in Genesis 18–19 were similarly possessed of sideral (elsewhere 'elemental') flesh, arguing from the silence of the text that they were able to take human flesh 'from nothing'. Yet despite presenting Apelles as having deserted Marcion's position, he also rejects any appeal by the latter to the same passage from Genesis, but as if it

18 Recovering Marcion's own views is made more complicated by Tertullian's apparent re-use of material from his argument in *Against the Jews* that the death of Jesus on the cross fulfilled prophecy: *AM* III. 18–19.

19 On Apelles' view see Tertullian, *AM* III. 11.2, 'Christ did indeed carry around flesh, but not from birth but *mutuatum* from the elements', and Greschat, *Apelles und Hermogenes*, 102–9, who relates it to Platonic ideas of the astral corporality of the soul, and who takes the different account of Epiphanius (that Jesus formed his body from earthly elements) as a subsequent assimilation to Church teaching. See also M. David Litwa, *We Are Being Transformed: Deification in Paul's Soteriology* (BZNW 187; Berlin: de Gruyter, 2012), 139–51, for the celestial transformation of the purified soul with reference also to 1 Cor. 15.49; Phil. 3.21. Perhaps for Marcion this again supported the view that the post-resurrection body helps determine the pre-resurrection body.

demonstrated that the angels were (like Christ) possessed of an 'illusory (*putativus*) flesh'; he protests that for the purposes of their visitation their flesh was 'of true and firm human substance', although by God's creative freedom alone it was not conditioned by the necessary qualities of birth and inevitable death.[20] It is not impossible that Marcion (and Apelles) did appeal to the same story, despite its provenance in the 'Old Testament', for it was well established in Christian apologetics, including as evidence of a pre-incarnate visitation of Christ, – perhaps offering Marcion an exercise in the same sort of turning of tables as Tertullian himself delights in. The story was also discussed more widely for the insights it might offer on the nature of angelic substantiality;[21] whether Marcion pursued this to the point of deciding whether Jesus could not only eat and drink but also eject – a disputed question in relation to angels – is not evident.[22]

Tertullian's preferred term to describe the Jesus of Marcion is *phantasma*; although not exclusive to the books against Marcion, it is predominantly found therein. Jesus cannot be 'believed a phantom' since the crowds sought to seize him; that he was able to elude them was because the crowd dispersed not because of his 'insubstantiality' (*caligo*; Tertullian, *AM* IV. 8.2–3; cf. Luke 4.30). For Tertullian the term denotes both mimicry and deception – hence his rhetorical question why did Jesus not adopt 'a *phantasm* of God'; it implies the 'illusory' (*putativus*) as opposed to the 'true' (*AM* III. 8.3; 11.1). Tertullian extracts considerable rhetorical mileage from the term: It allows him to associate Marcion's Christ with the 'illusory' goodness of his God, and the 'phantom' discipline that results from the absence of judge and judgement (*AM* I. 27.1); this also provides its dominant sense in his attack on Marcion in the *De Carne* (1.4; 5.2, 3, 9).[23] However, its recurrence in the polemical tradition elsewhere confirms that it might be traced to Marcion himself, and it may point to the importance of Luke 24.37–9 in the argument,

[20] Tertullian, *AM* III. 9; '*putativus*' might represent the Greek 'docetic', but it is only used by Tertullian in this context and may be his term rather than that of his opponent, if indeed the latter is Marcion.

[21] See also Markschies, *Valentinus Gnosticus*, 101 for the debates on this passage, including the capacity of angels not just to eat but also to digest and expel food. Braun, *Contre Marcion*, III, 280–2, argues that Tertullian has attributed to Marcion an argument made by Apelles in order to reuse the defence he had made in *De Carne*.

[22] Cf. Antonio Orbe, *Cristología Gnóstica: Introduccíon a la Soteriología de los siglos II y III* (Madrid: Bibliòteca de Autores Cristianos, 1976) II, 272; idem, 'El Hijo del hombre come y bebe (Mt 11,19, Lc 7,34)', *Gregorianum* 58 (1977), 523–55, 524–33. Marcion's text may have omitted Luke 24.42–3.

[23] Irenaeus does not use '*phantasma*' in the context of Christological error; where the term does occur in the Latin of the *Adversus Haereses* it either represents the Greek φαντασία (*AH* I. praef.; 8.1[v.l.]; II. 31.3; 32.3), or a post-mortem form of existence (II. 33.1).

where, as has been seen, in the text known to Marcion (and perhaps to Tertullian), the disciples feared they were seeing a *phantasma* (v. 37).

Contemporary readers would not have been surprised had the disciples encountered a 'phantasm' near the tomb of Jesus; that the dead do so appear had been stated by Plato and is reaffirmed by Origen, who explains that this is due to the soul subsisting in 'a so-called luminous body', but who denies that this sufficiently explains the resurrection experiences (Plato, *Phaedo* 81D; Origen, *C.Cels.* II. 60). '*Phantasm*' was also used of figures who appear in dreams and visions, although this still left considerable room for debate as to the nature of their substantial existence, and indeed whether they were to be trusted or taken as 'real'.[24] For example, Josephus describes the, certainly palpable, figure with whom Jacob wrestled as a '*phantasma*' (Josephus, *AJ* I. 20.2 [331–4]), while Philo follows a common trend in dismissing the apparitions, especially terrifying ones, that come in dreams as insubstantial and false (Philo, *De Somniis* II.23 [162]).[25] Strikingly, Luke omits the account of Jesus walking on the water and responding to his disciples, who are terrified at an apparent *phantasma*, with the theophanic, 'I am' (Mark 6.49; Matt. 14.26).

It remains uncertain whether Marcion considered that the disciples, regularly given to misunderstanding, were mistaken in thinking they saw a *phantasma*, or only in letting that terrify them, prior perhaps to a theophanic self-revelation. Much would depend on the alternative possibilities against which the term was pitted, and what models were being applied. For example, the *Treatise on Resurrection* affirms the resurrection as 'spiritual' and not 'fleshly', but denies that it is an illusion (*phantasia*) on the grounds of the appearance of Elijah and Moses ([*NH* I, 4] 48.3–19); conversely, a near-contemporary author on the same subject rejects those who appealed to Jesus' likening of the risen state to that of the angels (Luke 20.35–6), and who then claimed that the risen Jesus was 'spiritual only, no longer in flesh, but proffered an appearance (*phantasia*) of flesh', implying the equivalence of 'appearance' and 'spiritual' (Ps.Justin, *De Res.* 589).

24 See Patricia Cox Miller, *Dreams in Late Antiquity: Studies in the Imagination of a Culture* (Princeton, NJ: Princeton University Press, 1994), 35–65, for the various theories about the interrelationship of dream figures, the soul, and the daemons who inhabit the shadowy territory between divine and human.

25 This makes it difficult to sustain in these authors the difference between '*phantasma*', as having an objective dimension, and '*phantasia*', as situated more in the act of perception (so Diogenes Laertius, *Vit.Phil.* VII. 50). Justin, who does not use '*phantasma*', applies '*phantasia*' both positively to the divine epiphanies, and negatively as deceptive, with 'magical' (Justin, *Dial.* 69.7; 128.2).

A variant tradition of the Lukan resurrection appearance illustrates further the challenges of language. Strikingly, Ignatius knows a tradition of the risen Jesus saying to his disciples 'Touch me and see, that/for I am not an incorporeal demon (δαιμόνιον ἀσώματον)', which he takes to confirm his conviction that Jesus was 'in flesh' even after the resurrection, thus equating 'body' and 'flesh' (Ignatius, *Smyrn.* 3).[26] 'Incorporeal' (ἀσώματος) is also how Justin describes the appearance of Jesus to Moses in pillar of fire or as angel ('in incorporeal form'), while elsewhere he assumes that what is 'incorporeal' is also without suffering or passion (ἀπαθής) (Justin, *Apol.* 63.10, 16; *Dial.* 1.5).[27] All this demonstrates how scriptural narratives about forms of Divine manifestation, the ambiguities evident in the resurrection traditions concerning the nature of Jesus' risen persona and its continuity with his pre-mortem ministry, and debates about the intrinsic qualities of specifically human flesh, intersected with varying consequences, which should not be straightjacketed into a single model.[28] It also shows that such language need not of itself imply that *phantasma* or 'incorporeality' lacked any materiality; demons still occupy space, and according to some traditions can ingest smoke. In that sense they have bodies, although of a distinctive kind: '"the daemonic" is less a substantive than it is a situational category'.[29] Evidently mapping terminological differentiation upon substantial or spatial differentiation when it came to various categories of beings and the bodies they possessed allowed for considerable confusion.[30]

It does seem that for Marcion the resurrected form of Jesus provided the key to his pre-resurrected form: 'I am the same' (Luke 24.39).[31] As already noted, he used 'spirit' language both of the descended Christ and in a discussion of resurrection: 'the last Lord was made a life-giving spirit' (1 Cor. 15.45). Even so, it is difficult to know how this might relate to his

[26] A similar form is found in Origen, *De Princip.* I. praef. 8 ascribed to the *Preaching of Peter*: see above, p. 220, n. 107. Contrast Vinzent who attributes these traditions to an anti-Marcionite polemic: '"Ich bin kein körperloses Geistwesen"'.

[27] Harvey, *Sancti Irenaei*, I, 40, n.3, argues that ἀσώματος should be translated not as 'incorporeal substance' but as 'unorganised matter' (although 'unconstituted' seems better to express his point).

[28] As well illustrated by Tertullian, *De Carne.*

[29] Cox Miller, *Dreams*, 55; see also Gregory A. Smith, 'How Thin Is a Demon?', *JECS* 16 (2008), 479–512.

[30] Litwa, *We Are Being Transformed*, 119–36, demonstrates the presence of ideas of 'divine corporeality and the pneumatic body' in Graeco-Roman and Jewish thought of the period.

[31] See above, p. 219 on Marcion's text here; Epiphanius, *Pan.* 42.11.5, S78 omits these words. Apelles reportedly claimed that Jesus' demonstration of side and nail-prints (John 20.20!) proved he was no *phantasma*, but was still temporarily possessed of his 'elemental' flesh (Ps.Hippolytus, *Ref.* VII. 38.4).

apparent denial (*contra* Tertullian) that Jesus, after his resurrection, was 'a spirit without bones' (Luke 24.39).[32] Both the Transfiguration and the resurrection narratives were important for him, and the possible absence of 'flesh' in his text of the latter was perhaps of particular significance.

On the other hand, Pauline discussion undoubtedly also contributed to his understanding of types of flesh, and his exploitation of the ambiguities of flesh in Paul's reading in 1 Corinthians 15.35–41 probably provoked Tertullian's insistent but somewhat un-nuanced reading of that passage.[33] In addition, statements such as the sending of the Son 'in the likeness of flesh of sin' (Rom. 8.3) provided a challenge that all had to negotiate; no one wished to admit that Jesus was possessed of a 'flesh that was sinful', but they differed fundamentally when it came to 'likeness' and to the identification of wherein lay the 'substance' of flesh (Tertullian, *AM* V. 14.1–3). Tertullian denies that there is any equivalence between 'likeness' (*simulitudo*) and *phantasma*, and equally that there is any distinction between 'body' and flesh (cf. Rom. 7.4, 'dead to the law through the body of Christ'; *AM* V. 13.12). That Marcion did take these steps is suggested by the protests that Tertullian makes at Colossians 1.22, 24, verses that might be read as a denial of any simple identification of Jesus' body with flesh, and also at Philippians 2.6–8, a passage that is open to suggesting a distinction between 'form' or 'likeness' and the actuality of substance (Tertullian, *AM* V. 19.6; 20.3).[34]

Within this context the formulaic account of Marcion's Christology in Ps.Hippolytus, *Refutation* is certainly over-simplistic and misleading: 'that he appeared as (ὢς) man but was not man, and as enfleshed but (was) not enfleshed, and suffered in appearance (δοκήσις), but did not undergo birth/becoming (γένεσις) or suffering, except in semblance (δοκεῖν) (*Ref.* X. 19.3).[35]

32 See Orbe, 'Marcionitica', 223, who argues that for Marcion Jesus' body was 'from heaven'. Daniel A. Smith, 'Seeing a Pneuma(tic Body): The Apologetic Interests of Luke 24: 36–43', *CBQ* 72 (2010), 752–72, finds a challenge to the Pauline model of a transformed body in the Lukan account, but he decides that it is not specifically against Marcion.

33 See Francis Watson, 'Resurrection and the Limits of Paulinism', ed. J. Ross Wagner, C. Kavin Rowe, and A. Katherine Grieb, *The Word Leaps the Gap: Essays on Scripture and Theology in Honor of Richard B. Hays* (Grand Rapids, MI: Eerdmans, (2008), 453–71, on the readings by the *Treatise on Resurrection* and by Tertullian.

34 Antonio Orbe, 'Hacia la doctrina marcionítica de la redención', *Gregorianum* 74 (1993), 45–74, 68–70 notes the difficulty in following Marcion's position here; in idem, 'Entorno al modalismo de Marción', *Gregorianum* 71 (1990), 43–65, Orbe suggests that the preexistent Son was composed of divine substance and divine glory, but surrendered the latter to appear among humans, recovering it in ascension. See also Tertullian, *AM* V. 17.12–15 on Eph. 2.13–16, where Marcion perhaps read 'the hostility of flesh', omitting 'his'.

35 Contrast the earlier account in Ps.Hippolytus, *Ref.* VII. 31.5–6, 'without birth/becoming … unbegotten', which makes no reference to Christ's death. In *Ref.* VIII. 8–12 'those who call

To describe Marcion's views as 'docetic' on this basis is unhelpful, especially if it suggests his allegiance to an existing coherent doctrine about the nature of Christ's body or about his mode of presence in the human sphere. In fact, despite his rejection of 'becoming', *genesis*, Marcion does not seem to have been driven by the related desire to disassociate any form of suffering with the divine.[36] According to Ephraem if Jesus' adoption of a body did involve any deceit it was driven by concern for those he encounters: 'that he might hide his greatness and make them believe that he was corporeal because they were not capable of it'.[37]

Marcion would not have been alone in the second century in struggling to give a justified account of Jesus' human experience. The frequent insistence that 'Jesus Christ came in the flesh', or, more expansively, 'was truly born, ate and drank, was truly persecuted under Pontius Pilate, truly crucified and died … truly raised from the dead', undoubtedly articulates an anxiety, but it does not reveal its precise causes (1 John 4.2; Polycarp, *Phil.* 7.1; Ignatius, *Trall.* 9). Both the problem and the available solutions were far more complex than a simple opposition between 'flesh' and 'not flesh', or 'truly' and 'not truly', could articulate.

The strained language common in the second century reveals the tensions between theological precision and confessional conviction: These same authors do not hesitate to make God the subject of the experiences of the incarnate Jesus, including his suffering. Ignatius speaks of 'God appearing in human manner for the newness of eternal life': 'There is one God who manifested himself through Jesus Christ his son, who is his word proceeding from silence' (Ignatius, *Eph.* 19.3; *Magn.* 8.2).[38] Within the same tradition Melito famously declared, 'God has been murdered' (Melito, *Peri Pascha* §96, l.715). It would be wrong to ascribe such language, often labelled 'modalist' or even 'theopaschite', to a formal doctrinal position: It expresses a conviction as to what was happening in the story of Jesus, and it refuses any model that sees him only in prophetic terms or as an emissary of God. Couched within the rhetorical flourishes of contemporary second sophistic,

themselves Docetics' are treated as a separate heresy. See also Serapion of Antioch in Eusebius, *HE* VI. 12. 6 on the 'docetics' who make use of the *Gospel of Peter*. See J. G. Davies, 'The Origins of Docetism', ed. F. L. Cross, *Studia Patristica* 6 (Berlin: Akademie-Verlag, 1962) IV, 13–35.

36 See Paul Gavrilyuk, *The Suffering of the Impassible God: The Dialectics of Patristic Thought* (OECS; Oxford: Oxford University Press, 2004), 47–90.

37 Ephraem, *Comm. in Diat.* 11. 9 on Luke 11.27.

38 This translation follows the Armenian with most modern editors against the negative ('not proceeding') of the Greek and Latin, which is accepted by Hübner, *Paradox*, 192.

the effects could be startling: 'he who created the world was fixed with nails' (Melito, *New Frag.* II. 89). Yet, it could itself lead to precisely the same ambiguities as Ignatius denounced: 'This one, coming from heaven to the earth on account of the suffering one, put on himself that one through the womb of a virgin and proceeded as man; he accepted the sufferings of the suffering one through the body which was able to suffer and dissolved the sufferings of the flesh by the spirit which was not able to die and so killed death, the killer of humankind' (Melito, *Peri Pascha* §66, ll.451–58). In similar fashion, the author of the *Against Noetus* explicitly rejects any doctrine that makes God the subject of suffering, and yet himself uses somewhat constrained language, 'He was manifest coming forth into the world as God embodied (ἐνσώματος), coming forth as perfect man. For not in perception or manner of speaking, but truly having become man' (*C.Noet.* 17.5). That final emphasis testifies to the way in which familiar slogans such as 'truly man' could be reused and redirected in the many-faceted debate towards finding a way of articulating the nature of the incarnate Son of God.[39] Marcion's readiness to speak both of the descent of the Father and of the appearance of the Christ, however much lampooned, easily blends into such a context.

There are significant other driving forces on all sides of the argument; a primary one was the demands of the soteriological model adopted. In Marcion's case this did not require Jesus' humanity to be the same as that of the rest of humanity, as was demanded by the theologies of Irenaeus or of Tertullian. What the Saviour needs to be able to do is to descend without detection and to effect the rescue of some. Again Marcion was not alone; the *Ascension of Isaiah* describes a similar narrative: The son is sent in human 'appearance', clarified in the Ethiopic as, 'they will think that he is flesh and man' (*Asc.Isa.* 9.13). The son achieves this by descending through the heavens, transforming himself into the guise of the angels responsible for each level until he reaches the earth. Such a Christology of transformation is perhaps bound to be 'docetic', even if there is no deliberate theological rejection of any alternative.[40]

Further, tied up with reflection on Jesus' body was that concerning the bodily experience of believers. For example, reflection on the experience of

[39] Against Hübner, *Paradox*, who uses it as a stable touchstone for dating other texts (including Ignatius) that use a similar formula. On the authorship see above p. 99.

[40] See further Enrico Norelli, *Ascensio Isaiae: Commentarius.* (CC.SA 8; Turnhout: Brepols, 1995), 2, 461. A spurious prophetic testimonium states, 'Another prophet says, "Not born from the womb of a woman but he descended from a heavenly place"' (*Asc.Isa.* 23.6), but Norelli decides that this is Valentinian rather than Marcionite.

persecution readily intersected with that on Jesus' own suffering.[41] Yet this could work in more than one way; for Ignatius, the value of his own anticipated martyrdom depends on the reality of Jesus' own physical suffering. On the other hand, when the martyrs seemingly triumph already in the midst of their physical agonies, and their bodies refuse to be subject to the normal consequences of torture, this is because Christ suffers in them (Eusebius, *HE* V. 1.24); some might easily conclude that what they experienced was what the mortal Christ also experienced. More generally, the identification of the Church, or of its members, as the body of Christ brings the experience of believers and of Christ into dialogue: Marcion perhaps similarly concluded that as 'members of Christ' the bodies of believers will not rise (Tertullian, *AM* V. 7.4 on 1 Cor. 6.15, 19). An intra-textual reading of Luke 24.39 with Ephesians 5.30 in its longer form ('we are members of his body, of his flesh and of his bones'), which for Irenaeus establishes the capacity of flesh for God's gift (Irenaeus, *AH* V. 2.3), might in reverse redefine the true meaning of Christ's 'flesh and bones' as more ecclesiological than incarnational.[42]

THE WORK OF SALVATION

Origen claims that Celsus had drawn from an anti-Marcionite polemic a series of objections, and had mistakenly used them against the normative Christian position: 'Why does he secretly send to destroy the creations of this God? Why does he force his way in by stealth to beguile and lead astray? Why does he lead off those whom, as you say, the creator has condemned and cursed, and carry them away like a slave-dealer? Why does he teach them to escape from their master? Why should they flee to the Father? Why does he adopt them as his children without the consent of their father? Why does he lay claim to be the father of the strangers?' (Origen, *C.Cels.* VI. 53). Although Origen finds some of these objections somewhat crude and lacking in intellectual rigour, the positive principles they presuppose are already voiced by Irenaeus and Tertullian, and they recur in a number of accounts of Marcion's thought.[43]

Fundamental to such principles is that redemption entails rescue from the control of the Creator God; yet equally they presuppose that the redeemer

[41] See Gavrilyuk, *Suffering*, 69–75.

[42] As shall be seen, Marcion may have interpreted Eph. 5.28–9 as an exemplar model for Christian asexual marriage.

[43] See above, pp. 63, 155.

has no intrinsic connection with the Creator but also none with those whom he redeems. The widespread repetition of this last point underlines its distinctive note: Those who are saved do not already belong in some sense to the one who saves them; they are 'strangers' to him and he to them.[44] This establishes a fundamental and important contrast with those 'gnostic' systems that provide narratives of a spark of light or of the divine which has become entrapped under the power of the Demiurge, and which needs to be freed in order to recover a state that is natural to it. In that sense, within such gnostic systems those to be redeemed, whether all humanity or only some, are in their own right capable of salvation even if they cannot effect it on their own; for Marcion they are not. Yet the consequence is that, for Marcion, Jesus came equally to save the righteous and sinners (Ephraem, *PR* 2. 80,45–8).

Some modern interpreters have been quick to see here merely a radical, perhaps radically Pauline, expression of divine grace: that God saves freely and out of the divine self-giving nature, and is not bound by any obligation imposed either from without – such as by human merit – or from within.[45] For Marcion's opponents, however, from the perspective of the 'normative' Christian narrative, it is not only logically nonsense for the Father to redeem those for whom he has no responsibility; when such behaviour is treated on the model of human behaviour it is exposed as also morally objectionable, an act of theft of that to which he has no right.

Although the language of theft is deliberately derogatory, Marcion's model undoubtedly has earlier, including scriptural, precedent. Tertullian denies that the thief who comes at an unexpected hour (Luke 12.39) could refer to the Creator, but at the same time he takes the opportunity for a snide comment at Marcion's 'unexpected' redeemer, and so leaves it entirely opaque as to whether Marcion referred the verse to either protagonist (Tertullian, *AM* IV. 29.7–9). Perhaps more readily applicable to the redeemer was the parable of the 'stronger man' who overwhelms the apparently 'strong' and sequesters his booty (Luke 11.21–22): Ephraem quotes the sayings, 'The Stranger was able to come like a Mighty One' and 'The Just One is mighty, but the Good One is more mighty than him' (Ephraem, *PR* 1. 47,30–4; 2. 132,10–13).[46] If Marcion did apply the parable in this way, he

44 See above, p. 329.

45 See Hoffmann, *Marcion*, 226; Calvin J. Roetzel, 'Paul in the Second Century', ed. James D. G. Dunn, *The Cambridge Companion to Paul* (Cambridge: Cambridge University Press, 2003), 227–41, 233; contrast Verweijs, *Evangelium und neues Gesetz*, 263–7, 345–6.

46 The term is not that used in the Peshitta of Luke 11.20–1.

would again have been participating in a continuing exegetical debate as to how to determine both conqueror and conquered (Irenaeus, *AH* V. 21.3; 22.1; Origen, *C.Cels.* VIII. 15; Tertullian, *AM* IV. 26.12). Indeed, Justin Martyr had already debated the application of the scriptural epithet 'the strong man' to Jesus, recognizing that the title also evoked images of Heracles (Justin, *Apol.* 54.9; *Dial.* 69.1–4; cf. Ps. 115.4–8). Lines from Melito suggest that such language had become formulaic: 'I am the one who destroyed death and triumphed over the enemy, and trampled on Hades, and bound the strong one, and seized man up to the heights of heaven' (Melito, *Peri Pascha* §102, ll.760–4).[47] Ephesians 4.8, retained by Marcion probably lacking the quotation formula, would give Pauline reinforcement to this model of taking captives. Similar imagery is used in the *Odes of Solomon* 10.3–4: 'to bring back the souls of those who desire to come to him and to lead captive a good captivity for freedom, I was made mighty and strengthened and took the world captive'.[48] Michael Lattke argues that the two go back to a common source and argues that already in Ephesians it may represent an incipient Gnosticism.[49]

Marcion evidently also drew his imagery from elsewhere in his scriptural authorities: Ephraem mocks his opponents for apparently trying on the one hand to retain the language of 'might' but to deny that of 'violent robbery', and, on the other, to combine it with that of 'purchase in humble fashion' (Ephraem, *PR* 2. 132,30–6). Evidently Philippians 2.6–8 is playing a significant exegetical role here, while potential intra-textual links with the Gospel passages already cited are intriguingly suggestive.[50] Also fundamental is Galatians 3.13, together with Galatians 2.20 and 1 Corinthians 6.20, where Marcion found the language of purchase or ransom.[51] Tertullian triumphantly points out that Jesus must therefore have had a real body to exchange for those whom he redeems, conveniently forgetting that for Marcion it was the soul that was redeemed (Tertullian, *AM* V. 7.5). Ephraem, for his part, subjects to equally withering mockery the actualisation of the metaphor whereby the 'deal' is agreed with Moses and Elijah, presumably as

47 See Hall, *Melito of Sardis*, 59, n. 60, and also Fragment 13 (ibid., 80–1). See below, p. 383 on the link with the descent to Hades.

48 Translation from Lattke, *The Odes of Solomon*, 140–4.

49 Lattke, *Oden Salomos*, 1, 175–6.

50 In Greek, Phil. 2.6 links with the Matthaean version of the 'Mighty one' saying through the verb 'ἁρπάζειν' (Matt. 12.29; so also the citation from Melito, *Peri Pascha* §102 above), but this is not replicated in the Syriac (nor in either language in the Lukan version).

51 1 Cor. 6.20 '*empti enim magno*'; see above, p. 262, and p. 173 on Ephraem; Orbe, 'Haçia la doctrina', 57–9; Enrico Norelli, 'Note sulla soteriologia di Marcione', *Augustinianum* 35 (1995), 281–305.

representatives of the Creator God, on the mountain of Jesus' transfiguration.[52] The importance of that incident is confirmed by Tertullian's lengthy discussion, although he shapes it entirely around his favourite theme of 'the departure of the old and the succession of the new testament' (*AM* IV. 22.1–16). Already behind the Gospel accounts of the event themselves lies a network of associations of mountains and theophanies, as well as of the giving of the Law at Sinai, while, more generally, biblical geography often carries cosmological significance in early Jewish and Christian thought.[53] Marcion evidently used spatial categories to express the radical otherness of the God proclaimed by Jesus, so it would not be surprising if he saw in the Transfiguration a point of collision between that God and the Creator, and all that each represented.[54]

Again, Marcion would not be alone in exploiting such scriptural language and imagery: The *Gospel of Philip* also describes the Transfiguration as a moment of the revelation of Jesus' true identity, and it declares 'Christ came to ransom some, to save others, to redeem others. He ransomed those who were strangers and made them his own' (*NH* II.3. 52.35–53.3; 58.5–10).[55] Adopting a reverse geography, Jesus' 'descent to the Underworld' can be treated as a metaphor of his becoming as man 'to die as a ransom for your sin' (*Teaching of Silvanus* [*NH* VII.4] 103,30–104,15; 110,27–111,5).[56] Set alongside the allusions to the *descensus* as an image of the destruction of the enemy in Melito's *Peri Pascha* §102, cited above, Irenaeus' idiosyncratic reference to Marcion's teaching about Jesus' proclamation in Hades may be a misunderstanding of a parallel mythologisation of the rescue by Jesus of even the unrighteous from the Creator in his own domain.[57]

Marcion's dominant model was that of the battle over the forces that enslave humanity, and of victory won, namely a 'realized soteriology'. Again, a similar pattern appears in the *Ascension of Isaiah*, where the Son is sent by God to overcome the rebellion of the 'prince of death' and of the angels,

52 See above, p. 169; Drijvers, 'Christ as Warrior and Merchant'.

53 See in general James M. Scott, *Geography in Early Judaism and Christianity: The Book of Jubilees* (SNTS 113; Cambridge: Cambridge University Press, 2002).

54 See above p. 230 and Tardieu, 'Marcion depuis Harnack', 441–50, who sees this as a symbolic representation of two opposing worlds (world views).

55 See also above, p. 375 on the appeal to the appearance of Elijah and Moses in the *Treatise on Resurrection* (*NH* I, 4).

56 Compare Heracleon's interpretation of John 2.12, above, p. 369.

57 See above, p. 46; there may here be a challenge to, or from, the Jeremiah apocryphon as cited by Justin (*Dial.* 72.4), 'The Lord God remembered the dead of his [holy] Israel who were buried in the ground of soil and descended to them to proclaim their salvation' (see above, p. 370).

who claimed unique authority.[58] Salvation and judgement are effected by the concealed descent and glorious ascent of the Son, and there is no interest in – but not thereby a denial of – any future judgement. Within such a world of images, ideas of sin and forgiveness are unlikely to have played a leading role. Despite the attention that his opponents draw to Marcion's rejection of the Law, Irenaeus' association of Jesus' dissolution of the Law with that of the works of the Creator persuasively suggests that for Marcion the Law primarily represented the means by which the Demiurge exercises power (Irenaeus, *AH* I. 27.2).[59] Here again spatial categories take priority over temporal ones.

The problem was made acute when Marcion was read, as he is by his opponents, against a salvation-historical template in which the act of redemption is enacted over time and is appropriated by believers, who must then still live in present mortal conditions, and for whom resurrection, the final judgement, and the establishment of God's Kingdom lie in the future. Within such a scheme the future consummation of redemption is as important as whatever may have happened in the past, and it certainly becomes the measure of the validity of the latter. Set within this framework Marcion could be asked questions that he had little interest in answering. Tertullian rhetorically argues his Marcion into a corner where he has to acknowledge that the Father will judge people for their sins; he also forces him to conclude that the Creator will have his own system of punishment for those who persist in believing in him (Tertullian, *AM* I. 26–8). Ephraem similarly presses the logic where each deity will have to exercise final judgement or vindication (*PR* 2. 75,1–35; 112,20–113,39). Whether Marcion did envisage a continuing role for the Creator as judge for those who had not turned to the Son is difficult to determine; the parable of the rich man and Lazarus perhaps demanded some such interpretation.[60] But most probably this was simply not where Marcion's interest lay.

However, the point at which his opponents found Marcion most vulnerable was regarding that which is redeemed. Characteristic of Marcion's position, as already seen, was that those who will be redeemed, like the rest of humankind, are 'strangers' to the Good God; the Creator is responsible both for what they are as well as for their present dilemma. Unlike some contemporary 'gnostic' systems, Marcion therefore did not need to pay much attention to the nature and origins of human existence; he had no 'myth' to explain the 'human condition' or to predefine the potential for and

[58] See above, p. 379; Norelli, *Ascensio Isaiae*, 2, 38–44, 413–16. [59] See above, pp. 355–7.
[60] On the importance of this parable, see p. 211.

the goal of salvation, and neither did he require one: Salvation was not a return to origins. For him, to be human was to consist of body and soul, both being the work of the Creator. Yet, according to his detractors, he allowed only for the salvation of the soul, leaving the body behind (so already Irenaeus, *AH* I. 27). Surely, they reasoned, if the soul, without any prior disposition or appropriate origin, could be saved then so could the body. There was also a further concern: For these authors the resurrection of the fleshly body carried moral imperative since the body is the subject and sphere of moral action, as Tertullian works out in detail.

Whether Marcion himself explained the difference in salvific potential between body and soul is less clear. According to Irenaeus, the problem with the body for Marcion was that 'it was taken from the earth' (*a terra sit sumptum*). Ephraem echoes this when he surmises that the difference was that the body was from matter, whereas the soul was 'polluted', although the latter addition may be a subsequent rationalisation.[61] It would, perhaps, not be surprising if some of Marcion's followers, represented by Marcus in the *Dialogue of Adamantius*, introduced a tripartite division of the human being, in which the 'intellect' came from and found its natural destiny in the Good God. Yet Marcion's position can be understood as a response to Paul: If the subjunctive '*let us* bear the image of the heavenly one' is read, then believers are no longer defined by the 'earthly' body that tied them to the Creator (1 Cor. 15.47–9).[62] Moreover, in failing to offer any further precision, such as was supplied by his later followers and detractors, Marcion would only be following contemporary speculation about the origins of both body and soul or intellect. Even Plutarch had asserted that God did not beget the body but formed and filled it with the aid of Matter, whereas the soul was not simply a work of God but an actual portion (*Plat. Quaest.* 1001B–C). As has been seen, the first-person plural in Genesis 1.26 already prompted some to suggest that the body was created by angels (Justin, *Dial.* 62.3–4), while Philo even has the intermediary 'helpers' responsible for the mortal aspect of the human soul (Philo, *De Opif.* 24 [72–5]). In each case exegesis helps provide a solution to fundamental philosophical problems: What others explained by protology, Marcion perhaps explained through eschatology.

There may be a further exegetical level to Marcion's thinking. Just as he arguably interpreted Christ's own body in relation to the Church or to believers, so conversely he perhaps saw the redeemed as presently or

[61] See the English reconstruction at Mitchell, *Ephraim's Prose Refutations* 2, xliv–xlv; Drijvers, 'Christ as Warrior and Merchant', 79–81.

[62] On the text, see p. 265.

proleptically possessed of, or constituting, a different form of corporeality, one not defined by flesh but by soul. The bodies of the saved already are in some sense the limbs of Christ (cf. Tertullian, *AM* V. 7.4–5 [1 Cor. 6.15, 19]; 10.3–4 [1 Cor. 15.35–42]; 15.7–8 [1 Thess. 5. 23]). Indeed, it has been argued that Paul's own thought can be read within the framework of ancient conceptions of deification: Believers already partake in 'Christ's pneumatic corporeality', even though this may only be fully realized beyond death (Gal. 2.20; 1 Cor. 15.49).[63] At the very least this suggests that Marcion may have so read him. Despite attempts to see such views as determined by a philosophical position, perhaps a Stoic one, it seems more likely that again exegesis and dilemma are reciprocally engaged within a broad philosophical framework.[64] However, this was not just an abstract response to the philosophical problem of the nature of the body; to the mystification of his opponents, Marcion's own understanding of soteriology resulted in as rigorous an ethical imperative as did their own.

[63] Litwa, *We Are Being Transformed*, 161–6.

[64] See Orbe, 'Hacia la doctrina', who speaks of a 'psychic body'; Jérôme Alexandre, *Une chair pour la gloire. L'anthropologie réaliste et mystique de Tertullien* (Th.Hist. 115; Paris: Beauchesne, 2001), 199–225, does interpret Marcion in Stoic terms.

14

The principles of Marcion's thought and their context III: life and practice

There is little consistent information about the actual organisation of followers of Marcion, either in his lifetime or later, or about their lifestyle beyond certain standard caricatures. It is a standard heresiological topos that opponents adopt views and practices that self-evidently demonstrate their error while at the same time the unsuspecting may easily be deceived by their lack of difference. Justin already states that he does not know whether those like Marcion engage in nefarious practices, although that bare statement alone was perhaps intended to be enough to arouse suspicion in his imperial audience, but he is more confident that they are not persecuted or put to death – a claim that is contradicted by the evidence (Justin, *Apol.* 26.5). In the fourth century in Syria it was still possible for Ephraem to admit their superficial similarity to his own communities, while Cyril of Jerusalem warns of the danger of stumbling into a Marcionite gathering unawares. Theodoret's account of whole Marcionite villages similarly reflects a situation where community allegiance was based more on local custom and tradition than on recognised polemical convictions.[1] Although, under Constantine, Marcionites were forbidden to meet together and were decreed to lose their buildings, it is hard to know how effectively that could be implemented (Eusebius, *Vita Const.* 3.65). It is particularly striking that the inscription from Lebaba, dated to 318 CE, identifies their community (building) as the 'synagogue of the Marcionites', although, otherwise, it is only through an assiduously Marcionite lens that it appears any different from those erected by other Christian groups.[2] Such later

[1] See pp. 158, 179 and below, n. 32.

[2] *OGIS* 608; see above, p. 143. Harnack, *Marcion*, 341*–5*, attempts a 'Marcionite' reading of the inscription. Although the 'synagogue' was built after Constantine's edict, there was greater tolerance in the East under Licinius.

models presuppose a degree of ecclesial organisation that would be anachronistic in the second century. Marcion himself, as has been argued here, initially belongs in a 'school' setting rather than in one with clear communal structures. However, 'lifestyle' was an integral part of any such school, and was seen as a consequence of the philosophical teaching about the nature of being human in the world, and about the goals that might be properly aspired to. Marcion's teaching about the Demiurge, creation, and the function of Law, as also that about the revelation of the son sent by his High God to redeem the souls of the saved, undoubtedly had its correlates in the practices he espoused.

As has just been seen, it would seem that in some sense believers, in Marcion's system, already live the lives of the redeemed. On the other hand, the 'myth' of the deliverance of their souls and of their being brought into the realm of the Father God, although using the categories of space and time that his opponents ridiculed, had neither removed them from this earth nor rendered their continuing lives 'in the body' as of no significance. Here again, to Tertullian's consternation, they did not conclude that their actions were of no consequence: When he asks why their failure to fear God does not lead them into every kind of sensuous excess, and even into evasion of persecution, they reply with a horrified 'God forbid' (*absit*: *AM* I. 27.5). Their actual practice needs to be plotted between the two poles characteristic of his system, namely, first, the absence of fear of judgement as a motivating force, and, second, the intense hostility to the created order, and in particular to the flesh and its capacity for change.[3]

ASCETICISM

Attempts to ascribe any overt immorality to Marcion and his followers are at best bluster.[4] Instead, the most consistent theme in accounts of Marcion's practice is his rejection of marriage or at least of sexual intercourse, although already this alternative witnesses to some confusion.[5] Irenaeus' initial account is notably silent on the issue, but he subsequently traces the avoidance of marriage (ἀγαμία) by the so-called Encratites

[3] See Norelli, 'Paix, justice', 25–31.

[4] Heresiological accounts of Marcion's youthful seduction of a virgin are self-evidently spurious; see pp. 101–02. Jerome, *Epist.* 133, includes Marcion in a catalogue of heretics who used women to deceive women; surprisingly his account of Marcion sending a woman ahead to prepare the ground is accepted by Lampe, *From Paul to Valentinus*, 244.

[5] See below, p. 391; Tertullian, *AM* V. 7.6, says that Marcion prohibits 'sexual intercourse' (*concubitum*).

(ἐγκρατεῖς) to Saturninus and to Marcion, and he describes Tatian as also echoing these two when he disparaged marriage as 'corruption (φθορά) and fornication (πορνεία)' (*AH* I. 28.1).[6] However, although Irenaeus had stated previously that Saturninus saw marriage and procreation as originating from Satan, he has no such explanation for Marcion's position (*AH* I. 24.2). Indeed, by interpreting such 'encratite' views as tantamount to the condemnation of the one 'who made male and female for the generation (γένεσις) of humankind', he indicates that the issue was primarily driven by the need to avoid any association with procreation, 'becoming', and with death. At the same time, sexual extremism, at both ends of the spectrum, is evidently already becoming a polemical topos: Irenaeus immediately follows with a reference back to Basilides and Carpocrates who are accused of introducing indiscriminate sexual activity and multiple marriages (*AH* I. 28.2).[7] However, even though Irenaeus' polemical rhetoric undoubtedly shapes his account, it does seem likely that Marcion and his followers were already associated with sexual asceticism, and in particular with anxieties regarding procreation; certainly, this becomes a stable theme in later polemic.

Even so, it would be wrong to separate Marcion's position too sharply from a broader trend towards ascetic commitment, such as would locate him firmly in the midst of debates current in the second century. 'Self-discipline' or 'self-mastery' (ἐγκρατεία) was a widely paraded virtue, and was one that someone of philosophical aspirations could readily be expected to model.[8] Christians shared with contemporary philosophy the view that the sole legitimate purpose of sexual intercourse was the procreation of children, but the Apologists were proud to claim that many among their number avoided even that; indeed, Justin uses with approbation the term 'uncorrupted' (ἄφθορος) to describe such Christians (Justin, *Apol.* 15.6; 29.1–3; Minucius Felix, *Oct.* 31.5). That some Christians did adopt such abstinence even won the admiration of Galen, although he disparaged the fact that their behaviour was not driven by reason, namely

6 On the question of Tatian's 'encratism', see Naomi Koltun-Fromm, 'Re-imagining Tatian: The Damaging Effects of Polemical Rhetoric', *JECS* 16 (2008), 1–30, who decides that the origins and reliability of this accusation are uncertain.

7 See below, pp. 393–4.

8 See James A. Francis, *Subversive Virtue: Asceticism and Authority in the Second-Century Pagan World* (University Park, PA; The Pennsylvania State University Press, 1995). For Christian concerns see David G. Hunter, *Marriage, Celibacy, and Heresy in Ancient Christianity: The Jovinianist Controversy* (OECS; Oxford: Oxford University Press, 2007), 90–105.

by the overcoming of the passions by the will.[9] The actual driving forces for such behaviour obviously varied among different Christian groups, and were not always expressly articulated.

The Pauline tradition contributed its own dynamic to these tendencies, as is evidenced by two opposing second-century claims to reproduce Paul's own teaching: While the Pastoral Letters repeatedly urge a commitment to marriage and to the upbringing of children, the *Acts of Paul* represent the core of Paul's preaching as a 'self-discipline and the resurrection' that provokes at least one hearer, Thecla, into renouncing marriage.[10] Also within the 'Pauline' tradition, *1 Clement* and Ignatius warn that anyone who is able to remain continent should not boast of it, thereby implicitly assigning such practice a certain primacy; it is perhaps with deliberate irony that Ignatius declares that anyone who does so boast (other than to the bishop) is thereby 'corrupted' (*1 Clem.* 38.2; Ignatius, *Poly.* 5). Both authors reflect the extent to which the language of 'holiness' or 'chastity' (ἁγνεία) and 'self-discipline' (ἐγκρατεία) were coming to refer primarily to sexual abstinence, and they both regard such practice as directed 'to the flesh', although in Ignatius' case this is characteristically defined Christologically, 'in honour of the flesh of the Lord'.

It is likely that Paul's ambivalent teaching in 1 Corinthians 7 is already at play in these responses, and certainly it continued to provide a particular provocation. Marcion's own interpretation of the chapter is unclear, but this is only because Tertullian finds himself struggling to emphasise Paul's affirmation of marriage, betraying by the relative superficiality of his discussion his actual closeness to Marcion's own position, both by instinct and then, by the time of the writing of the *Against Marcion*, further reinforced by his attraction to Montanism.[11] Likewise, Tertullian agrees that 1 Corinthians 6.13 'dissuades us from fornication', but, strikingly, he ignores the appeal Paul makes there to Genesis 2.24, which is witnessed as present in Marcion's text by Epiphanius, perhaps because this might be used to justify the equation of marital intercourse with

[9] See Richard Walzer, *Galen on Jews and Christians* (London: Oxford University Press, 1949), 15–16.

[10] 1 Tim. 2.13; 3.4, 12; 5.4; *Acts of Paul* 5. See Markus Lau, 'Enthaltsamkeit und Auferstehung: Narrative Auseinandersetzung in der Paulusschule', ed. Martin Ebner, *Aus Liebe zu Paulus? Die Akte Thekla neu aufgerollt* (SBS 206; Stuttgart: Katholischen Bibelwerk, 2005), 80–90.

[11] See also *AM* I. 29.1–5. See Braun, 'Tertullien et l'exégèse de 1 Cor 7'; also Reynolds, *Marriage in the Western Church*, 189–200; however, Paul Mattei, 'Le Divorce chez Tertullien: Examen de la question à la lumière des developments que le De Monogamia consacre à ce sujet', *RevSciRel* 60 (1986), 207–34, argues that Tertullian is consistent in his antipathy to remarriage and merely expresses himself more economically against Marcion.

'fornication'.[12] Instead, Tertullian counters Marcion's reported argument that 'the limbs of Christ will not arise because they are no longer ours' with the assertion that Paul teaches the resurrection of the flesh. Other hints reinforce these apparent echoes of Marcion's own position: Tertullian leapfrogs from 2 Corinthians 5.17, 'if there is a new creation in Christ', to 7.1, 'Let us cleanse ourselves from the wickedness of flesh *and blood* [*sic*]', and thence to 11.2, with the allusive comment, 'if indeed he determines to assign the holy virgin, the church, to Christ, as also bride to groom, the image cannot be combined with hostility towards the actuality itself' (*AM* V. 12.6); this sequence may follow intra-textual connections that were already drawn by Marcion, rather than be driven only by Tertullian's 'desire to finish', as has been suggested.[13] Similarly, Marcion arguably understood Ephesians 5.28–9 to mean that believers should be married as Christ is to the church, namely asexually.[14] Each of these passages might be read as offering a further justification for a call to live the asexual life of the redeemed, even if in a married state, and Marcion may well not have been alone in making these exegetical deductions.[15]

The little snapshot provided by the account that Eusebius gives of the correspondence of Dionysius of Corinth in the second half of the second century is revealing both for the apparently more widespread concerns regarding sexual practice, and for the difficulty of unravelling any association with heresy, and with Marcion in particular (Eusebius, *HE* IV. 23). Reportedly, Dionysius provided the churches of Amastris and elsewhere in Pontus with encouragement 'concerning marriage and chastity (ἁγνεία)', while he combated 'the heresy of Marcion' in a letter to Nicomedia, further to the west. Crete was a particular focus of his concerns. His warning to one bishop, Pinytus of Knossos, 'not to impose a heavy burden as regards chastity', was received only coolly and as lacking in more demanding nourishment, while he encouraged another, Philip of Gortyna, later credited with a 'vigorous work against Marcion', to guard against 'the error of heretics'. It may well be, as suggested by Pierre Nautin, that the real issues

12 Tertullian, *AM* V. 7.4; Epiphanius, *Pan.* 42.12.3, R14.

13 As suggested by Braun, *Contre Marcion*, V, 252 n. 1. On the reading of 2 Cor. 5.17 see above, p. 264; that Marcion read 'and blood' (instead of 'and spirit') at 2 Cor. 11.2 is likely although not otherwise attested in the manuscript tradition.

14 See above, pp. 268–9.

15 Ekkehard Mühlenberg, *Altchristliche Lebensführung zwischen Bibel und Tugendlehre: Ethik bei den griechischen Philosophen und den fruhen Christen* (AGAW, Phil-Hist. 3.272; Göttingen: Vandenhoeck & Ruprecht, 2006), 104, identifies the combination of 1 Cor. 6.19 with Eph. 5.27 and of 2 Cor. 11.2 with Eph. 5.31–2 as basic justifications for sexual abstinence. See above, n. 5: Marcion perhaps required the rejection of intercourse within marriage.

in the region were to do with encratism and rigorism, and that charges of 'Marcionism' either were exchanged in the debates or were deduced by Eusebius himself.[16] Similar ambiguities are to be found further East. Ascetic tendencies seem to have been a particularly significant hallmark of 'Syrian' Christianity in its various forms, although the distinctive origin of these remains unclear.[17] Nonetheless, Ephraem, too, is hard put to distance Marcion from the outwardly similar behaviour adopted by some of his contemporaries (Ephraem, *CH* 45), while Eznik of Kolb also struggles with the similarities between Marcionites and members of his own Church, both of whom, it seems, claimed the title 'Covenanters' given to those dedicated to a greater ascetic discipline (*De Deo* 416).[18]

The problem clearly was that outwardly similar practices could be inspired by very different principles, and that similar principles could inspire different practices; so, too, those who did adopt the various patterns of behaviour may have interpreted what they were doing in a variety of ways, not necessarily in agreement either with those who praised or denounced them or with their immediate co-practitioners.[19] Given the prevalence of such concerns among all groups in the period it would be wrong to assume simply either that abstract principles determined the behaviour, or that the adoption of certain patterns of behaviour preceded their secondary justification through appeal to theological principles. The examples already cited point to a variety of factors, including different responses to a realised or to a future eschatology; an assimilation of the believer to the person of Christ; debates about the continuing relevance of the body, whether in the present or in some future state; varying constructions of 'flesh'; and the desire for more demanding expectations of total self-dedication to God, some of which may have had roots in earlier Jewish practice. To these should be added specific exegetical practices, whether focused on passages dealing with purity in the Scriptures, on traditions about Jesus, or on Paul's own, highly ambivalent, teaching. Certainly, factors in Marcion's case included his rejection of any suggestion that Jesus himself underwent human birth, and his appeal to Jesus' redefinition of family (Luke 8.20–1); bound up with this was his understanding of the nature of Jesus' bodiliness and of that of believers,

16 See Pierre Nautin, *Lettres et écrivains chrétiens des IIe et IIIe siècles* (Patristica II; Paris: Éd. du Cerf, 1961), 16–26.

17 See Griffith, 'Asceticism', and the monumental work of Arthur Vööbus, *History of Asceticism in the Syrian Orient. A Contribution to the History of Culture in the Near East* (3 vols.; CSCO 184, 197, 500, Subsidia 14, 17, 81; Louvain: Sec. CSCO/Peeters, 1955–1988).

18 See above, p. 177.

19 See Andrew McGowan, 'Marcion's Love of Creation', *JECS* 9 (2001), 295–311, 304–5.

for which his reading of Paul offered further evidence. However, it is less clear whether these exegetical positions inspired or justified a position that had its roots elsewhere.

Certainly a number of so-called gnostic texts also advocate asceticism, and in particular reject marriage, within the framework of their demiurgical systems.[20] Hence, it is not surprising that subsequent authors are explicit that Marcion's rejection of reproduction was a direct expression of his hatred of the Demiurge, although, as has been seen, the reverse is equally true, that the association of the Demiurge with change, and with 'generation', could be identified as what set the latter below the supreme God.[21] This might seem to distance Marcion from the more general widespread ascetical trends of the period, and associate him more closely with the 'cosmic alienation' often ascribed to such 'gnostic' or demiurgical positions. Vigorous arguments have been made on both sides of the debate as to whether the disparagement of the created order and its Creator was a secondary justification of a prior intense sexual asceticism, or whether the latter was the consequence of the former.[22] In Marcion's case his exegetical priorities only serve to complicate the issue further.

It seems likely that Marcion's 'asceticism' was not limited to matters of sexual practice and reproduction. In including concerns about aspects of diet he would have been similarly participating in contemporary trends. Again, it is only in his criticism of the Encratites that Irenaeus implicates Saturninus and Marcion in their 'introduction of the avoidance of those things they call "ensouled" (ἔμψυχος)'; again, for Irenaeus this helps provide a counterbalance to Basilides and Carpocrates who are accused of 'disregard towards the

20 Koschorke, *Die Polemik der Gnostiker*, 112–27. However, it is unlikely that Marcion's asceticism was driven by the desire to recover a pre-fall identity which knew no sexual differentiation with its consequences, a position that Han J. W. Drijvers, 'Apocryphal Literature in the Cultural Milieu of Osrhoene', *Apocrypha* 1 (1996), 231–47, argues for later Syriac asceticism.

21 See Ps.Hippolytus, *Ref.* X. 19.4; Clement of Alexandria, *Strom.* III. 4.25 (pp. 91, 130 above). On the more ambivalent account by Epiphanius, see p. 108.

22 Michael A. Williams, 'The Demonizing of the Demiurge: The Innovation of Gnostic Myth', ed. Michael A. Williams, Collett Cox, and Martin S. Jaffee, *Innovation in Religious Traditions: Essays in the Interpretation of Religious Change* (Religion and Society 31; Berlin: de Gruyter, 1992), 73–107, ascribes priority to the preoccupation with sexuality; similarly, Mühlenberg, *Altchristliche Lebensführung*, 106, suggests that early Christian exegetical and philosophical tendencies to asceticism prepared the ground for the gnostic exegesis including that of Marcion. Conversely, Tjitze Baarda, '"If you do not sabbatize the Sabbath..." The Sabbath as God or World in Gnostic Understanding (Ev. Thom., Log. 27)', ed. R. van den Broek, Tjitze Baarda, Jaap Mansfeld, *Knowledge of God in the Graeco-Roman World* (EPROER 112; Leiden: Brill, 1988), 178–201, argues for the priority of cosmological alienation there.

eating of food sacrificed to idols' (Irenaeus, *AH* I. 28.1–2). Once again, the wider second-century concern regarding self-control generally extended to matters of diet, with some recommending vegetarianism on the grounds of it being 'more natural to human beings'.[23] Ps.Hippolytus refers to Marcionite 'avoidance of foods', although this is part of his assimilation of Marcion to Empedocles (*Ref.* VII. 30.3), while Clement of Alexandria claims that Marcion forbade the use of 'what belongs to the world' (κοσμικοί: *Strom.* III. 4.25); yet, like the comparisons between him and the Cynics, the precise reference of such statements is unclear. Tertullian is notably even less informative: He accuses Marcion of hypocrisy in his disparagement of the Creator, since in his rites he uses water for baptism, oil for unction, milk and honey, probably for catechumens, and bread, 'by which he makes manifest his own body';[24] Marcion, he asserts, extracts the 'marrow (*medulla*)' of the earth for food, and the riches of the sea, 'which he considers a holier form of food' (Tertullian, *AM* I. 14. 3–4). This charge probably points to the avoidance of meat, but such practice would have offered Tertullian little polemical advantage, and he prefers to retort that Marcion would have been more consistent had he starved himself to death. Indeed, the repeated charge against him of ingratitude could be taken to indicate that Marcion was ready to make use of many if not all elements of the created order despite his refusal to honour their Creator, but, more probably, the charge is simply carried over from other polemics regardless of its strict applicability.[25] Later sources refer to the Marcionites as fasting, according to Epiphanius 'on the Sabbath', which might suggest that otherwise their diet was more conventional, although perhaps more probably this is a polemical mirroring of conventional Christian practice. They also attribute to them a distinctive Eucharistic diet; the use of water instead of wine, or, more problematically, of milk and honey: It is certainly possible that a Marcionite rejection of any process that could be linked to 'corruption' became institutionalised, and the use of diet, especially in a ritual context, to mark distinctive identity is a common phenomenon.[26] Theodoret of Cyr describes his encounter with

23 See Francis, *Subversive Virtue*, who cites Musonius Rufus, Epictetus and others (pp. 13, 18 etc.).

24 It is probably over-interpreting Tertullian's silence to deduce that Marcion avoided wine in the Eucharist.

25 For Marcion's ingratitude see Clement, *Strom.* III. 3.21. The assimilation to a Cynic way of life is a similar conventional polemic: Ps.Hippolytus, *Ref.* X. 19.4; cf. p. 96.

26 For fasting, see Ephraem, *CH* 28, and Epiphanius, *Pan.* 42.3.3 (on the Sabbath), although the latter's explanation that its purpose was to have nothing to do with 'the God of the Jews' who rested on the Sabbath is unconvincing (above p. 109). Ephraem's criticism of their use of milk and honey is surprising since this has positive associations in

a ninety-year-old Marcionite who would not take anything from the Creator but who admitted to compromising these principles in order to partake of the 'mysteries' – for Theodoret providing an occasion for mockery.[27]

Just as the sources give little evidence of the conceptual core inspiration of these 'world-denying' practices, so also they fail to reveal whether they also reflected sociopolitical responses to the reliable ordering of the world under imperial control.[28] However, within the ancient world dietary choices could carry a political dimension, a covert sign of resistance;[29] opponents of Christianity had long interpreted their family ethic as undermining society, and a community of those rejecting the social norms of marriage and family might certainly appear potentially subversive. It has been argued that the beneficient Demiurge of much second-century philosophy, with his role of ensuring cosmic harmony and stability, reflected and affirmed understandings of the similar role of the Emperor.[30] Marcion's disparagement of the Demiurge, as a source of evils, whose system of law and punishment is vigorously rejected, could be seen as profoundly counter-cultural.[31] It would be easy to imagine a Marcionite echoing the words attributed to Saturninus, one of the Scillitan martyrs (who were found carrying 'books and letters of Paul, a just man'): 'I do not recognise the dominion of this age' (*Acts of the Scillitan Martyrs* 6, 12). Yet the martyrs also protest their loyalty to the Emperor; as this example shows, straightforward lines between theological outlook, social practices, and political positioning are even more difficult to plot in the past than they are in the present.

COMMUNITY STRUCTURES

Contrary to their polemical intent, therefore, many of these charges imply that Marcionite communities appeared little different to those of their

earlier sources (Ephraem, *CH* 47.9; cf. *Odes of Solomon* 4.10; 40.1–2). McGowan, 'Marcion's Love of Creation', suggests that Marcion's attitude could be understood as one of reappropriation.

27 See above, p. 179. 28 See Norelli, 'Paix, justice'.

29 Hence the title of Francis, *Subversive Virtue*.

30 See Rebecca Flemming, 'Demiurge and Emperor in Galen's World of Knowledge', ed. Christopher Gill, Tim Whitmarsh, John Wilkins, *Galen and the World of Knowledge* (Cambridge: Cambridge University Press, 2009), 59–84. Woltmann, 'Geschichtliche Hintergrund', 32–3, presents Marcion as a reforming protest against the Stoic optimism of the period, that is also visible, for example, in *1 Clement*.

31 Drijvers, 'Apocryphal Literature', 238, sees the dispute between Bardaisan and Marcion as 'two lifestyles come into conflict', with Bardaisan's anthropology modelling the contemporary values of the 'cultural elite'.

opponents; the possibility that one might enter one unawares was probably not just a later phenomenon.[32] Despite Marcion's repudiation of the 'judaising' of the apostles and perhaps their heirs, and his claim to restore the Gospel, there is little evidence to suggest that he was the 'Reformer' of some more recent reconstructions, or that he sought to establish a 'reformed church' grounded on his rediscovered Pauline principles.[33] So too, contrary to the claims of Tertullian and of Epiphanius, accounts that assume either that he was expelled from 'the Roman church' or that he broke away from it to found his own community are largely anachronistic for the mid-second century.[34] Victor of Rome sought to 'cut off' whole churches in Asia, and he failed (Eusebius, *HE* V. 24.9); local acts of discipline would have been easier to enforce but only so far as any jurisdiction was recognised, which in Rome took time to establish.[35] The spread of those who claimed him as founder, however, does suggest that his movement quickly outgrew the model of a 'school' in which it may have originated, whether or not he deserves the frequent plaudits from modern interpreters for his 'institutional skills'.[36] More probably, he inspired teachers who took with them his interpretations of the world and of the Scriptures. If Theodoret's account of 'whole villages' is to be trusted, then presumably such teachers worked in parallel to the representatives of other forms of Christianity, each shaping the community where they settled. Although Marcion's opponents pay much attention to the disagreements found among some of his disciples, such as Apelles or Prepon, the long-lasting survival of a movement under his name, even when translated into new languages, indicates that for the most part he gave birth to a stable tradition of teaching and practice.

Undoubtedly, the spread of his movement was accompanied by the development of structures, although these appear to have been little different from those of other Christian groups or churches, perhaps suggesting a long period of co-existence or of blurred boundaries. Cyprian knows that converts from Marcionite groups 'seem already to have been baptised in the name of Jesus Christ', although he justifies baptising them (again) on the grounds that they do not hold the same Trinity (Cyprian, *Epist.* 73).

32 See Cyril of Jerusalem, *Catech.* 18.26, who warns against asking for directions to 'the church' without the explicatory epithet 'catholic'.

33 See p. 3.

34 See above, pp. 57, 106. That he took the initiative and broke away is argued by Langerbeck, 'Zur Auseinandersetzung', 173; Lüdemann, 'Zur Geschichte', 97.

35 See above, p. 304.

36 See above, p. 6 and, for example, Roetzel, 'Paul in the Second Century', 232–33.

Tertullian already claims that Marcion would only baptise the celibate, widows, and the divorced, although, as has been suggested, the first of these may have included those willing to commit to such practices within marriage. Moreover, even if they made particularly stringent demands of those who came for baptism, they may have allowed catechumens more leniency.[37] It was not in the interests of the polemicists to say on what terms those who were already married, and/or baptised, were received, but the very urgency of the polemic and efforts at differentiation must suppose that there were such. If some moved from the Marcionite fold into that of the Catholic church, then no doubt others moved in the opposite direction. While, as has been seen, Marcionite groups would not have been alone in upholding a level of attainment that not all would hope, or wish, to reach, that they did so may have been a source of attraction to some.

Marcionite communities were probably little different from their other counterparts in other ways, too. Epiphanius' claim that they allowed women to administer baptism is, as has been seen, merely an extrapolation from a more generic antiheretical topos, with no independent corroboration.[38] Contrary to Justin's assertion that Marcion and the others like him were not persecuted, it is evident from numerous references that they were just as likely to find themselves the objects of persecution and martyrdom. Narratives of martyrdom do not hesitate even to locate Marcionites alongside 'Catholics' in the arena, such as the elder Metrodorus whose martyrdom was apparently recounted with others from Smyrna like Polycarp and Pionius – and perhaps his death was also celebrated alongside theirs as well.[39] Indeed, the absence of specific accusations of flight, a frequent concern in the Church, suggests that they apparently made no efforts to avoid martyrdom. As has been seen, their opponents found this hard to explain, and, given no other ways of distinguishing them, had recourse only to vigorously discrediting the value of their acts.[40] In the eyes of outsiders, too, then they were, and could be labelled, 'Christians'.

37 Tertullian, *AM* I. 28.2; 29.1; IV. 11.8; cf. V. 7.6 where Tertullian professes ignorance about what was required of catechumens. On Epiphanius' account of their multiple washings see above, p. 108.

38 See above, p. 110. It cannot be correlated with the restrictions on women urged by the Pastoral Epistles (1 Tim. 2.12), and hence as supporting the anti-Marcionite character of these.

39 Eusebius, *HE* IV. 15.46; V. 16.21; *Mart.Pal.* X. 3.

40 Tertullian, *AM* I. 24.4; 27.5; Clement of Alexandria, *Strom.* IV. 4.18; Ephraem, *CH* 38. 9.

15

The principles of Marcion's thought and their context IV: the contradictions of the Gospel

The approach taken here has left until the end those features that have often been seen as the defining characteristics of Marcion's doctrine and of his impact on subsequent Christian development. The first of these is the pervasive emphasis on discontinuity, which readily crystallises around certain catchwords. There follows from this, secondly, the role of Paul, whether in Marcion's imagination or as a traceable influence on his thought. Linking these two, thirdly, are the understanding of, and the appeal to, a scriptural authority. The controlling term that holds these features together, albeit in different articulations, would be 'Gospel'.

LAW AND GOSPEL

Tertullian is adamant from the start that 'the separation of Law and Gospel is the characteristic and chief work of Marcion'; he claims that the 'Antitheses' are 'contrasted oppositions that attempt to establish the disparity of Gospel with Law, in order that they might also demonstrate a diversity of gods from the diversity of principles (*sententiae*) of each document (*instrumentum*)' (*AM* I. 19.4; cf. 21.5).[1]

Although only articulated quite so bluntly in these terms by Tertullian – it is, for example, absent from Ephraem – it has been widely accepted that Marcion's dualism was one of Law and Gospel. Adolf von Harnack expressed a further precision which again is echoed by many interpreters: 'The starting point of M's criticism cannot be missed in the tradition: It was provided in the Pauline opposition of Law and Gospel, malevolent, petty, and cruel penal justice on the one hand and compassionate love

[1] See above, p. 71; also Irenaeus, *AH* III. 12.12; IV. 12.3, although Marcion is not exclusively identified (see above, p. 41).

on the other'.[2] 'Starting point' may allow space for considerable further debate as to whether Marcion echoed, radicalised, seriously distorted, or had no substantive continuity with, the 'Pauline opposition'; indeed, each of these positions has been adopted by subsequent interpreters. Harnack's claim might also prompt discussion as to whether his own antithetical expansion of the opposition pertains only to its Marcionite form, or also, as is implied, to Paul's own thought. Certainly, his further assertion that 'Marcion had soaked himself in the basic thought of the Letters to the Galatians and to the Romans', reflects more about the status of those two letters in the interpretation of Paul in Harnack's own time than an independent analysis of Marcion's procedure, or indeed of reports about Marcion's thought. Subsequent understanding of Marcion has been hampered by the tendency to use 'Law and Gospel' as an all-encompassing framework for analysing and evaluating early Christian thought, whether as symbols of old and new covenant, of Old and New Testament, of modes of salvation before God, of early Christian attitudes to the Mosaic (and/or Oral) Torah, of the place and principles of ethics, or of life within the political framework of the state. Despite the undoubted importance of both terms 'Gospel' and 'Law' in Paul's thought, it is far from obvious that any early reader of Paul could, or should, have read Paul's letters by using them in such a framework of exclusive salvific categories.[3] Instead, Marcion's language and models need to be located within their own more immediate context, and with attention to the development of vocabulary as well as of concepts.

There are multiple strands in the early efforts to describe the significance of Jesus, and of those who believed in him, within the framework of the Scriptures and of Jewish experience, but it is only over a considerable period of time that these come to be expressed in regular formulations. In particular, the term 'Gospel', despite its adoption by Paul and its development as a distinctively 'Christian' concept, is initially only sporadically taken up. When Ignatius speaks of those who have not been persuaded by 'the prophets and the law of Moses, nor even now [by] the Gospel and our sufferings', the fourth component, 'our sufferings', makes it difficult to be confident precisely what he means by 'Gospel'; equally ambiguous is his

2 Harnack, *Marcion*, 30.

3 Contrast Victor E. Hasler, *Gesetz und Evangelium in der Alten Kirche bis Origenes: Eine auslegungsgeschichtliche Untersuchung* (Zurich: Gotthelf, 1953), who proceeds by tracing the exegesis of certain key Matthaean passages during the period, but who also uses the two terms as representing both historical and systematic entities. See also Verweijs, *Evangelium und neues Gesetz*.

encouragement to hold on 'to the prophets and particularly the Gospel in which the suffering is made plain to us and the resurrection completed' (Ignatius, *Smyrn.* 5.2; 7.2). Both passages suggest an unbroken harmony between prophets (and Law) and Gospel, although elsewhere Ignatius contrasts 'the archives', probably the Jewish Scriptures, with 'the Gospel' (*Philad.* 8.2). Yet Ignatius is alone even in this degree of contrast; it is striking that *Barnabas*, whose major preoccupation might be described as the proper interpretation of the Jewish Law, does not use the term 'law' itself to explore it – although it is a mark of scholarly preoccupation that the letter has been accused of 'misunderstanding the dialectical relationship of Law and Gospel'.[4] Similarly, although Justin can assert, 'we did not place our hope through Moses or through the law', he immediately continues with a declaration of 'the eternal and perfect law and faithful covenant' given through Christ; for him the term 'Gospel', infrequently used, needs explanation as a reference to specific texts (Justin, *Dial.* 10.2; 11.2; 100.1; *Apol.* 66.3). Even when Ptolemaeus argues for the status of the tripartite Law on the basis of the words of 'the Saviour', he nowhere uses the language of 'Gospel'.[5] There is little to suggest that the terminology of 'Law *versus* Gospel' had any resonance in this period, independently of the relevant authors' attitudes to what would become 'the Old Testament'.

Towards the end of the second century the picture changes. The most impressive example is provided by Melito of Sardis (fl. c. 160–80 CE), who develops an extended exposition of Passover and Exodus as a model or 'type' of the Passion of Jesus; the former serves like a craftsman's preliminary sketch or model, which in itself has no lasting function, particularly once the reality or intended construction is completed. The initial contrast is not only between elements within the two stories, the sheep and the Lord, but also between the two frameworks to which they belong: 'Old is the law but new the word; temporary is the model but eternal the grace; perishable the sheep but imperishable the Lord' (Melito, *Peri Pascha* §4, ll.19–24). In Melito's overall scheme, however, the first element in each pair is not dismissed as obsolete; in the second part of the homily the language of model is subsumed by the assertion that Christ was already active in Israel's past experience: 'It was he who guided you into Egypt and guarded you there and cared for

[4] See only *Barn.* 2.6, the 'new law of Christ', which is presumably opposed to 'their law' (3.6); 5.9 and 8.3 refer to those who 'preach [his] Gospel'. Contrast Johannes Klevinghaus, *Die theologische Stellung der Apostolischen Väter zur alttestamentlichen Offenbarung* (BFChTh 44.1; Gütersloh: Bertelsmann, 1948), 39; this whole study circles round the failure of these writers to maintain this right relationship between 'Law and Gospel'.

[5] See above, p. 356.

you; it was he who lit your way in a pillar and sheltered you in a cloud, who cut the Red Sea and led you through, and destroyed your enemy' (§84, ll.613–18). However, it is striking that as the first part moves towards its climax the language of Law and Gospel replaces that of Law and Word:

> As then in perishable examples so also in the imperishable; as in the earthly so also in the heavenly, for the salvation and the truth of the Lord were pre-modelled in the people and the decrees of the gospel were proclaimed beforehand by the law. Then the people became a model of a preliminary sketch and the law a writing of parable; but the gospel an exposition and fulfilling of law, and the Church a repository of the truth. The model was honourable before the truth and the parable was marvelous before the interpretation (ἑρμηνεία); that is, the people was honourable before the church arose and the law marvelous before the gospel came to light. When the church arose and the gospel came forth the model was emptied handing over its power to the truth and the law was fulfilled handing over its power to the gospel.
>
> (*Peri Pascha* §39–42, ll.255–72)

It is easy to see why this passage has been interpreted as refuting the view that the law and people were never possessed of any honour, a view identified as Marcionite because of the polarity of 'Gospel and Law'.[6] The unexpected introduction of 'Gospel' is striking, but so is the fact that the term is not used outside this section (which extends to §43, l.276), as neither is 'church'. Clearly Melito understands 'law' as, among other things, something that is written and that can be read;[7] whether the same is true of 'gospel' is less certain – 'interpretation' could apply either to written text or to oral exposition. For Melito law represents a narrative pattern whose ultimate subject and author is God – in whose activity Christ is also active; the unity of the divine actor is, therefore, a fundamental principle, whether or not polemically inspired. However, despite the contrast between 'command' (and by implication 'law') and 'grace' (§7, ll.40–3), there is no suggestion that these are two different ways of responding to God, or that there is any further tension between them. Moreover, even without any external impetus, Melito's own initial scheme of model and reality itself might provoke the question of whether the former as parable had any

6 That the *Peri Pascha* is in part directed against Marcion is argued by Wilson, *Related Strangers*, 253–5.

7 This follows from its being written (so also §6, ll.38, 66), but it also presupposes some connection with 'the writing of the Hebrew Exodus' whose reading opens the homily.

intrinsic value; since this was certainly not Marcion's own starting point, the response could only serve to refute him in an indirect way.

Irenaeus appears to represent a new position: When he specifically addresses the question of Law and Gospel he is explicitly responding to 'All those of evil disposition, who are driven by the giving of the law (*legisdatio*), which is according to Moses, and think that it is different from and contrary to the teaching of the Gospel – who still have not repented – and so who ask about the origins of the difference and of each testament/covenant'. In response, Irenaeus understands his task as to demonstrate that 'God the maker of the universe is one' and that 'the law which is according to Moses and the grace of the new testament, each being appropriate to the times, are established for the benefit of the human race by one and the same God' (Irenaeus, *AH* III. 12.10–12; cf. V. 22.1). Undoubtedly, when he finds himself compelled to deal with Jesus' attitude to the Law he understands it in terms of legal precepts, but there is little to suggest that he is struggling to articulate a primary relationship between Law and Gospel as concepts. Indeed, Matthew 13.52 allows him to bring together 'the giving of the law', as 'the old which was before', and 'the new', which is 'behaviour (*conversatio*) according to the Gospel'; even here he immediately continues with the affirmation of the primacy of the giving of the law in freedom, and to every race, over that given in slavery to one race alone (*AH* IV. 9.1–2).[8] In Irenaeus' eyes, the formulation 'Law *versus* (or *and*) Gospel' apparently belonged entirely to the vocabulary of his heretical opponents, including but not exclusively Marcion.[9] For him, however, such a formulation makes little sense, and he has no real inclination to rescue it for his own exploitation; he will find his own models for exploring continuity and difference elsewhere.

Undoubtedly Paul was a key figure for Irenaeus, but, although he takes from him the language of Law, works, justification, and faith – irrespective of whether he understands these in a 'Pauline' sense – he does not relate these to the language of 'Gospel' (IV. 34.1).[10] Certainly, too, he knows that Marcion and his followers claim that Jesus taught contrary to and so dissolved the Law; part of his riposte relies on the command to love God 'in the Gospel', but he expends greater attention on explaining in what senses the Law has been expanded and how obedience to it has been enabled through the gift of liberty (IV. 12.4–13.4).[11] However, it is the language of old and new

8 This could be seen as an exegesis of Gal. 4.24.
9 So Noormann, *Irenäus als Paulusinterpret*, 381.
10 Noormann, *Irenäus als Paulusinterpret*, 413–20.
11 ibid, 406–16.

covenant that best helps Irenaeus explore the relationship between God's past relationship with the people and the new dispensation in Christ.

Before returning to Tertullian, it is notable that Origen demonstrates the development of a formulaic opposition of the God of the Law and the God of the Gospel as a hallmark of the heretics. He assumes that Celsus has derived his purported contradictions between what is written in the Law and in the Gospel 'from those who say the God of the Gospel is different from the God of the Law' (Origen, *C.Cels.* VII. 25).[12] Yet Origen's response here, as elsewhere, is entirely textual, provoking explication both of the continuities between Old and New Testament and of the need to interpret the former spiritually. The issue is not one of patterns of religion or of salvation but of the character of God as evidenced by specific texts; this would be even clearer if Origen did in fact claim that he could show that 'the God of Law and of the *Gospels* is one and the same', although the plural may be due to his translator (*De Princip.* II. 4–5).[13] Whether Origen derived these oppositional categories directly from his opponents or whether they were by then part of a heresiological and apologetic tradition, they had come to serve as something of an epigrammatic code, denoting a more extensive hermeneutical agenda.

Unlike his predecessors Tertullian is not in principle uncomfortable with the antithesis of Law and Gospel: 'the destruction of the Law and the building up of the Gospel serve my cause in this letter also' (Tertullian, *AM* V. 2.2). He finds in the double-edged sword of Rev. 1.16 'the two testaments of Law and Gospel'; elsewhere he uses his own terminology of 'document' (*instrumentum*), indicating that the contrast is, at least in part, a textual one (*AM* III. 14.3; IV. 1.1). Yet he can also describe the apostles as 'turning aside from Judaism, when they exchanged the obligations and burdens of the Law for the liberty of the Gospel', and he can state that 'the whole issue at stake is this, whether the Law of the Creator should be excluded from the Gospel in the Creator's Christ' (III. 22.3; V. 2.3). For Tertullian, the issue that divides him from his opponents is whether

12 Compare *Comm. in Rom.* II. 10,116–20, where Origen says that the Scriptures are read among the heretics although they separate Law from the Gospels. However, it is possible that in his translation Jerome has intensified, or even introduced, a Law/Gospel contrast: Thus whereas Jerome refers to Marcion and others who proclaimed one God of the Law and another of the Gospel, Origen's catena commentary has 'those who dissect the deity and think that the prophets belong to one God and the apostles to another': see Ronald E. Heine, *The Commentaries of Origen and Jerome on St Paul's Epistle to the Ephesians* (OECS; Oxford: Oxford University Press, 2002), 139 on Eph. 2.19.

13 This follows a reference to the witnesses available from all the Gospels: '*Longum erit si ex omnibus Evangeliorum locis testimonia congregemus, quibus unus atque idem Deus legis et Evangeliorum esse doceatur*' (*De Princip.* II. 4.2).

the acknowledged difference points to a difference of deities; his own answer is that the divinity (*divinitas*) preached is the same, the discipline (*disciplina*) is different (V. 2.3). His extensive engagement with the polarity in *Against Marcion* certainly suggests that he is in part provoked by the language of his opponent: If the *Against the Jews* is earlier, it is striking that the phrase 'the two testaments of the ancient law and new law' there becomes 'the two testaments of Law and Gospel' in the later work (*AJ* 9.18; *AM* III. 14.3). Yet, although rare it is not totally absent from his other writings; writing on prayer he appeals to the parables of wineskins and garments, beloved by Marcion, to point to 'a new form of prayer for new disciples of a new covenant (testament)'; the Law is supplemented, prophecy fulfilled, and the Gospel added on. Earlier, in polemic against Hermogenes, he described 'the Gospel' as the supplement to the 'old *instrumentum*' or even to Scripture (*De Orat.* 1.1; *Adv.Herm.* 20.4; 22.3). He also contrasts the newness of the Gospel with what is old (*De Corona* 11.1; *De Pudic.* 12.1). Tertullian's scheme of a progression in justice, from the nursery stage of nature, to the law and prophets in infancy, to the Gospel in youth, and finally to the Paraclete in maturity, evidently reflects the convictions of what is often called his Montanist stage (*De Virg. Vel.* 1.10); but the underlying principle that the Law represents one element or stage in a structure whose consistent focus is 'discipline' is basic to his own thought.[14]

Unlike Irenaeus, Tertullian, it would seem, is reading Marcion through spectacles that share the same focus and are – perhaps as a consequence – profoundly sensitive to the distortions effected by a common set of tools. Given his own efforts to understand the place of Law within a scheme patent of new demands and even of new revelation, he may have identified the polarity of 'Law and Gospel' as the vulnerable point both of his own system and of that of his opponent. If the problem, then, was as much his own, for Marcion, it may have been but one element in a more complex argument. Indeed, Tertullian's own understanding of 'Law and Gospel' is so fluid, extending from 'document' or covenant/testament to articulation of discipline, that it obscures any precise referent that it may have had in Marcion's system.

Yet Tertullian's defensiveness may betray an echo of Marcion's concerns. No doubt these were anchored in Galatians, which Tertullian acknowledges as in particular addressing the question of Law and Gospel. Tertullian's defence of the position taken by Peter and the 'brethren' indicates that he

[14] See Bray, *Holiness and the Will of God*, 111–23.

is genuinely responding here to an opponent, although his own reading of Acts 15 alongside Galatians 2.1–7 aids his own definition of the question as 'obedience to the Law of Moses' (cf. Acts 15.5). Marcion presumably saw the issue in similar terms but without the interpretive lens of Acts, and he drew the conclusion that the Pauline rejection – as he understood it – of such adherence was a demonstration that Paul represented a deity other than the one who demanded it.[15] This is already a recurring theme in Tertullian's treatment of Marcion's 'Gospel': He imagines his opponent commenting on Jesus' prohibition of divorce, 'Do you see the difference of Law and Gospel, Moses and Christ?' (Luke 16.18; *AM* IV. 34.1). If this sounds very far from a Pauline dialectic, it cannot be blamed on Marcion for elevating and at the same time profoundly misunderstanding 'Gospel'. Tertullian makes a similar, probably deliberate, misrepresentation of his opponent when he hints that a prohibition of divorce hardly sounds like the work of one committed to the destruction of Moses' 'constitution'; here again he is imposing on Marcion his own reading of 'Law' as command.[16] Marcion's imagined riposte, however, does make sense in its own terms: Moses and Christ are two authorities, Law and Gospel the patterns of life they represent and demand.[17]

If indeed Marcion did read Luke 16.18 as exemplary of Law and Gospel, he was doing so in the light of the preceding verses, 'The Law and prophets [were] until John, from then [*or* whom] the kingdom of God has been preached ("gospelled", εὐαγγελίζεσθαι) … heaven and earth may pass away more swiftly than one accent of the [my] words' (Luke 16.16–17).[18] Tertullian's protest confirms the importance of the passage, even though in his Latin version the semantic link with 'Gospel' had been lost: 'As if we did not acknowledge that John established a form of boundary between old and new, at which Judaism ceased and from which Christianity began, but

15 Marcion would have been sympathetic to a recent response to a paper asking, 'Galatians 2:11–14 – Was Peter Right?': 'It is essential to recognise the sharp opposition into which Law and Gospel are set. The Law is tied up with death. Christ died to the Law. The Gospel, however, brings life. With the coming of Christ there came about a turn from darkness to light. There is no compromise between them': Eric Osborn (perhaps *in persona Pauli*), in the discussion following John McHugh, 'Galatians 2:11–14 – Was Peter Right?', ed. Martin Hengel and Ulrich Heckel, *Paulus und das antike Judentum: Tübingen-Durham-Symposium im Gedenken an den 50. Todetag Adolf Schlatters (19. Mai 1938)* (WUNT 58; Tübingen: Mohr Siebeck, 1991), 319–27 and 328–30, 329.

16 See Reynolds, *Marriage in the Western Church*, 189–200, who shares Tertullian's sense of the incongruity of Marcion's position.

17 See above, p. 281.

18 Tertullian's citation, 'words of the Lord', indicates that Marcion read 'my words' as in Luke 21.33; see p. 127.

not as if the cessation of law and prophets and the initiation of Gospel, in which is the reign of God, Christ himself, were made by another power' (Tertullian, *AM* IV. 33.8).[19] Both Tertullian and his opponent would seem to agree that the contrast, however understood, is a temporal one, 'until John'. Origen similarly criticises those ('the heterodox') who say that John belonged to another deity, the Demiurge, although he bases his own riposte on Mark 1.1 where John, although a type of the Old Testament or representative of its culmination, is still bound to the Gospel as its beginning (Origen, *Comm. in Joh.* I. 13). Law thus belongs to a historical period now past, 'the old'; Gospel belongs to the present, 'the new', although these adjectives are now firmly predicated of 'testaments'.

Old and new

The 'boundary between old and new' is therefore equally fundamental for the threat or misunderstanding that Marcion is seen as representing. However, 'newness' has an extensive reach. For Tertullian, the root folly of the Marcionites was their advocacy of a 'new God' (Tertullian, *AM* I. 8.1). As has been seen, 'newness' is fundamental to Tertullian's own logic of heresy, and is intrinsic to its definition.[20] Yet, once again, this marks territory that he navigates with extreme care: 'I do indeed acknowledge that one order was expressed in the old dispensation under the Creator, another in the new under Christ' (IV. 1.3). The detailed attention he expends on ridiculing 'newness' as he ascribes it to Marcion, while defending it in his own terms, obscures the precise extent to which 'new' served as a watchword in Marcion's own teaching. Certainly, Marcion's God was, as already explored, hitherto 'unknown', and even 'strange', to human knowledge, but any 'newness' thus implied was not that mocked by Tertullian. Undoubtedly the parable of the new wineskins (Luke 5.36–38) played a key role, as too, probably, did Paul's language of 'a new creation' (2 Cor. 5.17), and the effect of both these would be on radical discontinuity.[21] Yet, as Tertullian was forced to recognise, these passages already point to a tension that was integral to the very emergence of Christian thought.

Throughout Christian literature of the period 'newness' is both affirmed and denied. Probably without Pauline influence, *Barnabas* predicates

[19] In Tertullian's Latin the verb is 'announce', *adnuntio*.

[20] See above, p. 62; for Irenaeus, see p. 40.

[21] On these see above, pp. 231, 264; see also Tertullian, *AM* V. 17.15 on the 'new man' of Eph. 2.15. So also Epiphanius, above, pp. 105–06.

'the beginning of another world' and having 'become new' on the resurrection on 'the eighth day' (*Barn.* 15.8–9; 16.8), while Ignatius, in a passage quoted earlier, likens the incarnation to a totally 'new and unequalled star' (Ignatius, *Eph.* 19.2).[22] Yet 'newness' could also be an embarrassment in a world that valued antiquity above all else, as emerges particularly within an apologetic setting. The *Letter to Diognetus* takes as its starting point its reader's question why 'this new race or practice has come to life now and not previously' (*Diog.* 1). Celsus evidently made the same point: 'Is it only now after such a long age that God has remembered to judge the life of men? Did he not care before?' (Origen, *C.Cels.* IV. 7; cf. VI. 78). Yet more seriously, within political polemic 'newness' might suggest subversion and antisocial activity: Suetonius had labelled the Christians as 'a class of men given to a new and dangerous superstition' (*Nero* 16.2). In contrast to his practice in the *Dialogue*, in his *Apology* Justin avoids the language of newness; although he does claim for Christians some affinity with Socrates who was accused of introducing 'new daimonia', he prefers to emphasise the precedents, albeit corrupted, of Christian principles in Greek thought, and to argue for the antiquity of Moses and the prophets, whom Christians claimed for themselves, as well as of the activity of the Logos (Justin, *Apol.* 5.3; 21.1; 23.1; 2 *Apol.* 10.5).

On the other hand, 'newness' could bring apologetic benefits: The reply to Diognetus acknowledges 'newness' by exposing the intellectual folly of previous claims to know and worship God, both Jewish and Greek; the author presents God's 'late' intervention as a sign not of previous lack of concern, but of long-suffering kindness and as the final accomplishment of a long-planned purpose (*Diog.* 8). His identification of God as 'master and creator of all' and his insistence that this long-suffering God is and always has been 'without wrath' and 'alone good' could be read as a challenge to Marcion. However, it is equally likely that Marcion was in effect mounting an exposé of the difficulty in maintaining such a position while also affirming, as Diognetus also attempted to do, that 'before he came [no one] had any knowledge at all of what God might be' – a claim that might sound surprisingly like Marcion's own stance (*Diog.* 8.1).[23]

However, Tertullian gives this conventional topos a particular twist when he states that Marcion's separation of Gods or of Christs was based on 'the diversity of old and new testament' (Tertullian, *AM* IV. 6.1). The terminology is Tertullian's own, and 'newness' is, as has been seen,

[22] See above, p. 378.

[23] On the ambiguity of locating *Diognetus* in relation to Marcion see also p. 422.

a particular concern for him. It is he who identifies the Transfiguration as the cessation of the old and replacement by the new, each 'testament' having been ratified on a mountain (IV. 22.7, 11).[24] By contrast, Marcion, it would seem, was not concerned with the character of a complementary or parallel 'old' dispensation but with that of an entirely different one, defined by being under the Creator. His version of Jesus' words over the cup at the Last Supper may have spoken only of a 'covenant', without the adjective 'new' (*AM* IV. 40.4; cf. Luke 22.20). It would be anachronistic to assume that Marcion in the mid-second century used these terms in a documentary sense, and there is nothing to support the suggestion that it was he who first offered as a counterpart to a familiar 'old testament' an alternative scriptural authority, a 'new testament' consisting of his 'Gospel' and 'Apostolikon'.[25] At a later date, when the idea of the two testaments was firmly textualised in Christian thought, then only did Marcion come to be accused of pulling apart, or of cutting and pasting, what properly belonged together (Ephraem, *CH* 2, 19–20; 36, 8).[26]

Judaism and Christianity

Tertullian had already introduced the third pair in his comment on Luke 16.16, 'Judaism and Christianity', when he charged Marcion with establishing a divide between the Christ who came under Tiberius and the one yet to come, 'as great as that between just and good, between Law and Gospel, between Judaism and Christianity' (*AM* IV. 6.3). Although repeated elsewhere in the *Against Marcion*, this pair is not found outside it, and neither of the individual terms is common in Tertullian's work.[27] This, together with the Greek origin of the terms, makes it likely that its association with Marcion was not entirely Tertullian's invention, although Irenaeus' apparent ignorance of the polarity indicates that it did not function as a significant 'head-line' for the former.

Marcion most likely used the term 'Judaism' under the influence of Paul's reference to his 'past life in Judaism' (Gal. 1.13–14), and his voice may be

24 See above, p. 249 on 'testament' in Gal. 4.24.

25 So, rightly, Markschies, *Kaiserzeitliche christliche Theologie*, 253–8, against Kinzig, 'καινὴ διαθήκη'; see above, p. 2.

26 See pp. 167–9.

27 *PrH* 7.11 contrasts the '*dialecticum christianismum*' with the 'curiosity' of the philosophers. 'Those from Judaism who believe' in the *Against the Jews* (*AJ* 9.3) becomes 'Hebrew and Marcionite Christians' (*AM* III.12.3). In *De Pud.* 17, a late writing, he asks whether Paul might seem to be adopting an argument 'from Judaism'. See also *De Res.* 50.7, below.

heard behind Tertullian's affirmation, 'we also claim Galatians as a primary letter against Judaism' (*AM* V. 2.1). It would not be difficult to see how a reader of Galatians 1–2 might bring together Paul's own statement of his background in Judaism with his declaration that he had died to the Law, as well as with his defence of the Gospel that he had been called to proclaim through the revelation of God's son, and with the opposition to that Gospel, which focused on the need to be circumcised and on the Law. Here would fit his accusation, according to Tertullian, of the other apostles as being 'too close to Judaism', and of Luke's Gospel as having been corrupted 'by the protectors of Judaism' (IV. 4.4; V. 3.1). The assertion that the tax-collector 'was outside the Law and profane to Judaism' suggests that 'Judaism' and 'Law' were synonymous for Marcion (IV. 11.1 on Luke 5.27–28); similarly, Marcion may be among those whom Tertullian describes as identifying the 'flesh and blood' of 1 Corinthians 15.50, with the help of Galatians 1.16, as 'Judaism', defined in particular by circumcision (*De Res.* 50.7).[28] If Marcion did interpret 'Judaism' as a distortion present already in the time of Paul and represented by the other apostles, it would have been for him more a danger within the Church than embodied in some other outside group, such as the Jews of his own time. However, for Tertullian the term is tied to the 'old covenant' and perhaps to the Jewish tradition associated with it: He is able to conclude that if Paul had turned away from Judaism and was 'the destroyer of Judaism' (*AM* I. 20.3; V. 1.8; 5.1; 17.9), then so was Jesus himself (III. 6.10; 22.3).

It is more uncertain whether Marcion used 'Christianism' in opposition to 'Judaism' – Pauline precedent would have suggested 'Gospel'. Each of the occurrences in Tertullian's writing can be ascribed to himself: In addition to those already cited, it is he, not Marcion, who explains Paul's allegory in Galatians 4.22–24, 31 as 'the nobility of Christianity' against 'the legal servitude to Judaism' (*AM* V. 4.8; cf. 3.5).[29] The only indication that Tertullian might be drawing on earlier debates would be Ignatius of Antioch, who makes an uncompromising separation of 'Judaism' from 'Christianity': 'For Christianity did not direct its faith to Judaism but Judaism to Christianity' (Ignatius, *Magn.* 10.3; cf. 8.1; 10.1; *Philad.* 6.1). Prior to Ignatius and Paul, 'Judaism' appears in the Maccabean literature, where it mimics other more established words like 'hellenism',

28 Ignatius, *Philad.* 6.1 (see below), similarly identifies circumcision as the characteristic mark of Judaism.

29 See also *AM* V. 6.10 where Tertullian interprets Isa. 3.1–3 as referring to Paul's removal from Judaism (= Judaea) for the building up of Christianity.

'barbarism' (2 Macc. 2.21; 8.1; 14.38; cf. 4 Macc. 4.26); other connections between Ignatius and the Maccabean tradition perhaps point to local usage rather than deliberate borrowing. Further, given his partiality for 'christ-' compounds, '*christianismos*' is likely to be Ignatius's own coinage, a fact that in turn would explain its subsequent solitary appearance in the account of the trial of Polycarp, who had a role in collecting Ignatius' letters (Polycarp, *Phil.* 13.1; *Mart.Poly.* 10.1).[30] Given the other points of contact between the language of Ignatius and that of Marcion,[31] it remains possible that this polarity was in use in circles that emphasised discontinuity, even if it cannot be demonstrated for Marcion himself.

Evidently Marcion did express his theology through oppositions or 'antitheses', even if the literary formulation of these was not of overriding importance for him. It is also clear that certain key terms were foundational, reappearing in a range of polemical texts: 'good', 'just', 'unknown', 'Gospel', 'new'. However, these two facts are not to be combined overly simplistically: It seems likely that it is Tertullian who has epitomised Marcion's thought as a series of antithetical slogans, 'Law versus Gospel', 'old versus new', 'Judaism versus Christianity'. That he was successful in so doing was because of the appeal such epigrammatic summaries had for articulating continuing internal Christian anxieties. Projecting these upon the heretic allowed Christian writers to negotiate between them, and indeed to reapply them to other contested areas of thought and practice.

SCRIPTURES AND AUTHORITY

Law observance and prophetic fulfilment

It is within this process that the roots of the classic picture of Marcion as embodying and provoking Christian ambivalence about 'the Old Testament' are to be located.[32] In fact, much that could be said about the conventional depiction of him as representing an extreme stance regarding the continuing relevance of the 'Law and prophets' has already been discussed. That is because, as he has emerged here, Marcion did not belong, at least initially, within the trajectory of debates concerning the continuing obligation of believers in Jesus to obey the injunctions of Torah, or of those debates concerning interpretation of the prophetic passages; however, in time he,

30 See Lieu, *Christian Identity*, 108–9, 251–2. 31 See above, pp. 6, 407.

32 For example, Moll, *Arch-Heretic*, 135–58, identifies 'the Old Testament before Marcion' as the decisive theme to be considered under the heading 'Marcion's time'.

as 'remembered', does become entangled within these. The origins of that particular, multistranded, trajectory can be traced from the ambiguities regarding the Gospel accounts of Jesus' attitude towards Sabbath or purity observance, coupled with the conviction that in him not just prophets but also Law were 'fulfilled', passages that undoubtedly Marcion did find fruitful for his own purposes. It continues through Paul's anguished debates both over the obligations to be asked of non-Jewish believers and over the implications of this for the status and intention of 'the Law', which again attracted Marcion's creative exegesis. However, that others were struggling with these problems is demonstrated both by the very different models of that status and intention that are explored, for example, by Hebrews and by *Barnabas*, as well as by the complex pattern of attitudes towards those individuals or groups who did practice or advocate continuing adherence to some or all of the provisions of Torah.

The conclusion reached in *Barnabas* that the Jews ('they') totally lost the covenant when they broke the law at the making of the golden calf, with the consequence that Israel was abandoned (*Barn.* 4), demonstrates the close intersection between debates over the status of the Jewish Law, and later over 'the Old Testament', and attempts to define the place of 'the Jews', both past and present, in the overarching purposes of God. The two come together clearly in Justin Martyr, who is also forced to locate the continuing force of moral obligations that were to be found within the Law: the 'perfect law … which it is now necessary that all people should obey' (Justin, *Dial.* 11.2; cf. 43.1). For him, if blame is to be attributed, it is 'on account of your lawlessness and hardheartedness', which necessitated the imposition of the Law (*Dial.* 18.2; 19.6). Yet this aspect of the purpose of the Law is but one part of a threefold division that Justin draws which also distinguishes those commands that are directed towards 'piety and right practice' and those whose primary function is as a sign of 'the mystery of Christ' (*Dial.* 44.2).

These issues were evidently live ones in Christian thought from a number of different perspectives. Thus, Justin overtly has to defend Christian nonobservance of Sabbath and other Torah observances, and is aware of the variant practice and attitudes to be found among Christians (*Dial.* 10; 47). However, it is not at all evident that this was a major concern for his near-contemporary, Ptolemaeus, even though the latter also taught a division of the Law into three, and in explicit opposition against those who misjudged its origins. Presupposing that the character of Law must reflect the character of the legislator, and that the former is to be measured by 'the words of the Saviour', Ptolemaeus concludes that, since the Law is self-evidently imperfect, it cannot be attributed to 'the perfect God the

Father'. He explains the second and third subdivisions of the law as respectively the work of Moses and of the elders on their own initiative, while the first is to be ascribed to the God of justice who is also the Creator. Yet this first subdivision is itself tripartite, with part allegorical, part 'interwoven with inferiority and injustice', and so destroyed by the Saviour, and only part 'properly called Law', and fulfilled by the Saviour (Epiphanius, *Pan.* 33.4–5). The part intended to be allegorical of the spiritual is that 'dealing with offerings and circumcision and the sabbath and fasting and Passover and unleavened bread and other similar matters', but Ptolemaeus is not embarrassed to admit to still practising 'external (φαινόμενος)' fasting alongside 'spiritual', and there is little sense that he is addressing serious pressures regarding law-observance.[33] Finally, even this final part, identified as the Decalogue, which contains 'pure law-giving but not perfection, required fulfilment by the Saviour'.

Evidently, both the challenges of specific situations and explanatory logic demanded some interpretation of received traditions. There is no reason to suppose that Justin and Ptolemaeus specifically have Marcion in view, or even that they develop their own ideas under the pressure of the challenges he provoked. When Justin rejects those who criticise God for 'not always teaching the same things as righteous', the context is an apologetic one towards both outsiders and 'Jews' (Justin, *Dial.* 30.1). It has proved possible to identify Ptolemaeus both as arguing against Marcion, and, conversely, as adopting a fundamentally Marcionite position.[34] This ambiguity is demonstrated, on the one hand, by the way Ptolemaeus' argument moves from the nature of the law to the character of God, and hence to a distinction between two deities, as well as by the appeal to the words of Jesus as providing the criterion of authenticity, including Jesus' rejection of divorce and his exhortation to turn the other cheek in contrast to the *lex talionis*. On the other

[33] However, there continued to be areas where observance was a very pressing issue, as is exemplified by the Syriac *Didascalia*, which also adopts a division of the law into the eternal and the second legislation, the latter given after the Golden Calf incident, and which is clearly seeking to so justify a separation in practice from non-Christian Jews. See Charlotte Elisheva Fonrobert, 'The *Didascalia Apostolorum*: A Mishnah for the Disciples of Jesus', *JECS* 9 (2001), 483–509; W. C. van Unnik, 'The Significance of Moses' Law for the Church of Christ According to the Syriac Didascalia', *Sparsa Collecta* (NovTSup. 31; Leiden: Brill, 1983), 7–39, emphasises the difference from Ptolemaeus.

[34] See W. Löhr, 'La doctrine de Dieu dans la Lettre à Flora de Ptolémée', *RHPhR* 75 (1995), 177–91. The debate is complicated by the question whether this Ptolemaeus is to be identified with the Valentinian of the same name in Irenaeus. See also Herbert Schmid, 'Ist der Soter in Ptolemaüs *Epistula ad Floram* der Demiurg? Zu einer These von Christoph Markschies', *ZAC* 15 (2011), 249–71, who sees Marcion and Ptolemaeus as reflecting similar debates in the Roman context.

hand, unlike Marcion, for Ptolemaeus the relationship between these deities is one of inferiority but not one of hostility.

Most probably, each of these authors represents a different stance in more extensive debates, stimulated by internal as well as by external polemical and apologetic demands. Marcion may well have shared Ptolemaeus' philosophical starting point, but he was also constrained by his need to exegete Paul's own language. Perhaps this is in part why, even if his main concern was a contrast between the authority of the Creator and the grace brought by Christ, it would be difficult to avoid some temporal expression of this: '*then the law*, now the justice of God through faith of Christ' (Rom. 3.22).[35] Similarly, the language of fulfilment or goal had to be addressed, although he presumably found less contradiction in ascribing this to the adversarial work of another God (Rom. 5.21; Gal. 5.14; Tertullian, *AM* V. 4.12–13; 13.8–10).

The issues of observance and the nature of fulfilment were both related to but separate from those of the continuing place of Israel or 'Judaism' in the purposes of God. In fact, the latter appears less of a fraught concern than the former, and it has been argued that it is Marcion who did much to stimulate the debate.[36] However, unlike his mentor, Paul, who agonised over his relationship with 'his own family' (Rom. 9.1–5, not attested for Marcion), there is little to suggest that the question of the role of the Jews was a compelling issue for Marcion himself. He probably understood references to 'the rest of the Jews' (Gal. 2.13) and to 'Judaism' as labelling the apostles who opposed Paul. As has been seen, it is unlikely that he labelled the Creator, 'God of the Jews', and attempts to associate him with Jewish interpretations of Scripture are entirely a rhetorical device by Tertullian. Accounts of the yet-to-come Jewish Christ are confused and invite the suspicion that they may owe something to the antithetical imagination of Tertullian himself (*AM* III. 24.1–2).[37] They might also have developed under the duress of debate: Thus they do echo the interpretive tradition already found in Justin that separates those prophecies fulfilled in Christ's coming in humility, and those yet to be fulfilled in exaltation, when, asserts Justin, those of the circumcision who approach him in belief and seeking a blessing will be accepted and blessed by him (Justin, *Dial.* 31–4 [33.2]). At the same time Tertullian's protest that those who rejected the prophets of the Demiurge hardly deserved condemnation mirrors objections which defended the Serpent for bringing humankind knowledge

35 On the text here see p. 256. 36 So Brennecke, 'Die Kirche als wahres Israel'.

37 However, see above, p. 281 and n. 44, for the suggestion that this was an original 'antithesis'.

(*AM* IV. 22.8–10). These were issues easily raised in 'questions and answers', but there is little sense that they belong to the substructure of Marcion's position.

Tradition and corruption

Tertullian's initial references to the dating of Jesus' appearance under Tiberius are designed to mock the gaps that separated it from the appearance of Marcion, as well as the latter from Tertullian's own time. The second gap established the ineffectiveness of the revelation of Marcion's God, which still had nothing to show for itself; the former demonstrated that 'that which first came forth under Antoninus did not come forth under Tiberius, that is, the God of the reign of Antoninus was not of the reign of Tiberius' (Tertullian, *AM* I. 15.1; 19.2–3). In practice both parties would have to give some account of the time lag between their own period and that of Jesus, and would have to justify the authority with which they claimed correctly to represent his message.

Within the early Church there are two primary solutions to this problem, both of which claim the apostles as their legitimating starting point. One, already introduced by Irenaeus, traces back a continuous tradition to the apostles, partly manned by the shadowy 'elders'; the other claims a more immediate authenticated apostolic origin for their texts and practice.[38] However, these solutions could not of themselves decide between competing claims to represent authentic apostolic tradition or to possess the authoritative apostolic tradition in written form. Between the time of Marcion and of Tertullian the controversy over the nature and timing of the celebration of the Passion/Passover of the Lord had been waged through appeals and counter-appeals to apostolic heritage, and Irenaeus had pleaded that maintaining a difference of practice, which evidently went back to 'those before us', would not undermine a unity of faith (Eusebius, *HE* V. 23–4).

Tertullian, therefore, is appealing to an optimistic ideal more than to proven practice when he assumes that all will agree that 'that is from the beginning which is from the apostles', and even when he also recognises that it was still necessary to determine what is 'from the apostles', concluding that it is 'that which has been held as sacrosanct among the churches of the apostles', to which have to be added the churches not of apostolic foundation but in alliance with them. These churches can stand surety for the Gospels,

[38] See above, pp. 42–4.

and not just for Luke of which Marcion alone has taken note. Yet Tertullian knows that Marcion's 'Gospel' also has its churches; his bluster that a little investigation will reveal that they are 'apostatic rather than apostolic' is just that, bluster, and it probably betrays that Marcion made similar claims for the pedigree of his own 'Gospel' (*AM* IV. 5.1–3).[39]

According to Tertullian, Marcion emended the Gospel available to him because he thought it had been corrupted (*AM* I. 20.1). Such a claim was almost impossible to disprove: Tertullian can only appeal to Luke's conformity to the other Gospels, which Marcion had not claimed to be corrupted – since he had ignored them – although this appeal has its own obvious weaknesses (IV. 5.6). The details of Marcion's theory of falsification are difficult to untangle, partly perhaps because they were not systematically set out, partly because Tertullian is only concerned to provide an account of something he feels able to undermine. Crucial is the somewhat obscure suggestion: 'If indeed that Gospel which is attributed to Luke among us – we shall see whether it is for Marcion – is the same as that which through his Antitheses Marcion argued was falsified by the champions of Judaism to form a single body with the law and prophets, by which they might fabricate a Christ…' (IV. 4.4).[40] Marcion's complaint here is somewhat ambiguous, particularly since Tertullian's Latin 'form a single body' (*concorporatio*) is a neologism, the only other use of which does little to help (Tertullian, *De Bapt.* 8.1). Accepting Tertullian's assumption of a literary or documentary model, the 'single body' might refer to the association of the Gospel with the 'Old Testament', or, more probably, the inclusion within the Gospel of material from 'the law and prophets'; in support of the latter, Origen uses a Greek equivalent for reading the different statements in the Gospels as a single narrative (Origen, *Comm. in Joh.* VI. 22.120).[41] However, if Tertullian's language does echo that of Marcion – itself uncertain – the latter may have been referring not to the physical location or production of texts, but to the way they were being used. Justin's 'interactive' reading of Psalm 22

[39] Interpreters are too quick to conclude that Marcion's churches were new foundations and not established churches that had accepted his teaching.

[40] Cf. *AM* V. 3.2 where in similar terminology Tertullian rejects the activity of the false brothers as being '*interpolatione scripturae qua Christum Creatoris effingerent*'.

[41] See above, p. 189, n. 13. As noted there, Hays, 'Marcion vs. Luke', following LS s.v. 'union, harmony', rejects the translation 'into a body'; however, LS appears to be reliant on Tertullian, *AM* IV. 4, and their rendering is less appropriate for the nature of the relationship between the water of baptism and the spirit following the imposition of hands ('*concorporationem eorum*': *De Bapt.* 8.1). Subsequently the term is used for Christological and eucharistic union. Origen's verb is σωματοποιέω, but compare Eph. 3.6, and συσωματοποιέω of amalgamation (*PGL* s.v.).

(LXX 21.) 1–24 and a Gospel-like Passion narrative could well be described as 'the formation of a single body' (Justin, *Dial.* 97–106).[42]

Tertullian's counter-argument is that, by claiming to restore that which had supposedly been 'falsified', Marcion in effect admits the priority of the latter. Both sides are playing the same game in which the original is by definition superior. Other models of negotiating authenticity and the possibility of innovation would have been available: In a different context Tertullian himself allows that the Paraclete provides a progression beyond the Gospel and Christ when he acknowledges that there are ambiguities in Scripture; he even describes the activity of the new outpouring of the Paraclete as 'purging' the darkness of these (Tertullian, *De Res.* 63). Among the Montanists, with whom Tertullian is here most clearly allied, Maximilla describes herself as sent as 'an interpreter…to impart the knowledge of God' (Epiphanius, *Pan.* 48.13);[43] yet even they apparently felt constrained also to claim a prophetic continuity with the earliest church (Eusebius, *HE* V. 17.3–4). That this could lead to a confrontation over the authenticity of received scriptural sanction is evident when Eusebius charges the Montanist Themiso with composing 'a certain catholic letter in imitation of the apostle', possibly Paul, and of 'blaspheming the lord and the apostles and the holy church' (Eusebius, *HE* V. 18.5) – which may indicate that Themiso held the apostles responsible for the disappearance of the spirit in the Church.

Marcion's solution was not a narrative of the possibility of new revelation but one of the loss of the original by corruption. He was not alone in this; the *Gospel of the Egyptians* chooses rather to appeal to physical loss or hiding and then final discovery in order to explain why 'since the days of the prophets, and the apostles, and the preachers, the name [of Seth] has not at all arisen upon their hearts' (*NH* III.2. 68).[44] The same theme is found in the philosophy of the period: Numenius wrote a work tracing the successive failure of the Academy to remain true to the initial teaching of Plato.[45] Moreover, an appeal to the corruption of the text or tradition, whether wilful

[42] On this see Judith M. Lieu, 'Justin Martyr and the Transformation of Psalm 22', ed. Charlotte Hempel and Judith M. Lieu, *Biblical Traditions in Transmission. Essays in Honour of Michael A. Knibb* (JSJSup. 111; Leiden; Bill, 2006), 195–211. There is no reason to identify this as drawn from the 'Syntagma' against Marcion as does Enrico Norelli, 'Le Statut des Textes Chrétiens', ed. Enrico Norelli, *Receuils normatifs et canons dans l'Antiquité: Perspectives nouvelles sur la formation des canons juif et chrétien dans leur contexte culturel* (PIRSB 3; Prahins: Éd. du Zèbre, 2004), 175–82.

[43] Christine Trevett, *Montanism: Gender, Authority and the New Prophecy* (Cambridge: Cambridge University Press, 1996), 165–6, suggests that Maximilla may have understood her work as in opposition to heresy.

[44] For the echo of 1 Cor. 2.9 cf. p. 261.

[45] Numenius, *Frag.* 24–8.

or accidental, supplied a routine justification for the sort of textual 'emendation' or commentary characteristic of the period, and particularly associated with the philosophical 'schools'.[46]

Marcion's account, however, is a striking one. As just noted, those blamed were 'the champions of Judaism' (*protectores Iudaismi*); Marcion found in Galatians 1–2, supported by passages from 2 Corinthians (2.17; 4.2; 11.13–15), the narrative of how 'false apostles', closely allied if not identified with Peter and James, did indeed carry out what Paul most fears, namely 'turn aside' believers 'from the one who called them, to another Gospel' (Gal. 1.6).[47] By implication at least, however, they were inspired not only by a mistaken allegiance to Judaism but also by the Creator God or 'the God of this age' (2 Cor. 4.4), represented in Paul's language by the sort of 'angel from heaven' into which even Satan might transform himself (Gal. 1.8; 2 Cor. 11.14). Thus, Marcion's demiurgical cosmology, his reading of the (Jewish) Scriptures, his understanding of the significance of Jesus' person and ministry, his story of the Church, and his strategies of textual interpretation and legitimation, are inextricably intertwined; the thread which runs through, and perhaps which holds together, this interweaving is Paul.

PAUL AND GOSPEL ...

Were it not for the insistent presence in his thought of Paul, the embattled apostle of Jesus Christ and the writer of letters, Marcion might easily appear as another 'demiurgical Christian', albeit one who was striking because of his fascination with scriptural 'problems' rather than with cosmogonic elaboration. Even favouring a single Gospel would not give him the same degree of distinction, although his apparent linking of this Gospel to Paul was, in context, highly idiosyncratic even if internally logical. His opponents accused him of misrepresenting Paul, both textually as well as in regard to his relations with the other apostles, while also claiming 'that Paul alone knew the truth' – even if he were not alone in this claim (Irenaeus, *AH* III. 13.1). Contrary to their intent, in more recent scholarship this charge has become a key reference point within debates as to how extensively, sympathetically, or accurately Paul was remembered in the second century; more specifically, it has formed a cornerstone within constructions of

46 See above, p. 307.

47 See above, pp. 245–6; according to Tertullian, *AM* V. 3.1 Marcion saw Peter and James as 'too close to Judaism' (above, p. 246). In *Adam.* 88.31 [2.15]) the Marcionite Marcus blames 'Judaisers' (ἰουδαϊστής) for a 'misreading' of Matt. 5.17.

early Christianity as decisively marked by the opposing trajectories of Pauline and of Petrine or Jamesian Christianity with their roots in the conflicts reflected in Galatians 1–2.[48] While Irenaeus has certainly contributed to this picture, since he also challenges those who reject Paul (*AH* III. 15.1), Tertullian's reference to Paul as 'apostle of the heretics' (Tertullian, *AM* III. 5.4) is widely cited as if its author were documenting facts rather than mounting an irony-filled argument. Consequently this has prompted the further scholarly hypothesis that the 'Pauline trajectory' was largely ignored, misunderstood, or treated with suspicion in the second century, until such time as it was 'rescued' for 'Catholic' Christianity by Irenaeus.[49] Combined with the then-contemporary evocations of 'Law *versus* Gospel', already discussed, and the self-fulfilling tendency to read Marcion's teaching within this framework, it was inevitable that Adolf von Harnack's much-repeated assessment of Marcion as the one who alone was 'convinced that in all respects the truth was' to be found in Paul's Gospel, and who 'took pains to comprehend the real sense of Paul's statements', and yet whose finding had to be described 'a very imperfect solution', would become a lodestone in assessments of Marcion's primary inspiration and of his significance.[50]

Few would now subscribe to an account in which early Christianity was defined by the deep fissure represented, whether or not with historical justification, by an opposition between Paul and James or Peter – if only because that has been replaced by a far more complex 'diversity'. Similarly, claims regarding the submersion or loss of the Pauline heritage, or at least of an authentic one, by whomsoever defined, do not stand up to the close scrutiny of a broad range of sources. On the one hand, it is evident that Paul never represented a single, monolithic, force: Quite apart from the contested perceptions current in his own lifetime, the literary tradition swiftly presented different 'ideas' of Paul, as is canonically expressed not only in the collection of his letters but also in the Acts of the Apostles, and in those letters written in his name, not least the Pastoral Epistles.[51]

48 See Andreas Wechsler, *Geschichtsbild und Apostelstreit: Eine forschungsgeschichtliche und exegetische Studie über den antiochischen Zwischenfall (Gal 2,1l-14)* (BZNW 62; Berlin: de Gruyter, 1991), 30–280. Gerd Lüdemann, *Opposition to Paul in Jewish Christianity* (ET Minneapolis: Fortress, 1989), gives a brief history of research as a preface to his own historical analysis (1–32).

49 See also *AH* IV. 41.3 where Irenaeus identifies a particular task as addressing 'the teaching of Paul' because of the perverse use of it made by the heretics.

50 *History of Dogma*, 1, 282–83; see above, p. 3.

51 See Thomas Schmeller, *Schulen im Neuen Testament? Zur Stellung der Urchristentum in der Bildungswelt seiner Zeit* (mit einem Beitrag von Christian Cebulj zur johanneischen Schule)

To these would have to be added the Paul of other, eventually marginalised, texts such as *3 Corinthians*, the *Acts of Paul*, the *Prayer of Paul the Apostle* (*NH* I. 1), and the *Apocalypse of Paul* (*NH* V. 2). What these confirm is that there were undoubtedly traditions with specific interests or claiming particular authorities, but that there is little evidence to link these with circles or defined groups in conflict.[52]

Yet even without re-examining in detail the fate of Paul in the second century, Marcion's attention to him is not easily dismissed or fitted into wider trends. Two issues are intertwined: the key place occupied by a number of Pauline letters treated as a coherent corpus, and the narrative account of Paul that is read into or out of these, and that arguably has as much if not more importance in the period than any attempt at a reconstruction of a 'Pauline theology'. A number of studies have examined explicit references to Paul's letters as well as possible implicit allusions to their language or thought up to the middle of the second century; the latter are obviously more a matter of interpretation than the former, although even where the presence of either is agreed, disagreement is still possible as to how well the author knows or 'understands' Paul, however determined.[53] Certainly the Roman *1 Clement* expects its Corinthian readers to be able to 'take up' Paul's letter to them, whereas Ignatius similarly presupposes Paul's repeated references to the church at Ephesus – although a more critical reading might wonder whether he knew how many letters do *not* refer to them (*1 Clement* 47.1; Ignatius, *Eph.* 12.2; cf. *Trall.* praef.).[54] However, such references do not justify any confident account of how the Pauline corpus

(HBS 30: Freiburg: Herder, 2001); Christopher Mount, *Pauline Christianity: Luke-Acts and the Legacy of Paul* (NovTSup. 104; Leiden: Brill, 2002), 1–9. Suggestions that Acts or the Pastoral Epistles are to be dated contemporary with or later than Marcion complicate the issue.

52 See Michael Kaler, 'Towards an expanded understanding of Nag Hammadi Paulinism', *SR* 33 (2004), 301–17; similarly with reference to the writings associated with Peter, Enrico Norelli, 'Situation des Apocryphes Pétriniens', *Apocrypha* 2 (1991), 31–82.

53 Schneemelcher, 'Paulus in der griechischen Kirche'; Andreas Lindemann, *Paulus im ältesten Christentum: Das Bild des Apostels und die Rezeption der paulinischen Theologie in der frühchristlichen Literatur bis Marcion* (BHT 58; Tübingen: Mohr, 1979).

54 See also Polycarp, *Phil.* 3, whose reference to the 'letters (Paul) wrote to you' has been taken to indicate that he knew more than one, perhaps prior to the editorial combination that produced the canonical letter. Kenneth Berding, *Polycarp and Paul: An Analysis of their Literary and Theological Relationship in light of Polycarp's Use of Biblical and Extra-biblical Literature* (VCSup. 62; Leiden: Brill, 2002), 126–41, argues that Polycarp is intentionally imitating Paul but that this is for the specific purposes of this letter and permits no more general conclusion about Polycarp's 'Paulinism'. If *Phil.* 12.1 is a quotation from Eph. 4.26 and not from Ps. 4.5, then the reference as 'in these Scriptures' (*his scripturis*) is striking but inconclusive.

came into being, and whether this went through several stages. As has been seen, the text and order of the letters apparently used by Marcion perhaps constitute the best evidence available for determining what preceded him, with the inevitable consequent circularity of argument and demonstration.[55] Even Irenaeus does not unequivocally accord the Pauline letters the same status as the Gospels and prophets, and although he can appeal to 'all his letters' he rarely treats them as a corpus.[56]

The argued traces of Pauline language and thought do not substantially alter this conclusion. Depending on the criteria for detecting echoes, assessments will differ as to whether these presuppose general familiarity with a tradition of thought or specific literary association.[57] Yet, for an understanding of how Paul was viewed, unexpected absence or silence may be no less telling — for example, the failure to make use of Paul's arguments in 1 Corinthians 15 in the discussion of resurrection in *1 Clement*, and even in Athenagoras (*1 Clem.* 23 - 27; Athenagoras, *De Res.* 18.5, citing 1 Cor. 15.53).[58]

Particularly important for this question is the case of Justin Martyr; when he explicitly addresses the purpose of the Law of Moses as 'the old law and yours alone' in contrast to 'the eternal and perfect law and authentic covenant Christ gave us' (Justin, *Dial.* 11.2), Justin reaches back before Moses to Abraham and even to Enoch, who were faithful to God prior to the giving of the Law, and in particular of circumcision, citing for this purpose Genesis 15.6; 17.11, as also had Paul (*Dial.* 23; 92.3; cf. Rom. 4.3, 10–12). Subsequently, when defending Jesus' death by crucifixion, Justin appeals to Deuteronomy 27.26 and 21.23 in text forms closer to Galatians 3.10, 13 than to the Septuagint (*Dial.* 95.1; 96.1). If these are accepted as evidence of Justin's knowledge and use of Paul, then other examples can be adduced, although none are indisputable quotations.

55 See Lucetta Mowry, 'The Early Circulation of Paul's Letters', *JBL* 63 (1944), 73–86; Gamble, 'Redaction'; pp. 239–41 above.

56 *AH* III. 12.10; see Noormann, *Irenäus als Paulusinterpret*, 63–9. See also Andreas Lindemann, 'Die Sammlung der Paulusbriefe im 1. und 2. Jahrhundert', ed. Auwers and de Jonge, *Biblical Canons*, 321–51, for a cautious account down to and including Irenaeus.

57 Examples would include 'You must keep the flesh as the Temple of God'; 'the living church is the body of Christ' (*2 Clem.* 9.3; 14.2), and the appeal to Abraham's faith while uncircumcised in *Barn.* 13.7. See also the relevant discussions in Andrew Gregory and Christopher Tuckett, ed., *The Reception of the New Testament in the Apostolic Fathers* (NTAF; Oxford: Oxford University Press, 2005). The pattern of echoes begins within the New Testament with the 're-use' of Pauline material within the Pastoral Epistles.

58 1 Cor. 15.53 is also echoed by Justin, *Apol.* 19.4 and by Theophilus, *Ad Autol.* I. 7; however, a similar sentiment is found in *Odes Sol.* 15.8, and may be an independent aphorism.

On the other hand, Justin never suggests that he is quoting from an earlier source, and given that elsewhere his scriptural text frequently diverges from the LXX and probably depends on a 'Christian testimonia' tradition, dependence directly on Paul cannot be assumed.[59] Indeed, supposed evidence of Pauline influence is almost entirely restricted to shared citations from and paraphrases of Scripture, although Justin's understanding of the significance of the Law, which is dominated by observance of circumcision, Sabbath, washing and, to a lesser extent, of sacrifice, breathes a very different spirit from Paul's.[60] In some ways his approach to food sacrificed to idols and to observance of the Law by some Christians, especially Jewish Christians, even appears alien to Paul's attitude (*Dial.* 35; 47). All this may be readily attributed to his different background and context, particularly the context of attitudes to the Jewish Scriptures and Law in the second century as a whole.[61] Nonetheless, even if the judgement that 'the teaching of justification is missing; Pauline ecclesiology, eschatology, and anthropology find no echo'[62] reflects a later period's evaluation of the heart of Pauline theology, it is evident that Justin does not look to Paul as a revered authority, nor to his letters as providing a central means for addressing the questions he faces from without as well as from within – in contrast to his appeal to 'the Gospel' or the 'memoirs of the apostles', and most of all to Scripture (*Dial.* 100.1, 4). At the same time, there is nothing to support suggestions that his silence about Paul is compelled either by Marcion's adoption of the apostle or by a personal antipathy to him, whether for his theology or as an apostle. In the end, the evidence simply does not allow a confident conclusion as to whether or not Justin used Paul's letters directly as a literary source, or, if he did, as to their status for him.[63]

59 Lindemann, *Paulus*, 360 n. 103, in a footnote allows the possibility that Paul and Justin are dependent on a testimonia tradition for the catena of texts found in Rom. 3.11–17 and *Dial.* 27.

60 Rodney Werline speaks of 'The Transformation of Pauline Arguments in Justin Martyr's "Dialogue with Trypho"' (*HTR* 92 [1999] 79–93), but because he focuses on the narrow contexts where Pauline-type arguments from Scripture are used, the essay is a demonstration more of that Justin does something quite different from Paul than of Justin's deliberate procedure and attitude to Paul.

61 See above, pp. 411–12; David Rokeah, *Justin Martyr and the Jews* (JCPS 5; Leiden: Brill, 2002), does argue vehemently for a real and conscious continuity between Justin and Paul, but these arguments belong more to a this further discussion of attitudes to the law and to the place of the Jews.

62 Lindemann, *Paulus*, 366.

63 Although Lindemann, *Paulus*, 362, concludes that Justin obviously knew and referred to the Pauline letters the argument that leads to this is far more hesitant and qualified; it is a question of whether an accumulation of 'perhaps' produces greater or less certainty.

By contrast, the *Letter of Diognetus* has been seen as imbued both with Pauline language and with some sympathy with Pauline thought.[64] The former is expressed particularly in epigrammatic phrases interspersed with others of different origin: Christians 'are in flesh but do not live according to flesh; they spend their time on earth but are citizens of heaven; they are reviled and they give blessings; they are insulted and offer respect' (*Diog.* 5.8–15; cf. 2 Cor. 10.3; 1 Cor. 4.12). The latter is tantalising precisely because it uses its own language to offer what could almost be a paraphrase of Paul: 'convicted in the past by their own deeds so that they were unworthy of life', believers are found worthy in the present 'by the goodness of God'; God 'in mercy himself took on our sins, and he himself gave his own son as a ransom for us, the holy for the lawless' (*Diog.* 9.1–2). On the other hand, *Diognetus* is striking for the absence of any reference to or citation from the Jewish Scriptures; this is not entirely unparalleled in a follower of Paul, for the same might be said of Polycarp's *Letter to the Philippians*, but it is the more notable here given its adoption of a 'then/now' contrast.[65]

A continuing evocation of Paul, as one who was the recipient of a revelation regarding that original Gospel and yet was systematically opposed, is at least as, if not more, difficult to map as a coherent 'tradition'. Certainly his 'voice' is continued but with particular or new emphases. For example, his special calling as apostle to the Gentiles is celebrated often in stark contrast to his earlier activity as a persecutor (Col. 1.29; Eph. 3.7–10; 1 Tim. 1.13–14; 2 Tim. 1.11; *Epist.Apost.* 31), but there is far less sense of just how counter-intuitive and counter-cultural his approach to the Gentiles was for him and his associates; in Acts the real breakthrough comes with Peter rather than with Paul, and attempts to qualify any exclusive claim of Paul have been traced elsewhere.[66] In Acts his missionary journeys are remembered (cf. also 2 Tim. 3.10–11; *Acts of Paul*), but elsewhere their symbolic significance figures more than any geographical precision

64 See p. 407 for the ambiguous position of *Diognetus* in relation to Marcion also; to this should be added the debates about its date. See also Charles M. Nielsen, 'The Epistle to Diognetus and Its Relationship to Marcion', *AThR* 52 (1970), 77–91

65 See Charles M. Nielsen, 'Polycarp and Marcion. A Note', *ThSt* 47 (1986), 297–99, who argues that Polycarp 'was already stressing the Pauline corpus as Scripture to the near exclusion of the Old Testament', but that although this is partly shared with Marcion, Polycarp still opposes Marcion.

66 For example in the attribution of the founding of the Roman church to both Peter and Paul; cf. also Eph. 2.20. However, statements that the Gentiles responded to the teaching of the apostles (plural), who began from Jerusalem, probably repeat a well-established *topos*, even if it is one that accords poorly with Paul's account in Gal. 2.7–8 (Justin, *Apol.* 45.5; 53.3; *Epist.Apost.* 30; cf. Matt. 28.16–28).

(*1 Clem.* 5.7). The physical suffering that accompanied his activities becomes an established theme, and is joined seamlessly with his imprisonment and finally his death in Rome (Eph. 6.19–20; 2 Tim. 1.12, 17; 2.9; 4.16–18), although some ambiguity surrounds that death, and hints and allusions maintain the shadowy possibility that it had something to do with resentment from his fellow-Jews or even from other quasi- or former colleagues (2 Tim. 4.6–14; *1 Clem.* 5.5–6).

Opposition and even betrayal, as well as anticipated attempts to draw his churches away from the teaching he had given them, were embedded in the 'memory' of Paul (2 Thess. 3.14; 2 Tim. 1.15; 4.9, 14). The precise shape of such distortion is indistinct, although Pauline conflicts over circumcision and law continue to resound (Titus 1.10–14; 1 Tim. 1.6–9; Col. 2.11–16). However, whereas the Paul of Galatians or of 1 Corinthians is aggressively prepared to identify his difficulties not only with those who associated themselves with Peter or James, but even with those luminaries themselves, the remembered Paul is often far more circumspect (Col. 4.10). In the *Apocalypse of Paul*, which is clearly dependent on Galatians and 2 Corinthians but interprets them within the tradition of Jewish apocalyptic literature, Paul is greeted by the twelve apostles as he attains to each successive heaven, although whether he then alone goes beyond them to the tenth heaven is not entirely clear; he does however encounter an old man who attempts to restrain him in the seventh heaven, and who probably denotes the impotency of the ('gnostic') Demiurge (*NH* V.2. 22.25–23.29).[67] Although it is difficult to determine the context of that *Apocalypse*, it is obvious that such visionary experiences could be the foundation for claiming access to secretly transmitted teaching, and that it invited counter-claims: Irenaeus may reflect such when he challenges any interpretation of the apostle's journey that would take him beyond the Demiurge (Irenaeus, *AH* II. 30.8–9).[68]

Perhaps more striking is the fact that the texts from Nag Hammadi that elevate James or Peter do not reflect any hostility towards Paul.

[67] The *Prayer of the Apostle Paul* also reflects these traditions, but its original setting is equally unclear.

[68] See also Tertullian, *PrH.* 2; Michael Kaler, Louis Painchaud, Marie-Pierre Bussières, 'The Coptic *Apocalypse of Paul*, Irenaeus' *Adversus Haereses* 2.30.7, and the Second Century Battle for Paul's Legacy', *JECS* 12 (2004), 173–93, argue that Irenaeus is constructing a reading of 2 Cor. 12 in Valentinian mode in order to undermine it. In *AH* V. 5.1 Irenaeus makes his own passing appeal to Paul's experience. Trevett, *Montanism*, 164, with reference to Maximilla's statement in Epiphanius, *Pan.* 48.13, suggests that such passages may have been taken up in the 'new prophecy'.

This has to be set against the frequent appeal to the Pseudo-Clementine literature for such antipathy as widespread. In the source widely agreed to lie behind *Recognitions* 1.27–71, Paul is certainly to be identified as 'the enemy' or 'hostile person' who intervenes just as James is about to successfully evangelise and baptise the Jewish people, including the High Priest; his attempt to kill James probably mimics the death of Stephen in Acts and is followed by his commission by Caiaphas to go to Damascus seeking to destroy the church (*Rec.* 1.70–1). However, only in a restricted sense need this be seen as anti-Pauline, for Paul's own emphasis on his past as a persecutor is developed elsewhere even within the Pauline tradition, although the targeting of James could be seen as an anticipation of problems to come. Moreover, this source appears not to know of Paul's letters or to be concerned with his subsequent apostolic teaching about the Law.[69] Certainly, elsewhere in the Pseudo-Clementine literature Paul has often been seen as hiding behind Simon Magus with whom Peter engages in heated debate, and, indeed, who is the syzygy or negative counterpart to Peter. Yet this development of the tradition is later than the second century and may even reflect fourth-century concerns; rather than there being a simple equivalence between Simon and Paul it is more likely that Simon Magus, Marcion, and Paul, as each has been received in the tradition and, in the case of Marcion, as the system associated with him was currently experienced, are continually merging and separating.[70] Instead, Peter and Paul are routinely brought into harmonious agreement, an attempt some would find already in Acts (Acts 15.12–14, 22–6; 2 Peter 3.15–16; cf. also *1 Clem.* 5).

To the extent that this 'Paul legend' is also promoted through letters penned under his name or which to some degree mimic him, it clearly presupposes some knowledge of Paul as a letter writer, and of at least some of the letters he actually wrote. At some stage Paul as letter writer came to be cited simply as 'the apostle'. Irenaeus takes this for granted without any apology, and similar usage elsewhere has led to the assumption that this was

69 So F. Stanley Jones, *An Ancient Jewish Source on the History of Christianity. Pseudo-Clementine Recognitions 1.27–71* (Atlanta, GA.: Scholars, 1995), 165–6.

70 See Kelley, 'Problems of Knowledge'; Luigi Cirillo, 'L'antipaolinismo nelle Pseudoclementine. Un riesame della questione', ed. Giovanni Filoramo and Claudio Gianotto, *Verus Israel: Nuove prospettive sul giudeocristianesimo. Atti del Colloquio di Torino (4–5 novembre 1999)* (Biblioteca di cultura religiosa 65; Brescia: Paideia, 2001), 280–303. See, however, Jones, 'Marcionism in the Pseudo-Clementines', who has more confidence in the possibility of detecting behind the 'Basic Writing' both Marcionites and followers of the version espoused by Apelles, then current in Syria.

well-established before him.[71] Elsewhere such knowledge is less evident, most strikingly in the overt absence of any reference in Acts either to the letters or to Paul as 'apostle'.[72] Yet not only Acts, but also arguably the Pastoral Epistles and perhaps the *Acts of Paul*, draw on additional traditions about Paul, whatever their origin and reliability, and whether oral or written. At the same time sharp differences between (post-)'Pauline' texts, for example over the nature of the resurrection or over the role of women, point at the very least to differing interpretations of the shared Pauline memory (2 Tim. 2.18; Eph. 2.6; *Acts of Paul*).

What is striking throughout this is the uses to which Paul is being put. They give no grounds for a simple oppositional model or 'gnostic/heretical *versus* catholic' any more than for 'Pauline *versus* Petrine'. Any attempt to ascribe these various uses to the authors' desire to oppose Marcion or to distance themselves from him relies on silence and on hypothetical strategies that are far from self-evident. It may be possible to discern a growing awareness of the utility of Pauline material in polemical and apologetic contexts, although the passage of time, increasing circulation of Christian texts, and changing literary practice may account for that. Certain passages from Paul's letters easily attracted attention in debates of contested questions, particularly over resurrection. When Irenaeus fails to identify Marcion as responsible for the 'mis-punctuation' of 2 Corinthians 4.4 as 'God of this world', that may be because others had independently so read the verse, just as the later claims that Hegesippus had rejected contemporary appeals to 1 Corinthians 2.9 on the grounds that it contradicted Matthew 13.16, or that Tatian 'exegeted the apostle', taking 1 Corinthians 7.5 in the light of Matthew 6.24, cannot easily be dismissed.[73] Alongside this there may be some evidence that a number of groups in the second century 'were claiming the Pauline high ground'.[74]

71 So Noormann, *Irenäus als Paulusinterpret*, 41 with reference to the *Excerpts from Theodotus* and the *Letter to Rheginos*, and possibly also to Irenaeus, *AH* IV. 27–32, often assumed to be taken from a writing or homily by one of Irenaeus' predecessors.

72 Acts 14.4, 14, are the exceptions that prove the rule. On the broader problem see Daniel Marguerat, *Paul in Acts and Paul in His Letters* (WUNT 310; Tübingen: Mohr Siebeck, 2013).

73 Irenaeus, *AH* III. 7.1, see above, p. 44. On 1 Cor. 2.9 see above p. 261, and n. 88, and Lindemann, *Paulus*, 294–6; the charge against Hegesippus is made in Photius, *Bibl.* 232. On Tatian see Molly Whittaker, ed. and transl., *Tatian. Oratio ad Graecos and Fragments* (OECT; Oxford: Clarendon Press, 1982), 79–81 (frag. 5).

74 So Trevett, *Montanism*, 130, although her subjects 'catholic and Prophetic' could be expanded.

All these represent the environment in which Marcion developed his own picture of Paul, but equally they undermine attempts to locate him within an identifiable and continuous 'Pauline School'. However, in method and consequences his approach appears very different from these, and is not readily explained by them. His treatment of the corpus as such, reading the letters sequentially and intertextually and as giving rise not just to theological proof-texts but to a coherent narrative of the threats to the Gospel and its truth, as well as providing an integrated account of the nature of the revealer, the salvation he bought, and the destiny of believers, would seem to have little precedent in surviving sources.

There is some confirmation of this assessment in the much more systematic and unequivocally positive treatment of Paul that emerges only in Irenaeus. As noted earlier, Irenaeus explicitly addresses those who claim Paul as their own primary authority, although he is equally aware of those, primarily the Ebionites, who reject Paul altogether (*AH* III. 11.9; 15.1; IV. 41.4).[75] Alongside Peter, with whom he is credited the foundation of the Roman church, Paul stands above 'the other apostles' (*AH* III. 1.1).[76] Thus, Irenaeus takes for granted that Paul can be labelled simply as 'the apostle', but also defends at length his place alongside the other apostles, particularly through appeal to Acts: Irenaeus is the first to bring together the Paul of the letters and the Paul of Acts, although the lack of unequivocal evidence of the availability of Acts before Irenaeus renders this difficult to assess. It seems likely that the value of Acts as a challenge to Marcion's position secured it a role it had not previously held. Less probable is that it was written, or compiled in its present form, in the period between Marcion and Irenaeus, and as a response to the former; had it been a response to Marcion, some alternative account of the Pauline letters might be expected.[77]

Irenaeus also differs distinctively from his predecessors, and even his contemporaries, in the way that he reads Paul, and it is evident that what he does is inseparable from what he sees his opponents doing.[78] He closes the fourth book of the *Against Heresies* by promising to address the teaching of the apostle and its insane and fallacious interpretation by the heretics

[75] According to Jerome's commentary on Titus, Tatian rejected a number of Paul's letters, but not Titus – but this notice appears confused (see Whittaker, *Tatian*, 82–3). Eusebius, *HE* IV. 29.4–6, refers to the Severiani who blaspheme Paul and do not accept his letters, and reports that Tatian was said to have paraphrased some of Paul's statements.

[76] On this and what follows see Noormann, *Irenäus als Paulusinterpret*, 39–58.

[77] See above, p. 293, and below, p. 431.

[78] See Richard A. Norris, 'Irenaeus' Use of Paul in his Polemic Against the Gnostics', ed. Babcock, *Paul and the Legacies of Paul*, 79–98.

(*AH* IV. 41.4). What in practice he does is to tackle Paul's teaching about the body, and in particular the resurrection of the flesh (*AH* V. 1–15). He takes as his starting point 1 Corinthians 15, to which they also made appeal, but he responds by interweaving other passages, among others, from 2 Corinthians 12, Romans 8, and Colossians 2. His goal is to build a unified and coherent argument about the nature of human anthropology, the working of God in and through the human body, and the significance of Christ's body. This networking of passages allows him to demonstrate the logical and scriptural unity of God's purposes and of his own understanding of them, and to set out a proper framework for interpreting Paul which challenges the alternative readings of his opponents. Yet he is driven to do this by the polemical context in which he finds himself, in opposition to those who are developing different readings, perhaps prompted by different nexuses of texts.

The contrast with other authors who draw on very different arguments in support of resurrection could not be stronger.[79] Elaine Pagels has set out Valentinian exegesis of the Pauline letters in a sequential 'commentary' style, in a number of cases providing parallels to those identified in the polemical tradition against Marcion.[80] In practice, these may point to an engagement with Paul among Valentinus' successors rather than by he himself, and perhaps even to their disputes with Marcion and his followers.[81] Still, as D. Bingham remarks, 'The issue was the interpretive network. Exegesis, and therefore theology, is an issue of canonical connection in the second century'.[82]

In many ways the development of this holistic and intertextual way of reading Paul is more noteworthy than, and perhaps also prior to, the engagement with what might now be called 'Pauline theology'. It involves using Paul's letters not simply as a source for proof-texts to address disparate issues, but in order to interpret him by himself; it is not his words or isolated sentiments that are important, but his explanation of the different elements in the plan of salvation and of the interrelationship between them. Such an approach recognises that there are questions to be answered, for example, about the nature of the body or about the purposes of God stretching from the past into the present and the future, but it also assumes that these are to be addressed primarily not by an appeal to the natural order nor to the

79 See above, p. 266.
80 Elaine Pagels, *The Gnostic Paul: Gnostic Exegesis of the Pauline Letters* (Philadelphia, PA: Fortress, 1975).
81 On Valentinus' disciples, see Markschies, *Valentinus Gnosticus*, 392–402.
82 D. Jeffrey Bingham, 'Irenaeus reads Romans 8: Resurrection and Renovation', ed. Gaca and Welborn, *Early Patristic Readings of Romans*, 114–32, 129.

Scriptures, but by a faithful and close reading of Paul's writings. It is this major innovation in intellectual framework and method, as it emerges in the late second century, that still invites exploration and explanation even if it is shown that Paul was previously far from the pariah in 'orthodox' circles that he has sometimes been assumed to be. However, Irenaeus' failure to fulfil the expectations raised by his promise that he would expose Marcion's distortion from his own Scriptures may suggest that he found himself on uncharted territory. This itself perhaps indicates that the real innovation lay with Marcion, even if we do not know how this intertextual reading was carried out and taught, nor the degree to which it was anchored in the actual production of texts of Paul.[83]

. . . Gospel and Paul

In retrospect it may be easy to understand how a fascination with Paul, especially one anchored in the priority of the Letter to the Galatians, would alert someone to the idea of the Gospel, and even to the need to identify that Gospel, free of the distortions against which Paul had warned. Yet it is far from obvious that this would have been a natural step without some sort of precedent, still less that 'the Gospel' would have been presumed to be a written text, and indeed to be identified with one that nowhere uses the noun – as Luke does not.[84] However, the alternative possibility, that a prior commitment to this Gospel somehow led Marcion to adopt Paul poses equal if not greater challenges, and the third option, that the two were already associated before Marcion, seems unlikely.

There is little contextual evidence to establish any precedent even for the first of these possibilities, that it would be self-evident that Paul's 'Gospel' should be sought in a written text. Leaving aside the question of Paul himself, two lines of language and tradition converge in this dilemma. The first relates to the emergence of written texts concerning the life and (or) teaching of Jesus, perhaps culminating in his death and appearances to his disciples. The issue is not so much the controverted one of the dating of any given 'Gospel', but that of the process by which, once written, they acquired a certain pre-eminence over the oral traditions, which also continued to circulate. Further, was the predominant pattern one of a single Gospel having primary if not sole authority in any particular community or region?

83 So, for example, Schneemelcher, 'Paulus in der griechischen Kirche', 16–17, who identifies Marcion as the first to consciously want to think and speak in a Pauline manner.

84 See above, p. 405 on the use of the verb at Luke 16.16.

If so, at what stage, and in what areas, were two or more (and ultimately the four 'canonical') Gospels circulated together and read in relationship to each other? The second theme specifically concerns the term εὐαγγέλιον: When and where does it come to refer not to the message proclaimed by or about Jesus but specifically to a written document?[85] These two questions can be taken together because a key passage in addressing each is the *Didache*'s version of the Lord's Prayer, which is close to that in Matthew 6 and which is introduced by the words 'as the Lord commanded in his gospel' (*Did.* 8.2).[86] The plural, 'Gospels', would appear first to have been used by Justin Martyr, and then somewhat tentatively, when he cites the apostolic account of the words of institution to be found in the 'Memoirs produced by them, which are called Gospels' (Justin, *Apol.* 66.3).[87]

However, Justin also witnesses to the fluidity still characteristic of his time: He quotes the words of Jesus extensively elsewhere, but without identifying his source; indeed, the fact that his quotations often seem be an amalgam of forms familiar from the separate Synoptic Gospels has led to considerable debate as to whether he was dependent on oral tradition, or on a harmony, or whether he was responsible for one, perhaps as a predecessor to his disciple Tatian who was later credited with producing what came to be called the 'Diatessaron'. Justin's own practice, reinforced by the difficulties of determining the earliest form of the 'Diatessaron', prohibits any assumption that its composition presupposes a prior authority given to a corpus of the subsequently canonical four. Moreover, study of the textual history of Gospel traditions, both in relation to the canonical Gospels and with reference to the production of other 'Gospels' with an indeterminate relationship to the former, also testifies to their considerable fluidity throughout the period. Marcion's own supposed 'editing' of his Gospel is, as has been seen, a prime example of such fluidity, but to it might be added texts such as the *Gospel of Thomas*, the *Gospel of Peter*, Papyrus Egerton 2, and perhaps Basilides' intended revision of the Gospel of Luke.[88]

85 On this see James A. Kelhoffer, '"How Soon a Book?" Revisited: ΕΥΑΓΓΕΛΙΟΝ as a Reference to 'Gospel' Materials in the First Half of the Second Century', *ZNW* 95 (2004), 1–34.

86 See also *Did.* 11.3; 15.3,4; 2 *Clem.* 8.5.

87 Cf. Justin, *Dial.* 10.2, 'the injunctions in the so-called Gospel'; 101.1, 'in the Gospel it is written, saying ...'. Helmut Koester, 'The Text of the Synoptic Gospels in the Second Century', ed. William L. Petersen, *Gospel Traditions in the Second Century: Origins, Recensions, Text and Transmission* (Christianity and Judaism in Antiquity 3; Notre Dame, IN: University of Notre Dame Press, 1989), 19–37, 33, argues that Justin took the term from Marcion.

88 See above, pp. 209, 218.

Marcion, however, appears to represent two further steps: firstly, the combination of 'Gospel' and 'apostolic writing', and, secondly, the location of this in some sort of relationship to the received Scriptures, a pattern that would eventually be signalled by the term 'New Testament'. A corpus of single Gospel and apostolic Letters (including those within and structured by the Apocalypse) may lie behind Tertullian's reference to the 'Johannine instrument', but whether this is his own construction is unclear (Tertullian, *De Res.* 38). However, the most obvious parallel to Marcion's corpus is that produced by the combination of Luke with Acts, although these almost certainly share common authorship at some level. As has been indicated already, that Acts was composed as a companion to Luke, itself perhaps extended, in opposition to Marcion lacks any certain proof; any polemic is remarkably muted and requires considerable eisegesis to detect it, although Irenaeus and his successors swiftly found its benefits for their own polemics. On the other hand, the limited evidence for the circulation of Acts before the middle of the second century, and the degree of apology on its behalf even by Irenaeus, renders it difficult to argue that its authority was already established before Marcion, and that his only recourse was to delete it and replace it with his Pauline corpus and the narrative it provided.[89]

The most likely solution to this uncertainty is to locate Marcion among a number of attempts to 'extend' the written Gospel narrative into the time of the Church, attempts which were designed to address contemporary needs, and in particular to provide some legitimation among competing claims to authority. The most probable conclusion is that the Gospel Marcion worked with was anonymous, and that he associated it with 'the Gospel' defended by Paul in Galatians because it was the only 'Gospel' available to him.[90] Such a scenario is the best way of explaining both the focal authority accorded to Paul and his letters by Marcion, as well as the claims that the starting point for his more extensive 'cosmological' narrative was provided by the Lukan sayings regarding the good and bad trees, or the parables of wineskins and garments, as well as that it was the 'Gospel' which generated the 'Antitheses'.[91]

[89] That Marcion rejected Acts is claimed by Tertullian, *AM* V. 2.7 (although note the plural, 'you [pl.] repudiate]) and by Ps.Tertullian, *Adv.Omn.Haer.* 6. See above, p. 271 for a rejection of the claim that the 'Antitheses' were designed to take its place.

[90] Contra Jens Schröter, 'Die Apostelgeschichte und die Enstehung des neutestamentlichen Kanons: beobachtungen zur Kanonisierung der Apostelgeschichte und ihrer Bedeutung als kanonischer Schrift', ed. Auwers and De Jonge, *Biblical Canons*, 395–429, 411 who concludes that Marcion knew the Gospel as by Luke or as closely associated with Paul.

[91] Tertullian, *AM* I. 2.1 and above, p. 72; *Adam.* 56.14–17 [1.28]; above p. 275.

The identification of the author of that Gospel, and also of Acts, with an available character from Pauline tradition, Luke, belonged to the subsequent techniques of recuperation (Col. 4.14; Philem. 24; 2 Tim. 4.11; cf. Irenaeus, *AH* III. 14.1); this itself, however, confirms that by then a more direct apostolic claim would not have succeeded. Eventually, although a preference for trajectories predicated on a particular Gospel may have continued in some circles, an alternative strategy, the four-Gospel corpus championed by Irenaeus, was to displace them, disrupting their potentially exclusive narratives and demanding new, more harmonising, theories of tradition.[92]

The Pastoral Epistles undoubtedly also had a role in this process, although not one that is easily recoverable. Again, it seems most likely that Marcion was unaware of them, rather than that he consciously omitted them. They also serve to secure the reputation and authority of Paul for a later generation, reinforcing elements in the 'Paul legend' and claiming his authority for particular patterns of authority and lifestyle. As with Acts, they can only be read as targeted against Marcion through a degree of eisegesis, and by importing a model of Marcion that is not supported by the earliest sources.[93] It is more likely that they shortly predate him even if they reflect some of the same dilemmas. It was, once again, Irenaeus who helped secure their place as the lens through which Paul would subsequently be viewed, through his appeal to them, in particular against 'the falsely named knowledge' and in favour of the avoidance of 'a partisan person' (1 Tim. 6.20; Titus 3.10–11; Irenaeus, *AH* I. 16.3; III. 3.4). Yet, in origin, they too must be located among the various currents that Marcion helps make visible.

The designation 'New Testament' was also a term that did not originally refer to a textual entity. However, that Marcion was the first to introduce this usage already has been proven unlikely; so too has any suggestion that such a move was the obverse of his supposed 'rejection of the Old Testament'.[94] Given that the weaknesses of the Creator was pre-eminently displayed within it, and was crucial for his own narrative of God's revelation in Jesus Christ, the 'Old Testament' must, at least initially, have retained some necessary status. Yet even without any specific terminology, Marcion undoubtedly gave a pre-eminent authority to the 'Gospel' and 'Apostolikon',

92 See, for example, the growth of texts associated with Peter, and the placing of the *Apocalypse of Peter* immediately following the *Gospel of Peter* in the Akhmîm Codex: Paul Foster, *The Gospel of Peter. Introduction, Critical Edition and Commentary* (TENTS 4; Leiden: Brill, 2010), 91–7.

93 For example that Marcion promoted the role of women in his congregations; this only appears late: see above, p. 397.

94 See above, pp. 406–08.

for these provided for him the sole record of the revelation of God, as well as the evidence for the obfuscation of that record and the means of its recovery. To ask whether they therefore constituted 'Scripture' for Marcion, or even a 'Canon', and also whether the 'Antitheses' were included within this, is to impose anachronistic, and highly disputed, terminology and concepts; this is even more the case given that there is little evidence that he actively rejected any alternative writings that had an established authority among some groups. It is equally anachronistic to credit Marcion with 'inventing' the New Testament; if he can be described as a catalyst or turning point for that process,[95] it is only because of the response of Irenaeus who defends the fourfold Gospel and introduces the model of Marcion as 'cutting away' at a textual integrity which mirrors and protects the integrity of the Church (Irenaeus, *AH* IV. 33.7–8). This response, reinforced by Tertullian and others, ensured that textual or scriptural choices, whether affirmative or negative, became part of the ongoing debate about 'heresy'.[96]

A final ironic 'contradiction', however, is that while Marcion's 'Gospel' (together with his 'Apostolikon') continued to have iconic status as a symbol of schism and separation, in practice, in a world of actual textual and versional diversity, the real debates continued to be waged on the basis of *shared* scriptural narratives and of a *shared* conviction of their need and their potential for interpretation as revelatory about God, the world, and human salvation.

[95] See above, pp. 2, 5, 293–4. [96] See Lieu, 'Heresy and Scripture'.

16

Afterword: Marcion and the making of the heretic

Was Marcion a heretic? The answer lies in the title of this chapter, and of the book. 'Heresy', and therefore the idea of 'the heretic' and the identification of those who might qualify, is a construction of early Christian rhetoric within the processes of shaping some form of self-definition or identity. Marcion survives within the tradition as, and only as, a heretic; if he had not been so constructed his name would have long been forgotten. Although there evidently were those who would not have identified him as such, their voices are lost except as ventriloquised, for example, by Megethius and Marcus in the *Dialogue of Adamantius*; whether these others accepted the concept of 'heresy' but would have 'returned the compliment' is unknown, although the co-existence of groups in the Syriac East may suggest at least not immediately, and other models of competition after the truth were possible. Yet equally, without Marcion there may have been no 'heresy', no 'heretic'. The initial models of heresy are deeply rooted within the second century and within the social and intellectual context within which Marcion worked; the idea takes shape with him as one of the chief targets, albeit alongside others, such as Valentinus or Basilides. Although in due course the origins of heresy were traced back to Simon Magus, this is a retrospective view that does not sit entirely comfortably with the earliest traditions about him. Of course, polemic against 'others' who believe or behave differently while claiming the same heritage of faith long precedes Marcion, and indeed has roots within Jewish sectarian experience before Jesus.[1] Arguably, then, some form of more stable categorisation of opponents eventually would still have replaced the various 'false prophets', 'antichrists', 'licentious teachers',

1 This is the virtue of Robert M. Royalty, *The Origin of Heresy: A History of Discourse in Second Temple Judaism and Early Christianity* (New York: Routledge, 2013), although he is less effective in analysing the changes in such discourse.

'hypocrites', 'Nicolaitans', or followers of 'Jezebel', of earlier denunciation; but whether it would have adopted the language, characteristics, and strategies of philosophical competition must remain unknown, as too must whether Marcion would have immediately attracted fatal attention. The heresiological tradition 'made' Marcion, but so also Marcion (or at least the 'perceived' Marcion) perhaps made, or helped to do so, the 'idea' or profile of the heretic.

What 'made Marcion', as argued above, was also the mix of intellectual and social currents of the time, particularly as these offered possibilities or challenges to the articulation of the Christian message, together with his response to them. Conversely, therefore, Marcion has also proved a powerful lens for tracing these currents and their intersection. Before exploring them again it must also be repeated that Marcion is not simply a cipher for such currents, for this too would not account for the survival not just of his name but also of groups who looked to him and to the way he formulated the Christian message or Gospel. Rather than any appeal to the irrecoverable impact of his own personal experience,[2] it is the specific 'alchemy' of this formulation, and of its potential to give voice to and to provide a solution for the most pressing concerns of his audience, that must account for his longevity.

The Marcion who has emerged from the preceding pages is a product of his age and of its preoccupations, particularly preoccupations with the nature of God, of the created order, and of being human, and with the nature of the authority by which answers to those preoccupations could be given. He is also a thoroughly 'Christian' thinker, with an account of human need, with a proclamation of a divine intervention narrated through the life, death, and resurrection of one who alone could bring salvation because he was not constrained by the chains of that human need, and with a summons to those who responded to that proclamation to live in a way that demonstrated that they also were free from those same constraints. His authorities are, it would seem, the established authorities of Christian preaching and apologetic, the received Scriptures and the emergent yet sometimes competitive or contested writings that were increasingly shaping the network of Christian communities.

Thus far there is little that is exceptional. Where Marcion stands out is in his radical separation and degrading of the Creator. To some extent this is achieved by the combination of well-worn philosophical debates about the

[2] Such as Harnack's appeal to religious experience (see above, pp. 3, 285), or May's suggestion of the uncertainties and dangers of the ship-trader's profession ('Schiffsreeder', 61–2).

implications of change or 'becoming', with equally well-worn apologetic and hermeneutical debates about the propriety of the scriptural narratives of the Creator God. In doing this he does not stand, it would seem, in the tradition of discussion of the status of the Jewish Law for Christians, in particular for those of Gentile background, nor in that of debates, whether driven by personal commitment or by apologetic necessity, regarding God's intentions in the past or in the present for God's people, the Jews.[3] If his arguments overlapped with these, and if they were elided with these by future protagonists, that was because the common resource to which all appealed was the Jewish Scriptures. On the other hand, he did give expression to, and propose a solution to, the exegetical and apologetic challenges posed by the conviction shared by most early Christians that these Scriptures, and not, for example, the classical authorities of Greek culture, were and would retain their pre-eminent authority.[4] Even so, it might be remarked that whereas Justin, and perhaps Theophilus of Antioch, appears to have encountered these Scriptures as authoritative and revelatory primarily through the prophetic writings, for Marcion the narratives of Genesis and Exodus provided a starting point.

Here, too, however, there is a point of differentiation from some other interpreters of these Scriptures. It would seem that Marcion probably did not find in the Genesis narratives any grounds for cosmological speculation or cosmogonic myths; it remains most persuasive that the hints at any such developed myth, including 'Matter' as a generative principle, most probably belong to subsequent explication or to regional predilection. Marcion's interest in cosmology, however, remains opaque. Despite his supposed absolute separation between the Unknown God and the Creator or Demiurge, he had no account of their origins, nor, in any detail, of their final destiny; his system is not consistently dualist, although neither can it be shown to be fundamentally monist.[5] On the other hand, his consistent identification of the Demiurge as 'the God of this world', and the somewhat oblique references to powers or to 'Gods in nature' (e.g. Gal. 4.8–9), hint at some cosmological theory, if only as a way of explaining or expressing the nature of the human situation. This is where it becomes particularly difficult to determine how far Marcion's account of the Demiurge, which has been

3 Hence, there are no grounds for explaining Marcion in terms of the failure of the Bar Kochba revolt.

4 For this framework for understanding the place of the Bible in the development of early Christianity see Frances M. Young, *Biblical Exegesis and the Formation of Christian Culture* (Cambridge: Cambridge University Press, 1997) and pp. 63–7 on Marcion.

5 See above, p. 337.

given a quasi-metaphysical reality by his opponents, was fundamentally shaped to give mythic expression to the nature of human experience without or before the revelation and salvation of the Christian Gospel, namely to articulate a radically pessimistic view of that experience as plight.[6] 'Without or before [the revelation ...]' is used intentionally: Again, while Marcion's opponents read his account in a rigidly and literalistic temporal framework, which made it open to derision, mythic time may express contemporaneous possibilities.[7] Subsequent Christian interpreters would find in the Scriptures alternative mythic explanations of human and cosmic alienation from God, some of which were overtly more anthropological. It is not evident that Marcion for his part found in anthropology a satisfactory way of expressing the human problem or its solution, or at least this is not how his initial detractors read him. On the other hand, those detractors do represent his rejection of the Demiurge as being inseparable from a profound anthropological agenda, namely through a determined ascetic stance whose most marked element was the rejection of procreative activity.

Marcion is also a thoroughly Christian thinker in that for him his 'myth' or account of the need, solution, and response of salvation were to be found within the distinctively Christian authorities. It has been argued here that these authorities were those he had encountered as a Christian, and that there is no evidence that he rejected any other available ones. The narrative account of the ministry, death, and resurrection of Jesus most probably was already referred to as 'the Gospel', although that title was not identified exclusively with a particular text in written form; rather, it was he who so labelled the authentic version that he 'restored'. The written text with which he was familiar bore a strong resemblance to canonical Luke, particularly as attested within some surviving textual traditions, but likely it was in several respects shorter. More uncertain is the form in which Marcion encountered Paul's letters, and in particular whether or not these had already been collected together and treated as a unit, or, perhaps, whether he found others to add to a pre-existing smaller corpus. Certainly, Marcion is the first of whom we know, to read these letters as built upon a single narrative, or upon multiple intersecting narratives, of Paul, of Christ, of those who believe in Christ, and of the demiurgically inspired forces of opposition. Here again, his reading of these writings and his diagnosis of the state of the world and of human existence are so deeply intertwined that

6 Compare Mark Edwards' analysis of the Valentinian 'myth' in 'Pauline Platonism'.

7 Christian theology had to address the same dilemma, and does so through Trinitarian confession.

it is impossible to assign priority to one or to the other in the building of his system. Did he find in Paul and the Gospel a remarkable explanation of and solution to a position already reached on philosophical grounds, or in his struggle to make sense of the alien world view of the Gospel and Jewish Scriptures did he come to read them, as others read Homer, as conveying a philosophical message that was more radical than almost any of his contemporaries had conceived? Did Paul's letters, with their story of the perversion and obstruction of the Gospel, then confirm why those who first introduced him to the Christian message had not provided any more satisfactory marriage of contemporary preoccupation and the 'new superstition'? If there is no means of deciding on the sequence here perhaps that is because hermeneutical theory has made it clear that the interaction between patterns of interpretation and conscious or unconscious predilection almost always defies unravelling. Nonetheless, in this case it does seem likely that Marcion interpreted both narrative and parabolic language as alternative, 'mythic', expressions of philosophical analysis: the spatial imagery of the descent of the redeemer to the realm under the sway of the Demiurge, or of the events and exchanges on the mountain of Transfiguration; the symbolism of conquest, of the taking of spoils, of purchase or exchange, all metaphors that would readily resonate in the sociopolitical setting of the second century, more perhaps than would those of atoning sacrifice. Such an intervention may appear a highly idiosyncratic redefinition of the Platonic 'goodness' of the unknown God, but it is over-simplistic to assume that it was driven by an understanding of Pauline 'grace', and there is no foundation for then equating the latter with a grasp of 'the God of Love'.

Challenging the potential of Marcion's mythic reading of the Scriptures to be understood as reflective of a philosophical account certainly is his well-attested emphasis on the newness or suddenness of that intervention, modelled by the new wineskins or garment and by Paul's 'new creature' or 'new creation'. 'Newness' was already an established component in the scriptural semantics of early Christian preaching. For Marcion, however, it provides another articulation of how the incommensurability between the Unknown God and those whose identity and destiny inevitably belong to the created realm, or to the Demiurge, is overcome. Again, some contemporary scriptural exegetes had addressed similar questions through exploration of the twofold exercise by God of mercy and of justice. If Marcion was aware of such efforts he evidently found them unsatisfactory for they failed to overcome the charges of unpredictability in a God for whom it would be 'unfitting' to act so irrationally. For him, as in his scriptural examples and perhaps in evangelical preaching, justice meant the imposition of a judgement, and it was this that was problematic both if it was unequally distributed and because, within the structures of created and ordered existence, it was properly unavoidable. 'Newness', then, is not so much a temporal category, as an affirmation that the only one able to bring into effect knowledge of, and harmony with, the God who is untainted by and unconstrained by the structures that define human existence, and who is not bound by the necessity of judgement, can only be that very same God. In believing that this was actually possible, Marcion is again a thoroughly Christian thinker. It is from this conviction that, as has been argued, there follows Marcion's understanding of Christ, and of those who wished to live out that understanding.

Here, too, Marcion's voice sounds a credible note within the cross-questioning and experimentation of the time. The formulation of a sustained narrative account of Jesus, and one that does not simply conclude with an empty tomb as does Mark, impelled such cross-questioning. Affirmations of the appearance of Christ risen from the grave to his disciples (1 Cor. 15.4–8) provoke new challenges and new possibilities when attached to the stories about him before that death. Whereas, once established, it would be natural to take the latter stories as the measure of the 'real fleshliness' and to read accounts of the former in their light, it might seem as reasonable to reverse the logic, and so to reinforce the privileged position of the experience of the apostles: Thus the risen Jesus, like the transfigured Jesus, is revelatory of his true identity. The deep ambiguities that any reader of Paul would associate with 'flesh' would only exacerbate such conundrums, and again would provide a scriptural imperative for an interpretation that both reinforced the redeemer's total independence of the Demiurge's realm of change and begetting, and that challenged the endeavours of the latter, as 'the God of this age', to extinguish the effect of 'the illumination of the Gospel of the glory of Christ' (2 Cor. 4.4). As has been seen, all this could be woven into a tapestry of interpretation and reading of the texts, which no less provided a pattern for the life of believers, and offered a radical justification for its rigorous pursuance. Marcion again appears as one who channels many of the contemporary conceptual and hermeneutical practices, as well as those of conduct, but who does so within a potentially coherent unitary narrative, in both scriptural and philosophical register.

All this may explain something of the attraction of his particular interpretation among the various attempts to translate and re-translate the Christian message. It does so without needing to appeal to the language of 'reformer' or 'believer', or even without crediting him with the burden of laying bare the lurking crisis of second-century Christianity or of being the inimitable catalyst for the mechanisms that would characterise the third. Contextually, it might be better to see him as discovering a distinctive and even plausible solution to the fundamental challenge of the second century, namely of introducing the Christian message, rooted in the Scriptures and received tradition, to a new audience whose world view was shaped by the philosophical, and particularly by the popularised Platonic, tradition. Although his opponents portrayed him as inward looking, bent on eviscerating the Church and its texts, his own gaze may have been outward, apologetic- or mission-driven. He belongs not to the ecclesiastical or liturgical setting with its confessional formulae but to the school with its debates and its gifted teachers.

Yet there remain unsolved questions: whether he had any tutors in the alchemy to which we have referred, or only innocent suppliers of its ingredients; whether he achieved it through lengthy study or apprenticeship or by happenchance, perhaps with little awareness of its explosive by-products; whether, despite all that has been argued above, he knowingly offered a potentially subversive response to contemporary politics, one which would have little room for an apologetics of shared civic values. This Marcion, who is no less constructed, still retains his secrets.

Bibliography

Critical editions of major sources are listed here by editor and can also be traced by author through the index of ancient writings.

Aalders, Gerhard J. D., 'Tertullian's Quotations from St Luke', *Mnemosyne* 5 (1937) 241–82.

Aland, Barbara, 'Marcion (*ca. 85–160*) Marcioniten', *Was ist Gnosis?*, 318–40 (= *TRE* 22 [1992] 89–101).

'Marcion: Versuch einer neuen Interpretation', *Was ist Gnosis?*, 291–317 (= *ZThK* 70 [1973] 420–47).

Was ist Gnosis? Studien zum frühen Christentum, zu Marcion, und zur kaiserzeitlichen Philosophie (WUNT 239; Tübingen: Mohr Siebeck, 2009).

See also Ehlers, Barbara.

Alexandre, Jérôme, *Une chair pour la gloire. L'anthropologie réaliste et mystique de Tertullien* (Th.Hist. 115; Paris: Beauchesne, 2001) 199–225.

Allen, Joel S., *The Despoliation of Egypt in Pre-Rabbinic, Rabbinic and Patristic Traditions* (VCSup. 92; Leiden: Brill, 2008).

Allison, Dale C., 'Rejecting Violent Judgment: Luke 9:52–56 and Its Relatives', *JBL* 121 (2002) 459–78.

Alt, Karin, *Weltflucht und Weltbejahung. Zur Frage des Dualismus bei Plutarch, Numenios, Plotin* (Abhandlungen des Geistes- und Sozialwissenschaftlichen Klasse 8, 1993; Mainz: Akadamie der Wissenschaften und der Literatur; Stuttgart: Steiner, 1993).

American and British Committees of the International Greek New Testament Project, ed. *The New Testament in Greek: The Gospel According to Luke*, Part 1: Chapters 1–12 (Oxford: Clarendon Press, 1984).

Amir, Yehoshua, 'Philons Erörterungen über Gottesfurcht und Gottesliebe in ihren Verhältnis zum palästinischen Midrasch', *Die hellenistische Gestalt des Judentums bei Philon von Alexandrien* (Forschungen zum jüdisch-christlichen Dialog 5; Neukirchen-Vluyn: Neukirchener, 1983) 164–85.

Amit, Yairah, '"The Glory of Israel Does Not Deceive or Change His Mind": On the Reliability of Narrator and Speakers in Biblical Narrative', *Prooftexts* 12 (1992) 201–12.

Amphoux, Christian-Bernard, 'La revision du "Notre Père" de Luc (11, 2–4) et sa place dans l'histoire du texte', ed. R. Gryson and P.-M. Bogaert, Recherches sur l'Histoire de la Bible Latine (Cahiers de la Revue Théologique de Louvain 19; Louvain-la Neuve: Faculté de Théologie, 1987) 105–21.

'Les Premères Éditions de Luc I. Le Texte de Luc 5', *ETL* 67 (1991) 312–27.

'Les Premères Éditions de Luc II. L'Histoire de Texte au IIe Siècle', *ETL* 68 (1992) 38–48.

Amphoux, Christian-Bernard, and J. Keith Elliott, *The New Testament Text in Early Christianity: Proceedings of the Lille Colloquium, July 2000* (Histoire du Texte Biblique 6; Lausanne: Éditions du Zèbre, 2003).

Andía, Ysabel de, 'L'hérésie et sa refutation selon Irénée de Lyon', *Augustinianum* 25 (1985) 609–44.

Andresen, Carl, 'Justin und der mittlere Platonismus', ed. Zintzen, *Mittelplatonismus*, 319–68 (= *ZNW* 44 [1952/3] 157–95).

Armstrong, A. H., 'Gnosis and Greek Philosophy', ed. Barbara Aland, *Gnosis. Festschrift für Hans Jonas* (Göttingen: Vandenhoeck & Ruprecht, 1978) 87–124.

Athanassiadi, Polymnia, *La Lutte pour Orthodoxie dans le Platonisme Tardif de Numénius à Damascius* (Paris: Les Belles Lettres, 2006).

Auwers, Jean-Marie, and Henk J. de Jonge, ed., *The Biblical Canons* (BETL 163; Leuven: Peeters, 2003).

Azéma, Yvan, ed., *Théodoret de Cyr. Correspondance* II-III [SC 98, 111; Paris: Éditions du Cerf, 1964–65).

Aziza, Claude, 'La figure de Moïse chez Tertullien', *Annales de la Faculté des Lettres et Sciences Humaines de Nice* 35 (1979) 275–95.

Baarda, Tjitze, 'De korte tekst van het Onze Vader in Lucas 11:2–4: een Marcionitische corruptie?', *NTT* 44 (1990) 273–87.

'ΔΙΑΦΩΝΙΑ-ΣΥΜΦΩΝΙΑ: Factors in the Harmonization of the Gospels, Especially in the Diatessaron of Tatian', ed. Petersen, *Gospel Traditions in the Second Century*, 133–54.

'"If You Do Not Sabbatize the Sabbath…" The Sabbath as God or World in Gnostic Understanding (Ev. Thom., Log. 27)', ed. R. van den Broek, Tjitze Baarda, Jaap Mansfeld, *Knowledge of God in the Graeco-Roman World* (EPROER 112; Leiden: Brill, 1988) 178–201.

'Luke 12, 13–14: Text and Transmission from Marcion to Augustine', ed. J. Neusner, *Christianity, Judaism and Other Greco-Roman Cults: Studies for Morton Smith at Sixty, I. New Testament* (SJLA 12; Leiden: Brill, 1975) 107–62.

'Marcion's Text of Gal. 1:1: Concerning the Reconstruction of the First Verse of the Marcionite Corpus Paulinum', *VC* 42 (1988) 236–56.

Babcock, William S. ed., *Paul and the Legacies of Paul* (Dallas, TX: Southern University Methodist Press, 1991).

Bacon, Benjamin W., 'Marcion, Papias, and "the Elders"', *JTS* 23 (1922) 134–60.

'The Anti-Marcionite Prologue to John', *JBL* 49 (1930) 43–54.

Bainton, Ronald H., 'Basilidian Chronology and New Testament Interpretation', *JBL* 42 (1923) 81–134.

Bakhuyzen, W. H. van de Sande, *Der Dialog des Adamantius* (GCS; Leipzig, 1901).

Balás, David L., 'Marcion Revisited: A "Post-Harnack" Perspective', ed. W. Eugene March, *Texts and Testaments: Critical Essays on the Bible and Early Church Fathers.*

A Volume in Honour of Stuart Dickson Currie (San Antonio, TX: Trinity University Press, 1980) 95–108.

Baltussen, Han, 'From Polemic to Exegesis: The Ancient Philosophical Commentary', *Poetics Today* 28 (2007) 247–81.

Bammel, Caroline P. Hammond, *Der Römerbriefkommentar des Origenes. Kritische Aufgabe der Übersetzung Rufins* Buch 1–3 (VL.AGLB 16; Freiburg: Herder, 1990).

Der Römerbriefkommentar des Origenes. Kritische Aufgabe der Übersetzung Rufins Buch 4–6 (ed. H. J. Frede and H. Stanjek; VL 33; Freiburg: Herder, 1997).

Der Römerbriefkommentar des Origenes. Kritische Aufgabe der Übersetzung Rufins Buch 7–10 (ed. H. J. Frede and H. Stanjek; VL 34; Freiburg: Herder, 1998).

Bardy, Gustave, 'La littérature patristique des "*Quaestiones et Responsiones*" sur l'Ecriture Sainte', *RevBib* 41 (1932) 210–36, 341–69, 515–37; 42 (1933) 14–30, 211–29, 328–52.

Barnes, Timothy D., *Tertullian: A Historical and Literary Study* (Oxford: Clarendon Press, 1971).

Barton, John, 'An Early Metacommentary: Tertullian's *Against Marcion*', ed. J. Cheryl Exum and Hugh G. M. Williamson, *Reading from Right to Left. Essays on the Hebrew Bible in Honour of David J. A. Clines* (JSOTSup. 373; Sheffield: Sheffield Academic Press, 2003) 38–49.

Bassler, Jouette M., 'Cain and Abel in the Palestinian Targums', *JSJ* 17 (1986) 56–64.

Bastianini, Guido et al., ed., *Commentaria et Lexica Graeca in Papyris Reperta* (Leipzig/München: K. G. Saur, 2004).

Bauer, Walter, *Orthodoxy and Heresy in Earliest Christianity* (ET ed. from the 2nd German edn by Robert Kraft and Gerhard Krodel; Philadelphia, PA: Fortress Press, 1971).

Baur, F. Chr., *Das Markusevangelium nach seinem Ursprung und Charakter nebst einem Anhang über die Evangelium Marcion's* (Tübingen: Ludw.Friedr.Fuer, 1851).

Beck, Edmund, 'Bardaisan und seine Schule bei Ephräm', *Le Muséon* 91 (1978) 271–333.

'Die Hyle bei Markion nach Ephräm', *OCP* 44 (1978) 5–30.

ed. and trans., *Des heiligen Ephraem des Syrers Hymnen contra Haereses* (2 vols; CSCO 169, 170, Script.Syr. 76, 77; Louvain: Sec. du CSCO, 1957).

ed. and trans., *Des heiligen Ephraem des Syrers Hymnen de Virginitate* (2 vols.; CSCO 223, 224, Script.Syr. 94, 95; Louvain: Sec. du CSCO, 1962).

Becker, Adam, *Fear of God and the Beginning of Wisdom. The School of Nisibis and Christian Scholastic Culture in Late Antique Mesopotamia* (Philadelphia, PA: University of Pennsylvania Press, 2006).

BeDuhn, Jason, 'Biblical Antitheses, Adda, and the Acts of Archelaus', ed. Jason BeDuhn and Paul Mirecki, *Frontiers of Faith: The Christian Encounter with Manichaeism in the Acts of Archelaus* (NHMS 61; Leiden: Brill, 2007) 131–47.

The First New Testament: Marcion's Scriptural Canon (Salem, OR: Polebridge, 2013).

Bellinzoni, A. J., *The Saying of Jesus in the Writings of Justin Martyr* (NovTSup. 17; Leiden: Brill, 1967).

Benoit, André, 'Irénée et l'hérésie: Les conceptions hérésiologiques de l'évêque de Lyon', *Augustinianum* 20 (1980) 55–67.

Berding, Kenneth, *Polycarp and Paul: An Analysis of their Literary and Theological Relationship in Light of Polycarp's Use of Biblical and Extra-Biblical Literature* (VCSup. 62; Leiden: Brill, 2002).

van den Berg, Robbert M., 'God the Creator, God the Creation: Numenius' Interpretation of Genesis 1:2 (Frg. 30)', ed. George H. van Kooten, *The Creation of Heaven and Earth: Re-interpretations of Genesis I in the Context of Judaism, Ancient Philosophy, Christianity, and Modern Physics* (TBN VIII; Leiden: Brill, 2005) 109–23.

Betholo, Paolo, Alda Giambelluca Kossova, Claudio Leonardi, Enrico Norelli, Lorenzo Perrone, ed., *Ascensio Isaiae, Textus* (CCSA 7; Turnhout: Brepols, 1995) (see also Norelli).

Beyschlag, Karlmann, *Clemens Romanus und der Frühkatholizismus: Untersuchungen zu 1 Clemens 1–7* (BHT 35; Tübingen: Mohr Siebeck, 1966).

Simon Magus und die christliche Gnosis (WUNT 16. Tübingen: Mohr Siebeck, 1974).

Bianchi, Ugo, 'Marcion: Theologien biblique ou docteur gnostique', *VC* 21 (1967) 141–9.

'Origen's Treatment of the Soul and the Debate over Metensomatosis', ed. Lothar Lies, *Origeniana Quarta*, 270–81.

Bickermann, Elias J., 'Les deux erreurs du prophète Jonas', *RHPhR* 45 (1965) 232–64.

Bienert, W., 'Marcion und der Antijudaismus', ed. Gerhard May and Katharina Greschat, in association with Martin Meiser, *Marcion und seine kirchengeschichtliche Wirkung. Marcion and His Impact on Church History. Vorträge der internationalen Fachkonferenz zu Marcion, gehalten vom 15.-18. August 2001 in Mainz* (TU 150; Berlin and New York: de Gruyter 2002) 191–205.

Bilde, Per, '2 Cor. 4,4: The View of Satan and the Created World in Paul', ed. Bilde, Nielsen and Søvensen, *Apocryphon Severini*, 29–41.

Bilde, Per, Helge Hjaer Nielsen, and Jørgen Podeman Søvensen, *Apocryphon Severini Presented to Søren Giversen* (Aarhus: Aarhus University Press, 1993).

Bingham, D. Jeffrey, 'Irenaeus Reads Romans 8: Resurrection and Renovation', ed. Gaca and Welborn, *Early Patristic Readings of Romans*, 114–32.

Blackman, Edwin C., *Marcion and His Influence* (London: SPCK, 1948).

Blanchard, Monica J., and Robin Darling Young, *A Treatie on God Written in Armenian by Eznik of Kolb (floruit c. 430–50)* (Eastern Christian texts in translation; CSCO; Leuven: Peeters, 1998).

Blois, François C. de, 'Markiyûniyya', *Encyclopaedia of Islam, Supplement*, 599–601.

'Dualism in Iranian and Christian Traditions', *JRAS* 3, 10 (2000) 1–19.

'Review of *Iranian Turfan Texts in Early Publications [1904–1914]*: Photo edn; edited by Werner Sundermann (Corpus Inscriptionum Iranicarum. Supplementary Series, Vol. III. London: School of Oriental and African Studies, 1996)', *JRAS* 3, 8 (1998) 481–85.

Bobichon, Philippe, ed., *Justin Martyr. Dialogue avec Tryphon. Édition critique, traduction, commentaire* (2 vols.; Paradosis 47/1–2; Fribourg: Academic Press, 2003).

Bochet, Isabelle, 'Transcendance divine et paradoxe de la foi chrétienne. La polémique de Tertullien contre Marcion', *RSciRel* 96 (2008) 255–94.

Böhlig, Alexander, 'Das Böse in der Lehre des Mani und des Markion', *Gnosis und Synkretismus: Gesammelte Aufsätze zur spätantiken Religionsgeschichte* (WUNT 48; Tübingen: Mohr, 1989) 612–37.

Borgen, Peder, 'Philo of Alexandria as Exegete', ed. Alan J. Hauser and Duane F. Watson, *A History of Biblical Interpretation, Vol. 1: The Ancient Period* (Grand Rapids, MI: Eerdmans, 2003) 114–43.

Borleffs, J. W. Ph., 'Review of G. Quispel, De Bronnen van Tertullianus' *Adversus Marcionem*', *VC* 1 (1947) 192–8.

Borret, M., *Origène. Homélies sur L'Exode*, texte latin, introd., trad., notes (SC 321; Paris: Éd. du Cerf, 1985).

Origène. Homélies sur le Lévitique II (Hom. VIII–XVI), texte latin,. trad., notes et index (SC 287; Paris: Éd. du Cerf, 1981).

Bou Mansour, Tanios, 'La défense Éphrémienne de la liberté contre les doctrines marcionite, bardesanite et manichéenne', *OCP* 50 (1984) 331–46.

La Pensée symbolique de saint Ephrem le Syrian (Bibliothèque de l'Université Saint Esprit 16; Kaslik, Lebanon: Université Saint-Esprit, 1988).

Boys-Stones, George R., *Post-Hellenistic Philosophy: A Study of Its Development from the Stoics to Origen* (Oxford: Oxford University Press, 2001).

Brandhuber, P., 'Die sekundären Lesarten bei 1. Kor. 15,51: Ihre Verbreitung und Enstehung', *Biblica* 18 (1937) 303–33, 418–38.

Braun, Oscar *De Sancta Nicaena Synodo: Syrische Texte des Maruta von Maipherkat nach einer Handschrift der Propaganda zu Rom* (Kirchengeschichtliche Studien 4iii; Münster: Schöningh, 1898).

Braun, René, 'Chronica Tertullianía' *REAug* 42 (1996) 305–7.

Deus Christianorum: recherches sur le vocabulaire doctrinal de Tertullien (EAA 70; Paris: Études augustiniennes, 1977).

introd., texte critique, traduction et notes, *Tertullien: Contre Marcion* Livre I, II, III, IV, V (5 vols. [vols. 3, 4, 5, texte critique by Claudio Moreschini]; SC 365, 368, 399, 456, 483 Paris: Éditions du Cerf, 1991–2004).

'Le témoinage des Psaumes dans la polémique antimarcionite de Tertullien', *Augustinianum* 22 (1982) 149–63.

'Tertullien et l'exégèse de 1 Cor 7', ed. Jacques Fontaine and Charles Kannengiesser, *Epektasis: Mélanges patristiques offerts au Cardinal Jean Daniélou* (Paris: Beauchesne, 1972) 21–8.

Bray, Gerald L., *Holiness and the Will of God: Perspectives on the Theology of Tertullian* (London: Marshall, Morgan & Scott, 1979).

Brennecke, Hanns Christof, 'Die Kirche als wahres Israel. Ein apologetischer Topos in der Auseinandersetzung mit Markion und der Gnosis', ed. Christoph Schubert and Annette von Stockhausen, *Ad veram religionem reformare. Frühchristliche Apologetik zwischen Anspruch und Wirklichkeit* (Erlanger Forschungen A.109; Erlangen: Universitätsbund Erlangen-Nürnberg, 2006) 47–69.

'Marcion oder das philosophische Gottesbild in der Spannung zwischen Orthodoxie und Häresie', ed. Jürgen Dummer und Meinolf Vielberg, *Leitbilder im Spannungsfeld von Orthodoxie und Heterodoxie* (Altertumswissenschaftliches Kolloquium 19; Stuttgart: Steiner, 2008) 11–28.

Brent, Allen, *Hippolytus and the Roman Church in the Third Century: Communities in Tension Before the Emergence of a Monarch-Bishop* (VCSup. 31; Leiden: Brill, 1995).

Brock, Sebastian, *The Luminous Eye: The Spiritual World Vision of Saint Ephrem* (Cistercian Studies 124; Kalamazoo, MI: Cistercian Publications, 1992.

Broek, R. van den and Maarten J. Vermaseren, *Studies in Gnosticism and Hellenistic Religions: Presented to Gilles Quispel on the Occasion of His 65th Birthday* (EPROER 91; Leiden: Brill, 1981).

Brown, Raymond E. and John P. Meier, *Antioch and Rome: New Testament Cradles of Catholic Christianity* (London: Chapman, 1983).

Brox, Norbert, 'Mehr als Gerechtigkeit: Die außenseitenschen Eschatologie des Markion und Origenes', *Kairos* 24 (1982) 1–16.

'"Non huius aevi deus" (Zu Tertullian, adv.Marc. V 11,10)', *ZNW* 59 (1968) 259–61.

'Zum literarischen Verhältnis zwischen Justin und Irenäus', *ZNW* 58 (1967) 121–8.

Buchheit, Vinzenz, introd., ed., and comm., *Tyrannii Rufini Adamantii Origenis adversus haereticos interpretatio* (Studia et testimonia antiqua 1; Munich: Fink, 1966).

Bundy, David, 'Criteria for being *in communione* in the early Syrian Church', *Augustinianum* 25 (1982) 597–608.

'Marcion and the Marcionites in Early Syriac Apologetics, *Le Muséon* 101 (1988) 21–32.

'The Anti-Marcionite Commentary on the Lucan Parables (*Pseudo-Ephrem A*): Images in Tension', *Le Muséon* 103 (1990) 111–23.

'*The Life of Abercius*: Its Significance for Early Syriac Christianity', *Second Century* 7 (1989/90) 163–76.

Burkitt, F. C., 'The Exordium of Marcion's Antitheses', *JTS* 30 (1929) 279–80.

Burnyeat, Myles F., 'Platonism in the Bible: Numenius of Apamea on *Exodus* and Eternity', ed. Ricardo Salles, *Metaphysics, Soul, and Ethics in Ancient Thought. Themes From the Work of Richard Sorabji.* (Oxford: Clarendon Press, 2005) 143–69 (reprinted in ed. George H. van Kooten, *The Revelation of the Name YHWH to Moses: Perspectives from Judaism, the Pagan Graeco-Roman World, and Early Christianity* [Leiden: Brill, 2006], 139–68).

Butcher, Kevin, *Roman Syria and the Near East* (London: British Museum Press, 2003).

Cameron, Averil, 'How to Read Heresiology', *JMEMS* 33 (2003) 471–92.

Campenhausen, Hans von, *The Formation of the Christian Bible* (ET John Austin Baker; London: A&C Black, 1972).

Canivet, Pierre, and Alice Leroy-Molinghen, ed. *Théodoret de Cyr. Histoire des Moines de Syrie* (SC 257; Paris: Éditions du Cerf, 1979).

Carleton Paget, James, 'Marcion and the Resurrection: Some Thoughts on a Recent Book', *JSNT* 35 (2012) 74–102.

Carlson, Stephen C., '"For Sinai Is a Mountain in Arabia": A Note on the Text of Galatians 4.25', *ZNW* 105 (2014) 80–101.

Casey, Robert P., 'The Armenian Marcionites and the Diatessaron', *JBL* 57 (1938) 185–94.

Cerrato, J. A., *Hippolytus Between East and West: The Commentaries and the Provenance of the Corpus* (Oxford Theological Monographs; Oxford: Oxford University Press, 2002).

Chapot, Frédéric, 'L'hérésie d'Hermogène. Fragments et commentaire', *Rech.Aug.* 30 (1997) 3–111.

Cirillo, Luigi, 'L'antipaolinismo nella Pseudoclementine. Un riesame della questione', ed. Giovanni Filoramo and Claudio Gianotto, *Verus Israel: Nuove prospettive sul giudeocristianesimo. Atti del Colloquio di Torino (4–5 novembre 1999)* (Biblioteca di cultura religiosa 65; Brescia: Paideia, 2001) 280–303.

Clark, Elizabeth A., *The Origenist Controversy: The Cultural Construction of an Early Christian Debate* (Princeton, NJ: Princeton University Press, 1992).

Clements, Ruth, 'Origen's Readings of Romans in *Peri Archon*: (Re)Constructing Paul', ed. Kathy L. Gaca and Larry L. Welborn, *Early Patristic Readings of Romans* (New York: T&T Clark, 2005), 159–79.

Clivaz, Claire, 'The Angel and the Sweat Like "Drops of Blood" (Luke 22:43–44): P69 and f13', *HTR* 98 (2005) 419–40.

Colson, F. H., 'Two Examples of Literary and Rhetorical Criticism in the Fathers (Dionysius of Alexandria on the Authorship of the Apocalypse, and Tertullian on Luke VI)', *JTS* 25 (1924) 364–77.

Cook, John Granger, *The Interpretation of the Old Testament in Greco-Roman Paganism* (STAC 23; Tübingen: Mohr Siebeck, 2004).

Cosgrove, Charles H., 'Justin Martyr and the Emerging Christian Canon: Observations on the Purpose and Destinantion of the Dialogue with Trypho', *VC* 36 (1982) 209–32.

Couchoud, Paul-Louis, *The Creation of Christ: An Outline of the Beginning of Christianity* (2 vols. Trsl. C. Bradlaugh Bonner; London: Watts, 1939).

Crouzel, Henri, François Fournier, Pierre Périchon, introd., trad, et notes, *Origène. Homélies sur S. Luc. Texte Latin et Fragments Grec* (SC 87; Paris: Éditions du Cerf, 1962).

Crouzel, Henri, Gennaro Lomiento, Josef Rius-Camps, ed., *Origeniana: Premier colloque international des études origéniennes (Montserrat, 18–21 septembre 1973)* (Quaderni di Vetera Christianorum 12; Bari: Università di Bari, 1975).

Crouzel, Henri and Manlio Simonetti, trans., *Origène. Traité des Principes. Introduction, texte critique de la Philocalie et de la version de Rufin* (4 vols.; SC 252, 253, 268, 269; Paris: Éditions du Cerf, 1978–80).

Cullmann, Oscar, 'The Plurality of the Gospels as a Theological Problem in Antiquity', *The Early Church* (ed. A. J. B. Higgins; London: SCM, 1956) 39–54.

Dahl, Niels, 'Justin und die griechische Philosophie', ed. Zintzen, *Mittelplatonismus*, 369–96 (= *Philosophie und Christentum* [Acta Theologica Danica 9. Copenhagen: Munksgaard, 1966] 272–92).

'The Origin of the Earliest Prologues to the Pauline Letters', ed. David Hellholm, Vemund Blumkvist, Tord Fornberg, *Studies in Ephesians: Introductory Questions, Text- and Edition-Critical Issues, Interpretation of Texts and Themes* (WUNT 131; Tübingen, Mohr, 2000) 179–209 (= ed. W. A. Beardslee, *The Poetics of Faith: Essays offered to Amos Niven Wilder* [Semeia 12; Missoula, MT: Scholars Press, 1978] 233–77).

Dahl, Nils A. and Alan F. Segal, 'Philo and the Rabbis on the Names of God', *JSJ* 9 (1978) 1–28.

Davies, J. G., 'The Origins of Docetism', ed. F. L. Cross, *Studia Patristica* 6 (Berlin: Akademie-Verlag, 1962) IV, 13–35.

Dawson, David, *Allegorical Readers and Cultural Revision in Ancient Alexandria* (Berkeley, CA: University of California Press, 1992).

Deakle, David W., '*The Fathers Against Marcionism: A Study of the Methods and Motives in the Developing Patristic Anti-Marcionite Polemic*', unpublished PhD. St. Louis University, 1991.

'Harnack and Cerdo: A Reexamination of the Patristic Evidence for Marcion's Mentor', ed. May and Greschat with Meiser, *Marcion und seine kirchengeschichtliche Wirkung*, 177–90.

DeConick, April D., *The Original Gospel of Thomas in Translation : With a Commentary and New English Translation of the Complete Gospel* (Library of New Testament Studies. Early Christianity in context; 287; London and New York: T&T Clark, 2007).

Delobel, Joël, 'Extra-Canonical Sayings of Jesus: Marcion and Some "Non-Received" Logia', ed. Petersen, *Gospel Traditions in the Second Century*, 105–16.

'The Lord's Prayer in the Textual Tradition: A Critique of Recent Theories and Their Views on Marcion's Role', ed. Sevrin, *New Testament in Early Christianity*, 293–309.

'The Text of Luke-Acts: A Confrontation of Recent Theories', ed J. Verheyden, *The Unity of Luke-Acts* (BETL 142: Leuven: Peeters, 1999) 83–107.

Demoen, Kristoffel, 'A Paradigm for the Analysis of Paradigms: The Rhetorical *Exemplum* in Ancient and Imperial Greek Theory', *Rhetorica* 15 (1997) 125–55.

Dillon, John, transl., introd. and comm., *Alcinous. The Handbook of Platonism* (Clarendon Later Ancient Philosophers; Oxford: Clarendon Press, 1993).

'Numenius: Some ontological questions', ed. Sharples and Sorabji, *Greek and Roman Philosophy*, II. 397–402.

'Plutarch and God: Theology and Cosmogony in the Thought of Plutarch', ed. Dorothea Frede and André Laks, *Traditions of Theology: Studies in Hellensitic Theology, Its Background and Aftermath* (Ph.Ant. 89; Leiden: Brill, 2002) 223–37.

Dodd, Charles H., *The Bible and the Greeks* (London: Hodder & Stoughton, 1935).

Doutreleau, Louis, ed., *Origène. Homélies sur les Nombres I Homélies I-X, II Homélies XI–XIX* (SC 415, 442; Paris: Éditions du Cerf, 1996, 99).

Drijvers, Han J. W., 'Adam and the True Prophet in the Pseudo-Clementines', ed. Christoph Elsas and Hans G. Kippenberg, *Loyalitätskonflikte in der Religionsgeschichte. Festschrift für Carsten Colpe* (Würzburg: Königshausen & Neumann, 1990) 314–23.

'Apocryphal Literature in the Cultural Milieu of Osrhoene', *Apocrypha* 1 (1990) 231–47.

The Book of the Laws of the Countries: Dialogue on Fate of Bardaisan of Edeassa (Assen: Van Gorcum, 1964).

'Christ as Warrior and Merchant: Aspects of Marcion's Christology', ed. Elizabeth A. Livingstone, *Studia Patristica* 21 (Leuven: Peeters, 1989) 73–85.

'Die Oden Salomos und die Polemik mit den Markioniten im syrischen Christentum', *Symposium Syriacum 1976* (OCA 205; Rome: Pont.Inst. Orientalium Studiorum, 1978) 39–55.

'Edessa und das jüdische Christentum', *VC* 24 (1970) 4–33.

'Marcionism in Syria: Principles, Problems, Polemics', *Second Century* 6 (1987/88) 153–72.

'Marcion's Reading of Gal. 4,8: Philosophical Background and Influence on Manichaeism', ed. J. Duchesne-Guillemin, W. Sundermann, F. Vahman, *A Green Leaf: Essays in Honour of Professor Jes P. Asmussen* (Acta Iranica 28; Leiden: Brill, 1988) 339–48.

'Quq and the Quqites: An Unknown Sect in Edessa in the Second Century', *Numen* 14 (1967) 104–29.

Dunderberg, Ismo, 'Valentinian Teachers in Rome', ed. Jürgen Zangenberg and Michael Labahn, *Christians as a Religious Minority in a Multicultural City: Modes of Interaction and Identity Formation in Early Imperial Rome* (JSNTSup. 243; London: T&T Clark, 2004) 157–74.

Dungan, David L., *A History of the Synoptic Problem: The Canon, the Text, the Composition, and the Interpretation of the Gospels* (ABRL; New York: Doubleday, 1999).

'Reactionary Trends in the Gospel Producing Activity of the Early Church: Marcion, Tatian, Mark', ed. M. Sabbe, *L'Évangile selon Marc: Tradition et redaction* (BETL 34; Leuven: Leuven University Press, 1974) 179–202.

Dunn, Geoffrey D., *Tertullian's Adversus Iudaeos: A Rhetorical Analysis (NAPSPMS* 19; Washington, DC: Catholic University of America Press, 2008).

'Tertullian's Scriptural Exegesis in the *de praescriptione haereticorum*', *JECS* 14 (2006) 141–55.

Dunn, James D. G., *The New Perspective on Paul: Collected Essays* (WUNT 185; Tübingen: Mohr Siebeck, 2005).

Edwards, Mark, 'Atticizing Moses? Numenius, the Fathers and the Jews', *VC* 44 (1990) 64–75.

'Middle Platonism on the Beautiful and the Good', *Mnemosyne* 44 (1991) 161–67.

'On the Platonic Schooling of Justin Martyr', *JTS* 42 (1991) 17–34.

'Pauline Platonism: The Myth of Valentinus', ed. M. F. Wiles and E. J. Yarnold, with the assistance of P. M. Parvis, *Studia Patristica* 35 (Louvain: Peeters, 2001) 205–21.

Efroymson, David P., 'The Patristic Connection', ed. Alan Davies, *Antisemitism and the Foundations of Christianity* (New York: Paulist Press, 1979) 98–117.

Egan, George A., *An Analysis of the Biblical Quotations of Ephrem in "An Exposiiton of the Gospel" (Armenian Version)* (CSCO 443, Subsidia 66; Louvain: Peeters, 1983).

Saint Ephrem. An Exposition of the Gospel (CSCO 291-2, Script.Arm. 5–6; Louvain, Sec. du CSCO, 1968).

Ego, Beate and Helmut Merkel, *Religiöses Lernen in der biblischen, frühjüdischen und frühchristlichen Überlieferung* (WUNT 180; Tübingen: Mohr Siebeck, 2005).

Ehlers, Barbara, 'Bardaisan von Edessa: Ein syrischer Gnostiker', *ZKG* 81 (= 4.39) (1970) 334–51 (reprinted in Aland, *Was ist Gnosis?*, 355–74).

'Kann das Thomasevangelium aus Edessa stammen?: Eine Beitrag zur Frühgeschichte des Christentums in Edessa', *NovT* 12 (1970) 284–317.

Ehrman, Bart, 'Christ come in the Flesh', *Studies in the Textual Criticism of the New Testament* (NTTS 33; Brill: Leiden, 2006), 343-60 .

Eisele, Wilfried, *Ein unerschütterliches Reich: Die mittelplatonische Umformung des Parusiegedankens in Hebräerbrief* (BZNW 116; Berlin: de Gruyter, 2003).

El-Khoury, Nabil, *Die Interpretation der Welt bei Ephraem dem Syrer: Beitrag zur Geistesgeschichte* (Tübinger Theologische Studien; Mainz: Grünewald, 1976).

Elm, Susanna, Éric Rebilard, Antonella Romano, *Orthodoxie, Christianisme, Histoire/ Orthodoxy, Christianity, History* (Coll. de l'École française de Rome 270; Paris: École française de Rome, 2000).

Evans, Ernest, ed. and transl., *Tertullian Adversus Marcionem* (2 vols.; OECT; Oxford: Oxford University Press, 1972).

Ferrari, Franco, 'Der Gott Plutarchs und der Gott Platons', ed. Hirsch-Luipold, *Gott und die Götter bei Plutarch*, 13–25.

Ferreiro, Alberto, *Simon Magus in Patristic, Medieval and Early Modern Traditions* (SHCT 125. Leiden: Brill, 2005).

Fiey, Jean Maurice, 'Les Marcionites dans les Textes Historiques de l'Église Perse', *Le Muséon* 83 (1970) 183–87.

Finn, Richard, *Almsgiving in the Later Roman Empire: Christian Promotion and Practice 313–450* (Oxford Classical Monographs; Oxford: Oxford University Press, 2006).

Fitzgerald, John, Dirk Obbink and Glenn S. Holland, ed., *Philodemus and the New Testament World* (NovTSup. 111; Leiden: Brill, 2004).

Flemming, Rebecca, 'Demiurge and Emperor in Galen's World of Knowledge', ed. Christopher Gill, Tim Whitmarsh, John Wilkins, *Galen and the World of Knowledge* (Cambridge: Cambridge University Press, 2009) 59–84.

Fonrobert, Charlotte Elisheva, 'The *Didascalia Apostolorum*: A Mishnah for the Disciples of Jesus', *JECS* 9 (2001) 483–509.

Fontaines, Jacques, 'Sur un Titre de Satan chez Tertullien: *Diabolus Interpolator*', *Studi in onori di Alberto Pincherle* (Rome: Ed. dell'Ateneo, 1967) (= *Studie Materiali di Storia delle Religioni* 38 [1967]) 197–216.

Foster, Paul, *The Gospel of Peter. Introduction, Critical Edition and Commentary* (TENTS 4; Leiden: Brill, 2010).

Francis, James A., *Subversive Virtue: Asceticism and Authority in the Second-Century Pagan World* (University Park, PA; The Pennsylvania State University Press, 1995).

Frede, Michael, 'Numenius', *ANRW* II.36.2, 1034–75.

Fredouille, Jean Claude, *Tertullien et La Conversion de la Culture Antique* (Paris: Études augustiniennes, 1972).

Frick, Peter, *Divine Providence in Philo of Alexandria* (TSAJ 77; Tübingen: Mohr Siebeck, 1999).

Gaca, Kathy L. and Larry L. Welborn, *Early Patristic Readings of Romans* (New York: T&T Clark, 2005),

Gager, John G. Marcion and Philosophy', *VC* 26 (1972) 53–9.

Gamble, Harry, 'The Redaction of the Pauline Letters and the Formation of the Pauline Corpus', *JBL* 94 (1975) 403–18.

Gavrilyuk, Paul, *The Suffering of the Impassible God: The Dialectics of Patristic Thought* (OECS; Oxford: Oxford University Press, 2004).

Gemeinhardt, Peter, *Das lateinische Christentum und die antike pagane Bildung* (STAC 41; Tübingen: Mohr Siebeck, 2007).

Gershenzon, Rosalie and Elieser Slomovic, 'A Second Century Jewish-Gnostic Debate: Rabbi Jose ben Halafta and the Matrona', *JSJ* 16 (1985) 1–41.

Gibson, Craig A., *Interpreting a Classic: Demosthenes and His Ancient Commentators* (Berkeley, CA/London: University of California Press, 2002).

Grant, Robert M., *Gnosticism and Early Christianity* (2nd edn; New York and London: Columbia University Press, 1966).

Heresy and Criticism: The Search for Authenticity in Early Christian Literature (Louisville, KY: Westminster/John Knox Press, 1993).9

Gregory, Andrew, *The Reception of Luke and Acts in the Period before Irenaeus: Looking for Luke in the Second Century* (WUNT 2.169; Tübingen: Mohr Siebeck, 2003).

Gregory, Andrew, and Christopher Tuckett, ed., *The Reception of the New Testament in the Apostolic Fathers* (NTAF; Oxford: Oxford University Press, 2005).

Greschat, Katharina, *Apelles und Hermogenes: Zwei theologische Lehrer des zweitens Jahrhunderts* (VCSup. 48; Leiden: Brill, 2000).

'"Woher hast du den Beweis für deine Lehre?" Der altkirchliche Lehrer Rhodon und seine Auseinandersetzung mit den römischen Marcioniten', ed. M. F. Wiles, E. J. Yarnold, with the assistance of P. M. Parvis, *Studia Patristica* 34 (Leuven: Peeters, 2001) 82–7.

Greschat, Katharina and Martin Meiser, ed. *Gerhard May: Markion. Gesammelte Aufsätze* (Veröffentlichungen des Instituts für Europäische Geschichte Mainz 68; Mainz: Philipp von Zabern, 2005).

Griffith, Sydney H., 'Asceticism in the Church of Syria: The Hermenutics of Early Syrian Monasticism', ed. Vincent L. Wimbush and Richard Valantasis, *Asceticism* (New York: Oxford University Press, 1998) 220–45.

'Setting Right the Church of Syria: Saint Ephraem's *Hymns Against Heresies*', ed. William E. Klingshirn and Mark Vessey, *The Limits of Ancient Christianity: Essays in Late Antique Thought and Culture in Honor of R. A. Markus* (Ann Arbor, MI: University of Michigan, 1999) 97–114.

'The Marks of the "True Church" according to Ephraem's *Hymns Against Heresies*', ed. Gerrit J. Reinink and Alexander C. Klugkist, *After Bardaisan: Studies on Continuity and Change in Syriac Christianity in Honor of Professor Han J. W. Drijvers* (OLA 89; Leuven: Peeters, 1999) 125–40.

Gruenwald, Ithamar, 'The Problem of Anti-Gnostic Polemic in Rabbinic Literature', ed. van den Broek and Vermaseren, *Studies in Gnosticism and Hellenistic Religions*, 171–89.

Gunther, John J., 'Syrian Christian Dualism', *VC* 25 (1971) 81–93.

Haar, Stephen, *Simon Magus. The First Gnostic?* (BZNW 119. Berlin: de Gruyter, 2003).

Hägg, Henry F., *Clement of Alexandria and the Beginnings of Christian Apophaticism* (OECS; Oxford: Oxford University Press, 2006).

Hahn, Johannes, *Der Philosoph und die Gesellschaft: Selbstverständnis, öffentliches Auftreten und populäre Erwartungen in der hohen Kaiserzeit* (Weisbaden: Franz Steiner, 1989).

Hahnemann, Geoffrey M., *The Muratorian Fragment and the Development of the Canon* (Oxford Theological Monographs; Oxford: Clarendon Press, 1992).

Hall, Stuart George, text and transl., *Melito of Sardis.* On Pascha *and fragments* (OECT; Oxford: Clarendon Press, 1979).

Hamman, Adalbert G., 'Essai de chronologie de la vie et des Oeuvres de Justin', *Augustinianum* 35 (1995) 231–39.

Hanig, Roman, 'Der Beitrag der Philumene zur Theologie der Apelleianer', *ZAC* 3 (1999) 241–77.

Harnack, Adolf von, *Der Ketzer-Katalog des Bischofs Maruta von Maipherkat* (TU 4.3; Leipzig: Hinrichs'sche, 1899).

History of Dogma 1 (trsl. from the 3rd German edn; Neil Buchanon; London: Williams and Norgate, 1894).

Lehrbuch der Dogmengeschichte (4th edn; Tübingen: Mohr, 1909).

Marcion. Der Moderne Glaübige des 2. Jahrhunderts, der erste Reformator, Die Dorpater Preisschrift (1870) (ed. Friedemann Steck; TU 149; Berlin: de Gruyter, 2003) [=*Der Moderne Glaübige*].

Marcion: das Evangelium vom Fremden Gott; eine Monographie zur Geschichte der Gundlegung der katholischen Kirche (2nd corrected edn printed with *Neue Studien zu Marcion*; TU 45; Lleipzig: Hinrichs, 1924) [=*Marcion*].

Marcion. L'évangile du Dieu étranger. Une monographie sur l'histoire de la fondation de l'Eglise catholique. Traduit par Bernard Lauret et suivit de contributions de Barnard Lauret, Guy Monnot et Émile Poulat avec un essai de Michel Tardieu MARCION DEPUIS HARNACK (Patrimoines christianisme; Paris: Éditions du Cerf, 2003) [=*L'évangile du Dieu étranger*].

Marcion. The Gospel of the Alien God, trsl. John E. Steeley and Lyle Bierma (Durham, NC: Labyrinth Press, 1990) [= *Gospel of the Alien God*].

Harnack, Adolf von, *Neue Studien zu Marcion*: see *Marcion: Das Evangelium vom Fremden Gott.*

'Die Neuheit des Evangeliums nach Marcion [1929]', ed. Axel von Harnack, *Aus der Werkstatt des Vollendeten* (Giessen: Topelmann, 1930) 128–43.

Harrington, Daniel J. and Saldarini, Anthony J., *Targum Jonathan to the Former Prophets: Introduction, Translation and Notes* (Aramaic Bible 10; Edinburgh: T&T Clark, 1987).

Harris, James Rendel, 'Marcion's Book of Contradictions', *BJRL* 6 (1921/22) 289–309.

ed. and transl., The *Apology* of Aristides on Behalf of the Christians from a Syriac Ms. Preserved on Mount Sinai with an appendix containing the main portion of the original Greek text by J. Armitage Robinson (Texts and Studies 1; Cambridge: Cambridge University Press, 1891).

Harrison, P. N. *Paulines and Pastorals* (London: Villiers Publications, 1964).

Polycarp's Two Epistles to the Philippians (Cambridge: Cambridge University Press, 1936).

Hartog, Paul, *Polycarp and the New Testament: The Occasion, Rhetoric, Theme, and Unity of the Epistle to the Philippians and Its Allusions to New Testament Literature* (WUNT 2.134; Tübingen: Mohr, 2002).

Harvey, W. Wigan, ed., *Sancti Irenaei Episcopi Lugdunensis Libros quinque adversus Haereses* (2 vols.; Cambridge, 1857).

Hasler, Victor E., *Gesetz und Evangelium in der alten Kirche bis Origenes: Eine auslegungsgeschichtliche Untersuchung* (Zürich: Gotthelf, 1953).

Hays, M. Christopher, 'Marcion vs. Luke: A Response to the Plädoyer of Matthias Klinghardt', *ZNW* 99 (2008) 213–32.

Heckel, Theo K., *Der Innere Mensch; Die paulinische Verarbeitung eines platonischen Motivs* (WUNT 2,53; Tübingen: Mohr Siebeck, 1993).

Heil, Christopher, 'Arius Didymus and Luke-Acts', *NovT* 42 (2000) 358–93.

Heine, Ronald E., *The Commentaries of Origen and Jerome on St Paul's Epistle to the Ephesians* (OECS; Oxford: Oxford University Press, 2002).

Herrmann, Fritz-Gregor, 'φθόνος in the World of Plato's *Timaeus*', ed. David Konstan and N. Keith Rutter, *Envy, Spite and Jealousy: The Rivalrous Emotions in Ancient Greece* (Edinburgh Leventis Studies 2; Edinburgh: Edinburgh University Press, 2003) 53–83.

Heylen, F., ed., *Philastrius. Diversarum hereson liber* (CC.SL 9; Turnholt: Brepols, 1957).

Hidal, S., *Interpretatio Syriaca: die Kommentar des heiligen Ephräm des Syrers zu Genesis und Exodus mit besondere Berücksichtigung ihrer Auslegungsgeschichtlichen Stellung* (CB.OT 6; Lund: Gleerup, 1974).

Higgins, A. B. John, 'The Latin Text of Luke in Marcion and Tertullian', *VC* 5 (1951) 1–42.

Hilgenfeld, Adolf, *Kritische Untersuchungen über die Evangelien Justin's, clementinischen Homilien und Marcions* (Halle: Schwerschke & Sohn, 1850).

Hill, Charles E., *From the Lost Teaching of Polycarp. Identifying Irenaeus' Apostolic Presbyter and the Author of Ad Diognetum* (WUNT 186; Tübingen: Mohr Siebeck, 2006).

Hill, James Hamlyn, *The Gospel of the Lord: An Early Version which was circulated by Marcion of Sinope as the Original Gospel* (Guernsey: John Whitehead, 1893).

Hirsch-Luipold, Rainer, ed., *Gott und die Götter bei Plutarch: Götterbilder-Gottesbilder-Weltbilder* (Religionsgeschichtliche Versuche und Verarbeiten 54; Berlin: de Gruyter, 2005).

Hoek, Annewies van den, *Clement of Alexandria and His Use of Philo in the Stromateis: An Early Christian Reshaping of a Jewish Model* (Leiden: Brill, 1988).
Hoek, Annewies van den, ed., *Clément d'Alexandrie: Les Stromates IV*, transl. Claude Mondésert (SC 463; Paris: Éd. du Cerf, 2001).
Hoffmann, R.J., *Marcion: On the Restitution of Christianity* (Chico, CA: Scholars Press, 1982).
Hofius, Otfried, '"Die Wahrheit des Evangeliums": Exegetische und theologische Erwägungen zum Wahrheitsanspruch der paulinischen Verkündigung', *Paulusstudien II* (WUNT 143; Tübingen: Mohr Siebeck, 2002) 17–37.
'Gesetz und Evangelium nach 2. Korinther 3', in *Paulusstudien* (WUNT 51; Tübingen: Mohr Siebeck, 1989), 75–120.
Holl, Karl, *Epiphanius II. Panarion haer. 34–64* (2nd revised edn; Jürgen Dummer; GCS; Berlin: Akademie Verlag, 1980).
Hollander, W. Harm and Marinus de Jonge, *The Testaments of the Twelve Patriarchs: A Commentary* (SVTP 8; Leiden: Brill, 1985).
Holloway, Paul A., 'The Apocryphal *Epistle to the Laodiceans* and the Partitioning of Philippians', *HTR* 91 (1998) 321–5.
'Paul's Pointed Prose: The "Sententia" in Roman Rhetoric and Paul', *NovT* 40 (1998) 32–53.
Hübner, Reinhard. M., *Der Paradox Eine: Antignostischer Monarchianismus im zweiten Jahrhundert* (mit einem Beitrag von Markus Vinzent; VCSup. 50. Leiden: Brill, 1999).
Hunter, David G., *Marriage, Celibacy, and Heresy in Ancient Christianity: The Jovianist Controversy* (OECS; Oxford: Oxford University Press, 2007).
Inglebert, Hervé, *Interpretatio Christiana: Les mutations des savoirs (cosmographie, géographie, ethnographie, histoire) dans l'Antiquité chrétienne (30–630 après J.-C.)* (Coll. des étud.aug. Série Antiquité 166; Paris: Inst. d'études augustiniennes, 2001).
Isser, Stanley J., *The Dositheans: A Samaritan Sect in Late Antiquity* (SJLA 17; Leiden: Brill, 1976).
Jacob, Christian, 'Questions sur les questions: Archéologie d'une pratique intellectuelle et d'une forme discursive', ed. Annelie Volger and Claudio Zamagni, *Erotapokriseis: Early Christian Question-and-Answer Literature in Context* (CBET 37; Leuven: Peeters, 2004) 25–54.
Johnson, William A., *Readers and Reading Culture in the High Roman Empire: A Study of Elite Communities* (Oxford: Oxford University Press, 2010).
Jones, Stanley F., *An Ancient Jewish Source on the History of Christianity.* Pseudo-Clementine *Recognitions* 1.27–71 (Atlanta, GA.: Scholars, 1995).
'Marcionism in the Pseudo-Clementines', ed. Albert Frey and Rémi Gounelle, *Poussières de christianisme et de judaïsme antiques. Études réunies en l'honneur de Jean-Daniel Kaestli et Éric Junod* (PIRSB 5; Lausanne: Éditions du Zèbre, 2007) 225–44.
Jülicher, Adolf, ed., *Itala, das Neue Testament in altlateinischer Überlieferung III Lucas-Evangelium* (Berlin: de Gruyter, 1954).
Kaler, Michael, 'Towards an expanded understanding of Nag Hammadi Paulinism', *SR* 33 (2004) 301–17.
Kaler, Michael, Louis Painchaud, and Marie-Pierre Bussières, 'The Coptic *Apocalypse of Paul*, Irenaeus' *Adversus Haereses* 2.30.7, and the Second Century Battle for Paul's Legacy', *JECS* 12 (2006) 173–93.

Kalvesmaki, Joel, 'The Original Sequence of Irenaeus, *Against Heresies 1*: Another Suggestion', *JECS* 15 (2007) 407–17.

Kamesar, Adam, *Jerome, Greek Scholarship and the Hebrew Bible: A Study of the Quaestiones Hebraicae in Genesim* (Oxford: Clarendon Press, 1993).

'Philo, the Presence of "Paideutic" Myth in the Pentateuch, and the "Principles" or *Kephalaia* of Mosaic Discourse', *Stud.Phil.Ann.* 10 (1998) 34–65.

Kannengiesser, Charles, 'Origen, Systematician in De Principiis', ed. Robert J. Daly, *Origeniana Quinta. Papers of the Fifth International Origen Congress, Boston College 14–18 August 1989)* (BETL 105; Leuven: Leuven University Press/Peeters, 1992) 395–405.

Kasher, Rimon, 'The Palestinian Targum to Genesis 4:8: A New Approach to an Old Controversy', ed. Isaac Kalimi and Peter J. Haas, *Biblical Interpretation in Judaism and Christianity* (LHB/OTS 439; London: T&T Clark, 2006) 33–43.

Kaufman, Peter Iver, 'Tertullian on Heresy, History, and the Reappropriation of Revelation', *ChHist* 60 (1991) 167–79.

Kelhoffer, James A., 'Basilides's Gospel and *Exegetica (Treatises)*', *VC* 59 (2005) 115–34.

'"How Soon a Book?" Revisited: ΕΥΑΓΓΕΛΙΟΝ as a Reference to "Gospel" Materials in the First Half of the Second Century', *ZNW* 95 (2004) 1–34.

Kelley, Nicole, 'Problems of Knowledge and Authority in the Pseudo-Clementine Romance of Recognitions', *JECS* 13 (2005) 315–48.

Kim, Young Richard, 'Reading the *Panarion* as Collective Biography: The Heresiarch as Unholy Man', *VC* 64 (2010) 382–413.

Kinzig, Wolfram, *Harnack, Marcion und das Judentum. Nebst einer Kommentierten Edition des Briefwechsels Adolf von Harnacks mit Houston Stewart Chamberlain* (Arbeiten zu Kirchen- und Theologiegeschichte 13; Leipzig; Evangelische Verlagsanstelt, 2004).

'καινὴ διαθήκη: The Title of the New Testament in the Second and Third Centuries', *JTS* 45 (1994) 519–44.

Novitas Christiana: Die Idee des Fortschritts in der Alten Kirche bis Eusebius (FKD 58; Göttingen: Vandenhoeck & Ruprecht, 1994).

Kister, Menahem, 'Some Early Jewish and Christian Exegetical Problems and the Dynamics of Monotheism', *JSJ* 37 (2006) 548–93.

Klein, R., 'Christliche Glaube und heidnische Bildung', *Laverna* 1 (1990) 50–100.

Klevinghaus, Johannes, *Die theologische Stellung der Apostolischen Väter zur alttestamentlichen Offenbarung* (BFChTh 44.1; Gütersloh: C. Bertelsmann Verlag, 1948).

Klinghardt, Matthias, '"Gesetz" bei Markion und Lukas', ed. Dieter Sänger und Matthias Konradt, *Das Gesetz im frühen Judentum und im Neuen Testament. Festschrift für Christoph Burchard zum 75. Geburtstag* (NTOA 57; Göttingen: Vandenhoek & Ruprecht, 2006) 99–128.

'The Marcionite Gospel and the Synoptic Problem: A New Suggestion', *NovT* 50 (2008) 1–27.

Klingshirn, William E. and Mark Vessey, ed., *The Limits of Ancient Christianity: Essays in Late Antique Thought and Culture in Honor of R. A. Markus* (Ann Arbor, MI: University of Michigan, 1999).

Knox, John, *Marcion and the New Testament: An Essay in the Early History of the Canon* (Chicago, IL: University of Chicago Press, 1942).

'A Conjecture as to the Original Status of II Corinthians ans II Thessalonians in the Pauline Corpus', *JBL* 55 (1936) 145–53.

'On the Vocabulary of Marcion's Gospel', *JBL* 58 (1939) 193–201.

Koch, H., 'Philastrius', *PW* 38 (1938) 2125–31.

Koester, Helmut, 'The Text of the Synoptic Gospels in the Second Century', ed. Petersen, *Gospel Traditions*, 19–37.

Kolton-Fromm, Naomi, 'Re-imagining Tatian: The Damaging Effects of Polemical Rhetoric', *JECS* 16 (2008) 1–30.

van Kooten, George, *Cosmic Christology in Paul and the Pauline School: Colossians and Ephesians in the Context of Graeco-Roman Cosmology with a New Synopsis* (WUNT 2.171; Tübingen: Mohr Siebeck, 2003).

Koschorke, Klaus, *Die Polemik der Gnostiker gegen das kirchliche Christentum* (NHS 12; Leiden: Brill, 1978).

Hippolyt's Ketzerbekämpfung und Polemik gegen die Gnostiker: Eine tendenzkritische Untersuchung seiner "Refutatio omnium Haeresium" (GO 6. Hellenistica 4; Wiesbaden: Harrasowitz, 1975).

Kremer, Thomas, 'Ephräm versus Bardaisan: Das Ringen der syrischen Christenheit mit dem Erbe parthischer Kosmologie', ed. Jürgen Dummer and Meinolf Vielberg, *Leitbilder im Spannungsfeld von Orthodoxie und Heterodoxie* (Altertumswissenschaftliches Kolloquium 19; Stuttgart: Steiner, 2008) 119–55.

Kunze, Johannes, *De Historiae Gnosticismi Fontibus: Novae Quaestiones Criticae* (Lipsiae: Dörffling & Francke, 1894).

Laechuli, S., 'The Polarity of the Gospels in the Exegesis of Origen', *ChHist.* 21 (1952) 215–24.

Lampe, Peter, *From Paul to Valentinus: Christians at Rome in the first two centuries* (transl. Michael Steinhauser, ed. Marshall D. Johnson; London: T&T Clark, 2003).

Lange, Christian, 'Ephrem, his school and the Yawnaya: Some Remarks on the Early Syriac Versions of the New Testament', ed. Bas ter Haar Romeny, *The Peshitta: Its Use in Literature and Liturgy. Papers Read at the Third Peshitta Symposium* (Monographs of the Peshitta Institute Leiden 15; Leiden: Brill, 2006) 159–75.

Introd. and transl., *Ephraem der Syrer Kommentar zum Diatessaron* (FC 54,1–2; Turnhout: Brepols, 2008).

The Portrayal of Christ in the Syriac Commentary on the Diatessaron (CSCO 616, Subsidia 118; Louvain: Peeters, 2005).

Langerbeck, Hermann, *Aufsätze zur Gnosis. Aus dem Nachlaß herausgegeben von Hermann Dörries* (AAWG Phil-hist. 3.69; Göttingen: Vandenhoeck & Ruprecht, 1967).

'Die Anthropologie der alexandrinischen Gnosis', *Aufsätze zur Gnosis*, 38–82.

'Zur Auseinendersetzung von Theologie und Gemeindeglauben in der römischen Gemeinde in den Jahren 135–65', *Aufsätze zur Gnosis*, 167–79.

Lattke, Michael, *Oden Salomos. Text, Übersetzung, Kommentar* (3 vols.; NTOA 41/1–3; Fribourg: Academic Press/Göttingen: Vandenhoeck & Ruprecht, 1999–2005).

The Odes of Solomon. A Commentary (trsl. Marianne Ehrhardt; ed. Harold Attridge; Hermeneia; Minneapolis: Fortress, 2009).

Lau, Markus, 'Enthaltsamkeit und Auferstehung: Narrative Auseinandersetzung in der Paulusschule', ed. Martin Ebner, *Aus Liebe zu Paulus? Die Akte Thekla neu aufgerollt* (SBS 206; Stuttgart: Katholischen Bibelwerk, 2005) 80–90.

Lauret, Bernard, *Marcion. L'Evangile du Dieu Etranger. Une Monographie sur l'histoire de la fondation de l'eglise catholique* (Paris: Cerf, 2003). See Harnack, Adolf von.

Layton, Richard A., 'Recovering Origen's Pauline Exegesis: Exegesis and Eschatology in the *Commentary on Ephesians*', *JECS* 8 (2000) 373–411.

Le Bas, Philippe, *Voyage Archéologique en Grèce et en Asie Mineur. Inscriptions III i* (Paris: Firmin Didot Frères, 1870).

Le Boulluec, Alain, 'Le place de la Polémique antignostique dans le Peri Archôn', ed. Henri Crouzel, Gennaro Lomiento, Josef Ruis-Camps, *Origeniana*, 47–61.

La notion d'hérésie dans la littérature greque, IIe-IIIe siècles (2 vols.; Paris: Études augustiniennes, 1985).

'Le Problème de l'extension du canon des écritures aux premiers siècles', *RSR* 92 (2004) 45–87.

ed., *Clément d'Alexandrie: Les Stromates* V, (SC 279; Paris: Éd. du Cerf, 1981).

Lebreton, J., *Gnosticism, Marcionism, and Manichaeism* (London: CTS, 1934).

Leonhardt, Jutta, *Jewish Worship in Philo of Alexandria* (TSAJ 84; Tübingen: Mohr Siebeck, 2001).

Levine, Étan, *The Aramaic Version of the Bible: Contents and Context* (BZAW 174; Berlin: de Gruyter, 1988).

The Aramaic Version of Jonah (Jerusalem: Jerusalem Academic Press, 1975).

'Some Characteristics of Pseudo-Jonathan Targum to Genesis', *Augustinianum* 11 (1971) 89–103.

Levinson, John D., *The Death and Resurrection of the Beloved Son: The Transformation of Child Sacrifice in Judaism and Christianity* (New Haven, CT: Yale University Press, 1995).

Lewis, Agnes Smith, *Catalogue of the Syriac MSS in the Convent of S. Catharine on Mount Sinai* (Studia Sinaitica I; London: C. J. Clay & Sons, 1894).

Lies, Lothar, ed., *Origeniana Quarta: Die Referate des 4. Internationalen Origeneskongresses (Innsbruck, 1–6 September 1985)* (Innsbrucker theologische Studien 19; Innsbruck/Wien: Tyrolia, 1987).

Lieu, Judith M., '"As much my apostle as Christ is mine". The dispute over Paul between Tertullian and Marcion', *EC* 1 (2010) 41–59.

Christian Identity in the Jewish and Graeco-Roman World (Oxford: Oxford University Press, 2004).

'Heresy and Scripture', ed. M. Lang, *Ein neues Geschlecht? Entwicklug des frühchristlichen Selbstbewusstseins* (NTOA 105; Göttingen: Vandenhoeck & Ruprecht, 2013) 81–100.

Image and Reality: The Jews in the World of the Christians in the Second Century (Edinburgh: T&T Clark, 1996).

'Justin Martyr and the Trnsformation of Psalm 22', ed. Charlotte Hempel and Judith M. Lieu, *Biblical Traditions in Transmission. Essays in Honour of Michael A. Knibb* (JSJSup. 111; Leiden; Bill, 2006) 195–211.

'Marcion and the New Testament', ed. Andrew B. McGowan and Kent Harold Richards, *Method and Meaning. Essays on New Testament Interpretation in Honor of Harold W. Attridge* (SBL Resources for Biblical Study 67; Atlanta, GA: SBL, 2011) 399–416.

'Marcion and the Synoptic Problem', ed. P. Foster, A. Gregory, J. S. Kloppenborg, J. Verheyden, *New Studies in the Synoptic Problem* (BETL 239; Leuven: Peeters, 2011) 731–51.

Lindemann, Andreas, *Paulus im ältesten Christentum: Das Bild des Apostels und die Rezeption der paulinischen Theologie in der frühchristlichen Literatur bis Marcion* (BHT 58; Tübingen: Mohr, 1979).

'Paul in the Writings of the Apostolic Fathers', ed. Babcock, *Paul and the Legacies of Paul*, 25–45.

'Der Apostel Paulus im 2. Jahrhundert', ed. Sevrin, *New Testament in Early Christianity*, 39–67.

'Die Sammlung der Paulusbriefe im 1. und 2. Jahrhundert', ed. Auwers and de Jonge, *The Biblical Canons*, 321–51.

Lipsius, Richard A., *Zur Quellenkritik des Epiphanios* (Wien: Wilhelm Braumüller, 1865).

Die Quellen der ältesten Ketzergeschichte (Leipzig: Barth, 1875).

Litwa, M. David, *We Are Being Transformed: Deification in Paul's Soteriology* (BZNW 187; Berlin: de Gruyter, 2012).

Löhr, Winrich A., *Basilides und seine Schule: Eine Studie zur Theologie- und Kirchengeschichte des zweiten Jahrhunderts* (WUNT 83; Tübingen: Mohr, 1996).

'Did Marcion Distinguish between a Just God and a Good God?', ed. May and Greschat, with Meiser, *Marcion und seine kirchengeschichtliche Wirkung*, 131–46.

'Die Auslegung des Gesetzes bei Markion, den Gnostikern und den Manichäern', ed. G. Schölligen and C. Scholten, *Stimuli: Exegese und ihre Hermeneutik in Antike und Christentum. Festschrift für Ernst Dassmann* (JbACErg. 23; Münster: Aschendorff, 1996) 77–95.

'La doctrine de Dieu dans la lettre à Flora de Ptolémée', *RHPhR* 75 (1995) 177–91.

'Markion', *RAC* 24 (2010) 147–73.

Lüdemann, Gerd, *Opposition to Paul in Jewish Christianity* (ET. M. Eugene Boring; Minneapolis, MN: Fortress, 1989).

'Zur Geschichte des ältesten Christentums in Rom'. *ZNW* 70 (1989) 86–114.

Ludovici, Emanuele S., 'Sull' interpretazione di Alcuni Testi della *Lettera ai Galati* in Marcione e in Tertulliano', *Aevum* 46 (1972) 371–401.

Lukas, Volker, *Rhetorik und literarischer 'Kampf': Tertullians Streitschrift gegen Marcion als Paradigma der Selbstvergewisserung der Orthodoxie gegenüber der Häresie. Eine philologisch-theologische Analyse* (EH 23, Theologie 859; Frankfurt am Main: P. Lang, 2008).

Lyman, Rebecca J., 'Ascetics and Bishops: Epiphanius on Orthodoxy', ed. Elm, Rebilard, Romano, *Orthodoxie, Christianisme, Histoire*, 149–61.

'Hellenism and Heresy', *JECS* 11 (2003) 209–22.

Madelung, Wilfred, 'Abu 'Isa al Warraq über die Bardesaniten, Marcioniten und Kantäer', ed. Hans R. Roemer and Albrecht Noth, *Studien zur Geschichte und Kultur des Vorderen Orients: Festschrift für Bertold Spuler zum siebzigsten Geburtstag* (Leiden: Brill, 1981) 210–224.

Madsen, Jesper Majborn, *Eager to Be Roman: Greek Response to Roman Rule in Pontus and Bithynia* (London: Duckworth, 2009).

Mahé, Jean-Pierre, introd., texte critique, traduction et commentaire, *Tertullien. La Chair du Christ* (2 vols.; SC 216–17; Paris: Éditions du Cerf, 1975).

'Tertullien et l'epistula Marcionis', *RSR* 45 (1971) 358–71.

Mansfeld, Jaap, 'Bad World and Demiurge: A "Gnostic" Motif from Parmenides and Empedocles to Lucretius and Philo', ed. van den Broeck and Vermaseren, *Studies in Gnosticism and Hellenistic Religions*, 261–314.

Heresiology in Context: Hippolytus' Elenchos as a Source for Greek Philosophy (Ph.Ant. 56; Leiden: Brill, 1992).

Prolegomena: Questions to be Settled Before the Study of an Author, or a Text (Ph.Ant. 61; Leiden: Brill, 1994).

'Sources', ed. Keimpe Algra, Jonathan Barnes, Jaap Mansfeld, Malcolm Schofield, *The Cambridge History of Hellenistic Philosophy* (Cambridge: Cambridge University Press, 1999) 3–29.

Marcovich, Miroslav, ed., *Hippolytus Refutatio Omnium Haeresium* (PTS 25; Berlin and New York: de Gruyter, 1986).

Iustini Martyris Apolgiae pro Christianis (PTS 38; Berlin and New York: de Gruyter, 1994).

Iustini Martyris Dialogus cum Tryphone (PTS 47; Berlin and New York: de Gruyter, 1997) [First cited 'Justin' 4].

Marguerat, Daniel, *Paul in Acts and Paul in His Letters* (WUNT 310; Tübingen: Mohr Siebeck, 2013).

Mariès, Louis, *Le De Deo d'Eznik de Kolb connu sur le nom de "Contre les Sectes": Études de Critique Littéraire et Textuelle* (Paris: Impremerie Nationale, 1924).

Markschies, Christoph, *Kaiserzeitliche christliche Theologie und ihre Institutionen: Prolegomena zu einer Geschichte der antiken christlichen Theologie* (Tübingen: Mohr Siebeck, 2007).

'Kerinth: wer er war und was lehrte er?', *JbAC* 41 (1998) 48–76.

'Platons König oder Vater Jesu Christi? Drei Beispiele für die Rezeption eines griechischen Gottesepithetons bei den Christen in den ersten Jahrhunderts und deren Vorgeschichte', ed. Martin Hengel and Anna Maria Schwemer, *Königsherrschaft Gottes und himmlischer Kult im Judentum, Urchristentum und in der hellenistischen Welt* (WUNT 55; Tübingen: Mohr Siebeck, 1991) 385–439.

'Origenes und die Kommentierung des paulinischen Römerbriefs – einige Bermerkungen zur Rezeption von antiken Kommentar-techniken im Christentum des dritten Jahrhunderts und ihrer Vorgeschichte', ed. Glenn W. Most, *Commentaries – Kommentare* (Aporemata 4; Göttingen: Vandenhoeck and Ruprecht, 1999) 66–94 (= Markschies, Cristoph, *Origenes und sein Erbe: gesammelte Studien* [TU 160; Berlin: Walter de Gruyter, 2007] 63–90).

Valentinus Gnosticus? Untersuchungen zur valentinianischen Gnosis mit einem Kommentar zu den Fragmenten Valentins (WUNT 65; Tübingen: Mohr, 1992).

Marmorstein, Arthur, 'Philo and the Names of God', *JQR* 22 (1932) 295–306.

Marshall, John W., 'Misunderstanding the New Paul: Marcion's Transformation of the *Sonderzeit* Paul', *JECS* 20 (2012) 1–29.

Martikainen, Jouko, *Das Böse und der Teufel in der Theologie Ephraems des Syrers: Eine systematisch-theologische Untersuchung* (Publications of the Research Institute of the Åbo Akademi Foundation 32; Åbo, 1978).

'Gerechtigkeit und Güte Gottes bei Ephraem dem Syrer', ed. René Lavenant, *III Symposium Syriacum 1980: Les contacts du monde Syriaque avec les autres cultures* (OCA 221; Rome: Pontifical Institute Stud. Orient., 1983) 281–5.

Gerechtigkeit und Güte Gottes: Studien zur Theologie von Ephraem der Syrer und Philoxenos von Mabbug (GO I Syriaca 20; Wiesbaden: Harrassowitz, 1981).

Martin, Michael Wade, 'Defending the Western Non-Interpolations: The Case for an Anti-Separationist *Tendenz* in the Longer Alexandrian Readings', *JBL* 124 (2005) 269–94.

Martyn, J. Louis, *Theological Issues in the Letters of Paul* (Edinburgh: T&T Clark, 1997).

Mattei, Paul, 'Le divorce chez Tertullien: examen de la question à la lumière des dévеloppements que le De Monogamia consacre à ce sujet' *RevSciRel* 60 (1986) 207–234.

May, Gerhard, 'Apelles und dies Entwicklung der Markionitischen Theologie', [1984], ed. Greschat and Meiser, *Gerhard May: Markion*, 93–110.

'Der "Schiffsreeder" Markion', ed. Greschat and Meiser, *Gerhard May: Markion*, 51–62 (= ed. Elizabeth A. Livingstone, *Papers presented to the Tenth International Conference on Patristic Studies held in Oxford, 1987: Studia Patristica* 21 [Leuven: Peeters, 1989] 142–53).

'Der Streit zwischen Petrus und Paulus in Antiochien bei Markion', ed. Greschat and Meiser, *Gerhard May: Markion*, 35–41 (= ed. Walter Homolka and Otto Ziegelmeier, *Von Wittenburg nach Memphis, FS Reinhard Schwarz* [Göttingen: Vandenhoeck & Ruprecht, 1989] 204–11).

'Ein neues Markionbild?', *ThR* 51 (1986) 404–13.

'In welchem sinn kann Markion als der Begründer des neutestamentlichen Kanons angesehen werden', ed. Greschat and Meiser, *Gerhard May: Markion*, 85–91.

'Marcion in Contemporary Views: Results and Open Questions', ed. Greschat and Meiser, *Gerhard May: Markion*, 13–33 (=Second Century 6 (1987/88) 129–51).

'Markion in seiner Zeit' [1992], ed. Greschat and Meiser, *Gerhard May: Markion*, 1–12.

'Marcion ohne Harnack', ed May and Greschat, with Meiser, *Marcion und seine Kirchengeschichtliche Wirkung*, 1–7.

'Markions Bruch mit der Römischen Gemeinde', [2005], ed. Greschat and Meiser, *Gerhard May: Markion*, 75–83.

'Markions Genesisauslegung und die "Antitheses"', ed. Greschat and Meiser, *Gerhard May: Markion*, 43–50 (= ed. Dietmar Wyrwa, Barbara Aland, Christoph Schäublin, *Die Weltlichkeit des Glaubens in der Alten Kirche. Festschrift für Ulrich Wickert* [BZNW 85. Berlin: de Gruyter, 1997] 189–98).

'Markion und der Gnostiker Kerdon', ed. Greschat and Meiser, *Gerhard May: Markion*, 63–73 (= ed. Alfred Raddatz and Kurt Lüthi, *Evangelischer Glaube und Geschichte. Grete Mecenseffy zum 85. Geburtstag* [Vienna: Evangelischer Oberkirchenrat, 1984] 233–46).

'Platon und die Auseinandersetzungen mit den Häresien bei Klemens von Alexandrien', ed. Horst-Dieter Blume and Friedhelm Mann, *Platonismus und Christentum: Festschrift für Heinrich Dörrie* (JbAC Ergbd. 10; Münster: Aschendorff, 1983) 123–32.

May, Gerhard, and Katharina Greschat, with Martin Meiser, *Marcion und seine Kirchengeschichtliche Wirkung/Marcion and his Impact on Church History: Vorträge der Internationalen Fachkonferenz zu Marcion gehalten vom 15.-18. August 2001 in Mainz* (TU 150; Berlin: de Gruyter, 2002).

McGowan, Andrew, 'Marcion's Love of Creation', *JECS* 9 (2001) 295–311.

McHugh, John, 'Galatians 2:11–14–Was Peter Right?', ed. Martin Hengel, and Ulrich Heckel,*Paulus und das antike Judentum: Tübingen-Durham-Symposium im*

Gedenken an den 50. Todetag Adolf Schlatters (19. Mai 1938) (WUNT 58; Tübingen: Mohr Siebeck, 1991) 319–30.

McVey, Kathleen E., 'Were the earliest *Madrase* songs or recitations?', ed. Reinink and Klugkist, *After Bardaisan*, 185–99.

Méhat, André, *Étude sur les 'Stromates' de Clément d'Alexandrie* (Patristica Sorbonensia 7; Paris: Éd. du Seuil, 1966).

Meijering, E. P., 'Bemerkungen zu Tertullians Polemik gegen Marcion (Adversus Marcionem 1, 1–25)', *VC* 30 (1976) 81–108.

God Being History: Studies in Patristic Philosophy (Amsterdam, North Holland/New York: Elsevier, 1975).

Tertullian contra Marcion: Gotteslehre in der Polemik Adversus Marcionem I-II (Philosophia Patrum 3. Leiden: Brill, 1977).

Merkel, Helmut, *Die Widersprüche zwishen den Evangelien: Ihre polemische und apologetische Behandlung in der Alten Kirhe bus zu Augustin* (WUNT 13; Tübingen: Mohr Siebeck, 1971).

Merz, Annette, *Die fictive Selbstauslegung des Paulus: Intertextuelle Studien zur Intention und Rezeption der Pastoralbriefe* (NTOA 52; Göttingen: Vandenhoeck & Ruprecht/Fribourg: Academic Press, 2004).

Millar, Fergus, 'Theodoret of Cyrrhus: A Syrian in Greek Dress?', ed. Hagit Amirav and Bas ter Haar Romeny, *From Rome to Constantinople: Studies in Honour of Averil Cameron* (Leuven: Peeters, 2007) 105–25.

The Roman Near East 31BC – AD 337 (Cambridge, MA: Harvard University Press, 1993).

Miller, Patricia Cox, *Dreams in Late Antiquity: Studies in the Imagination of a Culture* (Princeton, NJ: Princeton University Press, 1994).

Minns, Denis and Paul Parvis, ed. with introd., transl., and comm., *Justin, Philosopher and Martyr. Apologies* (OECT; Oxford: Oxford University Press, 2009)

Mitchell, C. W., *S. Ephraim's Prose Refutations of Mani, Marcion, and Bardaisan* (2 vols. [vol. 2 completed by A. A. Bevan and F. C. Burkitt]; London and Oxford: Williams and Norgate, 1912, 1921)

Mitchell, Margaret M., 'Looking for Abercius: Reimagining Contexts of Interpretation of the "Earliest Christian Inscription"', ed. Laurie Brink and Deborah Green, *Commemorating the Dead. Texts and Artifacts in Context. Studies of Roman, Jewish, and Christian Burials* (Berlin and New York: de Gruyter, 2008) 304–35.

Moll, Sebastian, *The Arch-Heretic Marcion* (WUNT 250; Tübingen: Mohr-Siebeck, 2010).

'Three Against Tertullian: The Second Tradition About Marcion's Life, *JTS* 59 (2008) 169–80.

Mount, Christopher, *Pauline Christianity: Luke-Acts and the Legacy of Paul* (NovTSup. 104; Leiden: Brill, 2002).

Mowry, Lucetta. 'The Early Circulation of Paul's Letters', *JBL* 63 (1944) 73–86.

Muehlenberg, Ekkehard, *Altchristliche Lebensführung zwischen Bibel und Tugendlehre: Ethik bei den griechischen Philosophen und den fruhen Christen* (AGAW, Phil-Hist. 3.272; Göttingen: Vandenhoeck & Ruprecht, 2006).

'Marcion's Jealous God', ed. Donald F. Winslow, *Disciplina Nostra: Essays in Memory of Robert F. Evans* (PMS 6; Cambridge, MA: Philadelphia Patristic Foundation, 1979) 93–113.

Mueller, Ian, 'Hippolytus *Retractus*: A Discussion of Catherine Osborne, *Rethinking Early Greek Philosophy*', ed. Julia Annas, *Oxford Studies in Ancient Philosophy VII 1989* (Oxford: Clarendon Press, 1989) 233–51.

Munier, Charles, 'Les conceptions hérésiologiques de Tertullien', *Augustinianum* 20 (1980) 257–66.

Murray, Robert, 'Ephraem Syrus', *TRE* 9: 755–62.

Symbols of Church and Kingdom: A Study in Early Syriac Tradition (2nd edn; London: T&T Clark, 2006).

Nakano, Chiemi, 'Des Rapports entre les Marcionites et les Manichéens dans un corpus Éphrémien: *S. Ephrem's Prose Refutations of Mani, Marcion, Bardaisan*', ed. Mohammed Ali Amir-Moezzi, Jean-Daniel Dubois, Christelle Jullien and Florence Jullien, *Pensée Grecque et Sagesse d'Orient: Hommage à Michel Tardieu* (Bibliothèque de L' École des Hautes Études Sciences Religeuses 142; Brepols: Turnhout, 2009) 441–53.

Nau, François, ed., *La première Partie de l'histoire de Barhadbesabba 'Arabaïa* (PO 23.2; Paris: Firmin Didot, 1932).

Nautin, Pierre, 'Histoire des Dogmes et des Sacrements Chrétiens', *EPHE* Ve Section, 25 (1967–8) 162–7.

Hippolyte Contre les Hérésies. Fragment (Études et textes pour l'histoire du dogme de la Trinité 2; Paris: Éditions du Cerf, 1949).

Hippolyte et Josipe. Contribution a l'histoire de la littérature chrétienne de troisième siècle (Études et texts pour l'histoire du dogme de la Trinité 1; Paris: Éditions du Cerf, 1947).

Lettres et écrivains chrétiens des IIe et IIIe siècles (Patristica II; Paris: Éditions du Cerf, 1961).

'Patristique et Histoires des Dogmes: 1. Le livre Justin contre les hérésies', *EPHE* Ve Section, 90 (1981–82) 335–37.

Niehoff, Maren R., 'Circumcision as a Marker of Identity: Philo, Origen and the Rabbis on Gen 17:1–14', *JSQ* 10 (2003) 78–123.

'*Creatio ex Nihilo* Theology in *Genesis Rabbah* in Light of Christian Exegesis', *HTR* 99 (2006) 37–64.

'Homeric Scholarship and Bible Exegesis in Ancient Alexandria: Evidence from Philo's "Quarrelsome" Colleagues', *CQ (New Series)* 57 (2007) 166–82.

Jewish Exegesis and Homeric Scholarship in Alexandria (Cambridge: Cambridge University Press, 2011).

'Questions and Answers in Philo and Genesis Rabbah', *JSJ* 39.3 (2008) 337–366.

Nielsen, Charles M., 'The Epistle to Diognetus and its Relationship to Marcion', *AThR* 52 (1970) 77–91.

'Polycarp and Marcion. A Note', *ThSt* 47 (1986) 297–99.

Noormann, Rolf, *Irenäus als Paulusinterpret: Zur Rezeption und Wirkung der paulinischen und deuteropaulinischen Briefe im Werk des Irenäus von Lyon* (WUNT 2.66; Tübingen: Mohr, 1994).

Norelli, Enrico, *Ascensio Isaiae: Commentarius* (CCSA 8; Turnhout: Brepols, 1995). See also Betholo.

'La Funzione di Paolo nel Pensiero di Marcione', *Rivista Biblica* 34 (1986) 543–97.

'La Lettre aux Laodicéens: Essai d'interprétation', *Archivum Bobiense* 23 (2001) 45–90.

'Le Statut des Textes Chrétiens', ed. Enrico Norelli, *Receuils normatifs et canons dans l'Antiquité: perspectives nouvelles sur la formation des canons juif et chreetien dans leur contexte culturel* (PIRSB 3; Prahins: Éd. du Zèbre, 2004) 175–82.

'Marcione e gli gnostici sul libero arbitrio e la polemica di Origene', ed. Lorenzo Perrone, *Il cuore indurito del Faraone: Origene e il problema del libero arbitrio* (Genova: Marietti, 1992) 1–30.

'Marcione lettore dell' epistola ai Romani', *Cristianesimo nella storia* 15 (1994) 635–75.

'Marcion et les disciples de Jésus', *Apocrypha* 19 (2008) 9–42.

'Note sulla soteriologia di Marcione', *Augustinianum* 35 (1995) 281–305.

'Paix, justice, intégrité de la creation: Irenée de Lyon et ses adversaires', *Irenikon* 64 (1991) 5–43.

'Que pouvons-nous reconstituer du *Syntagma* contre les hérésies de Justin?', *RThPh* 139 (2007) 167–81.

'Situation des Apocryphes Pétriniens', *Apocrypha* 2 (1991) 31–82.

Norris, Richard A., 'Irenaeus' Use of Paul in his Polemic against the Gnostics', ed. William S. Babcock, *Paul and the Legacies of Paul* (Dallas, TX: Southern University Methodist Press, 1991) 79–98.

van Nuffeln, Peter, 'Pagan Monotheism as a Religious Phenomenon', ed. Stephen Mitchell and Peter van Nuffeln, *One God: Pagan Monotheism in the Roman Empire* (Cambridge: Cambridge University Press, 2010) 16–33.

Obbink, Dirk, 'Craft, cult, and canon in the books from Herculaneum', ed. Fitzgerald, Obbink and Holland, *Philodemus and the New Testament World*, 73–84.

Opsomer, Jan, 'Demiurges in early imperial Platonism', ed. Hirsch-Luipold, *Gott und die Götter*, 51–99.

'Plutarch on the One and the Dyad', ed. Sharples and Sorabji, *Greek and Roman Philosophy*, II. 379–95.

Orbe, Antonio, *Cristología Gnóstica: Introduccíon a la Soteriología de los siglos II y III* (Madrid: Biblìoteca de Autores Cristianos, 1976).

'El "Decensus ad inferos" y san Ireneo', *Gregorianum* 68 (1987) 485–522.

'El Hijo del hombre come y bebe (Mt 11,19; Lc 7,34)', *Gregorianum* 58 (1977) 523–55.

'Entorno al modalismo de Marción', *Gregorianum* 71 (1990) 43–65.

'Hacia la doctrina Marcionítica de la redención', *Gregorianum* 74 (1993) 45–74.

'Marcionitica', *Augustinianum* 31 (1991) 195–244.

Osborn, C. D., 'Methodology in identifying patristic citations in N.T. Textual criticism', *NovT* 47 (2005) 313–43.

Osborn, Eric, *Tertullian, First Theologian of the West* (Cambridge: Cambridge University Press, 1997).

Osborne, Catherine, *Rethinking Early Greek Philosophy: Hippolytus of Rome and the Presocratics* (London: Duckworth, 1987).

Pagels, Elaine, *The Gnostic Paul: Gnostic Exegesis of the Pauline Letters* (Philadelphia, PA: Fortress, 1975).

Palmer, Darryl W., 'Atheism, Apologetic, and Negative Theology in the Greek Apologists of the Second Century', *VC* 37 (1983) 234–59.

Parker, David C., *The Living Text of the Gospels* (Cambridge: Cambridge University Press, 1997).

Pastorelli, David, 'The Genealogies of Jesus in Tatian's *Diatessaron*. The Question of their Absence or Presence', ed. Claire Clivaz, Andreas Dettwiler, Luc Devillers,

Enrico Norelli, with the assistance of Benjamin Bertho, *Infancy Gospels: Stories and Identities* (WUNT 281; Tübingen: Mohr Siebeck, 2011) 216–30.

Pearson, Birger A., 'Egypt', ed. Margaret M. Mitchell and Frances M. Young, *The Cambridge History of Christianity I: Origins to Constantine* (Cambridge University Press: Cambridge, 2006) 331–50.

'Jewish Haggadic Tradition in *The Testimony of Truth* from Nag Hammadi (CG IX,3)', *HTR* 73 (1980) 311–19.

Pedersen, Nils Arne, 'Some Comments on the Relationship between Marcionism and Manichaeism', ed Bilde, Nielsen and Søvensen, *Apocryphon Severini*, 166–79.

Pelikan, Jaroslav, *What Has Athens to Do with Jerusalem? Timaeus and Genesis in Counterpoint* (Ann Arbor, MI: University of Michigan Press, 1997).

Perkins, Pheme, 'Irenaeus and the Gnostics: Rhetoric and Composition in Adversus Haereses Book One', *VC* 30 (1976) 193–200.

Petersen, Silke, 'Die Evangelienüberschriften und die Enstehung des neutestamentlichen Kanons', *ZNW* 96 (2006) 250–74.

Petersen, William L., ed., *Gospel Traditions in the Second Century: Origins, Recensions, Text and Transmission* (Christianity and Judaism in Antiquity 3; Notre Dame, IN: University of Notre Dame Press, 1989).

Tatian's Diatessaron: Its Creation, Dissemination, Significance, and History in Scholarship (VCSup. 25; Leiden: Brill, 1994).

'The Genesis of the Gospels', ed. A. Denaux, *New Testament Textual Criticism and Exegesis. Festschrift J. Delobel* (BETL 161; Leuven: Peeters, 2002) 33–65.

'What Text Can New Testament Textual Criticism Ultimately Reach', ed. Barbara Aland and Joël Delobel, *New Testament Textual Criticism, Exegesis and Church History: A Discussion of Methods* (CBET 7; Kampen: Kok, 1994) 136–51.

Pétré, Hélène, *L'Exemplum chez Tertullien* (Dijon: Imprimerie Darantière, 1940).

Pilhofer, Peter, 'Von Jakobus zu Justin: Lernen in den Spätschriften des Neuen Testaments und bei den Apologeten', ed. Ego and Merkel, *Religiöses Lernen*, 253–69.

des Places, Édouard, ed., *Numénius Fragments* (Paris: Les Belles Lettres, 1973).

Plese, Zlatko, *Poetics of the Gnostic Universe: Narrative and Cosmology in the Apocryphon of John* (NHMS52; Leiden: Brill, 2006)

Pohlenz, Max, 'το πρέπον: Ein Beitrag zur Geschichte der griechischen Geistes', *NGWGPh* (1933) 53–92.

Pollmann, Karla, introd., text, transl. and comm., *Das Carmen adversus Marcionitas. Einleitung, Text, Übersetzung und Kommentar* (Hypomnemata 96; Göttingen: Vandenhoeck & Ruprecht, 1991).

Possekel, Ute, 'Bardaisan of Edessa on the Resurrection: Early Syriac Eschatology in its Religious-Historical Context', *OrChr* 88 (2004) 1–28.

Evidence of Greek Philosophical Concepts in the Writings of Ephrem the Syrian (CSCO 580, Subsidia 102; Louvain: Peeters, 1999).

Pouderon, Bernard, 'Refléxions sur la formation d'une élite intellectuelle chrétienne au IIe siècle: Les "écoles" d'Athènes, de Rome et d'Alexandrie', ed. Pouderon and Doré, *Les Apologistes Chrétiens et la Culture Grecque*, 237–69.

Pouderon, Bernard and Joseph Doré, ed., *Les Apologistes Chrétiens et la Culture Grecque* (Théologie historique 105; Paris: Beauchesne, 1998).

Pourkier, Aline, *L'Hérésiologie chez Épiphane de Salamine* (Christianisme Antique 4; Paris: Beauchesne, 1992).

Pretty, Robert A., transl. and comm., *Adamantius, Dialogue on the True Faith in God* (ed. Garry W. Trompf; Gnostica 1; Leuven: Peeters, 1997).

Prigent, Pierre, *Justin et l'Ancien Testament* (Ét.Bib.; Paris: Libraire Lecoffre, 1964).

Quispel, Gilles, *De Bronnen van Tertullianus' Adversus Marcionem* (Burgersdijk & Niermans, 1943).

'Marcion and the Text of the New Testament', *VC* 52 (1998) 349–60.

'Review of *Tertullien contre Marcion, Tome IV* by René Braun; Claudio Moreschini', *VC* 56 (2002) 202–07.

Rakoczy, Thomas, *Böser Blick, Macht des Auges und Neid der Götter: Eine Untersuchung zur Kraft des Blickes in der griechischen Literatur* (Classica Monacensia 13; Tübingen: Gunter Narr, 1996).

Rankin, David, *Athenagoras: Philosopher and Theologian* (Farnham: Ashgate, 2009).

Raspanti, Giacomo, ed., *Commentarii in Epistulam Pauli Apostoli ad Galatas* (S. Hieronymi Presbyteri Opera Pars 1. Opera Exegetica 6; CC.SL 77A; Turnhout: Brepols, 2006).

Reed, Anette Yoshiko, 'ΕΥΑΓΓΕΛΙΟΝ: Orality, Textuality, and the Christian Truth in Irenaeus' *Adversus Haereses*', *VC* 56 (2002) 11–46

Regul, Jürgen, *Die Antimarcionitischen Evangelienprologe* (VL; AGLB 6. Freiburg: Herder, 1969).

Reinink, Gerrit J., and Alexander C. Klugkist, ed., *After Bardaisan: Studies on Continuity and Change in Syriac Christianity in Honor of Professor Han J. W. Drijvers* (OLA 89; Leuven: Peeters, 1999).

Reynolds, Philip L., *Marriage in the Western Church: The Christianization of Marriage during the Patristic and Medieval Periods* (VCSup. 24; Leiden: Brill, 1994).

Riedinger, Rudolf, 'Zur antimarkionitischen Polemik des Klemens von Alexandrien', *VC* 29 (1975) 15–32.

Riedl, Gerda, *Hermeutische Grundstrukturen frühchristlicher Bekenntnisbildung* (Theologische Bibliothek Töpelmann 123; Berlin: de Gruyter, 2004).

Rist, Martin, 'Pseudepigraphic Refutations of Marcionism', *JBL* 22 (1942) 39–62.

Rius-Camps, Josef, 'Origenes Y Marción: Carácter Preferentemente Antimarcionita del Prefacio y del segundo ciclo del Pari Archôn', ed. Crouzel, Lomiento, Rius-Camps, *Origeniana*, 297–312.

Roetzel, Calvin J., 'Paul in the Second Century', ed. James D. G. Dunn, *The Cambridge Companion to Paul* (Cambridge: Cambridge University Press, 2003) 227–41.

Rokeah, David, *Justin Martyr and the Jews* (JCPS 5; Leiden: Brill, 2002).

Ross, Steven K., *Roman Edessa: Politics and Culture on the Eastern Fringes of the Roman Empire, 114–242 CE* (London and New York: Routledge, 2001).

van Rossum-Steenbeek, Monique, *Greek Readers Digests? Studies in a Selection of Subliterary Papyri* (Mnem.Sup. 175; Leiden: Brill, 1998).

Roth, Dieter T., 'Marcion's Gospel and Luke: The History of Research in Current Debate', *JBL* 127 (2008) 513–27.

'Matthean Texts and Tertullian's Accusations in *Adversus Marcionem*', *JTS* 59 (2008) 580–97.

'Did Tertullian Possess a Greek Copy or Latin Translation of Marcion's Gospel?', *VC* 63 (2009) 429–67.

Rottenwöhrer, Gerhard, *Unde Malum? Herkunft und Gestalt des Bösen nach heterodoxer Lehre von Markion bis zu den Katharen* (Bad Honnef: Bock & Herchen, 1986).

Roukema, Riemer, 'Jews and Gentiles in Origen's Commentary on Romans III 19–22', ed. Lies, *Origeniana Quarta*, 21–25.

'The Good Samaritan in Ancient Christianity', *VC* 58 (2004) 56–74.

Roux, René, 'Antimarcionitica in the Syriac *Liber Graduum*: A Few Remarks', *Augustinianum* 53 (2013) 91–104.

Royalty, Robert M., *The Origin of Heresy: A History of Discourse in Second Temple Judaism and Early Christianity* (New York: Routledge, 2013).

van Ruiten, Jacques T.A.G.M., 'The Use of Deuteronomy 32:39 in Monotheistic Controversies in Rabbinic Literature', ed. Florentino García Martínez, Anton Hilhorst, Jacques T.A.G.M van Ruiten, Adam S. van der Woude, *Studies in Deuteronomy: In Honour of C. J. Labuschagne on the Occasion of his Sixty-fifth Birthday* (VTSup. 53; Leiden: Brill, 1994) 223–41.

Runia, David T., *Philo: On the Creation of the Cosmos according to Moses. Introduction, Translation and Commentary* (Philo of Alexandria Commentary Series 1; Atlanta, GA: SBL, 2001).

'Philo of Alexandria and the Greek Hairesis-Model', *VC* 53 (1999) 117–47.

Philo of Alexandria and the Timaeus of Plato (Ph.Ant. 44; Leiden: Brill, 1986).

Russell, Donald A. and Konstan, David, ed. and trans., *Heraclitus, Homeric Problems* (Leiden: Brill, 2005).

Salles, A., 'Simon le Magicien or Marcion', *VC* 12 (1958) 197–224.

Sanday, William, *The Gospels in the Second Century* (London: Macmillan, 1876).

Schäfer, Karl Th., 'Marcion und die ältesten Prologe zu den Paulusbriefen', ed. Patrick Granfield and Josef A. Jungmann, *Kyriakon: Festschrift J. Quasten* (Munster: Aschendorff, 1970) I, 135–50.

Schäfers, Joseph, *Eine altsyrische antimarkionitische Erklärung von Parabeln des Herrn und zwei andere altsyrische Abhandlungen zu Texten des Evangeliums: mit Beiträgen zu Tatians Diatessaron und Markions Neuem Testament* (Münster: Aschendorff, 1917).

Scheck, Thomas P., *Origen: Commentary on the Epistle to the Romans* (2 vols.; FOC 103–4; Washington, DC: Catholic University of America Press, 2001–2).

Schenke, Hans-Martin, *Der Gott 'Mensch' in der Gnosis: Ein religionsgeschichtlicher Beitrag zur Diskussion über die paulinischer Anschauung von der Kirche als Leib Christi* (Göttingen: Vandenhoek & Ruprecht, 1962).

'Das Weiterwirken des Paulus und die Pflege seines Erbes durch die Paulus-Schule', *NTS* 21 (1975) 505–18.

Scherbenske, Eric W., *Canonizing Paul: Ancient Editorial Practice and the Corpus Paulinum* (Oxford: Oxford University Press, 2013).

'Marcion's *Antitheses* and the Isagogic Genre', *VC* 64 (2010) 255–79.

Schleyer, Dietrich, transl. and introd., *Tertullian de Praescriptione Haereticorum. Vom Prinzipiellen Einspruch gegen die Häreticker* (FC 42; Turnhout: Brepols, 2002).

Schmeller, Thomas, *Schulen im Neuen Testament? Zur Stellung der Urchristentum in der Bildungswelt seiner Zeit* (mit einem Beitrag von Christian Cebulj zur johanneischen Schule) (HBS 30: Freiburg: Herder, 2001).

Schmid, Herbert, 'Ist der Soter in Ptolemaüs *Epistula ad Floram* der Demiurg? Zu einer These von Christoph Markschies', *ZAC* 15 (2011) 249–71.

Schmid, Ulrich, 'How can we access second century Gospel Texts? The Cases of Marcion and Tatian', ed. Amphoux and Elliott, *The New Testament Text in Early Christianity*, 139–50.

Marcion und sein Apostolos: Rekonstruktion und historische Einordnung der marcionitischen Paulusbriefausgabe (ANTF 25; Berlin: de Gruyter, 1995).

Schmidt, Carl, and Violet MacDermot, ed., *The Books of Jeu and the Untitled Text in the Bruce Codex* (NHS 13; Leiden: Brill, 1978).

Pistis Sophia (NHS 9; Leiden: Brill, 1978).

Schneemelcher, Wilhelm, 'Paulus in der griechischen Kirche des zweiten Jahrhunderts', *ZKG* 75 (1964) 1–20.

Schremer, Adiel, 'Midrash, Theology and History: Two Powers in Heaven Revisited', *JSJ* 39 (2008) 230–54.

Schoedel, William R., 'Enclosing, not Enclosed: The Early Christian Doctrine of God', ed. Willliam R. Schoedel and Robert L. Wilken, *Early Christian Literature and the Classical Intellectual Tradition* (ThHist. 53; Paris: Beauchesne, 1979) 75–86.

Schröter, Jens, 'Die Apostelgeschichte und die Enstehung des neutestamentlichen Kanons: Beobachtungen zur Kanonisierung der Apostelgeschichte und ihrer Bedeutung als kanonischer Schrift', ed. Auwers and de Jonge, *Biblical Canons*, 395–429.

Schüle, Ernst U., 'Der Ursprung des Bösen bei Marcion', *ZRGG* 16 (1964) 23–42.

Schwager, Raymond, 'Der Gott des Alten Testaments und der Gott des Grekreuzigten: Eine Untersuchung zur Erlösungslehre bei Markion und Irenäus', *ZKTh* 102 (1980) 289–313.

Scott, James M., *Geography in Early Judaism and Christianity: The Book of Jubilees* (SNTSMS 113; Cambridge: Cambridge University Press, 2002).

Sedley, David, *Creationism and Its Critics in Antiquity* (Sather Classical Lectures 66; Berkeley, CA: University of California Press, 2007).

'Philosophical allegiance in the Greco-Roman world', ed. Miriam Griffin and Jonathan Barnes, *Philosophia Togata I: Essays on Philosophy and Roman Society* (Oxford: Clarendon Press, 1989) 97–119.

Segal, Alan F., 'Dualism in Judaism, Christianity and Gnosticism: A Definitive Issue', ed. Alan F. Segal, *The Other Judaisms of Late Antiquity* (BJS 127; Atlanta, GA: Scholars Press, 1987) 1–40.

'Ruler of This World: Attitudes about Mediator Figures and the Importance of Sociology for Self-definition', ed. E. P. Sanders, *Jewish and Christian Self-Definition*, Vol. 2 (Philadelphia, PA: Fortress, 1981) 245–268 (= Segal, *Other Judaisms*, 41–77).

Two Powers in Heaven: Early Rabbinic Reports about Christianity and Gnosticism (Leiden: Brill, 1977).

Sevrin, Jean-Marie, *The New Testament in Early Christianity: La reception des écrits neotestamentaires dans le christinisme primitif* (BETL 86; Leuven: Peeters, 1989).

Sharples, Robert W. and Richard Sorabji, *Greek and Roman Philosophy 100BC – 200 AD* (2 vols.; BICSSup. 94; London: University of London, Institute of Classical Studies, 2007).

Shepardson, Christine, *Anti-Judaism and Christian Orthodoxy: Ephrem's Hymns in Fourth Century Syria* (NAPSPMS 20; Washington, DC: Catholic University of America Press, 2008).

Sider, Robert D., *Ancient Rhetoric and the Art of Tertullian* (Oxford Theological Monographs; London: Oxford University Press, 1971).

'Literary Artifice and the Figure of Paul in the Writings of Tertullian', ed. Babcock, *Paul and the Legacies of Paul*, 99–120.

Siegert, Folker and Jacques de Roulet, transl, notes and comm., with the assistance of Jean-Jacques Aubert and Nicolas Cochand, *Pseudon-Philon. Prédications Synagogales* (SC 435; Paris: Éditions du Cerf, 1999).

Sillett, Helen, 'Orthodoxy and Heresy in Theodoret of Cyrus' Compendium of Heresies', ed. Elm, Rebillard, Romano, *Orthodoxie, Christianisme, Histoire*, 261–73.

Skarsaune, Oskar, *The Proof from Prophecy: A Study in Justin Martyr's Proof-text Tradition* (NovTSup. 56; Leiden: Brill, 1987).

Smith, Daniel A., 'Seeing a Pneuma(tic Body): The Apologetic Interests of Luke 24: 36–43', *CBQ* 72 (2010) 752–72.

Smith, Gregory A., 'How Thin Is a Demon?', *JECS* 16 (2008) 479–512.

Smolar, Leivy and Aberbach, Moses, *Studies in Targum Jonathan to the Prophets* (New York: KTAV, 1983).

Snyder, H. Gregory, *Teachers and Texts in the Ancient World: Philosophers, Jews and Christians* (London and New York: Routledge, 2000).

Speigl, J., 'Tertullian Adversus Marcionem. Historische Notizen über die Erfassung des Göttlichen unter dem asschließlichen Aspekt der barmherzigen Liebe', ed. J. Auer, F. Mussner, G. Schwaiger, *Gottesherrschaft-Weltherrschaft. Festschrift Bischof Dr. Dr. h.c. Rudolf Graber* (Regensburg: F. Pustet, 1980) 243–50.

van Staalduine-Sulman, Eveline, *The Targum of Samuel* (SAIS I; Leiden: Brill, 2002).

Stein, Edmund, *Alttestamentliche Bibelkritik in der späthellenistischen Literatur* (Lwów: Związkowe Zakłady Graficzne, 1935).

Sterling, Gregory E., '"The School of Sacred Laws": The Social Setting of Philo's Treatises', *VC* 53 (1999) 148–64.

Tardieu, Michel, 'L'imitation du monde selon Marcion d'après les auteurs orientaux', ed. Philippe Gignoux, *Ressembler au Monde: Nouveaux documents sur la théme du macro-microcosme dans l'antiquité orientale* (Bibl. de l'École des Hautes Études: Section des Sciences Religeuses; Turnhout: Brepols: 1999) 41–53.

'Marcion depuis Harnack', in Harnack, Adolf von, *Marcion. L'évangile du Dieu étranger*, 419–561.

Teixidor, Javier, *Bardaisan d'Édesse: la première philosophie syriaque (Patrimoines christiansime*; Paris: Éditions du Cerf, 1992).

Temins, Peter, 'A Market Economy in the Early Roman Empire', *JRS* 91 (2001) 169–81.

Thoma, Clemens, 'Rabbinische Reaktionen gegen die Gnosis', *Judaica* 44 (1988) 2–14.

Thomassen, Einar, *The Spiritual Seed: The Church of the "Valentinians"* (NHMS 60; Leiden: Brill, 2006).

'Orthodoxy and Heresy in Second-Century Rome', *HTR* 97 (2004) 241–256.

Tloka, Jutta, *Griechische Christen, Christliche Griechen: Plausibilierungsstrategien des antikes Christentums bei Origenes und Johannes Chrystostomos* (STAC 30; Tübingen: Mohr Siebeck, 2005).

Tørjesen, Karen R., *Hermeneutical Procedure and Theological Method in Origen's Exegesis* (PTS 28; Berlin: de Gruyter, 1986).

Tränkle, Hermann, ed., *Q.S.F. Tertulliani Adversus Iudaeos: mit Einleting und kritischen Kommentar* (Weisbaden: Steiner, 1964).

Trapp, Michael. 'Neopythagoreans', ed., Sharples and Sorabji, *Greek and Roman Philosophy*, II. 347–63.

Philosophy in the Roman Empire: Ethics, Politics, Society (Aldershot: Ashgate, 2007).

Trevett, Christine, *Montanism: Gender, Authority and the New Prophecy* (Cambridge: Cambridge University Press, 1996).

Trigg, Joseph W. *Origen: The Bible and Philosophy in the Third-Century Church* (Atlanta, GA: John Knox, 1983).

Tsutsui, Kenji, 'Das Evangelium Marcions: Ein neuer Versuch der Textrekonstruktion', *AJBI* 18 (1992) 67–132

Die Auseinandersetzung mit den Markioniten im Adamantios-Dialog: Ein Kommentar zu den Büchern I-II (PTS 55; Berlin: de Gruyter, 2004).

Turnage, Marc, 'Is It the Serpent That Heals? An Ancient Jewish *Theologoumenon* and the Developing Faith in Jesus', ed. Kenneth E. Pomykala, *Israel in the Wilderness: Interpretations of the Biblical Narratives in Jewish and Christian Traditions* (TBN 10; Leiden: Brill, 2008) 71–88.

Turner, John D. 'Victorinus, *Parmenides* Commentaries and the Platonizing Sethian Treatises', ed. Kevin Corrigan and John D. Turner, *Platonisms: Ancient, Modern, and Postmodern* (Ancient Mediterranean and Medieval Texts and Contexts 4; Leiden: Brill, 2007) 55–96.

Tyson, Joseph B., *Marcion and Luke-Acts: A Defining Struggle* (Columbia, SC: University of South Carolina Press, 2006).

van Unnik, Willem C., 'Der Neid in der Paradiesgeschichte nach einigen gnostischen Texten', ed. Martin Krause, *Essays on the Nag Hammadi Texts in Honour of Alexander Böhlig* (NHS 3; Leiden: Brill, 1972) 120–32.

'Is 1 Clement 20 Purely Stoic?', *VC* 4 (1950) 181–89.

'The Significance of Moses' Law for the Church of Christ according to the Syriac Didascalia', *Sparsa Collecta: The collected essays of W. C. Van Unnik. Part Three* (NTSup. 31; Leiden: Brill, 1983) 7–39.

Usher, Mark D., 'Theomachy, Creation, and the Poetics of Quotation in Longinus Chapter 9', *Class.Philol.* 102 (2007) 292–303.

Vajda, George, 'Le Témoinage d' Al-Maturidi sur la Doctrine des Manichéens, des Daysanites et des Marcionites', *Arabica* 13 (1966) 1–38.

Vallée, Gérard, *A Study in Anti-Gnostic Polemics: Irenaeus, Hippolytus, and Epiphanius* (SCJ 1; Waterloo, ON: Wilfrid Laurier University Press, 1981).

Verweijs, P. G. *Evangelium und neues Gesetz in der ältesten Christenheit bis auf Marcion* (Studia Theologica Rheno-Traiectina 5; Utrecht: Kemink, 1960).

Vinzent, Markus, *Christ's Resurrection in Early Christianity and the Making of the New Testament* (Farnham: Ashgate Publishing, Ltd., 2011).

'"Ich bin kein körperloses Geistwesen": Zum Verhältnis von κήρυγμα Πέτρου, "Doctrina Petri", διδασκαλία Πέτρου und IgnSm 3', in Hübner, *Der Paradox Eine*, 241–86.

Marcion and the Dating of the Synoptic Gospels (Studia Patristica Supplement 2; Leuven: Peeters, 2014).

Vööbus, Arthur, *Literary Critical and Historical Studies in Ephrem the Syrian* (Papers of the ETSE 10; Stockholm: ETSE, 1958).

The Canons Ascribed to Maruta of Maipherqat (CSCO 439, Script.Syr. 191–2; Louvain: Peeters, 1982).

History of Asceticism in the Syrian Orient. A Contribution to the History of Culture In the Near East (3 vols.; CSCO 184, 197, 500, Subsidia 14, 17, 81; Louvain: Sec.CSCO/Peeters, 1955–88).

Wagenmann, Julius, *Die Stellung des Apostels Paulus neben den Zwölf in den ersten zwei Jahrhunderten* (BZNW 3; Giessen: Töpelmann, 1926).

Walker, William O., 'Romans 1.18 – 2.29: A Non-Pauline Interpolation?', *NTS* 45 (1999) 533–52.

'The Burden of Proof in Identifying Interpolations in the Pauline Letters', *NTS* 33 (1987) 610–18.

Walzer, Richard, *Galen on Jews and Christians* (London: Oxford University Press, 1949).

Wanke, Daniel, 'Irenäus und die Häretiker in Rom: Thesen zur geschichtlichen Situation von Adversus Haereses', *ZAC* 3 (1999) 202–40.

Waszink, Jan Hendrick, 'Bemerkungen zum Einfluß des Platonismus im frühen Christentum', ed. A Zintzen, *Der Mittelplatonismus*, 413–48 (= *VC* 19 (1965) 129–62.

Watson, Francis, 'Resurrection and the Limits of Paulinism', ed. J. Ross Wagner, C. Kavin Rowe, and A. Katheine Grieb, *The World Leaps the Gap: Essays on Scripture and Theology in Honor of Richard B. Hays* (Grand Rapids, MI: Eerdmans, 2008) 453–71.

Wechsler, Andreas, *Geschichtsbild und Apostelstreit: Eine forschungsgeschichtliche und exegetische Studie über den antiochischen Zwischenfall (Gal 2,11–14)* (BZNW 62; Berlin: de Gruyter, 1991).

Weiss, Hans-Friedrich, *Untersuchungen zur Kosmologie des hellenistischen und Palästinischen Judentums* (TU 97; Berlin: Akademie-Verlag, 1966).

Weiss, Herold, 'The Sabbath in the Writings of Josephus', *JSJ* 29 (1998) 363–90.

Werline, Rodney, 'The Transformation of Pauline Arguments in Justin Martyr's "Dialogue with Trypho"' *HTR* 92 (1999) 79–93.

Whittaker, John, 'Plutarch, Platonism and Christianity', ed. H. J. Blumenthal and R. A. Markus, *Neoplatonism and Early Christian Thought. Essays in honour of A. H. Armstrong* (London: Variorum, 1981) 50–63.

Whittaker, Molly, ed. and transl., *Tatian.* Oratio ad Graecos *and Fragments* (OECT; Oxford: Clarendon Press, 1982).

Wilken, Robert L., *John Chrysostom and the Jews* (Berkeley, CA: University of California Press, 1983).

Williams, Catrin H., *I Am He: The Interpretation of 'Anî Hû' in Jewish and Early Christian Literature* (WUNT 2.113; Tübingen: Mohr-Siebeck, 2000).

Williams, Daniel H., 'Harnack, Marcion and the Argument from Antiquity', ed. Wendy G. Hellerman, *Hellenization Revisited: Shaping a Christian Response within the Greco-Roman World* (Langham, MD: UPA, 1994) 223–40.

Williams, David S., 'On Tertullian's Text of Luke', *Second Century* 8 (1991) 193–99.

'Reconsidering Marcion's Gospel', *JBL* 108 (1989) 477–96.

Williams, Frank, transl., *The Panarion of Epiphanius of Salamis* (2nd revised edn; 2 vols. NHMS 63, 79; Leiden, Brill, 2009, 2013).

Williams, Michael A., *Rethinking "Gnosticisim": An Argument for Dismantling a Dubious Category* (Princeton, NJ: Princeton University Press, 1999).

'The demonizing of the demiurge: The innovation of Gnostic myth', ed. Michael A. Williams, Michael A., Collett Cox, and Martin S. Jaffee, *Innovation in Religious Traditions: Essays in the Interpretation of Religious Change* (RS 31; Berlin: de Gruyter, 1992), 73–107.

Williams, Rowan D., 'Origen between Orthodoxy and Heresy', ed. W. A. Bienert and U. Kühneweg, *Origeniana Septima: Origenes in den Auseinandersetzungen des 4. Jahrhunderts* (BETL 137; Leuven: Peeters/Leuven University Press, 1999) 3–14.

Willing, Meike, *Eusebius von Cäsarea als Häreseograph* (PTS 63; Berlin: de Gruyter, 2008).

Wilshire, L. E., 'Was Canonical Luke Written in the Second Century? – A Continuing Discussion', *NTS* 20 (1974) 246–53.

Wilson, Stephen G., *Related Strangers: Jews and Christians 70–170 C.E.* (Minneapolis, MN: Fortress Press, 1995).

Wisse, Frederick, 'Heterodidaskalia: Accounting for Diversity in Early Christian Texts', ed. Ian H. Henderson and Gibeon S. Oegema, *The Changing Face of Judasim, Christianity, and Other Greco-Roman Religions in Antiquity* (SJSHR 2; Gütersloher, 2006) 265–79

'The Nag Hammadi Library and the Heresiologists', *VC* 25 (1971) 205–223.

Wolfson, Harry, *Philo: Foundations of Religious Philosophy in Judaism, Christianity, and Islam* (Cambridge, MA: Harvard University Press, 1947).

Woltmann, Jörg, 'Der Geschichtliche Hintergrund der Lehre Markions vom "Fremden Gott"', ed. Ernst C. Suttner and Coelestin Patock, *Wegzeichen: Festgabe zum 60. Geburtstag von Prof. Dr. Hermengild M. Biedermann, O.S.A.* (Das östliche Christentum NF 25; Würzburg: Augustinus-Verlag, 1971) 15–42.

Woolf, Greg, 'Pliny's Province', ed. Tønnes Bekker-Nielsen, *Rome and the Black Sea Region: Domination, Romanisation, Resistance*, (BSS 8; Aarhus: Aarhus University Press, 2006) 93–108.

Wucherpfennig, Ansgar, *Heracelon Philologus: Gnostische Johannesexegese im zweiten Jahrhundert* (WUNT 142; Tübingen: Mohr Siebeck, 2002).

Wyrwa, Dietmar, *Die christliche Platonaneigung in den Stromateis des Clemens von Alexandrien* (Arbeiten zur Kirchengeschichte 53; Berlin: de Gruyter, 1983).

'Religiöses Lernen im zweiten Jahrhundert und die Anfänge der alexandrinischen Katechetenschule', ed. Ego and Merkel, *Religiöses Lernen*, 271–305.

Yarbro Collins, Adela, 'The Female Body as Social Space in 1 Timothy', *NTS* 57 (2011) 155–75.

Young, Frances M., *Biblical Exegesis and the Formation of Christian Culture* (Cambridge: Cambridge University Press, 1997).

'Did Epiphanius know what he meant by Heresy?', ed. Elizabeth A. Livingstone, *Studia Patristica* 17.3 (Oxford: Pergamon Press, 1982) 199–205.

Zahn, Theodor, *Geschichte des Neutestamentlichen Kanons. Volume II: Urkunden und Belege zum ersten und dritten Band*, Part 2 (Erlangen and Leipzig: A. Deichert, 1892).

Zeegers, Nicole, 'Les trois cultures de Théophile d'Antioche', ed. Pouderon and Doré, *Les Apologistes Chrétiens et la Culture Grecque*, 135–76.

Zintzen, Claus, ed., *Der Mittelplatonismus* (WF 70; Darmstadt: Wissenschaftliche Buchgesellschaft, 1981).

Index of ancient authors and sources

Ancient authors and sources are listed alphabetically, by title, author or conventional collections. Where appropriate the abbreviation used and editions cited as listed in the bibliography are given. Passages in Marcion's 'Apostolikon' and 'Gospel' are discussed under the canonical equivalents. References in footnotes are listed only where there is substantive discussion. I am grateful to Patrick Cook for help with the indices.

Index of subjects

For ancient authors and sources in general as well as specific citations see index of ancient authors and sources.

CPSIA information can be obtained
at www.ICGtesting.com
Printed in the USA
FSOW01n0725121017
39813FS